Lecture Notes in Computer Science 10407

Commenced Publication in 1973
Founding and Former Series Editors:
Gerhard Goos, Juris Hartmanis, and Jan van Leeuwen

More information about this series at http://www.springer.com/series/7407

Osvaldo Gervasi · Beniamino Murgante
Sanjay Misra · Giuseppe Borruso
Carmelo M. Torre · Ana Maria A.C. Rocha
David Taniar · Bernady O. Apduhan
Elena Stankova · Alfredo Cuzzocrea (Eds.)

Computational Science and Its Applications – ICCSA 2017

17th International Conference
Trieste, Italy, July 3–6, 2017
Proceedings, Part IV

 Springer

Editors
Osvaldo Gervasi 🆔
University of Perugia
Perugia
Italy

Beniamino Murgante 🆔
University of Basilicata
Potenza
Italy

Sanjay Misra 🆔
Covenant University
Ota
Nigeria

Giuseppe Borruso 🆔
University of Trieste
Trieste
Italy

Carmelo M. Torre 🆔
Polytechnic University of Bari
Bari
Italy

Ana Maria A.C. Rocha 🆔
University of Minho
Braga
Portugal

David Taniar 🆔
Monash University
Clayton, VIC
Australia

Bernady O. Apduhan
Kyushu Sangyo University
Fukuoka
Japan

Elena Stankova 🆔
Saint Petersburg State University
Saint Petersburg
Russia

Alfredo Cuzzocrea 🆔
University of Trieste
Trieste
Italy

ISSN 0302-9743   ISSN 1611-3349   (electronic)
Lecture Notes in Computer Science
ISBN 978-3-319-62400-6   ISBN 978-3-319-62401-3   (eBook)
DOI 10.1007/978-3-319-62401-3

Library of Congress Control Number: 2017945283

LNCS Sublibrary: SL1 – Theoretical Computer Science and General Issues

Printed on acid-free paper

This Springer imprint is published by Springer Nature
The registered company is Springer International Publishing AG
The registered company address is: Gewerbestrasse 11, 6330 Cham, Switzerland

Preface

These multiple volumes (LNCS volumes 10404, 10405, 10406, 10407, 10408, and 10409) consist of the peer-reviewed papers from the 2017 International Conference on Computational Science and Its Applications (ICCSA 2017) held in Trieste, Italy, during July 3–6, 2017.

ICCSA 2017 was a successful event in the ICCSA conference series, previously held in Beijing, China (2016), Banff, Canada (2015), Guimarães, Portugal (2014), Ho Chi Minh City, Vietnam (2013), Salvador, Brazil (2012), Santander, Spain (2011), Fukuoka, Japan (2010), Suwon, South Korea (2009), Perugia, Italy (2008), Kuala Lumpur, Malaysia (2007), Glasgow, UK (2006), Singapore (2005), Assisi, Italy (2004), Montreal, Canada (2003), (as ICCS) Amsterdam, The Netherlands (2002), and San Francisco, USA (2001).

Computational science is a main pillar of most present research as well as industrial and commercial activities and plays a unique role in exploiting ICT innovative technologies. The ICCSA conference series have been providing a venue to researchers and industry practitioners to discuss new ideas, to share complex problems and their solutions, and to shape new trends in computational science.

Apart from the general tracks, ICCSA 2017 also include 43 international workshops, in various areas of computational sciences, ranging from computational science technologies to specific areas of computational sciences, such as computer graphics and virtual reality. Furthermore, this year ICCSA 2017 hosted the XIV International Workshop on Quantum Reactive Scattering. The program also features three keynote speeches and four tutorials.

The success of the ICCSA conference series in general, and ICCSA 2017 in particular, is due to the support of many people: authors, presenters, participants, keynote speakers, session chairs, Organizing Committee members, student volunteers, Program Committee members, international Advisory Committee members, international liaison chairs, and various people in other roles. We would like to thank them all.

We would also like to thank Springer for their continuous support in publishing the ICCSA conference proceedings.

July 2017

Giuseppe Borruso
Osvaldo Gervasi
Bernady O. Apduhan

Welcome to Trieste

We were honored and happy to have organized this extraordinary edition of the conference, with so many interesting contributions and participants coming from more than 46 countries around the world!

Trieste is a medium-size Italian city lying on the north-eastern border between Italy and Slovenia. It has a population of nearly 200,000 inhabitants and faces the Adriatic Sea, surrounded by the Karst plateau.

It is quite an atypical Italian city, with its history being very much influenced by belonging for several centuries to the Austro-Hungarian empire and having been through several foreign occupations in history: by French, Venetians, and the Allied Forces after the Second World War. Such events left several footprints on the structure of the city, on its buildings, as well as on culture and society!

During its history, Trieste hosted people coming from different countries and regions, making it a cosmopolitan and open city. This was also helped by the presence of a commercial port that made it an important trade center from the 18th century on. Trieste is known today as a 'City of Science' or, more proudly, presenting itself as the 'City of Knowledge', thanks to the presence of several universities and research centers, all of them working at an international level, as well as of cultural institutions and traditions. The city has a high presence of researchers, more than 35 per 1,000 employed people, much higher than the European average of 6 employed researchers per 1,000 people.

The University of Trieste, the origin of such a system of scientific institutions, dates back to 1924, although its roots go back to the end of the 19th century under the Austro-Hungarian Empire. The university today employs nearly 1,500 teaching, research, technical, and administrative staff with a population of more than 16,000 students.

The university currently has 10 departments: Economics, Business, Mathematical, and Statistical Sciences; Engineering and Architecture; Humanities; Legal, Language, Interpreting, and Translation Studies; Mathematics and Geosciences; Medicine, Surgery, and Health Sciences; Life Sciences; Pharmaceutical and Chemical Sciences; Physics; Political and Social Sciences.

We trust the participants enjoyed the cultural and scientific offerings of Trieste and will keep a special memory of the event.

Giuseppe Borruso

Organization

ICCSA 2017 was organized by the University of Trieste (Italy), University of Perugia (Italy), Monash University (Australia), Kyushu Sangyo University (Japan), University of Basilicata (Italy), and University of Minho, (Portugal).

Honorary General Chairs

Antonio Laganà	University of Perugia, Italy
Norio Shiratori	Tohoku University, Japan
Kenneth C.J. Tan	Sardina Systems, Estonia

General Chairs

Giuseppe Borruso	University of Trieste, Italy
Osvaldo Gervasi	University of Perugia, Italy
Bernady O. Apduhan	Kyushu Sangyo University, Japan

Program Committee Chairs

Alfredo Cuzzocrea	University of Trieste, Italy
Beniamino Murgante	University of Basilicata, Italy
Ana Maria A.C. Rocha	University of Minho, Portugal
David Taniar	Monash University, Australia

International Advisory Committee

Jemal Abawajy	Deakin University, Australia
Dharma P. Agrawal	University of Cincinnati, USA
Marina L. Gavrilova	University of Calgary, Canada
Claudia Bauzer Medeiros	University of Campinas, Brazil
Manfred M. Fisher	Vienna University of Economics and Business, Austria
Yee Leung	Chinese University of Hong Kong, SAR China

International Liaison Chairs

Ana Carla P. Bitencourt	Universidade Federal do Reconcavo da Bahia, Brazil
Maria Irene Falcão	University of Minho, Portugal
Robert C.H. Hsu	Chung Hua University, Taiwan
Tai-Hoon Kim	Hannam University, Korea
Sanjay Misra	University of Minna, Nigeria
Takashi Naka	Kyushu Sangyo University, Japan

| Rafael D.C. Santos | National Institute for Space Research, Brazil |
| Maribel Yasmina Santos | University of Minho, Portugal |

Workshop and Session Organizing Chairs

Beniamino Murgante	University of Basilicata, Italy
Sanjay Misra	Covenant University, Nigeria
Jorge Gustavo Rocha	University of Minho, Portugal

Award Chair

| Wenny Rahayu | La Trobe University, Australia |

Publicity Committee Chair

Stefano Cozzini	Democritos Center, National Research Council, Italy
Elmer Dadios	De La Salle University, Philippines
Hong Quang Nguyen	International University (VNU-HCM), Vietnam
Daisuke Takahashi	Tsukuba University, Japan
Shangwang Wang	Beijing University of Posts and Telecommunications, China

Workshop Organizers

Agricultural and Environmental Big Data Analytics (AEDBA 2017)

| Sandro Bimonte | IRSTEA, France |
| André Miralles | IRSTEA, France |

Advances in Data Mining for Applications (AMDMA 2017)

Carlo Cattani	University of Tuscia, Italy
Majaz Moonis	University of Massachusettes Medical School, USA
Yeliz Karaca	IEEE, Computer Society Association

Advances Smart Mobility and Transportation (ASMAT 2017)

| Mauro Mazzei | CNR, Italian National Research Council, Italy |

Advances in Information Systems and Technologies for Emergency Preparedness and Risk Assessment and Mitigation (ASTER 2017)

Maurizio Pollino	ENEA, Italy
Marco Vona	University of Basilicata, Italy
Beniamino Murgante	University of Basilicata, Italy

Advances in Web-Based Learning (AWBL 2017)

Mustafa Murat Inceoglu   Ege University, Turkey
Birol Ciloglugil   Ege University, Turkey

Big Data Warehousing and Analytics (BIGGS 2017)

Maribel Yasmina Santos   University of Minho, Portugal
Monica Wachowicz   University of New Brunswick, Canada
Joao Moura Pires   NOVA de Lisboa University, Portugal
Rafael Santos   National Institute for Space Research, Brazil

Bio-inspired Computing and Applications (BIONCA 2017)

Nadia Nedjah   State University of Rio de Janeiro, Brazil
Luiza de Macedo Mourell   State University of Rio de Janeiro, Brazil

Computational and Applied Mathematics (CAM 2017)

M. Irene Falcao   University of Minho, Portugal
Fernando Miranda   University of Minho, Portugal

Computer-Aided Modeling, Simulation, and Analysis (CAMSA 2017)

Jie Shen   University of Michigan, USA and Jilin University, China
Hao Chenina   Shanghai University of Engineering Science, China
Chaochun Yuan   Jiangsu University, China

Computational and Applied Statistics (CAS 2017)

Ana Cristina Braga   University of Minho, Portugal

Computational Geometry and Security Applications (CGSA 2017)

Marina L. Gavrilova   University of Calgary, Canada

Central Italy 2016 Earthquake: Computational Tools and Data Analysis for Emergency Response, Community Support, and Reconstruction Planning (CIEQ 2017)

Alessandro Rasulo   Università degli Studi di Cassino e del Lazio
    Meridionale, Italy
Davide Lavorato   Università degli Studi di Roma Tre, Italy

Computational Methods for Business Analytics (CMBA 2017)

Telmo Pinto   University of Minho, Portugal
Claudio Alves   University of Minho, Portugal

Chemistry and Materials Sciences and Technologies (CMST 2017)

Antonio Laganà   University of Perugia, Italy
Noelia Faginas Lago   University of Perugia, Italy

Computational Optimization and Applications (COA 2017)

Ana Maria Rocha   University of Minho, Portugal
Humberto Rocha   University of Coimbra, Portugal

Cities, Technologies, and Planning (CTP 2017)

Giuseppe Borruso   University of Trieste, Italy
Beniamino Murgante   University of Basilicata, Italy

Data-Driven Modelling for Sustainability Assessment (DAMOST 2017)

Antonino Marvuglia   Luxembourg Institute of Science and Technology, LIST,
                          Luxembourg
Mikhail Kanevski   University of Lausanne, Switzerland
Beniamino Murgante   University of Basilicata, Italy
Janusz Starczewski   Częstochowa University of Technology, Poland

Databases and Computerized Information Retrieval Systems (DCIRS 2017)

Sultan Alamri   College of Computing and Informatics, SEU, Saudi
                          Arabia
Adil Fahad   Albaha University, Saudi Arabia
Abdullah Alamri   Jeddah University, Saudi Arabia

Data Science for Intelligent Decision Support (DS4IDS 2016)

Filipe Portela   University of Minho, Portugal
Manuel Filipe Santos   University of Minho, Portugal

Deep Cities: Intelligence and Interoperability (DEEP_CITY 2017)

Maurizio Pollino	ENEA, Italian National Agency for New Technologies, Energy and Sustainable Economic Development, Italy
Grazia Fattoruso	ENEA, Italian National Agency for New Technologies, Energy and Sustainable Economic Development, Italy

Emotion Recognition (EMORE 2017)

Valentina Franzoni	University of Rome La Sapienza, Italy
Alfredo Milani	University of Perugia, Italy

Future Computing Systems, Technologies, and Applications (FISTA 2017)

Bernady O. Apduhan	Kyushu Sangyo University, Japan
Rafael Santos	National Institute for Space Research, Brazil

Geographical Analysis, Urban Modeling, Spatial Statistics (Geo-and-Mod 2017)

Giuseppe Borruso	University of Trieste, Italy
Beniamino Murgante	University of Basilicata, Italy
Hartmut Asche	University of Potsdam, Germany

Geomatics and Remote Sensing Techniques for Resource Monitoring and Control (GRS-RMC 2017)

Eufemia Tarantino	Polytechnic of Bari, Italy
Rosa Lasaponara	Italian Research Council, IMAA-CNR, Italy
Antonio Novelli	Polytechnic of Bari, Italy

Interactively Presenting High-Quality Graphics in Cooperation with Various Computing Tools (IPHQG 2017)

Masataka Kaneko	Toho University, Japan
Setsuo Takato	Toho University, Japan
Satoshi Yamashita	Kisarazu National College of Technology, Italy

Web-Based Collective Evolutionary Systems: Models, Measures, Applications (IWCES 2017)

Alfredo Milani	University of Perugia, Italy
Rajdeep Nyogi	Institute of Technology, Roorkee, India
Valentina Franzoni	University of Rome La Sapienza, Italy

Computational Mathematics, and Statistics for Data Management and Software Engineering (IWCMSDMSE 2017)

M. Filomena Teodoro   Lisbon University and Portuguese Naval Academy,
                             Portugal
Anacleto Correia   Portuguese Naval Academy, Portugal

Land Use Monitoring for Soil Consumption Reduction (LUMS 2017)

Carmelo M. Torre   Polytechnic of Bari, Italy
Beniamino Murgante   University of Basilicata, Italy
Alessandro Bonifazi   Polytechnic of Bari, Italy
Massimiliano Bencardino   University of Salerno, Italy

Mobile Communications (MC 2017)

Hyunseung Choo   Sungkyunkwan University, Korea

Mobile-Computing, Sensing, and Actuation - Fog Networking (MSA4FOG 2017)

Saad Qaisar   NUST School of Electrical Engineering and Computer
                             Science, Pakistan
Moonseong Kim   Korean Intellectual Property Office, South Korea

Physiological and Affective Computing: Methods and Applications (PACMA 2017)

Robertas Damasevicius   Kaunas University of Technology, Lithuania
Christian Napoli   University of Catania, Italy
Marcin Wozniak   Silesian University of Technology, Poland

Quantum Mechanics: Computational Strategies and Applications (QMCSA 2017)

Mirco Ragni   Universidad Federal de Bahia, Brazil
Ana Carla Peixoto   Universidade Estadual de Feira de Santana, Brazil
  Bitencourt
Vincenzo Aquilanti   University of Perugia, Italy

Advances in Remote Sensing for Cultural Heritage (RS 2017)

Rosa Lasaponara   IRMMA, CNR, Italy
Nicola Masini   IBAM, CNR, Italy Zhengzhou Base, International
                      Center on Space Technologies for Natural and
                      Cultural Heritage, China

Scientific Computing Infrastructure (SCI 2017)

Elena Stankova   Saint Petersburg State University, Russia
Alexander Bodganov   Saint Petersburg State University, Russia
Vladimir Korkhov   Saint Petersburg State University, Russia

Software Engineering Processes and Applications (SEPA 2017)

Sanjay Misra   Covenant University, Nigeria

Sustainability Performance Assessment: Models, Approaches and Applications Toward Interdisciplinarity and Integrated Solutions (SPA 2017)

Francesco Scorza   University of Basilicata, Italy
Valentin Grecu   Lucia Dlaga University on Sibiu, Romania
Jolanta Dvarioniene   Kaunas University, Lithuania
Sabrina Lai   Cagliari University, Italy

Software Quality (SQ 2017)

Sanjay Misra   Covenant University, Nigeria

Advances in Spatio-Temporal Analytics (ST-Analytics 2017)

Rafael Santos   Brazilian Space Research Agency, Brazil
Karine Reis Ferreira Brazilian Space Research Agency, Brazil
Maribel Yasmina Santos University of Minho, Portugal
Joao Moura Pires   New University of Lisbon, Portugal

Tools and Techniques in Software Development Processes (TTSDP 2017)

Sanjay Misra   Covenant University, Nigeria

Challenges, Trends, and Innovations in VGI (VGI 2017)

Claudia Ceppi	University of Basilicata, Italy
Beniamino Murgante	University of Basilicata, Italy
Lucia Tilio	University of Basilicata, Italy
Francesco Mancini	University of Modena and Reggio Emilia, Italy
Rodrigo Tapia-McClung	Centro de Investigación en Geografía y Geomática "Ing Jorge L. Tamayo", Mexico
Jorge Gustavo Rocha	University of Minho, Portugal

Virtual Reality and Applications (VRA 2017)

Osvaldo Gervasi	University of Perugia, Italy

Industrial Computational Applications (WICA 2017)

Eric Medvet	University of Trieste, Italy
Gianfranco Fenu	University of Trieste, Italy
Riccardo Ferrari	Delft University of Technology, The Netherlands

XIV International Workshop on Quantum Reactive Scattering (QRS 2017)

Niyazi Bulut	Fırat University, Turkey
Noelia Faginas Lago	University of Perugia, Italy
Andrea Lombardi	University of Perugia, Italy
Federico Palazzetti	University of Perugia, Italy

Program Committee

Jemal Abawajy	Deakin University, Australia
Kenny Adamson	University of Ulster, UK
Filipe Alvelos	University of Minho, Portugal
Paula Amaral	Universidade Nova de Lisboa, Portugal
Hartmut Asche	University of Potsdam, Germany
Md. Abul Kalam Azad	University of Minho, Portugal
Michela Bertolotto	University College Dublin, Ireland
Sandro Bimonte	CEMAGREF, TSCF, France
Rod Blais	University of Calgary, Canada
Ivan Blečić	University of Sassari, Italy
Giuseppe Borruso	University of Trieste, Italy
Yves Caniou	Lyon University, France
José A. Cardoso e Cunha	Universidade Nova de Lisboa, Portugal
Rui Cardoso	University of Beira Interior, Portugal
Leocadio G. Casado	University of Almeria, Spain
Carlo Cattani	University of Salerno, Italy

Alexey Rodionov	Institute of Computational Mathematics and Mathematical Geophysics, Russia
Cristina S. Rodrigues	University of Minho, Portugal
Jon Rokne	University of Calgary, Canada
Octavio Roncero	CSIC, Spain
Maytham Safar	Kuwait University, Kuwait
Chiara Saracino	A.O. Ospedale Niguarda Ca' Granda - Milano, Italy
Haiduke Sarafian	The Pennsylvania State University, USA
Jie Shen	University of Michigan, USA
Qi Shi	Liverpool John Moores University, UK
Dale Shires	U.S. Army Research Laboratory, USA
Takuo Suganuma	Tohoku University, Japan
Sergio Tasso	University of Perugia, Italy
Ana Paula Teixeira	University of Tras-os-Montes and Alto Douro, Portugal
Senhorinha Teixeira	University of Minho, Portugal
Parimala Thulasiraman	University of Manitoba, Canada
Carmelo Torre	Polytechnic of Bari, Italy
Javier Martinez Torres	Centro Universitario de la Defensa Zaragoza, Spain
Giuseppe A. Trunfio	University of Sassari, Italy
Unal Ufuktepe	Izmir University of Economics, Turkey
Toshihiro Uchibayashi	Kyushu Sangyo University, Japan
Mario Valle	Swiss National Supercomputing Centre, Switzerland
Pablo Vanegas	University of Cuenca, Ecuador
Piero Giorgio Verdini	INFN Pisa and CERN, Italy
Marco Vizzari	University of Perugia, Italy
Koichi Wada	University of Tsukuba, Japan
Krzysztof Walkowiak	Wroclaw University of Technology, Poland
Zequn Wang	Intelligent Automation Inc., USA
Robert Weibel	University of Zurich, Switzerland
Roland Wismüller	Universität Siegen, Germany
Mudasser Wyne	SOET National University, USA
Chung-Huang Yang	National Kaohsiung Normal University, Taiwan
Xin-She Yang	National Physical Laboratory, UK
Salim Zabir	France Telecom Japan Co., Japan
Haifeng Zhao	University of California, Davis, USA
Kewen Zhao	University of Qiongzhou, China
Albert Y. Zomaya	University of Sydney, Australia

Additional Reviewers

A. Alwan Al-Juboori Ali	School of Computer Science and Technology, China
Aceto Lidia	University of Pisa, Italy
Acharjee Shukla	Dibrugarh University, India
Afreixo Vera	University of Aveiro, Portugal
Agra Agostinho	University of Aveiro, Portugal
Aguilar Antonio	University of Barcelona, Spain
Aguilar José Alfonso	Universidad Autónoma de Sinaloa, Mexico
Aicardi Irene	Politecnico di Torino, Italy
Alberti Margarita	University of Barcelona, Spain
Alberto Rui	University of Lisbon, Portugal
Ali Salman	University of Magna Graecia, Italy
Alvanides Seraphim	University at Newcastle, UK
Alvelos Filipe	Universidade do Minho, Portugal
Amato Alba	Seconda Università degli Studi di Napoli, Italy
Amorim Paulo	Instituto de Matemática da UFRJ (IM-UFRJ), Brazil
Anderson Roger	University of California Santa Cruz, USA
Andrianov Serge	Saint Petersburg State University, Russia
Andrienko Gennady	Fraunhofer-Institut für Intelligente Analyse- und Informationssysteme, Germany
Apduhan Bernady	Kyushu Sangyo University, Japan
Aquilanti Vincenzo	University of Perugia, Italy
Asche Hartmut	Potsdam University, Germany
Azam Samiul	United International University, Bangladesh
Azevedo Ana	Athabasca University, USA
Bae Ihn-Han	Catholic University of Daegu, South Korea
Balacco Gabriella	Polytechnic of Bari, Italy
Balena Pasquale	Polytechnic of Bari, Italy
Barroca Filho Itamir	Universidade Federal do Rio Grande do Norte, Brazil
Behera Ranjan Kumar	Indian Institute of Technology Patna, India
Belpassi Leonardo	National Research Council, Italy
Bentayeb Fadila	Université Lyon, France
Bernardino Raquel	Universidade da Beira Interiore, Portugal
Bertolotto Michela	University Collegue Dublin, UK
Bhatta Bijaya	Utkal University, India
Bimonte Sandro	IRSTEA, France
Blecic Ivan	University of Cagliari, Italy
Bo Carles	ICIQ, Spain
Bogdanov Alexander	Saint Petersburg State University, Russia
Bollini Letizia	University of Milano-Bicocca, Italy
Bonifazi Alessandro	Polytechnic of Bari, Italy
Bonnet Claude-Laurent	Université de Bordeaux, France
Borgogno Mondino Enrico Corrado	University of Turin, Italy
Borruso Giuseppe	University of Trieste, Italy

Bostenaru Maria   Ion Mincu University of Architecture and Urbanism, Romania
Boussaid Omar   Université Lyon 2, France
Braga Ana Cristina   University of Minho, Portugal
Braga Nuno   University of Minho, Portugal
Brasil Luciana   Instituto Federal Sao Paolo, Brazil
Cabral Pedro   Universidade NOVA de Lisboa, Portugal
Cacao Isabel   University of Aveiro, Portugal
Caiaffa Emanuela   Enea, Italy
Campagna Michele   University of Cagliari, Italy
Caniato Renhe Marcelo   Universidade Federal de Juiz de Fora, Brazil
Canora Filomena   University of Basilicata, Italy
Caradonna Grazia   Polytechnic of Bari, Italy
Cardoso Rui   Beira Interior University, Portugal
Caroti Gabriella   University of Pisa, Italy
Carravilla Maria Antonia   Universidade do Porto, Portugal
Cattani Carlo   University of Salerno, Italy
Cefalo Raffaela   University of Trieste, Italy
Ceppi Claudia   Polytechnic of Bari, Italy
Cerreta Maria   University Federico II of Naples, Italy
Chanet Jean-Pierre   UR TSCF Irstea, France
Chaturvedi Krishna Kumar   University of Delhi, India
Chiancone Andrea   University of Perugia, Italy
Choo Hyunseung   Sungkyunkwan University, South Korea
Ciabo Serena   University of l'Aquila, Italy
Coletti Cecilia   University of Chieti, Italy
Correia Aldina   Porto Polytechnic, Portugal
Correia Anacleto   CINAV, Portugal
Correia Elisete   University of Trás-Os-Montes e Alto Douro, Portugal
Correia Florbela Maria da   Instituto Politécnico de Viana do Castelo, Portugal
    Cruz Domingues
Cosido Oscar   University of Cantabria, Spain
Costa e Silva Eliana   University of Minho, Portugal
Costa Graça   Instituto Politécnico de Setúbal, Portugal
Costantini Alessandro   INFN, Italy
Crispim José   University of Minho, Portugal
Cuzzocrea Alfredo   University of Trieste, Italy
Danese Maria   IBAM, CNR, Italy
Daneshpajouh Shervin   University of Western Ontario, USA
De Fazio Dario   IMIP-CNR, Italy
De Runz Cyril   University of Reims Champagne-Ardenne, France
Deffuant Guillaume   Institut national de recherche en sciences et technologies pour l'environnement et l'agriculture, France
Degtyarev Alexander   Saint Petersburg State University, Russia
Devai Frank   London South Bank University, UK
Di Leo Margherita   JRC, European Commission, Belgium

Dias Joana	University of Coimbra, Portugal
Dilo Arta	University of Twente, The Netherlands
Dvarioniene Jolanta	Kaunas University of Technology, Lithuania
El-Zawawy Mohamed A.	Cairo University, Egypt
Escalona Maria-Jose	University of Seville, Spain
Faginas-Lago, Noelia	University of Perugia, Italy
Falcinelli Stefano	University of Perugia, Italy
Falcão M. Irene	University of Minho, Portugal
Faria Susana	University of Minho, Portugal
Fattoruso Grazia	ENEA, Italy
Fenu Gianfranco	University of Trieste, Italy
Fernandes Edite	University of Minho, Portugal
Fernandes Florbela	Escola Superior de Tecnologia e Gest ão de Bragancca, Portugal
Fernandes Rosario	USP/ESALQ, Brazil
Ferrari Riccardo	Delft University of Technology, The Netherlands
Figueiredo Manuel Carlos	University of Minho, Portugal
Florence Le Ber	ENGEES, France
Flouvat Frederic	University of New Caledonia, France
Fontes Dalila	Universidade do Porto, Portugal
Franzoni Valentina	University of Perugia, Italy
Freitas Adelaide de Fátima Baptista Valente	University of Aveiro, Portugal
Fusco Giovanni	Università di Bari, Italy
Gabrani Goldie	Tecpro Syst. Ltd., India
Gaido Luciano	INFN, Italy
Gallo Crescenzio	University of Foggia, Italy
Garaba Shungu	University of Connecticut, USA
Garau Chiara	University of Cagliari, Italy
Garcia Ernesto	University of the Basque Country, Spain
Gargano Ricardo	Universidade Brasilia, Brazil
Gavrilova Marina	University of Calgary, Canada
Gensel Jerome	IMAG, France
Gervasi Osvaldo	University of Perugia, Italy
Gioia Andrea	Polytechnic University of Bari, Italy
Giovinazzi Sonia	University of Canterbury, New Zealand
Gizzi Fabrizio	National Research Council, Italy
Gomes dos Anjos Eudisley	Universidade Federal da Paraíba, Brazil
Gonzaga de Oliveira Sanderson Lincohn	Universidade Federal de Lavras, Brazil
Gonçalves Arminda Manuela	University of Minho, Braga, Portugal
Gorbachev Yuriy	Geolink Technologies, Russia
Grecu Valentin	University of Sibiu, Romania
Gupta Brij	Cancer Biology Research Center, USA
Hagen-Zanker Alex	University of Surrey, UK

Hamaguchi Naoki	Tokyo Kyoiku University, Japan
Hanazumi Simone	University of Sao Paulo, Brazil
Hanzl Malgorzata	University of Lodz, Poland
Hayashi Masaki	University of Calgary, Canada
Hendrix Eligius M.T.	Operations Research and Logistics Group, The Netherlands
Henriques Carla	Inst. Politécnico de Viseu, Portugal
Herawan Tutut	State Polytechnic of Malang, Indonesia
Hsu Hui-Huang	National Chiao Tung University, Taiwan
Ienco Dino	La Maison de la télédétection de Montpellier, France
Iglesias Andres	Universidad de Cantabria, Spain
Imran Raheea	NUST Islamabad, Pakistan
Inoue Kentaro	National Technical University of Athens, Greece
Josselin Didier	Université d'Avignon et des Pays de Vaucluse, France
Kaneko Masataka	Kisarazu National College of Technology, Japan
Kang Myoung-Ah	Blaise Pascal University, France
Karampiperis Pythagoras	National Center of Scientific Research, Athens, Greece
Kavouras Marinos	University of Athens, Greece
Kolingerova Ivana	University of West Bohemia, Czech Republic
Korkhov Vladimir	Saint Petersburg State University, Russia
Kotzinos Dimitrios	University of Cergy Pontoise, France
Kulabukhova Nataliia	Saint Petersburg State University, Russia
Kumar Dileep	SR Engineering College, India
Kumar Lov	National Institute of Technology, Rourkela, India
Kumar Pawan	Institute for Advanced Study, Princeton, USA
Laganà Antonio	University of Perugia, Italy
Lai Sabrina	Università di Cagliari, Italy
Lanza Viviana	Lombardy Regional Institute for Research, Italy
Lasala Piermichele	Università di Foggia, Italy
Laurent Anne	Laboratoire d'Informatique, de Robotique et de Microélectronique de Montpellier, France
Lavorato Davide	University of Rome, Italy
Le Duc Tai	Sungkyunkwan University, South Korea
Legatiuk Dmitrii	Bauhaus University, Germany
Li Ming	University of Waterloo, Canada
Lima Ana	University of São Paulo (UNIFESP), Brazil
Liu Xin	École polytechnique fédérale de Lausanne, Switzerland
Lombardi Andrea	University of Perugia, Italy
Lopes Cristina	Instituto Superior de Contabilidade e Administracao do Porto, Portugal
Lopes Maria João	Instituto Universitário de Lisboa, Portugal
Lourenço Vanda Marisa	Universidade NOVA de Lisboa, Portugal
Machado Jose	University of Minho, Portugal
Maeda Yoichi	Tokai University, Japan
Majcen Nineta	Euchems, Belgium
Malonek Helmuth	Universidade de Aveiro, Portugal

Mancini Francesco	University of Modena and Reggio Emilia, Italy
Mandanici Emanuele	Università di Bologna, Italy
Manganelli Benedetto	Università degli studi della Basilicata, Italy
Manso Callejo Miguel Angel	Universidad Politécnica de Madrid, Spain
Margalef Tomas	Autonomous University of Barcelona, Spain
Marques Jorge	University of Coimbra, Portugal
Martins Bruno	Universidade de Lisboa, Portugal
Marvuglia Antonino	Public Research Centre Henri Tudor, Luxembourg
Mateos Cristian	Universidad Nacional del Centro, Argentina
Mauro Giovanni	University of Trieste, Italy
McGuire Michael	Towson University, USA
Medvet Eric	University of Trieste, Italy
Milani Alfredo	University of Perugia, Italy
Millham Richard	Durban University of Technoloy, South Africa
Minghini Marco	Polytechnic University of Milan, Italy
Minhas Umar	University of Waterloo, Ontario, Canada
Miralles André	La Maison de la télédétection de Montpellier, France
Miranda Fernando	Universidade do Minho, Portugal
Misra Sanjay	Covenant University, Nigeria
Modica Giuseppe	Università Mediterranea di Reggio Calabria, Italy
Molaei Qelichi Mohamad	University of Tehran, Iran
Monteiro Ana Margarida	University of Coimbra, Portugal
Morano Pierluigi	Polytechnic University of Bari, Italy
Moura Ana	Universidade de Aveiro, Portugal
Moura Pires João	Universidade NOVA de Lisboa, Portugal
Mourão Maria	ESTG-IPVC, Portugal
Murgante Beniamino	University of Basilicata, Italy
Nagy Csaba	University of Szeged, Hungary
Nakamura Yasuyuki	Nagoya University, Japan
Natário Isabel Cristina Maciel	University Nova de Lisboa, Portugal
Nemmaoui Abderrahim	Universidad de Almeria (UAL), Spain
Nguyen Tien Dzung	Sungkyunkwan University, South Korea
Niyogi Rajdeep	Indian Institute of Technology Roorkee, India
Novelli Antonio	University of Bari, Italy
Oliveira Irene	University of Trás-Os-Montes e Alto Douro, Portugal
Oliveira José A.	Universidade do Minho, Portugal
Ottomanelli Michele	University of Bari, Italy
Ouchi Shunji	Shimonoseki City University, Japan
Ozturk Savas	Scientific and Technological Research Council of Turkey, Turkey
P. Costa M. Fernanda	Universidade do Minho, Portugal
Painho Marco	NOVA Information Management School, Portugal
Panetta J.B.	Tecnologia Geofísica Petróleo Brasileiro SA, PETROBRAS, Brazil

Pantazis Dimos	Otenet, Greece
Papa Enrica	University of Amsterdam, The Netherlands
Pardede Eric	La Trobe University, Australia
Parente Claudio	Università degli Studi di Napoli Parthenope, Italy
Pathan Al-Sakib Khan	Islamic University of Technology, Bangladesh
Paul Prantosh K.	EIILM University, Jorethang, Sikkim, India
Pengő Edit	University of Szeged, Hungary
Pereira Ana	IPB, Portugal
Pereira José Luís	Universidade do Minho, Portugal
Peschechera Giuseppe	Università di Bologna, Italy
Pham Quoc Trung	HCMC University of Technology, Vietnam
Piemonte Andreaa	University of Pisa, Italy
Pimentel Carina	Universidade de Aveiro, Portugal
Pinet Francois	IRSTEA, France
Pinto Livio	Polytechnic University of Milan, Italy
Pinto Telmo	Universidade do Minho, Portugal
Pinet Francois	IRSTEA, France
Poli Giuliano	Université Pierre et Marie Curie, France
Pollino Maurizio	ENEA, Italy
Portela Carlos Filipe	Universidade do Minho, Portugal
Prata Paula	Universidade Federal de Sergipe, Brazil
Previl Carlo	University of Quebec in Abitibi-Témiscamingue (UQAT), Canada
Prezioso Giuseppina	Università degli Studi di Napoli Parthenope, Italy
Pusatli Tolga	Cankaya University, Turkey
Quan Tho	Ho Chi Minh, University of Technology, Vietnam
Ragni Mirco	Universidade Estadual de Feira de Santana, Brazil
Rahman Nazreena	Biotechnology Research Centre, Malaysia
Rahman Wasiur	Technical University Darmstadt, Germany
Rashid Sidra	National University of Sciences and Technology (NUST) Islamabad, Pakistan
Rasulo Alessandro	Università degli studi di Cassino e del Lazio Meridionale, Italy
Raza Syed Muhammad	Sungkyunkwan University, South Korea
Reis Ferreira Gomes Karine	Instituto Nacional de Pesquisas Espaciais, Brazil
Requejo Cristina	Universidade de Aveiro, Portugal
Rocha Ana Maria	University of Minho, Portugal
Rocha Humberto	University of Coimbra, Portugal
Rocha Jorge	University of Minho, Portugal
Rodriguez Daniel	University of Berkeley, USA
Saeki Koichi	Graduate University for Advanced Studies, Japan
Samela Caterina	University of Basilicata, Italy
Sannicandro Valentina	Polytechnic of Bari, Italy
Santiago Júnior Valdivino	Instituto Nacional de Pesquisas Espaciais, Brazil
Sarafian Haiduke	Pennsylvania State University, USA

Santos Daniel	Universidade Federal de Minas Gerais, Portugal
Santos Dorabella	Instituto de Telecomunicações, Portugal
Santos Eulália	SAPO, Portugal
Santos Maribel Yasmina	Universidade de Minho, Portugal
Santos Rafael	University of Toronto, Canada
Santucci Valentinoi	University of Perugia, Italy
Sautot Lucil	MR TETIS, AgroParisTech, France
Scaioni Marco	Polytechnic University of Milan, Italy
Schernthanner Harald	University of Potsdam, Germany
Schneider Michel	ISIMA, France
Schoier Gabriella	University of Trieste, Italy
Scorza Francesco	University of Basilicata, Italy
Sebillo Monica	University of Salerno, Italy
Severino Ricardo Jose	Universidade de Minho, Portugal
Shakhov Vladimir	Russian Academy of Sciences (Siberian Branch), Russia
Sheeren David	Toulouse Institute of Technology, France
Shen Jie	University of Michigan, USA
Silva Elsa	INESC Tec, Porto, Portugal
Sipos Gergely	MTA SZTAKI Computer and Automation Research Institute, Hungary
Skarga-Bandurova Inna	Technological Institute of East Ukrainian National University, Ukraine
Skoković Dražen	University of Valencia, Spain
Skouteris Dimitrios	SNS, Italy
Soares Inês Soares Maria Joana	Universidade de Minho, Portugal
Soares Michel	Federal University of Sergipe, Brazil
Sokolovski Dmitri	Ikerbasque, Basque Foundation for Science, Spain
Sousa Lisete	Research, FCUL, CEAUL, Lisboa, Portugal
Stener Mauro	Università di Trieste, Italy
Sumida Yasuaki	Center for Digestive and Liver Diseases, Nara City Hospital, Japan
Suri Bharti	Guru Gobind Singh Indraprastha University, India
Sørensen Claus Aage Grøn	University of Aarhus, Denmark
Tajani Francesco	University of Rome, Italy
Takato Setsuo	Kisarazu National College of Technology, Japan
Tanaka Kazuaki	Hasanuddin University, Indonesia
Taniar David	Monash University, Australia
Tapia-McClung Rodrigo	The Center for Research in Geography and Geomatics, Mexico
Tarantino Eufemia	Polytechnic of Bari, Italy
Teixeira Ana Paula	Federal University of Ceará, Fortaleza, Brazil
Teixeira Senhorinha	Universidade do Minho, Portugal
Teodoro M. Filomena	Instituto Politécnico de Setúbal, Portugal
Thill Jean-Claude	University at Buffalo, USA
Thorat Pankaj	Sungkyunkwan University, South Korea

Tilio Lucia	University of Basilicata, Italy
Tomaz Graça	Instituto Politécnico da Guarda, Portugal
Torre Carmelo Maria	Polytechnic of Bari, Italy
Totaro Vincenzo	Polytechnic University of Bari, Italy
Tran Manh Hung	University of Danang, Vietnam
Tripathi Ashish	MNNIT Allahabad, India
Tripp Barba Carolina	Universidad Autónoma de Sinaloa, Mexico
Tut Zohra Fatema	University of Calgary, Canada
Upadhyay Ashish	Indian Institute of Public Health-Gandhinagar, India
Vallverdu Jordi	Autonomous University of Barcelona, Spain
Valuev Ilya	Russian Academy of Sciences, Russia
Varela Leonilde	University of Minho, Portugal
Varela Tania	Universidade de Lisboa, Portugal
Vasconcelos Paulo	Queensland University, Brisbane, Australia
Vasyunin Dmitry	University of Amsterdam, The Netherlands
Vella Flavio	University of Rome, Italy
Vijaykumar Nandamudi	INPE, Brazil
Vidacs Laszlo	University of Szeged, Hungary
Viqueira José R.R.	Agricultural University of Athens, Greece
Vizzari Marco	University of Perugia, Italy
Vohra Varun	Japan Advanced Institute of Science and Technology (JAIST), Japan
Voit Nikolay	Ulyanovsk State Technical University Ulyanovsk, Russia
Walkowiak Krzysztof	Wroclaw University of Technology, Poland
Wallace Richard J.	University College Cork, Ireland
Waluyo Agustinus Borgy	Monash University, Melbourne, Australia
Wanderley Fernando	FCT/UNL, Portugal
Wei Hoo Chong	Motorola, USA
Yamashita Satoshi	National Research Institute for Child Health and Development, Tokyo, Japan
Yamauchi Toshihiro	Okayama University, Japan
Yao Fenghui	Tennessee State University, USA
Yeoum Sanggil	Sungkyunkwan University, South Korea
Zaza Claudio	University of Foggia, Italy
Zeile Peter	Technische Universität Kaiserslautern, Germany
Zenha-Rela Mario	University of Coimbra, Portugal
Zoppi Corrado	Università di Cagliari, Italy
Zullo Francesco	University of l'Aquila, Italy
Zunino Alejandro	Universidad Nacional del Centro, Argentina
Žemlička Michal	Univerzita Karlova, Czech Republic
Živković Ljiljana	University of Belgrade, Serbia

Sponsoring Organizations

ICCSA 2017 would not have been possible without the tremendous support of many organizations and institutions, for which all organizers and participants of ICCSA 2017 express their sincere gratitude:

University of Trieste, Trieste, Italy
(http://www.units.it/)

University of Perugia, Italy
(http://www.unipg.it)

University of Basilicata, Italy
(http://www.unibas.it)

Monash University, Australia
(http://monash.edu)

Kyushu Sangyo University, Japan
(www.kyusan-u.ac.jp)

Universidade do Minho
Escola de Engenharia

Universidade do Minho, Portugal
(http://www.uminho.pt)

Contents – Part IV

**Workshop on Interactively Presenting High-Quality Graphics
in Cooperation with Various Computing Tools (IPHQC 2017)**

Workshop on Geomatics and Remote Sensing Techniques for Resource Monitoring and Control (GRS-RMC 2017)

UAV-Borne Photogrammetric Survey as USAR Firefighter Teams Support

G. Caroti⑩, A. Piemonte$^{(\boxtimes)}$⑩, and Y. Pieracci

Dipartimento di Ingegneria Civile e Industriale – Sezione Vie,
Trasporti e Geomatica, Università di Pisa, Pisa, Italy
andrea.piemonte@unipi.it

Abstract. Fire Departments feature specialized teams for Urban Search And Rescue (USAR) activities, operating in case of disasters and in collapse contexts, where the actual situation no longer coincides with any previous survey. In this context, current UAV-borne photogrammetry may offer very effective methods, enabling achievement of to-date knowledge of the status quo. Their effectiveness in these contexts is due to the ability of drones to operate in triple-D areas (Dull, Dusty, Dangerous) and to the remote sensing features inherent in photogrammetry.

This article presents an experimental project exploring the potential of this kind of survey. The test survey dataset was collected at the USAR training facility of the Fire Brigade of Pisa. In particular, the analysis of the team intervention procedures on the disaster area and the survey methods used to obtain a quick but geometrically consistent survey, are presented.

Keywords: 3D surveying · Structure from motion · UAV · Photogrammetry · Map updating · USAR · Firefighter

1 Introduction

In Italy, the occurrence of natural disasters prompts the activation of the National Civil Protection Service [1], in order to safeguard lives, property, settlements and environment from present and/or threatening danger and the related damages. Anyway, technical operations requiring immediate response, highly specialized skills and suitable equipment are provided by CNVVF ('Comando Nazionale dei Vigili del Fuoco', Italian for National Firefighters Corps) [2].

Upon definition of the disaster area, known as 'cratere' (Italian for 'crater'), a crater Commander is designated, setting the allocation of each base camp, seat of a COA ('Comando Operativo Avanzato', Italian for Advanced Operating Centre), and assigning to each COA its own territorial jurisdiction. The commander is also in charge of specialized units, such as helicopter operators, divers, dog units, surveyors, search teams etc.

The establishment of a COA reproduces at crater level the management and operation of a local Firefighters Centre (Fig. 1).

The CNVVF have recently developed a field support activity based on surveying techniques and use of GIS (Geographic Information System) software, known as

© Springer International Publishing AG 2017
O. Gervasi et al. (Eds.): ICCSA 2017, Part IV, LNCS 10407, pp. 3–15, 2017.
DOI: 10.1007/978-3-319-62401-3_1

TAS ('Topografia Applicata al Soccorso', Italian for Rescue-Applied Topography). This service joins map knowledge and emergency rescue, offering a decision support in complex scenarios, and plays a key role in the reporting phase, which provides mapping of the disaster scene by way of collected information [3].

It is an effective and efficient operational tool for optimal planning of rescue interventions and increasing operator safety.

In urban environments, TAS faces the problem of collecting information referring to red zones, i.e. highly dangerous areas for disaster-induced structural failures. Accessing red zones exposes any operator to high risks, which can be reduced to acceptable levels only with the utmost care in planning and logistics and in defining the subsequent time requirements.

In case of events requiring search and rescue of victims involved in collapses in urban environment, trapped under debris, UN-approved INSARAG guidelines, describing the response mode of SAR (Search and Rescue) teams, apply [4].

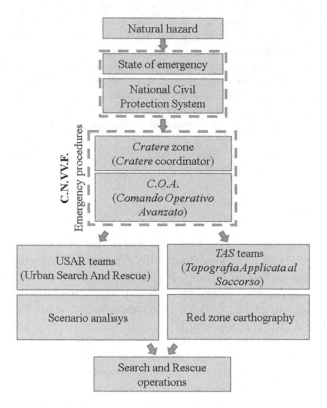

Fig. 1. Emergency procedures and cells flow chart.

Firefighters train teams specializing in urban environment collapse areas, called USAR (Urban Search and Rescue) [5–7].

These teams typically operate in scenarios where collapses and changes of the status quo can destroy or obliterate points previously used as direction references. Furthermore, disaster scenes typically undergo other changes due to further collapses or debris removal.

Assessment of these scenarios usually relies on visual recognition carried out by operators. Use of UAVs (Unmanned Aerial Vehicles) for video shooting of the disaster area in the last few years allowed for optimized recognition and reduced risk.

Compiling an up-to-date, large-scale map of the status quo would be extremely valuable [8, 9]. The present work contributes on this issue.

Thanks to the collaboration with the Pisa Headquarters of C.N.VV.F., the Authors have carried out some tests in order to assess an effective methodological approach aimed at attaining both speed and metric consistence in cartographic surveys

This paper presents some precision checks of models and maps achieved with the support of photogrammetry with UAV-borne imagery in emergency-like operating conditions.

2 Materials and Methods

Use of UAV-supported photogrammetry for large-scale cartography has been widely tested and applied in different contexts. In particular, the common approach to collecting and processing UAV-borne imagery has departed from classic photogrammetry and provides exploitation of modern techniques such as Structure from Motion (SfM) and Multi-View Stereo (MVS) [10, 11], which have expanded fields of use of image-based 3D surveys thanks to greater flexibility in image acquisition geometry, camera choice and GCP (Ground Control Point) layout [12, 13]. Besides, software houses have marketed several products able to process images and generate 3D (point clouds/mesh models, either textured or plain) and 2D (maps, orthophotographs) outputs [14].

Use of UAV-borne photogrammetry in emergency has long been the object of several researches [15–19].

Despite the availability of these tools, however, CNVVF's TAS units have not yet opted for their use in emergency operations, using UAVs just as means for shooting qualitative inspection videos. Several considerations stand behind this situation. Emergency operators promote the use of tools allowing maximum benefit for knowledge gain and minimum logistics complications. In these respects, UAV-supported photogrammetry performance is still unsatisfactory.

The present research, therefore, has tested a methodology allowing reduction of operating time for data collecting and processing, while keeping logistic requirements as low as possible.

In addition to internal orientation parameters, photogrammetric methods require to know external orientation parameters for each image. The two main methods for providing external orientation parameters are direct georeferencing and indirect georeferencing. The latter exploits airborne triangulation and requires an adequate amount of Ground Control Points (GCPs) well distributed across the photogrammetric block [20, 21].

Direct georeferencing provides that the UAV be fitted with GNNS (Global Navigation Satellite System) and IMU (Inertial Measurement Unit) sensors, whose measures, upon real-time integration, directly provide external orientation parameters. This methodology does not require contact with the survey area, a major advantage in unsafe areas. On the other hand, its accuracy depends on the quality of on-board sensors, and high-performance devices are as yet very expensive.

The current research did not involve this kind of systems, opting instead for an UAV fitted with only autopilot positioning sensors, and therefore unusable for direct georeferencing purposes. Several tests have been carried out in order to assess the influence of number and layout of GCPs on the accuracy of the 3D model and the orthophotograph of the survey area.

More specifically, this paper focuses on the comparison of results obtained with different configurations as regards GCP layout and flight parameters.

2.1   Test Area

Proposed survey methodologies have been checked by tests carried out at the USAR training facility at the Pisa CNVVF Headquarters. This covers about 1300 m^2 and reproduces the effects of an earthquake such as total or partial building collapse, including a debris-covered red zone (about 700 m^2) and a safe zone suitable for establishment of a COA (Fig. 2). In view of minimizing the logistic impact, TAS operators are admitted only to the safe zone; physical access to the red zone is forbidden.

Fig. 2. Test area

2.2   UAV and Photogrammetric System

Use of UAVs for specialized operations must comply with national regulations. Italy currently enforces ENAC (Ente Nazionale Aviazione Civile – National Body for Civil Aviation) Regulation of December 2016 [22]. This defines several restraints to UAV use in areas labelled as 'critical', i.e. with urban conglomerations, assemblages or relevant infrastructures. Use of UAVs in urban contexts for ordinary surveying purposes may not always be possible, involving lengthy bureaucratic actions and logistic complexity potentially beyond economic feasibility.

Use of these systems in emergency operations overcomes most of these restraints and CNVVF can operate in derogation to the rules. However, since research test work is not comparable to actual emergency, the Authors have opted to use an UAV whose specifications are not subjected to ENAC regulations. The UAV chosen for the survey is MicroGeo's BeeCopter quad-rotor, whose features include a miniAPM 3drobotics autopilot, timed shooting through a stripped-down GoPro Hero Black 4 with a 12 Megapixels 1/2.3″ CCD sensor and a modified f = 5.4 lens, removable storage, overall dimensions of 160 × 160 × 100 mm and maximum weight = 248 g.

The undeniable advantage of escaping ENAC regulations and the subsequent ability to operate in otherwise critical zones is, however, counterbalanced by extreme wind sensitivity and lack of a stabilized gimbal.

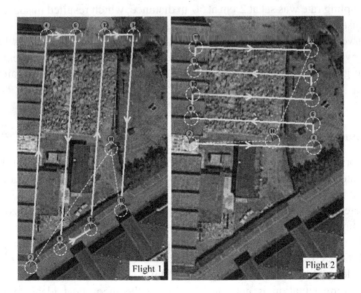

Fig. 3. Flight plans

As widely reported in literature, performing additional photogrammetric shootings at different levels and along orthogonal directions (Fig. 3) allows for better assessment of internal and external camera orientation parameters [21].

For this reason, the first flight took place at flight level = 30 m (Ground Sampling Distance – GSD = 9 mm) with nadiral shooting axis, and a second flight took place at flight level = 20 m (GSD = 6 mm) with 45° shooting axis. Flight plans provided theoretical overlap = 80%.

It is worth noting that performing additional flights does not affect emergency logistics, because operators can stay within the safe zone, remotely monitoring flights, and multi-rotor type UAVs do not need dedicated structures for take-off and landing.

2.3   Benchmark Surveys

As the present research aims at methodology assessment as regards both timing and attainable accuracy, a preliminary survey of the test area has been carried out in order to provide a reference for subsequent checks.

A total of 11 points have been signalized across the test area by means of dedicated targets affixed to the ground; their 3D coordinates have been measured via real-time differential GPS survey, based upon LeicaGeosystems' ItalPos network. Some of the points have been used as Ground Control Points (GCPs) and others as Control Points (CPs).

A laser scanning survey has also been carried out by means of a Leica ScanStation C10 in order to perform checks on surfaces, rather than just for discrete points.

The sampling rate was set at 2 cm at 50 m distance, which resulted in sub-centimeter sampling distance across the entire point cloud.

The survey of the object area required 5 stations. All the point clouds have been registered by means of common targets and cloud-constrain for subsequent refining. Finally, the global point cloud has been georeferenced by means of the available GPS points.

2.4   Ground Control Point and Images Processing Methods

While performing additional flights does not entail logistic complications for emergency operators, coordinate fixing requires operators to actually place sighting targets over ground points.

It is therefore obvious that, while ground placement of targets in safe zones poses no issues, any access to red zones must be avoided unless strictly necessary.

For this reason, a preliminary plan draft provided materialization of a minimum number of GCPs (#200, 201 and 202), placed exclusively in the safe zone, so to provide model scaling and referencing (Fig. 4 left).

The resulting situation is not consistent with the theoretical ideal layout for an efficient model constraining, as point distribution is uneven and decentralized.

Remaining points are not used as constraints and act as model-independent CPs.

Although processing was carried out using different configurations, this paper reports only those allowing to assess the influence of the use of point 106 as additional GCP and of concurrent vs. sequential processing of images collected in both flights.

Fig. 4. GCPs and CPs map

Table 1 shows the different configurations, detailing points acting as GCP and CP, as well as the number of flights used for image collection.

Table 1. Survey and processing cases

	Flight	GCPs	CPs
Case 1	1	200, 201, 202	101, 102, 103, 104, 105, 106, 107, 108
Case 3	1	200, 201, 202, 106	101, 102, 103, 104, 105, 107, 108
Case 6	1 + 2	200, 201, 202	101, 102, 103, 104, 105, 106, 107, 108
Case 7	1 + 2	200, 201, 202, 106	101, 102, 103, 104, 105, 107, 108

For each photogrammetric processing the constraints (in both 3 GCPs and 4 GCPs cases), due to their limited number and the presence on few images, have been used only for model rototranslation with scale factor but not for the optimization of computation of camera orientation parameters.

Besides, in the view of quick modelling, no tie points have been manually added to the images and computation of orientation parameters is based on software-detected tie points only.

3   Results and Discussion

Upon generation of models in the different cases, horizontal and vertical deviation at CPs were measured. Standard deviation, mean, and RMSE were subsequently derived by distribution of deviation.

The first row in Table 2 refers to "Case 1" configuration, which provides use of images acquired in flight 1 only for processing and the use of a minimum number of GCPs. It is apparent that the use of only three GCPs positioned in the secure zone entails errors ranging from several centimetres (plan) to several tens of centimetres (height).

The configuration referred to as "Case 3" shows how the addition of just a single GCP (106) diametrically opposite to the safe zone with respect to the survey area, reduces the planimetric error to about 1 cm and considerably cuts down the height error. The addition of such a point, however, could lead to logistic complications since its location may not be safely accessible to survey GCP coordinates.

As mentioned in Sect. 2.2, an additional image acquisition flight was carried out at a different flight level and in orthogonal direction with respect to the first one, aiming to maintain the minimum number of GCPs and use the images of both flights.

The latter working hypothesis was tested in the configuration referred to as "Case 6", reporting accuracy levels comparable to those of the "Case 3". These results suggest that the benefits deriving by the addition of GCP 106 are similar to those given by providing an additional flight. In case of emergency interventions with inaccessible areas, the addition of a flight is definitely the more favourable solution as regards logistics.

Table 2. Standard deviation and RMSE in the different configurations

	σ [m]			RMSE [m]		
	3D	XY	Z	3D	XY	Z
Case 1 3 GCPs	0.304	0.029	0.304	0.962	0.047	0.961
Case 3 4 GCPs	0.063	0.006	0.067	0.149	0.017	0.149
Case 6 3 GCPs	0.039	0.025	0.039	0.197	0.082	0.180
Case 7 4 GCPs	0.020	0.011	0.024	0.055	0.017	0.052

In the last tested configuration, named "Case 7", 2 flights were performed and point #106 was used as GCP. As expected, this configuration gave the best accuracy in both planimetry (RMSE = 1.7 cm) and height (RMSE = 5.2 cm) components.

In addition to the deviation checks on the CPs, some portions of photogrammetric model surface were also compared against the laser scanning-derived one.

These surfaces were selected in continuous, gap-free regions on both the laser and photogrammetric models by the same cutting polylines (Fig. 5 left). Once isolated, the surfaces were compared with Multiscale Cloud Model to Model Comparison (M3C2) algorithms. Figure 5 shows the RMSE values in cases 3, 6 and 7 as a function of the distance between safe zone and surface considered for the comparison, and then by 3 GCPs (200, 201, 202).

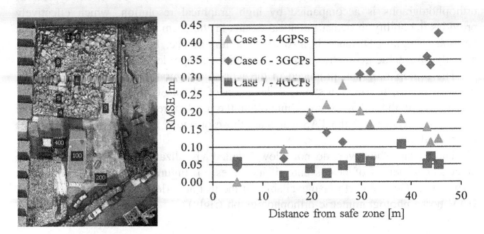

Fig. 5. Layout of point cloud comparison areas (left) and RMSE plotted as a function of distance from safe zone (right).

The checks carried out on the surfaces confirm the results obtained with the checks on individual CPs. Analysis of the RMSE value as function of the distance from the safe zone underlines that where the constraints are limited to the safe zone, errors increase with the distance. Instead, when using single-flight images and the additional 106 GCP, the error is greatest in the area equidistant from the latter and the safe zone, while in "Case 7" the error is low and constant throughout the surveyed area. This is an expected outcome, in part due to the precision of the methodology used for computation of GCPs coordinates. The real-time differential GPS is a very quick technique, which allows the determination of the coordinates in an absolute reference system, but has a horizontal theoretical accuracy $\approx$ 1–2 cm and a vertical theoretical accuracy $\approx$ 2–3 cm.

Figure 6 shows that a 2 cm relative vertical error between the two GCPs 201 and 202, placed at a distance of about 5 m from each other, entails a 20 cm error at 50 m distance from these GCPs.

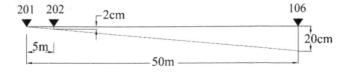

Fig. 6. Theoretical vertical error at 50 m from GCPs

As a further consideration, RMSE is an absolute error indicator, while the standard deviation is rather a relative error index.

In models and orthophotographs for USAR team intervention management, the relative accuracy has a greater importance. It is more important to be able to perform a measurement of a collapsed element (e.g. beam length, section, …) rather than placing it accurately in an absolute reference system.

The good relative accuracy, and therefore low standard deviation, typical of orthophotographs is accompanied by high graphical resolution, which effectively provides the ability to detect graphical details in the 1 cm range. For this reason, the Ground Sampling Distance is also of great importance, because, regardless of the actually obtainable geometric accuracy, it defines image detail level.

The orthophotograph produced in the worst configuration (Case 1 - 3GCPs + 1 imaging flight), featuring a standard deviation of about 30 cm, presents a graphical detail level of about 0.5–1.0 cm. Quite often, the most current orthophotographs of the crater zone available to the TAS teams are those provided by the well-known Google Earth platform.

These maps, however, do not allow detailed visualization of medium-small size objects (e.g. details of beams and pillars, pipes…). Figure 7 displays a comparison between the Google Earth map available for the test area (left) and an extract from the UAV-borne photogrammetric orthophotograph (right).

Fig. 7. Graphical resolution of Google Earth map (left) and Orthophotograph (right).

A final aspect considered in tests is the time required, in this operating context, to obtain a useful cartographic product, starting from the arrival of the survey team on the disaster scene. Table 3 lists survey, processing and map drawing phases with the time required for their execution.

The evidence is that time requirements to obtain an orthophotograph at 1:100 scale, ready for use in GIS software for intervention planning purposes, are in the range of 90 min.

Table 3. Required time in processing steps

Step	Required time [min]
Flight planning and image acquisition	30
Orientation parameters estimation	21
Dense cloud processing	24
Mesh processing	5
Texture processing	3
KMZ orthophotograph exporting	1
TIF orthophotograph exporting	2

4   Conclusions

The research highlighted the need for the USAR teams to have up-to-date maps of the state of the intervention area. Generation of these maps require methodologies granting the best results with the least logistics impact. In this sense, UAV-borne photogrammetry is a methodology that allows safe operation.

Photogrammetry requires the survey of the Ground Control Points, that in a theoretical configuration should be homogeneously distributed across the survey area. However, it has been shown that it is possible to operate only by surveying a minimum number of GCPs, positioned in the safe area, and providing flights at different levels for acquisition of additional images, obtaining the same final accuracy.

It was shown that the obtainable accuracy levels are in line with the needs of a large scale (approximately 1:100) and that the graphical resolution of the produced orthophotograph can also display smaller details than the obtainable accuracy. Finally, it was determined that the time required to produce a ready-to-use map is about 90'.

Acknowledgments. The authors would like to thank the Pisa CNVVF Provincial Command for the test area availability and for help in defining the operational phases of emergency management and the needs of USAR and TAS teams. Furthermore, the authors would like to thank Microgeo Srl for carrying out the photogrammetric survey by means of the BeeCopter multirotor and for granting use of its license for 3DZephir photogrammetric processing software.

References

1. Legge 24 Febbraio1992 n. 225: Istituzione del Servizio Nazionale della Protezione Civile (1992)
2. D.Lgs. 8 marzo 2006 n. 139: Ordinamento del Corpo nazionale dei vigili del fuoco (2006)
3. Cuzzocrea, F.P: Tecniche topografiche applicate al soccorso. GEOmedia n. 03 (2014)
4. Mazzotta, G., Romano, G.: INSARAG: International search and rescue advisory group - modalità operative in situazioni di crisi a seguito di disastri naturali - similitudini ed aspetti innovativi rispetto alle procedure adottate dal corpo nazionale dei vigili del fuoco (2011)
5. Circolare EM 05/2013: Qualificazione, composizione e dotazioni dei team USAR (2013)

6. Circolare EM-01/2011: Riorganizzazione delle Colonne Mobili Regionali e del dispositivo di mobilitazione per grande calamità (2011)
7. Corpo Nazionale dei Vigili del Fuoco: Sistema di Gestione Operativa L-USAR. Versione 1.0, settembre 2014
8. Caroti, G., Piemonte, A., Nespoli, R.: UAV-Borne photogrammetry: a low cost 3D surveying methodology for cartographic update. In: Proceedings of the International Conference on Advances in Sustainable Construction Materials & Civil Engineering Systems (ASCMCES-17), Sharjah, United Arab Emirates, MATEC Web of Conferences (2017)
9. Cramer, M., Bovet, S., Gültlinger, M., Honkavaara, E., McGill, A., Rijsdijk, M., Tabor, M., Tournadre, V.: On the use of RPAS in national mapping—the EuroSDR point of view. In: International Archives of the Photogrammetry, Remote Sensing and Spatial Information Sciences, vol. XL-1/W2, pp. 93–99 (2013)
10. Triggs, B., McLauchlan, P.F., Hartley, R.I., Fitzgibbon, A.W.: Bundle adjustment — a modern synthesis. In: Triggs, B., Zisserman, A., Szeliski, R. (eds.) IWVA 1999. LNCS, vol. 1883, pp. 298–372. Springer, Heidelberg (2000). doi:10.1007/3-540-44480-7_21
11. Barazzetti, L., Forlani, G., Remondino, F., Roncella, R., Scaioni, M.: Experiences and achievements in automated image sequence orientation for close-range photogrammetric projects. In: Proceedings SPIE 8085, Videometrics, Range Imaging, and Applications XI, 80850F, 23 May 2011, Munich (2011)
12. Nex, F., Remondino, F.: UAV for 3D mapping applications: a review. Appl. Geomatics 6(1), 1–15 (2014). doi:10.1007/s12518-013-0120-x
13. Caroti, G., Zaragoza, I.M.E., Piemonte, A.: Accuracy assessment in structure from motion 3D reconstruction from UAV-born images: the influence of the data processing methods. Int. Arch. Photogramm. Remote Sens. Spat. Inf. Sci. - ISPRS Arch. 40(1W4), 103–109 (2015). doi:10.5194/isprsarchives-XL-1-W4-103-2015
14. Remondino, F., Pizzo, S., Kersten, T.P., Troisi, S.: Low-cost and open-source solutions for automated image orientation – a critical overview. In: Ioannides, M., Fritsch, D., Leissner, J., Davies, R., Remondino, F., Caffo, R. (eds.) EuroMed 2012. LNCS, vol. 7616, pp. 40–54. Springer, Heidelberg (2012). doi:10.1007/978-3-642-34234-9_5
15. Huang, H., Long, J., Yi, W., Yi, Q., Zhang, G., Lei, B.: Method and application of using unmanned aerial vehicle for emergency investigation of single geo-hazard. Nat. Hazards Earth Syst. Sci. Discuss. (2017). doi:10.5194/nhess-2017-44
16. Verykokou, S., Doulamis, A., Athanasiou, G., Ioannidis, C., Amditis, A.: UAV-based 3D modelling of disaster scenes for urban search and rescue. In: Proceedings of IST 2016 - 2016 IEEE International Conference on Imaging Systems and Techniques, 7 November 2016, Article number 7738206, pp. 106–111 (2016). doi:10.1109/IST.2016.7738206
17. Dominici, D., Alicandro, M., Massimi, V.: UAV photogrammetry in the post-earthquake scenario: case studies in L'Aquila. Geomatics Nat. Hazards Risk (2016). doi:10.1080/19475705.2016.1176605
18. Gomez, C., Purdie, H.: UAV- based photogrammetry and geocomputing for hazards and disaster risk monitoring – a review. Geoenviron. Disasters 3, 23 (2016). doi:10.1186/s40677-016-0060-y
19. Boccardo, P., Chiabrando, F., Dutto, F., Tonolo, F.G., Lingua, A.: UAV Deployment exercise for mapping purposes: evaluation of emergency response applications. Sensors 15, 15717–15737 (2015). doi:10.3390/s150715717

20. Cramer, M.: On the use of direct georeferencing in airborne photogrammetry. In: Proceedings of the 3rd International Symposium on Mobile Mapping Technology, Cairo (2001)
21. Benassi, F., Dall'Asta, E., Diotri, F., Gianfranco, F., Morra di Cella, U., Roncella, R., Santise, M.: Testing accuracy and repeatability of UAV blocks oriented with GNSS-supported aerial triangulation. Remote Sens. **9**, 172 (2017). doi:10.3390/rs9020172
22. ENAC - Ente Nazionale Aviazione Civile: Mezzi aerei a pilotaggio remoto. Emendamento 2 Regolamento, 22 dicembre 2016

Calibration of the CLAIR Model by Using Landsat 8 Surface Reflectance Higher-Level Data and MODIS Leaf Area Index Products

Giuseppe Peschechera, Antonio Novelli[✉][iD], Grazia Caradonna[iD], and Umberto Fratino[iD]

Politecnico di Bari, via Orabona 7, 70125 Bari, Italy
peschechera.g@gmail.com,
{antonio.novelli,grazia.caradonna,umberto.fratino}@poliba.it

Abstract. This study proposes a method for the calibration of the semi-empirical CLAIR model, a simplified reflectance model used to estimate Leaf Area Index (LAI) from optical data. The procedure can be applied in case of lacking of both LAI field measurements and surface reflectance data by exploiting free of charge data as the novel high level Landsat 8 Operational Land Imager Surface Reflectance (OLISR) product and the MODIS LAI (MCD15A3H level 4 product). This last dataset was used as LAI reference within an iterative procedure based on the resampling, at the MODIS pixel size, of LAI estimated from OLISR data. The procedure generated LAI information consistent with the MCD15A3H LAI estimation. Lastly, the method was tested and statistically assessed in a territory characterized by an extremely heterogeneous and fragmented landscape (irrigation district "Sinistra Ofanto") located in the Apulia Region (Italy).

Keywords: Leaf Area Index · CLAIR model · Landsat 8 surface reflectance higher-level data · MCD15A3H

1 Introduction

Leaf Area Index (LAI) is defined as the one half of the total leaf area per unit ground area [1] and is a key parameter implemented in a large variety of climate, ecological and agricultural applications [2]. In particular, LAI is used as input parameter in many biophysical models for calculating vegetation parameters as evapotranspiration (e.g. [3,4]) and net primary production (e.g. [5]).

Direct measurements of LAI over large areas require continuous updates and can be extremely time-consuming and not cost-effective owing to its large spatial and temporal variability [6]. This is especially true over heterogeneous landscapes [7] in which the analysis of spatial/temporal data is required [8]. In these cases, passive remotely sensed observations covering the visible to shortwave infrared (SWIR) spectral region are a valid alternative to provide a rapid and non-destructive LAI estimation [9]. Several algorithms were developed during

© Springer International Publishing AG 2017
O. Gervasi et al. (Eds.): ICCSA 2017, Part IV, LNCS 10407, pp. 16–29, 2017.
DOI: 10.1007/978-3-319-62401-3_2

the past decades to estimate LAI from remote sensing. The procedures can be divided in four groups [10]: parametric regressions, non-parametric regressions, physical based approaches and hybrid methods. Parametric methods (e.g. [11]) assume an explicit relationship between LAI and spectral observations (typically a vegetation index) through a fitting function built by relying on statistical or physical knowledge of the variable and the spectral response. Among parametric methods, in this study was selected the semi-empirical CLAIR model (Clevers leaf area index by reflectance) [12]. The model estimates LAI of green canopy (vegetative stage) by means of an empirical logarithmic relationship of the Weighted Difference Vegetation Index (WDVI) [13]. Due to the WDVI, the model can compensate the errors related to soil background reflectance contribute [14].

CLAIR model LAI estimation requires the soil-line slope value to calculate the WVDI and to calibrate its own parameters: the asymptotic value of WDVI ($WDVI_\infty$) and the extinction and scattering coefficient (α). Although these parameters have a physical nature, they are estimated empirically from a set of LAI field measures [9, 15–17]. However, this practice requires special attention since field-measured and remote sensing data are different both in spatial resolution and accuracy [18, 19]. In case of lacking LAI and surface reflectance field measurements, the retrieval of model parameters could be performed collecting previous results (e.g. . [20–22]). This solution is hardly applicable because of a very great number of soil and crop type combinations with respect to the number of produced works. Nevertheless, for its easy conception, the CLAIR model is still utilized in many studies (e.g. [23–26]).

Image-based estimation of the model parameters can be useful to extend the applications of the CLAIR model, especially lacking *in situ* measurements. Literature has already shown that the soil-line slope can be retrieved from surface reflectance images [27] and used to estimate vegetation biophysical parameters or soil surface status [28]. With regard to the $WDVI_\infty$, image-based solutions assume it as the maximum WDVI value for vegetated areas retrieved within an image (e.g. [9, 16, 29, 30]). In this way, it is possible to estimate LAI in all the images. To filter out outliers, Akdim et al. [31] proposed $WDVI_\infty$ estimation from WDVI time series, as a linear combination of their mean value and the standard deviation retrieved in each image.

The extinction coefficient requires crop specific calibration [9] because it describes the canopy architecture and depends on the crop type and the corresponding Leaf Angle Distribution (LAD) value. Vuolo et al. [16] tested a procedure to derive site-specific values of α and $WDVI_\infty$ for two study areas in Italy and Austria. However, this solution partially solved the problem because each new test site needs field LAI measurements to infer α. Once calibrated, the model could be applied to the newly images without the need of new field measurements.

The main goal of this work is to define a procedure for the evaluation of the two parameters of CLAIR model using only surface reflectance and LAI retrieved from satellite data. The method exploits only free of charge data. In this way is possible to estimate LAI without expensive *in situ* measurements and satellite data acquisition.

For this purpose, Landsat 8 Operational Land Imager Surface Reflectance (OLISR) sensor data and the four days composite MODIS (Moderate Resolution Imaging Spectroradiometer) LAI products (MCD15A3H) were selected. In particular, Landsat 8 OLI datasets were used to implement the CLAIR model by applying different algorithms to perform the atmospheric correction (e.g. [15, 31, 32].

The proposed procedure generates LAI information consistent with the MODIS LAI product and characterized by a higher resolution. The featured geometric resolution is the same of the surface reflectance data used as input in the CLAIR model. The procedure does not require the knowledge of the crop species present in the considered area. In fact, by taking in account the mixture of all crop types, the estimated parameters can be considered site specific (and not crop specific). Lastly, the procedure was tested and statistically assessed in a study area located in the Apulia Region (Italy) and characterized by an extremely heterogeneous and fragmented landscape.

2 Study Area and Data

The study area (Fig. 1) falls within the Italian irrigation district "Sinistra Ofanto", a large cultivated area, characterized by an extremely heterogeneous landscape with the presence of vineyards, olive trees, orchards and cereals. The district is situated in the North of the Apulian Region and is delimited by the Ofanto river at the southeast and characterized by a typical Mediterranean climate with strong seasonal and inter-annual variability. The climate is semi-arid and the irrigation system (managed by the Consortium Capitanata) implements both reservoir and groundwater as often happens in other semi-arid Mediterranean regions (e.g. [33,34]). For this study Landsat 8 OLISR and MODIS LAI (MCD15A3H) product acquired in the 2013 crop year were used. Both datasets were retrieved from the U.S. Geological Survey (USGS) archives (https://earthexplorer.usgs.gov/). Landsat 8 OLISR data are developed for supporting land surface change studies. OLISR products include: Original Input Products (Level-1 data files, Quality Assessment Band file and metadata text file), Top of Atmosphere (TOA) Reflectance, Surface Reflectance (SR), Brightness Temperature products and Surface Reflectance-based Spectral Indices (such as NDVI, NDMI, NBR, SAVI, EVI). These data are obtained with the algorithm Landsat 8 Surface Reflectance Code (LaSRC). Although LaSRC is a new algorithm (that should be considered provisional), the first test carried out showed that the LaSRC OLISR product performed better than previous LEDAPS (Landsat Ecosystem Disturbance Adaptive Processing System) products [35]. This result was achieved by using the coastal aerosol band and auxiliary climate data from MODIS for the implementation of the radiative transfer model. OLISR products have inherited the properties of the previous Landsat 8 products: 30-meter spatial resolution with a 16-day temporal

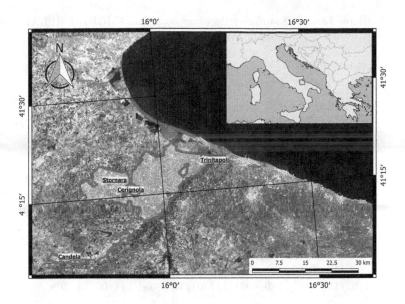

Fig. 1. The irrigation district "Sinistra Ofanto" (North of the Apulian Region Italy) as seen by a true color visualization of Landsat 8 (7 August 2013 - Reference System WGS 84).

resolution [36]. Further details related to the Landsat 8 OLISR product (e.g. data type, data range, correction coefficients, etc.) can be found in the "Provisional Landsat 8 surface reflectance code (LASRC)" (https://landsat.usgs.gov/landsat-surface-reflectance-high-level-data-products) product guide.

The site-specific CLAIR calibration was executed using the Cloud mask band (CFmask) and the surface reflectance Blue (Band 2), Green (Band 3), Red (Band 4) and Near Infrared (NIR - Band 5) bands. Moreover, the study area is included in two Landsat 8 frames, named by the notation Path-Row 189-031 and 188-031 of Landsat 8 Pre-Worldwide Reference System (WRS-2). The satellite acquisitions in these two frames are shifted by 7/9 days. For this reason, the temporal resolution of surface reflectance data for the study area is nearly doubled. In this study eleven Landsat 8 OLISR images, acquired from 05/19/2013 to 11/02/2013 without cloud contamination over the study area, were used. The complete scene list is reported in the Table 1.

The product MCD15A3H (level 4) is included in the latest version of MODIS LAI and Fraction of Photosynthetically Active Radiation (FPAR) products, Collection 6 (C6). It was derived from the combined use of Terra and Aqua satellite and generated with 500-meter spatial resolution and a temporal compositing period of 4 days. As remarked by Gao et al. using a four-day composite product can ensure a better temporal product, particularly during the period of rapid crop growth [2]. MCD15A3H data include 6 Science Dataset: LAI and FPAR with their standard deviation (LAI_500m, Fpar_500m, LaiStdDev_500m, FparStdDev_500m) and two quality assessment bands at the pixel level (FparLai_QC,

Table 1. Available Landsat 8 surface reflectance scenes and MCD15A3H LAI (M LAI) products over the study area for the 2013 crop year.

Landsat 8 OLISR			Prev. M LAI		Next M LAI	
Date	DOY	Path-Row	Date	DOY	Date	DOY
05/19/13	139	188 - 031	05/17/13	137	05/23/13	141
06/20/13	171	188 - 031	06/18/13	169	06/24/13	173
07/13/13	194	189 - 031	07/12/13	193	07/17/13	197
07/29/13	210	189 - 031	07/28/13	209	08/02/13	213
08/07/13	219	188 - 031	08/05/13	217	08/11/13	221
08/14/13	226	189 - 031	08/13/13	225	08/18/13	229
08/23/13	235	188 - 031	08/21/13	233	08/27/13	237
09/08/13	251	188 - 031	09/06/13	249	09/12/13	253
09/24/13	267	188 - 031	09/22/13	265	09/28/13	269
10/26/13	299	188 - 031	10/24/13	297	10/30/13	301
11/02/13	306	189 - 031	11/01/13	305	11/06/13	309

FparExtra_QC). The MODIS LAI algorithm consists of a main Look-Up-Table (LUT) based procedure. The LUT was generated using the 3D radiative transfer equation [37] and exploits the spectral information content of the MODIS red and NIR surface reflectance. When the LUT method fails, the algorithm utilizes the backup method based on empirical relationships between LAI and the Normalized Difference Vegetation Index (NDVI). Yang [38] demonstrated that the best quality is obtained from the main algorithm.

Among the datasets stored in the MCD15A3H product the following layers were used in this study: LAI (Lai_500m); Quality Control information band (FparLai_QC) that specifies the overall quality of the product (algorithm path and quality of the input data); Standard Deviation (LaiStdDev_500m) related to the uncertainty in the estimation of LAI. To consider LAI data close to the acquisition of the surface reflectance, for each Landsat surface reflectance data the previous and the successive MCD15A3H data were considered, as reported in Table 1.

3   Method

The semi-empirical CLAIR model (Eq. 1) is based on a simplified reflectance model that exploits an empirical logarithmic relationship between LAI and WDVI [13]:

$$LAI = -\left(\frac{1}{\alpha}\right) * \log\left(1 - \frac{WDVI}{WDVI_\infty}\right) \qquad (1)$$

WDVI is a vegetation index developed to consider the influence of soil background reflectance [14]. The WDVI (Eq. 2) is defined as a weighted difference between the measured NIR and Red reflectance (respectively ρ_{NIR} and ρ_{Red}) assuming as weighting factor the "soil-line slope" (a) defined (Eq. 3) as the ratio between NIR and red reflectance of bare soil ($\rho_{NIR,s}, \rho_{Red,s}$):

$$WDVI = \rho_{NIR} - (a * \rho_{Red}) \tag{2}$$

$$a = \frac{\rho_{NIR,s}}{\rho_{Red,s}} \tag{3}$$

In the next sections are described the image-based procedure proposed for the retrieval of the soil-line slope (a), necessary to calculate the WDVI, and the parameters of the model ($WDVI_\infty$ and α) for the selected study area.

3.1 Identification of the Soil-Line Slope (a) and Asymptotical Limiting Value of WDVI ($WDVI_\infty$)

The evaluation of the soil-line slope started from the selection of a Region Of Interest (ROI) corresponding to bare soil. This operation was performed for each surface reflectance image due to the variability of the land cover during the vegetative season. The selection was conducted by exploiting "natural color" (Red-Green-Blue) and "false color" (NIR-Red-Green) band combinations. In addition, an NDVI thresholding filter was applied. In this way the pixels wrongly interpreted as bare soil and with NDVI value major than 0.20 corresponding to shrub and grassland were eliminated from the ROI [39]. From each bare-soil ROIs, the scatter plot between Red and NIR surface reflectance was calculated: the value of soil-line slope, for the selected scene and accordingly to Eq. 3, was assumed equal to the angular coefficient of the fitting line of the scatter plot. For the CLAIR model, the soil-line slope of the study area does not depend from the soil water content and thus it was calculated as the mean value of all the retrieved ones.

As stated within the "Introduction" section, in image-based estimation the $WDVI_\infty$ is often equal to the maximum WDVI value found within the scene. In this way, LAI can be estimated since the argument of the logarithm in Eq. 1 results greater than zero. The respect of this condition is necessary to ensure future applications of the model to the newly images. For this reason, $WDVI_\infty$ was estimated by increasing of the 6% the greatest WDVI value retrieved among all the surface reflectance scenes. This assumption was a consequence of empirical and iterative tests and reduced the problem of LAI saturation when WDVI values approach $WDVI_\infty$.

3.2 Extinction Coefficient (α)

The calibration of the extinction requires a preliminary pre-processing phase of the MODIS LAI data to retrieve LAI values, with the best quality and the lowest uncertainty, close to the acquisition of the surface reflectance. In this phase, for each Landsat surface reflectance data, the previous and the successive MCD15A3H data were considered. The elaborations, proposed in this paper, were applied for each MODIS pixel of the study area, following the 3 steps:

- Selection of the pixels with overall good quality: LAI retrieved using the main algorithm and without index saturation and presence of significant clouds. This information was carried out by the layer Quality Control (FparLai_QC).
- Among the selected pixels, were selected the pixels with the minor uncertainty in the estimation of LAI. This selection was carried out using the Standard Deviation data (LaiStdDev_500m) and excluding pixels with ratio StdDev/LAI major than 0.25.
- Lastly, LAI data close to the acquisition of surface reflectance data were calculated as mean values, among the previous and the successive MODIS LAI data, and only for the pixels common for both the MCD15A3H scenes. In this way, a further quality selection of the data was performed. It was considered the mean value since surface reflectance data occurred in the middle of two MODIS acquisitions.

The procedure proposed for the calibration of the extinction coefficient (α) is based on a simple method, proposed by Gao et al. [2], to retrieve LAI from Landsat using MODIS LAI products as reference. They proposed two different solutions to match coarse-resolution MODIS LAI data: one is to first aggregate the Landsat surface reflectance (SR) to MODIS resolution and then compute LAI at that scale; another way is to compute LAI from Landsat data and then linearly aggregate these fine-scale LAI value to the MODIS resolution. This last solution was adopted in the proposed method in which for each MODIS pixel the Landsat LAI was aggregated following Eq. 4:

$$LAI_{MODIS} = \frac{\sum_{i=1}^{n} LAI_{Land,i}(\alpha)}{n} = \frac{\sum_{i=1}^{n} f(SR_{Land,i}(\alpha))}{n} \qquad (4)$$

Where f is the CLAIR model function (Eq. 1), i is the index associated with each Landsat pixel within a given MODIS pixel cell and n is the total number of Landsat pixels in the considered MODIS pixel cell.

The objective function (Eq. 5) of the iterative procedure is based on the difference between LAI MODIS and the LAI Landsat aggregate at the MODIS resolution, accordingly the previous equation. For each MODIS pixel (j), the objective function is shown in Eq. 5.

$$LAI_{diff,j}(\alpha) = LAI_{MODIS_{QC,i}} - \frac{\sum_{i=1}^{n} LAI_{Land,i}(\alpha, WDVI_{\infty}, WDVI_i)}{n} \qquad (5)$$

For the Landsat pixels with WDVI values negative, it was assumed LAI ($LAI_{Land,j}$) equal to 0 because in these cases the LAI retrieved with the CLAIR model is negative and therefor without physical meaning. The possible range of α values was extended from 0.10 to 0.80 with steps of calculation of 0.025.

The range of α values was selected by analyzing previous ones retrieved in literature and estimated by means of regression analysis between computed LAI and field LAI measurements. These results are synthetically reported in Table 2.

In this case, the selected test range was greater than the previous ones to extend the investigations with respect to similar studies. For each scene was selected the value of the α parameter that determines the minor Mean Absolute

Table 2. Soil-line slope, maximum WDVI and extinction coefficient for the CLAIR model retrieved in literature. Parameters were estimated by using field measurements of LAI and surface reflectance.

Reference	Soil-line slope (a)	$WDVI_\infty$	Extinction coefficient (α)
Vannino et al. [32]	-	0.55	0.39 (0.34–0.70)
Akdim et al. [31]	1.02–1.25	0.40–0.51	0.37
Vuolo et al. [16]	1.47 (1.41–1.64)	0.60 (0.57–0.61)	0.34
	1.35 (1.24–1.42)	0.52 (0.47–0.59)	0.35
Richter et al. [9]	1.2	0.50	0.8
Minacapilli et al. [25]	-	0.57	0.225 (0.120–0.515)
Vuolo et al. [24]	0.90–1.10	0.64–0.68	0.40 0.47
DUrso et al. [40]	0.97–1.16	0.51 (0.45–0.54)	0.42 (0.34–0.54)
Clevers et al. [23]	-	0.579 0.686	0.25–0.53

Difference (MAD (6)) computed between α Landsat retrievals, resampled at the MODIS resolution, and MODIS LAI products. MAD was calculated over the MODIS grid.

$$MAD = \frac{\sum_{j=1}^{m} LAI_{diff,j}(\alpha)}{m} \tag{6}$$

where m is the total number of MODIS pixels used for the calibration procedure.

Lastly, the α value (valid for the whole crop season) was calculated as the average value of the extinction coefficients retrieved among all the surface reflectance scenes.

4   Results and Discussion

The CLAIR model parameters for each image were retrieved following the procedure described in the last sections. Table 3 resumes the results of the calibration.

The soil-line slope values retrieved during the season were between 1.22 and 1.38 with an average value of 1.31. This range of values results in line with previous similar scientific studies (Table 3).

With the computed soil-line slope value, it was possible to calculate the WDVI for the study area and for each image. This operation was carried out both using the mean seasonal soil-slope (a_{mean}, see Table 3) and the image specific soil-slope values (a_i, see Table 3) with the purpose to estimate the difference in the maximum WDVI retrieved. The differences were not significant since in both the cases the maximum WDVI retrieved ($WDVI_{MAX}$), within the study area, was equal to 0.61. This result is in line with the values retrieved in literature as reported in Table 2. Vanino et al. [32], retrieved WDVI value of 0.55 for a vineyard situated within the irrigation district Sinistra Ofanto. However, this value was crop specific and was calculated to create a correspondence of pixels with maximum vegetation cover. In order to ensure future applications of the

Table 3. Soil-line slope, maximum WDVI and extinction coefficient values retrieved for each satellite image in the study area using the proposed image-based method. For each scene, the maximum WDVI was retrieved both using the corresponding soil-line slope ($f(a_i)$) and the seasonal mean soil-line slope value ($f(a_{mean})$).

Soil-line slope		WDVI$_{MAX}$		Extinction coefficient (α)				
n. pixel				n. pixel		WDVI$_\infty = 0.61$		WDVI$_\infty = 0.65$
ROI	a_i	$f(a_{mean})$	$f(a_i)$	LAI reference	α	MAD	α	MAD
267	1.22	0.44	0.45	967	0.33	0.18	0.31	0.18
477	1.40	0.61	0.61	1287	0.38	0.26	0.35	0.26
265	1.38	0.57	0.56	1096	0.35	0.30	0.32	0.29
269	1.29	0.51	0.51	1285	0.33	0.27	0.30	0.27
950	1.36	0.57	0.57	1299	0.37	0.26	0.34	0.26
770	1.34	0.55	0.55	1258	0.34	0.26	0.32	0.26
1282	1.28	0.54	0.55	1177	0.37	0.24	0.34	0.24
1315	1.24	0.52	0.52	1172	0.34	0.24	0.32	0.23
3838	1.27	0.55	0.55	1269	0.37	0.23	0.34	0.22
1522	1.30	0.60	0.60	687	0.39	0.15	0.37	0.15
2012	1.37	0.56	0.56	426	0.37	0.12	0.35	0.12
mean	1.31				0.36	0.23	0.33	0.291
max		0.61	0.61					

model to the newly images, WDVI$_\infty$ was estimated by increasing of the 6% the greatest WDVI value retrieved among all the surface reflectance scenes. Therefore WDVI$_\infty$ was assumed equal to 0.65.

The calibration of the extinction coefficient, achieved adopting the proposed iterative procedure, was executed after the soil-slope and the WDVI$_\infty$ retrieval. The results depicted that the calibrated CLAIR is able to produce LAI values consistent with MODIS data. The maximum MAD value retrieved along all the scenes was equal to 0.29 (Table 3). The MAD was close to the range of MODIS LAI accuracy reported in the Standard Deviation layer, being the possible MODIS LAI standard deviations errors variable from 0 to 1 for LAI values included in the range 0–4. The scatterplots between the LAI MODIS (reference) and the LAI Landsat (Fig. 2), shows that the model tends to underestimate LAI. This is more evident for higher LAI values (greater than 2).

In order to verify the effects of the hypothesis adopted for the estimation of WDVI$_\infty$, the calibration procedure was iterated also with WDVI$_\infty$ equal to the mean value of WDVI$_{MAX}$ (0.61). In both cases the estimated extinction coefficient values are included in the range value found in literature (Table 2). It is important to underline that an increment of the 6% of the WDVI$_\infty$ value corresponds, for each scene, to a mean reduction of the 8% of the α values. The overall MAD values retrieved were very similar for the two parameter sets.

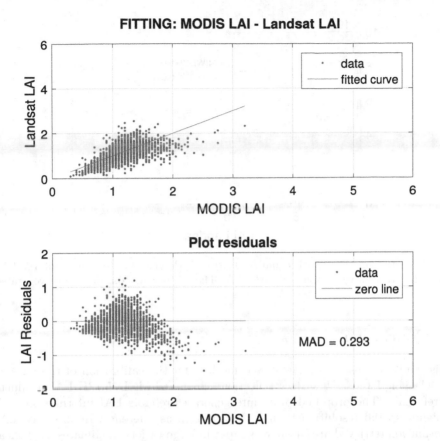

Fig. 2. Scatter plot between LAI MODIS and LAI Landsat retrieved using the CLAIR model and aggregated to the MODIS pixel resolution for the surface reflectance acquisition of the 07/13/2013 (DOY 194).

It globally ranges from 0.12 and 0.30 with a mean value of 0.23. The MAD results, between Landsat retrievals and MODIS LAI products, are in lines with the ones showed by Gao et al. [2]. They found MAD values in the range 0.07–0.80 for the High-Quality MODIS LAI pixels used as training sample.

Moreover, for each scene was analyzed the distribution of LAI values retrieved using the two sets of parameters. Figure 3 shows the histogram related to the scene with the highest WDVI value found (0.61). This condition was selected since it highlights LAI saturation problems. The histograms show that by adopting a $WDVI_\infty$ values major than the maximum one, the distribution of LAI remains the same whereas the differences, in terms of MAD, are non-significant. The most important consequence is that the maximum LAI value retrieved within the image ranges from 20.79 to 8.42. However, this occurs for a very little number of saturated pixels. In this way is possible t o reduce LAI saturation problems and further extend the future application of the model for the newly images.

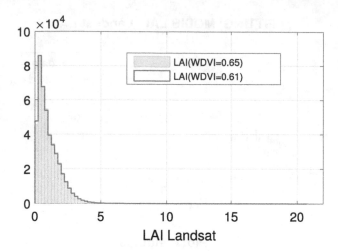

Fig. 3. Histogram (bin width equal to 0.25) of LAI related to the maximum WDVI values for the entire season (06/20/2013). The histogram considers only vegetated areas.

5 Conclusion

This study proposes an image-based method for the calibration of the CLAIR model using Landsat 8 surface reflectance data and MCD15A3H LAI products as reference. The proposed procedure generates reliable LAI information with a higher spatial resolution than LAI data used as reference. In this way, LAI information retrieved are suitable as input in large variety of climates, ecological and agricultural applications (e.g. crop yield prediction, evapotranspiration estimation). The procedure can be applied in case of lacking both LAI and surface reflectance field measurements and moreover it is not required the knowledge of crops present in the investigated area. In fact, the estimated parameters of the model can be considered site specific (and not crop specific) because during the calibration procedure were considered the mixture of all crop types present in the selected area. For its characteristics, image-based calibration represents a valid solution to extend the field of application of the CLAIR model.

The method was tested and statistically assessed in a territory of the irrigation district Sinistra Ofanto (Apulia region - Italy). Despite the extremely heterogeneous and fragmented landscape of the study area, the obtained results depict that, once calibrated, the CLAIR model is able to produce results conform to the MODIS data. In fact, MAD values were close to the range of MODIS LAI retrieval accuracy over all the considered scenes. Furthermore, the proposed calibration procedure can be furtherly tested by using others surface reflectance (e.g. Sentinel products) and LAI datasets.

References

1. Chen, J.M., Black, T.: Defining leaf area index for non-flat leaves. Plant, Cell Environ. **15**(4), 421–429 (1992)
2. Gao, F., Anderson, M.C., Kustas, W.P., Wang, Y.: Simple method for retrieving leaf area index from landsat using modis leaf area index products as reference. J. Appl. Remote Sens. **6**(1), 063554–1 (2012)
3. Duchemin, B., Hadria, R., Erraki, S., Boulet, G., Maisongrande, P., Chehbouni, A., Escadafal, R., Ezzahar, J., Hoedjes, J., Kharrou, M., et al.: Monitoring wheat phenology and irrigation in central Morocco: on the use of relationships between evapotranspiration, crops coefficients, leaf area index and remotely-sensed vegetation indices. Agric. Water Manag. **79**(1), 1–27 (2006)
4. Anderson, M.C., Kustas, W.P., Norman, J.M., Hain, C.R., Mecikalski, J.R., Schultz, L., González-Dugo, M.P., Cammalleri, C., d'Urso, G., Pimstein, A., Gao, F.: Mapping daily evapotranspiration at field to continental scales using geostationary and polar orbiting satellite imagery. Hydrol. Earth Syst. Sci. **15**(1), 223–239 (2011)
5. Jégo, G., Pattey, E., Liu, J.: Using leaf area index, retrieved from optical imagery, in the stics crop model for predicting yield and biomass of field crops. Field Crops Res. **131**, 63–74 (2012)
6. Bréda, N.J.: Ground-based measurements of leaf area index: a review of methods, instruments and current controversies. J. Exp. Bot. **54**(392), 2403–2417 (2003)
7. Martinez, B., Cassiraga, E., Camacho, F., Garcia-Haro, J.: Geostatistics for mapping leaf area index over a cropland landscape: efficiency sampling assessment. Remote Sens. **2**(11), 2584–2606 (2010)
8. Tarantino, E., Figorito, B.: Extracting buildings from true color stereo aerial images using a decision making strategy. Remote Sens. **3**(8), 1553–1567 (2011)
9. Richter, K., Vuolob, F., D'Ursoa, G., Dini, L.: Evaluation of different methods for the retrieval of LAI using high resolution airborne data. In: Proceedings of SPIE, the International Society for Optical Engineering, Society of Photo-Optical Instrumentation Engineers, p. 67420E–1 (2007)
10. Verrelst, J., Rivera, J.P., Veroustraete, F., Muñoz-Marí, J., Clevers, J.G., Camps-Valls, G., Moreno, J.: Experimental sentinel-2 LAI estimation using parametric, non-parametric and physical retrieval methods-a comparison. ISPRS J. Photogramm. Remote Sens. **108**, 260–272 (2015)
11. Balacco, G., Figorito, B., Tarantino, E., Gioia, A., Iacobellis, V.: Space-time lai variability in Northern Puglia (Italy) from spot vgt data. Environ. Monit. Assess. **187**(7), 434 (2015)
12. Clevers, J.: Application of a weighted infrared-red vegetation index for estimating leaf area index by correcting for soil moisture. Remote Sens. Environ. **29**(1), 25–37 (1989)
13. Clevers, J.: The derivation of a simplified reflectance model for the estimation of leaf area index. Remote Sens. Environ. **25**(1), 53–69 (1988)
14. Baret, F., Jacquemoud, S., Hanocq, J.: The soil line concept in remote sensing. Remote Sens. Rev. **7**(1), 65–82 (1993)
15. Vanino, S., Nino, P., De Michele, C., Bolognesi, S.F., Pulighe, G.: Earth observation for improving irrigation water management: a case-study from Apulia region in Italy. Agric. Agric. Sci. Proc. **4**, 99–107 (2015)

16. Vuolo, F., Neugebauer, N., Bolognesi, S.F., Atzberger, C., D'Urso, G.: Estimation of leaf area index using Deimos-1 data: application and transferability of a semi-empirical relationship between two agricultural areas. Remote Sens. 5(3), 1274–1291 (2013)

17. Clevers, J.: Application of the WDVI in estimating LAI at the generative stage of barley. ISPRS J. Photogramm. Remote Sens. 46(1), 37–47 (1991)

18. Novelli, A., Tarantino, E., Fratino, U., Iacobellis, V., Romano, G., Gentile, F.: A data fusion algorithm based on the Kalman filter to estimate leaf area index evolution in durum wheat by using field measurements and modis surface reflectance data. Remote Sens. Lett. 7(5), 476–484 (2016)

19. Novelli, A.: A data fusion kalman filter algorithm to estimate leaf area index evolution by using Modis LAI and PROBA-V top of canopy synthesis data. In: Fourth International Conference on Remote Sensing and Geoinformation of the Environment. International Society for Optics and Photonics (2016). 968813

20. Clevers, J., Vonder, O., Jongschaap, R., Desprats, J.F., King, C., Prévot, L., Bruguier, N.: Using spot data for calibrating a wheat growth model under mediterranean conditions. Agronomie 22(6), 687–694 (2002)

21. Apollonio, C., Balacco, G., Novelli, A., Tarantino, E., Piccinni, A.F.: Land use change impact on flooding areas: the case study of Cervaro Basin (Italy). Sustainability 8(10), 996 (2016)

22. Novelli, A., Tarantino, E., Caradonna, G., Apollonio, C., Balacco, Gabriella, Piccinni, Ferruccio: Improving the ANN classification accuracy of landsat data through spectral indices and linear transformations (PCA and TCT) aimed at LU/LC monitoring of a river basin. In: Gervasi, O., et al. (eds.) ICCSA 2016. LNCS, vol. 9787, pp. 420–432. Springer, Cham (2016). doi:10.1007/978-3-319-42108-7_32

23. Clevers, J., Vonder, O., Jongschaap, R., Desprats, J., King, C., Prévot, L., Bruguier, N.: A semi-empirical approach for estimating plant parameters within the reseda-project. Int. Archives Photogramm. Remote Sens. 33, 272–279 (2000). B7/1; Part 7

24. Vuolo, F., Dini, L., D'Urso, G.: Assessment of LAI retrieval accuracy by inverting a RT model and a simple empirical model with multiangular and hyperspectral CHRIS/PROBA data from SPARC. In: Proceedings of the 3rd CHRIS/Proba Workshop (2005)

25. Minacapilli, M., Iovino, M., D'Urso, G., Osann Jochum, M., Moreno, J.: Crop and irrigation water management using high resolution remote sensing and agrohydrological models. In: AIP Conference Proceedings, vol. 852, pp. 99–106. AIP (2006)

26. Neugebauer, N., Vuolo, F.: Crop water requirements on regional level using remote sensing data-a case study in the marchfeld region berechnung des pflanzenwasserbedarfs für sommerfeldfrüchte mittels fernerkundungsdaten. eine fallstudie in der marchfeld-region. Photogramm. Fernerkund. Geoinf. 2014(5), 369–381 (2014)

27. Yoshioka, H., Miura, T., Demattê, J.A., Batchily, K., Huete, A.R.: Soil line influences on two-band vegetation indices and vegetation isolines: a numerical study. Remote Sens. 2(2), 545–561 (2010)

28. Balenzano, A., Satalino, G., Lovergine, F., Rinaldi, M., Iacobellis, V., Mastronardi, N., Mattia, F.: On the use of temporal series of L-and X-band SAR data for soil moisture retrieval. capitanata plain case study. Eur. J. Remote Sens. 46(1), 721–737 (2013)

29. Aquilino, M., Novelli, A., Tarantino, E., Iacobellis, V., Gentile, F.: Evaluating the potential of geoeye data in retrieving LAI at watershed scale. In: SPIE Remote Sensing. International Society for Optics and Photonics (2014). 92392B–92392B

30. Tarantino, E., Novelli, A., Laterza, M., Gioia, A.: Testing high spatial resolution worldview-2 imagery for retrieving the leaf area index. In: Third International Conference on Remote Sensing and Geoinformation of the Environment. International Society for Optics and Photonics (2015). 95351N

31. Akdim, N., Alfieri, S.M., Habib, A., Choukri, A., Cheruiyot, E., Labbassi, K., Menenti, M.: Monitoring of irrigation schemes by remote sensing: phenology versus retrieval of biophysical variables. Remote Sens. **6**(6), 5815–5851 (2014)

32. Vanino, S., Pulighe, G., Nino, P., De Michele, C., Bolognesi, S.F., D'Urso, G.: Estimation of evapotranspiration and crop coefficients of tendone vineyards using multi-sensor remote sensing data in a mediterranean environment. Remote Sens. **7**(11), 14708–14730 (2015)

33. Giordano, R., Milella, P., Portoghese, I., Vurro, M., Apollonio, C., D'Agostino, D., Lamaddalena, N., Scardigno, A., Piccinni, A.: An innovative monitoring system for sustainable management of groundwater resources: objectives, stakeholder acceptability and implementation strategy. In: 2010 IEEE Workshop on Environmental Energy and Structural Monitoring Systems (EESMS), pp. 32–37. IEEE (2010)

34. Giordano, R., DAgostino, D., Apollonio, C., Scardigno, A., Pagano, A., Portoghese, I., Lamaddalena, N., Piccinni, A.F., Vurro, M.: Evaluating acceptability of groundwater protection measures under different agricultural policies. Agric. Water Manag. **147**, 54–66 (2015)

35. Vermote, E., Justice, C., Claverie, M., Franch, B.: Preliminary analysis of the performance of the landsat 8/OLI land surface reflectance product. Remote Sens. Environ. **185**, 46–56 (2016)

36. Roy, D.P., Wulder, M., Loveland, T., Woodcock, C., Allen, R., Anderson, M., Helder, D., Irons, J., Johnson, D., Kennedy, R., et al.: Landsat-8: science and product vision for terrestrial global change research. Remote Sens. Environ. **145**, 154–172 (2014)

37. Knyazikhin, Y., Glassy, J., Privette, J., Tian, Y., Lotsch, A., Zhang, Y., Wang, Y., Morisette, J., Votava, P., Myneni, R., et al.: Modis leaf area index (LAI) and fraction of photosynthetically active radiation absorbed by vegetation (FPAR) product (MOD15) algorithm theoretical basis document. Theoretical Basis Document. NASA Goddard Space Flight Center, Greenbelt, MD 20771 (1999)

38. Yang, W., Shabanov, N., Huang, D., Wang, W., Dickinson, R., Nemani, R., Knyazikhin, Y., Myneni, R.: Analysis of leaf area index products from combination of modis terra and aqua data. Remote Sens. Environ. **104**(3), 297–312 (2006)

39. Weier, J., Herring, D.: Measuring Vegetation (NDVI & EVI) (2011)

40. D'Urso, G.: Simulation and Management of On-Demand Irrigation Systems: A Combined Agrological and Remote Sensing Approach [sn] (2001)

The Use of Geomorphological Descriptors and Landsat-8 Spectral Indices Data for Flood Areas Evaluation: A Case Study of Lato River Basin

Vincenzo Totaro⊙, Andrea Gioia(✉)⊙, Antonio Novelli⊙,
and Grazia Caradonna⊙

Politecnico di Bari, via Orabona 4, 70125 Bari, Italy
{vincenzo.totaro,andrea.gioia,antonio.novelli,grazia.caradonna}@poliba.it

Abstract. In the last few years, the scientific community has dedicated a strong effort for the rapid identification and mapping of flood risk. Last generation models have often taken advantage (even without of in-situ measurements) of the distributed information provided from remotely sensed data. In this work is proposed a multidisciplinary approach to reproduce maps of flooded areas. The method compared spectral descriptors to estimate the areas at risk of flooding in the Lato river basin (Puglia region - Southern Italy) using the ground effects caused by flood events. The inundated areas, obtained with a 2D hydraulic model, were used as reference for Landsat-8 spectral indices. The selection of the most appropriate spectral index was achieved using the binary classifiers test. Lastly, the adopted procedure provided also the calibration of different geomorphological descriptors for a rapid identification of areas at risk of flooding by using Digital Elevation Models.

Keywords: Geomorphological descriptors · Flooded areas · Spectral indices · Landsat-8 imagery

1 Introduction

The application of European Directive 2007/60/EC, on the assessment and management of flood risks, compels a necessary upgrade of theoretical means so far used to map the hydraulic hazard level of the territory, with the purpose to mitigate and contain the effects that floods have on the surrounding areas. In this context, challenge and responsibility of the scientific community is to improve and develop new techniques to provide a rapid identification and mapping of areas exposed to flood inundations, in order to satisfy the needs of recent legislation and the increasing requirements of end users for practical applications (i.e. numerical analyses, risk-reduction programs for human life and public safety or for insurance companies that have a growing interest in the identification of the assets and population at risk).

© Springer International Publishing AG 2017
O. Gervasi et al. (Eds.): ICCSA 2017, Part IV, LNCS 10407, pp. 30–44, 2017.
DOI: 10.1007/978-3-319-62401-3_3

The delineation of areas exposed to flood risk should deal with the complex problem regarding the definition of flood events and flood wave propagation (e.g. [1–3]). In recent years, much effort has gone into the identification of flood-risk areas through the use of hydrological and hydraulic models with different level of accuracy (e.g. [4,5]). These latter are, in more cases, difficult to be applied for their parameterization that needs to be calibrated and/or validated in areas with limited availability of hydrological information, due to the difficulty of performing adequate monitoring campaigns. Indeed, several researchers have addressed the prediction of floods at ungauged sites by operating a transfer of hydrologic information using regionalization methods (e.g. [6–10]).

In the last few year the availability of new technologies for the measurement of surface elevation (i.e. global positioning systems [GPS], synthetic aperture radar [SAR] interferometry, radar and laser altimetry) and the increasing availability of digital terrain models (DTMs) has given a strong impulse to the development of DTM-based hydrogeomorphic models (e.g. [1,11,12]); in this regard were relevant the recent improvements achieved for flood susceptibility, especially with the application of DTM-based models (e.g. [12–17]). Although these methodologies implement only geomorphological information, they allow to obtain indices that can provide reliable information on the tendency of areas to be flooded; in particular, geomorphologic/topographic indices can be correlated to areas exposed to flood inundation.

Moreover, significant advances in this field were performed in the latest decades through the combination of hydrology with other contiguous disciplines dealing with the sophisticated earth observation techniques (e.g. [18–26]). Remote sensing techniques are able to monitor the evolution of terrestrial phenomena and play a fundamental role in the availability of distributed information for hydrological application, such as extensive and reliable maps of vegetation cover (e.g. [27–32]) even in territories where there is limited availability of the data measured in situ.

In the context of the multidisciplinary approach, we propose a comparison between the maps obtained through the definition of the more appropriate spectral index, derived from a remote sensor, and those obtained by applying DTM-based models, in order to demonstrate the applicability of the two methodologies for an a-priori flood susceptibility evaluation. Specifically, by using Landsat-8 images, was evaluated the capability, of different spectral descriptors, to estimate the areas subjected to flood risk of the valley of the Lato river, located in Puglia region - Southern Italy. The inundated areas, obtained with a 2D hydraulic model, were used for the selection of the most performant spectral index and DTM-based basin descriptor, exploiting the linear binary classifiers test, introduced by Degiorgis et al. [14].

2   Case Study

The best spectral and geomorphological indices, for the identification of floodable areas (given a meteoric event), were derived over the Lato river basin (Fig. 1).

This river born from the union of the Lama river and the Talvo river at Masseria Sant 'Andrea Grande and can be considered as the recipient of the water coming from the ravines of Castellaneta, Laterza and Palagianello. His length is about 5 km and his basin area has an extension of about 670 km². Lato river is located in the province of Taranto and flows into the Gulf of Taranto (Ionian Sea), in a locality called Torre del Lato. The analysis was performed on a flood event that affected the valley part of the Lato river (6/7 October 2013) for which a Landsat-8 scene was available.

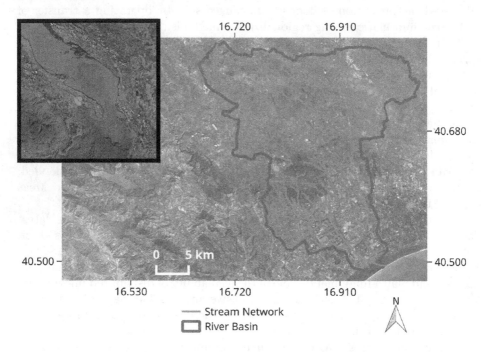

Fig. 1. Study area. Coordinate system WGS 84 decimal degree.

3   Methodologies

In the following section are illustrated: the basin morphological descriptors (synthetic and composite) used for the reconstruction of floodable areas; the hydrologic/hydraulic approach for the definition of the reference map of flooded areas; the binary classifiers method for the selection of the spectral index and the most appropriate basin descriptor; the methodologies of correction and sampling of satellite images.

3.1   Morphological Descriptors of Basin

The morphology of a river basin is the basic element that allows the identification of the effects of the runoff distribution, resulting from the occurrence of meteoric stresses as input to the basin itself. The synthetic and composite morphological descriptors analyzed in this paper were obtained from a DTM provided by the Puglia Region Informative System (SIT-Puglia), with a spatial resolution of $8 * 8$ m. As observed in [17], an important role is played from the characteristics of DTM, that provides a relevant influence on results analysis. In the following, we analyzed some of the descriptors shown in [33].

Synthetic Descriptors

- upslope contributing area, A_s $[m^2]$;
- elevation to the nearest stream, H $[m]$;
- distance from the nearest stream, D $[m]$;
- surface curvature, $\nabla^2 H [\ ]$;
- local slope, S $[-]$.

It is worth noting that these descriptors take into account both the morphological structure of the basin and its hydrological characteristics (fundamental for the analysis).

Composite Descriptors

- modified topographic index, TI_m:

$$TI_m = ln\left[\frac{A_d^n}{tan(\beta)}\right] \tag{1}$$

being A_d the drainage area per unit contour length, $tan(\beta)$ the local gradient and n a dimensionless parameter with values lesser than 1.
- downslope index, DW_i, defined as:

$$DW_i = tan(\alpha_d) = \frac{d}{L_d} \tag{2}$$

this index aims to describe the length (L $[m]$) of the flow path which deprives the particle of water a given amount of potential energy d $[m]$. We imposed d = 5 m (as stated in [16]).
- $ln\left[\frac{h_l}{H}\right]$: this index relates, in each point, water depth h with the synthetic descriptor H, where h can be defined for each basin location with the following relationship:

$$h_l \cong bA_l^n \tag{3}$$

with A_l $[m^2]$ upslope contributing area at the point of interest, b a scale factor usually set equal to 10^{-2} and n a dimensionless exponent set equal to 0.3 as stated in [17].
- Geomorphic Flood Index (GFI) $ln\left[\frac{h_r}{H}\right]$: this index is different from the previous, because the upslope contributing area A_r is evaluated on the cell belonging to the hydrographic network hydraulically nearest to the considered cell.
- $\frac{[h_r - H]}{D}$: an evolution of the previous one is obtained introducing the distance from the nearest stream (D).

3.2   Hydrologic/hydraulic Modeling

The inundated areas, obtained with a 2D hydraulic model, were used as reference flooding map for the selection of the most performant spectral index and DTM-based basin descriptor; in particular, this reference map was determined by exploiting a two-dimensional hydraulic modeling (FLO-2D [34]) coupled to the CN SCS hydrological model [35] for the estimation of the flood hydrograph consequent to the investigated meteorological event. The numerical simulation was performed over the computational grid of the selected DTM elevations. The flood event was reproduced introducing the simulated hydrograph (obtained using the hydrological model) as boundary condition. The hydraulic modeling has been calibrated by means of a comparison with flooded areas corresponding to return periods of 30 and 200 years, extracted from the database of the Basin Authority of Puglia for the investigated study area (e.g. http://www.adb.puglia.it/public/news.php).

3.3   Linear Binary Classifiers Method

The method of binary classifiers is widely used for the identification of flood-prone areas. As noted by Degiorgis et al. [14], the implementation of this methodology involves a preliminary processing, by scaling and normalizing the descriptor in the range $[-1, 1]$; to find the optimum value of the descriptor, a calibration procedure is performed using a moving threshold; therefore, for each assigned threshold the map of the geomorphological descriptor is converted into binary type (using 0 for non-flooded cells and 1 for inundated ones) and compared with the reference map (preliminarily converted in binary type), providing the following classification:

- TP (True Positive): the classifier correctly identifies a flooded element reported on the reference map;
- FP (False Positive): the cell is inundated for the classifier, but the flood reference map does not identify it as an element of a flood prone area;
- TN (True Negative): the classifier correctly identifies a not flooded element;
- FN (False Negative): the cell is not inundated for the classifier, but the flood reference map identifies it as an element of a flood prone area.

The best value of the threshold is obtained by minimizing the following objective function:

$$OB = r_{fp} + (1 - r_{tp}) \tag{4}$$

In which the true positive rate r_{tp} and false positive rate r_{fp} are:

$$r_{tp} = \frac{TP}{TP + FN} \tag{5}$$

$$r_{fp} = \frac{FP}{FP + TN} \tag{6}$$

3.4   Correction and Sampling Methodologies of Satellite Imagine

For this study a Landsat-8 satellite image was downloaded. The scene was retrieved in the U.S. Geological Survey (USGS) archives from the online Earth Explorer page (https://earthexplorer.usgs.gov/). The satellite data was selected in order to consider an acquisition close to the considered event and with a modest cloud cover. For these purposes, was chosen a LANDSAT-8 scene acquired on 10/10/2013 at 09:37:07. Particularly were used only Operational Land Imager (OLI) Landsat-8 data without considering the thermal information stored in the Thermal Infrared Sensor (TIRS) bands [36] more useful in other fields (e.g. surface temperature retrieval [37]).

The Landsat-8 OLI dataset was constituted by terrain corrected data (Level 1T) with 30 m of geometric resolution, a dynamic range of 12-bit and the following bands: coastal aerosol (430–450 nm), blue (450–510 nm), green (530–590 nm), red (640–670 nm), near infra-red (NIR, 850–880 nm), shortwave infrared-1 (SWIR1, 1570–1650 nm), shortwave infrared-2 (SWIR2, 2110–2290 nm), cirrus (1360–1380 nm) and a panchromatic band (PAN 500–680 nm).

The OLI digital numbers of the two Landsat-8 images were linearly converted to sensor Top of Atmosphere (TOA) reflectance and then corrected for the sun angle using gains, offsets and local sun elevation values stored in each scene metadata. The following equation (Eq. 7) was used to convert the original digital numbers of the two scenes to top of atmosphere reflectance (TOA) values.

$$\rho\lambda' = M_\rho \times Q_{cal} + A_\rho \tag{7}$$

Where $\rho\lambda'$ is the TOA reflectance, without correction for the solar angle; M_ρ is the band-specific multiplicative rescaling factor from the metadata; A_ρ is the band-specific additive rescaling factor from the metadata and Q_{cal} is the quantized and calibrated standard product pixel digital number value. The TOA reflectance was corrected with Eq. 8 by considering the sun elevation angle (from metadata).

$$\rho\lambda = \frac{\rho\lambda'}{sin(\theta_{SE})} \tag{8}$$

Where $\rho\lambda$ and θ_{SE} are respectively the TOA reflectance and the local sun elevation angle (as defined in the Landsat 8 (L8) Data User Handbook). TOA reflectance values were converted in ground reflectance values by using the so-called Dark Object subtraction (DOS) image-based atmospheric correction algorithm [38]. In particular, this algorithm exploits the basic idea to find a surface whose reflectance is so low that its contribution to the signal recorded by a sensor, can be considered negligible if compared with the radiance diffused by the atmosphere. Lastly, the Gram-Schmidt pan-sharpening algorithm [39] was used to fuse the multi-spectral information with the enhanced geometric accuracy of the PAN band. Thus, the subsequent computation was executed with pan-sharpened multi-spectral bands with a geometric resolution of 15 m.

3.5 Evaluation of Spectral Indices: The Procedure Used for the Definition of Flooded Areas

The use of spectral indices (such as the Simple Ratio (SR) index, the Normalized Difference Vegetation Index (NDVI), the Land Surface Water Index (LSWI), the Optical Water Index (OWI) and the Automated Water Extraction Index (AWEI)), reported in Lillesand et al. [40], was tested to find out the flooded areas from satellite image. The reference map, used to assess the quality of the spectral indices results, was obtained by the application of a two-dimensional hydraulic model, as described in Sect. 3.2. This was necessary for the lack of an accurate monitoring campaign of the ground effects of the investigated flood events.

The SR index (Eq. 9) is defined as the ratio between the reflectance values in the near infrared or NIR and RED bands.

$$SR = \frac{\rho_{NIR}}{\rho_{RED}} \tag{9}$$

The SR is very close to 0 and 1 in the presence of soil and water.

The $NDVI$, given by the normalized difference of the reflectance values in the NIR and the RED, is defined by Eq. 10.

$$NDVI = \frac{\rho_{NIR} - \rho_{RED}}{\rho_{NIR} + \rho_{RED}} \tag{10}$$

Where ρ_{NIR} and ρ_{RED} are respectively the reflectance in the NIR and in the red bands. It ranges between -1 and 1, and negative values are indicative of the presence of water.

The LSWI index implements shortwave infrared (SWIR) reflectance band values:

$$LSWI = \frac{\rho_{NIR} - \rho_{SWIR2}}{\rho_{NIR} + \rho_{SWIR2}} \tag{11}$$

The OWI index, which is particularly sensitive to the presence of water in the soil [41], is closely related to two other indices: the Enhanced Vegetation Index (EVI) and the Global Vegetation Moisture Index (GVMI) through the relationship Eq. 12:

$$\begin{aligned} OWI &= \quad\quad 0 \quad\quad && if \ EVI \geq 0 \\ OWI &= GVMI - EVI && if \ EVI < 0 \end{aligned} \tag{12}$$

The EVI [42] and GVMI [43] equations are shown in Eq. 13 and Eq. 14 respectively.

$$EVI = G \times \frac{\rho_{NIR} - \rho_{RED}}{\rho_{NIR} + C_1 \times \rho_{RED} - C_2 \times \rho_{BLUE} + L} \tag{13}$$

$$GVMI = \frac{(\rho_{NIR} + 0.1) - (\rho_{SWIR2} + 0.02)}{(\rho_{NIR} + 0.1) + (\rho_{SWIR2} + 0.02)} \tag{14}$$

In this case, were implemented the EVI MODIS (Moderate Resolution Imaging Spectroradiometer) parameters $L = 1$ (soil correction factor); $C_1 = 6$ and $C_2 = 7.5$ to consider the presence of atmospheric aerosol; $G = 2.5$ (gain factor). The AWEI index tends to bring out the contrast between water and other dark surfaces, implementing a linear combination, of reflectance values of known bands, able to increase the sensitivity of the index for liquid surfaces [44]. For this index, we referred to the present formulation:

$$AWEI = 4 \times (\rho_{BLUE} - \rho_{NIR}) - (0.25 \times \rho_{RED} + 2.75 \times \rho_{SWIR2}) \tag{15}$$

Where ρ is the reflectance value of the spectral bands of the Landsat-8 satellite.

4   Results and Discussion

In this section are reported the comparisons between flooding maps obtained by using spectral indices and geomorphological descriptors evaluated with reference to the flood event occurred on October 2013 on the Lato river basin. In particular, in the following subsections, the best spectral index and the best geomorphological descriptor results are described, highlighting the behavior of the different indices/descriptors examined.

4.1   Spectral Index Selection

The selection of the most suitable index has been realized exploiting the linear binary classifier test with the aim to minimize the overlay error between the floodable footprint, reconstructed by processing of satellite images, and the imprint, considered as reference map, obtained by hydraulic model. Several binary maps were created, by thresholding the considered indices, before performing this test.

The tests performed have allowed to calibrate, for each used spectral index, a numerical threshold to the detection of flooded areas. In Fig. 2 is shown the map of flooded areas (with the identified threshold value) evaluated by using the OWI index which has featured the best performance among the chosen indices.

The detection of the spectral index that best identifies the flooded areas was performed by minimizing the objective function (defined in Sect. 3.3). Table 1 summarizes the results of the conducted analysis and shows that the OWI is the

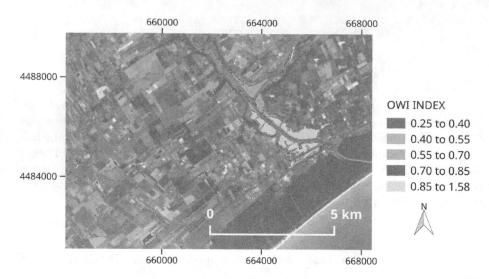

Fig. 2. Flooding map obtained from the OWI index ($OWI > 0.25$). Coordinate System UTM WGS84 zone 33N.

best spectral index with a threshold equal to 0.25. In particular, for this index, the test returned a minimum value of the objective function equal to 0.444, of which the 0.166 is due to false positive errors and 0.288 is due to false negative errors (the false negative error is equal to one minus the true positive rate). The result appears satisfying, as qualitatively deduced from Fig. 2, since the applied threshold $OWI > 0.25$ leads to an overestimation of 16.6% (due to false positive errors) and to an underestimation of the 28.8% (due to false negative errors) of the flooded area.

Table 1. Implemented thresholds values (τ), linear binary test results and objective function value related to the considered spectral indices.

Indices	τ	r_{fp}	r_{tp}	OB
SR	1.000	0.013	0.473	0.540
NDVI	0.000	0.013	0.473	0.540
LSWI	0.450	0.038	0.458	0.580
OWI	0.250	0.166	0.712	0.444
AWEI	0.000	0.035	0.534	0.491

4.2   Evaluation of Geomorphological Indices

The calibration based on geomorphological descriptors was carried out by seeking the τ value, of the threshold, that minimized the objective function (see Table 2). The implemented reference was derived by the hydraulic modeling (see Fig. 3).

Table 2. Results of the linear binary classification test for synthetic and composite calibrated descriptors.

Indices	τ	r_{fp}	r_{tp}	OB
A_s	−0.999	0.035	0.073	0.962
D	0.552	0.530	0.808	0.632
$\nabla^2 H$	0.45	0.623	0.899	0.724
H	−0.975	0.051	0.941	0.110
S	−0.993	0.111	0.676	0.435
TI_m	−0.260	0.119	0.691	0.428
DW_i	−0.992	0.130	0.877	0.253
$ln\left[\frac{h_l}{H}\right]$	−0.437	0.122	0.946	0.176
$ln\left[\frac{h_r}{H}\right]$	−0.231	0.057	0.846	0.211
$\frac{[h_r-H]}{D}$	0.668	0.073	0.073	0.300

The calibration of the morphological descriptors on the basin of Lato river was carried out in an area close to the outlet of the river basin: this choice is justified by the criticalities here verified after intense rainfall events. Moreover, being the 2D Hydraulic model applied on the main stream of the Lato river basin, the minor order stream and the tributaries were not considered in the hydraulic simulation and thus removed from the calibrated area. The performances of the investigated methodologies were evaluated by comparing flooding image obtained using the geomorphological descriptor with that obtained by processing the spectral index. Figure 4 shows the comparison between the flooded area identified by the GFI descriptor and the flooded area evaluated from the spectral index OWI that, as mentioned above, is better suited for the identification of the flooded area. This reinforces the ability of the satellite descriptor to represent the effect on the ground of a meteoric event.

In particular, the comparison between the results obtained using the two methodologies and their ability to reproduce the flood-prone areas, confirms the high reliability of these approaches to carry out a priori estimations of the ground effect of a meteoric event, especially when it is very expensive for end users to extend numerical analysis from small to large scale.

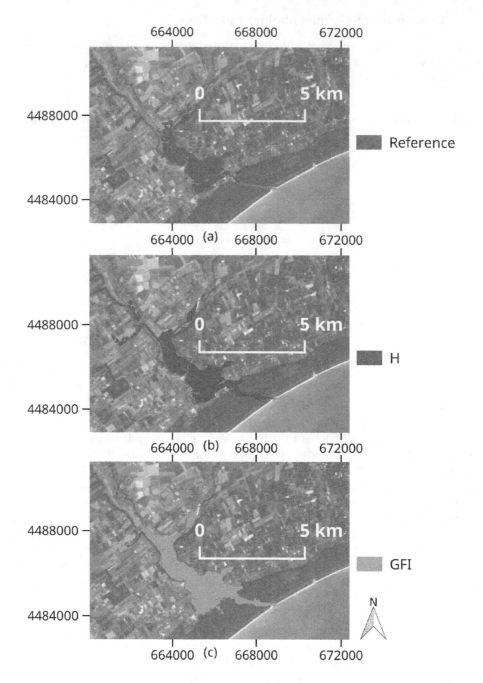

Fig. 3. Calibration: comparison between the reference flooded map (a) and the flooded area identified by the H (b) and GFI (c) composite descriptors for the event of October, 2013. Reference System UTM WGS84 zone 33N.

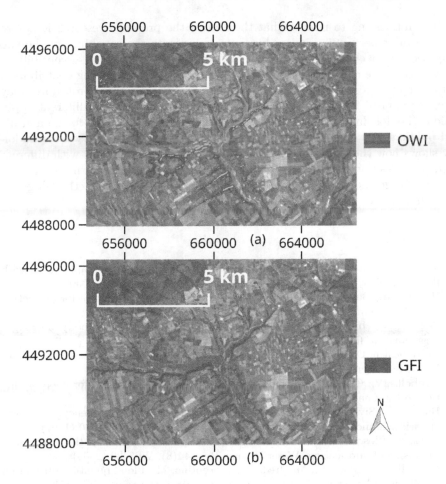

Fig. 4. Comparison between the flooded area identified by spectral index OWI (a) and by the descriptor GFI. Reference System UTM WGS84 zone 33N.

5 Conclusion

In this manuscript, two methodologies were compared to locate, at first approximation, the flooded areas following a given meteoric event. The observation of the figures above-reported shows that the two methods (the first based on geomorphological descriptors and the second on spectral indices derived from remote sensing), albeit conceptually different, give comparable results.

This was true except for the areas close to the outlet of the river basin in which the geomorphological indices fail to consider a number of human interventions, limiting the field of applicability of these procedures, as already observed by Manfreda et al. [45].

It is interesting to remark that the aim of the proposed research is not to find the most performing index, but is to investigate the capability of the two proposed approaches in order to evaluate areas exposed to flood susceptibility.

Moreover, we can affirm that the proposed work gives a strong contribution to the scientific research in this field, showing how the described procedures may be easily applied for an priori evaluation of inundated areas for different applications (i.e. for flood risk analysis or for risk-reduction programs for human life and public safety or for insurance companies). Finally the proposed methodology shows how the extension of DTM-based procedures to basins with different characteristics, supported by satellite images (in order to confirm the results achieved by geomorphological descriptors), can be an objective methodology for a new qualitative mapping of flooding risk on a large scale.

References

1. Marks, K., Bates, P., et al.: Integration of high-resolution topographic data with floodplain flow models. Hydrol. Process. **14**(11–12), 2109–2122 (2000)
2. Horritt, M., Bates, P.: Evaluation of 1d and 2d numerical models for predicting river flood inundation. J. Hydrol. **268**(1), 87–99 (2002)
3. Werner, M., Hunter, N., Bates, P.: Identifiability of distributed floodplain roughness values in flood extent estimation. J. Hydrol. **314**(1), 139–157 (2005)
4. De Wrachien, D., Mambretti, S.: Mathematical models for flood hazard assessment. Int. J. Saf. Secur. Eng. **1**(4), 353–362 (2011)
5. Iacobellis, V., Castorani, A., Di Santo, A.R., Gioia, A.: Rationale for flood prediction in karst endorheic areas. J. Arid Environ. **112**, 98–108 (2015)
6. Blöschl, G., Sivapalan, M.: Process controls on regional flood frequency: coefficient of variation and basin scale. Water Resour. Res. **33**(12), 2967–2980 (1997)
7. Merz, R., Blöschl, G.: Flood frequency hydrology: 1. temporal, spatial, and causal expansion of information. Water Resour. Res. **44**(8), W08432 (2008)
8. Iacobellis, V., Gioia, A., Manfreda, S., Fiorentino, M.: Flood quantiles estimation based on theoretically derived distributions: regional analysis in southern italy. Nat. Hazards Earth Syst. Sci. **11**(3), 673–695 (2011)
9. Fiorentino, M., Gioia, A., Iacobellis, V., Manfreda, S.: Regional analysis of runoff thresholds behaviour in southern italy based on theoretically derived distributions. Adv. Geosci. **26**, 139–144 (2011)
10. Gioia, A., Manfreda, S., Iacobellis, V., Fiorentino, M.: Performance of a theoretical model for the description of water balance and runoff dynamics in southern italy. J. Hydrol. Eng. **19**(6), 1113–1123 (2013)
11. Gallant, J.C., Dowling, T.I.: A multiresolution index of valley bottom flatness for mapping depositional areas. Water Resour. Res. **39**(12), 1347–1360 (2003)
12. Nardi, F., Vivoni, E.R., Grimaldi, S.: Investigating a floodplain scaling relation using a hydrogeomorphic delineation method. Water Resour. Res. **42**(9), W09409 (2006)
13. Dodov, B., Foufoula-Georgiou, E.: Floodplain morphometry extraction from a high-resolution digital elevation model: a simple algorithm for regional analysis studies. IEEE Geosci. Remote Sens. Lett. **3**(3), 410–413 (2006)
14. Degiorgis, M., Gnecco, G., Gorni, S., Roth, G., Sanguineti, M., Taramasso, A.C.: Classifiers for the detection of flood-prone areas using remote sensed elevation data. J. Hydrol. **470**, 302–315 (2012)

15. De Risi, R., Jalayer, F., De Paola, F., Giugni, M.: Probabilistic delineation of flood-prone areas based on a digital elevation model and the extent of historical flooding: the case of ouagadougou. Bol. Geol. Min. **125**(3), 329–340 (2014)
16. Manfreda, S., Samela, C., Gioia, A., Consoli, G.G., Iacobellis, V., Giuzio, L., Cantisani, A., Sole, A.: Flood-prone areas assessment using linear binary classifiers based on flood maps obtained from 1d and 2d hydraulic models. Nat. Hazards **79**(2), 735–754 (2015)
17. Samela, C., Manfreda, S., Paola, F.D., Giugni, M., Sole, A., Fiorentino, M.: Dem-based approaches for the delineation of flood-prone areas in an ungauged basin in Africa. J. Hydrol. Eng. **21**(2), 1–10 (2015)
18. Bates, P., Horritt, M., Smith, C., Mason, D.: Integrating remote sensing observations of flood hydrology and hydraulic modelling. Hydrol. Process. **11**(14), 1777–1795 (1997)
19. Horritt, M., Mason, D., Luckman, A.: Flood boundary delineation from synthetic aperture radar imagery using a statistical active contour model. Int. J. Remote Sens. **22**(13), 2489–2507 (2001)
20. Mattia, F., Satalino, G., Balenzano, A., D'Urso, G., Capodici, F., Iacobellis, V., Milella, P., Gioia, A., Rinaldi, M., Ruggieri, S., et al.: Time series of cosmo-skymed data for landcover classification and surface parameter retrieval over agricultural sites. In: Geoscience and Remote Sensing Symposium (IGARSS), 2012 IEEE International, pp. 6511–6514. IEEE (2012)
21. Balenzano, A., Satalino, G., Belmonte, A., D'Urso, G., Capodici, F., Iacobellis, V., Gioia, A., Rinaldi, M., Ruggieri, S., Mattia, F.: On the use of multi-temporal series of cosmo-skymed data for landcover classification and surface parameter retrieval over agricultural sites. In: Geoscience and Remote Sensing Symposium (IGARSS), 2011 IEEE International, pp. 142–145. IEEE (2011)
22. Iacobellis, V., Gioia, A., Milella, P., Satalino, G., Balenzano, A., Mattia, F.: Inter-comparison of hydrological model simulations with time series of sar-derived soil moisture maps. Eur. J. Remote Sens. **46**(1), 739–757 (2013)
23. Balenzano, A., Satalino, G., Iacobellis, V., Gioia, A., Manfreda, S., Rinaldi, M., De Vita, P., Miglietta, F., Toscano, P., Annicchiarico, G., et al.: A ground network for sar-derived soil moisture product calibration, validation and exploitation in southern italy. In: Geoscience and Remote Sensing Symposium (IGARSS), 2014 IEEE International, pp. 3382–3385. IEEE (2014)
24. Tarantino, E., Novelli, A., Laterza, M., Gioia, A.: Testing high spatial resolution worldview-2 imagery for retrieving the leaf area index. In: Proceedings of SPIE - The International Society for Optical Engineering, vol. 9535 (2015)
25. Trombetta, A., Iacobellis, V., Tarantino, E., Gentile, F.: Calibration of the aquacrop model for winter wheat using modis lai images. Agric. Water Manag. **164**, 304–316 (2016)
26. Aquilino, M., Novelli, A., Tarantino, E., Iacobellis, V., Gentile, F.: Evaluating the potential of geoeye data in retrieving lai at watershed scale. In: Proceedings of SPIE - The International Society for Optical Engineering, vol. 9239 (2014)
27. Olang, L.O., Kundu, P., Bauer, T., Fürst, J.: Analysis of spatio-temporal land cover changes for hydrological impact assessment within the nyando river basin of Kenya. Environ. Monit. Assess. **179**(1), 389–401 (2011)
28. Pattison, I., Lane, S.N.: The link between land-use management and fluvial flood risk: a chaotic conception? Prog. Phys. Geogr. **36**(1), 72–92 (2012)
29. Balacco, G., Figorito, B., Tarantino, E., Gioia, A., Iacobellis, V.: Space-time lai variability in Northern Puglia (Italy) from spot vgt data. Environ. Monit. Assess. **187**(7), 434 (2015)

30. Apollonio, C., Balacco, G., Novelli, A., Tarantino, E., Piccinni, A.F.: Land use change impact on flooding areas: the case study of Cervaro basin (Italy). Sustainability **8**(10), 996 (2016)

31. Novelli, A., Tarantino, E., Caradonna, G., Apollonio, C., Balacco, G., Piccinni, F.: Improving the ANN classification accuracy of landsat data through spectral indices and linear transformations (PCA and TCT) aimed at LU/LC monitoring of a river basin. In: Gervasi, O., Murgante, B., Misra, S., Rocha, A.M.A.C., Torre, C., Taniar, D., Apduhan, B.O., Stankova, E., Wang, S. (eds.) ICCSA 2016. LNCS, vol. 9787, pp. 420–432. Springer, Cham (2016). doi:10.1007/978-3-319-42108-7_32

32. Novelli, A., Tarantino, E., Fratino, U., Iacobellis, V., Romano, G., Gentile, F.: A data fusion algorithm based on the kalman filter to estimate leaf area index evolution in durum wheat by using field measurements and modis surface reflectance data. Remote Sens. Lett. **7**(5), 476–484 (2016)

33. Samela, C., Troy, T.J., Manfreda, S.: Geomorphic classifiers for flood-prone areas delineation for data-scarce environments. Adv. Water Resour. **102**, 13–28 (2017)

34. O'brien, J., Julien, P., Fullerton, W.: Two-dimensional water flood and mudflow simulation. J. Hydraul. Eng. **119**(2), 244–261 (1993)

35. Mockus, V.: National Engineering Handbook Section 4, Hydrology. NTIS (1972)

36. Roy, D.P., Wulder, M., Loveland, T., Woodcock, C., Allen, R., Anderson, M., Helder, D., Irons, J., Johnson, D., Kennedy, R., et al.: Landsat-8: science and product vision for terrestrial global change research. Remote Sens. Environ. **145**, 154–172 (2014)

37. Tarantino, E.: Monitoring spatial and temporal distribution of sea surface temperature with tir sensor data. Italian J. Remote Sens. **44**(1), 97–107 (2012)

38. Mandanici, E., Franci, F., Bitelli, G., Agapiou, A., Alexakis, D., Hadjimitsis, D.: Comparison between empirical and physically based models of atmospheric correction. In: Proceedings of SPIE - The International Society for Optical Engineering, vol. 9535 (2015)

39. Maurer, T.: How to pan-sharpen images using the gram-schmidt pan-sharpen method-a recipe. Int. Arch. Photogramm. Remote Sens. Spat. Inf. Sci. **XL–1/W1**, 239–244 (2013)

40. Lillesand, T., Kiefer, R.W., Chipman, J.: Remote Sensing and Image Interpretation. Wiley, New York (2014)

41. Guerschman, J.P., Van Dijk, A., McVicar, T.R., Van Niel, T.G., Li, L., Liu, Y., Peña-Arancibia, J.: Water balance estimates from satellite observations over the murray-darling basin. Report to the Australian Government from the CSIRO Murray-Darling Basin Sustainable Yields project (2008)

42. Huete, A., Didan, K., Miura, T., Rodriguez, E.P., Gao, X., Ferreira, L.G.: Overview of the radiometric and biophysical performance of the modis vegetation indices. Remote Sens. Environ. **83**(1), 195–213 (2002)

43. Ceccato, P., Gobron, N., Flasse, S., Pinty, B., Tarantola, S.: Designing a spectral index to estimate vegetation water content from remote sensing data: part 1: theoretical approach. Remote Sens. Environ. **82**(2), 188–197 (2002)

44. Feyisa, G.L., Meilby, H., Fensholt, R., Proud, S.R.: Automated water extraction index: a new technique for surface water mapping using landsat imagery. Remote Sens. Environ. **140**, 23–35 (2014)

45. Manfreda, S., Di Leo, M., Sole, A.: Detection of flood-prone areas using digital elevation models. J. Hydrol. Eng. **16**(10), 781–790 (2011)

C_AssesSeg Concurrent Computing Version of AssesSeg: A Benchmark Between the New and Previous Version

Antonio Novelli[1], Manuel A. Aguilar[2], Fernando J. Aguilar[2], Abderrahim Nemmaoui[2], and Eufemia Tarantino[1(✉)]

[1] Politecnico di Bari, Via Orabona 7, 70125 Bari, Italy
{antonio.novelli,eufemia.tarantino}@poliba.it
[2] Department of Engineering, University of Almería, 04120 Almería, Spain
{maguilar,faguilar,an932}@ual.es

Abstract. This paper presents the capabilities of a command line tool (.exe) created to assess the quality of segmented digital images. The executable source code, called AssesSeg (Assess Segmentation), was written in Python 2.7 using only open source libraries. AssesSeg implements a modified version of the supervised discrepancy measure named Euclidean Distance 2 (ED2) and was tested on different satellite images (Sentinel-2, Landsat 8, WorldView-2 and WorldView-3). The segmentation was applied to plastic covered greenhouse detection in the south of Spain (Almería). AssesSeg 2.0 was compared with the previous version computing time. The comparisons showed how the new version can benefit from modern multi-core CPU.

Keywords: AssesSeg · Segmentation quality · Sentinel-2 Multi Spectral Instrument (MSI) · Landsat 8 Operational Land Imager (OLI) · WorldView-2 (WV2) · WorldView-3 (WV3)

1 Introduction

Environmental assessment and modeling, spatial planning and ecosystem preservation can benefit from the availability of information and tool designed to exploit remote sensing data [1]. This is especially true when the considered data are processed with tools that simplify the analysis of remotely sensed data and the extracted information has an economic relevance.

In the last decade, passive satellite data were analyzed by means of different approaches that can be classified into two big categories: pixel-based and (Geographic) object-based image analysis (OBIA). According to Blaschke et al. [2], the pixel-based approach was increasingly criticized since the late nineties, although it was the dominant approach with passive remotely sensed data. Particularly, Blaschke et al. [2] focused their attention on the geometric resolution of the data stating that, for objects composed of many pixels, could be more

© Springer International Publishing AG 2017
O. Gervasi et al. (Eds.): ICCSA 2017, Part IV, LNCS 10407, pp. 45–56, 2017.
DOI: 10.1007/978-3-319-62401-3_4

relevant the analysis of their spatial patterns than the classic statistical analysis of single pixels. This statement is confirmed by the increasing amount of OBIA studies, performed especially with very high resolution (VHR) data for environmental/anthropic resources assessment (e.g. [3–8]).

A crucial step, in the OBIA workflow, is the image segmentation carried out by aggregating pixels that respect homogeneity criteria. In particular, scientific literature identifies four different segmentation methods [9]: thresholding techniques, boundary-based techniques, region-based techniques and hybrid techniques. Starting from the segmentation, the image classification can be performed on segments by exploiting different kind of spatial/spectral information stored inside them (e.g. spectral value, spectral indices, texture, etc.) in order to handle more complex image classification tasks [1,2,10]. Analyzing the current development of VHR sensor data (e.g. GeoEye-1, WorldView-2; WorldView-3, etc.) and medium resolution (e.g. Landsat-8 and Sentinel-2), the probability that significant objects can be described by many pixels is extremely higher than before. In these cases, the segmentation quality plays a key role in the quality of the final result [11,12] and a particular attention should be paid in order to considering segmentation biasing factors such as the objects represented by the scene, the geometric resolution, number of bands and overall image quality [13,14].

In this work, the segmentation of satellite images datasets used was performed by means of the multi-resolution segmentation (MRS) algorithm available from the eCognition software (Trimble, Sunnyvale, California, United States). Scientific literature describes the MRS as one of the most used segmentation algorithms (e.g. [1,15,16]). A proper description of the algorithm is shown in [17,18]. In particular, the most important user-editable parameters for the algorithm are scale, shape, compactness and band combinations often selected after a trial and error approach (e.g. for plastic greenhouses [8,19]).

In the last years, a few tools have been proposed to help users in the selection of optimum MRS parameters. Among them, the Estimation of Scale Parameter (ESP) tool was developed to deal both with single band and multiband image unsupervised MRS scale parameter estimation [13,20]. The authors of this paper have proposed, recently, AssesSeg (Assess Segmentation) by creating a free of charge command line tool (.exe for 64 bit Microsoft © Windows systems) to assess the quality of segmented digital images [21]. The tool is not dependent on the specific segmentation algorithm and it implements a modified version of the supervised discrepancy Euclidean Distance 2 (ED2) described, for the first, time by Liu et al. [22]. AssesSeg demonstrated its usefulness in [23], through the ability on estimating the ideal segmentation parameters, for greenhouses detection, from Sentinel-2 (S2), Landsat-8 (L8) and WorldView-2 (WV2) imagery by using the MRS algorithm.

This paper describes and shows the performance of the new version of the tool AssesSeg that exploits the modern multi-core CPU architectures capabilities. The execution times of new and previous version will be compared for the same datasets to highlight the differences in computation time. It is important to underline that the development of the tool was occurred in the frame

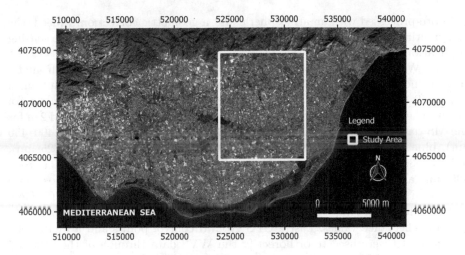

Fig. 1. Reference-Spanish (R-S) and Target-Spanish (T-S) scenes used in this study. Coordinate System UTM WGS 84 zone 30N.

of a project aimed at greenhouse detection from satellite imagery (Greenhous-eSat, website: https://www.ual.es/Proyectos/GreenhouseSat/). Indeed, the ED2 parameter has proved its effectiveness in two previous works [23,24]. The L8, S2 and WV2 satellite imagery datasets, already described in [21], together with the WorldView-3 (WV3) image dataset, implemented in [25], were used in order to carry out the comparison between the two aforementioned As-sesSeg versions. It is worth noting that these datasets were segmented several hundred times by means of the eCognition MRS algorithm.

2   Study Area and Dataset

2.1   Study Area

The test area falls in the so-called Sea of Plastic (Mar de Plástico), in the province of Almería (Southern Spain) Fig. 1. The main economic activity is agriculture under plastic covered greenhouses that implements different types of plastic materials to cover greenhouse structures. The climate is semi-arid and plastic covered greenhouses are coupled with the use of groundwater for irrigation [26], as often happens in other semi-arid Mediterranean regions (e.g. [27,28]).

2.2   Dataset: Satellite Data

The dataset developed for the two previous works were used for this comparison: the segmentation dataset obtained from a L8 scene, a S2 scene and a WV2 scene [21] together with the segmentation dataset produced from a WV3 scene [25]. In particular, the scenes were not affected by cloud cover. All the satellite data were pre-processed with an atmospheric and a geometric correction. Indeed, the orthorectification of VHR satellite imagery plays a crucial role in remote sensing applications [29,30].

The WV2 scene (5 July 2015) was a bundle combination of panchromatic (PAN) and MultiSpectral (MS) images. In fact, the radiometric resolution of the WV2 (in: Ortho Ready Standard Level-2A (ORS2A) format) data was of 11 bit, whereas the geometric resolution was 0.5 m for the PAN image and 2 m for the MS data. The MS data is made of the following bands: coastal (C, 400–450 nm), blue (B, 450–510 nm), green (G, 510–580 nm), yellow (Y, 585–625 nm), red (R, 630–690 nm), red edge (RE, 705–745 nm), near infrared-1 (NIR1, 760–895 nm) and near infrared-2 (NIR2, 860–1040 nm). The ATCOR atmospheric correction algorithm, provided by the software Geomatica v. 2014 (PCI Geomatics, Richmond Hill, ON, Canada), was used to convert digital numbers into ground reflectance values. Lastly GPS ground control points and a digital elevation model were used to orthorectify the WV2 data through of the software Geomatica v. 2014.

The free of charge L8 data (8 January 2016, Path 200 and Row 34) was downloaded from the USGS EROS website as terrain corrected (L1T) product with a geometric resolution 30 m and 16-bit dynamic range. The L8 data was constituted by the following bands: coastal aerosol (C, 430–450 nm), blue (B, 450–510 nm), green (G, 530–590 nm), red (R, 640–670 nm), near infrared (NIR, 850–880 nm), shortwave infrared-1 (SWIR1, 1570–1650 nm), shortwave infrared-2 (SWIR2, 2110–2290 nm), and cirrus (CI, 1360–1380), a PAN band and two thermal infrared bands. Particularly the L8 PAN and thermal bands were not used.

The free of charge S2 dataset (12 January 2016, orbit R051- T30SWF granule) was downloaded from the Copernicus Scientific Data Hub website. The S2 dataset was characterized by 12-bit dynamic range, top of atmosphere reflectance values and it was distributed as Level 1C (L1C) product with UTM/WGS84 projection. The S2 dataset was made of by thirteen bands with three different geometric resolutions (60 m, 20 m and 10 m): Costal (C, 443 nm), water vapor (WV, 1375 nm) and cirrus (CI, 1376) at 60 m resolution; Red edge/NIR bands with four different central wavelength at 705 nm, 740 nm, 783 nm and 865 nm respectively, short wave infrared-1 (SWIR1, 1610 nm) and short wave infrared-2 (SWIR2, 2190 nm) at 20 m resolution; Blue (B, 490 nm), Green (G, 560 nm), Red (R, 665 nm) and Near Infrared (NIR, 842 nm) at 10 m resolution. The S2 bottom of atmosphere reflectance dataset was attained by means of the Sen2Cor algorithm [31]. S2 bands with a geometric resolution of 60 m were not considered. Lastly, the L8 and S2 datasets were geometrically corrected by using the VHR WV2 PAN image as reference. In fact, when a study involves more than one sensor data a very accurate spatial matching is needed to carry out geometrically unbiased comparisons [32,33].

The WV3 dataset (5 July 2016) was composed of a PAN and a MS dataset with 0.31 m and 1.24 m geometric resolution at nadir. The data were in Ortho Ready Standard Level-2A (ORS2A) format and with a dynamic range of 11 bit.

The MS image is composed of the above-described WV2 MS bands. In fact, the WV3 image was used to generate three dataset by using accurate ground control points and a digital elevation model [25]: PAN orthoimage with 0.3 m GSD and retaining the original digital numbers in its single band; MS orthoimage with 1.2 m GSD and retaining the original digital numbers in all the 8 bands; MS-ATCOR orthoimage with 1.2 m GSD and atmospherically corrected (ground reflectance) by using the ATCOR (atmospheric correction) module included in Geomatica v. 2016.

3   The New AssesSeg and Experimental Design

3.1   C_AssesSeg (Concurrent Computing Version of AssesSeg)

AssesSeg, in its original conception, was designed as a standalone command line tool (.exe - for 64 bit Microsoft © Windows systems). Its source code was written with open source Python 2.7 libraries (e.g., Gdal, NumPy, SciPy) to implement the rules of a modified ED2 index. Particularly, a description of the ED2 original design can be found in [22], whereas a description of the modified ED2 implemented in AssesSeg can be found in [12,21]. The software can process the widely used ESRI polygon shapefile, a very common output for segmentation data, and does not depend on the segmentation software/algorithm. Moreover, the software stores, in a .xlsx spreadsheet file, a record for each processed segmentation shapefile in which are shown all the data used to compute the quality assessment index. Since a supervised index is the main output, the software requires two different typologies of input to perform calculations: a reference data shapefile and segmentation shapefiles (at least composed by one single file). A proper description of the executable output can be found in [21].

Although the first version of the software was packaged for 64-bit systems, the computing algorithm was not designed to exploit multi-core CPU computation capabilities. This resulted in a sub-optimal management of modern CPU resources. In the new version of AssesSeg, C_AssesSeg (or AssesSeg 2.0), the function designed to compute the ED2 was rewritten to exploit the Python multiprocessing package (https://docs.python.org/2/library/multiprocessing.html). The multiprocessing package supports spawning processes using an API (Application programming interface) and offers both local and remote concurrent execution by using subprocesses instead of threads. Due to this, multiprocessing module allows to fully leverage multiple processors on a given machine. By exploiting the multiprocessing package C_AssesSeg implements the capability to split the working load among a prefixed number of processes (set by the user). The splitting of the working load is made by assigning to each process a random extraction of the file to process. This was necessary in order to increase the probability to equally distribute the working load among the activated processes avoiding the occurrence of a single process with several large files to analyze. Lastly, C_AssesSeg produces the same output of the previous version. The two versions, together with the corresponding user guide and test material, can be found at: https://www.ual.es/Proyectos/GreenhouseSat/index_archivos/links.htm.

3.2   Ground Truth Data and Experimental Design

The datasets used in this work were acquired to produce research results within the framework of the plastic covered greenhouse extraction (required by the GreenhouseSat project). In this sense, and just regarding the segmentation purposes, was considered only the plastic greenhouse delineation. Up to 400 polygons, representing individual greenhouses, were manually digitized over the whole study area. In particular, the 400 reference polygons were slightly different for the two datasets. The one referred to [21] was digitized on the corrected WV2 PAN image whereas the other, referred to [25], was digitized on the WV3 PAN orthoimage also exploiting the data contained in the WV3 MS orthoimage. Both reference data were uniformly distributed in the study area. In the above mentioned studies the reference geometries were used both to study the influence of the number of references on the segmentation quality assessment and to estimate the optimal MRS segmentation parameters for plastic greenhouses detection by using AssesSeg. Thanks to AssesSeg the number of reference polygons is no more a problem. In this regards, it is important to highlight that only 30 polygons per class were considered in previous segmentation quality studies (e.g. [11,22]).

Table 1 describes the data used for benchmark purposes between the previous and the new version of AssesSeg. Since the two versions output are exactly the same, the yardstick used to evaluate computational improvement was the execution time. The computations were executed with a desktop workstation based on an Intel© Xeon© E-1620 v3. This CPU is characterized by 4 cores, 8 threads and processor base frequency 3.50 Ghz. The comparisons were made starting from the initial AssesSeg version (one only process) to 12 simultaneously concurrent AssesSeg processes initialized by the new AssesSeg version.

Table 1. The dataset for the benchmark: Landsat-8 (L8), Sentinel-2 (S2), WorldView-2 (WV2), WorldView-3 (WV3) Multi Spectral (MS original digital number), WV3 Panchromatic (PAN original digital number) and WV3 MS-ATCOR (atmospherically corrected reflectance values).

Dataset	Number of segmentation files (*.shp)	Size [MB]
L8	111	396
S2	111	291
WV2	294	7340
WV3 MS	247	20225
WV3 MS-ATCOR	259	11551
WV3 PAN	35	11236

Although in [21] several bands combinations were used to research purposes, in this case are taken into account segmentations that involve only all the MS bands of the four satellite datasets (see Sect. 2.2) and also the PAN band of the

WV3 dataset. This choice was made in order to reduce the page length of the manuscript and to provide a benchmark related to the whole selected dataset.

4   Results and Discussion

Figures 2, 3 and 4 show the results of the benchmark experiment grouped according to the size of the dataset tested.

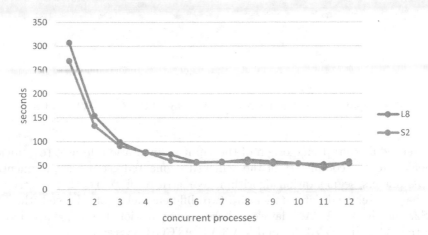

Fig. 2. Computing time for the L8 and S2 datasets.

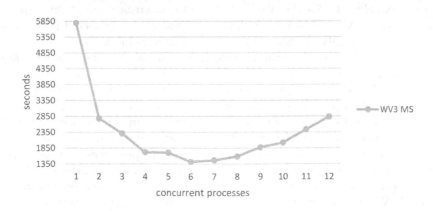

Fig. 3. Computing time for the WV3 MS dataset.

The figures clearly depict that the implementation of the multiprocessing package is coupled to a significant decrease in computing time. This is true for all the tested datasets. The figures show that each dataset has a specific variation rate of computating time. Particularly, it is clear that the computation time

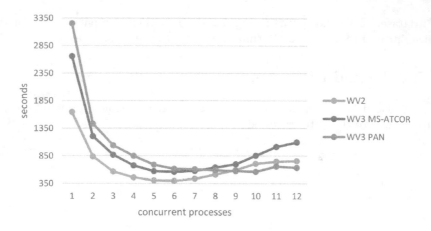

Fig. 4. Computing time for the WV2, WV3 MS-ATCOR and WV3 datasets.

is influenced by the specific origin of the input segmentation dataset (e.g. mean shapefile size, the complexity of the achieved segmented geometries, segmentation parameters, segmentation algorithm, geometric resolution of the image, etc.) and that the selected datasets feature two different behaviors. Indeed, the L8, the S2, and the WV3 PAN datasets share a computational time path different from the WV2, the WV3 MS and WV3 MS-ATCOR datasets.

The maximum time reduction ratio (maximum recorded execution time divided by the minimum recorded execution time), achieved for the L8, the S2, and the WV3 PAN datasets, was almost equal to 6. The computing time reduction ratio was almost 5 for the WV3 MS-ATCOR, whereas it was slightly greater than 4 for the WV2 and WV3 MS datasets. This was an expected result since the used CPU has only 4 core, and a minimum time reduction ratio lesser than 4 could be linked to a sub-optimal working-load division among the activated concurrent processes.

The L8, S2, and WV3 PAN datasets are characterized by a similar behavior. They reached their respective minimum computation time with a number of concurrent processes greater than the CPU threads number (respectively at 11 concurrent processes for the L8 and S2 datasets and 10 concurrent processes for the WV3 PAN dataset). Moreover, from 6 concurrent processes, the computing time variation rate between two consecutive computations is almost equal to 1: this means that the computing time is almost stable from 6 concurrent processes.

The WV2, WV3 MS and WV3 MS-ATCOR datasets feature a similar behavior in the benchmark experiment. In particular, they reached their minimum computation time with a number of concurrent processes lesser than the CPU threads number (at 6 concurrent processes). Moreover, from 6 concurrent processes, the computing time variation rate between two consecutive computations is lesser than 1: this means that the computing time tends to increase starting from 6 concurrent processes.

In a nutshell, all the six datasets feature a similar behavior up to 6 concurrent processes, with a very high decreasing rate of computing time between 1 and 4 concurrent processes. The different behavior between the two datasets groups, i.e. presenting minimum computing time for a number of concurrent processes greater or lesser than the number of threads, could depend on the MRS algorithm settings used to create each segmentation file. Moreover, differences could also be linked to the Python function, that was written to assign the working load to each concurrent process. Indeed, starting from the AssesSeg algorithm implemented in its first version, the fastest way to address this problem was to create a function that randomly selects an equal (when the number of files can be divided from the number or user selected concurrent processes) number of inputs for each process. This selection criterion was implemented to avoid an overload (many big files) for only a single active process among the active ones. However, its random behavior can generate slight changes (in equal computational conditions, no more than a couple of seconds for the used CPU) in computing time even by using the same number of concurrent processes.

5   Conclusions

The aim of this work is to present the performance of the new version of the tool AssesSeg, originally presented in [21], to the technical and research communities. The new version and the previous one can be downloaded at: https://www.ual. es/Proyectos/GreenhouseSat/index_archivos/links.htm.

Thanks to the improvements introduced in this new version, the tool can exploit the modern multi-core CPU architectures capabilities. This is combined with an impressive capability to execute the same amount of calculations with a reduced amount of time. The results showed that for some datasets a number of concurrent processes greater than the number of CPU threads could lead to a very small computing time reduction. However, this did not occur for all the tested datasets. For this reason, the authors do not suggest to set a number of concurrent processes that exceeds the number of the CPU threads.

Future development will be characterized by the implementation of a graphical interface for the command line tool and in the development of new supervised discrepancy measures to be implemented in a new and more performant version of AssesSeg.

Acknowledgement. This work was supported by the Spanish Ministry of Economy and Competitiveness (Spain) and the European Union FEDER funds (Grant Reference AGL2014-56017-R). It takes part of the general research lines promoted by the Agrifood Campus of International Excellence ceiA3.

References

1. Blaschke, T.: Object based image analysis for remote sensing. ISPRS J. Photogram. Remote Sens. **65**(1), 2–16 (2010)
2. Blaschke, T., Hay, G.J., Kelly, M., Lang, S., Hofmann, P., Addink, E., Feitosa, R.Q., van der Meer, F., van der Werff, H., van Coillie, F., et al.: Geographic object-based image analysis-towards a new paradigm. ISPRS J. Photogram. Remote Sens. **87**, 180–191 (2014)
3. Caprioli, M., Tarantino, E.: Identification of land cover alterations in the Alta Murgia National Park (Italy) with VHR satellite imagery. Int. J. Sustain. Dev. Plann. **1**(3), 261–270 (2006)
4. Pu, R., Landry, S., Yu, Q.: Object-based urban detailed land cover classification with high spatial resolution Ikonos imagery. Int. J. Remote Sens. **32**(12), 3285–3308 (2011)
5. Stumpf, A., Kerle, N.: Object-oriented mapping of landslides using random forests. Remote Sens. Environ. **115**(10), 2564–2577 (2011)
6. Figorito, B., Tarantino, E., Balacco, G., Fratino, U.: An object-based method for mapping ephemeral river areas from WorldView-2 satellite data. In: SPIE Remote Sensing, International Society for Optics and Photonics, p. 85310B (2012)
7. Fernández, I., Aguilar, F.J., Aguilar, M.A., Álvarez, M.F.: Influence of data source and training size on impervious surface areas classification using VHR satellite and aerial imagery through an object-based approach. IEEE J. Sel. Top. Appl. Earth Obs. Remote Sens. **7**(12), 4681–4691 (2014)
8. Chaofan, W., Jinsong, D., Ke, W., Ligang, M., Tahmassebi, A.R.S.: Object-based classification approach for greenhouse mapping using Landsat-8 imagery. Int. J. Agric. Biol. Eng. **9**(1), 79 (2016)
9. Fan, J., Yau, D.K., Elmagarmid, A.K., Aref, W.G.: Automatic image segmentation by integrating color-edge extraction and seeded region growing. IEEE Trans. Image Process. **10**(10), 1454–1466 (2001)
10. Marpu, P., Neubert, M., Herold, H., Niemeyer, I.: Enhanced evaluation of image segmentation results. J. Spat. Sci. **55**(1), 55–68 (2010)
11. Witharana, C., Civco, D.L.: Optimizing multi-resolution segmentation scale using empirical methods: exploring the sensitivity of the supervised discrepancy measure Euclidean Distance 2 (ED2). ISPRS J. Photogram. Remote Sens. **87**, 108–121 (2014)
12. Novelli, A., Aguilar, M.A., Nemmaoui, A., Aguilar, F.J., Tarantino, E.: Performance evaluation of object based greenhouse detection from Sentinel-2 MSI and Landsat 8 OLI data: a case study from Almería (Spain). Int. J. Appl. Earth Obs. Geoinf. **52**, 403–411 (2016)
13. Drăguţ, L., Csillik, O., Eisank, C., Tiede, D.: Automated parameterisation for multi-scale image segmentation on multiple layers. ISPRS J. Photogram. Remote Sens. **88**, 119–127 (2014)
14. Belgiu, M., Drguţ, L.: Comparing supervised and unsupervised multiresolution segmentation approaches for extracting buildings from very high resolution imagery. ISPRS J. Photogram. Remote Sens. **96**, 67–75 (2014)
15. Neubert, M., Herold, H., Meinel, G.: Assessing image segmentation quality-concepts, methods and application. In: Blaschk, T., Lang, S., Hay, G.J. (eds.) Object-Based Image Analysis, pp. 769–784. Springer, Heidelberg (2008)
16. Tong, H., Maxwell, T., Zhang, Y., Dey, V.: A supervised and fuzzy-based approach to determine optimal multi-resolution image segmentation parameters. Photogram. Eng. Remote Sens. **78**(10), 1029–1044 (2012)

17. Baatz, M., Schäpe, A., et al.: Multiresolution segmentation: an optimization approach for high quality multi-scale image segmentation. Angewandte geographische informationsverarbeitung XII **58**, 12–23 (2000)

18. Tian, J., Chen, D.M.: Optimization in multi-scale segmentation of high-resolution satellite images for artificial feature recognition. Int. J. Remote Sens. **28**(20), 4625–4644 (2007)

19. Tarantino, E., Figorito, B.: Mapping rural areas with widespread plastic covered vineyards using true color aerial data. Remote Sens. **4**(7), 1913–1928 (2012)

20. Drguţ, L., Tiede, D., Levick, S.R.: ESP: a tool to estimate scale parameter for multiresolution image segmentation of remotely sensed data. Int. J. Geogr. Inf. Sci. **24**(6), 859–871 (2010)

21. Novelli, A., Aguilar, M.A., Aguilar, F.J., Nemmaoui, A., Tarantino, E.: Assessega command line tool to quantify image segmentation quality: a test carried out in Southern Spain from satellite imagery. Remote Sens. **9**(1), 40 (2017)

22. Liu, Y., Bian, L., Meng, Y., Wang, H., Zhang, S., Yang, Y., Shao, X., Wang, B.: Discrepancy measures for selecting optimal combination of parameter values in object-based image analysis. ISPRS J. Photogram. Remote Sens. **68**, 144–156 (2012)

23. Aguilar, M.A., Aguilar, F., García Lorca, A., Guirado, E., Betlej, M., Cichon, P., Nemmaoui, A., Vallario, A., Parente, C.: Assessment of multiresolution segmentation for extracting greenhouses from WorldView-2 imagery. Int. Arch. Photogramm. Remote Sens. Spat. Inf. Sci. 145–152 (2016)

24. Aguilar, M.A., Nemmaoui, A., Novelli, A., Aguilar, F.J., García Lorca, A.: Object-based greenhouse mapping using very high resolution satellite data and Landsat 8 time series. Remote Sens. **8**(6), 513 (2016)

25. Aguilar, M.A., Novelli, A., Nemmaoui, A., Aguilar, F.J., García Lorca, A., González-Yebra, Ó.: Optimizing multiresolution segmentation for extracting plastic greenhouses from WorldView-3 imagery. In: De Pietro, G., Gallo, L., Howlett, R.J., Jain, L.C. (eds.) KES-IIMSS 2017. SIST, vol. 76, pp. 31–40. Springer, Cham (2018). doi:10.1007/978-3-319-59480-4_4

26. Van Cauwenbergh, N., Pinte, D., Tilmant, A., Frances, I., Pulido-Bosch, A., Vanclooster, M.: Multi-objective, multiple participant decision support for water management in the Andarax catchment, Almeria. Environ. Geol. **54**(3), 479–489 (2008)

27. Giordano, R., Milella, P., Portoghese, I., Vurro, M., Apollonio, C., D'Agostino, D., Lamaddalena, N., Scardigno, A., Piccinni, A.: An innovative monitoring system for sustainable management of groundwater resources: objectives, stakeholder acceptability and implementation strategy. In: 2010 IEEE Workshop on Environmental Energy and Structural Monitoring Systems (EESMS), pp. 32–37. IEEE (2010)

28. Giordano, R., DAgostino, D., Apollonio, C., Scardigno, A., Pagano, A., Portoghese, I., Lamaddalena, N., Piccinni, A.F., Vurro, M.: Evaluating acceptability of groundwater protection measures under different agricultural policies. Agric. Water Manag. **147**, 54–66 (2015)

29. Aguilar, M., Agüera, F., Aguilar, F., Carvajal, F.: Geometric accuracy assessment of the orthorectification process from very high resolution satellite imagery for common agricultural policy purposes. Int. J. Remote Sens. **29**(24), 7181–7197 (2008)

30. Aguilar, M.A., Nemmaoui, A., Aguilar, F.J., Novelli, A., García Lorca, A.: Improving georeferencing accuracy of very high resolution satellite imagery using freely available ancillary data at global coverage. Int. J. Digit. Earth 1–15 (2017)

31. Muller-Wilm, U., Louis, J., Richter, R., Gascon, F., Niezette, M.: Sentinel-2 level 2a prototype processor: architecture, algorithms and first results. In: Proceedings of the ESA Living Planet Symposium, Edinburgh, UK, pp. 9–13 (2013)
32. Townshend, J.R., Justice, C.O., Gurney, C., McManus, J.: The impact of misregistration on change detection. IEEE Trans. Geosci. Remote Sens. **30**(5), 1054–1060 (1992)
33. Barzaghi, R., Carrion, D., Pepe, M., Prezioso, G.: Computing the deflection of the vertical for improving aerial surveys: a comparison between EGM2008 and ITALGEO05 estimates. Sensors **16**(8), 1168 (2016)

An Optimized Fuzzy System for Coastal Water Quality Mapping Using Remote Sensing Data

Bahia Lounis[✉] and Aichouche Belhadj-Aissa

Laboratory of Image Processing and Radiation, Faculty of Electronics and Computer Science,
USTHB University, BP 32, El-Alia–Beb-Ezzouar, 16111 Algiers, Algeria
lounisbahia@yahoo.fr, h.belhadj@mailcity.com

Abstract. In this paper, we propose coastal water quality mapping process using the combination of in-situ measurements and remote sensing data. Water maps is processed by an hybridization of fuzzy model and genetic algorithm which exploits remotely sensed multispectral reflectances to estimate coastal water quality. The relation between the water parameters and the subsurface reflectances is modeled by a set of fuzzy rules extracted automatically from the data through two steps procedure. First, fuzzy rules are generated by unsupervised fuzzy clustering of the input data. In the second step, genetic algorithm is applied to optimize the rules. Our contribution has focused on the use of several water parameter maps to construct a graphical tool named Pollution Signature Draw (PSD) in order to characterize the water quality. Water characterization is then evaluated by analyzing several types of PSDs related to typical sites selecting the most representatives' ones. After, the selected PSDs are introduced in a classifier system to generate a pollution map (PM) associated the studied area. The proposed approach was tested on Algiers bay and has highlighted four pollution levels corresponding to High Pollution (HP), Medium Pollution (MP), Low Pollution (LP) and Clear Water (CW).

Keywords: Remote sensing data · Fuzzy clustering · Genetic optimization · Pollution signature · Coastal water classification

1 Introduction

Under the pressure of the human and industrial activities, the Algerian coast had undergone profound environmental changes affecting the quality of its water. The current environment's ministry methods for establishing water pollution are analysis and measurements done in laboratories. These techniques are very accurate, however they remain insufficient and very expensive for assessing and monitoring water quality on Algerian coast that extends on 1200 km [1]. Actually, remote sensing can overcome this constraint by providing an alternative for water quality monitoring over a range of temporal and spatial scales. Imagery from recent satellites with improved spectral and spatial resolution and the integration of the Geographic Information System (GIS) technologies offer a valuable tool for developing management plans for water pollution and thus allowing quicker and more effective actions to be taken. In this work, we are interested to this

© Springer International Publishing AG 2017
O. Gervasi et al. (Eds.): ICCSA 2017, Part IV, LNCS 10407, pp. 57–67, 2017.
DOI: 10.1007/978-3-319-62401-3_5

type of data to, first, map water quality indices. Then construct Pollution Signature Draw PSD in order to characterize the quality of this water. Finally, we propose a new water quality classification to highlight most polluted sites of Algiers bay.

Remote sensing of water quality monitoring is evaluated by several substances which affect its optical properties. Conventionally, three main components are used to estimate marine water quality in coastal areas. These components are: Suspended Particulate Matters "SPM", chlorophylls "Chl" and dissolved organic matter "DOM" [2]. To these components, we are also interested to water Turbidity (Turb) and its transparency measured by Secchi Disk Depth (SDD).

Various approaches have been developed to estimate coastal water quality parameters from remote sensing data. Due to the simultaneous presence of the three main water components, the relation between water components and remotely subsurface reflectances is complicate and is considered as no-linear. So, the first developed algorithms were empirical and semi-analytical models [3, 4]. With the increase of spectral information and the complexity to solve the inverse model, new estimation algorithms inspired from natural phenomena have emerged. Neural networks were successfully used to implement the inverse model and to properly address the non-linearity problem [5]. Besides neural networks, fuzzy systems have proved to be particularly effective in identifying non-linear models too [6]. The most popular approach to fuzzy modeling is based on the identification of fuzzy rules, which describe in linguistic terms the water parameters concentration/marine subsurface reflectance relationship. Furthermore, an optimization process is usually added to tune these fuzzy rules so that the fuzzy method implements the desired inverse model. Using this approach, a mapping process of coastal water classification is proposed in order to estimate the boundaries of coastal zones according to different water types. To attend this goal, we have followed the next steps (see Fig. 1):

- **Water quality estimation maps:** water quality maps are estimated using fuzzy systems. It consists of identifying fuzzy rules [7] which describe the relationship between water quality parameters and their corresponding reflectance. These rules, extracted from unsupervised clustering of training data, determine the actions that water parameter must perform if some conditions on multispectral reflectance are satisfied. After, an accurate definition of the rules coefficients is assigned to genetic algorithm (GA). This latter searches the best chromosomic structure that codifies the different parts of the fuzzy rules to give best optimization results.
- **PSD analysing:** in this part, we focused our interest on the use of PSD tool to water quality characterization which is evaluated by analysing several types of PSDs related to typical sites in order to select the most representative's ones [1].
- **Pollution map:** the main PSDs of typical sites are selected and introduced in maximum likelihood classifier in order to generate a pollution map related to Algiers bay. For this site, four pollution levels corresponding to "High pollution", "Medium Pollution", "Few Pollution" and "Clear Water" are considered.

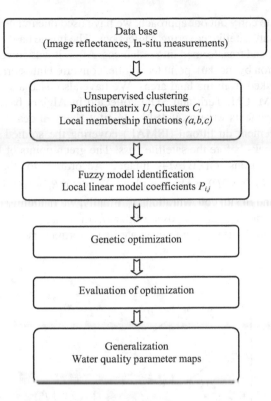

Fig. 1. Flowchart of estimation map process.

Our paper is structured as follows; in Sect. 2 the estimation principle of water parameters maps is described where an hybridization of fuzzy model and genetic algorithm is used. The PSD tool and water characterization are outlined in Sect. 3. Water pollution map is presented in Sect. 4. Finally, in Sect. 5, conclusions on the developed process are presented in order to show the contribution of remote sensing data to monitor the coastal water pollution.

2 Water Quality Estimation Maps

In the fuzzy estimation, Takagi Sugeno Kang (TSK) model was adapted to our application where the relation between water component concentration y_i and marine Subsurface reflectance R_i is considered as locally linear [8] (see Fig. 2). Thus, the input space is divided into crisp subspaces or clusters C_i. In each cluster C_i, y_i is assumed as a linear local function that models the variation of R_i in this cluster ($y_i = p_{i,0} + p_{i,1}R_i$, where $p_{i,0}, p_{i,1}$ are real numbers). The global model Y connects y_1 and y_2 according to their local activation degrees β_i and gives $Y = \beta_1 y_1 + \beta_2 y_2$. Whereas, in the optimization step, the fuzzy coefficients are applied to a genetic algorithm in order to tune them and improve the estimation map results. To implement this monetization, we took the following steps:

- Processed data: to carry out our approach, we have used one image corresponding to ETM+ of Landsat7 satellite covering Algiers bay. The image has been, first, geometrically corrected and transformed into radiances. After, it was corrected from atmospheric contribution by the dark point technique, converted into corresponding reflectance R and masked from the land areas. We have also used a set of in-situ measurements of SPM, Chl, Turb and SDD collected in Algiers bay. 300 samples of punctual measurements were provided by Institut National des Sciences de la Mer et de l'Aménagement du littoral (ISMAL) covering the studied area. They were collected two weeks before the satellite pass. The green points of Fig. 3 show their geographical locations on ETM+ image. According to the available data $y_i = (SPM, Chl, Turb, SDD)$, we have built a set of data (R_i, y_i) relevant to subsurface reflectances R_i and in situ concentrations y_i. Finally, we randomly split the data into two subsets, the training-set composed of the 2/3 of initial data is used to define the fuzzy model whereas the test-set to evaluate its performances.

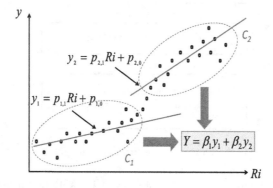

Fig. 2. Fuzzy estimation principle (Takagui-Sugeno-Kang model)

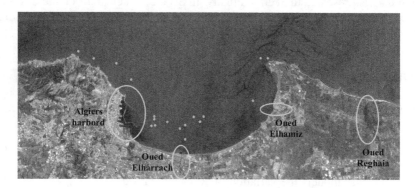

Fig. 3. Composed color of ETM + image (Red: TM1, Green: TM2, Blue: TM3) acquired on Algiers bay. (Color figure online)

- Determination of fuzzy input subspaces: using the Weighted Fuzzy C-means (WFCM) algorithm, we divide the training data-base into crisp subspaces or clusters C_i which share the same spectral characteristics [8]. To each cluster C_i, we define a fuzzy set A_i and associate a triangular membership function characterized by its parameters (a, b, c), where b corresponds to the abscissa of triangle vertex and a and c are deduced as the intersection of the abscissas axis with the lines on the left and the right sides of b;

- Determination of fuzzy model coefficients: To each cluster C_i, the output y_i of in-situ concentration variation is assumed to be locally linear and expressed as following relation: $y_i = p_{0,i} + p_{i,1}R_1 + p_{i,2}R_2 + \dots + p_{i,M}R_M$, where R_M are the M subsurface reflectances and $(p_{i,0}, p_{i,1}, p_{i,2}, \dots, p_{i,M})$ are real numbers. The estimation model is, then, expressed as a set of conditions which assign each pixel to a water type under the form of Takagi-Sugeno-Kang (TSK) rules. The premises of these rules depend on the fuzzy sets $A_{i,j}$ defined on the reflectance domain and the consequences present the local linear y_i model form, like shown by Eq. 1 [8].

$$
\begin{aligned}
&\text{Rule}_i \text{: If } (R_1 \text{ is } A_{i,1}) \ \& \ \dots \ \& (R_M \text{ is } A_{i,M}) \\
&\text{Then } y_i = p_{i,0} + p_{i,1}R_1 + \dots + p_{i,M}R_M
\end{aligned}
\tag{1}
$$

- Each local model is associated with a degree of activation β_i expressed as $\beta_i = \min(u_{A_{i,1}}(R_1), u_{A_{i,2}}(R_2), \dots, u_{A_{i,M}}(R_M))$, where $u_{A_{i,j}}(R_j)$ is the membership function associated to the fuzzy set $A_{i,j}$. The global Y concentration is, then, computed by aggregating the conclusions inferred from r individual rules as followed:

$$
Y = \frac{\sum_{i=1}^{r} \beta_i . y_i}{\sum_{i=1}^{r} \beta_i}
\tag{2}
$$

- Optimization of fuzzy coefficients: the obtained fuzzy coefficients are applied to genetic algorithm. For our application, the chromosome codifies the membership function (a, b, c) of the fuzzy sets coefficients [1]. We defined the fitness value as the inverse of the Mean Square Error MSE. Also, we apply the arithmetic crossover and the uniform mutation operators to generate a new population [9]. Chromosomes to be mated are chosen by using the well-known roulette wheel selection method, which associates to each chromosome a probability proportional to its fitness value. We fixed the probability of crossover and mutation to 0.9 and 0.1, respectively. When the average of the fitness values of all the individuals in the population is greater than 99% of the fitness value of the best individual or a prefixed number of iterations has been executed, the GA is considered to have converged.

- Generalization: After optimization, we used the optimum coefficients found and applied them to the total images to generate water maps related to each water parameter [8].

The estimation process of Fig. 1 was implemented in Interactive Data Language (IDL) and applied to Algiers bay Landsat7 ETM+ image acquired on 03 june 2001 to generate water maps related to each water parameter.

Table 1 presents an example of statistics results of SPM estimation before and after optimization. We estimated the SPM concentrations and evaluated the performances of the fuzzy model by calculating the mean square error MSE and the correlation coefficient ρ. We noticed that fuzzy estimation gives satisfactory results. Furthermore, the optimization process improves these results, the correlation coefficient is increased from 91% to 98%.

Table 1. Statistic comparison of SPM estimation process.

	Fuzzy model		Genetic optimization	
	MSE	ρ	MSE	ρ
Training data	0.0081039	0.9142	0.0015308	0.9842
Test data	0.0084515	0.9093	0.0021842	0.9762

After optimization, the fuzzy coefficients were applied to full ETM image. The resulting maps represent the spatial variability of water constituents (SPM, Chl, Turb and SDD) in coastal and marine surfaces. To examine this variability, we present in Fig. 4 the maps in pseudo-colours.

For all maps, it is obvious notice that the high parameters values are located near the coast and this phenomenon is more important for the Algiers bay. For example, the concentration of the SPM parameter is closed to 1300 mg/l near the coast. In fact, the data partition revealed nine clusters (C_i) which correspond to 9 nine rules (Eq. 1). This means that this site has a high risk of pollution and presents a complex system requiring a high number of rules to interpret this wide variability. This information motivates us to exploit the results maps and propose a new tool to characterize the water quality, to localize the sources of pollution and identify the most polluted sites of Algiers bay.

3   PSD Analysing

The pollution signature draw exploits the obtained maps of Fig. 4 and provides a tool to evaluate the water quality at any point of the bay. This signature gathers in the same graph the marine indices in the following order: SPM, Chl, Turb and SDD and presents the normalized concentration of each index.

Figure 5(a) shows an example of PSD taken at different distances of Oued Elharrach. In the same graph, we reported a PSD taken at the large of the bay and considered as a reference PSD (purple color). Compared to this latter, we note high concentrations of SPM, Chl, Turb recorded just at the embouchure of the oued. The discharges poured at the oued are transported at several meters, and even kilometres from their source as it is illustrated by the PSDs taken at 300 m, 900 m, 1500 m and 3000 m from the oued.

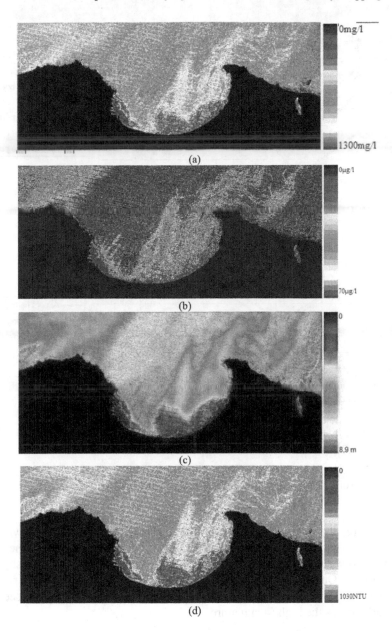

Fig. 4. Coastal water indices maps for Algiers bay. (a) SPM map, (b) Chl map, (c) SDD map and (d) Turb map.

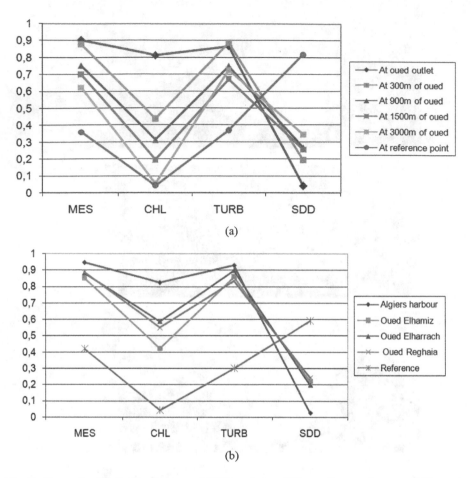

Fig. 5. Example of pollution signature. (a) PSDs taken at different distance from oued Elharrach, (b) PSDs taken at different sites.

Furthermore, the comparison between the PSDs of different sites provides an appreciation of water quality by its degree of pollution and hence, allows the detection of the risky sites. Figure 5(b) shows the average PSDs taken at risky sites (Algiers harbour, Oued Elharrach, oued Elhamiz and oued Reghaia). We also reported in the same graph a reference PSD taken at the large of the bay. It can be seen that Algiers harbour has the highest signature.

4   Pollution Map

Water classification based on the nature of waters components was proposed by Morel and Prieur [10]. Waters of the Case-I are those for which phytoplankton has a role in determining the water optical properties. Whereas the Case-II are determined or strongly influenced by the particulate and dissolved organic matter including the main water constituents as SPM, Chl and DOM. This classification is widely used until nowadays. In this context and from forementioned findings, we typify Algiers Bay coastal waters on the basis of the PSD characterization.

4.1 Selection of Risky Sites

According to the PAC's reports, Algiers's bay gathered about 70% of industrial and urban dismissals of PAC's basins [11]. It is considered as point of meting of all rejects of rivers (Oued el-harrach, Oued El-Hamiz and Oued Reghaia). Around 110.4 Hm3/year of domestic wastewater are discharged in this bay. Add to this, 5.4 millions m3/an of industrial wastewater coming from industrial cities which surround the bay (Hussein Dey, Bordj ElKiffan, Elhamiz and Rouiba). It should be noted that the water purification rate is around 47% for PAC region and it mainly concern Réghaia and Rouiba basin's without missing the oil pollution due to Algiers's harbour. These remarks reveal a high risk on some sites which need the integration of remote sensing tool in order to follow as well temporal as spatial of their pollution degree.

4.2 PSD Analysis

The analysis of some PSD related to risky sites (Fig. 5(b)) allows the evaluation of the pollution degree of these sites. Indeed, the PSDs of oued Elharrach and Oued Reghaia are similar. These sites are characterized by the same type of discharges (industrial discharges and wastewater). Also, oued Elhamiz has a low PSD value compared to those of oued Elharrach and oued Reghaia, but it remains significant when compared to the reference PSD. Thus, Algiers harbour is assigned to case-I (Strong Pollution), Oued Elharrach and Oued Reghaia are affected to the case-II (Average Pollution) while Oued Elhamiz is considered as case-III (Slight Pollution).

From risky sites relevant to different cases of water quality (Strong pollution, Average Pollution and Slight Pollution), we have selected some ROIs (region Of Interest) and extract their corresponding value in SPM, Chl, SDD and Turb images (see Fig. 6(a)). Also, we selected an ROI in clear water and urban area to construct a training data of five classes. Using Maximum Likelihood [12], the classification result is shown in Fig. 6. The pollution map highlights the most affected sites which present a high pollution risk. To evaluate our results and with a lake of ground realty, we compare our map to PAC (Plan d'Action Cotier) reports established on Algiers bay [11]. The obtained map highlights the risky sites which are cited in PAC reports.

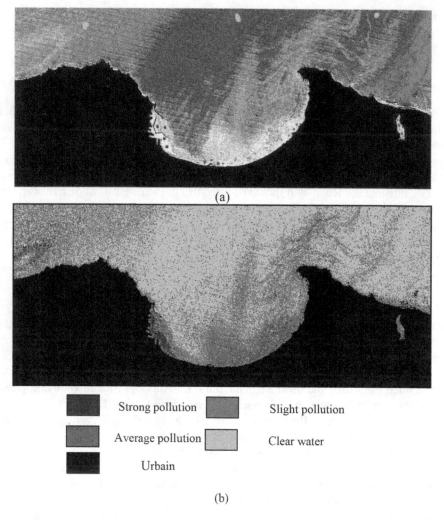

Fig. 6. Algiers bay water classification. (a) ROIs selection, (b) Pollution map

5   Conclusion

In this work, we proposed a coastal water quality using the combination of multispectral imagery and in-situ measurements. The first part is focused on the estimation and mapping of coastal water indices using an hybridization of fuzzy modeling and genetic optimization. The generalization of this hybridization to full images provides a map representing the spatial variability of water indices in the coastal and marine areas. Second and from these maps, Pollution Signature Draw "PSD" is constructed to characterize the water quality and to determine the boundaries of coastal zones with different water types. Finally, the comparison of some PSDs taken at risky sites of Algiers bay highlighted the pollution degree of each site and allowed a water quality classification. The latter was coherent with the ground truth of the studied site. Moreover, and using multi-temporal remote sensing images, a PSDs analysis can give an important information for coastal water quality monitoring in order to determine seasonal and yearly changes. These objectives are under consideration for future works.

References

1. Lounis, B., Belhadj Aissa, A., Rabia, S., Ramoul, A.: Hybridisation of fuzzy systems and genetic algorithms for water quality characterisation using remote sensing data. Int. J. Image Data Fus. **4**(2), 171–196 (2013). doi:10.1080/19479832.2011.617318. ISSN 1947-9832 (Print), 1947-9824 (Online)

2. Sathyendranath, S.: Remote Sensing of Ocean Colour in Coastal, and Other Optically-Complex Waters, IOCCG Report Number 3, Edited by Bedford Institute of Oceanography, Canada (2000)

3. Froidefond, J.M., Doxaran, D.: Télédétection optique appliquée à l'étude des eaux côtières. Télédétection **4**(2), 579–597 (2004)

4. Acker, J., Ouillon, S., Gould, R., Arnone, R.: Measuring marine suspended sediment concentrations from space: history and potential. In: 8th International Conference on Remote Sensing for Marine and Coastal Environments, Halifax, Canada, 17–19 May 2005

5. Zhang, Y., Pulliainen, J., Koponen, S., Hallikainen, M.: Application of an empirical neural network to surface water quality estimation in the Gulf of Finland using combined optical data and microwave data. Remote Sens. Environ. **81**, 327–336 (2002)

6. Cococcioni, M., Corsini, G., Lazzerini, B., Marcelloni, F.: Approaching the ocean color problem using fuzzy rules. IEEE Trans. Syst. Man Cybern. Part B Cybern. **34**(3), 1360–1373 (2004)

7. Takagi, T., Sugeno, M.: Fuzzy identification of systems and its application to modeling and control. IEEE Trans. Syst. Man Cybern. **15**, 116–132 (1985)

8. Lounis, B., Rabia, S., Ramoul, A., Belhadj Aissa, A.: An adaptive method using genetic fuzzy system to estimate suspended particulates matters SPM from Landsat and MODIS data. In: Fourth International Conference on Image and Signal Processing, ICISP 2010, Trois-Rivières, Québec, Canada (2010). ISBN 364213680-X, 9783642136801

9. Man, K.F., Tang, K., Kwong, S., Halang, S.: Genetic for Control and Signal Processing. Springer, London (1997)

10. Morel, A., Prieur, L.: Analysis of variations in ocean color. Limnol. Oceanogr. **22**(4), 709–722 (1977)

11. Mohamed, L.: Analyse de durabilité dans le cadre du PAC: Zone côtière algéroise (Algérie). Rapport du 4ème atelier, Alger, pp. 16–17, mai 2004. www.planbleu.org/publications/pac_alger_atelier4.pdf

12. Cocquerez, J.P., Philipp, S.: Analyse d'images: filtrage et segmentation, Edition Masson (1997)

MMS and GIS for Self-driving Car and Road Management

Vincenzo Barrile[1](✉) ⓘ, Giuseppe Maria Meduri[1] ⓘ, Maira Critelli[1],
and Giuliana Bilotta[2](✉) ⓘ

[1] DICEAM Department, Università Mediterranea di Reggio Calabria, Reggio Calabria, Italy
vincenzo.barrile@unirc.it, ing.giuseppemariameduri@gmail.com,
maira.critelli.910@studenti.unirc.it
[2] Planning Department, Università IUAV di Venezia, Venice, Italy
giuliana.bilotta@iuav.it

Abstract. More and more often, there is talk of autonomous cars or "intelligent guidance" that can detect and navigate without human intervention. The proposed system is a vehicle equipped for the Mobile Mapping System (MMS) with sensors that fathom the environment with radar techniques, LIDAR, GPS and cameras, capable of tracking paths, identify obstacles, and recognize road signs for the detailed knowledge of road network. This system supports both the user in the automatic driving systems via the creation/update of maps, both the public administrations with the help of GIS platforms and/or more additional sensors, in order to have databases and references regarding road maintenance, mitigating the risk of accidents, maintaining higher levels of safety.

We are trying an experimentation on a "rudimental" equipped vehicle; it is therefore only a rudimentary vehicle for testing and experimentations, which are still at an early stage.

Keywords: Mobile mapping systems · Geographical information systems · Mobile computing

1 Introduction

In recent years, many researches have been carried out to develop the so-called "intelligent vehicles", whose objective is to ensure the standard of driving more comfortable and safer. For this purpose, it is of fundamental importance, besides the use of ever more sophisticated and reliable sensors, the implementation of algorithms that make it possible to handle and interpret the amount of information coming from the external environment. As well as communication systems that very quickly must allow extremely rapid acquisition and renovation of what is available in the databases [1] and GIS platforms for MMS.

Particularly interesting, studying aspects of intelligent guidance, once it is chosen by the driver the route to be performed, it is all that relates to the interaction of the vehicle and its trajectory both with the road infrastructure on which it is located both with vehicles present on it. So, in terms of comfort and above all of safety in order to avoid road accidents, special importance take both the interpretation of the signs present on the infrastructure both the trajectory control and lane changes.

© Springer International Publishing AG 2017
O. Gervasi et al. (Eds.): ICCSA 2017, Part IV, LNCS 10407, pp. 68–80, 2017.
DOI: 10.1007/978-3-319-62401-3_6

In the article, therefore, it will be discussed first the two problems of tracking trajectories and traffic sign recognition [2]. In fact, whatever the system, the analysis of the characteristics of the road structure and the interaction with the traffic flow, which lead to certain trajectories of the vehicle, are key factors to implement automatic devices that help increase the safety and reduce congestion traffic. Moreover, these factors lead to the creation/update continuously databases and maps in support of technology; It is subsequently described the instrumental equipment.

2 Tracking of Trajectories

The research that we propose refers to the selection of paths and the identification of road signs, in view of organizing a complete system.

The standard instrumental equipment (Fig. 1) for such surveys consists of:

- Cameras that can perform images and movies and allow to acquire and possibly subsequently categorize signage, furniture, driveways, house numbers and road topography, location pad and type of containers for the collection of urban waste, integration to the mapping of the networks technology in the area (water, sewer, electric, telephone, gas, etc.);
- Odometer and GPS;
- Laser Scanners for 3D urban reconstruction, street furniture and road, vertical elements;
- Profilometer laser, which allows to detect the IRI parameter in real time and the parameters relating to rutting, macrotexture and longitudinal and transverse geometry, the presence of holes;
- GPR (Ground Penetrating Radar) for underground utilities.

Fig. 1. Equipped vehicle

We would like to upgrade it. The combination of use will depend on the type of survey or result to be achieved.

Any tracking system relies on the use of GPS data and an exchange of information between the vehicle and the processing center. Among the various configurations, we made a comparison between European Geostationary Navigation Overlay System (EGNOS) and the Real Time Kinematic (RTK) method to check their performance (Fig. 2).

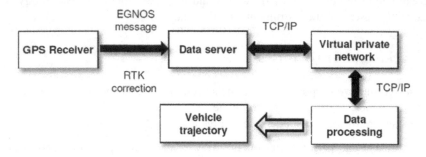

Fig. 2. Operational schema of the implemented architecture

The technological components of the system are a device for detecting the position (GPS), a transmission device (mobile phone) and a data processing center with GIS platform. The vehicle sends the position data and the instantaneous speed (in addition to other information as a function of active sensors on the vehicle) to a processing point that manages a database of the road network. In specific stretch of road, we have analyzed and processed information and track the vehicles by correlating information about the vehicle position to the road network graph.

However, the sensors used for the location of vehicles are affected by measurement errors that significantly reduce the accuracy of the position. The use of digital maps continually updated, enables us to correct and improve the position measurements through algorithms map matching [3] combining the position and trajectory of the vehicle identified by the sensors with the routes available on the digital map. Simultaneously, the information sent from the vehicle with the various sensors used allows updating the maps in terms of routes, road signs, characteristics of the infrastructure, traffic accidents, road works, etc.

To obtain the position of the vehicle, we made a comparison between two different methods: EGNOS and RTK. The EGNOS system [4] provides immediately location data, while the RTK method [5] however requires a real-time data processing to calculate the position object. RTK is more accurate than EGNOS, but requires more computational efforts. In terms of hardware instrumentation and software, the use of EGNOS depends on available commercial devices, while RTK method requires customized software architectures.

We therefore performed field tests in which precision of RTK is compared with the simplicity and speed of EGNOS to verify potential, future application where, for example when overtaking, the speed of calculation may be more relevant than the accuracy.

Regarding communication systems, the possibility of using a Wi-Fi network has advantages in terms of costs and speed thanks to the very low latency, but has also disadvantages for the limits of distance between the antennas and signal quality. Generally, the limit of distance is no more 100 m in good weather with a clear line of sight between antennas and the absence of obstacles between them. The signal quality is influenced by parameters such as the type of antenna adopted and potential interference.

Instead, the use of the mobile phone net has as advantage the complete independence among stations/vehicles, greater reliability because it does not require compliance with minimum distances and remote data processing capability. As disadvantages, it has higher costs, because each device has to be equipped with a mobile network modulus and a SIM card with a specific data plan or a phone contract, significantly higher latencies.

By using a RTK GPS suitably implemented to estimate the percentage of points relocated that deviates from the road side by a known quantity, we estimate the precision concerning measure and location - punctually and in real-time. In addition, to detect and reduce the effect of errors or unstable traffic flow conditions, we adopted some filters:

- All the measures, whose speed values are under a pre-fixed threshold, have to be removed;
- All the measures realized at less than 20 m from a crossroad have to be removed;
- All the measures with an absolute value of acceleration greater than 2 m/s², probably caused by location errors or unstable traffic conditions, have to be removed;
- All the speed measures, whose difference from the average value in the road section is greater than the typical deviation, have to be removed;
- All the road sections where typical deviations are greater than 10 km/h have to be analysed carefully. Such roads have to be split in smaller segments in order to evaluate the speed spatial distribution more in details.

By using such criteria, we excluded from the analysis anomalous data associated to speed reduction caused by traffic lights in congested traffic conditions, pedestrian crossings, crossroads, bottlenecks.

Figure 3(a) shows the map-matching obtained by using EGNOS (right side: path in magenta and green dots) and RTK (left side: path in yellow and blue dots) for a test

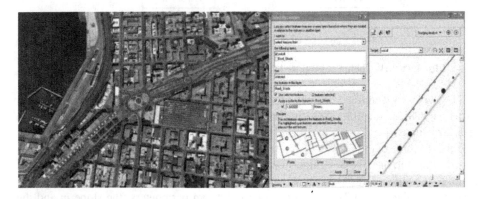

Fig. 3. (a) Positioning errors depicted by using a suitable GIS function; (b) Points reproduced by EGNOS (on the right) and RTK (on the left)

vehicle moving. The picture shows, as expected, that RTK provides points closer to the real, ideal trajectory followed by the test-vehicle (e.g., right line in the middle of the lane). Furthermore, data have been depicted by using a GIS function, which localizes points whose distance from the ideal trajectory (lane centre line) is greater than a prefixed threshold value. Figure 3(b) shows the results obtained with both EGNOS (on the right side) and RTK (on the left side). As we can see, RTK provides better results than EGNOS, although with a major computational effort.

3   Road Signs Recognition

The problem of detection of road signs both vertical and horizontal within the framework of intelligent guidance is of fundamental importance in order to regulate the movement of vehicles and ensure the necessary safety standards. In this sense, a key aspect is that the rapidity of response of the methodology used, as there are several methods, which, although automated, require onerous processing procedures with consequent delays in delivering the result.

We compared two approaches still being optimized.

3.1   Standard Hough Transform Algorithm

The first involves the use of a rapid economic survey method and self-sufficient that uses the Standard Hough Transform (SHT) algorithm [6]. It detects the type of signage within the macro-class of signals and then, with a particular car pack implemented in Matlab, characterizes it specifically with an extended version of the SHT, known as Generalized HT (GHT) for detecting the specific sign in its macro-class previously established. Figure 4 shows a schematic representation of the implemented method [7].

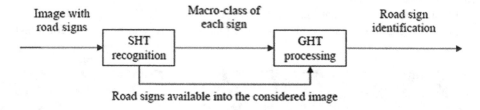

Fig. 4. Block schema of proposed approach to recognize road signs in raw images

The HT is a technique of forms extraction from digital images that, in its classical expression SHT, identifies lines in the image, but has been extended to identify also arbitrary shapes [8]. To achieve this objective, it must be able to detect group of pixels that lie on a line or curve.

For this purpose, the SHT algorithm uses an array called accumulator whose size is equal to the number of unknown parameters. For example, in the case of a straight line $y = mx + b$ the Hough Transform has two unknown parameters: the slope m and the intercept b. For each pixel and around it, SHT algorithm determines whether there are sufficient indications that pixel belongs to a straight line; if so, it calculates the parameters of this line, and then looks at other set points that meet those parameters increasing the number of points that constitute the line.

The GHT (Generalized Hough Transform) is an extension of SHT (Standard Hough Transform), used to detect forms that cannot be described by simple analytical formulas. Instead, a more complex representation is used, such as arrays or other mathematical constructs that represent patterns, shapes or vectors.

The basic idea for the search of forms is based on the "validation" hypothesis in which is defined the curve that you want to search in the scene, for each point of the image are calculated the parameters of all the curves that could pass for that point. Are then increased its cells of an n-dimensional space (with n number of parameters) that correspond to the different curves. This therefore generates a function of accumulation within the domain of the parameter space. The result obtained (the forms we are searching at the start) will be constituted by the maximum of the accumulation function.

At a computational level, the GHT roughly consists in making each examined pixel in an image to "project" a copy of the searched pattern at various angles and scales. Generally, projection and comparison takes place starting from the center of a certain object, but, under special conditions, it is possible to start elsewhere. Then keeping track of how many pixel matches for a given scale and angle occurred between the "projection" and the tested image. Therefore, the most general algorithm definition says to do exactly that: creating a special reference data structure (usually a binary image, in the form of a table, called R-Table) and essentially comparing its "boundary" or "contour" with groups of pixels (having a central or boundary pixel for reference) [9]. For further details, let us firstly consider to have a fixed orientation and size of in study object (see Fig. 5). Here, we pick a so called reference point (x_c, y_c), where:

$$x = x_c + x'$$
$$y = y_c + y'$$

(1)

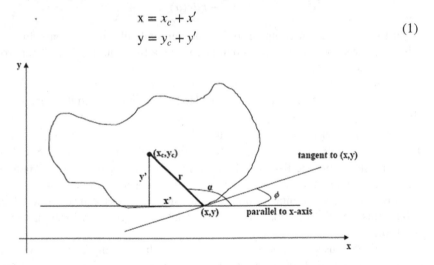

Fig. 5. Geometric schema of GHT determination for an object having fixed orientation and size

Fig. 6. Sample frame at a resolution 800 × 600 pixels in 8-bit format

On the other hand, we know that:

$$\cos(\pi - \alpha) = \frac{y'}{r} \Rightarrow y' = r\cos(\pi - \alpha) = -rsin(\alpha)$$
$$\sin(\pi - \alpha) = \frac{x'}{r} \Rightarrow x' = r\sin(\pi - \alpha) = -rcos(\alpha)$$

(2)

Combining Eqs. (1) and (2), we have:

$$x_c = x + rcos(\alpha)$$
$$y_c = y + rsin(\alpha)$$

(3)

In this way we can compute Φ, i.e. the perpendicular to gradients direction, and subsequently store the reference point (x_c, y_c) as a function off Φ: in other words, we can build the R-table.

The R-table allows us to use the contour edge points and gradient angle to recompute the location of the reference point. We need to build a separate R-table for each different object.

Summing up, after a quantization of the image space P $[x_{cmin}, \ldots, x_{cmax}] [y_{cmin}, \ldots, y_{cmax}]$, for each edge point (x, y) and using the gradient angle Φ, we retrieve from the R-table all the (α, r) values indexed under Φ. Then, for each (α, r), we compute the candidate reference point according to Eq. (3).

Now, we increase a suitable counter measuring the votes for the considered reference point. Thus, possible locations of the object contour are given by local maxima in $P[x_c]$ $[y_c]$ [10].

The images used for our experiments are captured using cameras with which is equipped the vehicle. They were controlled by an odometer so that it could set a sampling of images every x meters.

In a first case, each image has been passed to the block recognition SHT whose procedure is described in Fig. 7.

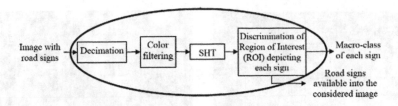

Fig. 7. Subschema of the SHT block

To obtain satisfactory results it is necessary to perform before the transformation, some preliminary steps in order to lighten the content for which it is decimated to expedite the procedure, thus reducing the resolution to 200 × 150 pixels and then filtered with a self-implemented color filter.

The color filter has the function of reducing the amount of information in the image because the road signal has a certain color on a background of another color, and then it is necessary for identifying a color domain useful for signal discrimination within the database.

Figure 8 shows the decimated and filtered version of the image in Fig. 6. Thus, the SHT can be applied to the considered image, e.g. to frame 4155. Here, it has been possible to recognize the shape of the pictured signs by the following considerations on the accumulator:

- for a triangular object, the maximum number of lines that cross 1 point is lower than three times the median value of the number of lines that cross the same point;
- for a squared object, numbers of lines that cross 1 point, 2 points,…, until *n* points, in which *n* is approximately the length of the square, is almost the same;
- for a rounded object, numbers of lines that cross 1 point, 2 points,…, until *n* oints, where *n* is approximately the diameter of the rounded object, exponentially increase.

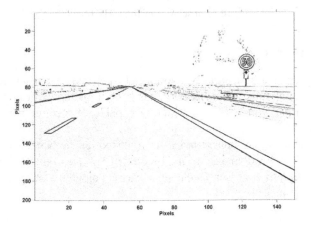

Fig. 8. The filtered version of the decimated image shown in Fig. 6

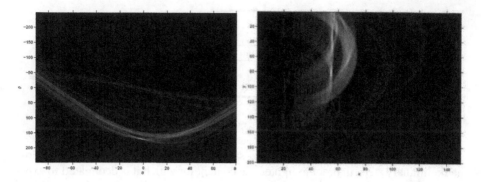

Fig. 9. (a) SHT accumulator into the Hough domain, (b) SHT accumulator into the image domain

Once the shape of the road sign has been detected, the result and its macro-class are passed to the GHT sub-block (see Fig. 10). Here, the ROI is compared with a set of templates, which are organized and queried according to the macro-class membership (Fig. 9).

At the end of the procedure, a message identifying the road sign appears to the user.

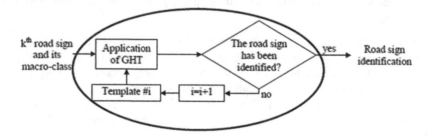

Fig. 10. Subschema of the GHT block

3.2 Neural Networks

The second approach uses Neural Networks [11, 12] and in particular, in order to streamlining the computational complexity, has been implemented using in a modular way more Neural Networks, each of which is capable of recognizing not the entire symbol but part of it.

The signal elements are considered a set of "frontier elements" (triangle, circle, rhombus, etc.), of "color domains" of the border, of "image contained in the border" (internal image). In turn, the "frontier elements" are considered a composition of predefined geometric elements (Fig. 11).

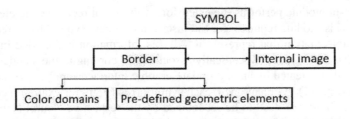

Fig. 11. Breakdown of a road sign or a superficial defectiveness of the street plan

As before stated, we developed the application that we refer in this work with a modular approach: it, in the first instance, can be seen as the union of four software modules (see Figs. 4, 5, 6, 7 and 8), each of which is devoted to the fulfilment of specific functions:

1. The module Plug-in has the aim to extend the number of recognizable and classifiable signals;
2. The kernel, real direction of the application, coordinates the various modules, pre-processes and post-processes the I/O data of the same modules, and interacts with the user;
3. The NNS (Neural Network Simulator) Form is a DLL (Dynamic Link Library software) developed by 'University of Tübingen and freely usable, has the task of processing the algorithm which implements the neural network trained to recognize the elements of interest;
4. The I/O (Input/Output) GIS manages the interface with the GIS software.

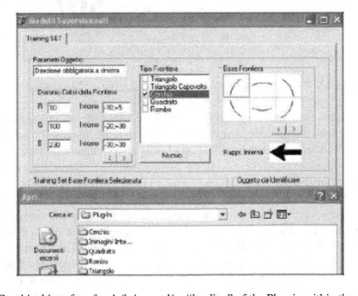

Fig. 12. Graphical interface for defining and/or "loading" of the Plug-in within the application

The Plug-in module performs the extension of the set of recognizable elements, as mentioned. This module requires, for the insertion of a new symbol to be recognized, of all those information that represent it. All this information is included in an XML file, which has a "language" specifically associated, according to the standard for this format. The file is created by an appropriate graphic interface supplied with the application itself (Fig. 12). As mentioned, each symbol (road sign, for example) consists of several parts, those that need to be recognized by the respective Neural Networks are the primitive elements, namely the geometrical elements constituting the borders and the internal symbols to it (Text "Stop", image "Speed bymp", etc.). The related "training set" (set of exemplary data, useful training) are created from an image built with any graphic editing tool, which is processed by the first module of the software object of this work (Fig. 13 particularized specifically for the case of recognition of the "speed limit" signal) and then creates a file compatible with JNNS.

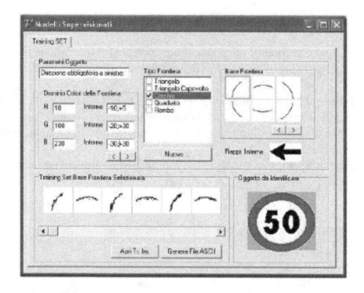

Fig. 13. Generation of the "training set" for the signal "Speed Limit"

The algorithm that underlies the recognition of symbols is constituted by three macro-phases; with the first, we have a pre-processing of the images, the second makes use of Neural Networks for the classification of primitive elements, and finally the third is concerned with identifying the road signs starting from the information obtained. The components are processed the following steps: (1) Decimation. (2) Color Filter: with the color pixels not belonging to the "color domains", identifying a given border, they are converted to a single default color, obviously not belonging to any domain of useful color. (3) Partitioning: the image is divided into sub matrices 7×8 that constitute the inputs of Neural Networks. (4) Recognition: Scan of the submatrices and calculation output of Neural Networks; this operation is possible through the operation link (connection) between the software used and the JNNS kernel (Dynamic Link Library). (5) Border Identification: Through a simple proximity, analysis of the various submatrices in which has been recognized a geometric element; it determines the type of the border. (6) Identification symbol: the relative area at a given recognized border is passed to the neural network for the recognition of internal images. It is shown in Figs. 14(a) and (b). Both recognition methods have provided appreciable results.

Fig. 14. (a) Rutting; (b) Segmented border of the rutting

Road signals are made up of several parts; the ones that need to be recognized by the neural networks are the primitive elements, i.e. the geometric elements constituting the frontiers and the internal symbols to it.

Neural networks used to classify individual geometric boundary elements are feed-forward networks [12] neuronal connections are unidirectional, signals propagate cascading from input to output); Neurons adopt the sigmoid transfer function; Are given an input layer of x neurons and a single neuron for output. Specifically, it is assigned value 1.0 if the symbol to which the network is associated is recognized or 0 otherwise.

In addition, we implemented a software, which is still being tested, for the management of the various equipment and applications supplied to the vehicle. It allows, depending on the type of survey, to activate the required sensors\tools with their settings

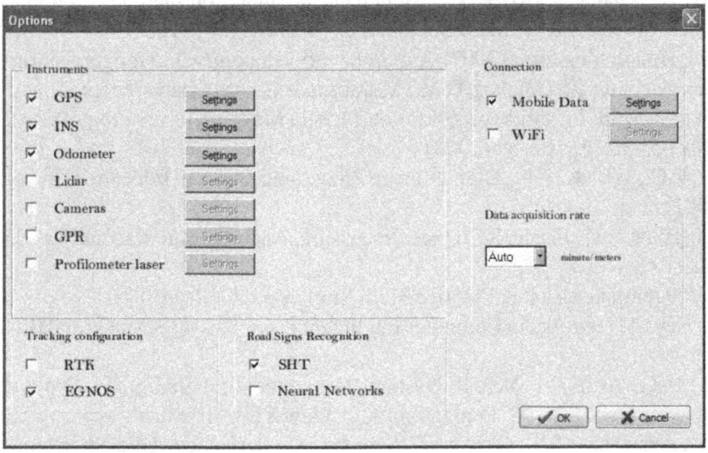

Fig. 15. Draft of the management software mask

as well as tracking mode, recognition signals mode and connection type to be used for communication with the data center, GIS platform and with databases (Fig. 15).

4   Conclusions

Recognizing of road signs is an important starting point to implement on-board vehicle devices aimed to improve safety.

This experimental work shows that the use of GIS functions, combined with the good performances of RTK methods [13], open promising scenarios for monitoring urban roads and then adopting efficient solutions to reduce traffic negative impacts. Although this RTK solution is more expensive and complex to realize than the simpler EGNOS, whose main advantage is in the computing speed, however the RTK solutions are more interesting for their accuracy. Moreover, the approach based on Neural Networks has proven its effectiveness.

However, it should be considered that the aim of this work, still raw and experimental, is the realization of a self-driving car and therefore not just for GPS and traffic. In fact, based on the work already we done on this subject, we are preparing the necessary for the realization of a self-driving car.

References

1. Wolf, P., DeWitt, B.A.: Elements of Photogrammetry with Applications in GIS. McGraw-Hill, New York (2000)
2. Barrile, V., Postorino, M.N.: Un approccio GPS and GIS per la ricostruzione delle traiettorie veicolari in ambito urbano. LaborEst **13**, 38–43 (2016)
3. Quddus, M.A., Ochieng, W.Y., Noland, R.B.: Integrity of map matching algorithms. Transp. Res. C-Emer. **14**(4), 283–302 (2006)
4. Chen, R., Toran-Marti, F., Ventura-Traveset, J.: Access to the EGNOS signal in space over mobile-IP. GPS Solut. **7**(1), 16–22 (2003)
5. Al-Shaery, A., Zhang, S., Rizos, C.: An enhanced calibration method of GLONASS inter-channel bias for GNSS RTK. GPS Solut. **17**(2), 165–173 (2013)
6. Wikipedia: Hough transform (2007). http://en.wikipedia.org/wiki/Houghtransform
7. Barrile, V., Cacciola, M., Meduri, G.M., Morabito, F.C.: Automatic recognition of road signs by hough transform. In: 5th Symposium on Mobile Mapping Technology ISPRS Archives, vol. XXXVI-5/C55, pp. 62–67 (2008)
8. Gonzalez, R.C., Woods, R.E.: Digital Image Processing. Pearson Education, Inc., Englewood Cliffs (2002)
9. Sonka, M., Hlavac, V., Boyle, R.: Image Processing, Analysis, and Machine Vision. Springer, New York (1998)
10. Ballard, D.: Computer Vision. Prentice-Hall, Englewood Cliffs (1982)
11. Fu, L.M.: Neural Networks in Computer Intelligence, pp. 101–130. McGraw-Hill, New York (1994)
12. Simpson, P.K: Artificial Neural Systems-Foundations, Paradigms, Applications, and Implementations, pp. 80–103. Pergamon Press, New York (1990)
13. Barrile, V., Postorino, M.N.: GPS and GIS methods to reproduce vehicle trajectories in urban areas. Proc. Soc. Behav. Sci. **223**, 890–895 (2016)

Hyperspectral Data Classification
to Support the Radiometric Correction
of Thermal Imagery

Gabriele Bitelli[1], Rita Blanos[2], Paolo Conte[1],
Emanuele Mandanici[1(✉)], Paolo Paganini[2], and Carla Pietrapertosa[3]

[1] Department of Civil, Chemical, Environmental and Materials Engineering
(DICAM), University of Bologna, viale Risorgimento 2, Bologna, Italy
emanuele.mandanici@unibo.it
[2] National Institute of Oceanography and Experimental Geophysics,
Borgo di Grotta Gigante, Trieste, Italy
[3] Institute of Methodologies for Environmental Analysis (IMAA),
National Research Council (CNR), c/da S.Loja, 85050 Tito Scalo, PZ, Italy

Abstract. The derivation of surface temperature from thermal images requires
a proper modelling of the spectral characteristics of the observed surfaces, in
particular emissivity. Several possible approaches have been developed in literature. A first category of methods relies on the availability of multiple bands in
the thermal region, while a second family of methods, which can be applied also
with a single channel sensor, requires the derivation of emissivity values from
ancillary data.

The methodology, discussed in the present paper, involves the use of
hyperspectral images acquired by an AISA Eagle 1 K sensor installed on board
an aircraft platform. Data are composed of 61 bands in the visible and
near-infrared region. A supervised classification approach was adopted to derive
a map of the main materials appearing in the scene, with special attention to
roofing materials. The presented analyses were performed in a portion of the
urban area of Treviso (Italy), where two aerial surveys, one with a thermal
sensor and the second with the AISA sensor, were carried out in 2011.

All the presented activities were conducted in the framework of the European
project "EnergyCity - Reducing energy consumption and CO_2 emissions in
cities across Central Europe".

Keywords: Thermal imagery calibration · Hyperspectral image classification ·
Aerial thermography · EnergyCity project

1 Introduction

For an appropriate quantitative evaluation of surface temperatures at building scale,
several processing phases are necessary in order to process high resolution thermo-
graphic imagery, that are influenced by different factors. Above all, the effects of the
acquisition geometry, the topography of the investigated area, the influence of the
atmosphere on the radiation received by the sensor and the physical-chemical

© Springer International Publishing AG 2017
O. Gervasi et al. (Eds.): ICCSA 2017, Part IV, LNCS 10407, pp. 81–92, 2017.
DOI: 10.1007/978-3-319-62401-3_7

properties of the different materials lying on the ground strongly influence the registered temperature; the values of apparent temperature acquired by the thermal sensor must be thus corrected for the corresponding effects [1].

Among the above mentioned error sources, the most relevant appear to be the properties of the investigated surfaces related to the thermal portion of the electromagnetic spectrum: this effect can be taken into account through the correction for the different emissivities, that requires a proper assessment of the emissivity values for each surface emitting (or reflecting) thermal radiation. The emissivity value of a surface can range from zero to one, and is expressed in respect to the behavior of a blackbody, which has emissivity equal to unity and is considered a perfect emitter.

In previous studies, it has been demonstrated that a variation of 1% in emissivity produce a variation in temperature of about 0.3 °C [2], that may reach an error of 0.6 K for dry atmosphere conditions [3]. Moreover, in an urban environment a large variability of materials (and emissivities) usually occurs; in addition, the multiple reflections effect among the complex texture of this type of environment can induce differences between the effective emissivity and the emissivity of the single materials investigated [4]. Finally, emissivity values can be different even for the same material, due to ageing and weathering [5, 6]. Thus, emissivity is likely to be the major source of uncertainty in surface temperature mapping [1].

Emissivity values should be assessed for a surface in any case because, even with multi-spectral sensors with N thermal channels, the system composed of N radiative transfer equations (one for each channel) remains mathematically unsolvable, because there will always be N + 1 unknowns corresponding to the N emissivities in each wavelength and the surface temperature [7, 8].

As reported in literature, several methods can be used to separate the effects of both emissivity and temperature on the radiance at ground level, and thus deriving accurate temperature values for the investigated surfaces: the choice of the most appropriate method depends mainly on the number of thermal bands available, but also from other considerations such as the spatial resolution of the thermal imagery and the availability of ancillary data.

Apart from the number of channels, infrared systems can be categorized in different groups according to several criteria [9]. The primary difference is related to the spectral range in which infrared detectors are sensitive to thermal radiation; considering that in the thermal infrared region the main atmospheric windows are located between 3–5 µm and 8–14 µm, infrared systems can be divided in medium-wave (MW) and long-wave (LW) devices. Systems can be furtherly divided in single, linear and array detectors depending on the detector unit arrangement; focal plane arrays do not require mechanical scanning parts, because the detectors acquire at the same time the entire thermal frame. A further categorization of thermal infrared systems is related to the presence of a detector's cooling system: devices using a refrigerator unit are cooled infrared cameras, while uncooled ones operate at ambient temperature. Uncooled sensors are commonly employed in the LW band, where most of the infrared energy is emitted by targets at temperatures typical of the Earth's surface.

On the basis of the number of thermal infrared channels available, the methods to derive the land surface temperature have been categorized in four main groups [10]: single-channel, double-channel (or split-window), two-angle methods and other methods developed for sensors operating in more than two infrared channels or based on different techniques. Single channel methods generally require the assessment of surface emissivities in order to compute surface temperatures, although for new Land Surface Temperature (LST) retrieval methods the Land Surface Emissivity (LSE) is not strictly necessary [3]. In addition, they are very sensitive to atmospheric effects: in a previous work [10], the authors conclude that they become almost unusable with high water vapor contents in the atmosphere column (higher than 1 g/cm^3 for flights at an height of approximately 1000 m above the ground).

The methods to derive the land surface emissivity from space have been divided in three groups in more recent classifications [3, 8]: (semi) empirical methods, multi-channel Temperature/Emissivity Separation (TES) methods, and physically based methods. Even if in most investigations the importance and potential impacts of urban LSE have been ignored, often due to data unavailability, for accurate quantitative temperature analysis they must necessarily be considered.

When using a single thermal channel, only empirical methods can be applicable in practice for the estimation of surface emissivity [3]: generally, this category can be furtherly divided in classification-based methods and spectral index-based methods, also if hybrid procedures combining them both have also been applied. For the former category, the accuracy of classification and the representativeness of the emissivity values associated to the different classes result very important.

In literature, several spectral libraries containing emissivity values for several man made materials are available and could be used (such as the ASTER Spectral Library version 2.0 [11] and the spectral library of impervious urban materials at London Urban Micromet Data Archive – LUMA [5]). Actually, they don't completely represent the variety of anthropogenic materials present in urban areas and, moreover, they are generally sensor dependent; thus, especially for satellite analysis, an "A priori" knowledge of the materials (and their surface conditions) present in a specific urban area is suggested as a more suitable way if compared to spectral libraries [3], and described as definitely beneficial for LSE estimation. In this viewpoint, a supervised classification of the principal roof materials present on the test area, and a consequent assessment of the emissivity value of each class on the basis of spectral libraries has been followed in the present work to overcome the emissivity assessment problem.

Hyperspectral sensors may be a valuable data source for the classification of materials [12], since they can provide detailed spectral/spatial signatures for different materials by collecting data in many narrow bands distributed in an almost continuous wavelength range. They can be mounted on both aircraft and satellite platforms.

The various types of hyperspectral devices can be distinguished in several ways, including spectral and spatial resolution, number of bands, electronic design and scanning geometry. Commercially available hyperspectral sensors generally acquire images in the spectral range from 400 to 2500 nm and can acquire from tens to hundreds of bands with a band width as narrow as a few nanometers.

All the presented activities were conducted in the framework of the European project "EnergyCity - Reducing energy consumption and CO_2 emissions in cities across Central Europe", funded by Central Europe. The project (ended in 2013) involved the survey of seven cities across Central Europe (Bologna, Budapest, Ludwigsburg, Munich, Prague, Treviso, Velenje), with the aim of addressing the lack of user-friendly methods and processes to analyze in a multi-criteria Spatial Decision Support System (SDSS) the energy efficiency of buildings and renewable measures to reduce the carbon dioxide output generated in urban areas. Image analyses were carried out in all the seven cities; however, this paper discusses in detail only the processing for the city of Treviso (Italy). Anyway, the SDSS with the produced thermal maps and an energy classification of buildings for all the seven cities involved in the project are available at http://energycity2013.eu/webgis.php.

2 Materials and Methods

Hyperspectral images were acquired through the AISA Eagle 1 K system (developed by Spectral Imaging Ltd, Specim), composed of a push-broom sensor capable of collecting data within a spectral range from 400 to 970 nm, a data-acquisition unit in a PC, a GPS receiver, and an inertial navigation system (200 Hz). The hyperspectral sensor can acquire any band combination ranging from few multispectral bands to full hyperspectral data sets of 244 bands in the Visible Near Infrared (VNIR) spectrum.

Thermal images were acquired through a system composed by a thermal camera NEC TS9260, a data-acquisition unit in a PC, a GPS receiver, and an inertial navigation system (200 Hz). The camera has a spectral range of 8–13 μm and resolution of 640 × 480 pixels.

Obtaining high quality aerial images depends on several environmental and meteorological factors, including clouds, snow, wind, sun angle. Ideal conditions are clear sky and absence of strong winds that can cause upper air turbulence which makes difficult to maintain the planned direction. Hyperspectral surveys must be carried out during day; the optimum sun angle is between 25° and 45° above the horizon. Angles above 30° provide enough reflective light and minimize the effects of long shadows.

Thermal surveys, conversely, must be carried out at night; this is because during daytime, sunlight (both direct and diffused) causes infrared reflections which may interfere with the radiation emitted from the target. Ideally the survey should be carried out in cold conditions; the greater the difference between the exterior of the house and the outside air temperature, the more clearly the heat emission will be seen.

Aerial acquisitions are made overflying the ground along parallel lines called strips by taking images that have to be overlapped to each other; thermal and hyperspectral images acquisition require a detailed flight plan through which we obtain the necessary parameters of the aerial survey such as the height and the speed of the aircraft, the overlap between the photograms in each strip, the number of the strips and the overlap between them. Image frames must have a minimum forward overlap of 60%, and an overlap of 20% between parallel flight lines.

The area chosen for the experimentation regards the town of Treviso, in North-East Italy: the area is almost trapezoidal, has an extension of about 40 km^2 and includes the whole historic center of the city, part of the suburbs and some rural areas (Fig. 1). The generation of the thermal orthomosaic and the radiometric correction have interested only a smaller part of the test area, with an extension of about 10 km^2, centered on the historic center.

Fig. 1. Area covered by the aerial flight (blue) and test area (red). (Color figure online)

The thermal survey was performed on the 19th of February 2011 with adequate atmospheric conditions (slow winds, clear sky, air temperature <10 °C); considering a shot frequency of 30 images/minute, in order to obtain a Ground Sampling Distance (GSD) of 0.50 m and two overlapping factors of 60% and 20% in forward and transversal direction respectively, a flight height of about 850 m and a flight speed of about 110 knots were planned. The whole surveyed area was covered with 26 strips in OE direction, for a total of 2368 thermal frames.

Simultaneously to the thermal flight, a ground survey was performed in order to collect some ground truth data about the temperature and emissivity of some ground-level surfaces, and to measure some atmospheric parameters necessary for the radiometric correction of the thermal imagery of the test area. This survey was carried out using a FLIR P620 thermal camera, with a spatial resolution of 640 × 480 pixels operating in almost the same thermal band of the infrared sensor used for the aerial survey. For the measurements of air temperature and relative humidity a psychrometer was used.

Surface temperatures and emissivities were collected with a standard "non-contact" procedure at ground level, in correspondence of homogeneous pavements easily recognizable on thermal imagery, in locations uniformly scattered over the test area but easily accessible in the limited time span of the aerial survey: in total, ground truths of both surface temperature and emissivity values were collected in 12 locations (Fig. 2). Even if the presented analysis is focused on the estimation of roof temperatures, the validation sites are located at the ground level mainly for logistic reasons and to ensure a reasonable number of points. The geographic positions of the targets were computed

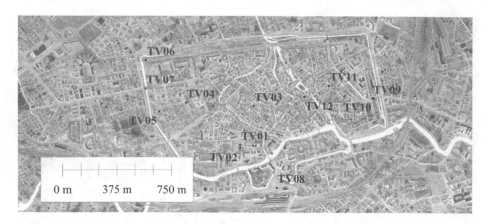

Fig. 2. A portion of the thermal mosaic of Treviso with the position of the ground surveys.

through post processing techniques using geodetic GNSS receiver recordings, in combination with data from a permanent GNSS station.

The hyperspectral survey was carried out on September 13, 2011 (Fig. 3). In this case, desired GSD has been set to 0.75 m, obtaining a planned value of 1250 m for the flight height and of 110 knots for the platform speed with the same transversal overlapping factor of 20%. The surveyed area was entirely covered with 12 parallel strips in OE direction and one strip in NS direction; the number of hyperspectral bands was set to 61 in order to limit the amount of digital data to be processed in the subsequent phases.

Fig. 3. True color composite of a portion of the hyperspectral mosaic of Treviso.

The acquired hyperspectral dataset was radiometrically and geometrically corrected using Caligeo software (Specim spectral imaging). The radiometric calibration transforms the raw data to radiance (mW/cm^2/sr/μm), using the dark data frame and the instrument calibration file that is prepared according to calibration measurements and source response. The geometric correction removes the aircraft waving effect from the image data and calculates ground coordinates to each image pixel using navigation and attitude data collected during the flight; to improve the georeferencing accuracy boresight calibration was applied. Afterward, the calibrated and georeferenced data were processed to remove the influence of the atmosphere using FLAASH (Fast Line-of-sight Atmospheric Analysis of Hypercubes, developed by Spectral Sciences, Inc.) [13] as implemented in the ENVI software package, which incorporates the MODTRAN4 radiation transfer code. The Mid-Latitude Summer atmospheric profile and the Urban aerosol/haze type (visibility 40 km) were used respectively to model the atmosphere. The 820 nm water absorption feature was used for water vapor retrieval, while no aerosol retrieval was set because the dataset does not cover all the necessary wavelengths.

Masks were applied to every image in order to eliminate the vegetation pixels. The masks were built by calculating the Normalized Different Vegetation Index (NDVI) and applying a threshold (>0.3) to eliminate the vegetation pixels; the application of this threshold was sufficient.

The atmospheric corrected and vegetation free hyperspectral data were classified using the pixel-based supervised approach Spectral Angle Mapper (SAM). SAM classification algorithm has the advantage of not to be strictly dependent on solar illumination; in fact, SAM is a spectral classification that treats each spectrum (the observed and the reference) as a vector in a space with dimensionality equal to the number of bands. The algorithm determines the spectral similarity between observed and reference spectra by calculating the angle between them; smaller angles represent more similar spectral characteristics.

The first classification step was to collect roof spectral signatures of different materials on the acquired images (Fig. 4). The spectral library was obtained from several Region Of Interest (ROI) drew on the images; each ROI represents a different material and was built using more than one polygon on the images. Identification of different materials was based on photointerpretation and some truths on the ground. In this preliminary study, three macro classes that represent the large part of roofs in this urban context have been identified: terracotta tiles, metal roofs, bituminous sheaths. The metal roofs class often includes cars, while the sheaths class includes asphalt roads. For these reasons, a mask based on the technical cartography of the Municipality of Treviso was used to exclude all pixels not belonging to roofs. The unclassified class therefore includes only unknown roofing materials, which correspond, anyway, to a limited portion of the roofs in the test area.

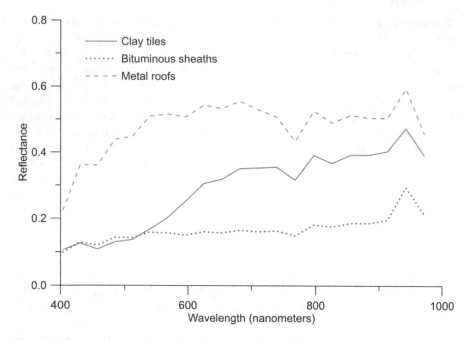

Fig. 4. Average spectral signatures of training regions extracted from AISA Eagle images.

3 Results

The classification process applied to hyperspectral images and described in the previous section resulted in a map of the three major types of roofing materials. A portion of the map is showed in Fig. 5. Some roofs remained unclassified, because their spectral signatures appear too different from those defined by the training dataset.

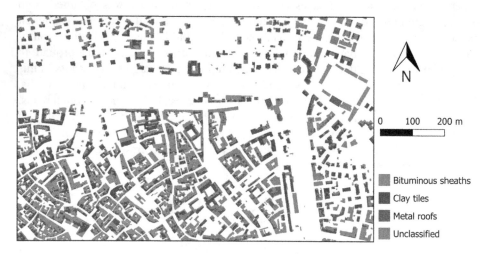

Fig. 5. A portion of the classification of the hyperspectral data cube (in white, areas not belonging to roof covers).

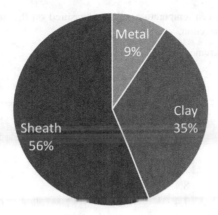

Fig. 6. Percentage of the total classified area belonging to each major roofing type.

Among the classified surfaces, however, the dominant roofing material appears to be sheaths, which include bituminous, slated or other reinforced sheaths (Fig. 6). This class covers about 56% of the total classified roof area. The second most employed roofing cover are clay tiles, which are largely adopted in the city center and in almost all historical buildings. Finally, only 9% of the classified roof area is covered by metal sheets.

An emissivity value derived from literature data [2] was assigned to each class, thus deriving an emissivity map from the classification. To check the accuracy of the emissivity correction, the temperature observed in the thermal images and measured on the ground were compared for the twelve locations where ground surveys were performed. As reported in Table 1, the difference between temperature observed in the raw images and measured on the ground is about 1.2 °C in average, while the same difference using calibrated thermal images decreases to about 0.4 °C in average.

As reported in Fig. 7, the histogram of the roofs cover temperatures shows a multimodal distribution. The peaks corresponding to the modes of the two most occurring materials (clay tiles and bituminous sheath) are evident. The metal class, instead, is less identifiable, since they represent only 9% of the total area, and shows a higher mean temperature value with a significantly larger variance. This effects may be related to the fact that this class is likely to include a range of metal materials with similar spectral characteristics in the visible and near-infrared spectral range, but different emissivity properties in the longwave thermal infrared.

Table 1. Comparison between temperature values measured on the field and observed on the images before and after correction.

Point	Field measurements		Raw images		Corrected images	
	ε	T	T	ΔT	T	ΔT
TV01	0.97	5.4	4.9	0.5	4.1	1.3
TV02	0.98	5.2	5.9	−0.7	5.2	0
TV04	0.91	8.8	6.6	2.2	8.9	−0.1
TV05	0.95	6.5	5.1	1.4	5.3	1.2
TV06	0.94	5.8	4.9	0.9	5.2	0.6
TV07	0.95	7.6	6.4	1.2	7	0.6
TV08	0.91	8.4	7.6	0.8	10.5	−2.1
TV10	0.9	7.4	4.6	2.8	6.5	0.9
TV11	0.97	5.9	5.9	0	5.5	0.4
TV12	0.91	9	6.3	2.7	8.4	0.6

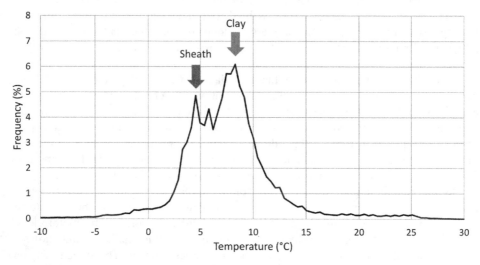

Fig. 7. Histogram of roof temperatures extracted from the corrected thermal map. Arrows indicate the peaks representative of the major roofing materials.

4   Conclusions

The presented work highlights the importance of the radiometric correction of aerial thermal imagery, in order to perform quantitative analyses involving temperature values. In this perspective, the effects of surface emissivity appear to be one of the major issues affecting the measurements. This is especially true for urban environments where different materials with a wide range of possible emissivity values occur.

To perform atmospheric and emissivity corrections with single channel instruments, ancillary data are necessary. Among the possible data sources, hyperspectral images appear promising for the discrimination of different roofing materials. At this stage only three major classes has been considered, but a finer separation in more specific subclasses will be possible when a sufficient number of training sites verified on the field become available.

Acknowledgements. The work was primarily performed in the framework of Central Europe project 2CE126P3 "EnergyCity - Reducing energy consumption and CO_2 emissions in cities across Central Europe" (PI T. Csoknyai).

References

1. Mandanici, E., Conte, P., Girelli, V.A.: Integration of aerial thermal imagery, LiDAR data and ground surveys for surface temperature mapping in urban environments. Rem. Sens. **8**, 880 (2016). https://doi.org/10.3390/rs8100880
2. Bitelli, G., Conte, P., Csoknyai, T., Franci, F., Girelli, V.A., Mandanici, E.: Aerial thermography for energetic modelling of cities. Remote Sens **7**, 2152–2170 (2015). https://doi.org/10.3390/rs70202152
3. Chen, F., Yang, S., Su, Z., Wang, K.: Effect of emissivity uncertainty on surface temperature retrieval over urban areas: investigations based on spectral libraries. ISPRS J. Photogram. Remote Sens. **114**, 53–65 (2016). https://doi.org/10.1016/j.isprsjprs.2016.01.007
4. Yang, J., Wong, M.S., Menenti, M., Nichol, J.: Modelling the effective emissivity of the urban canopy using sky view factor. ISPRS J. Photogram. Remote Sens. **105**, 211–219 (2015). https://doi.org/10.1016/j.isprsjprs.2015.04.006
5. Kotthaus, S., Smith, T.E.L., Wooster, M.J., Grimmond, C.S.B.: Derivation of an urban materials spectral library through emittance and reflectance spectroscopy. ISPRS J. Photogram. Remote Sens. **94**, 194–212 (2014). https://doi.org/10.1016/j.isprsjprs.2014.05.005
6. Adderley, C., Christen, A., Voogt, J.A.: The effect of radiometer placement and view on inferred directional and hemispheric radiometric temperatures of an urban canopy. Atmos. Meas. Tech. **8**, 2699–2714 (2015). https://doi.org/10.5194/amt-8-2699-2015
7. Mandanici, E., Conte, P.: Aerial thermography for energy efficiency of buildings: the ChoT project. In: Proceedings of SPIE 10008, Remote Sensing Technologies and Applications in Urban Environments, 1000808 (2016). https://doi.org/10.1117/12.2241256
8. Li, Z.L., Wu, H., Wang, N., Qiu, S., Sobrino, J.A., Wan, Z., Tang, B.H., Yan, G.: Land surface emissivity retrieval from satellite data. Int. J. Remote Sens. **34**(9–10), 3084–3127 (2013). https://doi.org/10.1080/01431161.2012.716540
9. Minkina, W., Dudzik, S.: Infrared Thermography: Errors and Uncertainties. Wiley, Chichester (2009)
10. Sobrino, J.A., Jiménez-Muñoz, J.C., Zarco-Tejada, P.J., Sepulcre-Cantó, G., De Miguel, E.: Land surface temperature derived from airborne hyperspectral scanner thermal infrared data. Remote Sens. Environ. **102**(1–2), 99–115 (2006). https://doi.org/10.1016/j.rse.2006.02.001
11. Baldridge, A.M., Hook, S.J., Grove, C.I., Rivera, G.: The ASTER spectral library version 2.0. Remote Sens. Environ. **113**, 711–715 (2009). https://doi.org/10.1016/j.rse.2008.11.007

12. Salem, F., Kafatos, M., El-Ghazawi, T., Gomez, R., Yang, R.: Hyperspectral image assessment of oil-contaminated wetland. Int. J. Remote Sens. **26**(4), 811–821 (2005). https://doi.org/10.1080/01431160512331316883
13. Cooley, T., Anderson, G.P., Felde, G.W., Hoke, M.L., Ratkowskia, A.J., Chetwynd, J.H., Gardner, J.A., Adler-Golden, S.M., Matthew, M.W., Berk, A., Bernstein, L.S., Acharya, P. K., Milled, D., Lewise, P.: FLAASH, a MODTRAN4-based atmospheric correction algorithm, its application and validation. In: IEEE International Geoscience and Remote Sensing Symposium, vol. 3, pp. 1414–1418. IEEE (2002). https://doi.org/10.1109/IGARSS. 2002.1026134

Evaluation of the Laser Response of Leica Nova MultiStation MS60 for 3D Modelling and Structural Monitoring

Roberta Fagandini[1], Bianca Federici[2], Ilaria Ferrando[2],
Sara Gagliolo[2], Diana Pagliari[1(✉)], Daniele Passoni[2], Livio Pinto[1],
Lorenzo Rossi[1], and Domenico Sguerso[2]

[1] DICA – Geodesy and Geomatics Section, Politecnico di Milano,
Piazza Leonardo da Vinci 32, 20133 Milan, Italy
{roberta.fagandini, diana.pagliari, livio.pinto,
lorenzol.rossi}@polimi.it
[2] DICCA – Laboratory of Geodesy, Geomatics and GIS,
Università degli Studi di Genova, Via Montallegro 1, 16145 Genoa, Italy
{bianca.federici, domenico.sguerso}@unige.it,
ilaria.ferrando@edu.unige.it,
saragagliolo@hotmail.it,
daniele.passoni@dicca.unige.it

Abstract. The use of Terrestrial Laser Scanner (TLS) is quite common for architectural surveys, however it requires to arrange special targets on the scanned object and to acquire several overlapping scans, which have to be aligned and edited externally. Recently, Leica released on the market a new kind of instrument, known as MultiStation (MS). It includes both the main characteristics of a TLS and of a Total Station (TS), meaning that no targets are required for the scan alignment, since the whole survey can be directly georeferenced. In this paper, some analyses about the use of this instrument for 3D modelling applications are discussed. First of all, the laser signal response is evaluated considering different materials, acquired using several combinations of distances and incidence angles. Then, the survey of the Casalbagliano Castle is presented and analyzed. All the performed tests show the great potentiality of the MS, allowing to reach accuracies of the order of few millimeters.

1 Introduction

Terrestrial Laser Scanner (TLS) is commonly used for architectural surveys because of its high data acquisition frame rate and high accuracy. Usually, TLSs allow to acquire also high-resolution images during the scanning, resulting in colored point clouds. They have to be georeferenced recognizing at least three non-aligned targets, whose geometry and radiometric properties allow an automatic identification. Alternatively, the point clouds can be aligned using the Iterative Closest Point (ICP) algorithm, which iteratively estimates the rototraslation between two scans, minimizing their distances. The algorithm works very well in case of high overlapping and complex geometries, allowing minimizing the number of targets to be placed on the scene.

© Springer International Publishing AG 2017
O. Gervasi et al. (Eds.): ICCSA 2017, Part IV, LNCS 10407, pp. 93–104, 2017.
DOI: 10.1007/978-3-319-62401-3_8

Leica Geosystem has recently released on the market a new instrument [1], whose design and weight are very similar to those of a Total Station (TS). It matches both the characteristics of TLSs and of automatic TSs, allowing acquiring 3D point clouds that are already georeferenced, by transferring the coordinates and the orientation of the station points. This family of instruments is known as MultiStation or Scanning Station and includes Leica Nova MS50 and MS60 models and Trimble SX10. Likewise other Total Stations, this kind of instruments can be also connected to a Global Navigation Satellite System (GNSS) receiver to directly georeference the surveyed points.

In this paper, the accuracy of the Leica Nova MS60 MultiStation (MS) used in scanning mode is evaluated by performing some experimental tests. This instrument has been recently acquired by Politecnico di Milano – Piacenza Campus. MS is very suitable for accurate surveys, such as those intended for infrastructure monitoring. It is characterized by an angular accuracy of 3^{cc}, a distance accuracy of 1 mm + 1.5 ppm using reflective prisms and 2 mm + 2 ppm in case of reflecting surfaces. The MS is equipped with two digital 5 Megapixel CMOS cameras, an overview and a telescope coaxial camera. The former is characterized by a 21 mm focal length and a field of view equal to 19°.4 (diagonal), while the latter has a focal length equal to 231 mm and a field of view of 1°.5 (diagonal). In order to acquire point clouds, the instrument automatically moves the telescope with a constant angular step, resulting in scanning the full area. Consequently, the time requested for a scan is higher if compared to those requested by a TLS. In fact, the maximum scanning acquisition rate is equal to 1000 points/s, when the distance is shorter than 300 m and in case of optimal reflectance properties of the investigated surface (Kodak White 90%). The acquisition rate decreases quickly as the distance increases, reaching 1 point/s for distances farther than 500 m. Nevertheless, the small size of the laser beam (8 mm × 20 mm at a distance equal to 50 m) and the precision of the measured coordinates (1 mm at 50 m) make the MS an interesting choice in case of architectural surveys and monitoring applications. Its wavelength is equal to 658 nm, which guarantees a good signal response from the investigated materials [2, 3], even if this value is lower respect to those that usually characterize a TLS. In this regard, the characteristics of the MS response have been studied by the manufacturer and by a number of researcher [1, 4–10]. Noticeable is the work presented in [4], in which the author investigated the scanning characteristics in case of a dam survey, presenting tests carried out at different distances (100 and 200 m) and evaluating the effect of the incidence angle on the laser beam by scanning a sloping surface. Zámečníková et al. [6] investigated the scanning error varying the incidence angle in case of short distances (between 3 and 5 m), demonstrating that it can be described using a non-linear stochastic model.

The tests discussed in Sect. 2 have been realized to evaluate the response of the Leica Nova MS60 laser beam as a function of the distance between the object and the instrument and of the incidence angle. Different distances in the range from 5 to 450 m have been considered, combined with various incidence angles (between 0 and 80°). The investigated object is a wooden panel with 12 squares of different materials. The selected samples are the ones commonly used for constructions (plywood or plaster), metals (shiny and crosshatch metal sheet) and cladding materials (cork, PVC, felt, polypropylene and polystyrene with different colors and thickness). In Sect. 3, MS survey has been compared with TLS survey in a real scenario. The acquisition was performed at the

Casalbagliano Castle (Alessandria, Italy). The castle consists in ruins; currently only the two towers and a part of the external walls are not collapsed. Finally, in the last section some clues useful for the planning of architectural survey using MS are given.

2   Leica Nova MS60 Response on Different Materials

In order to evaluate the laser beam response on different materials and different acquisition geometries (i.e. various combinations of distances and incidence angles), a panel with different materials has been scanned. The panel was realized in plywood and eleven different square samples (0.2×0.2 m^2) of various materials have been located on it. The selected samples have been considered representative of the most common materials that can be encountered when using the MS in Architecture or Civil Engineering.

We considered three different categories: metal (shiny and crosshatch metal sheet), construction materials (plywood and plaster) and cladding materials (cork, PVC, felt, black and neutral polypropylene, synthetic glass, polystyrene with thickness equal to 8 and 28 mm). Four checkerboard targets were located at the four corners of the panel and their centers have been used to georeference the different scans.

In order to have a reference point cloud to be used for evaluating the quality of the MS response, a photogrammetric model of the panel has been created, as shown in Fig. 1. The photogrammetric block was composed by 35 images (5520×3680 pixel resolution), acquired by a Nikon D800 camera with a fixed focal length of 20 mm, following a convergent geometry. This guarantees high overlapping and good intersections. An average distance of 1 m from the object has been maintained, resulting in an average Ground Sample Distance (GSD) of 0.6 mm. The four Ground Control Points (GCPs) measured with the MS (TS mode) in correspondence of the

Fig. 1. The dense point cloud created with the photogrammetric survey and used as a reference model

checkerboard centers were used to georeference the photogrammetric block. The convergent acquisition geometry ensured high quality and rigidity of the reference model, even if the used GCPs were coplanar.

The images have been processed using Agisoft Photoscan (version 1.2.6) [11], using the highest quality processing parameters, for both the external orientation and the dense cloud reconstruction phase. The residuals on the GCPs were in the order of 1.6 mm, in line with the accuracy of the MS scan in case of ideal surfaces.

The panel has been placed on a tripod and scanned with the MS, acquiring 1 point/cm^2 and considering different combinations of distances and angles. In particular, distances equal to 5, 25, 50, 75, 100, 200, 450 m, and incidence angles equal to 0, 20, 40, 60 and 80° have been analyzed, as shown in Fig. 2.

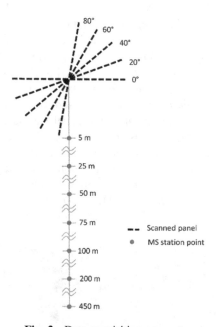

Fig. 2. Data acquisition geometry

In the case of a distance equal to 450 m, it was not possible to perform acquisitions at 60° and 80°, while in the case of 200 m it was not possible to scan the panel at 80°, because of the bad acquisition geometry. Before proceeding with further statistical analysis, all the scans have been roto-translated in a common reference frame, defined by the four centers of the checkerboard targets and used for the solution of the photogrammetric block too. The reference frame has been defined with the x-axis directed as the width of the panel, the z-axis perpendicular to the panel itself and the y-axis to complete the right handed Cartesian reference frame. The differences have been computed by searching the nearest neighbor in the photogrammetric point cloud, in terms of Euclidean distance, for every single point of MS scans. The comparisons with the photogrammetric reference data were performed considering only the central area of each sample (using a 0.16×0.16 m^2 surface), in order to avoid possible boundary effects, which are quite evident in case of high incidence angles. The statistical analyses have been conducted for all the combinations of distances, angles and materials, however only the results obtained for some angles and distances, considered particularly significant, are discussed here.

In Fig. 3, the results obtained for the plywood (chosen as reference material) are shown. The standard deviations between the different MS scans and the photogrammetric point cloud are reported, as a function of the distance and of the incidence angle between the instrument and the panel.

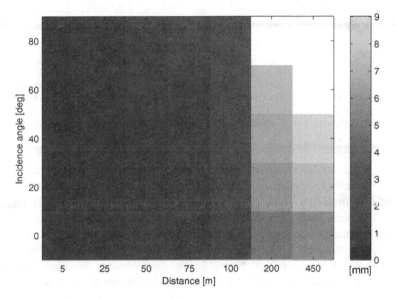

Fig. 3. Standard deviations between MS and photogrammetric point cloud for plywood, as a function of the acquisition distance and the incidence angle

From the given representation, it is quite evident that the standard deviation increases going farther from the station point. It is also interesting to notice that the laser response is quite independent from the incidence angle, in case of distances lower than 100 m. For greater distances there is a noticeable worsening when the incidence angle increases, until having no response for 80° and 60° (this last only at 450 m).

Figure 4 shows the computed standard deviations for each material as a function of the distance between the instrument and the scanned object, in case of null incidence angle. Please note that in all the analyses discussed from now on, the shiny metal sheet has been excluded, because the material reflected too much, thus the laser beam was not able to measure this kind of surface. The value of the standard deviation increases with the distance and it remains below 2 mm for distances up to 100 m and below 6 mm for distances between 100 m and 450 m, apart from few materials such as black polypropylene and cork.

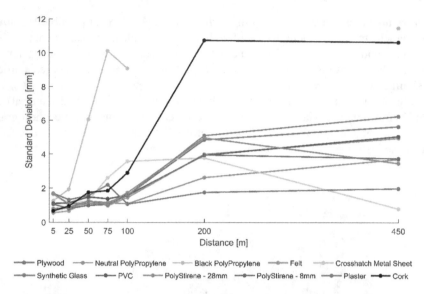

Fig. 4. Standard deviation of differences between the MS and the photogrammetric point cloud for null incidence angle

In Fig. 5, the ratio between the number of reflected points for each material and the number of the reflected points for the chosen reference material (plywood) is reported in case of null incidence angle. This ratio is always between 0.9 and 1.1 for all the measured distances, apart from the crosshatch metal sheet, which is characterized by a very unstable number of responses. The maximum variation in the number of points of about 10%, registered for all the materials, is not significant and could be related to the scanning resolution of 1 point/cm^2. Figure 6 shows the standard deviations between the reference photogrammetric scan and the MS scans, acquired under different incident

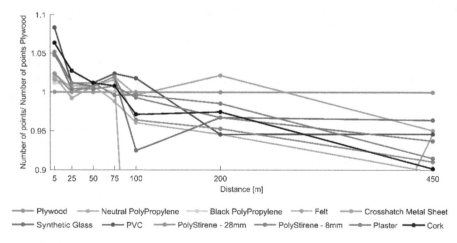

Fig. 5. Ratio between the number of reflected points for each material and the number of reflected points for the reference material (plywood)

angles, at a distance equal to 100 m. The results prove that the laser response is quite independent from the viewing angle; in fact, the standard deviations remain under 3 mm also for incidence angles equal to 80°, pointing out a slight worsening. The only materials that do not follow this rule are the black polypropylene and the crosshatch metal sheet. During the performed tests, it has clearly emerged how it is critical to have responses from these materials, starting from incidence angles equal to 20 and 40°, respectively.

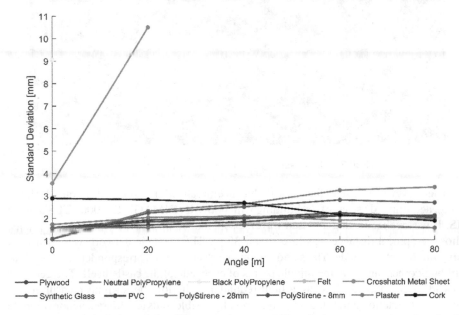

Fig. 6. Standard deviation of the differences between MS and photogrammetric point clouds considering an acquisition distance equal to 100 m

3 The Survey of the Castle of Casalbagliano

A second test has been realized in order to evaluate the MS response in case of an application that could be quite common in Architecture or Civil Engineering, such as the monitoring of a building or a collapsed structure. The chosen case study is the Castle of Casalbagliano (Alessandria province, Piedmont region, Italy). It was built in 1280 and it is characterized by a square map, which is quite typical in case of fortified medieval buildings. It was originally constructed using bricks, but it was restored several times and recently some structural enforcements using concrete were realized. In 1994, the flood of the Tanaro river caused a worsening of the situation. In 1998 one of its parts collapsed. Now, the castle is in a state of neglect. It is an unstable ruin, overrun by climbing plants that have almost completely invaded the inner courtyard and the Northern walls (Fig. 7).

Fig. 7. The Casalbagliano Castle from an aerial view

The survey of Casalbagliano Castle has been realized in a single day (on 17 March 2016), acquiring 3D scans of the building with both a Z+F IMAGER® 5006h TLS and the MS. It was realized using a closed traverse scheme, composed by eight station points, whose reciprocal distance was lower than 35 m. The geodetic network was measured using the MS in TS mode. The station points were chosen in correspondence of the four building corners and near the middle points of each side of the castle itself. The geodetic network was realized following a high redundant criterion, performing measurements among all the station points that were reciprocally visible, thus resulting in a more reliable scheme with respect to a classical closed traverse (Fig. 8). The reference system has been

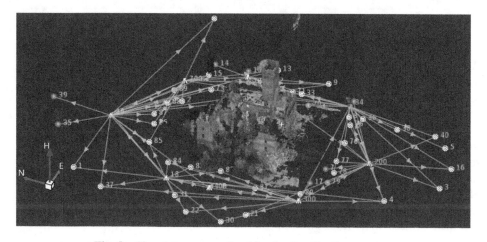

Fig. 8. Closed traverse realized for the Casalbagliano survey

defined locally, with the origin in the first station point, the y-axis oriented towards the last point of the network (parallel to one of the perimeter walls), the z-axis oriented as the vertical and the x-axis to complete the right handed Cartesian reference frame. The geodetic network has been adjusted using the Leica Infinity® software, supplied by the MS manufacturer and the closing angle error was equal to 50 cc.

The maximum distances between the walls and the station points were about 35–40 m. In order to obtain a spacing of 1 cm at a distance equal to 35 m (the maximum Z+F IMAGER® 5006h operative nominal distance is 79 m), the TLS scans have been realized with a resolution defined "superhigh", equal to 20,000 points/360°. For the MS a maximum horizontal spacing of 0.10 m has been used, while the vertical spacing has been set equal to 0.05 m. These values were imposed considering the farthest point, resulting that the final point cloud density is higher. The network has been measured together with the acquisition of the MS scans. The station points were used also for the TLS scanning. The point clouds acquired with the MS have been oriented, pre-processed and exported using the Leica Infinity® software. Instead, the point clouds acquired with the TLS have been pre-processed, oriented and exported using Z+F LaserControl®, the software supplied by Zoller+Fröhlich. The TLS scans have been aligned using at least 8 targets and refined using the ICP algorithm. Since the coordinates of the targets have been acquired also with the MS, the two final point clouds were directly co-registered in the same reference frame. Both the MS and the TLS models were manually edited in CloudCompare [12], in order to remove some noise due to the presence of trees and vegetation.

The accuracy of the point clouds produced by the MS was evaluated comparing each point with the correspondent one in the reference model obtained with the TLS, selected considering the shortest Euclidean distance. In Table 1, the statistics computed from this comparison are reported. The points located at distances greater that 0.1 m have been excluded, because they have been considered outliers due to the presence of the vegetation (creepers). The excluded points were 12.665 that correspond to less than 2% of the scanned points.

Table 1. Comparison between the MS and the TLS point clouds for the Casalbagliano Castle

	X [mm]	Y [mm]	Z [mm]
Mean	0.2	0.2	0.1
Standard deviation	9.0	9.2	8.8

The results underline that there is a great agreement between the 3D models obtained with the two instruments. The standard deviation values could be explained considering the errors introduced by the vegetation. In Fig. 9, the point cloud acquired with the MS is shown. The color scale corresponds to the Euclidean distance with respect to the reference TLS scan. As already stated before, the noticeable errors can be attributed to the vegetated areas. The same analysis has been performed also isolating the part of the point clouds corresponding to the main tower, which is the best-preserved area of the castle. The statistics of the differences are reported in Table 2, while a graphic representation is given in Fig. 10.

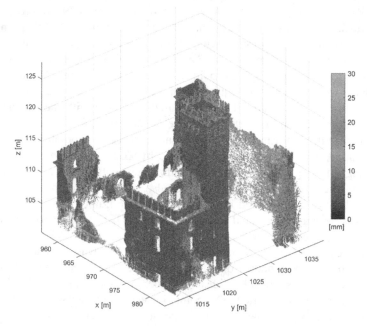

Fig. 9. Differences between the MS and the TLS point clouds for the Casalbagliano Castle

Table 2. Comparison between the MS and the TLS point clouds for the main tower of Casalbagliano Castle

	X [mm]	Y [mm]	Z [mm]
Mean	0.1	0.2	0.1
Standard deviation	5.9	6.0	5.8

The comparisons prove the quality of the data delivered by the MS when used in scanning mode, in great agreement with the TLS point clouds. These results are in accordance with the results discussed in previous Sect. 2.

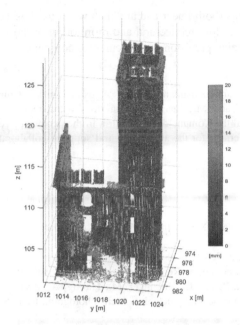

Fig. 10. Differences between the MS and the TLS point clouds for the main tower of the Casalbagliano Castle

4   Conclusion and Final Remarks

In this paper, the characteristics and the accuracy of the Leica Nova MS60 MultiStation (MS) have been investigated, paying particular attention to the laser beam response when the instrument is used in scanning mode. The signal response has been evaluated in terms of standard deviation considering various materials and combinations between different distances and incidence angles. A value of 2 mm has been obtained for almost all the investigated materials, in case of distance equal to 100 m, which could be considered representative in case of monitoring applications. A survey of the partially collapsed Casalbagliano Castle was realized too, with the aim to evaluate the use of the MS for architectural and structural monitoring purposes, compared with Z+F IMAGER® 5006h Terrestrial Laser Scanner (TLS).

From all the performed tests emerged that the MS delivers high quality scans, with standard deviations in the order of few millimeters with respect to the reference data (photogrammetry or TLS point clouds).

The great advantage of the MS is that all the acquired scans are co-registered and directly aligned in the geodetic network by the instrument, meaning that no targets are required. Moreover, the survey can be directly georeferenced in a global reference system, if a GNSS antenna is available and used to define the coordinates of at least two station points. For all these reasons, combined with the high quality of the performed measurements (both linear and angular) when used as Total Station, the MS is an excellent instrument for architectural and monitoring purposes, from the metrical point of view, guaranteeing precisions and accuracies comparable to those of a TLS for surface inspections.

Acknowledgments. The authors thank the students Agostini Cristian, Chinchella Enrico, Ferrari Eugenio, Riccio Simone and Mr. Spagnoli Maurizio for the technical support during the Casalbagliano survey, and the Comune di Alessandria in the persons of Arch. Marco Genovese and Geom. Gianfranco Ferraris for the availability and supplied collaboration.

References

1. Grimm, D.E.: Leica Nova MS50: the world's first multistation. GeoInformatics **16**(7), 22 (2013)
2. Pfeifer, N., Briese, C.: Geometrical aspects of airborne laser scanning and terrestrial laser scanning. Int. Arch. Photogram. Rem. Sens. Spat. Inf. Sci. **36**(3/W52), 311–319 (2007)
3. Pfeifer, N., Höfle, B., Briese, C., Rutzinger, M., Haring, A.: Analysis of the backscattered energy in terrestrial laser scanning data. Int. Arch. Photogram. Rem. Sens. Spat. Inf. Sci. **37**, 1045–1052 (2008)
4. Atkinson, M.J.A.: Dam deformation surveys with modern technology. Doctoral dissertation. University of Southern Queensland (2014)
5. Milinković, A., Ristić, K., Tucikešić, S.: Modern technologies of collecting and presentation of geospatial data. Geonauka **2**(2), 19–27 (2014)
6. Wagner, A., Huber, B., Wiedemann, W., Paar, G.: Long-range geo-monitoring using image assisted total stations. J. Appl. Geodesy **8**(3), 223–234 (2014)
7. Zámečníková, M., Wieser, A., Woschitz, H., Ressl, C.: Influence of surface reflectivity on reflectorless electronic distance measurement and terrestrial laser scanning. J. Appl. Geodesy **8**(4), 311–326 (2014)
8. Sepasgozar, S.M.E., Lim, S., Shirowzhan, S., Kim, Y.M., Nadoushani, Z.M.: Utilisation of a new terrestrial scanner for reconstruction of as-built models: a comparative study. In: ISARC Proceedings of the International Symposium on Automation and Robotics in Construction, Vilnius Gediminas Technical University, Department of Construction Economics & Property, vol. 32, p. 1 (2015)
9. Holland, D.A., Pook, C., Capstick, D., Hemmings, A.: The topographic data deluge-collecting and maintaining data in a 21st century mapping agency. Int. Arch. Photogram. Rem. Sens. Spat. Inf. Sci. **41**, 727 (2016)
10. Pagliari, D., Rossi, L., Passoni, D., Pinto, L., De Michele, C., Avanzi, F.: Measuring the volume of flushed sediments in a reservoir using multi-temporal images acquired with UAS. Geomatics Nat. Hazards Risk **8**(1), 1–17 (2016)
11. Agisoft Photoscan. http://www.agisoft.com/
12. CloudCompare, 3D point cloud and mesh processing software Open Source Project. http://www.cloudcompare.org/

A Low-Cost Solution for the Monitoring of Air Pollution Parameters Through Bicycles

Irene Aicardi[1]([✉]) [iD], Filippo Gandino[2] [iD], Nives Grasso[1] [iD],
Andrea Maria Lingua[1] [iD], and Francesca Noardo[1] [iD]

[1] DIATI, Politecnico di Torino, 11, c.so Duca degli Abruzzi 24, 10129 Turin, Italy
{irene.aicardi,nives.grasso,francesca.noardo}@polito.it
[2] DAUIN - Department of Control and Computer Engineering, Politecnico di Torino,
c.so Duca degli Abruzzi, 24, 10129 Turin, Italy
filippo.gandino@polito.it

Abstract. The monitoring of air quality parameters is a fundamental requirement for smart cities development and it is of primary importance for the quality of human life. In fact, the knowledge of air quality parameters along the days and in different areas of the city is essential to monitor its behavior and to take some preventive measurements to limit the concentration. Especially in big cities, it is very hard to have widespread updated data about pollutants and air quality parameters since normally only few air quality monitoring stations are available. In Piedmont (Italy), the reference public body for this kind of information is the ARPA (Regional Agency for the Protection of the Environment) which is responsible for the collection and the disclosure of environmental data. However, the number of monitoring stations along the city is limited and they have fixed positions. A solution through mobile sensors would be preferable to have a more comprehensive description of the phenomenon. In this paper, the authors describe the implementation of a new solution based on a mobile system to house environmental air quality and imaging sensors (since also the knowledge of the shape of the environment is a fundamental aspect). In particular, a bicycle is adopted and the paper describes all the analyses involved in the choice of the more appropriate sensors and their evaluation and behavior in a real environment. Finally, the collection and management of the acquired data is analyzed through the implementation of a dedicated GIS (Geographical Information System).

Keywords: Environmental monitoring · Low-cost sensors · Pollution · Semantic data management · Dynamic scenes

1 Introduction

Air quality in urban scenarios is considered one of the greatest threat to human health since it is fundamental to support the human life [3, 6, 11, 15, 19]. Especially in a densely populated urban environment, it is very difficult to manage this aspect since everyday activities contribute to increase the degree of pollution of the cities. The number of cars is significantly increasing and the streets are full of busses and motorbikes that are a

© Springer International Publishing AG 2017
O. Gervasi et al. (Eds.): ICCSA 2017, Part IV, LNCS 10407, pp. 105–120, 2017.
DOI: 10.1007/978-3-319-62401-3_9

source of air pollution (in terms of fossil fuel combustion). Moreover, also the heating systems of the buildings are a relevant source of pollutants in urban areas.

In this scenario, the knowledge of the pollution distribution along the days and the areas can be an important source of information, which allows people to make their own choice about the use of transports and their daily life [9]. To date, most of the information in Piedmont are acquired by fixed stations (usually located by the ARPA). These data are really accurate, but the use of fixed stations means not having the capability to perform dynamic analyses and having widespread information to observe the distribution of pollution along the whole urban area. In fact, a pervasive knowledge of the air quality can help to understand how it changes during the day and how it is spread. This kind of knowledge can derive from spatially and temporally accurate and well-distributed data about the air quality.

This information is one of the fundamental points for smart cities development. In fact, a lot of big cities are introducing the monitoring of multiple parameters along the urban areas through the use of wireless sensors networks (WSNs). This kind of technology uses low-cost sensors devices well spread along the area of interest that can collect data at the same time and send them to control stations, which perform the analyses. These technologies are then used to improve the services offered by the city and to increase the quality of life. An example of the use of this approach is reported in [16] where a WiFi-based system is adopted to collect the acquired data and transmit them to a neural network, which processes the data, extracts the information and publishes the results on a dedicated web page. Also [10] tried to use WSNs systems to monitor the air pollution in Mauritius through the use of static sensors. The technology is described in details and the use of the network is deeply investigated through different simulations.

However, many static sensors would be required in order to provide a dense coverage. For this reason, different mobile systems have been investigated over the years by the scientific community. In order to have widespread data, different studies began to incorporate low-cost sensors across the cities. For example, [12] proposed a monitoring system made by fixed and mobile sensors also mounted on public vehicles, such as buses, taxis and other public transport. Also, in this case, data were collected through a wireless transmission and managed through a data mining technique, whose analyses were made through simulations. Moreover, also [8] tested the possibility to use public transports to house mobile sensors and to have a more sophisticated spatio-temporal resolution of the data. The use of bicycles was already investigated by [5] to monitor pollution parameters through dynamic sensors easily installable on them. The main idea is to have a system that people can easily use by their own in a participatory framework. Following this idea, [4] proposed a dynamic monitoring system based on handheld devices that people can use to measure pollutants in the air and whose data constitute a network to monitor specific areas. In this regards, also [7] proposed a participatory system where the devices were directly connected to smartphones. This approach allowed to have very widespread data, but with the difficulty to identify problems related to the accuracy of the use of these low-cost sensors integrated in low-cost smartphones.

Another fundamental information that is correlated to pollution is the three-dimensional shape of the analyzed environment. For this reason, the simultaneous creation of a 3D model can be the best approach to cover this lack of information. 3D models of the buildings are often realized starting from laser scanner techniques, which, however, are expensive in terms of both time and costs. For this reason, in recent years, photogrammetric techniques based on images have been investigated and used to 3D models generation. The advantages of these techniques are the acquisition speed of the data and the low-cost instrumentation (photographic cameras). Moreover, the advantage of these systems is their ability to be mounted on mobile systems allowing rapid and dynamic acquisitions. The models thus created can be used as bases in the 3D mapping database.

In this scenario, the idea is to develop a low-cost system for the continuous, dense and frequent monitoring of air quality. The proposed system would be integrated on low-impact vehicles (such as bicycles), it would be used to get information useful for urban planning and the data would be real-time available on the Web and accessible by users. The proposed system is a part of the 'Cyclair' project included in the Torino Living Lab with the aim to promote the use of bicycles as a mean of urban transport and to raise awareness about the link between air pollution and transportation also through the direct involvement of users. A student team (Policycle) financed by the Politecnico di Torino is involved in the implementation of the system and in its application. The project is subdivided into two levels of detail:

- the development of an acquisition system installable on low-cost and low-impact vehicles: it allows to acquire all the necessary data to collect air pollution and environmental parameters. It is constituted by:
  - navigation sensors for the positioning and attitude estimation of the system;
  - imaging sensors (such as digital cameras or panoramic cameras) for the acquisition of visible information useful to describe the context;
  - environmental sensors for the collection of air pollution and quality data;
  - data storage systems and real time wireless communication platform to broadcast the acquired data;
- a dynamic spatial database for the management of air quality data: it is based on the Open Geospatial Consortium (OGC) CityGML standard, extended to handle dynamic environmental parameters. The developed platform is able to:
  - realize post-processing operation to integrate the acquired environmental data;
  - store the data on a GIS platform;
  - perform real time analyses and visualizations;
  - carry out analysis to estimate qualitative air quality indicators.

The paper describes the developed systems, the used sensors and the methodologies to verify the data and the implementation of a spatial database for the data management. The system is finally applied to a real case study in Torino where imaging and air pollution data were collected.

2   Implemented Dynamic System

The main benefit of a mobile monitoring system is to increase the spatial density of the collected measures. Therefore, with respect to a static system, it is possible to use fewer sensors to cover the same area. Our attention was more focused on the use of public and shared vehicles (daily used by citizens), on which is possible to install a monitoring system. The advantages in the use of bicycles are mainly two: they do not produce pollutants and they are very flexible monitoring systems, able to access areas not open to cars or busses. Moreover, the system for the air quality monitoring should be able to: monitor a large area, collect pervasive data, guarantee a proper level of accuracy, and involve limited costs. For these reasons, the acquisition system for air quality monitoring data has been mounted on a bicycle equipped with:

- navigation sensors for the position (GNSS) and attitude (IMU) definition;
- environmental sensors (temperature, humidity, pressure, PM10, PM2.5, PM1 and ozone);
- imaging sensors (digital cameras, webcams and panoramic 360° cameras).

Regards to the navigation sensors, two different systems were adopted:

- a Microstrain 3DM-GX3® - 35 (Fig. 1 left);
- a Ublox EVK-M8T (Fig. 1 right).

The Microstrain system (Table 1) allows to independently acquire accelerometers, gyroscopes and magnetometers data that can be synchronized thanks to an internal GNSS receiver (u-blox system). This allows to have a positioning solution with a metrical level of accuracy (since no Kalman filter is applied) [14]. The device was selected for its weight (23 g) and size (44.2 mm × 24.0 mm × 13.7 mm), very interesting for bicycles.

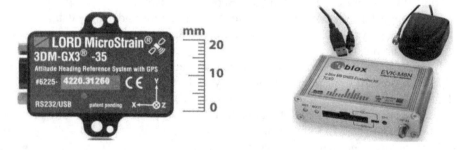

Fig. 1. Microstrain 3DM-GX3-35 (on the left) and Ublox EVK-M8T (on the right).

Table 1. Main features of Microstrain 3DM-GX3–35 [14].

	Accelerometer	Gyro
Measurement range	±5 g (standard)	300°/s (standard)
Non-linearity	±0.1% fs	±0.03% fs
Bias instability	±0.04 mg	18°/h
Initial bias error	±0.002 g	±0.25°/s
Noise density	80 µg/$\sqrt{Hz}$	0.03°/s/$\sqrt{Hz}$
Sampling rate	30 kHz	30 kHz

The Ublox EVK-M8T device was used to have positioning information of the acquired images. In fact, it was directly connected to the webcam to acquire synchronized data. It is connected to an active antenna able to collect GPS/GLONASS/BeiDou data and it is really user-friendly, in order to be easily managed also by no expert users.

For the pollution data, it is fundamental to define a system with the capability to be cheap, easy to use and able to produce reliable data to effectively develop a low-cost monitoring system. Looking at the systems available on the market and in the research field, the Waspmote Plug & Sense from Libelium has been selected [21]. It has been adopted also for other international research projects: for example, in Pisa (Italy) as monitoring system [1] and in industrial and urban areas [13] as air quality monitoring system. Its main evaluated characteristics are:

- compliance with ground level dust and ozone sensors;
- compliance with complementary sensors, such as ammoniac, nitrogen dioxide, atmospheric parameters and noise;
- possibility to integrate wireless communication systems (e.g., Zigbee, WiFi);
- easy programmability through the C++ language for Arduino;
- international protection level IP65, compliant with outdoor deployment;
- low cost, required for a pervasive network composed by many sensors.

The mobile stations were equipped with sensors for the acquisition of data related to ozone, pm10, pm2.5, pm1, temperature, humidity and pressure. Each station is able to work autonomously, acquiring new data every 30 s.

Finally, in order to assess the possibility of creating a photogrammetric 3D model of the urban environment, spherical images were acquired with the camera NCTech iSTAR (Fig. 2 rectangle 5).

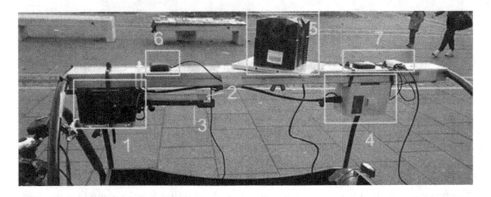

Fig. 2. Acquisition system mounted on the bicycle: 1. Wapmode Plug & Sense; 2. temperature, humidity and pressure sensors; 3. Ozone detection sensor; 4. fine particles detection sensor; 5. NCTech iSTAR; 6. Ublox antenna; 7. Microstrain 3DM-GX3-35 and its antenna.

Georeferenced images acquired by this sensor can be used to assess the state of the roads or the bike path or for the generation of the 3D model of the environment.

Each sensor has its own system to collect and store the data. Webcams were directly connected to a computer for the acquisition and data collection, the panoramic camera was managed by a dedicated computer, while the Waspmode autonomously collects data that can be downloaded through a WiFi connection.

3 Sensors Evaluation: Experimental Analysis

3.1 Air Quality Monitoring System

The main goal of the air quality monitoring system is to provide a quantitative information of the dust and ozone concentrations with a high spatial and temporal data density. However, the implementation of a distributed network of sensors does not allow using expensive sensors. Therefore, a mobile distributed system can provide a larger quantity of information with respect to fix stations, but with a lower accuracy. In order to evaluate the reliability of the achieved data [20] some tests have been executed and Fig. 3 shows the results of two OPC-N2 particle sensors with identical characteristics. Without an accurate calibration, a large offset is expected between the two set of data, that can be drastically reduced through a standardization process.

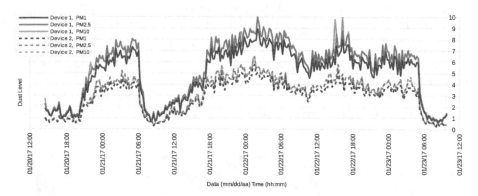

Fig. 3. Dust levels captured by two devices.

The experiment was performed over 3 days in a room with a forced air system able to filter the dust. Both the sensors performed a measure for 15 min. Every datum is related to the dust analyzed during 5 s. Each sensor collected 270 measures. It is possible to observe that the dust filter was active between the morning and the evening of January 20, 21 and 23, while it was inactive during the nights and on January 22. Both the sensors were able to sense all the transitions.

In order to obtain a better comparison, a standardization was executed on the first 135 records used for training. For each sensor the average and the variance of the training records was calculated, then the average was subtracted and the resulting data were divided by the deviation. Figure 4 shows the standardized data. It is possible to observe that, for all the lines, the average over the first 135 records is zero and the variance is one. The standardized data are very similar, as shown in the chart. The last 135 records were used for the test. The average and the deviation computed on the training data were used to modify also the last part of the chart. It is easy to observe that the average of the last 135 records is over zero. Although the standardization was based on other data, it provided good results even on the records used for the test. The results of this test show that it is possible to use mathematical formulas to compare the data.

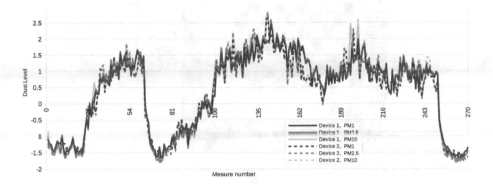

Fig. 4. Normalized dust levels.

Finally, the collected data were sorted according to the intensity of the particulate measured by the first device (Fig. 5). Although the data collected by the second device are not steady, they clearly identify the increasing trend.

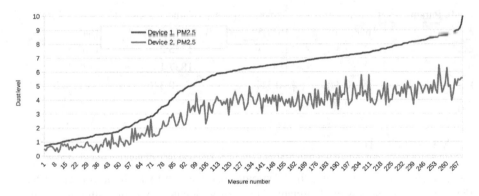

Fig. 5. PM2.5 data sorted by intensity level captured by device 1.

3.2 Imaging Sensors Calibration

To generate the 3D model of the environment through images, a panoramic camera NCTech iStar was adopted. It is able to simultaneously acquire 4 images that can be subsequently stitched to generate a spherical image.

Before using the system, it is necessary to calibrate it. This means to know the parameters with which the images were taken, to study the acquisition geometry of the system and to check and verify the synchronization of the 4 integrated cameras.

To get this data, a Matlab tool ("Camera Calibrator" (Fig. 6), [22]) was used, which allows to obtain these parameters from images taken from the camera. For the procedure, checkerboards panels with known dimensions need to be used. In our case, they were attacked on a wooden panel to limit their deformations.

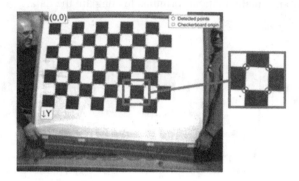

Fig. 6. Wooden panel with checkerboards for the camera calibration.

The procedure then suggests carrying out a series of photos of the panel from different points of view, which can then be inserted in Matlab. 20 photos were acquired for each camera and the application allowed to extract the parameters (Table 2).

Table 2. Estimated values of intrinsic parameters.

Calib. Param.	Camera 1 [pixel]	Camera 2 [pixel]	Camera 3 [pixel]	Camera 4 [pixel]
c	1646,5	1652.5	1646.8	1645.7
ξ_0	1393.4	1363.4	1375.2	1362.6
η_0	1798.9	1840	1837.1	1848.2
k_1	−0.348	−0.347	−0.346	−0.342
k_2	0.141	0.112	0.113	0.106

4   A Case Study

The area chosen as a test site is the 'Campidoglio' District in Turin, northwest of Italy (Fig. 7 left). This area is predominantly residential, located in semi-central location of the City, and characterized by the presence of commercial facilities, as well as public places and services, such as schools. The activities were aimed at the implementation of a medium-scale 3D metric documentation of a block of the 'Campidoglio' district (Fig. 7 right) by means of terrestrial laser scanning survey with the capabilities to associate pollution data. The generated 3D model can be used as reference for the spatial information system, which will be structured in an interoperable database.

Fig. 7. The Campidoglio district (left) and the buildings block selected for the analyses (right).

This test site was selected for different reasons:

- it has lots of features: buildings, schools, roads, cycle and public transport paths;
- it is rounded by streets having different kind of traffic intensity (from one-direction street to multiple lanes avenues, part of the principal traffic artery of the city);
- it is possible to easily survey the district by bike;
- the air pollution can change significantly during the day according to the work and school time. So it can be very useful to monitor the pollution behavior at different times of the day;
- the area is full of stable features useful to create a good reference 3D model and acquire laser scanner and imaging data.

The activities described below refer to a fist acquisition made to test the system, the available sensors and the implemented structure for the storage and management of the data in a spatial database.

4.1 Data Acquisition and Processing

The beginning step has involved the construction of a topographic network composed by five vertices (Fig. 8 red). The survey was made through a GNSS double frequency and multi-constellation receiver in static modality standing on each point for about 1 h, since in that place the GNSS coverage was not so good.

The coordinates of these points were determined in a post-processing approach, considering a single-base solution (through the Leica Geo Office® software v.8.3) with the Torino permanent station of the Regione Piemonte CORSs (Continuous Operating Reference Stations) network as reference. The coordinates were estimated with a high level of accuracy ($\sigma_M = 3$ mm) and the phase ambiguity was fixed for all points, which has guaranteed a high level of precision for the georeferencing step.

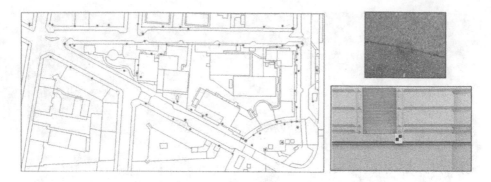

Fig. 8. Vertices distribution along the area (red) and position of the markers for the laser data georeferencing (blue). On the right, two examples of the used points: a network vertex (top) and a paper marker (bottom). (Color figure online)

Starting from the reference network, it was possible to acquire the position of some reference points (markers, Fig. 8 blue) using a total station and a prism. All measurements were subsequently adjusted with the MicroSurvey StarNet v.7.0 software, in order to obtain the final coordinates: the root mean square (RMS) of the estimated coordinates is less than 1 cm.

Then, terrestrial laser scanning surveys were performed to obtain a reference model for the pollution spatial information. The georeferencing of the scans took place through the pre-signalization of the markers measured by topographic techniques.

To cover the entire block, 14 scans were acquired using the laser Faro Cam2 Focus 3D (Fig. 9). It is a system with a range of acquisition from 0.6 m to 130 m, which is also able to acquire images through an integrated camera in order to color the point cloud. Each scan was acquired with 1/4 of resolution (÷ 1 point every 7 mm at 5 m), and it requires about 7 min for cloud acquisition and 1 min for images collection. The laser data were processed using Scene (v. 5.2), which is the own software developed by FARO. The process follows these steps:

1. scans integration and visualization: it is the first step where the scans can be visualized in the project space;
2. scans georeferencing: the software has an internal database that allows to automatically detect the markers in the cloud. Since the markers were topographically acquired, it was possible to insert in Scene their coordinates in the chosen reference system and georeference the whole model. To assess the registration reliability, it is possible to have a look at the errors contained in the ScanFit report;
3. data filtering and coloring: sometimes unnecessary data are recorded, but they can be manually deleted in order to reduce the point cloud and to facilitate the data processing. Then the point clouds can be colored through the acquired images.

The elaboration required about 7–8 h for the entire process (PC: Windows 7, Intel Core i7, 8 GB RAM) and the result is a colored 3D point cloud composed by 300 million points (Fig. 9).

Fig. 9. Final 3D model generated through the laser scanner technology (FARO FOCUS 3D at the bottom right of the image).

For the imaging and environmental data (described above in paragraph 2), a cargo bicycle was adopted to house all the sensors (Fig. 10).

Fig. 10. Acquisition system equipped with all the imaging and environmental sensors.

The acquired spherical images were processed with the commercial software Agisoft PhotoScan that allows, quickly and easily, to obtain three-dimensional models from images. The photos were initially aligned, founding correspondences between them to determine their position at the time of acquisition, and a first point cloud was generated. Subsequently, the dense cloud was realized. It has allowed to obtain a more detailed description of the area as reported in the final cloud shown in Fig. 11.

Fig. 11. Final 3D model generated through spherical images in the PhotoScan software.

4.2   Management of Dynamic Data in GIS

The data obtained from the used sensors (Fig. 12) were structured on a dynamic spatial database for the management of air quality data. It is based on a data model compliant with the OGC CityGML standard [17, 18], with a proposed extension for what concerns the dynamic environmental parameters. The open source GIS platform (based on PostgreSQL/PostGIS, QGIS) is able to perform the pre-processing steps to integrate the

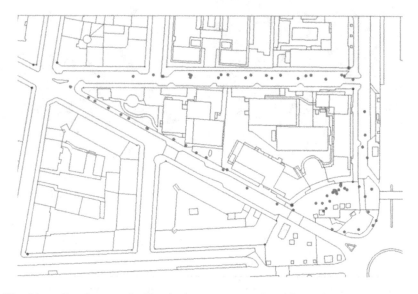

Fig. 12. Air quality data acquired by the sensors mounted on bikes. The red dots represent the acquisition points of the data concerning the air quality. (Color figure online)

acquired data, to store the data, to be able to carry out real-time analysis, and to perform analysis to estimate the qualitative indicators of air quality.

The database schema chosen for building the GIS is an extension of CityGML for representing the information about air quality: the CityGML Air Quality Application Domain Extension (AQADE) [2]. A synthesis of the CityGML extension is shown in Fig. 13. Analyzing the monitored data in association with their location in the 3D city model and further parameters (such as traffic at the moment of the survey, building usage, heating periods and so on) it could be possible to do some considerations (e.g. what are the main sources of air quality pollution and what are the main affected objects). This information can be stored in the database compliant with CityGML AQADE model, remaining as documentation for some kind of decision by administrators, operators, researchers or simple citizens.

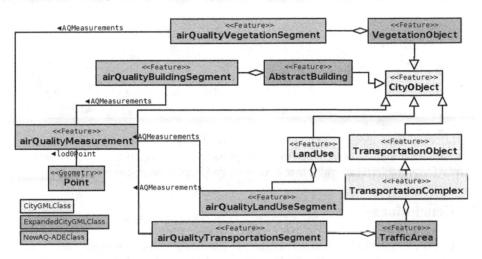

Fig. 13. The general UML schema of the CityGML AQADE.

It is possible to manage the so-structured data using different strategies. In particular, the first alternative is to use GML in order to represent and share the data; this can offer the advantage to maintain the object-oriented structure of the GML models and not to lose definition in the data complexity and interconnection. Moreover, the possibilities to manage the 3D data are wider. On the other hand, the tools to manage and analyze dynamic data in GML are still in a development phase, and the so-structured wide data-sets could result computationally heavy.

The second strategy has been used here: the translation of the model in an SQL database. The passage to an object-relational model permits to manage in an easier way the data, maintaining some important relations. For the management of the data in the so-structured database PostgreSQL-PostGIS was used, and QGIS was used as a GIS software tool as a support for both a graphical interface and analysis tools.

The information can be managed, visualized and analyzed in GIS for obtaining useful information (statistics, spatial queries). Moreover, a map of the pollution of the city can be generated by the interpolation of the measured points [2] (Fig. 14).

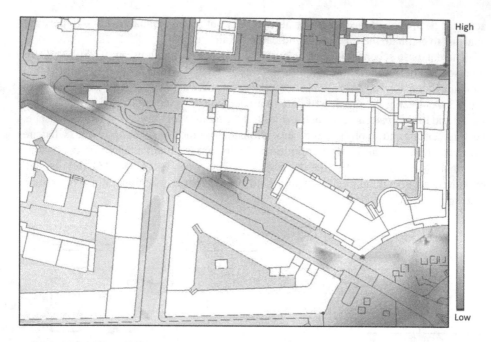

Fig. 14. Generation of the map of the presence of particulate (PM 2.5) in the study area, deriving from the interpolation of the measured values conducted on the GIS platform, using the method 'Inverse Distance Weighted' with power 2, as was tested in previous researches [2].

5   Conclusions

The proposed system allows to survey the 3D geometry of the city using mobile and low-cost sensors. This is very helpful for rapidly and accurately updating the maps (from both the geometrical and the semantic points of view). Moreover, the acquired information can be effectively managed in standardized GIS, useful for supporting a number of queries and analysis for different aims.

The main benefits of the tested acquisition system for pollution data are: negligible production of pollutants; limited alteration of the sensed environmental data (i.e., ground dust and ozone levels) due to the low speed of the bicycle (i.e., ~15 km/h); possibility to collect data from different locations without additional costs (if the devices are mounted on bicycles of a bike-sharing system or on private bicycles); cheapness. The main drawbacks are: lower accuracy than fixed, standard air quality sensors; exposure of the devices to physic shocks (e.g., holes and uneven ground), which can produce malfunction; sensibility of the sensors to atmospheric phenomena (e.g., rain, hailstorm, direct sunlight); risk of theft and vandalism. The low-cost device allows many nodes over the urban area to be deployed. Moreover, installing the devices on bicycles, these can be moved within the urban area without additional costs. Therefore, pervasive data distributed over the area of interest can be provided by the proposed system and the knowledge of the environment through the generation of a 3D model from images is fundamental to understand the pollution behavior in relation to fixed infrastructures along the area. The generated 3D model derives from the panoramic camera, but it can be extracted also from the webcam installed on the bicycles. This solution will be further analyzed to assess the reliability of images acquired with a very low-cost system easily replicable in multiple vehicles.

References

1. Anastasi, G., Bruschi, P., Marcelloni, F.: 'U-Sense', a cooperative sensing system for monitoring air quality in urban areas. In: Smart Cities, vol. 34 (2014)
2. Arco, E., Boccardo, P., Gandino, F., Lingua, A., Noardo, F., Rebaudengo, M.: An integrated approach for pollution monitoring: smart acquirement and smart information. In: 1st International Conference on Smart Data and Smart Cities, 30th UDMS, Split (Croatia), 7–9 September 2016, pp. 67–74 (2016)
3. Bates, D.V., Bell, G.M., Burnham, C.D., Hazucha, M., Mantha, J., Pengelly, L.D., Silverman, F.: Short-term effects of ozone on the lung. J. Appl. Physiol. **32**(2), 176–181 (1972)
4. Dutta, P., Aoki, P.M., Kumar, N., Mainwaring, A., Myers, C., Willett, W., Woodruff, A.: Common sense: participatory urban sensing using a network of handheld air quality monitors. In: Proceedings of the 7th ACM Conference on Embedded Networked Sensor Systems, pp. 349–350 (2009)
5. Eisenman, S.B., Miluzzo, E., Lane, N.D., Peterson, R.A., Ahn, G.S., Campbell, A.T.: BikeNet: a mobile sensing system for cyclist experience mapping. ACM Trans. Sensor Netw. (TOSN) **6**(1) (2009). Article 6
6. Fann, N., Lamson, A.D., Anenberg, S.C., Wesson, K., Risley, D., Hubbell, B.J.: Estimating the national public health burden associated with exposure to ambient PM2.5 and ozone. Risk Anal. **32**(1), 81–95 (2012)
7. Hasenfratz, D., Saukh, O., Sturzenegger, S., Thiele, L.: Participatory air pollution monitoring using smartphones. In: Mobile Sensing (2012)
8. Hasenfratz, D., Saukh, O., Walser, C., Hueglin, C., Fierz, M., Arn, T., Beutel, J., Thiele, L.: Deriving high-resolution urban air pollution maps using mobile sensor nodes. Pervasive Mob. Comput. **16**, 268–285 (2015)
9. Kheirbek, I., Wheeler, K., Walters, S., Kass, D., Matte, T.: PM2.5 and ozone health impacts and disparities in New York City: sensitivity to spatial and temporal resolution. Air Qual. Atmos. Health **6**(2), 473–486 (2013)
10. Khedo, K.K., Perseedoss, R., Mungur, A.: A wireless sensor network air pollution monitoring system. Int. J. Wirel. Mob. Netw. **2**(2), 31–45 (2010)
11. Lippmann, M.: Health effects of ozone a critical review. Japca **39**(5), 672–695 (1989)
12. Ma, Y., Richards, M., Ghanem, M., Guo, Y., Hassard, J.: Air pollution monitoring and mining based on sensor grid in London. Sensors **8**(6), 3601–3623 (2008)
13. Mansour, S., Nasser, N., Karim, L., Ali, A.: Wireless sensor network-based air quality monitoring system. In: 2014 International Conference on Computing, Networking and Communications (ICNC), pp. 545–550. IEEE (2014)
14. Piras, M., Dabove, P.: Comparison of two different mass-market IMU generations: bias analyses and real time applications. In: Position, Location and Navigation Symposium (PLANS), 2016 IEEE/ION, pp. 34–41. IEEE (2016)
15. Pope III, C.A., Dockery, D.W.: Acute health effects of PM10 pollution on symptomatic and asymptomatic children. Am. Rev. Respir. Dis. **145**(5), 1123–1128 (1992)

16. Postolache, O., Pereira, M., Girao, P.M.B.S.: Smart sensor network for air quality monitoring applications. In: Proceedings of the IEEE Instrumentation and Measurement Technology Conference, IMTC 2005, vol. 1, pp. 537–542. IEEE (2005)
17. Prandi, F., De Amicis, R., Piffer, S., Soavea, M., Cadzowb, S., Boix, E.G., D'Hondt, E.: Using CityGML to deploy smart-city services for urban ecosystems. In: International Archives of the Photogrammetry, Remote Sensing and Spatial Information Sciences, vol. 4 (2013)
18. Soave, M., Devigili, F., Prandi, F., de Amicis, R.: Visualization and analysis of CityGML dataset within a client sever infrastructure. In: Proceedings of the 18th International Conference on 3D Web Technology, pp. 215–215 (2013)
19. Spektor, D.M., Lippmann, M., Lioy, P.J., Thurston, G.D., Citak, K., James, D.J., Hayes, C.: Effects of ambient ozone on respiratory function in active, normal children. Am. Rev. Respir. Dis. **137**(2), 313–320 (1988)
20. Tsujita, W., Ishida, H., Moriizumi, T.: Dynamic gas sensor network for air pollution monitoring and its auto-calibration. In: Proceedings of IEEE Sensors, pp. 56–59. IEEE (2004)
21. Velasco, A., Ferrero, R., Gandino, F., Montrucchio, B., Rebaudengo, M.: On the design of distributed air quality monitoring systems. In: 11th International Conference of Computational Methods in Sciences and Engineering (ICCMSE 2015), Athens (Greece) (2015)
22. Zhang, Z.: A flexible new technique for camera calibration. IEEE Trans. Pattern Anal. Mach. Intell. **22**(11), 1330–1334 (2000)

High Temperature Fire Experiment for TET-1 and Landsat 8 in Test Site DEMMIN (Germany)

Erik Borg[1], Olaf Frauenberger[1,2], Bernd Fichtelmann[1],
Christian Fischer[2], Winfried Halle[2], Carsten Paproth[2],
Holger Daedelow[1], Frank Renke[1], Hans-Hermann Vajen[1],
Jens Richter[1], Gregoire Kerr[3], Eckehardt Lorenz[2], Doris Klein[3],
Jan Bumberger[4], Peter Dietrich[4], and Harald Scherntanner[5](✉)

[1] German Aerospace Center, German Remote Sensing Data Center,
Kalkhorstweg 53, 17235 Neustrelitz, Germany
{Erik.Borg, Bernd.Fichtelmann, Holger.Daedelow,
Frank.Renke, Hans-Hermann.Vajen, Jens.Richter}@dlr.de
[2] German Aerospace Center (DLR), German Remote Sensing Data Center
(DFD), Rutherfordstraße 2, 12489 Berlin, Germany
{Olaf.Frauenberger, Christian.Fischer, Carsten.Paproth,
Eckehardt.Lorenz}@dlr.de
[3] German Aerospace Center, German Remote Sensing Data Center,
Oberpfaffenhofen, Postfach 1116, 82230 Wessling, Germany
{Gregoire.Kerr, Doris.Klein}@dlr.de
[4] Department Monitoring and Exploration Technologies,
UFZ - Helmholtz-Centre for Environmental Research, Permoser Str. 15,
04318 Leipzig, Germany
{jan.bumberger, peter.dietrich}@ufz.de
[5] University Potsdam, Institute of Earth and Environmental Science,
Karl-Liebknecht-Strasse 24/25, 14476 Potsdam, Germany
hschernt@uni-potsdam.de

Abstract. In 2012, the German Aerospace Center (DLR) launched the small satellite TET-1 (Experimental Technology Carrier) as a test platform for new satellite technologies and as a carrier for the Multi-Spectral Camera System (MSC) with five spectral bands (Green, Red, Near Infrared, Middle Infrared, and Thermal Infrared). The MSC has been designed to provide quantitative parameters (e.g. fire radiative power, burned area) observing high-temperature events. The detection of such events provides information for operational support to fire brigades, to change detection of hotspots, to assess CO_2 emissions of burning vegetation, and, finally, contributes to the monitoring programs that support climate models. In order to investigate the sensitivity and accuracy of the MSC system, a calibration and validation fire campaign was developed and executed, to derive characteristic signal changes of corresponding pixels in the

G. Kerr—Since November 1, 2016 – Ascending Technologies, Intel Deutschland, 82152 Krailling.

O. Gervasi et al. (Eds.): ICCSA 2017, Part IV, LNCS 10407, pp. 121–136, 2017.
DOI: 10.1007/978-3-319-62401-3_10

MWIR and LWIR bands. The planning and execution of the validation campaign and the results are presented.

Keywords: Thermal infrared remote sensing · High-temperature event · Fire radiative power · TET-1 · FireBIRD · Landsat 8 · DEMMIN

1   Introduction

Thermal remote sensing (RS) is useful to monitor low-temperature events and their spatio-temporal dynamic for deriving environmental information, or to detect man-made or environmental high-temperature events, their expansion and distribution.

In the low-temperature range RS is used to monitor, e.g. the temperature of sea and lakes [1], urban structures [2, 3], air [4], buildings such as dykes, dams, bridges [5], or agricultural or irrigated regions [6], and hot-spots for climate studies [7].

High temperature applications are e.g. the identification and monitoring of artificial and natural hotspots like fires [8], volcanoes [9], and wildfires [10] with manifold and far-reaching environmental, economic, and social consequences like devastating forests and agricultural land, destroying settlements, existence-threatening change of environmental conditions for animals and human life, and having in medium and long term negative consequences to climate and biodiversity [11–14].

In order to obtain valuable information, a combination of measurements in the middle infrared[1] (MWIR), long-wave infrared (LWIR), red (RED), and/or near infrared (NIR) are optimal, e.g. to detect wild fires. Characteristic temperatures of these events are between 800 K and 1200 K and have a maximum of 1800 K [12].

In comparison with optical and radar missions, there is currently only a small number of satellite-based remote systems available with a band combination of RED, NIR, MWIR, LWIR, and medium ground resolution. Some of the reasons for this are: e.g. high development costs, because thermal systems need a cooling system, have a lower ground resolution in comparison to optical sensors recording reflectance or to radar sensors; and difficulties of the interpretation by unknown emission factors.

Currently, operational earth observation missions with coverage in LWIR spectral range are e.g. the EOS Terra and Aqua, National Oceanic and Atmospheric Administration (NOAA) Satellites, Metop, Suomi NPP, Landsat, and SENTINEL-3. To close this gap in the MWIR range, the DLR developed the BIRD mission, which was launched on October 22, 2001 and placed in a sun-synchronous orbit at a height of 573 km. The payload of the BIRD-satellite consisting of the WAOSS-B camera (0.6–0.67 μm and 0.84–0.9 μm), a MWIR sensor (3.4–4.2 μm), and a LWIR sensor (8.5–9.3 μm) is optimally designed for experimental fire detection systems.

The follow-on satellite TET-1 is part of the FireBIRD satellite constellation, which was developed as small satellite for the on-orbit verification program of new technologies in space. The German Aerospace Center (DLR) is supporting the different

---

[1] Use: near infrared NIR (0.75–1 μm), short wave infrared SWIR (1–2.7 μm), middle infrared MWIR (3–5 μm), long wave infrared LWIR (8–14 μm).

experiments and is operating the experiment N15 "Thermal Sensor". The TET-1 system was launched on July 22, 2012 in Baikonur (Russia), and the follow-up satellite BiROS on June 22, 2016 in Sriharikota (India).

The physics of thermal RS has been described by, e.g. [14–17]. Experimental investigations were carried out by Zhang et al. [18] in order to understand the imaging process of coal fires by means of thermal RS. The investigations focused on the analysis of spatio-temporal behavior of coal fires, in order to interpret this in RS data.

Nevertheless, it is important to calibrate and validate the physical relationship. Thus, this paper gives a detailed description of the development of a fireplace design for MWIR and LWIR cal/val activities, based on computer simulations and fire experiments. These investigations were the precondition for the fire design, reaching and holding its maximum temperature at a defined time. The defined time interval was the time-parallel overflight of the experimental satellite TET-1 and the Landsat 8. Furthermore, the paper discusses some aspects of the in-field experiments for RS hotspot detection.

2 Theoretical Background

Objects, having a temperature above absolute zero (0 K; –273.15 °C), emit electromagnetic radiation in relation to their intrinsic temperature. This fact is described by Planck's law for an idealized blackbody and describes the relation of spectral radiance to kinetic temperature T [K] and wavelength λ [m]:

$$L_{BB}(\lambda, T) = \frac{2hc^2}{\lambda^5} \left(\frac{1}{e^{\frac{hc}{\lambda kT}} - 1} \right) \tag{1}$$

with spectral radiance of a perfect emitter L_{BB} [Wm^{-2}m^{-1}], Planck's constant h [Js], Boltzmann's constant k [JK^{-1}], speed of the light in vacuum c [ms^{-1}].

The variation of the spectral radiant emittance, depending on the wavelength and blackbody temperature, is shown in Leblon et al. [12]. Here, it can be seen that a rise in temperature results in a shifting of the peak of spectral radiant emittance towards shorter wavelength. The dominant wavelength in the electromagnetic spectrum, which gives valuable information about an object as function of temperature, is described by Wien's Displacement Law. For example, solar radiation (sun temperature: approx. 6000 K) reflected by Earth's surface reaches a maximum in the visible domain (0.480 μm) whereas the typical Earth's surface emittance (temperature: approx. 300 K) reaches the radiation peak in the thermal domain (9.7 μm). In the case of hot temperature events (e.g. wild fires) with temperatures between 800 K and 1000 K, the radiant flux peaks at the MWIR spectral region between 3.7 μm and 4.6 μm. In particular, this shift is exploited to discriminate between normal and high-temperature phenomena.

Hence reflective and emissive spectral domain can be used to independently derive complementary surface information. For the thermal domain (LWIR), the basic radiative transfer Eq. (2) is given as:

$$L_{as}^e(\lambda) = L_{path}^e(\lambda) + \tau^e(\lambda) * L_{ag}^e(\lambda) + \tau^e(\lambda) * [1 - \varepsilon(\lambda)] * \frac{F^e(\lambda)}{\pi} \tag{2}$$

where $L_{as}^\varepsilon(\lambda)$ is the total thermal radiance at sensor, $L_{path}^e(\lambda)$ is the thermal path radiance emitted by the atmospheric layer between ground and sensor, $\tau^\varepsilon(\lambda)$ is the ground-to-sensor atmospheric thermal transmittance, $L_{ag}^\varepsilon(\lambda)$ is the ground emitted radiance, $\varepsilon(\lambda)$ is the ground surface emissivity, and $F^\varepsilon(\lambda)$ is the down-welling thermal sky flux at the ground [19].

Based on this, passive optical sensors record either electromagnetic radiation reflected by Sun-illuminated Earth's surface (NIR, SWIR), and emitted electromagnetic radiation (LWIR), or a mixture of both in MWIR. The temperature of Earth's surface is influenced by object-dependent (e.g. thermal inertia, density of stationary ground heat flux, albedo, and emittance) and object-independent factors (e.g. global radiation intensity, meteorological conditions, morphology, and vegetation cover).

For retrieval of ground based temperature from thermal radiance, taking the variability of the atmosphere into account, several methods have been described. A simple estimator based on empirical parameter is the split-window method, relaying on at least two separate spectral bands in the thermal region. The basics for this method are described by Merchant [20]. It is based on a simplified assumption, that the transmission of the atmosphere is basically dependent on atmospheric water vapor, where the transmission varies with the wavelength $\tau_{H2O}^e(\lambda)$.

To address the requirements of a RS sensor, the concept for detection and quantification of fire parameters by using the radiative energy (expressed as fire radiation power – FRP), was introduced [21]. Different authors have successfully used this concept to interpret RS data, e.g. [10, 14].

The Stefan–Boltzmann law describes the total power radiation P of a black body with respect to the Stefan–Boltzmann constant σ, its area A, and temperature T. In contrast to this, the radiation power of natural materials P_{nm}, or fires FRP, is additionally described by the emissivity ε (Eq. 3).

$$P_{nm} = FRP = \varepsilon A \sigma T^4 \tag{3}$$

Emissivity values of different natural materials are exemplarily shown by Brooks [22] and Baldrige et al. [23].

3   Test Site, Data, and Material

3.1   Calibration and Validation Test Site DEMMIN

The calibration and validation test site DEMMIN[2] is located in the federal state Mecklenburg–Western Pomerania. Detailed descriptions of DEMMIN are given by

---

[2] DEMMIN – Durable Environmental Multidisciplinary Monitoring Information Network is a registered trade mark of DLR.

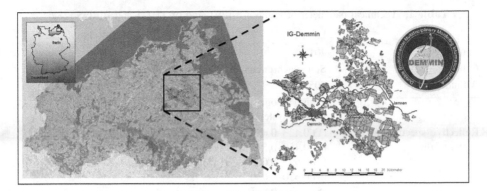

Fig. 1. Calibration and validation test site DEMMIN in Mecklenburg–Western Pomerania (left site, red rectangle) and agricultural fields of the farmers cooperating with DLR (right) [25] (Color figure online)

Gerighausen et al. [24], Borg et al. [25]. The area extends from 54°05′ N, 12°42′ E, upper left corner, to 53°41′ N, 13°30′ E lower right corner (Fig. 1).

The northern German lowland was formed during the Pleistocene (approx. 10,000 B.C.). The climate is described by long-term measurements (period: 1961–90) of the German Weather Service (DWD), with the weather station Demmin[3] (53°54′ N, 13°01′ E, height above NN: 17 m) of a mean precipitation of 555.2 mm/yr and the climate station Teterow (53°45′ N, 12°37′ E, height above NN: 46 m) of 544.0 mm/yr, and a mean temperature of 8.1 °C (variation of the annual mean temperature: 7.4–10.2 °C) is delivered for both stations [26, 27].

The landscape is characterized by agricultural land, interrupted by green land and forests as well as wetland around the river Peene.

Permanent in-situ data are measured by, e.g. an environmental measurement network of 23 DEMMIN stations (DLR) and 20 TERENO stations (GeoResearch Center Potsdam – GFZ). All stations are hosted and operated by DLR. The stations include, e.g. pyrano- and pyrgeometers to measure up- and down-welling short-wave and long-wave radiation. In addition, each station has sensors for measuring air moisture, temperature, leaf moisture, wind direction and speed, rain rate, as well as soil moisture and soil temperature at different depths. The measurement interval is 15 min.

3.2   In-Situ and Remote Sensing Data

The fire experiment was synchronously carried out with the data acquisitions by TET-1 (planned overpass: 11:56–12:05 MEST – Mean European Summer Time) and Landsat 8 (path/row: 194/22, planned overpass: 12:03–12:17 MEST) on August 17, 2013. The characteristics of TET-1 and Landsat 8 are shown in Table 1.

An in-situ campaign was synchronously carried out with the overpasses of both satellites. In the immediate vicinity of the fire experiment, the temperatures of the fire

---

[3] Demmin is a town in Mecklenburg–Western Pomerania.

Table 1. Technical parameter of Landsat 8 [29], and of TET-1 and BiROS [28]

	Landsat 8	TET	BiROS
Launch	2013	2012	2016
Orbit	Sun synchronous	Sun synchronous	Sun synchronous
Altitude	705	445	517
Type	Whisk-broom scanner-system	Push broom scanner system	Push broom scanner system
Reflective spectral band - Wavelength [μm]	(1) 0.433–0.453 (2) 0.450–0.515 (3) 0.525–0.600 (4) 0.630–0.680 (5) 0.845–0.885 (6) 1.560–1.660 (7) 2.100–2.300 (9) 1.360–1.390	(1) 0.460–0.560 (2) 0.565–0.725 (3) 0.790–0.930	(1) 0.460–0.560 (2) 0.565–0.725 (3) 0.790–0.930
Panchromatic band - Wavelength [μm]	(8) 0.500–0.680		
Emissive band - Wavelength [μm]	(10) 10.30–11.30 (11) 11.50–12.50	(4) 3.4–4.2 (5) 8.5–9.3	(4) 3.4–4.2 (5) 8.5–9.3
Ground resolution (m)	Bands 1–7, 9: 30 Band 8: 15 Bands 10, 11: 100 (30[a])	Bands 1–3: 36 Bands 4, 5: 325 (GSD 162[b])	Bands 1–3: 39 Bands 4, 5: 335 (GSD 167)

[a]Ground resolution of LWIR-bands: 100 m, delivered data products resampled to 30 m.
[b]Ground Sampling Distance.

and background have been measured using handheld Heitronics thermal sensor systems (temperature range: 8–14 μm, signal-to-noise ratio: S/N 1115, temperature range: −50 to +1000 °C, emissivity set to 1.0). In the broader environment of the fire, the soil temperature and moisture were measured using the environmental measurement stations described above.

4   Method

4.1   Work Flow of Fire Experiment

A general processing scheme of the experiment and results are given in Fig. 2. The experiment included: phase 1 "The preliminary consideration for fire campaign" (including computer simulations, small fire experiments, and draft of the fire site layout); phase 2, "Experiment (including the construction, execution of the experiment, and the in-situ measurements)", and phase 3 "Evaluation" (including interpretation of the TET-1 data and derivation of fire parameters, as well as the comparison of the results with in-situ data, and the improvement of the pre- and/or thematic processing, and, if necessary, the information distribution).

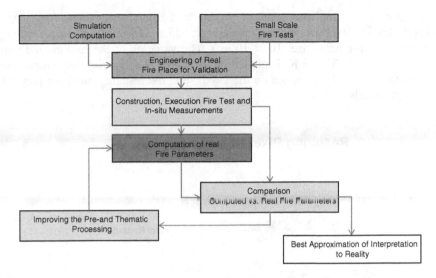

Fig. 2. Scheme of the work flow of the fire experiment in DEMMIN

4.2 Preliminary Consideration for Fire Campaign

Fire Simulation Computation. With respect to the experiment design, a fire with a realistic and feasible size, taking the individual pixel resolution of the TET-sensor into account, is difficult to realize. Mixed pixels include more than one land cover type (with individual properties: e.g. A, T, ε). In this case, the FRP_P of a pixel is a sum of different radiation powers P_i of n different sub-areas:

$$FRP_P = \varepsilon_P A_P \sigma T_P^4 = \sum_{i=1}^{n} P_i = \sum_{i=1}^{n} \left(\varepsilon_i A_i \sigma T_i^4 \right) \tag{4}$$

where i is the index of a land cover type.

If Eq. 4 is transformed to the temperature T_P and if FRP_P can be expressed as the sum of the background radiation power P_B and the fire radiation power FRP (with $A_P = A_F + A_B$) Eq. 5 can be derived:

$$T_P = \sqrt[4]{\frac{FRP_P}{\sigma \varepsilon_P A_P}} = \sqrt[4]{\frac{\left\{ (\varepsilon_F A_F T_F^4) + (\varepsilon_B (A_P - A_F) T_B^4) \right\}}{\varepsilon_P A_P}} \tag{5}$$

If ε_F and ε_B are set to 1, Eq. 5 can be used to compute different simulations by varying the parameters A_F, T_F, and T_B. The results deliver information to the required target temperature and its size to stimulate the recording by the sensor.

Figure 3 shows a simulation result of varying background temperature for a single TET-pixel (defined pixel size without staggering[4]: 325 × 325 m^2), including a varying temperature of a fire area (size: 10 × 10 m^2). The variation of the background temperature (273.16 K to 373.16 K) is plotted on the x-axis. The varying fire temperature (273.16 K to 1273.16 K) is shown on the y-axis, and the resulting radiation power is shown on the z-axis.

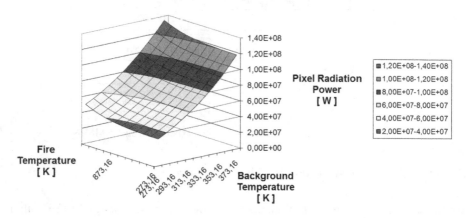

Fig. 3. Relationship between varying fire temperature, resulting temperature of the total pixel size of 325 × 325 m^2 and a fire area of 10 × 10 m^2

The influence of a fire on the increase of the radiation power in the temperature range 273.16 K to 763.16 K is very small. At temperatures $T > 763.16$ K a non-linear increase of the radiation performance of mixed pixel can be observed caused by the 4th power of the fire temperature. Therefore, it was necessary to achieve a temperature in the order of 763.16 K in minimum.

Small Scale Fire Experiments. In order to ensure a successful implementation of RS campaign, it was necessary to examine the thermal as well as the temporal behavior of the inflammation and combustion of different (available) materials.

In addition, an optimized design of the fireplace had to be developed in order to achieve the nearly maximum peak temperature of the fire with respect to the satellite overpass.

The results for wood and charcoal fire experiments, using a grill of size 40 × 30 cm^2, are summarized in Table 2.

---

[4] Real ground resolution of TET-1 is 325 × 325 m^2. Staggered detector assembly and double sampling along track allows a computed ground resolution of 162 × 162 m^2. The method is described in Skrbek and Lorenz [30].

Table 2. Temperature dynamic of a wood fire (exp. 1) and a charcoal fire (exp. 2)

Time	Experiment 1: Layer of timber (20 cm) (01.08.2013, 07:09–08:09 a.m.)			Experiment 2: Layer of charcoal (10 cm) (31.07.2013, 09:46–10:41 a.m.)		
	Border of fire [°C]	Center of fire [°C]	Max [°C]	Border of fire [°C]	Center of fire [°C]	Max [°C]
00:00	19	36	–	83	83	–
00:05	23	71	–	–	136	–
00:10	40	403	640	–	102	550
00:15	125	380	712	–	180	700
00:20	233	654	796	–	224	799
00:25	208	606	882	–	487	834
00:30	579	629	816	–	738	835
00:35	533	654	794	630	670	904
00:40	536	702	820	624	735	940
00:45	487	714	873	635	712	850
00:50	524	706	771	584	722	853
00:55	496	698	824	566	645	825
01:00	488	733	733	–	–	–

Design of the Fire Experiment. The fire campaign was conducted to support the commissioning phase of the TET-1 mission. The aim of the experiment was to design a fire plot which can be detected in the sub-pixel scale with a defined dimension and a homogeneous surface temperature. Therefore, the computer simulations with an experimental burned area of 10×10 m^2 based on available pre-launch parameters of TET-1 (estimated pixel resolution: 330×330 m^2).

However, during the campaign a fire area of 11×13 m^2 was realized. The reasons for it lay on: (i) the Euro palettes size (1.2 m $\times$ 0.8 m, respective 13×10 palettes inclusive gaps between it), (ii) uncertainties in reaching the postulated peak fire temperature for the whole fire area in 45 min which was necessary to stimulate the detector pixel, and (iii) the uncertainties in reaching the mission parameters, e.g. sensitivity and PSF[5]. Therefore, an additional fire area of 43 m^2 was used as a precaution. The change of the surface in this order of magnitude leads then to a higher temperature of 4 K, when assuming a fire temperature of 1000 K and a background temperature of 300 K.

Figure 4a shows schematically the experimental setup of the fire plot. According to this design, the burn plot was implemented in DEMMIN (Fig. 4b) with following details: Euro-palettes were used as basis. Thus, a continuous air flow similar to a furnace could be produced so that firstly an uniform inflammation was made possible within the complete fire area and then a homogeneously distributed high-temperature of the fire was achieved. In addition, a thin straw layer of approx. 50 cm thickness was installed on the pallets to guarantee homogeneous start conditions for the inflammation. An approx. 30 cm thick layer of beech wood (about 23 solid cubic meters) was implemented over the straw layer. Furthermore, an additional third layer of charcoal

---

[5] PSF – point spread function describes the response of an imaging system to a point source or point object.

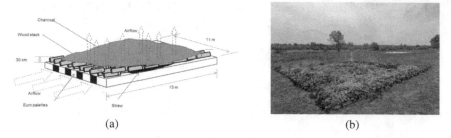

(a)   (b)

Fig. 4. Schematic presentation of the fireplace design (a) and the installed real fire plot in the DEMMIN test site (b)

(about 2500 kg) was placed on top to guarantee a maximum of surface temperature. In order to facilitate the fire inflammation, also solid fire starters (26 kg) were homogenously distributed within the different layers. Finally, the top layer was moistened with liquid fire lighter (10 L) for ignition. The fire was started using a gas burner 45 min before overpassing of TET-1. An intervention in the process was not possible after the start because of high temperature in the environment of the fire. For safety, fire brigade and fire engine were stationed at the fire location.

Table 3 compares the ground-truth data of the in-situ measurement campaign with the interpretation results of TET-1 data. The temperature T and area A, derived from the TET-1 data on August 26, 2013, have relatively large differences to the real set up. After improving the radiometric pre-processing the values were recomputed on February 15, 2017 (last column of Table 3). Although the fire took only 0.13% of the pixel area of TET-1, it could raise the brightness temperature from about 290 K to 323 K significantly above the noise level, allowing a clear detection and quantification. The results demonstrate that the dimension of the fire in temperature T and area A could be approximated to the real set up. On the other hand, the estimation of the FRP is more stable. The re-processing of the TET-1 data to derive fire parameters, using an adapted bi-spectral method [31], based on [32], yielded the following parameters: $T_F = 728$ K, $A_F = 141$ m^2, and $FRP = 2.24$ MW.

Table 3. Comparison of measured in-situ data and computer-based interpretation of TET-1 data on August 26, 2013 first draft, and on February 15, 2017, after modification of pre- and the thematic processing (measured flame temperature T and burnt area A)

Parameter	Unit	In-situ measurement	Computer-based interpretation (Aug. 26, 2013)	Computer-based interpretation (Feb. 15, 2017)
T_{min}	K	300 (Background)	490	488,3
T_{mean}	K	940	727,4	720,4
T_{max}	K	approx. 1150	1500	1500
AF_{min}	m^2	–	9	8,91
AF	m^2	143	141	148,3
AF_{max}	m^2	–	1733	1821,4
FRP	MW	1,36	2.24	2,27

Results of RS Data Interpretation. The TET-1 RGB image with RED: MWIR band, GREEN: LWIR band, and BLUE: RED band shows a clear signal of the fire (Fig. 5). But, as demonstrated in Fig. 6b, the fire could not be detected on the basis of the visible spectral bands. The reason for this could be that the fire had already reached the glowing state and the surface was overlaid by an ash layer.

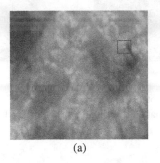 

(a)   (b)

Fig. 5. RGB image of TET, with RED: MWIR band, GREEN: LWIR band, and BLUE: RED band, shows the region of the fire marked by a red circle (a), and the detail with fire (b). Due to the staggered lines and double sampling in time, four fire pixels are visible and due to a non-rectangular point spread function (PSF) neighboring pixel are also affected

The TET-1 fire signal is based on MWIR spectral range (Fig. 6c), while the LWIR remains almost unaffected compared to the background. In comparison to the ground pixel size of 348×348 m^2 (increased due to off-nadir pointing, computed for the target), the fire plot represents a point source, covering only a fraction of 0.13% of the pixel area, but raising the signal from about 0.4 Wm^{-2}sr^{-1}μm^{-1} to about 1.2 Wm^{-2}sr^{-1}μm^{-1}, which can be clearly distinguished. Neighboring pixels show only little variations in MWIR band since the fire is not located in the center and due to a non-rectangular PSF.

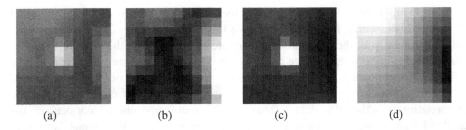

(a)   (b)   (c)   (d)

Fig. 6. RGB image of the TET-1 nadir looking bands with RED: MWIR band, GREEN: LWIR band, and BLUE: RED band (a); and as gray scale images the individual bands with RED band (b); MWIR band (c); and LWIR band (d). The variability of the background can be seen, as well as the effect of clouds on the right side of the scene (*see also* Fig. 5).

In contrast, the fire is clearly visible in Figs. 7a to c on the basis of the Landsat 8 image. The yellow cross in Fig. 7a is only caused by the signal in the SWIR band. The fire was recorded by one pixel of thermal band 11. Thus, it is clear that the fire of a size of 11 m × 13 m has stimulated the larger area of the Landsat pixel.

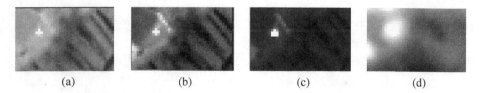

| (a) | (b) | (c) | (d) |

Fig. 7. Segment of Landsat 8 image of the same fire plot: RGB image with Red: NIR band, Green; SWIR band (band 6), and BLUE: RED band (a), band 6 (b), band 7 (c), and LWIR band 11 (d)

Figure 8 is a focused presentation of the fire without the surrounding situation shown in Fig. 7, to demonstrate the spatial allocation of the corresponding pixels of the fire plot. The comparison of the individual bands shows that the pixel with the highest value in the LWIR band (at the center of Fig. 8d) belongs to that pixel which is located at the top right to the cross center in Fig. 8a.

| (a) | (b) | (c) | (d) |

Fig. 8. The corresponding section of Fig. 7 in higher geometric resolution

Normal Temperature Validation. Since the correct estimation of the background temperature is essential for the estimation of the *FRP*, it is necessary to compare the real temperature with the brightness temperature measured with the satellite.

A comparison between satellite-based and ground-based measurements is provided in Table 4. Additionally, the background temperatures of the in-situ measurements of the automated environmental measurement system in DEMMIN can be used for the interpretation of the RS data (Table 5). Without atmospheric correction, the satellite-based values show significantly lower temperatures. Using atmospheric correction algorithms, based on the split-window algorithm (SWA), the difference is reduced, but still significant. The fire has raised the temperature in the Landsat 8 image, but it is not visible in the TET-1 thermal data.

Since the sky was overcast with relatively transparent clouds during the overpass, the estimated brightness temperatures show variations in the radiance received by the satellite, which might be the cause for the low-temperatures estimated. Such variations

Table 4. Comparison of in-situ measurements with satellite-based measurements in thermal infrared bands of TET-1 LWIR and Landsat B10 top of atmosphere (TOA) and atmospheric corrected with ATCOR using split-window method [20, 33]

Area	In-situ data	TET1 LWIR (TOA)			Landsat B10 (TOA)			SWA temperature retrieval - atmospheric corrected		
	T [°C]	T [°C]	ΣT [K]	ΔT [K]	T [°C]	ΣT [K]	ΔT [K]	T [°C]	ΣT [K]	ΔT [K]
Fire	670.0	9.6	0.9	−660	18.0	0.39	652.0	24.1	0.89	−645.9
Fire surrounding	27.0	8.2	4.6	−18.7	16.1	0.59	−13.9	20.1	0.96	−9.9
Field northwest	27.0	15.3	0.8	−11.6	22.5	1.22	−7.5	28.7	1.5	−1.3
Greenland southeast	24.2	8.4	0.54	−15.8	14.2	0.59	−10.0	18.2	1.12	−6.0

Table 5. Temperatures measured in meteorological stations close to the fire (13.1 E, 53.9 N)

Station	Longitude	Latitude	T [°C]		
			11:45 h	12:00 h	12:15 h
Karlshof	13.1	53.9	25.5	24.9	26.5
Rustow	13.1	54.0	23.2	23.4	23.7
Zeitlow	13.1	54.0	23.2	22.8	23.4
Seedorf	13.0	54.0	21.5	21.7	22.0

have been observed as well at the meteorological stations as variations of the air temperatures as shown in Table 5.

5 Conclusion

The understanding of environmental processes requires measurements adequate to the corresponding spatio-temporal process dynamics. Although thermal RS is considered an important source for environmental information, currently only a comparable small number of operational MWIR observation missions is available.

A successful validation of these missions based on in-field experiments is an important aspect for future operational monitoring concepts. Validation can be used to monitor the correct calibration of thermal products, provide an estimate of the accuracy of RS products, and give support for better understanding of signal generation at sensor. The retrieval of in-situ data for the calibration and validation of RS is very complex and cost-intensive. Accordingly, it is of key importance that the most relevant fire parameters, e.g. fire size and burning parameter, are well known. This is a pre-requisite for further data analyses and for the derivation of image-based relevant HTE parameter reference.

In different applications thermal data in the spectral range of 8–14 μm were used successfully to detect fire. But in order to detect fire and to quantify its properties as FRP, temperature, and fire area size, the MWIR band is more optimal for fire monitoring. In contrast to this, the spectral range of 8–14 μm is more optimal for land surface temperature retrieval. Both aspects can be explained by Planck's law (see Eq. 1) and Wien's Displacement Law.

This study demonstrates the feasibility of an experiment under real conditions during the overpass of satellites using a standardized experiment set-up and the temporal adjustment to satellite overflights, e.g. of TET-1 and Landsat 8.

For this, numerical simulations and burning experiments of different materials were operated to design a fire plot. The intended parameters of the fire could be obtained during the experiment and at the time of the overpass by TET-1 and Landsat 8. It could be shown that the results of the subpixel-evaluation of TET-1 data with the dual-band-method agree very well with the measured values of the in-situ-campaign. The size of the fireplace could be determined with 141 m^2 (in-situ-measurement: 143 m^2) and the temperature with 728 K (in-situ-measurement: 940 K).

The results were used, in order to improve the radiometry of the processing. The new computed values are 148 m^2 for the size of the fire plot and a temperature of 720 K. The difference between the RS data and the in-situ data can be correlated with thin cirrus clouds leading to an underestimation of the background signal.

A substantial aspect, which is to be considered during the execution of campaigns, is the spatio-temporal dynamic of environmental processes during the experiment. Here the question always arises, whether a measured in-situ value can be correlated with the RS data. This is important for very fast varying processes like fires.

But, if the quantity and quality of the experimental data (e.g. temperature, duration) can be guaranteed and if the data are well documented, the experimental data can be used for national and international validation activities [34–36]. Ongoing activities focus on further improvement of the FRP algorithm, taking information from different mapped HTE into account. This includes reliable estimations of the individual background temperatures. In addition, cross-validation activities by using VIIRS and Sentinel-3 data are starting.

Acknowledgements. The authors would like to thank Mr. Leddig and Mr. Baals (Rustower Service Company) for supporting the experiment. We thank the colleagues of Mr. Küthe (Ordnungsamt Demmin); Mr. Daedelow and Mr. Maier of the Umweltamt/Abfallrecht und Immissionsschutz, Waren–Müritz, Mrs. Klemm, advisor of the Umweltamt/Naturschutz, Landschaftspflege, Eingriffsregelungen, Biotopschutz Demmin. And last but not least we thank Mr. Rohleder, head of voluntary fire brigade (Freiwillige Feuerwehr) Demmin, and his colleagues for fire test assessing.

References

1. Wloczyk, C., Richter, R., Borg, E., Neubert, W.: Sea and lake surface temperature retrieval from Landsat thermal data in Northern Germany. Int. J. Remote Sens. **27**, 2489–2502 (2006)
2. Van, T.T., Trungand, L.V., Lan, H.L.: Application of thermal remote sensing in study on surface temperature distribution of Ho Chi Minh City. In: 7th FIG Regional Conference Spatial Data Serving People: Land Governance and the Environment – Building the Capacity, Hanoi, Vietnam, 19–22 October 2009

3. Weng, Q.: Thermal infrared remote sensing for urban climate and environmental studies: methods, applications, and trends. ISPRS J. Photogrammetry Remote Sens. **64**, 335–344 (2009)
4. Wloczyk, C., Borg, E., Richter, R., Miegel, K.: Estimation of instantaneous air temperature above vegetation and soil surfaces from Landsat 7 ETM+ data in northern Germany. Int. J. Remote Sens. **32**, 9119–9136 (2011)
5. Schnebele, E., Tanyu, B.F., Cervone, B.F., Waters, N.: Review of remote sensing methodologies for pavement management and assessment. Eur. Transp. Res. Rev. **7**, 1–19 (2015)
6. Ishimwe, R., Abutaleb, K., Ahmed, F.: Applications of thermal imaging in agriculture—a review. Adv. Remote Sens. **3**, 128–140 (2014)
7. Voogt, J.A., Oke, T.R.: Thermal remote sensing of urban climates. Remote Sens. Environ. **86**, 370–384 (2002)
8. Rosema, A., van Genderen, J.L., Veld, H., Vekerdy, Z., Ten Katen, A.M., Prakash, A.: Manual of coal fire detection and monitoring; report of the project: development and implementation of a coal fire monitoring and fighting system in China. Institute of Applied Geoscience (NITG), Delft, The Netherlands (1999)
9. Ramsey, M.S., Harris, A.J.L.: Volcanology 2020: how will thermal remote sensing of volcanic surface activity evolve over the next decade? J. Volcanol. Geoth. Res. **249**, 217–233 (2013)
10. Wooster, M.J., Zhukov, B., Oertel, D.: Fire radiative energy for quantitative study of biomass burning: derivation from the BIRD experimental satellite and comparison to MODIS fire products. Remote Sens. Environ. **86**, 83–107 (2003)
11. Gude, P., Jones, K., Rasker, R., Greenwood, M.C.: Evidence for the effect of homes on wildfire suppression costs. Int. J. Wildland Fire **22**, 537–548 (2013)
12. Leblon, B., Bourgeau-Chavez, L., San-Miguel-Ayanz, J.: Use of remote sensing in wildfire management. In: Curkovic, S. (ed.) Sustainable Development - Authoritative and Leading Edge Content for Environmental Management, Rijeka, Croatia, pp. 55–82 (2012)
13. Rábade, J.M., Aragoneses, C.: Social impact of large-scale forest fires. In: Proceedings of the Second International Symposium on Fire Economics, Planning, and Policy: A Global View. General Technical report PSW-GTR-208, Station, pp. 23–33 (2008)
14. Zhukov, B., Lorenz, E., Oertel, D., Wooster, M., Roberts, G.: Experience of detection and quantitative characterization of fires during the experimental small satellite mission BIRD. DLR-Forschungsbericht 2005-04 (2005)
15. Idso, S.B., Schmugge, T.J., Jackson, R.D., Reginato, R.J.: The utility of surface temperature measurements for the remote sensing of surface soil water status. J. Geophys. Res. **80**, 3044–3049 (1975)
16. Quattroch, D., Luvall, C.: Thermal Remote Sensing in Land surface Processes. CRC Press LLC, Boca Raton (2004)
17. Gillespie, A., Rokugawa, S., Matsunaga, T., Cothern, J., Hook, S., Kahle, A.: A temperature and emissivity separation algorithm for advanced spaceborne thermals emission and reflection radiometer (ASTER) images. IEEE Trans. Geosci. Remote Sens. **36**, 1113–1126 (1998)
18. Zhang, J., Kuenzer, C., Tetzlaff, A., Oertel, D., Zhukov, B., Wagner, W.: Thermal characteristics of coal fires 2: results of measurements on simulated coal fires. J. Appl. Geophys. **63**, 135–147 (2007)
19. Richter, R., Coll, C.: Bandpass-resampling effects for the retrieval of surface emissivity. Appl. Opt. **41**, 3523–3529 (2002)
20. Merchant, C.J.: Thermal remote sensing of sea surface temperature. In: Kuenzer, C., Dech, S. (eds.) Thermal Infrared Remote Sensing, pp. 287–314 (2013)

21. Kaufman, Y., Remer, L., Ottmar, R., Ward, D., Rong, R.L., Kleidman, R., Fraser, R., Flynn, L., McDougal, D., Shelton, G.: Relationship Between Remotely Sensed Fire Intensity and Rate of Emission of Smoke: SCAR-C Experiment in Global Biomass Burning, pp. 685–696. MIT Press, Cambridge (1996). Levine, J. (ed.)

22. Brooks, F.A.: An introduction to physical microclimatology. Associated Students Store. University of California, Davis (1959)

23. Baldrige, A.M., Hook, S.J., Grove, C.I., Rivera, G.: The ASTER spectral library version 2.0. Remote Sens. Environ. **113**, 711–715 (2009). https://speclib.jpl.nasa.gov/

24. Gerighausen, H., Borg, E., Wloczyk, C., Fichtelmann, B., Günther, A., Vajen, H.-H., Rosenberg, M., Schulz, M., Engler, H.-G.: DEMMIN – a test site for the validation of remote sensing data products. In: Proceedings on AGRISAR and EAGLE Campaigns Final Workshop, ESA/ESTEC, Noordwijk, Netherland, 15–16 October, pp. 1–9 (2007)

25. Borg, E., Lippert, K., Zabel, E., Löpmeier, F.J., Fichtelmann, B., Jahncke, D., Maass, H.: DEMMIN – Teststandort zur Kalibrierung und Validierung von Fernerkundungsmissionen. In: Rebenstorf, R.W. (ed.) 15 Jahre Studiengang Vermessungswesen – Geodätisches Fachforum und Festakt, Neubrandenburg, 16–17 January, pp. 401–419 (2009)

26. DWD/Deutscher Wetterdienst: Download of Mean Precipitation. Period 1961–1990 (2006). http://www.dwd.de/bvbw/appmanager/bvbw/dwdwwwDesktop?nfpb=true&_pageLabel= dwdwww_start&T3200039671164966383319gsbDocumentPath=Navigation% 2FOeffentlichkeit%2FKlima__Umwelt%2FKlimadatenzentren%2FNKDZ%2Fkldaten__akt %2Fausgabe__mittelwerte__node.html__nnn%3Dtrue. Accessed 14 Feb 2006

27. DWD/Deutscher Wetterdienst: Download of Mean Temperature. Period 1961–1990 (2007). http://www.dwd.de/bvbw/appmanager/bvbw/dwdwwwDesktop?nfpb=true&_pageLabel= dwdwww_start&T3200039671164966383319gsbDocumentPath=Navigation% 2FOeffentlichkeit%2FKlima__Umwelt%2FKlimadatenzentren%2FNKDZ%2Fkldaten__akt %2Fausgabe__mittelwerte__node.html__nnn%3Dtrue. Accessed 05 Dec 2007

28. ESA. https://directory.eoportal.org/web/eoportal/satellite-missions/t/tet-1. Accessed 09 2015

29. USGS. http://landsat.usgs.gov/band_designations_landsat_satellites.php. Accessed 09 2015

30. Skrbek, W., Lorenz, E.: HSRS – an infrared sensor for hotspot detection. Proc. SPIE Infrared Spaceborne Remote Sens. VI **3437**, 167–176 (1998)

31. Zhukov, B., Lorenz, E., Oertel, D., Wooster, M., Roberts, G.: Spaceborne detection and characterization of fires during the bi-spectral infrared detection (BIRD) experimental small satellite mission (2001–2004). Remote Sens. Environ. **100**, 29–51 (2006)

32. Dozier, J.: A method for satellite identification of surface temperature fields of subpixel resolution. Remote Sens. Environ. **11**, 221–229 (1981)

33. Richter, R., Schläpfer, D.: ATCOR Manual. Atmospheric/Topographic Correction for Satellite Imagery, (ATCOR-2/3 User Guide 9.0.2, March 2016).- DLR DLR-IB 565-01/15.- 263

34. Frauenberger, O., Börner, A., Borg, E., Halle, W., Lorenz, E., Mitchell, S., Paproth, C., Säuberlich, T., Terzibaschian, T., Wohlfeil, J.: Results on verification and validation of OOV-TET1 multi-spectral camera observations within the FireBIRD project. In: 10th IAA Symposium Small Satellites for Earth Observation, Berlin, Germany, 20–24 April, pp. 163–166. Wissenschaft und Technik Verlag, Berlin (2015)

35. Fischer, C., Klein, D., Kerr, G., Stein, E., Lorenz, E., Frauenberger, O., Borg, E.: Data validation and case studies using the TET-1 thermal infrared satellite system (ISRSE36-617). In: 36th International Symposium on Remote Sensing of Environment ISRSE36 International Archives of the Photogrammetry, Remote Sensing and Spatial Information Sciences, vol. XL-7/W3, Berlin, Germany, 11–15 May 2015, pp. 1177–1182 (2015)

36. Schroeder, W., Oliv, P., Giglio, L., Quayle, B., Lorenz, E., Morelli, F.: Active fire detection using Landsat-8/OLI data. Remote Sens. Environ. **185**, 210–220 (2016)

Ground-Based Real-Aperture Radar for Deformation Monitoring: Experimental Tests

Marco Scaioni[1,2,3(✉)], Fabio Roncoroni[2], Mario Ivan Alba[2,4], Alberto Giussani[1,2], and Mattia Manieri[1]

[1] Department of Architecture, Built Environment and Construction Engineering, Politecnico di Milano, Via Ponzio 31, 20133 Milan, Italy
marco.scaioni@polimi.it
[2] Politecnico di Milano, Polo Territoriale di Lecco, Via G. Previati 1/c, 23900 Lecco, Italy
[3] Department of Surveying and Geo-Informatics, Tongji University, 1239 Siping Road, 200092 Shanghai, People's Republic of China
[4] Cimolai, Corso L. Zanussi, 26, 33080 Porcia, PN, Italy

Abstract. This paper describes a series of six experiments to assess the potential of the Ground-Based Interferometric Real-Aperture Radar sensor IBIS-S (IDS Company, Pisa, Italy). In particular, attention focuses on long-term quasi-static deformation monitoring, because the measurement of dynamic deformation has been already treated by many authors. The use along with artificial corner reflectors, the repositioning mode, the mitigation of atmospheric effects, as well as the use from multiple stations ('stereo-radar') to help the recognition of targets and to improve the geometric definition of spatial displacements are the main subjects of these experiments. The results have shown the high potential of this kind of instrumentation for concurrent monitoring of several points of a complex structure, even though further research is needed to be fully operational and competitive against consolidated monitoring techniques.

Keywords: Deformation measurement · Interferometry · Microwave · Real-Aperture Radar · Structure and infrastructure monitoring

1 Ground-Based Real-Aperture Radar

During the last decades radar interferometry has achieved a primary relevance in Remote Sensing. In particular, the application for long-term deformation measurement based on the use of spaceborne [1] and ground-based sensors [2] is now a quite consolidated research domain whose outcomes have largely followed up to industry, professionals, public authorities and administrations.

Here the attention focuses on the ground-based radar sensors. On one side, Ground-Based Synthetic Aperture Radar sensors (GBSAR – [3]) have gained popularity for the measurement of slow deformations in civil structures [4], ground slopes [5, 6], and glaciers [7]. On the other side, less attention has been paid to Ground-Based Interferometric Real-Aperture Radar sensors (InRAR), as reported in [8]. These instruments have been designed to provide high-precision measurements (even better than 1/10 mm) for

© Springer International Publishing AG 2017
O. Gervasi et al. (Eds.): ICCSA 2017, Part IV, LNCS 10407, pp. 137–151, 2017.
DOI: 10.1007/978-3-319-62401-3_11

monitoring of civil structures and infrastructures, which are usually made of materials and geometric patterns able to provide a high-reflection to the radar signal. The main limitation of InRAR technology is the capability of operating only along the Line-of-Sight (LoS), whilst GBSAR also offers a cross-range resolution. For the sake of completeness, other ground-based radar systems based on different operating principles have been developed, as reported in [3, 9].

The InRAR IBIS-S instrument has been developed by IDS Company (Pisa, Italy, www.idscorporation.com) in cooperation with the Department of Electronics and Tele-communications of the University of Florence, Italy [10, 11]. IBIS-S has two different operational modes for measurement of quasi-static and dynamic displacements. The literature reports several applications of the 'dynamic' deformation measurement mode, especially for the modal analysis of civil structures [12], bridges [13], and historical buildings [14]. Not so many papers can be found on the 'quasi-static' deformation measurement mode: this is mainly due to the spatial ambiguities of InRAR measurements, which may lead to prefer other instruments (for example, robotic theodolites [15], laser trackers [16], and terrestrial laser scanners [17]) with similar performances but fewer limitations. Pieraccini et al. [18] reports about an experiment of static monitoring of a bridge with InRAR.

As shown in Fig. 1, IBIS-S is made of a Sensing Unit (including the antenna) devoted to generation, emission and recording of a coherent radar bandwidth, a Control Unit installed on an industrial laptop, and an Energy Supply Unit. In Table 1 some technical features of IBIS-S are shown. This sensor can locate and simultaneously track a set of targets in the portion of space illuminated by the radar signal. However, only one target can be detected inside each 'range bin,' which is the volume of the radar wavefront included between distances R and $R + \Delta R$ from the sensor (see Fig. 2), with ΔR the range resolution that is independent from range R. This involves that, if a strong reflecting element (belonging to the structure or installed on purpose – i.e., a corner reflector) is predominant in the range bin, this point will be effectively tracked within time. In all the other cases, it will not be possible to extract meaningful information about target displacements from the returned signal.

Fig. 1. The InRAR sensor IBIS-S (IDS Company, Pisa, Italy) installed on a topographic tripod.

Table 1. Main technical properties of the IBIS-S sensor.

Radar type	SFCW, interferometric
Operating frequency bandwidth	Band Ku (12–18 GHz)
Operating range	20–1000 m
Range resolution	0.5 m in radial direction
Precision of relative displacement measurement	0.01–0.1 mm
Sampling frequency	Up to 100 Hz (in 'dynamic' mode)
Size of Sensing Unit	$40 \times 40 \times 15$ cm (L $\times$ P $\times$ H)
Weight of Sensing Unit	12 kg

In order to accomplish the measurement process two radar processing techniques are implemented in the sensor. Continuous Wave Step Frequency (CWSF) and Differential Interferometry. While the readers may refer to the literature for more details about these techniques [19], here we limit ourselves to report two main operational features that are important for the applications described in the paper.

The transmitted coherent radar signal is on the frequency modulation of a stepped sequence covering a bandwidth between 12–18 GHz. This results in a range integer ambiguity ($\lambda_{amb} = 0.25\lambda$) that depends on the wavelength (λ) corresponding to the central frequency of the adopted bandwidth ($\lambda = 17.6$ mm). In the case of the IBIS-S sensor, the integer ambiguity is $\lambda_{amb} = 0.25\lambda = 4.4$ mm. In addition, the spatial resolution is constrained to the range bins, each of them featuring a typical depth $\Delta R = 0.5$ m. The recorded signal consists of a 'range profile' (see Fig. 2), showing the amplitude of the reflected radar signal in each range bin. The other information recorded per each range bin is the phase of the radar signal, which is used within the differential interferometry technique to determine the relative displacement of the potential target between consecutive observation epochs.

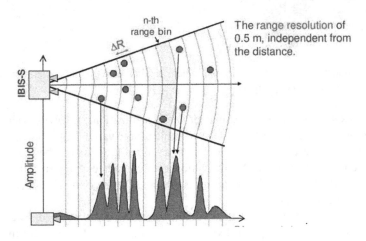

Fig. 2. Example of 'range profile' and 'range bins' obtainable with IBIS-S InRAR sensor.

The temporal resolution depends on the desired sampling rate. The range relative displacement (Δr) is a function of the phase shift ($\Delta\phi = \phi_{i+1} - \phi_i$) between two observation epochs i and $i + 1$:

$$\Delta r \propto -\frac{\lambda}{4\pi}\Delta\phi \tag{1}$$

where λ è is the wavelength of the broadcasted radar sequence.

The aim of this paper is to investigate the performances of the IBIS-S InRAR sensor for monitoring 'quasi-static' deformations of civil structures. The results of some tests carried out at Politecnico Milano university are reported in Sects. 2, 3, 4, 5 and 6 and discussed in Conclusions (Sect. 7).

2   Assessment of Range Displacement Measurement Precision

The first series of experiments (Exp. 1) has concerned the evaluation of IBIS-S instrumental accuracy of relative displacements along the LoS (range direction). This task has been accomplished by comparing a set of observed displacements against benchmarking values. The latter have been set up by using a high-precision micrometric slide ($\pm 10\,\mu$m positional accuracy). These tests have been carried out in uncontrolled outdoor environment to reproduce real operating conditions, see Fig. 3.

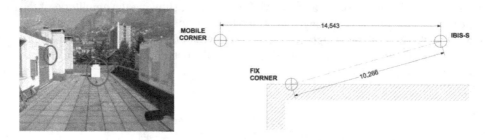

Fig. 3. Experiment 1: experiment site (left), where red circles highlight the corner reflectors; layout of the experiment set up (right).

The InRAR sensor has been used in continuous acquisition mode within short measurement sessions (maximum 30 min each), to avoid a large variability of outer conditions and to keep high coherence in the reflected radar signal [20]. As can be seen in Fig. 3, a couple of corner reflectors has been positioned to guarantee a proper radar response. One of them ('Mobile Corner') has been installed on the micrometric slide to set up a series of known displacements.

A set of four independent measurement sessions have been repeated. Each of them has entailed displacement steps of diverse size: 1 cm, 1 mm, 100 μm, 10 μm. During each step, 60 observations have been recorded using a sampling rate of 5 s. Preliminary processing of all experimental data sets has been done to remove some outliers (2% of total observations, mainly concentrated in the initial stage of Exp. 1), and to correct measurements at 1 cm step when the phase ambiguity gap was overcome. Results have confirmed the accuracy stated by IDS Company, since the root mean square error (RMSE) of mean errors of displacement steps and the root mean square (RMS) of respective standard deviations are 17 μm and 22 μm, respectively (Table 2). In addition, the normal distribution of errors around the benchmarking values has been always verified. It is important to report that the same experiments have been also repeated in indoor environment, obtaining much worse results, probably because of multipaths and interferences due to multiple reflections.

Table 2. Statistics on the experiments carried out when comparing observed and benchmarking displacements (RMSE/RMS: root mean square error/root mean square).

Step [mm]	RMSE of mean values per each step [mm]	RMS of std. dev.'s per each step [mm]
10.00	0.016	0.027
1.00	0.015	0.028
0.10	0.022	0.010
0.01	0.013	0.022
Total	0.017	0.022

3   Influence of the Environment on InRAR Measurements

In this section the attention is focused on the analysis of the influence of outer environmental parameters on the accuracy of IBIS-S measurements. In fact, the potential of this InRAR sensor, as demonstrated in Experiment 1, cannot be fully exploited when it operates in real environments for long measurement sessions. Under such conditions, the variability of local atmospheric temperature and pressure may result in a degraded quality of the observations.

To evaluate the amount of environmental effects on IBIS-S's measurements, a new series of experiments (Exp. 2) has been conducted. The IBIS-S sensor has been fixed on a stable support in a courtyard. Four points to be monitored have been localized in the scene illuminated by the instrument. In correspondence of three of them, three corner reflectors (FC1, FC2, MC1) have been installed to maximize the amplitude of the reflected signal. Corner reflector MC1 has been fixed on the high-precision slide used in Experiment 1. A fourth corner reflector (FC3) has been positioned in a farther location on the perimeter fence of the courtyard. This choice has been motivated by the large observed Signal-to-Noise ratio (S/N) in correspondence of this location. The distance from the radar sensor to each corner was 43 m (FC1), 96 m (FC2), 93 m (MC1), and 125 m (FC3).

Three similar measurement sessions have been repeated in three days, lasting from morning to evening. During these sessions the relative displacements along the LoS have been measured for points FC1, FC2 and FC3. The sensor has been operated in continuous acquisition mode, recording one observation every minute. In the case of point MC1, cycles of given displacements have been repeated during the session time. At the end of each session, the high-precision slide has been moved back to the initial position.

Concurrently, meteorological data have been recorded at a weather station located at approximately 500 m from the courtyard. In Fig. 4 a typical range profile recorded during one measurement session is shown. The peaks of amplitude in the profile corresponding to artificial reflectors can be clearly seen. The identification of such peaks in the practice is quite straightforward when artificial corner reflectors are used. Indeed, the distance from the radar sensor to each corner can be measured and sought for in the range profile.

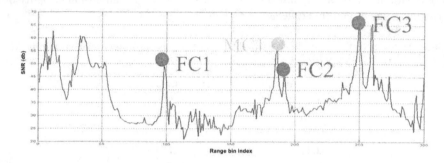

Fig. 4. Range bin profile of a typical measurement session in Experiment 2.

In the following the results obtained from the first measurement session are presented, since a higher variability of the environmental conditions has occurred during that time. For the sake of completeness, the outcomes from the other two measurement sessions were in full agreement with the ones discussed here. Looking at the results reported in Table 3, significant discrepancies between radar outputs and reference displacements can be observed. For instance, in the case of corner reflectors FC1, FC2 and FC3 that have not been moved, discrepancies up to approximately 3.5 mm have been found.

Table 3. Statistics on the results from Experiment 2, which refer to discrepancies between real and measured displacements on fixed (FC1, FC2, FC3) and mobile (MC1) corner reflectors.

Target	Mean of errors [mm]	Std. dev. of errors [mm]	Max error [mm]
FC1	−0.0785	0.6208	1.508
FC2	−0.1049	1.1066	2.721
FC3	−0.1985	1.4078	3.495
MC1	−0.9285	0.9742	2.756

The magnitude of these discrepancies is to a certain extent correlated to the recorded relative humidity (0.77 linear correlation), which justifies the application of a method for compensating atmospheric effects. In the literature, Monserrat et al. [3] reviews several methods that are reported for correcting GBSAR data. Here three different approaches have been tried:

- Use of at least one stable Ground Control Point ('GCP Method'): this simple technique relies on the selection of a fixed target in the scene, which may be either a natural or an artificial reflector. The observed discrepancies from zero displacement recorded on this point can be used for correcting other points;

- 'Zebker & Rosen Method' [21]: since the signal wavelength is modified by the changes of the atmospheric refraction, this model links this effect to the absolute pressure, to the partial vapor pressure and to the absolute atmospheric temperature; and

- 'Empirical polynomial regression Method': an empirical polynomial regression is used to model displacements on the basis of humidity, air pressure and temperature records; a few points located in stable positions are then used for model calibration.

All data sets collected for investigating the influence of atmospheric effects on IBIS-S measurements have been corrected using these three methods. In all cases, a beneficial offset could be observed. However, the 'GCP Method' provided the best corrections, both in term of error minimization, and by considering that no environmental parameters were needed. On the other hand, this method may work only if at least one stable target can be found (or installed on purpose) in the illuminated scene. The accuracy obtained after the correction based on the 'GCP Method' are better than 1/10 mm. 'Zebker & Rosen Method' also provided good corrections, even though at a lower level of accuracy than with the 'GCP Method'. Opposite to the previous technique, here stable reference points are not necessary, but the accurate knowledge of local environmental parameters is required to feed the model. The last method based on the estimate of an empirical regression requires both environmental parameter records and fixed points. Results provided less accurate corrections to corner reflector displacements than with the other two methods. One possible reason for this lower performance may be sought in the distance between the weather station and the test field, resulting in a less precise determination of local environmental parameters. This problem might have been also responsible for the non-optimal results achieved with the 'Zebker & Rosen Method.'

4   Analysis of the Influence of Design Parameters on Final Accuracy

In the previous section, the use of 'GCP Method' for correcting those observations affected by environmental parameter changes has been demonstrated to be a key-point to reduce the measurement uncertainty of IBIS-S. The influence of parameters controlling the design of a specific application is analyzed. In particular, the case when artificial corner reflectors are needed due to the absence of natural reflectors is considered in this section. The list of the analyzed parameters is:

- Distance instrument-target;
- Size of corner reflectors;
- Maximum acquisition range, to be set up before any measurement operations; and
- Angle between the LoS direction w.r.t. a specific target and the normal direction of the sensor.

To better understand these problems, a third series of experiments (Exp. 3) have been carried out in a university courtyard. During different testing sessions, squared corner reflectors of size 10 cm, 15 cm, 20 cm, 25 cm and 30 cm have been used. Each target has been positioned at different locations and measured along a time $\Delta T = 120$ s using a sampling rate equal to 1 Hz. The following sessions have been operated:

- Test Session 3.1: corner reflectors have been placed at three different distances from the radar sensor (50 m, 100 m, 150 m) along the normal direction in front of it;
- Test Session 3.2: corner reflectors have been positioned along an arc at 50 m from the sensor, starting from the normal direction and at regular steps of 5° rightwards; and
- Test Session 3.3: a corner reflector has been installed at 100 m distance from the radar sensor. Measurements have been repeated by setting a different maximum acquisition range to 110 m, 200 m, 300 m, 400 m. This option results in increasing the number of range bins and consequently to improve the signal gain.

From the analysis of results from Test Session 3.1, it can be noticed that the measurement accuracy is inversely proportional to the distance target-sensor and to the corner reflector size. An anomalous case has been observed in the case of the corner reflector of size 30 cm: in this case the accuracy improves as the distance from the sensor grows. From the results of Test Session 3.2, the best accuracy was obtained when targets were illuminated within the aperture radius of the antennas. A degradation of the accuracy was recorded when corner reflectors were placed outside. Eventually, Test Session 3.3 has revealed the independency between the accuracy and the maximum acquisition range that was set up.

5   Repositioning of the Radar Sensor

When slow deformations have to be monitored over time, and the instrument cannot be left installed and in function, the only possibility of keeping going the measurements is the repositioning of the IBIS-S sensor. This option is similar to the 'discontinuous monitoring mode' operated with GBSAR sensors [22]. Of course, the link to the previous measurements is lost after any interruptions of data acquisition, since IBIS-S provides only relative displacements. The aim of next Experiment 4 is then limited to assess whether the same targets can be consistently measured at multiple observation epochs. The accurate mechanical replacement of the sensor on the same position is the

Fig. 5. The basement plate designed for repositioning the IBIS-S sensor: on a topographic tripod (left), fixed to a wall (right).

prerequisite for applying the repositioning mode. In order to do this, a special basement plate has been designed, which can be installed on a topographic tripod or fixed to a wall as shown in Fig. 5.

A new series of experiments (Exp. 4) has been operated by installing two corner reflectors of size 15 cm in front of the sensor. One of them (CM) has been installed on the micrometric slide, while the other (CF) has been kept stable. Furthermore, three natural reflectors (NC1, NC2, NC3) showing a high S/N have been observed. The layout of the experiment field is shown in Fig. 6. To verify the quality of repositioning, five measurement sessions have been executed in different days. During each session, the same input parameters have been set up. The following operational steps have been repeated the same way during each day:

- Step 1: the radar sensor has been connected to the basement plate in Fig. 5 and a 5-minute long measurement session using a sampling rate of 5 s has been done;
- Step 2: the radar sensor has been disconnected from the basement plate and then repositioned on it. The corner reflector CM has been given a displacement of 3 mm along the LoS; a new 5-minute long measurement session has been repeated; and
- Step 3: corner CM has been reset to the initial position. A final 5-minute long measurement session has been operated.

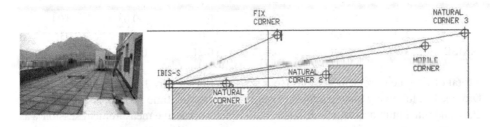

Fig. 6. Experiment 4: experiment site (left); layout of the experiment set up (right).

Results shown in Table 3 reveal small repositioning errors in all the sessions and for all the targets (RMSE = 0.06 mm and 0.21 mm, respectively). In Session 3 larger errors have been obtained (RMSE = 0.21 mm), anomaly that could have been caused by the change of the environmental parameters on the corresponding day. These results have confirmed in general the effectiveness of the tool designed for repositioning the IBIS-S sensor (Table 4).

A successive series of experiments (Exp. 5) have been conducted to assess the re-positioning mode in real operating conditions that could be met in standard structural monitoring applications. The same basement plate shown in Fig. 5 has been used and installed on a topographic tripod, which in turn has been rigidly connected to the ground. A drawing of the façade used as target during Experiment 5 is shown in Fig. 7. The position of the radar sensor w.r.t. the façade has been determined by measuring the 3D coordinates of 14 points on the façade itself and four points on the top of the sensor outer case. A theodolite has been used for this purpose: in the former case, the reflector-less mode has been adopted, in the latter four high-precision topographic reflectors have been put on the sensor case. The experiment spanned over two consecutive days on October 2016, consisting on

Table 4. Statistics of repositioning errors for all targets during different sessions of Experiment 4; measurements at each Step 1 have been considered as reference in each session. The upper part of the table reports mean errors during each step, while the line at the bottom reports RMSE's.

Day		1	1	1	1	2
Target	Step	Session 1 [mm]	Session 2 [mm]	Session 3 [mm]	Session 4 [mm]	Session 5 [mm]
NC1	1	–	–	–	–	–
	1–2	0.03	0.06	−0.11	0.07	0.07
	2–3	0.05	0.13	−0.11	0.19	0.11
CF	1	–	–	–	–	–
	1–2	−0.02	−0.05	−0.32	0.07	0.08
	2–3	0.05	−0.09	−0.27	−0.11	0.09
NC2	1	–	–	–	–	–
	1–2	0.07	0.03	−0.18	−0.07	0.07
	2–3	0.10	0.00	−0.18	0.08	0.07
NC3	1	–	–	–	–	–
	1–2	0.01	0.03	−0.15	−0.02	0.09
	2–3	0.06	−0.02	−0.18	0.04	0.07
CM	1	–	–	–	–	–
	1–2	0.03	0.04	0.23	−0.03	−0.04
	2–3	0.07	0.06	−0.24	0.01	0.03
RMSE		0.06	0.06	0.21	0.09	0.08

a total of five measurement sessions (four sessions during Day 1 and one session during Day 2). The following input parameters were set up: session time 30 min; acquisition time 10 s; and maximum acquisition distance 75 m. Each successive measurement session was postponed from the previous one by 1 h. This choice has allowed to have varying environmental conditions, as it occurs during a real monitoring session. During breaks, sensor IBIS-S has been removed and re-installed on the fixed basement plate. Environmental parameters (temperature, atmospheric pressure and relative humidity) was recorded during the experiment time by using a weather station located in the proximity of the radar set up. A point in stable position was used for correcting the effect of the environmental conditions change with the 'GCP Method.' The analysis of range profiles obtained from different sessions has highlighted the following aspects:

- The range profiles have kept quite unchanged during different sessions, since they only depended upon the returned intensity;
- Some of the local maxima in the range profile were always observed in the same range bins during different sessions, including the ones in Session 5 on Day 2;
- The correction based on the 'GCP Method' significantly improved the range profiles, but residual noise survived;
- By computing the regression of relative displacements in corresponding range bins, in many cases a correlation with the recorded relative humidity was observed. Anyway, these results could not be generalized; and

- Small relative displacements of the same magnitude (in the range of a few 1/100 mm) were observed during Sessions from 1 to 4 on Day 1. Session 5 on Day 2 resulted in larger displacements. This is caused by the larger temperature variability recorded during Day 2, being the temperature the main responsible for deformation in the monitored building.

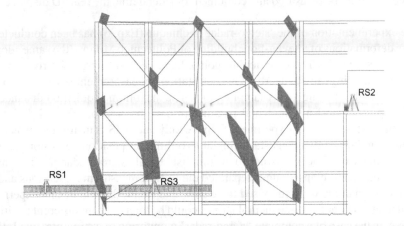

Fig. 7. University building adopted in Experiments 5 and 6. Green areas show the intersection of footprints corresponding to range bins where points measured by a theodolite should be located (RS: radar station) (Color figure online)

These outcomes have confirmed the validity of the adopted repositioning method when operating in real environment as well. In particular, when using corner reflectors – as in Experiment 4 – coupled with a high-precision mechanical repositioning system and the correction for the environmental effects, the performances of IBIS-S can be optimized. The high reflection capability of corner reflectors results in the easier detection of corresponding local maxima in the range profile, since the ratio S/N is higher.

6 Quasi-Static 'Stereo-Radar' Monitoring

The application of artificial corner reflectors for monitoring structure and infrastructures is not always feasible neither economically convenient. On the other hand, provided that the monitored construction might offer natural reflectors, the spatial ambiguity in the recognition of targets may limit the application of the InRAR technique. The knowledge of the illuminated scenario's geometry may help discriminate targets as well as detect which is the spatial direction of the observed displacements. This is possible thanks to the known positions of potential targets and to the overlap with footprints of the illuminated areas. In the case of some object typologies (e.g., bridges or construction developing along a prevalent direction), the typical geometry they feature help recognize targets. However, this is not generally possible.

To overcome the problem of the geometric ambiguity of target recognition, a new 'stereo-radar' monitoring technique has been applied. This technique is based on the use of the InRAR sensor from at least two stations located at different spatial positions. Such methodology should help detect the observed targets in individual range bins, since the intersection of the illuminated areas from multiple radar stations could reduce the footprint on the object corresponding to each range bin. Moreover, given that the same natural reflector is recognized in the range profiles from different stations, more displacement vectors could be measured and combined to better define the real 3D displacement vector.

The experimentation of the 'stereo-radar' technique (Exp. 6) has been conducted to measure deformations of a seven-floor building of Politecnico Milano (the same adopted in Exp. 5, see Fig. 7). Three stationing points have been set up on the roofs of two university's buildings in the nearby. On each station a measurement session of 25 min has been carried out using a 10 s sampling rate. The maximum acquisition distance has been set up to 75 m. Environmental parameters have been also recorded during the measurement sessions as in Experiment 5. Since only one IBIS-S instrument was available and then the simultaneous stationing at two different positions was not possible, the aim of this experiment was not to accomplish a real 'stereo-radar' measurement. However, since short elapsed times separated the InRAR measurement sessions and the building deformations were supposed to be slow and small, the aim of this experiment was to detect whether the same natural targets could be tracked from different positions. Of course, in the case of a complete 'stereo-radar' monitoring of a structure, two InRAR sensors should be placed to allow quasi-simultaneous data acquisition. In fact, also a perfect simultaneity should be avoided to limit possible interferences between concurrent radar signals from multiple sensors.

A first analysis of range profiles and footprints of projected range bins on the building façade has shown some differences depending on the considered station. Moreover, a very limited number of regions on the building façade corresponded to range bins with high-amplitude peaks (i.e., over a fixed threshold) in more than one range profile. These outcomes have prevented the use of such a methodology for analysing the deformations behaviour of this façade. Consequently, the analysis could not be limited to those areas corresponding to local maxima of S/N over the threshold in at least two range bins. In fact, other points of the façade have resulted in range bins with local maxima featuring quite high S/N, though below the fixed threshold. The following approach was then used. First, range bins of natural features whose 3D coordinates had been measured using a theodolite have been looked for. Secondly, footprint of these range bins have been projected on the façade, as shown in Fig. 7. Furthermore, some GCP's have been selected in stable positions to compensate for the effects of environmental parameters' change. By using this approach, 12 'double' points have been identified out of 14 points measured by the theodolite. As can be seen in Fig. 7, the spatial distribution of these points allows to reconstruct the deformation trend of this façade.

The atmospheric corrections based on the 'GCP Method' provided good results on relative displacements measured from Radar Station (RS) 1. Residuals in the average magnitude of 0.05 mm have been left. The other stations showed larger residuals after correction. In the case of RS 2, the adopted GCP was located on the border of the façade, and consequently it might have not been representative for the whole data set. In the case of RS 3, the amplitude of the range bin corresponding to the adopted GCP has been lower than the one of the other range bins to correct. This might have affected the accuracy of the correction process. By comparing the displacement trends to the recorded environmental temperature, a good correlation has been found. This result confirmed the mere dependency of displacements upon the thermal deformation. The Experiment 6 carried out to assess the chance to track the same natural targets on a building façade from different point of view could be retained quite successful. However, the necessity of operating an initial identification of potential targets (for example, crossing points between horizontal and vertical features on the façade pattern) as well as the measurement of their initial 3D coordinates by a theodolite has been considered a crucial point.

7   Conclusions and Future Developments

A series of six experiments carried out to assess the metrological performances of the interferometric real aperture radar (InRAR) sensor IBIS-S (IDS Company, Pisa, Italy) in applications focused on deformation monitoring of civil constructions have been reported.

First of all, the obtainable accuracy when using artificial corner reflectors has been evaluated. Experiment 1 has confirmed the performances reported by the vendor, i.e., an accuracy better than ±0.1 mm when IBIS-S is applied in continuous acquisition mode. Nevertheless, the corner reflectors' size and shape, as well as their position in the radar-illuminated scenario might significantly influence the outcome of monitoring operations, see Experiment 2. In particular, when the instrument is used in uncontrolled environment, the atmospheric conditions result in degrading the accuracy. Three different methods to compensate for the atmospheric effects have been tested in Experiment 3. The 'Ground Control Points (GCP) Method' has provided the best results, although it is the most complex to operate in the real practice.

Eventually, two other measurement approaches have been analysed: the discontinuous monitoring based on the high-precision mechanical repositioning of the InRAR sensor (Exp.'s 4 and 5), and the 'stereo-radar' monitoring of quasi-static deformations (Exp. 6). The former application is based on the adoption of a connection basement plate that allows the repositioning of the IBIS-S sensor at different epochs. Thanks to this device and the use of the 'GCP Method' for compensating the atmospheric effects, an accuracy slightly better than ±0.1 mm was achieved. Anyway, the continuity of the deformation trend cannot be tracked, since the initial phase-shift is always lost when the sensors is switched off. The use of this modality is meaningful only when displacements of the same targets and along the same directions are required at different epochs. This chance demonstrated to be practically feasible with the IBIS-S sensor.

Some interesting outputs also come from the 'stereo-radar' approach. Indeed, some factors influencing the effectiveness of this method could be recognized: position and attitude of sensors and the structure to monitor; amplitude of reflected signal; and size of each range bin's footprint on the structure. The preliminary identification of some features that could play as potential natural radar reflectors offered the opportunity to identify corresponding range bins in the range profiles at both adopted radar stations. This has allowed the reconstruction of the deformation trend of the investigated façade.

The closer is the time gap between data acquisition from both sensors, the higher is the accuracy obtainable. This solution may be practically obtained by using a couple of radar sensors, which may alternatively record observations to avoid interferences.

On the side of IBIS-S hardware improvement, a device to directly measure the spatial attitude of the sensor would be quite important for precisely computing footprints of range bins on the façade.

Acknowledgements. The authors would like to express their acknowledgment to the GICARUS laboratory of Politecnico Milano, Lecco Campus, for providing the facilities during the experimental phase. Also we would like to thanks our colleagues Salvatore Castrovinci and Elena Bogani for supporting logistic aspects during the experiments, and Dr. Riccardo Paolini for providing meteorological data.

References

1. Soergel, U., Gens, R., Crosetto, M.: Editorial theme issue: innovative applications of SAR interferometry from modern satellite sensors. ISPRS J. Photogram. Remote Sens. **73**, 1–2 (2012)
2. Caduff, R., Schlunegger, F., Kos, A., Wiesmann, A.: A review of terrestrial radar interferometry for measuring surface change in the geosciences. Earth Surf. Processes. **40**, 208–228 (2005)
3. Monserrat, O., Crosetto, M., Luzi, G.: A review of ground-based SAR interferometry for deformation measurement. ISPRS J. Photogram. Remote Sens. **93**, 40–48 (2014)
4. Alba, M., Bernardini, G., Giussani, A., Ricci, P.P., Roncoroni, F., Scaioni, M., Valgoi, P., Zhang, K.: Measurement of dam deformations by terrestrial interferometric techniques. Int. Arch. Photogram. Remote Sens. Spatial Inf. Sci. **37**(B1), 133–139 (2008)
5. Crosetto, M., Monserrat, O., Luzi, G., Cuevas, M.: Deformation monitoring using ground-based SAR data. In: Engineering Geology for Society and Territory, pp. 137–140 (2015)
6. Bardi, F., Raspini, F., Frodella, W., Lombardi, L., Nocentini, M., Gigli, G., Morelli, S., Corsini, A., Casagli, N.: Monitoring the rapid-moving reactivation of earth flows by means of GB-InSAR: the April 2013 Capriglio Landslide (Northern Appennines, Italy). Remote Sens. **9**, 20 pages (2017). Paper No. 165
7. Luzi, G., Pieraccini, M., Mecatti, D., Noferini, L., Macaluso, G., Tamburini, A., Atzeni, C.: Monitoring of an Alpine Glacier by means of ground-based SAR interferometry. IEEE Geosci. Remote Sens. Lett. **4**, 495–499 (2007)
8. Pieraccini, M.: Monitoring of civil infrastructures by interferometric radar: a review. Sci. World J., 9 pages (2013). Paper No. 786961
9. Pieraccini, M., Papi, F., Rocchio, S.: Interferometric RotoSAR. Electr. Lett. **51**, 1451 (2015)
10. Luzi, G.: Ground-based radar interferometry: a novel tool for geoscience. In: Imperatore, P., Riccio, D. (eds.) Geoscience and Remote Sensing New Achievements. InTech, Vukopvar, Croatia (2010)
11. Montuori, A., Luzi, G., Bignami, C., Gaudiosi, J., Stramondo, S., Crosetto, M., Buongiorno, M.F.: The interferometric use of radar sensors for the urban monitoring of structural vibrations and surface displacements. IEEE J-STARS **9**, 3761–3776 (2016)
12. Luzi, G., Crosetto, M., Cuevas-Gonzales, M.: A radar-based monitoring of the Collserola tower (Barcelona). Mech. Syst. Sign. Process. **49**, 234–248 (2014)

13. Gentile, C., Bernardini, G.: Output-only modal identification of a reinforced concrete bridge from radar-based measurements. NDT & E Int. **41**, 544–553 (2008)
14. Saisi, A., Gentile, C., Ruccolo, A.: Pre-diagnostic promt investigation and static monitoring of a historic bell-tower. Constr. Build. Mater. **122**, 833–844 (2016)
15. Scaioni, M., Alba, M., Giussani, A., Roncoroni, F.: Monitoring of a SFRC retaining structure during placement. Eur. J. Environ. Civil Eng. **14**, 467–493 (2010)
16. Barazzetti, L., Giussani, A., Previtali, M., Roncoroni, F.: Laser tracker technology for static monitoring of civil infrastructure. Lasers Eng. **32**, 263–294 (2015)
17. Lindenbergh, R., Pietrzyk, P.: Change detection and deformation analysis using static and mobile laser scanning. App. Geomatics **7**, 65–74 (2015)
18. Pieraccini, M., Parrini, F., Fratini, M., Atzeni, C., Spinelli, P., Micheloni, M.: Static and dynamic testing of bridges thourgh microwave interferometry. NDT & E Int. **40**, 208–214 (2007)
19. Pieraccini, M., Fratini, M., Parrini, F., Macaluso, G., Atzeni, C.: High-speed CW step-frequency coherent radar for dynamic monitoring of civil engineering structures. Electron. Lett. **40**, 907–908 (2004)
20. Ferretti, A., Monti-Guarnieri, A., Prati, C., Rocca, F., Massonet, D.: InSAR Principles: Guideline for SAR Interferometry Processing and Interpretation. ESA Publication TM-19, Noordwijk (2007)
21. Zebker, H.A., Rosen, P.A., Scott, H.: Atmospheric effects in interferometric synthetic aperture radar surface deformation and topographic maps. JGR-Solid Earth **102**, 7547–7563 (1997)
22. Crosetto, M., Monserrat, O., Luzi, G., Cuevas, M., Devanthéry, N.: Discontinuous GBSAR deformation monitoring. ISPRS J. Photogram. Remote Sens. **93**, 136–141 (2014)

Cultural Heritage Management Using Analysis of Satellite Images and Advanced GIS Techniques at East Luxor, Egypt and Kangavar, Iran (A Comparison Case Study)

Abdelaziz Elfadaly[1,2,3], Rosa Lasaponara[1(✉)], Beniamino Murgante[4], and Mohamad Molaei Qelichi[5]

[1] Italian National Research Council, C.da Santa Loja, Tito Scalo, Potenza, Italy
Rosa.lasaponara@imaa.cnr.it
[2] National Authority for Remote Sensing and Space Sciences, Cairo, Egypt
[3] Department of European and Mediterranean Cultures, University of Basilicata, Matera, Italy
[4] School of Engineering, University of Basilicata, 85100 Potenza, Italy
[5] Faculty of Geography, University of Tehran, Tehran, Iran
molaei1@ut.ac.ir

Abstract. Nowadays; the new technology like remote sensing techniques play an important role in cultural heritage management. Urban and agriculture crawling have become a universal problem in the developing countries like Egypt and Iran. This study deals with the spatial characterization over three times 1963, 1984 and 2017 of the buildup and vegetation indices around two important areas; east Luxor (Egypt) and Kangavar (Iran). For the both of investigated sites, environmental changes will detect using satellite Images indices in Thematic Mapper (TM) imagery and Sentinel 2 2016 available for free charge from the USGS Earth Explorer. The past and current urban and agricultural areas have been extracted by using consolidated remote sensing and GIS techniques. Analyses and quantification of the spatial dimension of the urban expansion show for both of the study sites in a significant percentage. As a whole, outputs from our investigations will clearly highlight of the environmental monitoring, and detect the changes between the indices of the both areas to observe and quantify urban and land use changes from a global view down to a local scale to protect the archaeological areas.

Keywords: Cultural heritage management · Satellite images · Advanced GIS techniques · Luxor · Kangavar

1 Introduction

Earth Observation (EO) technologies can enable advanced performance and new operational applications specifically addressed to security and risk (see, for example Copernicus program and Sentinel missions) also including the discovery, documentation, risk monitoring and preservation of heritage sites (1–11).

EO techniques can provide operative tools for supporting heritage protection, conservation and presentation identifying and monitoring factors that can adversely affect the property (http://whc.unesco.org/en/factors/). In this context, UNESCO in partnership with some space agencies in the world (NASA, ESA, DLR, ASI, CNES) over the years has strongly

© Springer International Publishing AG 2017
O. Gervasi et al. (Eds.): ICCSA 2017, Part IV, LNCS 10407, pp. 152–168, 2017.
DOI: 10.1007/978-3-319-62401-3_12

promoted the use of space technologies to assess the state of conservation of cultural and natural heritage sites. In particular, detecting temporal changes by observing surfaces at different times is one of the most important applications of satellite sensors because they can provide multidate imagery at short interval on global scale. National and international agencies provide long time series of the above mentioned products obtained from MODIS, Landsat TM, Sentinel data useful to obtain assessment of environmental degradation and capture changes from global to local scale change detection analyses.

Detecting regions of change in images of the same scene taken at different times is of widespread interest due to a large number of applications in diverse disciplines. Important applications of change detection include remote sensing (see for example, Bruzzone and Prieto 2002; Collins and Woodcock 1996; Huertas and Nevatia 2000), civil infrastructure (see, for example Landis et al. 1999; Nagy et al. 2001), underwater sensing (see, for example, Edgington et al. 2003; Singh 1989).

2 Study Area

2.1 Luxor Area

Luxor and Karnak temples are situated on the east side of the Nile, within the modern city of Luxor (Weeks et al. 2006). Thebes (east Luxor) ancient Greek name for the Upper

(a) Egypt by the world map (http://ontheworldmap.com/)

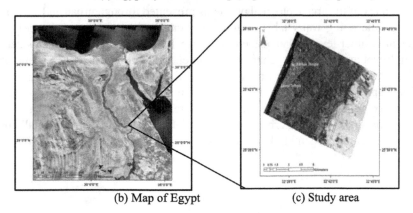

(b) Map of Egypt   (c) Study area

Fig. 1. Study area and Egypt map by Sentinel 2 (Composite RGB 4, 3, 2), and the world map.

Egyptian town of Nut or Waset (Redford 2001). Thebans were located close to the east banks of the Nile, lies the temple of Luxor and the temple of Karnak (DMS Long 32° 36′ 22.6932″ E, DMS Lat 25° 43′ 14.0748″ N) (Sullivan 2008). Karnak Temple and Luxor temple are within 'world heritage' sites (Rashed 1989) (Fig. 1).

2.2 Kangavar Area

A most and largest famous temple in Iran is Anahita which situated in "Kangavar" (Kermanshah province in Iran) (34° 30′ N, 47° 58′ E) (Tahmouri 2013). There is not precise information on the form of the temples and how religious cults were performed the Achaemenian era. According to the historians, in the Parthian era temples were built for the three gods among whom Anahita and Mithra temples were most known temples (Tahmasbi 2012) (Fig. 2).

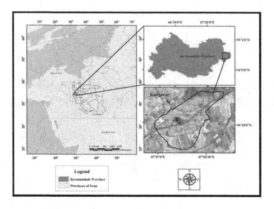

Fig. 2. Study area of Anahita temple, Iran (Landsat 8)

3 Problem Definition

Recently, most of the archaeological problems presented through urban and agriculture sprawling. The rising water tables (salty water can be harmful on sandstone) or the changes in weather levels. One of the most critical reasons in the monuments deterioration in Egypt and Iran is the urban encroachment which unfortunately became widespread phenomenon. Including Luxor temple (Fig. 3a), Karnak temple (Fig. 3b) and Anahita temple "Kangavar area" (Fig. 4a and b), many of the changes carried out in the landscape spaces in the last years. High groundwater depth, sewages, new roads, rubbish are known-results as result of urban sprawling around the monuments, especially in the developments countries similar Egypt and Iran.

(a) Luxor temple   (b) Karnak temple

Fig. 3. Urban sprawling around the archaeological areas in east Luxor.

(a)   (b)

Fig. 4. Urban sprawling around Anahita temple (a, b).

4 Material and Methodology

4.1 Materials

The collection of satellite imagery for the study area involves USGS Earth Explorer (Coronaj-3 1963), TM 1984, and Sentinel 2 (2016, 2017) data images. The ground truth data using Global Positioning System (GPS). Processing the images interpretation is done in Envi 5.1 software and Arc GIS 10.4.1.

4.2 Methodology

Corona data were geometrically corrected, in order to remove the effect of the atmosphere for the images of 1984, 2016, and 2017 comparable. To this aims, the dark object subtraction was applied. The obtained Images are analyzed to detect the changes in the land use and land cover on the past and present data. Some of the band combinations were carried out to detect the changes in the images between 1984 and 2016. Environmental modeling is based on creating a new method by Arc GIS software Suggests a new innovation solution using GIS modeling to protect the monuments.

4.2.1   Classification of the Images

The unsupervised classified technique has been used by Envi 5.1 software. A preliminary step for reference and understanding the statistical changes of the pixels with different digital numbers. ISODATA clustering algorithm has been used by 10 classes. Maximum likelihood is one of the widely used algorithms in the supervised classification technique. Images classification based on the training sets (signatures) provided by the user on the previous study area knowledge. Most popular metric Kappa statistic has been used in the accuracy assessment of the classification process. By comparing the classification results with the ROIs information by confusion matrix (post classification) using the software of Envi 5, the accuracy assessment has been calculated. The classification finally gives the diverse categorizations in the classes obtained for each year (1963, 1984, and 2016) investigated.

4.2.2   Band Combinations in TM and Sentinel 2 Data
NDVI

NDVI index was sensitive primarily to the highly absorbing red reflectance band (Huete et al. 1997). In the electromagnetic spectrum, the red and near-infrared bands are used in the Normalized Difference Vegetation Index that refers to a numerical indicator (Holm et al. 1987). NDVI index depends on the combination of the bands 3 and 4 in TM, and 4, 8 in Sentinel 2, as in formula 3 (Table 1).

Table 1. Equation of NDVI

Index	Satellite image
$NDVI_{L5} = (Band_4 - Band_3)/(Band_4 + Band_3)$	Landsat 4, 5 TM
$NDVI_{S2} = (Band_8 - Band_4)/(Band_8 + Band_4)$	Sentinel 2 MSI

NDBI

The Normalized Difference Build-up Index (NDBI) introduces one of the important land cover types, build-up areas (Hua and Qinhuo 2014). The mechanism of Normalized Difference Built-Up Index is demonstrated through the extraction of urban built-up lands from Landsat TM/ETM (Xu 2007), and Sentinel 2 images. NDBI index depends on the integrate between the bands 4, 5 in TM and 8, 11 in Sentinel 2. Presented by (Zha et al. 2003), as following equation (Table 2):

Table 2. Equation of NDBI

Index	Satellite image
$NDBI_{L5} = (Band_5 - Band_4)/(Band_5 + Band_4)$	Landsat 4, 5 TM
$NDBI_{S2} = (Band_{11} - Band_8)/(Band_{11} + Band_8)$	Sentinel 2 MSI

BRBA

In this study, the built-up areas have been also measured from BRBA. The BRBA proposed by Waqar et al. (2012) was applied to the Landsat TM image using bands 3 and 5 and 4, 11 in Sentinel 2. The BRBA is as (Bouzekri et al. 2015) (Table 3):

Table 3. Equation of BRBA

Index	Satellite image
$BRBA_{L5} = (Band_3)/(Band_5)$	Landsat 4, 5 TM
$BRBA_{S2} = (Band_4)/(Band_{11})$	Sentinel 2 MSI

NBAI

Normalized Built-up Area Index (NBAI), one of the more effectively estimates built-up area. NBAI depended on the integrate between the bands 2, 5, and 7 in TM (Anqi 2014), and 3, 11, and 12 in Sentinel 2 (Table 4).

Table 4. Equation of NBAI

Index	Satellite image
$NBAI_{L5} = (Band_7 - Band_5)/(Band_2)$	Landsat 4, 5 TM
$NBAI_{S2} = (Band_{12} - Band_{11})/(Band_3)$	Sentinel 2 MSI

5   Results

5.1   The Changes in the Urban Area

The changes have been captured by the differences revealed from supervised classification applied to the scenes acquired at different times for both Luxor and Kangavar area. The results obtained from the classification images of the three dates are used to calculate the area of change related to different land covers. In particular, the analysis of Landsat TM and Sentinel 2 imagery in Luxor revealed that the urban area increased about 20.138 km^2 from 1963 and 1984, and 2.173 km^2 from 1984 and 2017. In the other hand, the urban area in Kangavar increased about 2.523 km^2 from 1963 and 1984, and

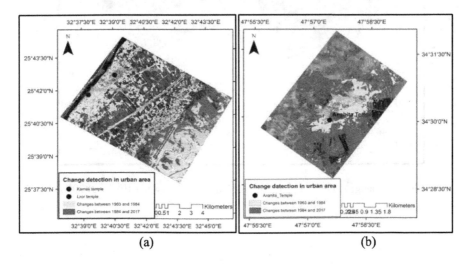

Fig. 5. Total changes spaces in the urban area around the archaeological area in east Luxor (a), and Kangavar (b) between 1963 and 2017.

about 4.702 km² from 1984 and 2017 (Table 5, Fig. 5a and b). As a whole, over time between 1963 and 2017, the urban area clearly increased for both of the two investigated areas.

Table 5. Total changes in the urban area by Km² in (Luxor and Kangavar)

Study area	1963	Change detection ± KM2	1984	Change detection ± KM2	2017
Luxor	8.444 km²	20.138 km²	28.582 km²	2.173 km²	30.755 km²
Kangavar	.445 km²	2.523 km²	2.978 km²	4.702 km²	7.680 km²

5.2   Band Combinations

Band combination analysis was taking place in both of the study areas in order to measure the effects of urban sprawling in the soil and vegetated areas. In Luxor area, the NDVI value highlighted and identified that the change in the vegetation value from 1984 to 2016 was enormous. . These effects are very clear in the agricultural land around the urban area from 1984 to 2017 (Fig. 6). Also, in Kangavar area, the NDVI value the change in the vegetation value from 1984 to 2017 was enormous that highlighted and identified (Fig. 7).

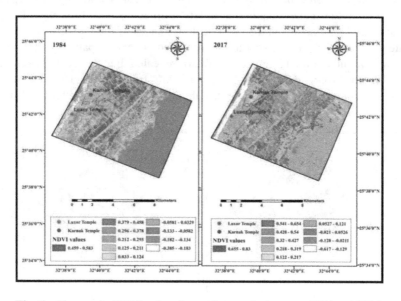

Fig. 6. Changes in NDVI values in east Luxor city between 1984 and 2016.

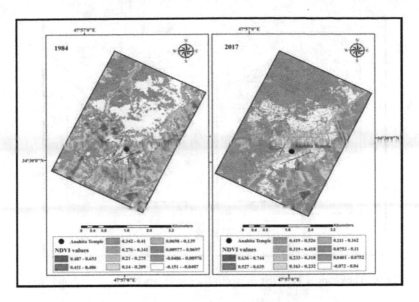

Fig. 7. Changes in NDVI values in Kangavar city between 1984 and 2016.

NDBI index results indicated that there is a development in both cities similar to the results. NDBI value Clearfield that the change in the built-up value from 1984 to 2017 was clear. These effects are very clear in the built-up around the archaeological area in east Luxor from 1984 and 2017 (Fig. 8). In the other hand, in Kangavar area, the NDBI value identified the change in the built-up value from 1984 to 2017 was enormous (Fig. 9).

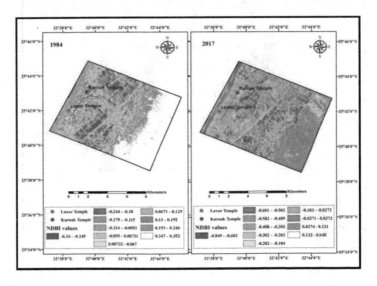

Fig. 8. The changes in NDBI values in east Luxor city between 1984 and 2017

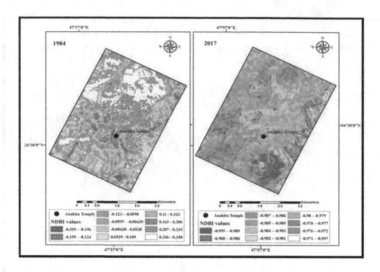

Fig. 9. The changes in NDBI values in Kangavar city between 1984 and 2017

BRBA index results indicated that there is increase in both cities. BRBA value highlighted and identified that the change in the built-up value from 1984 to 2017 was clear. These effects are very clear in the vegetation around the archaeological area from 1984 and 2016 (Fig. 10). In the other hand, in Kangavar area, the BRBA value the change in the built-up value from 1984 to 2017 was enormous that highlighted and identified (Fig. 11).

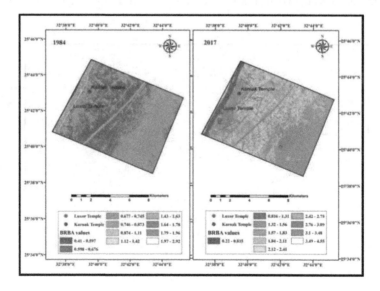

Fig. 10. The changes in BRBA values in east Luxor city between 1984 and 2017.

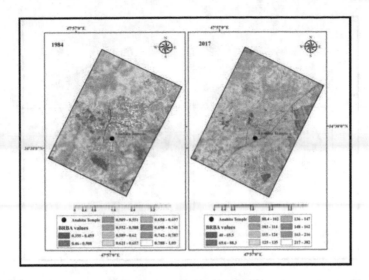

Fig. 11. The changes in BRBA values in Kanagvar city between 1984 and 2017.

Like the previous results in the indices, NBAI index results indicated that there is a development in both cities. NBAI value clearfield that the change in the built-up value from 1984 to 2017 was enormous. These effects are very clear in the built-up in east Luxor around the archaeological area from 1984 and 2017 (Fig. 12). In the other hand, in Kangavar area, the NBAI value identified the change in the built-up value from 1984 to 2017 was enormous (Fig. 13).

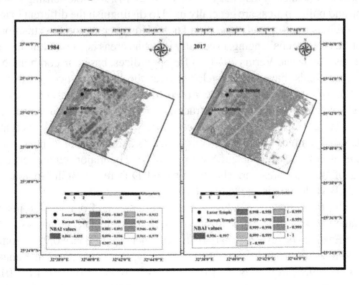

Fig. 12. The changes in NBAI values in east Luxor city between 1984 and 2017.

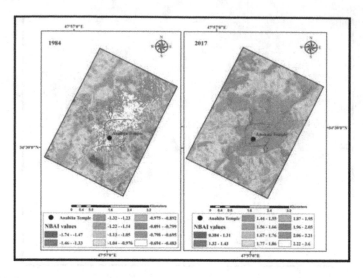

Fig. 13. The changes in NBAI values in Kanagvar city between 1984 and 2017.

6 Discussion

Remote sensing techniques are the very important tool for monitoring desertification, forest fragmentation, vegetation health and density as well as monitoring landform processes (Chandra 2011). Using RS and GIS techniques in the cultural heritage management as a tool is more ancient than the 1970s (Smith 2014). Remote sensing based indices in vegetation and built-up areas are generally used to distinguish the different in urban land use features such as built-up and vegetation lands. However, accurate extraction of these land use features is very challenging, especially in urban areas because of high intermixing between classes (Sinha and Verma 2016). Different indices, based on combinations of two or more spectral bands, have been developed over the last three decades (Schmidt and Karnieli 2001). Spectral indices are widely used for monitoring, analyzing, and mapping temporal and spatial variations in many structures as well as certain biophysical parameters (Gitelson et al. 2002). NDVI index has been widely recognized as an important method for the studies of dynamics at regional to global scales and the land biosphere characteristics (Susaki et al. 2005; Takeuchi and Yasuoka 2004). The major remote sensing indices for mapping of built-up areas are the Normalized Difference Built-Up Index (NDBI, NBAI, and BRBA) (Kaimaris and Patias 2016).

In this study, the comparison between the urban changes from satellite images taken forms the same scene at different acquisition dates. In particular, the analysis of satellite images in the East Luxor revealed that urban land increased about 90.98% from 1964 to 1984, and about 9.20% from 1984 to 2017. Similarly, the urban areas in Kangaver area increased about 34.92% from 1964 to 1984, and about 65.8% from 1984 to 2017. These means that the increase in urban area has different way between Luxor and Kangavar. It's very clear that the increase in the Luxor area between 1963 to 1984 has very high percentage 90.98%. In another hand the increase between 1984 to 2017 has the high level in Kangavar

65.8% than East Luxor 9.20%. Our suggestion that this increase related to the economic situation. Also, the increase in the urban area in the both study areas has, unlike direction. It's observed that the encroachment in the urban land in east Luxor was in the boundary near to the desert. In the other hand, the urban sprawling in Kangavar focused in the centre around the Anahita temple. In this study, a familiar technique is applied for the extraction of the urban built-up area from Landsat and Sentinel 2 data based on new image derived from three thematic indices, enhanced built-up (NDBI, BRBA, and NBAI), vegetation (NDVI). The method is demonstrated through the extraction of the vegetation and urban built-up area from Landsat TM and Sentinel 2 images for 1984 and 2017 and clarified the changes in the vegetation and built-up areas between 1984–2016 periods. The major result of the band's combination in NDVI, NDBI, BRBA, and NBAI showed that the urban sprawling was very clear around the study areas. With the same result from 1963 to 2017, the indices proved that the urban sprawling was the major trend in the both areas. Also, the direction of the encroachment has, unlike direction, near to the desert in Luxor but focused in the Centre in Kangavar.

7   Recommendations

Uncontrolled development and urbanization caused the increasing in the vulnerability of heritage sites. If there are no maintenance approaches, there is restoration, the site is affected by, there is a loss of local knowledge, and a lack of management systems for the archaeological site (Paolini et al. 2012). Using aerial photographs and other remote sensing techniques have been used for both research and heritage management. These have demonstrated the benefits for archaeology and landscape studies, also developed best practices (Cowley 2010).

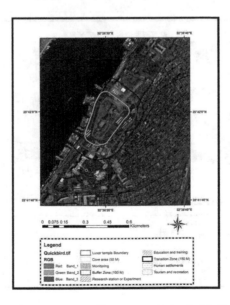

Fig. 14. Suggested zonation areas around Luxor temple by Quick bird satellite image 2005

Remote sensing and GIS techniques can be met by a Zonation System in east Luxor and Kangavar that applies different management policies to different boundary zones. The distances have been chosen as a result of the environmental situation in both areas. The archaeological area must be surrounded by three areas. The first one is between the temple and core area (monitoring 50 M). The second boundary is between the core area

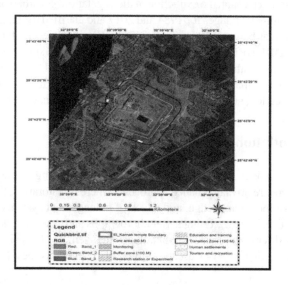

Fig. 15. Proposed zonation areas around Karnak temple by Quick bird satellite image 2005

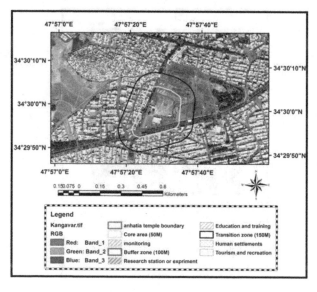

Fig. 16. Proposed zonation areas around Anahita temple by Google earth plus 2016.

and buffer zone (education, training-human settlements and research station or experiment 50 M). The last is between the buffer zone and transition zone (tourism and recreation 50 M) (Lasaponara et al. 2017) (Figs. 14, 15 and 16).

With annual average values about 5 to 30 cm/year, the groundwater level in the whole Luxor area is in continuous rising. The highest rise in the study area is recorded at El Karnak temple area. Generally, the maximum depth of the groundwater under the ground level is recorded (7.2 M) at the east of Luxor City (Selim et al. 2000). Drainage systems can be proposed to withdrawal the groundwater through digging up some of the trenches at spaced distances of the temple (related to GIS modeling), to withdraw the wastewater slowly. The wastewater will be transferred for these trenches with tubes to water recycle station. Finally, this water can be used as pure in the irrigation system (Lasaponara et al. 2016) (Fig. 17a and b).

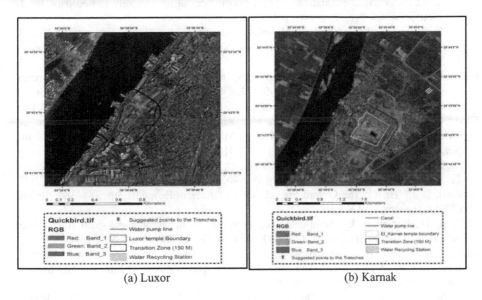

(a) Luxor   (b) Karnak

Fig. 17. Proposed GIS-modelling around temples by Quick bird satellite image 2005

8   Conclusions

This study presents the possibility of using the modern technologies tools in terms of design and planning a sustainable use of cultural heritage resources. Moreover, unlike the traditional methods, this proposal gave an example for the availability of using remote sensing data and GIS techniques in the new field. The aims of this study were focused on measurement the result of urban crawling, which appeared clearly in the both study areas in the images classification and extracted indices. This urban sprawling affected the archaeological area, so the working to create some of the innovation methods with supporting of space images and GIS techniques were critical. We can conclude that; observing and monitoring the changes from a global view down to a local scale is current availability from long term satellite time series as an excellent tool. Using an

active and passive satellite data from Sentinel 1 with additional improvement are
expected to be obtained in the future.

References

Anqi, F.: Urban growth and LULC change dynamics using Landsat record of region of Waterloo
  from 1984 to 2013. UWSpace (2014). http://hdl.handle.net/10012/8271
Bouzekri, S., Lasbet, A.A., Lachehab, A.: A new spectral index for extraction of built-up area
  using Landsat-8 data. J. Indian Soc. Remote Sens. **43**(4), 867–873 (2015). https://doi.org/
  10.1007/s12524-015-0460-6
Campos, E.: A groundwater flow model for water related damages on historic monuments-case
  study West Luxor Egypt. Vatten **65**, 247–254 (2009)
Chandra, P.: Performance evaluation of vegetation indices using remotely sensed data. Int. J.
  Geomatrics Geosci. **2**(1), 231–240 (2011)
Cigna, F., Tapete, D., Lasaponara, R., Masini, N.: Amplitude change detection with ENVISAT
  ASAR to image the cultural landscape of the Nasca Region, Peru. Archaeol. Prospection
  20(2), 117–131 (2013)
Cigna, F., Tapete, D., Lasaponara, R., Masini, N., Milillo, P., Tapete, D.: Persistent scatterer
  interferometry processing of COSMO-SkyMed StripMap HIMAGE time series to depict
  deformation of the historic centre of Rome, Italy. Remote Sens. **6**(12), 12593–12618 (2014)
David, C.: Heritage management heritage management remote sensing for of farmed and forested
  archaeological heritage landscapes in Europe Management. Occasional Publication of the
  Aerial Archaeology Research Group 3, 1–22 (2010)
Davis, E.S., Dodson, K., Hamilton, E.: Conservation of inscribed sandstone fragments at Luxor
  Temple in Egypt: case study (2014). http://mapio.net/pic/p-11229861/
Redford, D.B., (Hrsg.): The Oxford Encyclopedia of Ancient Egypt III, pp. 384–388. Oxford
  (2001). The temple of Karnak
Figorito, B., Tarantino, E.: Semi-automatic detection of linear archaeological traces from
  orthorectified aerial images. Int. J. Appl. Earth Obs. Geoinf. **26**, 458–463 (2014)
Gabriel, A., Ashraf, B.: Comprehensive Development Plan for the City of Luxor, Egypt –
  Investment Project #4, Investment Portfolio for the Development of Infrastructure Serving
  New Luxor and El Toad, pp. 1–126 (2000)
Ghanghermeh, A., Roshan, G., Orosa, J.A., Calvo-Rolle, J.L., Costa, A.M.: New climatic
  indicators for improving urban sprawl: a case study of Tehran city. Entropy **15**(3), 999–1013
  (2013)
Gitelson, A.A., Kaufman, Y.J., Stark, R., Rundquist, D.: Novel algorithms for remote estimation
  of vegetation fraction. Remote Sens. Environ. **80**(1), 76–87 (2002). doi:10.1016/
  S0034-4257(01)00289-9
Holme, A., Burnside, D.G., Mitchell, A.A.: The development of a system for monitoring trend in
  range condition in the arid shrublands of Western Australia. Aust. Rangeland J. **9**, 14–20 (1987)
http://jon-atkinson.com/Karnak.html
Huete, A.R., Liu, H.Q., Batchily, K., Van Leeuwen, W.: A comparison of vegetation indices over
  a global set of TM images for EOS-MODIS. Remote Sens. Environ. **4257**(1), 440–451 (1997)
Javidinejad, M.: Operation of Bishapur Anahita Temple - without any ceiling. Bull. Georgian
  Natl. Acad. Sci. **8**(2), 3–6 (2014)
Kaimaris, D., Patias, P.: Identification and area measurement of the built-up area with the Built-
  up Index (BUI). Int. J. Adv. Remote Sens. GIS **5**(6), 1844–1858 (2016)

Lasaponara, R.: Inter-comparison of AVHRR-based fire susceptibility indicators for the Mediterranean ecosystems of Southern Italy. Int. J. Remote Sens. **26**(5), 853–870 (2005)

Lasaponara, R., Nicola, M.: Image enhancement, feature extraction and geospatial analysis in an archaeological perspective. In: Satellite Remote Sensing, pp. 17–63. Springer, Amsterdam (2009)

Lasaponara, R., Nicola, M.: Full-waveform airborne laser scanning for the detection of medieval archaeological microtopographic relief. J. Cult. Heritage **10**, 78–82 (2009)

Lasaponara, R., Elfadaly, A., Attia, W.: Low cost space technologies for operational change detection monitoring around the archaeological area of Esna-Egypt. In: International Conference on Computational Science and Its Applications, pp. 611–621 (2016)

Lasaponara, R., Murgante, B., Elfadaly, A., Qelichi, M.M., Shahraki, S.Z., Wafa, O., Attia, W.: Spatial open data for monitoring risks and preserving archaeological areas and landscape: case studies at Kom el Shoqafa, Egypt and Shush, Iran. Sustainability **9**(4), 572 (2017). doi:10.3390/su9040572

Liu, Q., Li, H.: Comparison of NDBI and NDVI as indicators of surface urban heat island effect in MODIS imagery. In: International Conference on Earth Observation Data Processing and Analysis (ICEODPA) (2014). doi:10.1117/12.815679

Masini, N., Lasaponara, R.: Satellite-based recognition of landscape archaeological features related to ancient human transformation. J. Geophys. Eng. **3**(3), 230 (2006)

Masini, N., Lasaponara, R., Orefici, G.: Addressing the challenge of detecting archaeological adobe structures in Southern Peru using QuickBird imagery. J. Cult. Heritage **10**, 3–9 (2009). doi:10.1016/j.culher.2009.10.005

Novelli, A., Aguilar, M.A., Nemmaoui, A., Aguilar, F.J., Tarantino, E.: Performance evaluation of object based greenhouse detection from Sentinel-2 MSI and Landsat 8 OLI data: a case study from Almerьa (Spain). Int. J. Appl. Earth Obs. Geoinf. **52**, 403–411 (2016)

Rashed, Y., Hanan, A.: Cultural heritage and tourism: Luxor of Egypt? Las Vegas?, June 1989. http://ontheworldmap.com/

Schmidt, H., Karnieli, A.: Sensitivity of vegetation indices to substrate brightness in hyper-arid. Int. J. Remote Sens. **22**(17), 3503–3520 (2001)

Selim, S.A., Khedr, E.S., Falasteen, A.W., Kamel, E.R.: Reasons of local rise in groundwater level at Luxor city area, upper physical setting climate geomorphology. In: 5th International Conference on the Geology of the Arab World, Cairo University, February 2000, pp. 901–910 (2000)

Sinha, P., Verma, N.K.: Urban built-up area extraction and change detection of Adama municipal area using time-series Landsat images. Int. J. Adv. Remote Sens. GIS **5**(8), 1886–1895 (2016)

Smith, C.: Encyclopedia of Global Archaeology, Springer, New York, pp. 3631–4147 (2014)

Sullivan, E.A.: Visualising the size and movement of the portable festival barks at Karnak temple. Br. Museum Stud. Anc. Egypt Sudan **19**, 1–37 (2012)

Susaki, J., Pothithep, S., Ooka, R., Yasuoka, Y., Endo, T., Kawamoto, Y.: Extraction of parameters from remote sensing data for environmental indices for urban sustainability. Trimble Geospatial, 1–10 (2005)

Tahmasbi, E.: The Architecture and Status of Iranian Temples in the Sasanian Era (2012)

Tahmouri, A.: Study about presence of nature in Iranian architecture with analytical approach on water. World Appl. Program. **3**(9), 406–416 (2013)

Takeuchi, W., Yasuoka, Y.: Development of Normalized Vegetation, Soil and Water Indices Derived from Satellite Remote Sensing Data, pp. 1–20. IIS/UT, Japan (2004)

Tapete, D., Cigna, F., Masini, N., Lasaponara, R.: Prospection and monitoring of the archaeological heritage of Nasca, Peru, with ENVISAT ASAR. Archaeol. Prospection **20**(2), 133–147 (2013)

Tarantino, E., Figorito, B.: Extracting buildings from true color stereo aerial images using a decision making strategy. Remote Sens. **3**(8), 1553–1567 (2011)

Waqar, M.M., Mirza, J.F., Mumtaz. R., Hussain, E.: Development of new indices for extraction of built-up area & bare soil from Landsat data. Sci. Rep. **1**, 136 (2012)

Weeks, K.R., Hetherington, N.J., Jones, L.T.: The Valley of the Kings, Luxor, Egypt Site Management Masterplan. Theban Mapp. Proj., p. 4 (2006)

Xu, H.: Extraction of urban built-up land features from Landsat imagery using a thematic-oriented index combination technique. Photogram. Eng. Remote Sens. **73**(12), 1381–1391 (2007)

Zha, Y., Gao, J., Ni, S.: Use of normalized difference built-up index in automatically mapping urban areas from TM imagery. Int. J. Remote Sens. **24**(3), 583–594 (2003)

Zhang, Y., Balzter, H., Liu, B., Chen, Y.: Analyzing the impacts of urbanization and seasonal variation on land surface temperature based on subpixel fractional covers using Landsat images. IEEE Geosci. Remote Sens. Soc. **10**(4), 1–13 (2016)

High Frequency GNSS Measurements
for Structural Monitoring Applications

Raffaela Cefalo[1]([✉]) [iD], Giorgio Manzoni[†], Salvatore Noè[2] [iD],
and Tatiana Sluga[1]

[1] GeoSNav Lab, University of Trieste, Via Valerio 6/2, 34127 Trieste, Italy
raffaela.cefalo@dia.units.it
[2] Department of Engineering and Architecture,
University of Trieste, Trieste, Italy
noe@units.it
tatiana.sluga@gmail.com

Abstract. Dynamic deformation monitoring of structures such as long bridges, towers, and tall buildings, for the purpose of determining structural vibrations, is possible using Global Navigation Satellite System (GNSS) (Lovse et al. 1995).

Starting from 1998, high frequency GNSS measurements have been performed at the Department of Civil Engineering, University of Trieste, Italy, on special civil engineering structures: chimneys, bridges, wind-power towers simulators for the analysis of dynamic behavior and structural vibration monitoring.

Using 10, 20 and 50 Hz GPS and GPS+GLONASS receivers, different tests have been performed using simulators built on purpose for the experiments and in real conditions on high structures.

A report of the tests performed on a 100 m chimney in Trieste, Italy during strong wind conditions from 1998 to 2002 and using a simulator of elliptical movements for applications to wind-powers vibrations monitoring, in the framework of Italian COFIN98 Aerogen Project, in the years 2008–2010, are herein reported.

Keywords: GNSS · Dynamic deformation · Structural monitoring

1 Introduction

The dynamic deformation behaviour of engineering structures has been subject of concern to engineers for many years. Examples of dynamic deformation behaviour in engineering structures are vibrations in structures as long bridges, towers, and tall buildings. In these structures, the harmonic frequencies typically range from 0.1 Hz to 10 Hz D'ASdia and Noè (1996), D'Asdia and Noè (1998), and amplitudes from 10 mm to 200 mm (Lovse et al. 1995; Cefalo et al. 1998).

Interest in vibrations in civil engineering structures increased considering the growing number of long and tall structures and their higher flexibility.

Standard methods used for measuring structural vibrations are: accelerometers, laser interferometers and EDM (Electromagnetic Distance Measurement) instruments.

Accelerometers can be very light and compact having thus a minimal effect on the properties of the vibrating system but they require direct contact with the structure and

© Springer International Publishing AG 2017
O. Gervasi et al. (Eds.): ICCSA 2017, Part IV, LNCS 10407, pp. 169–180, 2017.
DOI: 10.1007/978-3-319-62401-3_13

wiring is required to link them to a central recording unit. The wiring adds noise to the signals from the accelerometers, especially if they are very long. Furthemore, placing the accelerometers on a structure may be difficult. Laser interferometry gives high resolution (1 μm or better) in the measurement of distance changes, measured from an external fixed point, with sampling rates up to 2,000 Hz or higher. EDM measurements can be carried out using much less expensive equipment but the resolution of the changes in distance (typically 1 mm) and the sampling rate (usually less than 10 Hz) are much lower, thus permitting to monitor frequencies limited to 5 Hz or less.

GNSS geodetic measurements in theory can give millimetric resolution.

The accuracies are normally worst due to undifferencible errors mainly related to signal propagation in the atmosphere and local errors due to multipaths. Special care in antennas location, an accurate choice of the instrumental components and data filtering allow to obtain accuracies near to the instrumental resolution (Cefalo et al. 1997; Manzoni et al. 1997; Cefalo et al. 2000).

The first part of the paper describes the experimental activities carried out some years ago, on a 100 m chimney in Trieste, Italy, using 2 Hz and 5 Hz recording frequency GPS receivers, to verify the possibility to use GNSS techniques to monitor the top displacements Celebi (1998), Manzoni (1996), Manzoni and Noè (1998). GPS data were compared with the simultaneous accelerometer ones.

The experiments objectives were: (a) the feasibility control from a technical point of view; (b) the optimization of the acquisition and data processing techniques; (c) the determination of the obtainable resolution. The second part, reports a series of experimental tests performed using a simulator for applications to wind-power towers for the analysis of dynamic behavior and structural vibration monitoring.

2   Case Study and Experimental Results

The analyzed chimney belongs to a waste incineration plant, Province of Trieste, Italy.

The chimney, in reinforced concrete, has a perfectly cylindrical external surface and is 100 m tall. The external diameter is 6.3 m. The frequency corresponding to the first vibrating mode is 0.375 Hz. The maximum expected displacements, under wind action, are in the order of some centimeters.

On the chimney top a Trimble Dome antenna (Fig. 1) was installed, linked to a Trimble SSE geodetic GNSS receiver through a 110 m cable with a preamplifier. The master receiver was located at the University of Trieste, nearly 5.5 km away.

For GPS data acquisition a sample rate of 2 Hz and 5 Hz was used. Contemporaneously to GPS data acquisition, the accelerations in correspondence of the mean part and the top of the chimney have been measured using 2 PCB 393B12 accelerometers, with horizontal sensitivity axes perpendicular to each other. Accelerometric signals were filtered before their acquisition by a low-pass filter with a 20 Hz cutoff frequency. Wind data were collected by an anemometer (mod. Young 05103). Data were recorded on a personal computer, via a National Instruments AT-MIO-16E-10 card with 20 Hz sampling frequency. Before starting each session, the accelerometers data were synchronized to the GPS ones.

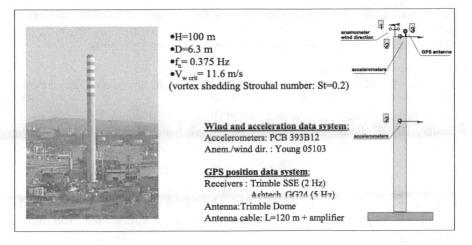

Fig. 1. The location of sensors (accelerometers and GPS antenna)

Like introduced in the first section, the targets to be reached were to:

- Verify the feasibility from a technical and an operational point of view;
- Test data acquisition and processing techniques; and
- Verify the achievable accuracy.

The carrier phase measurements and the pseudorange ones, recorded at every epoch, i.e. 0.5 s, were processed through the continuous kinematic processing technique, implemented by OTF (On The Fly) algorithm to compute ambiguities. Ambiguities are used to compute three dimensional vector components from the GPS antenna of the master to the chimney antenna (rover); the ambiguity parameters are very useful during cycle slips (lack of GPS signal, due either to the eclipses of satellites or physical obstructions).

The solutions accuracy thus obtained depends on several elements:

- Cycle slip duration time;
- Number of satellites in sight during the survey session, before and after the cycle slip; and
- The value of statistical parameters: PDOP (Positioning Dilution Of Precision) and mainly RDOP (Relative Dilution Of Precision), both depending on the satellite geometric configuration during the measurement session and the direction of the vector linking the two GPS antennas.

After calculating the positions by means of this technique, the ellipsoidal WGS84 coordinates were transformed into the ellipsoidal ED50 ones using the Molodenskij formulas, and projected into the UTM plane coordinates through the Gauss-Boaga formulas (Fig. 2).

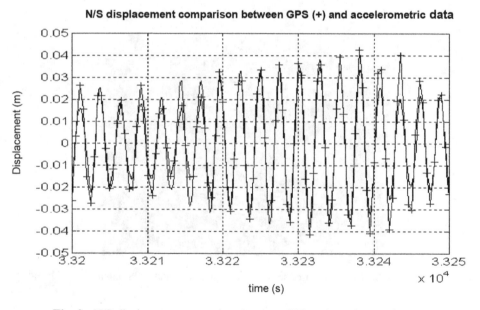

Fig. 2. N/S displacement comparison between GPS and accelerometric data

Using the digital filter transmission band 0.15 ÷ 3.00 Hz for the GPS signal it is possible to obtain the movement centered respect to a zero axis (Fig. 3a). It is thus possible to compare the displacements measured by the GPS receiver with those deduced from the accelerometers (Fig. 3c).

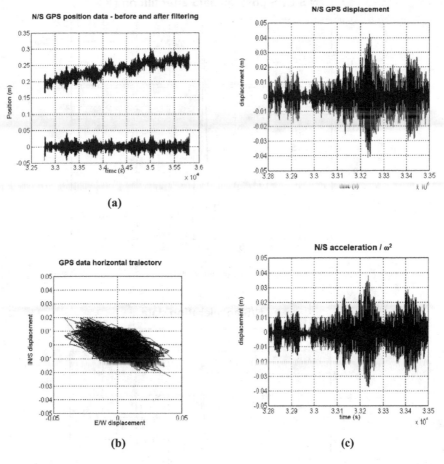

Fig. 3. (a) N/S GPS positions before and after data filtering; (b) GPS data horizontal trajectory; (c) N/S GPS displacements and accelerations

Acceleration signals in N/S and E/W directions have been obtained by projecting the signals recorded on these directions.

Figure 3b shows the horizontal trajectory described by the GPS antenna. Maximum displacement from the zero position is about 4 cm. The main oscillation perpendicular to the wind direction (Bora, from 30°N) due to vortex shedding is evident.

Figure 3c shows that the plot of the N/S displacement obtained from the GPS signal is in agreement with the one obtained from accelerometric data divided by $\omega_n^2 = 5.55$ (supposing chimney movements being a harmonic motion with f_n frequency). A magnification and a superimposition of the two plots relative to the displacement are given in Fig. 2, where the sign "+" on the GPS data shows, epoch by epoch, the position (centred with respect to a zero axis) collected by the GPS receiver.

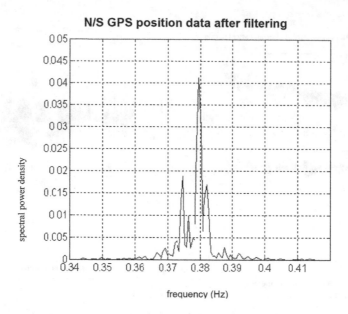

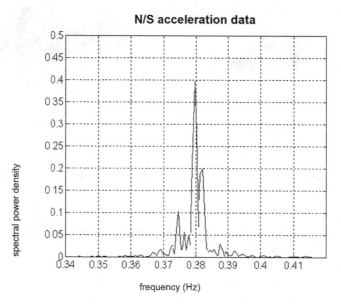

Fig. 4. The spectral power density obtained from filtered GPS and accelerometric data

Figure 4 shows how the spectral power density obtained from GPS filtered data and accelerometric data agree. They have the main peak at the same frequency, a little higher than the chimney first natural frequency.

Similar diagrams have been obtained considering the E/W direction.

In the second set of experiments, Ashtech GG24 receivers were used, recording GPS+GLONASS data at a sampling rate of 5 Hz. Due to the instrumental change another software was used for data processing.

The carrier phase measurements and the pseudorange ones (only for GPS signals) recorded at every epoch, i.e. 0.2 s, were processed using the "supersmoothed" option of the AOS (Ashtech Office Suite for Survey) v. 1.05, software.

This option makes use of an algorithm that takes all data between cycle slips and uses it equally for all epochs. So, the precision remains at the same high level starting from the first epoch. For the last epoch of a data range without cycle slip, the precision is identical to a hatch filter, i.e. the DGPS smooth. The positions computed through the super-smooth DGPS algorithm result in a very high relative precision between successive epochs. That means that, even if the absolute positions of two epochs might be wrong by a few decimeters, the difference between the positions is typically good at centimetric level. This is a valuable feature also for this type of application, where the use of carrier phase data is essential to obtain the desired accuracies.

After the position was calculated by this technique, the obtained data were analyzed as far as concerns accuracy, evaluating the statistical RDOP (Relative Dilution of Precision) parameter that gives a good idea of the obtained accuracy of the results, and eventually eliminating data with too a high RDOP parameter. The ellipsoidal WGS84 coordinates were then transformed into the ellipsoidal ED50 ones using the Molodenskij formulas, and projected into the UTM plane coordinates.

Figures 5 and 6 show the N/S displacements comparison between GPS and accelerometric data and GPS data horizontal trajectory, giving results similar to the first experience.

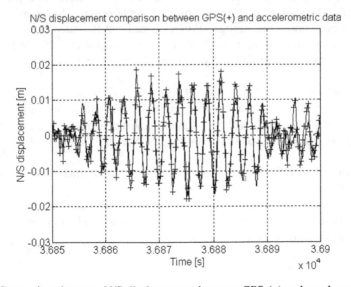

Fig. 5. Comparison between N/S displacements between GPS (+) and accelerometric data

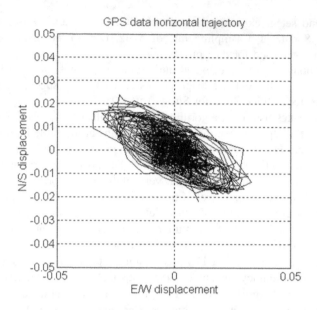

Fig. 6. Horizontal trajectory

3 Kinematic Experiments Applied to Wind-Powers Vibration Monitoring

Some years after these first experiments, a new set of tests have been performed at GeoSNav Lab, Department of Engineering and Architecture, University of Trieste, Italy, in the framework of the Aerogen Project, a national Research Project funded by MIUR (national coordinator Prof. F. Borri, local coordinator Prof. S. Noè), to verify GNSS (Global Navigation Satellite System) applicability to wind-powers vibrations monitoring.

The test have been carried out using a Topcon HyperPro and a Legacy GPS+GLO-ONASS geodetic receiver with a sampling rate of 20 Hz and a simulator of elliptical movements (Fig. 7), equipped with two stators. Another series of test have been performed using like master a Novatel Millennium GNSS receiver with a choke ring antenna (Fig. 8).

The kinematic GNSS data processing have been performed in post-processing using Topcon software tools.

In Fig. 9 Easting and Northing UTM – WGS84 coordinates of the GNSS rover antenna are displayed, showing the initial fixed session, used to compute the phase ambiguities, and the subsequent kinematic sessions.

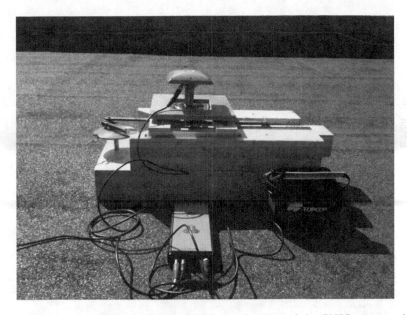

Fig. 7. The test simulator used for the GNSS experiments and the GNSS rover receiver

Fig. 8. The fixed choke ring GNSS antenna

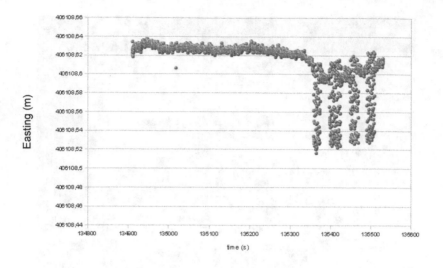

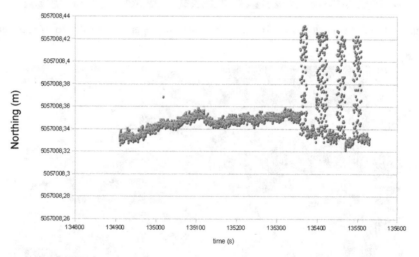

Fig. 9. Easting and Northing UTM – WGS84 coordinates of the GNSS rover antenna showing the static and dynamic phases

In Fig. 10 the GNSS horizontal elliptic trajectory is displayed. The two dense spots in the lower part of the trajectory correspond to the static phases used to compute the GPS+GLONASS phase ambiguities.

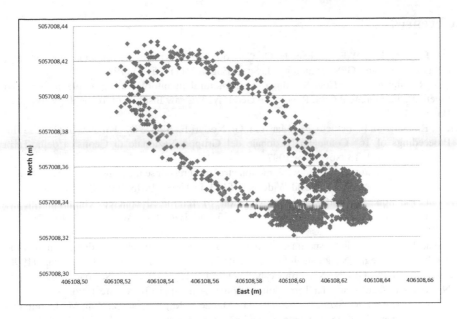

Fig. 10. The elliptical trajectory of the GNSS rover antenna

4   Conclusions

In the first reported experiences, relative to a 100 m chimney monitoring in Trieste, Italy, during strong wind conditions, the displacement measurements accuracies were at the millimetric range.

The two experiences reported in the first part (the one at 2 Hz and the one at 5 Hz) agree, demonstrating in this case that the 2 Hz sampling data frequency is sufficient to monitor structures having a low value of natural frequency.

The use of high sampling frequencies improves data quality and allows to extend GPS method employment in this area, thanks to a relatively simple installation and completely automatic operation. The GPS performed data spectral analyses shows a good agreement with the contemporaneous accelerometer data acquisition.

The second series of test have been performed in order to analyze GNSS applications to wind-powers vibrations monitoring.

2 Topcon GPS+GLONASS receivers, capable to acquire GNSS signal at an acquisition rate of 50 Hz, and a simulator of elliptical movements, have been used.

Repeated test showed a high level of accuracy and repeatability. A further improvement can be obtained applying kalman filtering to GNSS data.

Acknowledgements. The authors give thanks to the City Authority of Trieste to have authorized the first part of the experimentation. The second part of the tests were performed in the framework of the Aerogen Project, a national Research Project funded by MIUR (Italian Minister of University and Scientific Research).

References

Lovse, J.W., Teskey, W.F., Lachapelle, G., Cannon, M.E.: Dynamic deformation monitoring of tall structure using GPS technology. J. Surv. Eng. **121**(1), 35–40 (1995)

Cefalo, R., Manzoni, G., Noè, S., Sluga, T.: Structural monitoring using accelerometers and kinematic interferential GPS. Reports on Geodesy, Warsaw Institute of Technology, Warsaw, Poland (1998)

Cefalo, R., Daradin, F., Fernetti, M., Manzoni, G., Nodari F., Sluga, T.: DGPS+DGLONASS. In: Proceedings of 16° Convegno Nazionale del Gruppo Nazionale di Geofisica della Terra Solida, Roma, 11–13 Novembre 1997

Çelebi, M.: GPS and/or strong and weak motion structural response measurements – case studies. In: Structural Engineering World Wide, ref. T193-1 (1998). ISBN 0-08-042845-2

D'Asdia, P., Noè, S.: Vortex induced vibration of reinforced concrete chimneys: in situ experimentation and numerical previsions. J. Wind Eng. Ind. Aerodyn. **74–76**, 765–776 (1998)

D'Asdia, P., Noè, S.: Rilievo sperimentale della risposta all'azione del vento di una ciminiera in c.a. In: 4° Convegno Nazionale di Ingegneria del Vento - IN-VENTO-96, Trieste, Italy (1996)

Manzoni, G.: GPS+GLONASS: Primi esperimenti. In: 15° Convegno Nazionale del Gruppo Nazionale di Geofisica della Terra Solida, Roma, Atti, 11–13 novembre 1996

Manzoni, G., Cefalo, R., Skerl, G., Fernetti, M., Manzoni, M., Peressi, G., Zini, M.: Differential and interferential GNSS for precise navigation and road survey. In: XII EGS General Assembly, G14 Symposium, Vienna, 21–25 Aprile 1997, Reports on Geodesy No. (2) 25, 1997. Warsaw University of Technology, Institute of Geodesy and Geodetic Astronomy (1997)

Manzoni, G., Noè, S.: Impiego del metodo satellitare GPS (Global Positioning System) per la registrazione delle oscillazioni di una ciminiera. In: Proceedings of 5° Convegno Nazionale di Ingegneria del Vento - IN-VENTO-98 (1998)

Cefalo, R., Greblo, S., Manzoni, G., Noè, S., Pagurut, R., Sluga, T.: GPS and GLONASS application researches at the University of Trieste. In: Proceedings of the 6th Geodetic Millennium Meeting Poland-Italy, Krakow, Poland, 29 June–1 July 2000, Reports on Geodesy No. 8 (54), 2000, pp. 41–45. Warsaw Institute of Technology, Institute of Geodesy and Geodetic Astronomy, Warsaw University of Technology (2000)

Extraction of Road Geometric Parameters from High Resolution Remote Sensing Images Validated by GNSS/INS Geodetic Techniques

Raffaela Cefalo[1](✉) (iD), Giulia Grandi[2], Roberto Roberti[3] (iD), and Tatiana Sluga[1]

[1] GeoSNav Lab, University of Trieste, Via Valerio 6/2, 34127 Trieste, Italy
raffaela.cefalo@dia.units.it, tatiana.sluga@gmail.com
[2] Centre of Excellence for the Research in TeleGeomatics and Spatial Information,
University of Trieste, Trieste, Italy
giu.grandi@gmail.com
[3] Department of Engineering and Architecture, University of Trieste, Trieste, Italy
roberto.roberti@dia.units.it

Abstract. Roadway geometric data, user behavior and crash data provide the main input for developing existing highway safety evaluations. In particular, roadway geometric data can be useful in providing a quantitative guidance for alignment consistency and for having an initial indication of critical point presence along a road.

Furthermore the article 13 of the Italian Road Code requires an implementation of Road Cadastre for which it is necessary to know the planimetric and altimetric alignments.

This paper presents a methodology to obtain geometric road information from high resolution images using automatic techniques for the extraction of road geometric parameters.

The paper starts from the Road Cadastre characteristics and definitions and the analysis of the existing studies regarding remote sensing methodologies. Then two strategies, tested on road sections in Italy, are presented. The first one is based on the concept of spectral signature, while the second one is based on the Fractal Dimension of the image treated only as a numerical matrix.

The results were validated by GNSS/INS geodetic techniques, using also real time kinematic data.

Keywords: Road cadastre · High resolution satellite images · Geographical information system · GNSS · INS

1 Introduction

Roadway geometric data, user behavior and crash data provide the main input for developing existing highway safety evaluations. As regard user behavior, several studies have highlighted some relationships linking the driver behavior to the road geometric features.

The parameter chosen to represent the user behavior was the operating speed. Based on numerous speed surveys, some models were obtained to predict the operating speed

© Springer International Publishing AG 2017
O. Gervasi et al. (Eds.): ICCSA 2017, Part IV, LNCS 10407, pp. 181–195, 2017.
DOI: 10.1007/978-3-319-62401-3_14

of the vehicles as a function of the main horizontal geometric features of the road. In particular, interesting regression equations were studied to predict the environmental speed as a function of the CCR (curvature change rate), which represents the general characteristics of an homogenous section belonging to the road. The geometric characteristics of the roads used to develop the prediction models of the operating speed were obtained from the original design plan or from the analysis of the high resolution digital cartography. However, when the design plan is not available and the alignment is very long, a new methodology to obtain quick horizontal geometric road information with high precision could be extremely useful.

Moreover, the Road Administrations have also the necessity to know the as-built data of their roads to program the road maintenance and to improve the travelling safety. For this scope, a new quick methodology for the reconstruction of the road geometry could be useful to the writing of a road cadastre (Ministry of Public Works 2001) that, if constantly updated, could be a fundamental device for the improvement of the road safety evaluation.

In summary road geometric characteristics and in particular the geometrical characteristics of the road axis, the width of the roadway and the shoulders, are essential both for road safety studies and Cadastre.

Technical cartography is not a good tool because these elements cannot be extracted with high accuracy, moreover it is not possible to reconstruct the signing from cartography.

Moreover for example the Ministerial Act 01/06/2011 (Modalities of institution and updating of the Road Cadastre) does not give expressly a definition of road axis, but only "an illustrative definition" from which it is possible to give an enumerative definition:

- In the case of road cross section organized in a single carriageway with two run directions, the road axis is given by the separation axis between the internal lanes with opposite run directions (that does not necessarily coincide with the geometric axis of the roadway, nor with the section geometrical axis);
- In the case of a road cross section organized in a single carriageway with one run direction, the road axis is given by the geometric axis of the roadway (that does not necessarily coincide with the geometric axis of the section);
- In the case of road cross section organized on two separate carriageways, and if one decides to represent the road segment with a single road element, the road axis is given by the axis of the median.

Thus for Italian Road Cadastre the definition of road axis depends on road typology (category) and lane numbers for every sense of running, while for ministerial decree 05/11/2001 (Ministero delle Infrastrutture e dei Trasporti), "Functional and Geometric rules for road construction", the geometric axis of the road is the central point of the part of carriageway.

From these definitions it is possible to make some consideration of practical interest, namely: to be able to correctly detect the road axis, the signing must be complete and present (Fig. 1). Not always the road geometric axis coincides with the road sign of the axis, also because sometime the axis sign does not exist.

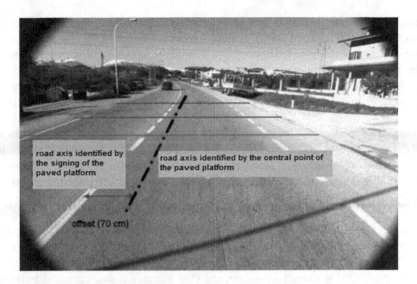

Fig. 1. Comparison between the road axis identification by means of the pavement signing and of the central point of the paved platform.

The remaking of the signing, can invalidate a pre-existing Cadastre (also in the cases in which the other parameters interesting for the Cadastre, like the roadway width, travel direction and the number of lanes, are not changed).

Being the materializations of the axis points not foreseen, it is necessary to give a documentation of the road situation at the time of the surveys together with the data given for allowing the operation of testing that will consist in a "congruence check with the national geodetic networks".

To obviate this it is possible to apply techniques that allow extracting the axis and signing width both using directly and indirectly techniques.

The techniques used till now for these aims foresee the use of instrumented vehicles running along the road; the vehicle positions, surveyed by GNSS (Global Navigation Satellite System), allow to reconstruct the geometric parameters of the elements (including signing measurements).

Besides of this technique, the authors experimented the potentiality of the geometric characteristic survey using the analysis of high resolution satellite images.

This technique allows surveying also the signing, thus overcoming the uncertainty deriving for instance from the analysis of cartography and reducing in the same time the acquisition time to respect to the GNSS surveying. Furthermore, this technique could be used to verify the accuracy of the signing layout.

2   Existing Studies

The extraction of roads from spatial data sources like aerial or satellite images has been in scope of research for more than thirty years. Many approaches are based upon techniques like edge detection or texture analysis (Dial et al. 2001). Other methods use dynamic programming or LSB-Snakes improving the results of the road extraction process (Grüen 1997), Gruen and Li (1995).

The use of knowledge-based approaches seemed to gain more importance by means of rules and models (Hinz et al. 2001).

Predefined information is acquired at a generic global level (e.g. connectivity) and at a local level (e.g. context), respectively (Hinz and Baumgartner 2002; Vosselmann 1997).

Valuable properties can be derived from other existing spatial data sources like vector data (Zhang et al. 2001). Some work has been done on the extraction of continuous surfaces like roads from laser scanning surveys; (Pattnaik et al. 2003), Hatger and Brenner (2003) suggest the use of laser scanning data to gather information on road inventory. Mobile Mapping Systems (MMS) use also laser scanner technology in order to collect dense and precise three-dimensional point clouds that gather both geometric and radiometric information of the road network. A methodology for the automatic detection and classification of road signs from point cloud and imagery data provided by a LYNX Mobile Mapper System, have been presented by Soilán et al. (2016).

Yang et al. (2015) extract urban objects (for instance poles, cars and buildings) segmenting a super voxel structure and classifying the segments according to a series of heuristic rules. Serna and Marcotegui (2014) classified up to 20 different objects using Support Vector Machines (SVM).

Other works focus on the detection of a single object class within a point cloud. Street lights (Yu et al. 2015), curbs (Zhou and Vosselman 2012; Wang et al. 2015) or trees (Reitberger et al. 2009) can be detected using LiDAR data. Regarding traffic signs, Pu et al. (2011) distinguished several classes of planar shapes corresponding to the possible shapes of traffic signs. Riveiro et al. (2015) used a linear regression model based on a raster image for classifying traffic signs based on their shapes. However, the resolution of a point cloud is not enough to distinguish the specific meaning of a traffic sign, therefore these analyses need to be integrated by the study of optical images.

Wen et al. (2015) detect traffic signs based on their retro reflectivity, and project the 3D data on 2D images in order to classify the previously detected traffic signs. There exists a vast literature regarding traffic sign recognition in RGB images. The Traffic Sign Recognition Benchmark (GTSRB) (Stallkamp et al. 2012) gathered more than 50,000 traffic sign images and established a classification challenge. The best results were achieved by Cireşan et al. (2012). They combined various Deep Neural Networks (DNN) into a Multi-Column DNN, getting a recognition rate of almost 99.5% (Sermanet and Lecun 2011).

Information from a street database was acquired to set up predefined regions along roads. Subsequently, least squares regression was applied to those regions in order to compute appropriate values for longitudinal and transversal slopes. Apart from that, few approaches investigate discontinuities like breaklines and introduce constraints like curvature or slope for the extraction of linear features.

The availability of images at resolutions close to that of aerial photographs make them suitable for a variety of applications ranging from water quality monitoring to monitoring of urban changes.

The excellent characteristics of such data, like its high resolution (1 m), real time data availability, three-dimensional measuring possibility by stereographic observations, flexibility of data acquisition, the high sensitivity and the availability of multi-spectrum covering up to NR (near infrared), improved the use of satellite remote sensing images in roads and in new technological areas (Kumagai et al. 2001).

Derivation of data like the road network data can be of use in the car navigation systems. So far, the extraction of the road information was mostly carried out manually by the operators, resulting in rather high costs.

The possibilities of automating process of road parameters extraction have been studied by many authors. One possibility is to divide the image of the aerial photograph into meshes considering that the contrast in the shade values between the road and the surroundings is quite strong. Using the Maximum A Posteriory probability technique and a Dynamic Programming technique for each mesh, the features of the road are extracted.

Various researches include the tracing of the starting segments of the roads in the mesh with the road feature to extract the major roads automatically.

Kumagai et al. (2001) carried out the process of automatic extraction of roads in regions containing some areas and road features, by applying some techniques of the image processing technology.

Grüen and Li (1997) proposed a semi-automated system for road extraction based on dynamic programming and least squares B-spline (LSB) snakes. The automatic completion of road networks based on the generation and verification of link hypoteses given in (Wiedemann and Ebner 2000; Wallace et al. 2001) present an approach designed for a wide variety of imagery. It is based on an object-oriented database which allows the modelling and utilization of relations between roads as well as other objects. Road extraction using statistical modelling in the form of point processes and Reversible Jump Markov Chain Monte Carlo was proposed by Stoica et al. (2004).

Some of the proposed techniques are suitable for the extraction of roads in mostly agricultural as well as arid areas, the latter also comprising mountainous regions, based on line/edge extraction, generation and verification of connection hypotheses and global grouping detailing.

Generally, due to the large differences in the appearance of roads in different areas, a single model for automatic road extraction is not sufficient. It could be useful to distinguish between agricultural, mountainous, and desert areas Bacher (2004).

In mountainous areas the roads are strongly affected by the topography. Roads often turn with a large curvature or even with sharp bends. In the images the roads are mostly represented as bright and only seldom by dark lines.

In desert areas roads mostly appear as bright or dark lines with few disturbing objects. The distinction from other linear objects is often difficult.

In agricultural areas roads appear as elongated structures. They often have no bar-shaped profiles in the images, but can be seen directly as collinear edges of field borders.

Other authors propose the extraction of linear features using the Steger sub-pixel line and edge extractor. The extracted features are split into segments with curvature values below a given threshold. Then the resulting lines and edges from all image channels are fused to single data sets and the connections are constructed from them.

Goemann et al. (2005) use polynomial interpolation to determine pixels belonging to road structures in the satellite images, for the lines detection. This is a standard method for ridge detection. The image is regarded as a function I (i, j). Lines are detected as ridges and ravines in this function by locally approximating the image function by its second order Taylor polynomial. The polynomial is used to approximate first and second order derivatives of the image function from the Hessian matrix of the Taylor polynomial.

The gradient and curvature information characterizing each pixel are used to classify a pixel in a number of topological classes based on their sign or magnitude. Line points are mainly characterized by a high second directional derivative, i.e. a high curvature perpendicular to the line direction.

The performance of the detector for a given dataset and the according parameter set that gives optimal results can be found. Furthermore the error propagation can be used to analyze the influence that perturbations on the intensity values have on the estimation of the parameters.

3   Method Case Studies

3.1   Road Geometry Survey Using a Mobile Mapping System (MMS)

The road geometry survey using a MMS, for the compilation of the Road Cadaster, has been performed initially as prototype, by the Centre of Excellence for the Research in TeleGeomatics and Spatial Information, University of Trieste, Italy, as required by the Friuli Venezia Giulia Region Manzoni et al. (2004). Sample roads have been surveyed in any of the four Regional Provinces.

Several public administrations adopted the same techniques in order to draw up the Road Cadastre in the areas of their competence, assigning the surveys to firms equipped with MMS.

The aim of the research presented in this paper was to compare the road geometric parameters computed from GNSS/INS road surveys by using "GIGI-One", the GeoSNav Lab, University of Trieste, MMS, with the ones extracted from high-resolution satellite images and the relative project values.

For the absolute positioning, the Mobile Mapping System uses the POS LV (Position and Orientation System for Land Vehicles) System of Applanix Corporation, a fully integrated, Position and Orientation System, utilizing GNSS positioning integrated by inertial technology to generate stable, reliable and repeatable positioning solutions for land-based vehicle applications (Fig. 2). Designed to operate under the most difficult GNSS conditions in urban and suburban environments, it enables accurate positioning for road geometry, pavement inspection, GIS database and asset management, road surveying and vehicle dynamics.

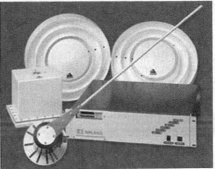

Fig. 2. The MMS of the GeoSNav Lab, University of Trieste, and the Applanix Corporation POS LV© system components mounted on board the vehicle.

This integrated GNSS/INS (Global Navigation Satellite System/Inertial System) system is able to give, instant by instant, the position and asset of the vehicle.

Besides two GNSS receivers and the Inertial System, an odometer mounted on the back left wheel of the vehicle, is present, measuring the travelled distance.

The integration of each sensor data is performed by a Kalman filter, allowing to gain in any instant the best solution. GNSS data has a 1 Hz acquisition rate, while the odometer and the inertial system send data to the System CPU at a 200 Hz rate.

The centre of the footprint of the back left tire was used as reference point for the MMS positioning data.

Kinematic tests were carried out to assess the repeatability of surveyed trajectories by driving the MMS without any constraint, keeping the vehicle on the centre of the lane.

The tests have been performed both in situations of nearly contemporaneous trajectories (few minutes between a passage and the subsequent one, in order to maintain the similarity on the satellite geometries) than in different days and with different satellite constellations: the maximum differences between the so surveyed trajectories are in the order of 50 cm.

In the case of motorways with two or more lanes, as well as when the road is double tracked, to determine the road axis, the road must be travelled in both directions, on symmetrical lanes with respect to the axis, maintaining the MMS in the centre of the lane and calculating the axis as the average of the detected trajectories.

When the white line, on a single carriageway road, materializes the road axis, the survey can easily be accomplished by keeping the reference wheel on the line.

Should signing not be present, it is possible to choose to have the output of the positioning data in correspondence of a predefined point along the vehicle axis, keeping the vehicle as much as possible in the centre of the lane during the survey.

Different drivers, following the guidelines outlined above, also run the same trajectories: this did not have a relievable influence on the captured data sets.

Each trajectory is materialized by a seeding of points, obtained by interpolating every 1-meter the data coming out from any component of the surveying system at its own acquisition frequency. For each point of the seeding, the plane coordinates in the chosen reference system are provided, as well as the ellipsoidal heights; the progressive distance from the starting point, the longitudinal and transversal slopes and the curvature expressed as punctual attribute, are associated.

In the present study, the radius determination was performed, point by point, based on the geometric construction of the circumference through three points: the central is the examined point, the forward and backward points are at a distance of 20 m from it. This choice - instead of considering three following points of the seeding- allows smoothing the driving effects.

The trajectory surveyed by the MMS is in fact never perfectly superimposable to the road geometries, but repeated runs showed it to be a good index of the "most likely" one.

The radius determined in this way, and consequently the curvature values, are thus affected by a certain level of noise needed to be filtered.

A null curvature is assigned to the points where the curvature value is less than a threshold (in the examined cases $k_s = 0.001$ m^{-1}). A null curvature value associated to consecutive points identifies straight roads segments.

For each point of the surveyed trajectories, the Easting and Northing coordinates, the ellipsoidal height, the radius and the curvature (computed as the inverse of the radius) are available, ordered by the progressive distance from a starting point.

A filtering technique was set up by the Authors in order to detect arches with constant curvature from the points' seeding, where present; in this way, it was possible to assign the "*curvature*" attribute to each segment.

The axis has been determined as the mean of two trajectories, so that the assigned radius value is the one resulting from the mean of the two starting values.

The progressive distance values of the first and the last point of each straight segment allow to calculate its length; the initial and final progressives of the elements with a curvature different from zero are also identified. Curved sections needed to be analysed one by one. The radius, as a function of the progressive distance, was considered point by point. By definition, the first derivative of the radius function has to be null where the radius is constant. This does not happen in practise due to the noise of the points' seeding identifying the trajectory, related to the driving uncertainty and the described methodology used for the punctual radius determination. The first derivative is not zero, but it fluctuates around the zero value due to the radius punctual value variations. It is necessary to assume a threshold for the first derivative, below which its value is consider null (first derivative < 12 in the performed test). If the first derivative of the radius function is zero, the radius value and the initial and final points of the constant-radius arc have to be estimated.

The radius can be calculated as the mean value of the punctual radii in the central half of the considered arc. Then the centre of the circle having R radius crossing two points of the seeding, whose punctual radius values have been used for the calculation of the mean radius, can be identified.

Knowing the C circle centre coordinates and the equations of the two straight lines (preceding and following the examining curve) calculated as linear regression of the surveyed points, the distances of the C centre from the straight lines can be computed.

Each of these distances $D_i = R + \Delta R_i$ can be determined and the A_i parameter can be calculated for the clothoid connecting each straight segment to the constant radius arc:

$$A_i = \sqrt[4]{24R^3 \Delta R_i \left(1 + \frac{3\Delta R_i}{14R} \right)} \tag{1}$$

The lengths S_1 and S_2 of the curves having variable radius, and the curvilinear abscissa at the beginning and end of the arc having constant curvature, can be obtained from equation $RS_i = A_i^2$.

The described methodology was applied to curves with known parameters, both in case of curves with constant radius connected by clothoids, and in case of curves with constant radius directly inserted on the straight lines.

The computed radius values resulted to be the same ones as in the project in both the cases.

In a first test phase, the equation of the two straight sections preceding and following the curve has been graphically determined by using the geometric construction of the line passing through two points of the seeding, instead of the linear regression of the points belonging to the same straight line. Using this approximation, the accuracy in the ΔR computation, and consequently in the clothoid parameter and its length, was smaller. Nevertheless, the so obtained values are very close to project ones.

A vehicle, driven on the road, runs a variable radius curve, even where it is not really designed and constructed. In such cases, the obtained ΔR values were in the order of $20 \div 30$ cm. It is possible to introduce a threshold to reduce the ΔR value to zero, thus excluding the presence of a variable radius curve where not really existing, by improving the algorithm used to determine the straight line equations like linear regressions of the points seeding.

3.2   Road Parameters Extraction from High Resolution Satellite Images

The availability of a large number of HR (High Resolution) satellite images gives a new instrument to extract road features using semi-automatic techniques.

These images give a resolution from 60 cm to 1 m, near to the one of the aerial photographs usually adopted for cartography.

One of the goals of this paper is to test HR images capability to provide information about road conditions and characteristics.

Two QuickBird images with a geometric resolution of 60 cm have been used for the tests. Their spectral resolution is 4 bands (three in the visible spectrum - blue, green and red - and a band in the near infrared wavelength). The chosen color depth is 8 bit/pixel.

Two strategies for road extraction have been tested: the first one based on the concept of spectral signature, and the second one based on the Fractal Dimension of the image, treated like a numerical matrix.

The "spectral signature" is the core concept of all remote sensing techniques. It is based on the idea that each object has a peculiar reflectance that can be observed and analyzed looking at the Digital Number that the object has on each recorded band. In particular, it is quite easy to separate non-vegetated areas from the vegetated ones using their great difference in reflectance in red and near-infrared (NIR) bands.

A combination of these two bands gives the NDVI (Normalized Difference Vegetation Index) index, largely used in remote sensing techniques to perform a separation of green and non-green areas Altobelli et al. (2004). NDVI is calculated as follows:

$$NDVI = \frac{NIR - RED}{NIR + RED} \tag{2}$$

where RED and NIR stand for the spectral reflectance measurements acquired in the red (visible) and near-infrared regions, respectively.

The Authors used it to have a basis on which being able to separate roads from the other kind of soil uses, considering that in the studied area the main roads built inside a largely wooded area have been analyzed. After this index calculation, it was possible to use it as a basis for a typical classification using a single band (the newly calculated NDVI "band") or a bias value that can separate vegetation from roads. Both this techniques were useful because of the peculiar soil use of the area; where more types of non-vegetated land are present, it is necessary to use of a multi spectral classification, otherwise it would be very difficult to separate roads from other soil coverage that are typical of urban areas like roofs, concrete, bare soils etc.

An unsupervised classification of the NDVI map was applied for this project, using an Euclidean Distance algorithm and then an isolation of road representing class, into a black and white map (Fig. 3).

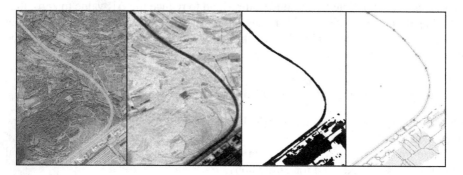

Fig. 3. Road extraction through NDVI map classification.

Even the Fractal Dimension of this area has been calculated on the NDVI map, because it represents a combination of band, so it has inside a larger quantity of information than a single band. The FD will be considered a measurement of the complexity of digital number distribution over: within the scale of the image used for this study, we expected a regular distribution of values on the artificial soil coverage (as roads are) and a more irregular distribution on the natural areas.

If the FD is regarded as a measure of input data roughness, the DN matrix can be imagined as a topographic surface, where higher or lower reflectance values (or NDVI) can be found as peaks or valleys: the bigger the differences in value between near pixels, the higher the fractal dimension of this area.

The "Triangular prism surface method (TPSA)" was applied to calculate the area fractal dimension (Fig. 4). The "topographic surface" is split up into cells, according to a regular grid, and each area is measured. Each cell is not considered as a plane surface but calculated as a prism where z coordinates of base vertexes are the DN of the pixel located on the corner of the cell, and prism height is the mean of the corner values.

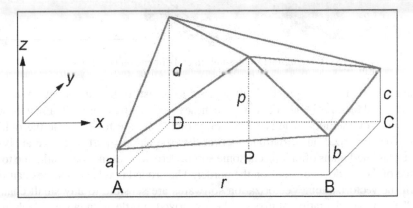

Fig. 4. Triangular prism surface method.

The area is calculated many times, according to grids of different scales so that the bases of the prisms have different numbers of pixels every time. The calculated area is then expressed through a logarithmic scale by means of a proper software routine developed by Altobelli and Pucci Poppi in 1998, and correlated with the respective dimensions of the cells on which it was calculated. The so obtained regression line coefficient is related to the Fractal Dimension as expressed below:

$$FD = 2 - b \tag{3}$$

where b is the linear regression coefficient. Roads are expected to have a lower FD respect to other kind of soil coverage in the used images, so that it is easy to separate them from other areas.

What was initially not considered is that the highest difference in the Digital Numbers occurs exactly around the road margins, describing the change of soil usage, from artificial coverage to vegetation.

A classification based on fractal dimension thus leads to the identification of road borders, rather than to an identification of the road path from which the road axes can be obtained, as happens with the classification based only on spectral signature (Fig. 5).

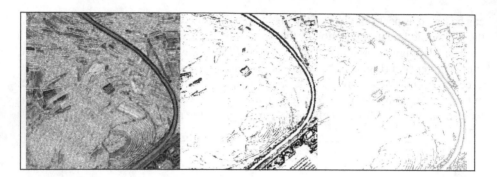

Fig. 5. Road extraction through fractal dimension techniques.

The last step of this road identification process consists of the vectorization of some of the extracted features in order to compare these results with the ones obtained through the other survey methods. The types of comparable data are for example the radii of curves. The vectorization of the map is probably the hardest part of image analyses, because classified maps often present some sort of "erosion" of the road path, due to the presence of the shadows of trees on the border. The eroded pixels sometimes cause an error in the vectorization. Vectorization softwares are sensible to any small changes towards the main orientation of pixels to be vectorized, a little abundance or lack in the road border therefore leads to an interruption in the direction of the extracted lines, or to a misinterpretation of it, such as in tracts where junctions with side roads are present. The map that should be provided to the vectorizing software therefore needs a quite important "cleaning" job, to avoid this problem as much as possible, being careful not to change the real road aspect.

Another aspect of roads that could be observed and obtained from satellite images is relative to road horizontal signings. These lines are clearly visible in high resolution images, even if the nominal pixel dimension could not theoretically permit it. This is possible because of the high difference in reflectance between the white lines and the black asphalt. The digital number of a pixel containing a line can be considered as a weighted mean of the values of the asphalt alone and the line alone. The radiometric difference is so high that the influence of a thin white area in the pixel causes a remarkable increase of the DN (note that in our case, with 8 bit images, a low reflectance is converted into a DN value near 0 and a high reflectance has a DN near 255).

The easiest way to extract this type of road feature for geometric purposes is through its manual digitalization. The image is georeferenced in the used coordinate projection system using proper GIS software functions, and the road lines are digitalized in a vector file. Otherwise, they can be extracted through a spectral based classification: another raster file can be obtained, which is a qualitative representation of the road signing characteristics, and could be particularly useful to check the signing aspect, e.g. brightness, straight positioning etc. (Fig. 6). This type of file cannot be used to precisely control the geometric characteristics of road signing, because the size of the pixel in the input map - as explained above - is wider than the extension of the signs themselves, so line positioning inside the pixels is not certain.

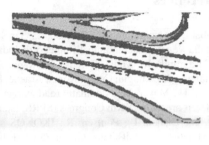

Fig. 6. Particular of road signings extraction.

In Table 1 the geometric road parameters derived from MMS surveys and Remote Sensing analysis are compared with the design project values, thus showing the agreement in curve radius extraction.

Table 1. Comparative values between design alignment, MMS and remote sensing surveys

	Curve radius	First clothoid parameter	First clothoid length	Second clothoid parameter	Second clothoid length
Project Information	250 m	160	102,4	160	102,4
MMS survey	250 m	154	95 m	161	104 m
Remote Sensing survey	252 m	Not detected	Not detected	Not detected	Not detected

4 Conclusions

The aim of this paper was to test and compare different road survey methods in order to select the more suitable one under certain conditions.

Mobile Mapping System (MMS) surveys can lead to a complete description of curve geometries with a very good accuracy, even when curvature radii are variable (clothoid), as frequently happens on motorways.

Similar results were obtained in radius determination through Remote Sensed Images where the radius is constant, and the expected accuracy was reached considering the image geometric resolution.

The analysis of road geometries through Remote Sensing Images could be useful when on site surveys are not possible. Up to now, the exact ending point of the straight lines could not be found by means of remote sensing data, and clothoids parameters could not be calculated. The adopted software and techniques need to be optimized in order to calculate these types of parameters. On the other hand, satellite images can provide further information such as road signing distribution or condition.

References

Altobelli, A., Napolitano, R., Bressan, E., Ganis, P., Feoli, E.: Analisi dell'informazione spettrale della vegetazione tramite l'impiego di indici ottenuti da immagini satellitari Landsat. In: Casagrandi, R., Melià, P. (eds.) Ecologia. Atti del XIII Congresso Nazionale della Società Italiana di Ecologia, Como, Roma, Aracne, 8–10 settembre 2003 (2004)

Bacher, U., Mayer, H.: Automatic road extraction from IRS satellite images in agricultural and desert areas. In: XXth Congress ISPRS, Istanbul, Turkey, 12–23 July 2004

Dial, G., Gisbon, L., Poulsen, R.: IKONOS satellite imagery and its use in automated road extraction. In Baltsavias, Gruen, Gool (Eds.) Automatic Extraction of Man-Made Objects From Aerial and Space Images (III). A.A. Balkema Publishers (2001)

Goeman, W., Martinez-Fonte, L., Bellens, R., Gautaman, S.: Automated verification of road network data by VHR satellite images using road statistics. In: Proceedings of IPSRS Workshop: High Resolution Earth Imaging for Geospatial Information, Hannover, Germany (2005)

Gruen, A., Li, H.: Road extractions from aerial and satellite images by dynamic programming. ISPRS J. Photogram. Remote Sens. 50(4), 111–120 (1995)

Grüen, A., Li, H.: Linear feature extraction with 3-D LSB-snakes. In: Automatic Extraction of Man-Made Objects from Aerial and Space Images (II), pp. 287–298. BirkhäuserVerlag, Basel (1997)

Hatger, C., Brenner, C.: Extraction of road geometry parameters from laser scanning and existing databases. In: Proceeding of ISPRS Workshop: 3D Reconstruction from Airborne Laserscanner and InSAR DATA, Dresden, Germany, 8–10 October 2003

Kumagai, J., Zhao, H., Nakagawa, M., Shibasaki, R.: Road extraction from high resolution commercial satellite data. In: Proceedings of the 22nd Asian Conference on Remote Sensing, Singapore, 5–9 November 2001

Manzoni, G., Bolzon, G., Martinolli, S., Pagurut, R., Rizzo, R.G., Sluga, T.: Ultimi risultati del rilevamento di strade con MMS e sue applicazioni interdisciplinari, Società Italiana di Fotogrammetria e Topografia - Convegno Nazionale "Attuali metodologie per il rilevamento a grande scala e per il monitoraggio", Chia Laguna, Cagliari, Italia, 22–24 Settembre 2004, Bollettino della Società Italiana di Fotogrammetria e Topografia, pp. 99–108 (2004)

Ministero delle Infrastrutture e dei Trasporti - D.M. 01/06/2001: Modalità di istuzione e aggiornamento del catasto delle strade - Gazzetta Ufficiale della Repubblica Italiana, n. 5, 07/01/2002 (2002)

Stoica, R., Descombes, X., Zerubia, J.: A Gibbs point process for road extraction from remotely sensed images. Int. J. Comput. Vis. 57(2), 121–136 (2004)

Wallace, S., Hatcher, M., Priestnall, G., Morton, R.: Research into a framework for automatic linear feature identification and extraction. In: Automatic Extraction of Man-Made Objects from Aerial and Space Images (III), pp. 381–390. Balkema Publishers, Lisse (2001)

Wiedemann, C., Ebner H.: Automatic completion and evaluation of road networks. Int. Arch. Photogram. Remote Sens. 33(B3/2), 979–986 (2000)

Soilán, M., Riveiro, B., Martínez-Sánchez, J., Arias, P.: Automatic road sign inventory using mobile mapping systems. In: The International Archives of the Photogrammetry, Remote Sensing and Spatial Information Sciences, 2016 XXIII ISPRS Congress, vol. XLI-B3, Prague, Czech Republic, 12–19 July 2016

Hinz, S., Baumgartner, A., Mayer, H., Wiedemann, C., Ebner, H.: Road extraction focussing on urban areas. In: Baltsavias, Gruen, Gool (eds.) Automatic Extraction of Man-made Objects From Aerial and Space Images (III), pp. 255–265. A.A. Balkema Publishers (2001)

Hinz, S., Baumgartner, A.: Urban road net extraction integrating internal evaluation models. In: International Society for Photogrammetry and Remote Sensingpp, Graz, Austria, pp. 255–265 (2002)

Vosselmann, G., de Gunst, M.: Updating road maps by contextual reasoning. In: Gruen et al., pp. 267–276 (1997)

Zhang, C., Baltsavias, E., Gruen, A.: Updating of cartographic road databases by image analysis. In: Baltsavias, Gruen, Gool (eds.) Automatic Extraction of Man-made Objects From Aerial and Space Images (III), pp. 243–253. A.A. Balkema Publishers (2001)

Pattnaik, S.B., Hallmark, S., Souleyrette, R.: Collecting road inventory using LIDAR surface models. In: Proceedings Map India (2003)

Yang, B., Dong, Z., Zhao, G., Dai, W.: Hierarchical extraction of urban objects from mobile laser scanning data.ISPRS J. Photogrammetry Remote Sens. **99**, 45–57 (2015)

Serna, A., Marcotegui, B.: Detection, segmentation and classification of 3D urban objects using mathematical morphology and supervised learning. ISPRS J. Photogrammetry Remote Sens. **93**, 243–255 (2014). Elsevier

Yu, Y., Li, J., Guan, H., Wang, C., Yu, J.: Semiautomated extraction of street light poles from mobile LiDAR point-clouds. IEEE Trans. Geosci. Remote Sens. **53**(3), 1374–1386 (2015). doi:10.1109/TGRS.2014.2338915

Zhou, L., Vosselman, G.: Mapping curbstones in airborne and mobile laser scanning data. Int. J. Appl. Earth Obs. Geoinf. **18**, 293–304 (2012)

Liu, J., Liang, H., Wang, Z., Chen, X.: A framework for applying point clouds grabbed by multi-beam LIDAR in perceiving the driving environment. Sensors **15**(9), 21931–21956 (2015). doi: 10.3390/s150921931

Reitberger, J., Schnörr, C., Krzystek, P., Stilla, U.: 3D segmentation of single trees exploiting full waveform LIDAR data. ISPRS J. Photogrammetry Remote Sens. **64**, 561–574 (2009)

Pu, S., Rutzinger, M., Vosselman, G., Elberink, S.O.: Recognizing basic structures from mobile laser scanning data for road inventory studies. ISPRS J. Photogrammetry Remote Sens. **66**(6), 28–39 (2011)

Riveiro, B., Diaz-Vilarino, L., Conde-Carnero, B., Soilan, M., Arias, P.: Automatic segmentation and shape-based classification of retro-reflective traffic signs from mobile LiDAR data. IEEE J. Sel. Top. Appl. Earth Obs. Remote Sens. (2015). doi:10.1109/JSTARS.2015.2461680

Wen, C., Li, J., Member, S., Luo, H., Yu, Y., Cai, Z., Wang, H., Wang, C.: Spatial-related traffic sign inspection for inventory purposes using mobile laser scanning data. IEEE Trans. Intell. Transp. Syst. **17**, 27–37 (2015). doi:10.1109/TITS.2015.2418214

Stallkamp, J., Schlipsing, M., Salmen, J., Igel, C.: Man vs. computer: benchmarking machine learning algorithms for traffic sign recognition. Neural Netw. **32**, 323–332 (2012). https://doi.org/10.1016/j.neunet.2012.02.016

Cireşan, D., Meier, U., Schmidhuber, J.: Multi-column deep neural networks for image classification. Neural Netw. **32**, 333–338 (2012)

Sermanet, P., LeCun, Y.: Traffic sign recognition with multi-scale convolutional networks. In: The 2011 International Joint Conference on Neural Networks (IJCNN). IEEE (2011)

Workshop on Interactively Presenting High-Quality Graphics in Cooperation with Various Computing Tools (IPHQC 2017)

Using Tangible Contents Generated by CindyJS and Its Influence on Mathematical Cognition

Masataka Kaneko[(✉)]

Toho University, Miyama 2-2-1, Funabashi, Japan
masataka.kaneko@phar.toho-u.ac.jp

Abstract. Included among other mathematical software, dynamic geometry software has the great advantage of enabling teachers and learners to visualize and interactively control mathematical models. However they are not used in real classrooms as widely as expected. One reason is that it is not so easy for ordinary teachers and learners to install those software onto personal computers and to master the skills needed to operate them appropriately. As a result, teachers do not have enough knowledge about the theme and the manner in which those software will be used effectively. To overcome this difficulty, the extensions associated with some dynamic geometry software are being developed so that the teaching materials generated by them can be adapted to plugin-less web technology. In this paper, the author explains some case studies which illustrate the software's influence on learners' mathematical cognition. The method to identify the above mentioned influence will be applicable to wide range of researches concerning the interaction between learners' reasoning processes and information technology.

1 Introduction

In order to visualize mathematical phenomena that contain variables, dynamic presentations of them should be helpful. In fact, some excellent dynamic geometry software have been developed. Among them, most popular ones are Cabri (http://www.cabri.com), Cinderella (https://cinderella.de), and GeoGebra (https://www.geogebra.org/) [1–3]. They enables us to generate mathematical objects (like points, lines, circles, function graphs, and areas) and move them by interactively controlling the variables on a PC screen through clicking or dragging of mouse. Though these programs are sometimes used in mathematics education [4,5], a great deal of effort is needed for learners to install these programs and to master the skills to operate them appropriately. Moreover mathematical activities that use finger tracing have been demonstrated to ease the burdens on learners' working memories in some cases [6]. Therefore, in the cases of Cinderella and GeoGebra whose underlying technology is Java, some extensions are being developed so that the resulting mathematical contents can be exported in the format of plugin-less web technology like JavaScript, HTML5 and WebGL [7–10]. Using these extensions, teachers can generate mathematical contents which can be used not only on PCs but also on touch devices

© Springer International Publishing AG 2017
O. Gervasi et al. (Eds.): ICCSA 2017, Part IV, LNCS 10407, pp. 199–215, 2017.
DOI: 10.1007/978-3-319-62401-3_15

like iPads and tablets. These contents enable learners to handle mathematical models without installing and mastering extra software. Learners' handling of mathematical models with their own hands (or fingers) can be regarded as a sort of "active learning". As illustrated in some previous research [11,12], learners' achievement can be greatly improved in classes that utilize active learning and interactive engagement techniques. However, it has also been illustrated that their achievement can vary from theme to theme. Therefore, from an educational point of view, it is crucial to obtain knowledge about the following points:

1. Which aspects of learners' reasoning processes are influenced when they use tangible contents?
2. How can tangible contents be generated and operated to maximize their effects?

In this paper, the author shows the methods and results of his attempts to clarify these points by conducting 10 individual case studies. The tangible contents are generated by using CindyJS (https://cindyjs.org/) which is the above mentioned extension of Cinderella. The polynomial approximation of some irrational function was chosen as the theme since it is expected that learners' interactively moving the graphs of polynomial functions on touch devices can help them to clearly observe the approximating procedure at their own pace. In these case studies, the reasoning processes of the subjects were detected through ethnomethodological study. In fact, the subjects' verbal behavior and their operation on the iPad screen were videotaped and the changes in their strategies for searching for an optimal approximation were detected by coding the movement on the iPad screen chronologically. The analysis of the results suggests that learners' cognition of mathematical models containing multi variables was substantially changed through interactive operation of tangible contents on touch screen devices.

2   Cinderella and CindyJS

While Cinderella has a graphical user interface (Cinderella screen) to generate and move geometric objects, it also has a command line user interface with a well-organized scripting language (CindyScript) which includes commands to generate and control analytic objects [13]. CindyScript also allows some programming that makes generation and control efficient.

For instance, Fig. 1 shows geometric objects generated on a Cinderella screen which are used to explain the geometric structure of complex number multiplication. Here, three points, A, B, and C corresponding to complex numbers, are generated by pushing buttons in the top menu of the screen. To keep the relationship in which point C corresponds to the complex number zw while points A and B correspond to z and w respectively, we input the commands in CindyScript as shown in Fig. 2. When we move points A or B by dragging the mouse, point C also moves accordingly. Thus learners can use the objects generated on the screen to find out the geometric rule for determining the position of point C in accordance with those of points A and B.

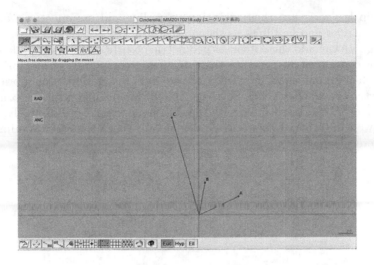

Fig. 1. Cinderella screen

Fig. 2. Commands in CindyScript

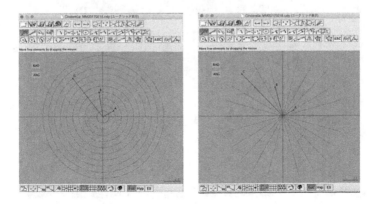

Fig. 3. Supplementary items in Cinderella screen

To help learners turn their attention to radius and argument, we can add concentric circles and half lines as shown in Fig. 3.

Though we can add these items as geometric objects on the Cinderella screen, it is more convenient to generate them by using commands of loop programming which are input into CindyScript as shown in Fig. 4. Conditional branching here is activated when we click buttons "RAD" (associated with the command num=1;) and "ANG" (associated with the command num=2;) respectively. In this manner, we can display either only circles or only half lines correspondingly on the Cinderella screen.

```
1 O=[0,0];
2 C.xy=(A.x*B.x-A.y*B.y,A.x*B.y+A.y*B.x);
3 draw([O,A]); draw([O,B]); draw([O,C]);
4
5 if(num==1,
6   forall(1..10,k,
7     plot(k*[cos(t),sin(t)],start->0,stop->2*pi+0.1,dashtype->3);
8   );
9 );
10
11 if(num==2,
12   forall(0..23,k,
13     draw([O,10*[cos(k*pi/12),sin(k*pi/12)]],dashtype->3);
14   );
15 );
```

Fig. 4. Programming in CindyScript

Once Cinderella content is generated, we can easily export it to CindyJS. In fact, we only need to choose "Export to CondyJS" from the file menu in the Cinderella screen as shown in Fig. 5, and the program does the rest.

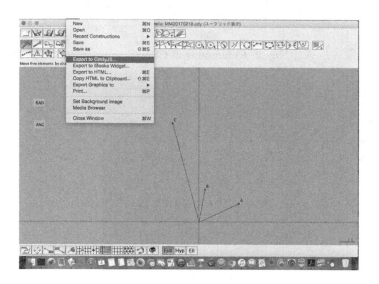

Fig. 5. Exporting CindyJS content

Figure 6 shows the image of content generated by CindyJS as displayed via Google Chrome. The contents can also be displayed via any ordinary web browser like Safari or Internet Explorer. As in the case of Cinderella, we can freely move the points A and B. Also the buttons work similarly as on the Cinderella screen. Some part of the background HTML script is shown in Fig. 7.

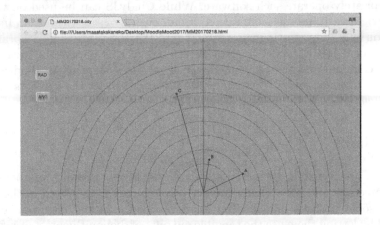

Fig. 6. CindyJS content exported from Cinderella

Fig. 7. Commands converted into HTML format

As seen in Figs. 4 and 7, the commands in CindyScript are converted without any modifications. Also the libraries to interpret these commands are imported into the browsing software. Moreover the geometry of the objects generated on the Cinderella screen is automatically described in the HTML output which leads to the resulting visualization via the graphical style "CSCanvas" specialized for CindyJS use.

Thus, no installation of software and no knowledge about the scripting language are needed for learners to use CindyJS contents. From an educational point of view, this characteristic of CindyJS is extremely important since it cannot be expected that almost all of the learners will be familiar with dynamic geometry software like Cinderella and the curriculum of mathematics classes cannot always afford to spend time getting learners to master the skills needed to appropriately operate such software. While CindyJS can be used on various touch devices with internet connection, it can even be used without an internet connection simply by putting the contents and the above mentioned libraries in the same local file system. For the case studies in this paper, the author put CindyJS contents and the libraries in the local file system of an iPad via the application "Documents 5" (https://readdle.com/) and let the subjects operate the contents without an internet connection.

3   Methods

Unless we use dynamic geometry software, we cannot display mathematical objects precisely and move them interactively. Moreover, as stated in the introduction, some positive influence on learners' mathematical cognition can be expected by letting them use the tangible outputs of dynamic geometry software.

Therefore, to help students improve their mathematical cognition of polynomial approximation of some functions, the author generated teaching material with CindyJS for use on an iPad. The screen image of the main CindyJS teaching material and part of the HTML script used to generate it are shown in Figs. 8 and 9 respectively.

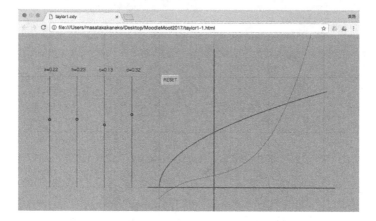

Fig. 8. Screen image of the main CindyJS teaching material (Color figure online)

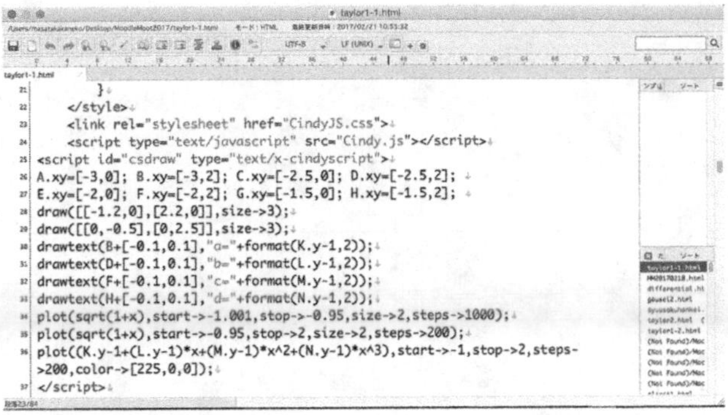

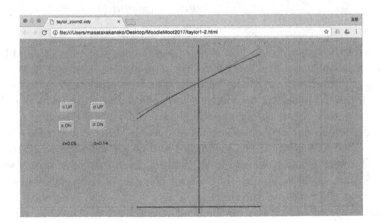

Fig. 9. Script in HTML file

In Fig. 8, the blue curve is the graph of the irrational function $y = \sqrt{x+1}$ and the red curve is the graph of the polynomial function $y = a + bx + cx^2 + dx^3$. Here the coefficients a, b, c, d are interactively determined by dragging the red points in the blue segments on the touch panel of the iPad. Also, as the red point for each coefficient is dragged along the slider, their values at each position are displayed on the screen. The shape of the red curve changes according to the specified values of a, b, c, d. When we touch the button "RESET" on the screen, the initial state in which $a = b = c = d = 0$ is recovered.

Figure 10 is another example of teaching material generated with CintyJS displaying the enlarged image of the region near the point $(0, 1)$ in Fig. 8.

Fig. 10. Enlargement of Fig. 8

While the values of a and b are fixed as 1 and 0.5 respectively, those of c and d can be interactively changed, this time not by dragging points but by touching buttons.

Supplementary CindyJS materials in Fig. 11 were also prepared to demonstrate the notion of the radius of convergence.

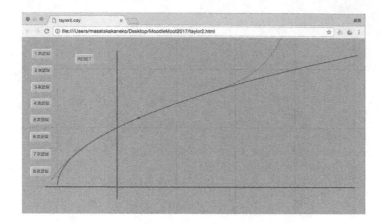

Fig. 11. Supplementary CindyJS material

Here the center of the approximation which is indicated by the red point can be moved by dragging it on the blue curve. Also the degree of the approximating polynomial can be changed by touching the buttons.

As subjects of the case studies, the author recruited ten first grade (19 years old) students from his university. Their major is not mathematical science but pharmaceutical science. They had already learned the formula for the Taylor expansion of a function $f(x)$ near $x = 0$:

$$f(x) = f(0) + f'(0)x + \frac{f''(0)}{2}x^2 + \frac{f'''(0)}{6}x^3 + \cdots$$

At the time of the case studies, half a year passed since the subjects had learned this formula in the calculus classroom. So, it could be assumed that most of them forgot the precise form of the formula. The case studies were executed one subject at a time. Therefore, no consultation between students was possible.

First, they were asked to use the main material in Fig. 8 to find the values a, b, c, d with which the red curve best fits into the blue curve near the point $(0, 1)$. No advice was given at the beginning and they were allowed to touch the "RESET" button as many times as they liked. If the subject took too much time, the author asked some questions about the role of the coefficients a and b in determining the graph of the function $y = a + bx + cx^2 + dx^3$. As shown in Fig. 12, the subjects' operations on the iPad screen were captured by connecting the iPad to the MacOS and by using QuickTime. Also the physical and verbal behaviors of the subjects were videotaped as shown in Fig. 13.

Second, they were asked to compute the coefficients a, b, c, d using the above cited formula. After computing them, they compared the result computed by hand with the result obtained by using CindyJS material in Fig. 8. When they claimed that these two results differ, they were asked about the reason for it. Also they were encouraged to move the content in Fig. 10 to observe the influence of the values c and d on the graph of the approximating polynomial function.

Fig. 12. Capturing iPad screen via QuickTime

Fig. 13. Record of subjects' behavior

Moreover, they were recommended to move the content in Fig. 11 to observe how the radius of convergence varied when the position of the central point was changed.

The recorded video image of the subjects' moving elements on the iPad screen in the first step was analyzed chronologically via the SportsCode system.

https://www.hudl.com/elite/sportscode

In fact, we coded each time interval in which the subjects moved the four red points respectively on some time lines. Combined with the videotaped verbal behavior of the subjects which were synchronized via the SportsCode system, the changes in the subjects' cognitive processes were detected and evaluated.

4 Results

Since it is well known that the coefficients a and b of the function $y = a + bx$ specify the intercept on the y-axis and the slope of its graph respectively, it was expected that the subjects would move the points corresponding to a and b first and then fix them at the appropriate positions so that the graph of $y = a + bx$ is tangent to the graph of $y = \sqrt{x+1}$ at the point $(0,1)$ while they were moving the points corresponding to c and d. Thus the expected result of the coding via the SoprtsCode system is shown in Fig. 14.

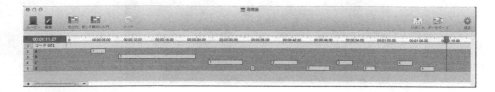

Fig. 14. Model result of the coding

However, the actual results are fairly different from the expectation shown above. In fact, Fig. 15 shows the results of how each subject moved the points. Here, the time intervals in which the subjects moved each point are charted onto 10 individual time lines. Each time line contains rows corresponding to a, b, c, d and RESET arranged from top to bottom. Also Table 1 shows the resulting values of a, b, c, d reported by the subjects.

Table 1. The coefficients reported by subjects

Subject	a	c	c	d
A	1	0.57	−0.2	0.05
B	1	0.49	−0.1	0.02
C	0.99	0.5	−0.07	−0.01
D	1	0.56	−0.17	0.04
E	1	0.53	−0.18	0.06
F	1	0.51	−0.16	0.06
G	1	0.51	−0.09	0.02
H	1	0.5	−0.2	0.07
I	1	0.56	−0.14	0.02
J	1	0.49	−0.15	0.07

At the second stage, all subjects could compute the coefficients a, b, c, d as follows by using the Taylor expansion.

$$a = 1, \quad b = 0.5, \quad c = -0.125, \quad d = 0.0625$$

The fact that this result is different from those in Table 1 illustrates that the subjects did not use the Taylor expansion in the first step. They compared this result obtained by using the Taylor expansion with the results they obtained by moving points on a CindyJS material (shown in Table 1). Their statements

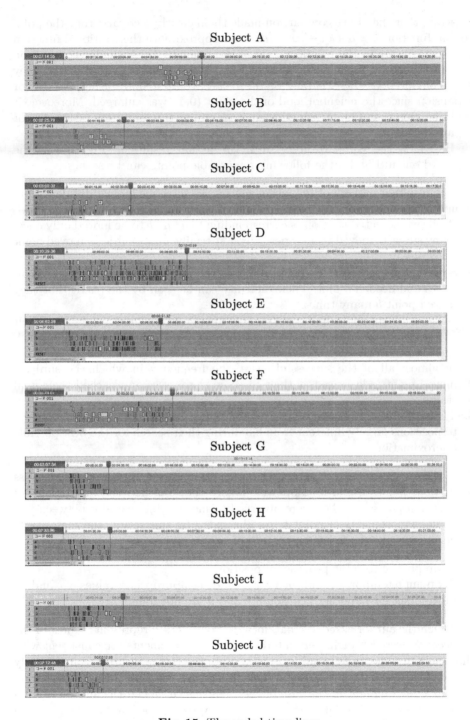

Fig. 15. The coded time lines

illustrate that the above comparison made them clearly recognize that the polynomial function $y = a + bx + cx^2 + dx^3$ can approximate the irrational function $y = \sqrt{x+1}$ only in the neighborhood of the point $(0,1)$. A similar comparison was also made by touching buttons in Fig. 10. Some subjects stated that they were convinced of the accuracy of the results computed by using the Taylor expansion since the neighborhood of the point $(0,1)$ was enlarged. Moreover, it could be seen that Fig. 11 helped them understand the limitation of the Taylor expansion.

Based on the comparison between the actual results in Fig. 15 and the expected one in Fig. 14, the following remarkable points can be seen.

1. The resulting pattern of the movement on the screen is largely different from subject to subject.
2. While we expected the points corresponding to a and b to be moved only once, many subjects moved them repeatedly. Especially, many subjects moved point b frequently.
3. Some subjects (E and F) could not find the appropriate strategy by themselves and needed a hint. Their difficulty can be seen by the result that they moved point b many times.
4. Other subjects could find a reasonable answer by themselves at last. Their success can be seen by the pattern of their movement in the last stage, which was similar to the expected pattern in Fig. 14.
5. In almost all of the successful cases, the frequency in which the subjects moved point b decreased as their reasoning processes approached their final stages.
6. Though values of b near 0.5 are listed in Table 1, many subjects moved point b to positions largely different from 0.5 during their search for the best possible approximation.

As a whole, successful subjects, those other than E and F, moved point b less often than points c and d. Moreover, before they reached the final stages of their search processes, they were observed to move points c and d between two contiguous movements of point b. As illustrated by this result, the majority of subjects repeated the following pattern of search processes.

1. Move point b to some provisional position.
2. Fix point b temporally and then try to find the appropriate values of c and d.
3. Move point b to another position if c and d are not found.

When the author asked, "What does the coefficient a represent?" most of the subjects answered "height" or "intercept". These statements are consistent with the result that most of the subjects moved point a to the position 1 at the early stages of their search processes and they did not move it after that. The situation is completely different in the case of the coefficient b. When the author asked a similar question, almost all of the subjects answered "slope" and they never used the terms "touch" or "differential". Moreover, no subject tried to select the values of a and b by making the line $y = ax + b$ touch the graph of the function $y = \sqrt{x+1}$

at $(0, 1)$. Instead of considering the tangent line, they simply tried to make these two graphs be overlapped. In fact, many subjects could fix b near the position 0.5 after making several trials with different values for b.

5   Discussions

On the one hand, enabling learners to compute the coefficients a, b, c, d based on the precise formula of the Taylor expansion is important. On the other hand, it is also important for learners to interpret mathematically what the computed coefficients are. In the cognitive processes of their interpreting these coefficients, the followings should be the main targets to be understood.

1. The function $y = a + bx + cx^2 + dx^3$ can be regarded as the result of the superposition of the four functions $y = a$, $y = bx$, $y = cx^2$, and $y = dx^3$.
2. The functions cx^2 and dx^3 are infinitesimals of higher order than the function bx near $x = 0$ regardless of the coefficients b, c, d.
3. In particular, the differential of the function $y = a + bx + cx^2 + dx^3$ at $x = 0$ depends not on the coefficients c, d but only on b.
4. On the contrary, cx^2 and dx^3 become dominant parts over bx in the region far from $x = 0$.

Since multi variables are involved, it is expected that the learners' interactive operations on the graphs created by using dynamic geometry software will go a long way in helping learners understand these targets. With regard to the change in the subjects' understanding these targets through the process of their interactive operations, the results of our case studies allows us the following evaluation. For this evaluation, it is necessary for us to observe not only the result of coding but also the videotaped image of the learners' operations on an iPad screen.

As stated in the last section, most subjects did not consider the tangent line at $(0, 1)$ and moved point b to a position largely different from 0.5 at first nevertheless they used the term "slope" in their answers to questions about coefficient b. This result implies that the subjects had previously not been able to identify the slope of a curve and the slope of its tangent line. For instance, subject C once fixed b to the position at 0.62 and moved c and d at an early stage as shown in Fig. 16(I). Then in the following stage, C gradually moved b to 0.58 and then to 0.5 as shown in Fig. 16(II)(III). The situation is quite similar to the case of subject H as shown in Fig. 17(I)(II)(III).

Through the subjects' repeating this pattern in their search process, they can be seen to have recognized that whether or not the slopes of the two curves at the point $(0, 1)$ were equal was not influenced by the fluctuation of c and d. This progress can be interpreted as the subjects' intuitive understanding of points 2 and 3 stated above.

Both infinitesimals of higher order in point 2 and infinites of higher order in point 4 are involved with the notion of limit. However, there are some substantial differences between them. As a matter of fact, the former is related to the case

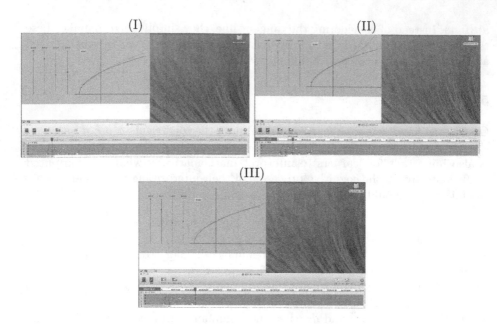

Fig. 16. Operations by subject C

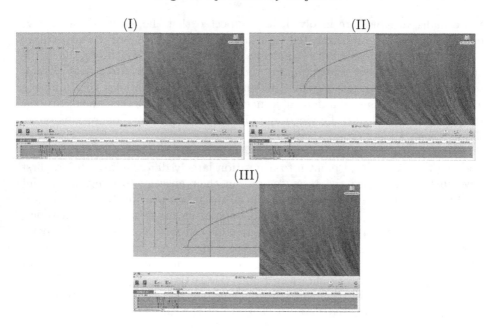

Fig. 17. Operations by subject H

$x \to 0$ and the latter is related to the case $x \to \infty$. Moreover, lower degree terms are dominant in the former case and higher degree terms are dominant in the latter case. Explanation of these notions using only mathematical expressions

(I)   (II)

(III)   (IV)

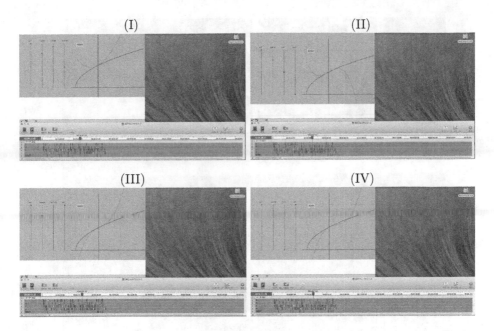

Fig. 18. Operations by subject D

and static graphic seems powerless to help learners acquire a clear image of the differences between them; however, a dynamic presentation of the continuous change in variables and coefficients will help learners to appreciate them. For instance, Fig. 18 shows the trial of subject D to observe how the shape of the graph changes when c and d are moved.

As is easily seen in Fig. 18, this trial enabled subject D to observe that the change in values of c and d had a great influence on the part of the graph far from $x = 0$ while it had little influence on the part of the graph in the neighborhood of $x = 0$. In fact, when D was asked to compare the values derived from the simulation on the iPad with that obtained by the computation based on the formula, he stated, "Even if the change in values of c and d is not so large, the shape of the graph changes greatly in the part far from $x = 0$ unlike its neighborhood." When he made this statement, he pointed to the region far from $x = 0$ on the screen of the iPad (right side) with his finger and moved his hand upward and downward as shown in Fig. 19. After making several trials as above, he could attain his final result successfully following the expected pattern of operation shown in Fig. 14. This tendency can also be seen in the operations of all subjects other than F. This progress can be interpreted as the subjects' intuitive understanding of infinitesimals of higher order.

Since many subjects inferred that a and b should be the intercept and slope of the graph at the early stages of their operating processes, the author thought that the "RESET" button could be programmed to show $a = 1$, $b = 0.5$, $c = d = 0$ as original state. Though the author proposed this change to the subjects after they

Fig. 19. Reaction of subject D

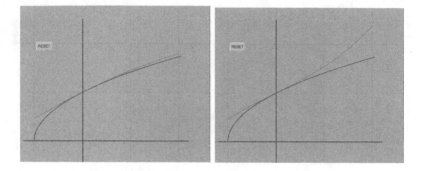

Fig. 20. Operations under the condition $a = 1$, $b = 0.5$

completed the task, almost all of them responded negatively. The reason, they stated, is that it would be easier to observe the influence of the fluctuations of c and d under the condition $a = b = 0$ compared to the condition $a = 1$, $b = 0.5$. In fact, Fig. 20 shows the graphs in case when $a = 1$, $b = 0.5$. The value of c is slightly changed from 0 in the left figure, and the value of d is slightly changed from 0 in the right figure. Because of the slope, it seems difficult for learners to see the above mentioned influence in this case.

It is obvious that the subjects regarded the function $y = a + bx + cx^2 + dx^3$ as the superposition of four monomial functions, which is point 1 mentioned at the beginning of this section, when they made the above statement. Since all subjects other than C and D did not try to move points c and d under the condition $a = b = 0$, it can be seen that their preference regarding the RESET button as stated above was stimulated through their operating processes.

6   Concluding Remarks

From the author's teaching experience, the size of the cognitive load on working memories and the amount of time required to translate the perceived image into a mathematical model are the factors having a great influence on the extent to which each individual learner can grasp mathematical concept. The results of this research strongly indicate that learners' interactive operations on the tangible contents generated by dynamic geometry software can lead their reasoning processes in desirable directions with minimal cognitive load and at their preferred pace. Since the method in this research seems to serve some convincing means to evaluate the learners' reasoning processes, more extensive study using it should be carried out.

Acknowledgements. The author is grateful to Professor Takeo Noda for proposing the theme and the contents used in this research. The author is also grateful to Professor Jürgen Richter-Gebert, Professor Ulrich Kortenkamp, and their colleagues for their great efforts to develop Cinderella and CindyJS.

This work was supported by JSPS KAKENHI (15K01037).

References

1. Laborde, C.: Experiencing the multiple dimensions of mathematics with dynamic 3D geometry environments: illustration with Cabri 3D. Electron. J. Math. Technol. **2**(1), 38–53 (2008)
2. Richter-Gebert, J., Kortenkamp, U.: Interactive Geometry with Cinderella. Springer, Heidelberg (2012)
3. Hohenwater, M., Preiner, J.: Dynamic mathematics with GeoGebra. J. Online Math. Appl. **7** (2007). Article ID 1448
4. Fest, A., Hiob, M., Hoffkamp, A.: An interactive learning activity for the formation of the concept of function based on representation transfer. Electron. J. Math. Technol. **5**(2), 169–176 (2012)
5. Lavicza, Z.: Integrating technology into mathematics teaching: a review. ZDM Int. J. Math. Educ. **42**(1), 105–119 (2010)
6. Ginns, P., Hu, F.T., Byrne, E., Bobis, J.: Learninng by tracing worked examples. Appl. Cogn. Psychol. **30**, 160–169 (2016)
7. von Gagern, M., Kortenkamp, U., Richter-Gebert, J., Strobel, M.: CindyJS. In: Greuel, G.-M., Koch, T., Paule, P., Sommese, A. (eds.) ICMS 2016. LNCS, vol. 9725, pp. 319–326. Springer, Cham (2016). doi:10.1007/978-3-319-42432-3_39
8. von Gagern, M., Richter-Gebert, J.: CindyJS Plugins. In: Greuel, G.-M., Koch, T., Paule, P., Sommese, A. (eds.) ICMS 2016. LNCS, vol. 9725, pp. 327–334. Springer, Cham (2016). doi:10.1007/978-3-319-42432-3_40
9. Montag, A., Richter-Gebert, J.: CindyGL: authoring GPU-based interactive mathematical content. In: Greuel, G.-M., Koch, T., Paule, P., Sommese, A. (eds.) ICMS 2016. LNCS, vol. 9725, pp. 359–365. Springer, Cham (2016). doi:10.1007/978-3-319-42432-3_44
10. Ancsin, G., Hohenwater, M., Kovacs, Z.: GeoGebra goes mobile. Electron. J. Math. Technol. **5**(2), 159–168 (2012)
11. Hake, R.R.: Interactive-engagement versus traditional methods - a six-thousand-student survey of mechanics test data for introductory physics courses. Am. J. Phys. **66**(1), 64–74 (1998)
12. Hoellwarth, C., Moelter, M.J.: The implications of a robust curriculum in introductory mechanics. Am. J. Phys. **79**(5), 540–545 (2011)
13. Richter-Gebert, J., Kortenkamp, U.: The power of scripting: DGS meets programming. Acta Didactica Napocensia **3**(2), 67–78 (2010)

Analysis of the Use of Teaching Materials Generated by KeTCindy as an Aid to the Understanding of Mathematics

Koji Nishiura[1](✉), Shunji Ouchi[2], and Kunihito Usui[3]

[1] National Institute of Technology, Fukushima College,
Taira, Iwaki-shi 970-8034, Japan
nishiura@fukushima-nct.ac.jp
[2] Shimonoseki City University, Daigaku-cho, Shimonoseki-shi 751-8510, Japan
ouchi@shimonoseki-cu.ac.jp
[3] National Institute of Technology, Kisarazu College, Kiyomidai-higashi,
Kisarazu-shi 292-0041, Japan
usui@d.kisarazu.ac.jp

Abstract. In this paper, we analyze how the accurate use of mathematical graphics in teaching materials contributes to an understanding of mathematics. We describe an experimental study used to verify the educational effect of teaching materials including mathematical graphics, and outline a method to analyze the experimental results. The mathematical software KeTCindy was used to make the teaching materials including mathematical artworks, and to process data collected using a cognitive detection clicker system which we created. The results suggest that careful use of mathematical artworks produced with a system such as KeTCindy can help improve student understanding of mathematical problems.

1 Introduction

In primary and early secondary education, extensive research on the lack of understanding of mathematical concepts has been conducted and applied to the improvement of teaching methods [1]. In contrast, within upper secondary and higher education, it is still unclear as to which aspects of mathematics students find difficult, with a lack of research into areas which students find problematic. Research aimed at uncovering answers here should aid in the development of better teaching materials, and ideally contribute to improvements in the classroom. In upper secondary and higher mathematical education, such teaching materials as mathematical visuals are essential to ensure adequate student understanding. Since diagrammatic presentations afford visual understanding of a concept, they play an important part in learning. However, we have yet to grasp the effectiveness of such teaching materials in raising learner understanding. In this paper, we analyze how the accurate use of mathematical graphics in teaching materials can contribute to a better grasp of mathematical concepts. We describe an experimental study verifying the educational effect of teaching materials, specifically mathematical graphics, and outline a method to analyze the experimental

O. Gervasi et al. (Eds.): ICCSA 2017, Part IV, LNCS 10407, pp. 216–227, 2017.
DOI: 10.1007/978-3-319-62401-3_16

results. The mathematical software KETCindy was used for the production of high-quality teaching materials.

We started with the creation of high-quality teaching materials incorporating graphics with KETCindy. These can be used to promote awareness of key mathematical concepts through problem-solving. These materials were then trialled with students at a technical college. Participants were given a number of problems derived from the teaching materials and asked to provide answers to the problems. Answers were recorded using a Cognitive Detection Clicker (CDC), a device of our making which allows for recording of students' responses along with response times. This allows for the measurement of the effect on understanding of the teaching materials. The data collected by the CDC can then be visualised with KETCindy, which is also provides a platform for statistical analysis of the results.

2   KETCindy

TEX is a popular tool used for the creation of teaching materials for mathematics. However the process of producing high-quality graphics in TEX documents can be challenging for many teachers. One possible way to simplify the process is with KETpic which was developed to help with the creation of teaching materials including mathematical graphics [2,3]. Along with drawing functionality, it incorporates layout and table creation functions. With KETpic, it is possible to make high-quality teaching materials including mathematical graphics. At the beginning of its development, KETpic programming required CUI (Commandline User Interface) input, which was often difficult for TEX beginners to work with. However, in recent years, the mathematical software KETCindy was developed to serve as an interface between KETpic and the dynamic geometry software Cinderella [4,5]. KETCindy uses the Cinderella screen as a GUI (Graphic User Interface) input for KETpic, and CindyScript as the CUI input of KETpic. In addition, it is possible to generate PDF output of materials produced in Cinderella using TEX and Scilab. By using KETCindy, even TEX beginners can easily make mathematical graphics as required, and we can also import and work with comma-separated values (CSV) data. In other words, with KETCindy we have a powerful system for the development of teaching materials including mathematical graphics, and the manipulation of data. In this research, we draw on these two functions of KETCindy.

3   Cognitive Detection Clicker System

The clicker system is a device that can aggregate students' answers to questions in real time. It utilises a personal computer as a master device and a clicker as a slave device. As we were unable to find a suitable clicker system that recorded the information required for the study, we created the CDC system, which records the question number and the answer, as well as the timing of the button press [6]. Although some clicker systems have these functions, the cost of such devices was too prohibitive given the number required to run the experiment [7]. Therefore a decision was made to build a cheaper alternative for the purposes of this research.

Figure 1 shows the CDC slave device. Figure 2 shows the block diagram of the slave device. The slave device has 4 Question-buttons and 4 Answer-buttons. A record of the button choice and response timing is saved as a CSV file on the linked personal computer. Data communication between the master device and the slave device is through a ZigBee module.

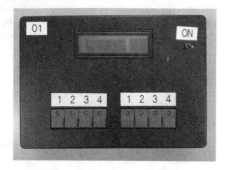

Fig. 1. CDC slave device

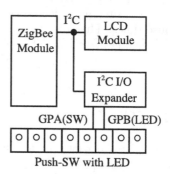

Fig. 2. Block diagram

4   Experimental Study

The following subsections outline the experiment conducted to test the usefulness of the materials created using KETCindy. Creation of the teaching material, its implementation, and the results will be covered.

4.1   Teaching Materials

Students often have trouble in changing the order of integration when calculating a multiple integral, so this seemed a suitable area to focus on in creating and testing the efficacy of graphical learning materials. To this end, teaching materials based around a number of problems expressing the region by inequalities were created.

The teaching material shown in Fig. 3 was made using KETCindy; the questions were originally in Japanese. This teaching material consists of seven problems, A1 to A7. Each problem consists of two or three multiple-choice questions, each with four possible choices. Problems A1 and A2 were given to the students prior to the training session, and A6 to A7 were administered after the training period. The key point to note is that the problem used for A6 is a replication of A1, while that for A7 replicates A2. A3 to A5 are problems designed to clarify the problem-solving process for A1 and A2. Our interest was with the extent of change in student responses to the original problems, A1 and A2, once they had completed working with problems A3 to A5.

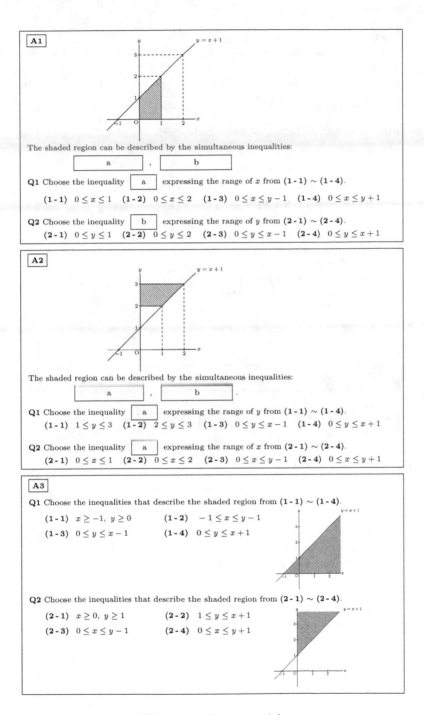

Fig. 3. Teaching materials

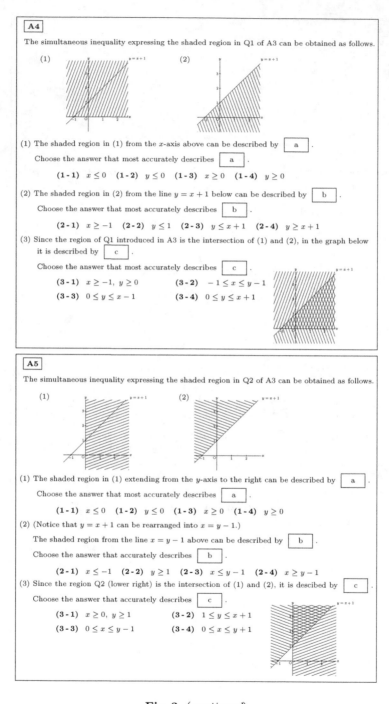

A4

The simultaneous inequality expressing the shaded region in Q1 of A3 can be obtained as follows.

(1)   (2)

(1) The shaded region in (1) from the x-axis above can be described by [a].

   Choose the answer that most accurately describes [a].

   (1-1) $x \leq 0$ **(1-2)** $y \leq 0$ **(1-3)** $x \geq 0$ **(1-4)** $y \geq 0$

(2) The shaded region in (2) from the line $y = x + 1$ below can be described by [b].

   Choose the answer that most accurately describes [b].

   (2-1) $x \geq -1$ **(2-2)** $y \leq 1$ **(2-3)** $y \leq x + 1$ **(2-4)** $y \geq x + 1$

(3) Since the region of Q1 introduced in A3 is the intersection of (1) and (2), in the graph below it is described by [c].

   Choose the answer that most accurately describes [c].

   (3-1) $x \geq -1, \ y \geq 0$ **(3-2)** $-1 \leq x \leq y - 1$
   (3-3) $0 \leq y \leq x - 1$ **(3-4)** $0 \leq y \leq x + 1$

A5

The simultaneous inequality expressing the shaded region in Q2 of A3 can be obtained as follows.

(1)   (2)

(1) The shaded region in (1) extending from the y-axis to the right can be described by [a].

   Choose the answer that most accurately describes [a].

   (1-1) $x \leq 0$ **(1-2)** $y \leq 0$ **(1-3)** $x \geq 0$ **(1-4)** $y \geq 0$

(2) (Notice that $y = x + 1$ can be rearranged into $x = y - 1$.)

   The shaded region from the line $x = y - 1$ above can be described by [b].

   Choose the answer that accurately describes [b].

   (2-1) $x \leq -1$ **(2-2)** $y \geq 1$ **(2-3)** $x \leq y - 1$ **(2-4)** $x \geq y - 1$

(3) Since the region Q2 (lower right) is the intersection of (1) and (2), it is descibed by [c].

   Choose the answer that accurately describes [c].

   (3-1) $x \geq 0, \ y \geq 1$ **(3-2)** $1 \leq y \leq x + 1$
   (3-3) $0 \leq x \leq y - 1$ **(3-4)** $0 \leq x \leq y + 1$

Fig. 3. (*continued*)

4.2 Implementation

The experiment was carried out in early November, 2016 at Fukushima National College of Technology, Japan. These kind of colleges were established during Japan's growth period of the 1960s to train engineers. Students enter at the age of 15 or 16, which is the same as the age for the 1st year of a Japan senior high school, and study for a minimum of 5 years, graduating at what would be the equivalent to the 2nd year of university. The participants in this study were 36 4th-year students from the Department of Electrical Engineering, with the majority aged around 19 years old. The experimental session took 50 min. At the beginning of the experimental session, CDCs and teaching materials were distributed to each student. Students were shown how to use the CDC, and then given time to familiarise themselves with its operation. Students were next instructed to solve the 7 problems from A1 to A7, recording their answers on the CDC. They were given 2 minutes per question to record their answers; multiple answers were allowed during this timeframe in case students wished to change their responses. At the end of the 2 min, the students were required to turn to the next problem. Figure 4 shows the experiment in process.

Fig. 4. Student answering using CDC

4.3 Results

The CSV data from the CDC included the CDC number, the time at which the button was pressed, and the answer selected. Scripts for processing the data were written in KeTCindy, which charted the responses of the participants showing the pattern of the answers over time. This is shown in Fig. 5, in comparison to A1 and A2 there is a clear indication of an increase in the correct answer rate for A6 and A7, with a corresponding decrease in the time to answer. A statistical analysis of the data will be made in Sect. 5.

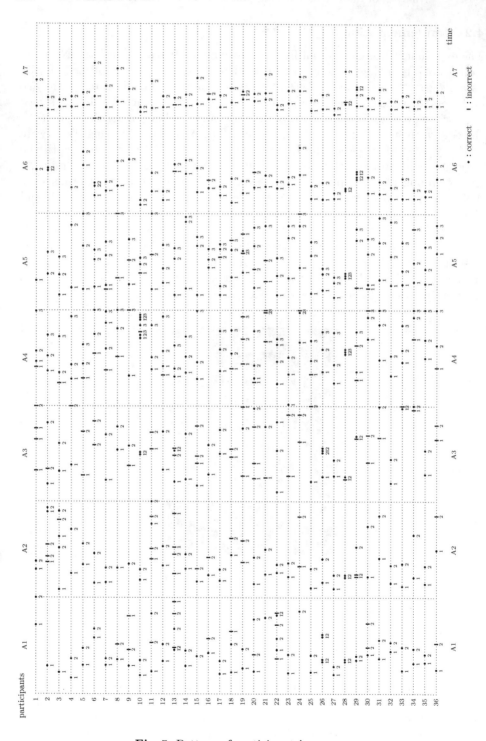

Fig. 5. Pattern of participants' responses

5   Statistical Analysis of CDC Data

In this section we will give an analysis of participants' responses, considering the proportions of correct answers, the changes in responses over time, and the nature of the incorrect answers given.

5.1   Comparison of Proportions of Correct Answers

As noted in Sect. 4.1, A6 is a replication of A1, and A7 replicates A2. A3, A4 and A5 are problems designed to clarify the problem-solving process for A1 and A2. Looking at changes in the participants' answers gives us one measure of the effect arising from solving A3 to A5. Table 1 shows the overall proportions of correct answers for A1 and A6 as well as A2 and A7. As can be seen from the results, the proportions increased for both questions, markedly so in the case of Q2 where there was a 19 ($\simeq \frac{0.89-0.75}{0.75} \times 100$)% and 21 ($\simeq \frac{0.94-0.78}{0.78} \times 100$)% increase for A1 and A2 respectively.

Since all participants in the experiment answered both A1 and A6 along with A2 and A7, their responses were paired. The paired responses are summarized in Tables 2 and 3. The numbers in the "correct × incorrect" cell (i.e. those who changed their original incorrect response to a correct response after working with the teaching materials) warrant special attention, as it appears that there was an overall improvement in participants' answers.

5.2   Comparison of Response Times for Correct Answers

Here we consider whether the time required for giving correct answers decreased after solving the three problems A3 to A5. We carried out a paired t-test to test the null hypothesis, H_o, of no change in the mean times required for giving correct answers. The results of the t-test are given in Table 4. Here the p-values are shown in the third row of Table 4 for the test of H_o against the alternative

Table 1. Proportion of correct answers for each question

A1		A6		A2		A7	
Q1	Q2	Q1	Q2	Q1	Q2	Q1	Q2
0.81	0.75	0.86	0.89	0.86	0.78	0.94	0.94

Table 2. Cross table of paired responses, A1 & A6

Q1		A1		Totals	Q2		A1		Totals
		Correct	Incorrect				Correct	Incorrect	
A6	Correct	25	7	32	A6	Correct	25	7	32
	Incorrect	0	1	1		Incorrect	2	1	3
Totals		25	8	33	Totals		27	8	35

Note: Non-respondents are excluded from the counts in the tables above.

Table 3. Cross table of paired responses, A2 & A7

Q1		A2		Totals	Q2		A2		Totals
		Correct	Incorrect				Correct	Incorrect	
A7	Correct	31	3	34	A7	Correct	28	6	34
	Incorrect	0	1	1		Incorrect	0	2	2
Totals		31	4	35	Totals		28	8	36

Note: Non-respondents are excluded from the counts in the tables above.

Table 4. Result of the analysis of changes in response rates

A1 $\longrightarrow$ A6		A2 $\longrightarrow$ A7	
Q1	Q2	Q1	Q2
0.00783**	0.000159***	0.000117***	2.46e-5***

p-value range: ** (.001, .01], *** [0, .001]

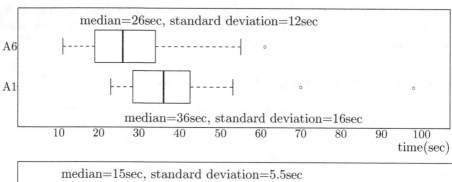

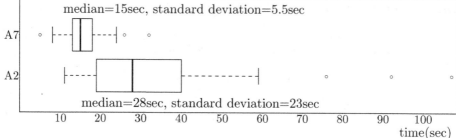

Fig. 6. Boxplot of changes in response times for correct answers

hypothesis that there will be a decrease in the time to answer correctly. Figure 6 shows boxplots of the times required for giving correct answers in Q1 of A1, A6 and A2, A7. These results show that there was a statistically significant difference in the time taken for all questions.

5.3   Analysis of Incorrect Answers

In this subsection, we compare the nature of incorrect responses of the before and after conditions to examine the change in participants' responses to the original problems once they had completed working with problems A3 to A5. Looking first at the answers for Q1 of A1 and A6, in Table 5 for Q1 we see for choice (1-3) a decrease in incorrect answers from 3 to 1. Most of the participants who chose (1-3) in A1 appeared to have learned that the range of x does not depend on y. For Q2 of A1 and A6, the number of answers choosing the incorrect choice (2-2) decreased from 7 to 2 (Table 5-Q2). This suggests that the participants learned through the training session that the upper limit of the range of y depends on x.

In the case of Q1 of A2 and A7, both incorrect choices of (1-3) and (1-4) in A2 decreased when answering A7 (Table 6-Q1). All of the participants who chose (1-3) in A2 seemed to have learned that the range of y does not depend on x. For the incorrect choices selected for Q2 of A2 and A7, the 8 incorrect choices initially selected for (2-2) decreased by 7 when answering A7 (Table 6-Q2). However, incorrect choices for (2-4) saw an increase of 1 (Table 6-Q2). Here, it would appear that through the training session the participants were able to learn that the upper limit of the range of x depends on y.

We now look at the comparison of two corresponding problems, A3 Q1 and A4 (3). A3 Q1 consisted of 1 problem; this was then broken down into separate steps which make up the three sections of A4. A4 (1) and (2) are questions designed to guide students to the final answer of A4 (3), which is the same as that for A3 Q1. Therefore, looking at the answers for both A3 Q1 and A4 (3) gives us one measure of the effect arising from the use of the graphics to solve (1) and (2) of A4. Table 7 shows the count of incorrect choices for A3 Q1 and

Table 5. Count of incorrect answers, A1 & A6

Q1	A1	A6	Q2	A1	A6
Incorrect choices	No. of answers	No. of answers	Incorrect choices	No. of answers	No. of answers
(1-2)	0	0	(2-1)	1	0
(1-3)	3	1	(2-2)	7	2
(1-4)	1	0	(2-3)	1	1

Table 6. Count of incorrect answers, A2 & A7

Q1	A2	A7	Q2	A2	A7
Incorrect choices	No. of answers	No. of answers	Incorrect choices	No. of answers	No. of answers
(1-1)	0	0	(2-1)	0	0
(1-3)	2	0	(2-2)	8	1
(1-4)	2	1	(2-4)	3	4

Table 7. Count of incorrect answers, A3 & A4

A3 Q1		A4 (3)	
Incorrect choices	No. of answers	Incorrect choices	No. of answers
(1-1)	6	(3-1)	3
(1-2)	8	(3-2)	2
(1-3)	3	(3-3)	1

Table 8. Count of incorrect answers, A3 & A5

A3 Q2		A5 (3)	
Incorrect choices	No. of answers	Incorrect choices	No. of answers
(2-1)	4	(3-1)	1
(2-2)	8	(3-2)	2
(2-4)	2	(3-4)	2

A4 (3). Those for A3 were mainly for the first and 2nd choices, but these decreased when students attempted A4. This decrease was especially drastic for choice 2. We suggest these improvements are the result of participants having solved (1) and (2) of A4.

Q2 of A3 and A5 are set up in the same manner as Q1 of A3 and A4; i.e. A5 is Q2 divided into three stages. As above, the answers for both A3 Q2 and A5 (3) should help us understand the effectiveness of the first two parts of A5. As shown in Table 8, at first, the biggest incorrect choice was (2-2), but by the time the students had worked through A5 most of them were getting part 3 correct. In particular, the change between (2-2) and (3-2) is noticeable. It would appear that the participants who first chose the incorrect answer (2-2) developed an understanding of how to describe the required region by a inequality of x, showing an understanding that the upper limit of the inequality was $y - 1$.

For A3, the proportions of correct answers for Q1 and Q2 are low in comparison to other questions, at $0.53 (= 19/36)$ and $0.61 (= 22/36)$ respectively. 57% of incorrect answers were (2-2) as shown in Table 8. As well as the low proportion of correct answers for A3 Q1, a similar outcome was found for A4 (1); although the correct proportion here was $0.72 (= 26/36)$ it was low in comparison to other answers. Common to these two questions is that the x-axis bounds the region. It would appear that a number of participants did not understand the equation x-axis is $y = 0$.

Our expectation prior to the experimental class was that we would see a low number of correct responses for A2 and A3 Q2, but a high number of correct responses for A3 Q1. In fact, the correct response rate for A3 Q1 was low. One cause for this may be that the students did not understand exactly the interactions of the inequalities.

6   Concluding Remarks

While it is possible that the changes in response we are seeing is due to students having completed problems A3 to A5, and applying the information they used in these questions to the subsequent analysis of problems A6 and A7, we have to also be open to alternative explanations. It may be that a practice effect from answering problems A1 and A2 contributed to the decrease in response times and higher success rates. Therefore, one consideration for future research relates to the type of questions used in the pre- and post experimental conditions. While we used the same questions in both parts of our study, it may be better to use questions that are similar but different enough to require the students to more deeply think about how to apply the information gained in the trial period.

This research has demonstrated how it is possible to use KeTCindy throughout the entire research process, from creating the teaching materials to analysing and visualising the data recorded on the CDC devices by the participants. It provides a strong illustration of the power of KeTCindy.

However, one challenge for effective application is to develop a system allowing for the easy use of KeTCindy in the creation of appropriate teaching materials to use in the training sessions.

References

1. Kokuritu Kyouiku Seisaku Kenkyujo [National Institute for Educational Policy Research], Zenkoku Gakuryoku·Gakusyu Jyoukyo Chosa no 4nenkan no Chosa Kekka kara Kongo no Torikumi ga Kitaisareru Naiyou no Matome ~Jido-Seito eno Gakushu Sidou no Kaizen·Jujitu ni Mukete~, Tokyo Kyoiku Shuppan (2012)
2. Sekiguchi, M., Kaneko, M., Tadokoro, Y., Yamashita, S., Takato, S.: A new application of CAS to LATEX plottings. In: Shi, Y., Albada, G.D., Dongarra, J., Sloot, P.M.A. (eds.) ICCS 2007. LNCS, vol. 4488, pp. 178–185. Springer, Heidelberg (2007). doi:10.1007/978-3-540-72586-2_26
3. Ouchi, S., Maeda, Y., Kitahara, K., Hamaguchi, N.: Creating interactive graphics for mathematics education utilizing KETpic. In: Hong, H., Yap, C. (eds.) ICMS 2014. LNCS, vol. 8592, pp. 607–613. Springer, Heidelberg (2014). doi:10.1007/978-3-662-44199-2_91
4. Kaneko, M., Yamashita, S., Kitahara, K., Maeda, Y., Nakamura, Y., Kortenkamp, U., Takato, S.: KETpic collaboration of Cinderella and KETpic reports on CADGME 2014 conference working group. Int. J. Technol. Math. Educ. **22**(4), 179–185 (2015)
5. Kaneko, M., Yamashita, S., Makishita, H., Nishiura, K., Takato, S.: Collaborative use of KETCindy with other small tools. Electron. J. Math. Technol. (in press)
6. Kitahara, K., Usui, K., Kaneko, M., Takato, S.: Neuroscientific consideration of the educational effect achieved using illustrated course materials. ScientiaeMathematicaeJaponicae, 205–315 (2014)
7. Vosaic: iCoda-Video Analysis Software Open Coding Framework. https://vosaic.com/products/vosaic-icoda. Accessed 8 May 2017

Active Learning with Dynamic Geometry Software

Yoichi Maeda[✉]

Department of Mathematics, Faculty of Science, Tokai University,
4-1-1, Kitakaname, Hiratsuka, Kanagawa 259-1292, Japan
maeda@tokai-u.jp

Abstract. As described in this paper, we present the usefulness of dynamic geometry software for education and research in mathematics. Active learning with dynamic geometry software sometimes leads to discoveries of beautiful constructions. Dynamic geometry software is also effective for the visualization of mathematical objects. We attempt to visualize special linear group $SL(2, \mathbb{R})$ in three-dimensional Euclidean space.

Keywords: Dynamic geometry software · Construction problem · visualization

1 Introduction

As described in this paper, we show that dynamic geometry software (DGS) is useful not only for education, but also for research in mathematics. What is the strong point of DGS? Animation command of DGS is extremely useful to find an invariant object under the animation, for example a fixed point. Animation command is also useful to taking a limit and to find a relation among mathematical objects, for example a relation between a circle and a line. The following examples are good demonstrations for students to grasp some mathematical facts intuitively with neither logical arguments nor proofs.

Example 1. **Homothetic center.** Figure 1 portrays a method of constructing the external homothetic center of two circles. Let C_1 and C_2 respectively represent two circles centered at O_1 and O_2. First, draw a pair of parallel lines L_1 and L_2 passing respectively through O_1 and O_2. Next, draw line L_3 passing through $C_1 \cap L_1$ and $C_2 \cap L_2$ as shown in Fig. 1. Then, let us rotate L_1 around O_1 with the animation command by pulling the animation spring at P as shown in Fig. 1 (left). One can find out that a fixed point exists on L_3, i.e., the external homothetic center of the two circles O_1 and O_2. This construction can be derived from a simple fact that the homothetic center is a center of similarity.

© Springer International Publishing AG 2017
O. Gervasi et al. (Eds.): ICCSA 2017, Part IV, LNCS 10407, pp. 228–239, 2017.
DOI: 10.1007/978-3-319-62401-3_17

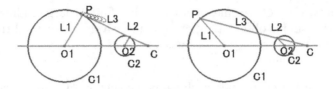

Fig. 1. Construction of the external homothetic center.

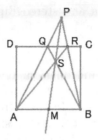

Fig. 2. Construction of the midpoint using a ruler.

Example 2. **Midpoint.** Let ABCD be a square as shown in Fig. 2. Take any point P in the plane. Let Q be the intersection of lines AP and CD. Let R be the intersection of lines BP and CD. Let S be the intersection of lines AR and BQ. Let M be the intersection of lines AB and PS. Then, move point P as desired. In this case, one can find out that M is the fixed point, which is the midpoint of A and B. This construction is an application of Ceva's theorem.

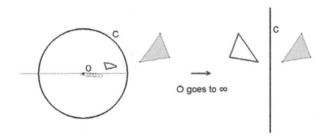

Fig. 3. Reflection in line as a limit of inversion.

Example 3. **Relation between inversion and reflection.** The inversion command is very useful in DGS because inversion of a point with respect to circle requires eight steps by ruler construction. Combining the inversion command with the animation command, one can understand that reflection in line is regarded as a limit of inversion as shown in Fig. 3. The left of Fig. 3 is the inversion of a triangle with respect to circle *C*. If one takes the center of *C* to point at infinity, then C becomes a circle with infinitely large radius, which is a line. With this simple observation, one can intuitively understand the relation between inversion and reflection in line. This fact is a piece of evidence that inversion preserves angles.

In this way, using commands in dynamic geometry software effectively, one can discover many facts from results of simple experiments. As described in this paper, we review two-dimensional geometry and three-dimensional geometry from the aspect of inversion and stereographic projection. In Sect. 2, we introduce several construction problems. These problems are good for education. Students sometimes discover the best and most beautiful construction. Section 3 presents summary of the relations among Euclidean transformations: reflection, translation, rotation, and dilation. Inversion and stereographic projection are fundamental in the sense that Euclidean transformations are given by inversion or stereographic projection. In the latter part of this paper, we show that DGS is useful for studies. In Sect. 4, we investigate a space curve on the unit sphere. The curve is a generator of five planar curves connected by orthogonal projection and stereographic projection. In Sect. 5, we describe our attempt to visualize special linear group $SL(2, \mathbb{R})$ in the three-dimensional Euclidean space. The space curve in Sect. 4 plays an important role. All figures in this paper are drawn using dynamic geometry software Cabri II plus, Cabri3D, and Geogebra.

2   Beautiful Constructions

Beautiful constructions always contain a certain important mathematical fact. We can start from the next easiest construction problem.

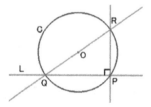

Fig. 4. Construction of perpendicular with one circle ($P \in L$).

Example 4. **Perpendicular line.** Let P be a point on line L. How can we construct the line perpendicular to L passing P under the restriction that we use a compass only once? The simplest solution is the following as shown in Fig. 4: First, draw a circle C centered at any point O not on L passing through P. Let Q be another intersection of C and L. Let R be another intersection of C and OQ. Then, line PR is the perpendicular we want to construct.

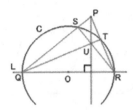 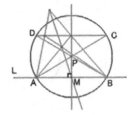

Fig. 5. Constructions of perpendicular with one circle (P $\notin$ L).

The construction above is an application of Thales' theorem, which is a special case of the inscribed angle theorem.

The next example is a beautiful construction as an application of the existence of the orthocenter of a triangle.

Example 5. **Perpendicular line.** Let P be a point not on line L. How can we construct the line perpendicular to L passing P under the restriction that we use a compass only once? A simple solution is the following: First, draw a circle C centered at any point O on L such that circle C does not pass through P, as shown in Fig. 5 (left). Let Q and R be intersections of C and L. Let S be another intersection of PQ and C; also, let T be another intersection of PR and C. Let U be the intersection of QT and RS. Then, line PU is the perpendicular that we wish to construct.

Figure 5 (right) shows another solution of the construction problem in Example 5. In this construction, a circle is drawn centered at P intersecting with L at A and B. Then, the construction problem is reduced to the construction of midpoint of A and B. Quadrangle ABCD in Fig. 5 (right) is a rectangle. Therefore, we can use the technique in Example 2 in the earlier section. However, it is not the best construction.

In general, all Euclidean geometric constructions can be conducted with a ruler alone if, in addition, one is given the radius of a single circle and its center. The fact is called Poncelet–Steiner Theorem which was suggested by Poncelet in 1822 and was proved by Steiner in 1833. The constructions as shown in Examples 4 and 5 are typical constructions of Poncelet–Steiner Theorem.

The next construction is a beautiful construction of the radical axis with inversion.

Example 6. **Radical axis.** Let C_1 and C_2 be two circles centered respectively at O_1 and O_2. Let O_1^* be inversion of O_1 with respect to C_2. Let O_2^* be inversion of O_2 with respect to C_1. Then, the perpendicular bisector of O_1^* and O_2^* is the radical axis of C_1 and C_2.

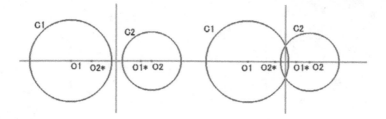

Fig. 6. Constructions of radical axis with inversion.

By observing Fig. 6 (right) in which the position of circle C_2 is changed so that two circles intersect in two points, the construction above can be verified. Nozomi Watanabe, one of the author's students, discovered this construction by chance. This discovery suggests that many chances exist for learners to find out an original construction with dynamic geometry software.

3   Relations Among Six Transformations

In this section, let us review Euclidean transformations from the viewpoint of inversion and stereographic projection ([1] p. 260, [2] p. 74, [3] pp. 74–77, [4] pp. 30–32). We learn the following fundamental transformations through high school: translation, rotation, reflection, and similarity transformation. As presented already in Example 3, reflection in line is regarded as a limit of inversion. Figure 7 shows that both translation and rotation are given by the composition of two reflections ([3] pp. 8–10). In fact, every translation is a composition of reflections with parallel lines. The displacement is double the distance between the two parallel lines. Similarly, every rotation is a composition of reflections with intersecting lines. The angle of rotation is double the angle subtended by two intersecting lines. How about similarity transformation? Similarity transformation is not isometry but angle preserving (conformal). Similarity transformation is a composition of inversions with concentric circles as shown in Fig. 8. The ratio of dilation is the square of the ratio of two circles' radii.

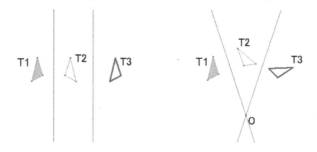

Fig. 7. Translation and rotation as a composition of two reflections.

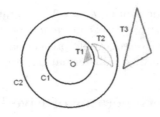

Fig. 8. Similarity transformation as a composition of inversions.

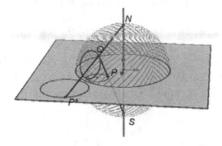

Fig. 9. Inversion by the combination of stereographic projections.

Figure 9 presents the relation between stereographic projection and inversion. Inversion is given as composition of stereographic projection. For point P on the XY-plane, take an inverse of stereographic projection from the south pole $(0, 0, -1)$. Then point P is projected to Q on the unit sphere as shown in Fig. 9. Taking a stereographic projection from the north pole $(0, 0, 1)$, point Q is projected to P*, which is the inversion of P with respect to the equator of the unit sphere.

Next, we summarize the relation among six transformations.

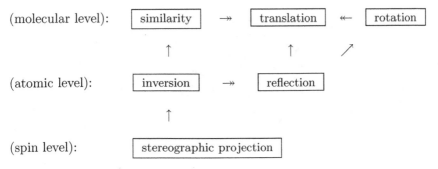

In the diagram above, arrow "→" represents the limit such that the center of the circle or the center of rotation goes to infinity. The arrow "↑" shows a combination of the transformation. At the atomic level, orientation is reversed by a single operation. At the molecular level, orientation is preserved by two orientation reversals. In this way, we can review and summarize high school geometry with inversion and stereographic projection. Stereographic projection is conformal. Therefore, other five transformations are also conformal.

4   Space Curve as a Generator of Five Planar Curves

In the latter part of this paper, we show that dynamic geometry software is effective for research. In this section, let us study a space curve C_0 on the unit sphere given by the following parametric equation:

$$(x, y, z) = (\sin \theta, \ \sin \theta \cos \theta, \ \cos^2 \theta). \tag{1}$$

This space curve plays an important role in a visualization of special linear group $SL(2, \mathbb{R})$ which we investigate in the next section. Curve C_0 is a generator of five planar curves: circle, parabola, hyperbola, lemniscate, and a Lissajous curve:

$$y^2 + \left(z - \frac{1}{2} \right)^2 = \left(\frac{1}{2} \right)^2,$$
$$z = -x^2 + 1,$$
$$x^2 - y^2 = 1,$$
$$x^2 - y^2 = \left(x^2 + y^2 \right)^2,$$
$$x^2 - y^2 = x^4.$$

These planar curves are given by orthogonal projection and stereographic projection as shown in Fig. 10.

By Eq. 1,

$$x^2 + z = \sin^2 \theta + \cos^2 \theta = 1,$$

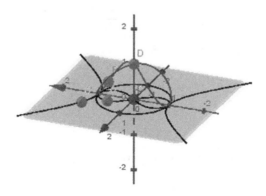

Fig. 10. Space curve as a generator of five planar curves.

the orthogonal projection of C_0 to the XZ-plane is a parabola $z = -x^2 + 1$. Equation 1 is also written as

$$(x, y, z) = \left(\sin\theta, \ \frac{1}{2}\sin 2\theta, \ \frac{1}{2}(1 + \cos 2\theta) \right). \tag{2}$$

Therefore, the orthogonal projection of C_0 to the XY-plane is a Lissajous curve determined as

$$(x, y) = \left(\sin\theta, \ \frac{1}{2}\sin 2\theta \right),$$

or, equivalently, $x^2 - y^2 = x^4$. As for the orthogonal projection of C_0 to the YZ-plane, Eq. 2 implies that

$$y^2 + \left(z - \frac{1}{2} \right)^2 = \frac{1}{4}\sin^2 2\theta + \frac{1}{4}\cos^2 2\theta = \left(\frac{1}{2} \right)^2$$

which means that C_0 is an intersection curve of the unit sphere and the 1-inch diameter cylinder, with passage through the center of the sphere.

Next, let us consider the stereographic projection from N $= (0, 0, 1)$ to the XY-plane. Then,

$$(X, \ Y) = \frac{(x, \ y)}{1 - z} = \frac{(\sin\theta, \ \sin\theta\cos\theta)}{1 - \cos^2\theta} = \frac{(1, \ \cos\theta)}{\sin\theta}.$$

Therefore,

$$X^2 - Y^2 = \frac{1 - \cos^2\theta}{\sin^2\theta} = 1,$$

which is a hyperbola. On the other hand, the stereographic projection from S $= (0, 0, -1)$ to the XY-plane is the lemniscate. In fact,

$$(X, \ Y) = \frac{(x, \ y)}{1 + z} = \frac{(\sin\theta, \ \sin\theta\cos\theta)}{1 + \cos^2\theta}.$$

Therefore,

$$X^2 - Y^2 = \frac{\sin^2\theta\left(1 - \cos^2\theta\right)}{(1 + \cos^2\theta)^2} = \frac{\sin^4\theta}{(1 + \cos^2\theta)^2}$$

$$X^2 + Y^2 = \frac{\sin^2\theta\left(1 + \cos^2\theta\right)}{(1 + \cos^2\theta)^2} = \frac{\sin^2\theta}{1 + \cos^2\theta},$$

and $X^2 - Y^2 = (X^2 + Y^2)^2$, which is the lemniscate. Hyperbola $X^2 - Y^2 = 1$ and lemniscate $X^2 - Y^2 = (X^2 + Y^2)^2$ are connected by inversion with respect to the unit circle. This inversional relation can be derived from the fact that the combination of stereographic projections from N and S is inversion with respect to the equator of the unit sphere, as shown in Fig. 9.

In the next section, we present visualization of a mathematical object $SL(2, \mathbb{R})$ in three-dimensional Euclidean space. In the visualization, lemniscate $X^2 - Y^2 = (X^2 + Y^2)^2$ is related to the set of matrices with 2 in trace, and hyperbola $X^2 - Y^2 = 1$ is related to the set of matrices with -2 in trace.

5   Visualization of Special Linear Group

In this section, we visualize the following special linear group

$$SL(2, \mathbb{R}) = \{A \in M(2, \mathbb{R}) \mid \det A = 1\}$$

in the three-dimensional Euclidean space. By the definition above, $SL(2, \mathbb{R})$ is a three-dimensional manifold in $\mathbb{R}^4$. The idea of an embedding $SL(2, \mathbb{R})$ into $\mathbb{R}^3$ is the following: First, we consider a map from $SL(2, \mathbb{R})$ to the three-dimensional unit sphere S^3. Next, we consider the stereographic projection from S^3 to $\mathbb{R}^3$. Let $S^3 \backslash \{u = 0\} = \{(u, v) \in \mathbb{C}^2 \mid |u|^2 + |v|^2 = 1, u \neq 0\}$ be an open subset of S^3 taking off a great circle $\{u = 0\}$. For $(u, v) \in S^3 \backslash \{u = 0\}$, let us consider the following 2×2 matrix:

$$A = \begin{pmatrix} a & b \\ c & d \end{pmatrix} = \frac{1}{|u|^2} \begin{pmatrix} \mathrm{Re}(u) + |u|\mathrm{Re}(v) & \mathrm{Im}(u) + |u|\mathrm{Im}(v) \\ -\mathrm{Im}(u) + |u|\mathrm{Im}(v) & \mathrm{Re}(u) - |u|\mathrm{Re}(v) \end{pmatrix}.$$

This matrix A is an element of $SL(2, \mathbb{R})$ because

$$\det A = \frac{1}{|u|^4} \left((\mathrm{Re}(u))^2 - |u|^2(\mathrm{Re}(v))^2 + (\mathrm{Im}(u))^2 - |u|^2(\mathrm{Im}(v))^2 \right)$$

$$= \frac{1}{|u|^4} \left(|u|^2 - |u|^2|v|^2 \right) = \frac{1}{|u|^2} \left(1 - |v|^2 \right) = 1.$$

In this way, we have defined a map from $S^3 \backslash \{u = 0\}$ to $SL(2, \mathbb{R})$.

Conversely, let us determine u, v by four elements a, b, c, d of $A \in SL(2, \mathbb{R})$. Because

$$a + d = \frac{2}{|u|^2}\mathrm{Re}(u), \quad a - d = \frac{2}{|u|}\mathrm{Re}(v),$$

$$b - c = \frac{2}{|u|^2}\mathrm{Im}(u), \quad b + c = \frac{2}{|u|}\mathrm{Im}(v), \tag{3}$$

the following equality holds:

$$(a + d)^2 + (b - c)^2 = \frac{4}{|u|^4}|u|^2 = \frac{4}{|u|^2}.$$

By setting $r = \sqrt{(a + d)^2 + (b - c)^2}$, then,

$$|u| = \frac{2}{r}. \tag{4}$$

It is noteworthy that $r = \sqrt{(a - d)^2 + (b + c)^2 + 4} \geq 2$. Using Eqs. 3 and 4, we obtain the following representations:

$$\begin{cases} u = \dfrac{2}{r^2}\{(a + d) + (b - c)i\}, \\ v = \dfrac{1}{r}\{(a - d) + (b + c)i\}. \end{cases}$$

In this way, we have obtained one-to-one correspondence between $S^3\backslash\{u=0\}$ and $SL(2,\mathbb{R})$.

The stereographic projection of S^3 from the South Pole $(u,v)=(-1,0)$ to $\mathbb{R}^3$ is given by the following formulae:

$$(X,Y,Z) = \frac{(\mathrm{Re}(v),\mathrm{Im}(v),\mathrm{Im}(u))}{1+\mathrm{Re}(u)} = \frac{(r(a-d),r(b+c),2(b-c))}{r^2+2(a+d)}. \tag{5}$$

In this projection, the exceptional set $\{u=0\}$ $(|v|=1)$ corresponds to the unit circle on the XY-plane, which means that $SL(2,\mathbb{R})$ is not simply connected.

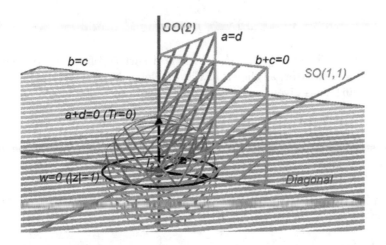

Fig. 11. Stereographic projection of $SL(2,\mathbb{R})$.

By Eq. 5, the XY-plane corresponds to the set of symmetric matrices $(b=c)$. Similarly, the YZ-plane corresponds to the set of $a=d$. The ZX-plane corresponds to the set of $b+c=0$ as shown in Fig. 11. The unit sphere corresponds to the set of matrices with 0 in trace $(\mathrm{Tr}(A)=a+d=0)$ because the unit sphere is the equator of S^3, which is the set of $\mathrm{Re}(u)=0$, equivalent to $a+d=0$ by Eq. 3. Particularly the X-axis, Y-axis, and Z-axis respectively correspond to the set of the matrices of following types:

$$\pm\begin{pmatrix} e^t & 0 \\ 0 & e^{-t} \end{pmatrix}, \quad \pm\begin{pmatrix} \cosh t & \sinh t \\ \sinh t & \cosh t \end{pmatrix}, \quad \begin{pmatrix} \cos t & \sin t \\ -\sin t & \cos t \end{pmatrix}.$$

The identity matrix I_2 is at the origin $(X,Y,Z)=(0,0,0)$, and $-I_2$ is at infinity.

In this way, we can visualize every element of $SL(2,\mathbb{R})$ as a point in $\mathbb{R}^3$. Now, let us investigate the surfaces of constant trace. Actually, the surfaces of constant trace are surfaces of revolution around the Z-axis. For example, if $\mathrm{Tr}(A)=-2$, then, $\mathrm{Re}(u)=-|u|^2$ by Eq. 3. Therefore, by setting $R=\sqrt{X^2+Y^2}$ and by Eq. 5,

$$R^2 = X^2 + Y^2 = \frac{|v|^2}{(1+\mathrm{Re}(u))^2} = \frac{1-|u|^2}{(1-|u|^2)^2} = \frac{1}{1-|u|^2},$$

$$Z^2 = \frac{\mathrm{Im}(u)^2}{(1+\mathrm{Re}(u))^2} = \frac{|u|^2 - \mathrm{Re}(u)^2}{(1-|u|^2)^2} = \frac{|u|^2 - |u|^4}{(1-|u|^2)^2} = \frac{|u|^2}{1-|u|^2}.$$

Therefore, $R^2 - Z^2 = 1$, which is a hyperboloid of one sheet. Similarly, if $\mathrm{Tr}(A) = 2$, then, $\mathrm{Re}(u) = |u|^2$ by Eq. 3. Then,

$$R^2 = \frac{1-|u|^2}{(1+|u|^2)^2}, \quad Z^2 = \frac{|u|^2(1-|u|^2)}{(1+|u|^2)^2},$$

hence,

$$R^2 + Z^2 = \frac{1-|u|^2}{1+|u|^2}, \quad R^2 - Z^2 = \frac{(1-|u|^2)^2}{(1+|u|^2)^2}.$$

Therefore, $R^2 - Z^2 = (R^2 + Z^2)^2$, which is a surface of revolution with the lemniscate as a generator, as shown in Fig. 12 (left). More generally, if $\mathrm{Tr}(A) = 2t$, then the surface is given by the following equation:

$$(t+1)(Z^2 + R^2)^2 + 2t(Z^2 - R^2) + t - 1 = 0.$$

To understand this surface, let us consider a stereographic projection of the generator $(t+1)(Z^2 + Y^2)^2 + 2t(Z^2 - Y^2) + t - 1 = 0$ on the YZ-plane from $(x, y, z) = (-1, 0, 0)$ to the unit sphere. By the relation

$$(Y, Z) = \frac{(y, z)}{1+x},$$

one can obtain

$$\left(x - \frac{1}{2t}\right)^2 + z^2 = \left(\frac{1}{2t}\right)^2,$$

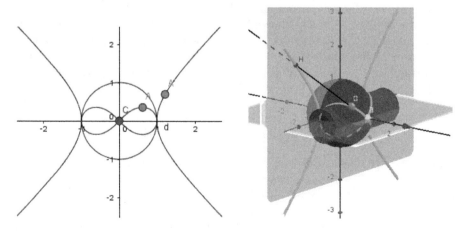

Fig. 12. Generators of surface of revolution.

which means that the generator of surface of revolution is given by the stereographic projection of a space curve, which is the intersection curve of a cylinder and the unit sphere as shown in Fig. 12 (right).

6   Conclusion

This paper has presented many geometric pictures with dynamic geometry software. DGS is a wonderful tool with which we can draw pictures, explore conjectures, make experiments, and discover geometric facts. Constructions are good exercises for students because the algorithm of construction is important to construct pictures similar to the algorithm of programming. Inversion is a fundamental operation. Euclidean geometry is reviewed with inversion. Furthermore, stereographic projection is more fundamental operation. With DGS, we can understand an important relation between inversion and stereographic projection. On the other hand, DGS must become increasingly important for studies. Visualization of mathematical objects provides intuitive images, which is expected to be useful for learners to understand abstract mathematical objects.

References

1. Berger, M.: Geometry I. Springer, Heidelberg (1987)
2. Berger, M.: Geometry II. Springer, Heidelberg (1987)
3. Jennings, G.: Modern Geometry with Applications. Springer, New York (1994)
4. Sved, M.: Journey into Geometries. The Mathematical Association of America, Washington, D.C (1997)

Data Processing with KETCindy

Yasuyuki Kubo[✉]

National Institute of Technology, Yuge College, Ehime, Japan
kubo@gen.yuge.ac.jp

Abstract. KETCindy is helpful not only for making TEX documents needing mathematically precise artwork but also for performing data processing efficiently. Furthermore, graphs obtained using KETCindy can be used in TEX documents without conversion.

1 Introduction

Spreadsheet software, such as Excel, is convenient for checking simple statistics and calculations. Entries can be easily typed into corresponding cells, and by selecting a range, such things as data number, average, and total can be displayed on the status bar and confirmed immediately. Scatter charts and line graphs can also be displayed on the screen if selected from the menu. However, as this report will show, KETCindy [1] can be used to handle complicated data processing with greater efficiency than spreadsheets such as Excel.

The advantage of KETCindy for data processing can be illustrated with an example from a project the author participated in. The project analyzed pollutants found in a certain area since 2013 onwards. Figure 1 shows part of the data (April 1st 2015 to February 29th 2016) as displayed in an Excel spreadsheet. The names of pollutants are displayed in the first row, e.g. PM2.5, PM10, etc.

To obtain the average level of each pollutant measured in ppm over the period, the following formula

```
=AVERAGE(B2..B336)
```

was entered in cell B337 of the Excel file and applied to all cells to the right.

Also, in order to obtain the moving average [2] of PM2.5, the following formula

```
=AVERAGE(B2,B8)
```

was entered in cell J8 and applied to all the other cells in the column. By applying

```
=IF(MOD(ROW(B7),7)=0,AVERAGE(B2:B8),"")
```

to the column, the average of every week could be displayed in every 7th cell.

© Springer International Publishing AG 2017
O. Gervasi et al. (Eds.): ICCSA 2017, Part IV, LNCS 10407, pp. 240–250, 2017.
DOI: 10.1007/978-3-319-62401-3_18

	A	B	C	D	E	F	G	H	I	J
1	date	PM2.5	PM10	OBC	O3	NO2	NO	NOx	SO2	
2	4.01				23.90417	21.425	14.47917	35.925	2.826087	
3	4.02				60.4625	6.858333	0.4625	7.316667	0.383333	
4	4.03				20.6087	18.625	1.983333	20.60417	0.5125	
5	4.04	10.15536	18.98452	0.25875	28.23333	10.17083	1.558333	11.7375	0.6	
6	4.05	20.67721	28.37721	0.496958	18.28333	17.36667	6.016667	23.38333	1.525	
7	4.06	19.34827	25.84827	0.585875	16.61667	14.89167	2.3875	17.2875	0.279167	
8	4.07	6.928.03	16.328.03	0.220833	45.53333	3.4625	0.345833	3.821833	0.208333	

332	2.25	7.522139	13.70547	0.019625	38.45	4.65	0.545833	5.183333	1.740909	
333	2.26	15.72195	29.50112	0.1405	41.6	6.5	0.729167	7.216667	2.370833	
334	2.27	34.47456	53.71208	0.317583	37.90833	9.53913	1.213043	10.73913	2.825	
335	2.28	44.6392	66.84753	0.369542	28.70833	14.35	1.591667	15.9375	3.9	
336	2.29	19.70227	31.0481	-0.02621	42.41667	5.704167	0.625	6.320833	1.4375	
337										

Fig. 1. Table of pollutants

However, it was not easy to make an average list every week. For example, by entering either

```
=AVERAGE(INDIRECT(ADDRESS(2+7*(ROW(C1)-1),2)&":"&ADDRESS(1+7*
(ROW(C1)),2)))
```

or

```
=AVERAGE(OFFSET($B$2,(ROW(B2)-2)*7,0,7,1))
```

in cell J2 and copying down, the formula tended to be more error prone and difficult to correct. Furthermore, calculation of the monthly average was made more difficult because the number of days of each month varied. In the case of Excel, a macro can be used but with difficulty.

To avoid the above difficulties encountered while attempting to use Excel, the author turned to Cinderella in order to complete the task more efficiently. Cinderella is a type of DGS (dynamic geometry software) developed by J. R-Gebert and U. Kortenkamp [3]. Unlike other DGS, it incorporates CindyScript, an easy-to-use programming language. CindyScript handles data in addition to numerical values and character strings called lists. A vector (sequence data), for example, can be expressed as `vec=[1,3,5]`. In addition, a matrix (table data) can be expressed as a double nested list. For example, `mat=[[1,3,5],[2,4,6]]` is a matrix of 2 rows and 3 columns. Also we can use functions of CindyScript to handle lists as explained in [4]. The following is some samples of functions in CindyScript which are subsequently used to define new functions in this paper.

`int1..int2`	lists integers from `int1` to `int2`
	Ex : `3..7=[3,4,5,6,7]`
`list_int`	takes the `int`-th element of `list`
	Ex : `[2,5,7,1]_3=7`

append(list,expr)	adds expr to list such as list++[expr] Ex1 : append([1,2],5)=[1,2,5] Ex2 : append([1,2],[5])=[1,2,[5]]
apply(list,oper)	applies the operation oper to all elements of list Ex : apply(3..5,f(#)])=[f(3),f(4),f(5)]
select(list,bool)	selects the elements of list that are true Ex : select(3..7,isodd(#))=[3,5,7]
sum(list)	sums all the elements of list if they are all numbers Ex : sum(-1..3)=5
row(mat,int)	gives the int-th row of mat, if mat is a matrix Ex : row([[1,3,5],[2,4,6]],2)=[2,4,6]
column(mat,int)	gives the int-th column of mat, if mat is a matrix Ex : row([[1,3,5],[2,4,6]],2)=[3,4]
transpose(mat)	transposes a matrix mat Ex : transpose([[1,3,5],[2,4,6]]) =[[1,2],[3,4],[5,6]]

Here # represents the running variable, successively taking the value of all elements in the list.

While KETCindy was developed as a Cinderella plug-in to generate LATEX source code for high quality mathematical artwork [5], it can perform several data processing functions as well. Data processing with KETCindy is in fact quite easy and very flexible as the next sections show.

2   Data Handling with KETCindy

2.1   Data Input, Output and Display

The following is an example of how KETCindy can be used to handle data. First, KETCindy converts the csv file (file.csv in this case) as shown in Fig. 2

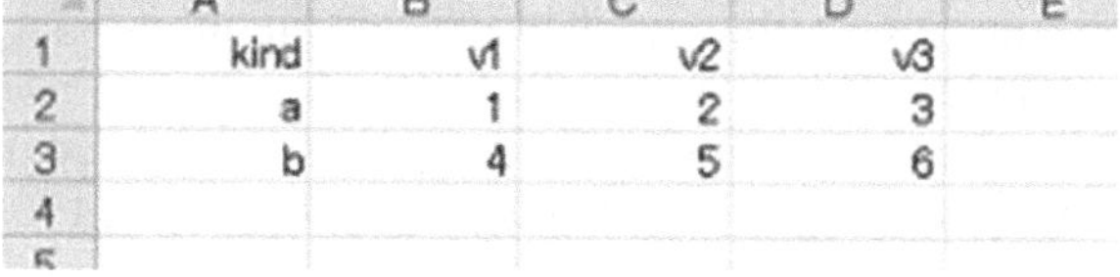

	A	B	C	D	E
1	kind	v1	v2	v3	
2	a	1	2	3	
3	b	4	5	6	
4					
5					

Fig. 2. View in excel

into the data named dt by the command

```
dt=Readcsv("file.csv");
```

if `file.csv` exists in a working directory. Also this command takes `dt` from the directory and arranges it into a matrix. Inputting and executing the command

```
println(dt);
```

on the edit area (the area on the top right of Fig. 3), the resulting matrix is displayed on the console (lower right of Fig. 3).

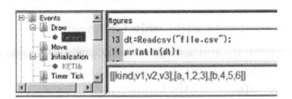

Fig. 3. Readcsv and println

Substituting `Dispmat(dt)` for `println(dt)`, the matrix is displayed as tab-separated strings on the console, as shown in Fig. 4.

```
12 dt=Readcsv("file.csv");
13 Dispmat(dt);
```

kind	v1	v2	v3
a	1	2	3
b	4	5	6

Fig. 4. Readcsv and Dispmat

Conversely, tab-separated strings can be translated into a matrix using the command, `Tab2list`. For example, Fig. 5 shows the data copied from the Excel window in Fig. 2 onto a CindyScript screen.

Here the data, in double quotes following `dt`, is converted into a list using the command `Tab2list`. Figure 6 shows the matrix which is made from `dt` and displayed on the console.

When the amount of data is large, it is necessary to scroll down the screen and look for the start and end of data to select and copy the range, which might cause mistakes. On the other hand, the command `Readcsv` is useful because it automatically selects the data and copies it into the edit area.

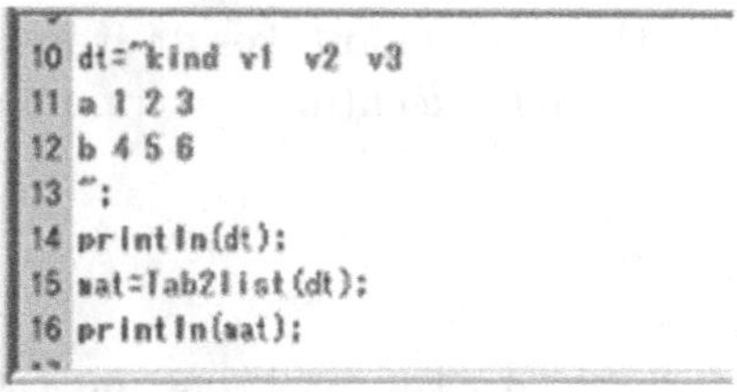

```
10 dt="kind v1 v2 v3
11 a 1 2 3
12 b 4 5 6
13 ";
14 println(dt);
15 mat=Tab2list(dt);
16 println(mat);
```

kind	v1	v2	v3
a	1	2	3
b	4	5	6

[[kind,v1,v2,v3],[a,1,2,3],[b,4,5,6]]

Fig. 5. Tab2list (edit area) 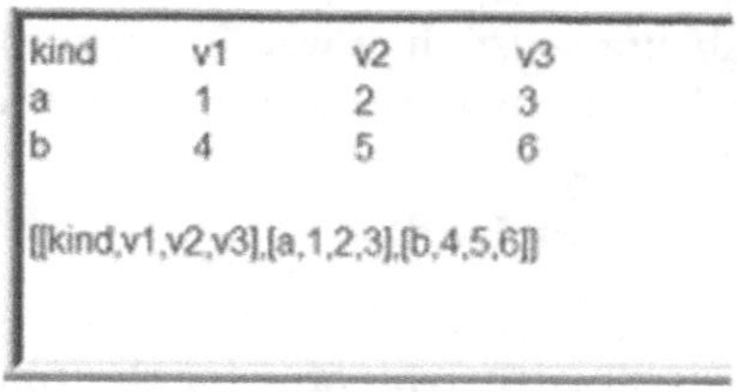   **Fig. 6.** Tab2list (console)

2.2   Data Processing with KETCindy Commands

While it is necessary to scroll down the window to select a wide data range in Excel, the commands Nrow and Ncol added by the author enable us to select it automatically in KETCindy. Also, the translation of row data into column data is accomplished simply by using the CindyScript command transpose. Moreover, we can easily keep or delete some part of a large table simply by using KETCindy commands prepared to store and substitute variables. Time consuming cell-by-cell work is needed to accomplish these tasks in Excel. Thus, much labor can be saved by adding commands to KETCindy.

The author will introduce the commands added to KETCindy using file.csv as an example. Commands beginning with lower case letters were of Cindyscript origin. Those newly defined by the author in KETCindy begin with capital letters like other commands in KETCindy. The commands added to KETCindy to handle matrices are as follows

Nrow(mat)	returns the number of rows of matrix mat
Ncol(mat)	returns the number of columns of matrix mat
RemoveR(mat,list)	removes the n-th row from mat if n is in list
RemoveC(mat,list)	removes the n-th column from mat if n is in list
AddR(mat,int,list)	adds list to int-th row of mat
AddC(mat,int,list)	adds list to int-th column of mat

For example, let dt be the data of file.csv obtained using the command

```
dt=Readcsv("file.csv");
```

We can easily delete the first row of dt with the command

```
dt1=RemoveR(dt,[1]);
```

Also we can easily find the number of rows and columns in `dt1` using the following commands (left side of Fig. 7) whose result is on the right of Fig. 7.

```
dt=Readcsv("file.csv");
dt1=RemoveR(dt,[1]);
println(Nrow(dt1));
println(Ncol(dt1));
```

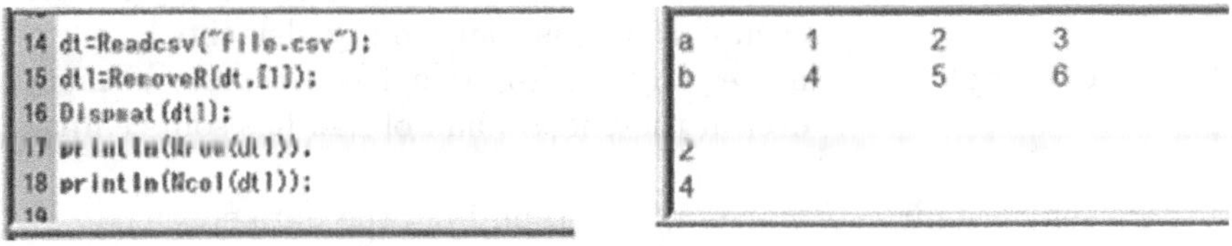

Fig. 7. Remove 1st Row and Return Nrow, Ncol

Similarly, the results obtained by the following commands

```
dt2=RemoveC(dt,[1,3]);     //remove 1st and 3rd columns
println(Nrow(dt2));
println(Ncol(dt2));
```

can be seen on the right of Fig. 8.

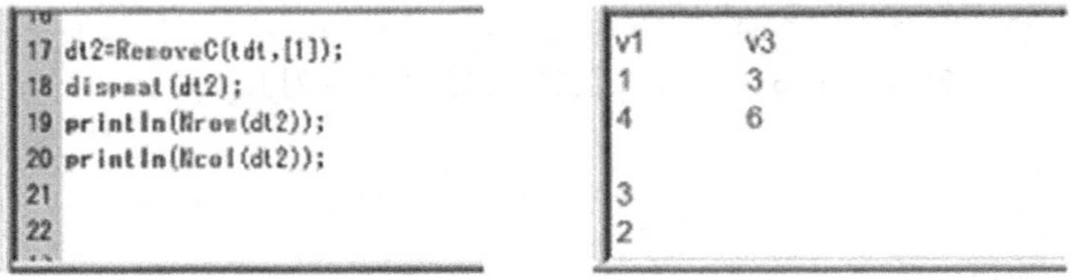

Fig. 8. Remove 1st and 3rd Columns, and Return Nrow, Ncol

Also the command, `Removemat` was added by the author. The combination of `RemoveR` and `RemoveC` returns the same results as `Removemat`. The following commands

```
dt3=RemoveR(dt,[1]);
dt4=RemoveC(dt3,[1,3]);
```

create the matrix dt4, [[1,3],[4,6]], and the next command

```
dt5=Removemat(dt,[1],[1,3]);
```

creates a matrix dt5 identical to dt4. Furthermore, the command Submat was added which leaves the specified part of the matrix.

Important commands that draw and label graphs are defined as follows

Linedata(list)	makes a list of lists that have no empty element, even if list has some empty elements
Linedata2(mat)	makes a list of lists that has no empty element, even if the 2nd column of mat has some empty elements
Linegraph(...list...)	makes a line graph from the data specified
Bargraph(...list...)	makes a bar graph from the data specified
Putlabel(...list...)	puts labels on a graph from the data specified

Here the commands Linegraph, Bargraph, and Putlabel have many arguments as explained below.

For example, let dt be the list [21,"",22,23,"","",24,25,26,"",27, 28,""].

Then, the following command

```
dt1=Linedata(dt);
```

produces dt1 which consists of four lists

[[21,1]],   [[22,3],[23,4]],
[[24,7],[25,8],[26,9]],   [[27,11],[28,12]].

Furthermore, let ma be the matrix made by the following command

```
ma=transpose([101..113,dt]);
```

which consists of [101,1], [102,""], [103,3], [104,4], [105,""], [106,""], [107,7], [108,8], [109,9], [110,""], [111,11], [112,12], [113,""]. Then, ma1 made by

```
ma1=Linedata2(ma);
```

consists of four lists

[[1,101]],   [[3,103],[4,104]],
[[7,107],[8,108],[9,109]],   [[11,111],[12,112]].

Based on these commands, the commands `Linegraph`, `Bargraph` and `Putlabel` were defined to generate line graphs and bar graphs from data like `dt1` and create graph labels from data like `mat1`. Both `Linegraph` and `Bargraph` take the following arguments: "name", "hscale", "vscale" and, "valuelist" which has the structure of `dt1`. `Linegraph` connects points that are continuously measured, while points with gaps are not connected. The argument "hscale" gives the horizontal scale of the graph, while "vscale" gives the vertical scale. `Putlabel` takes the following arguments: "gap", "scale", "depth", and "labellist" which has the structure of `mat1` whose element is a list consisting of pairs of natural numbers and labels (strings or real numbers). If there are too many labels, labels can be skipped by specifying gaps between the labels. Finally, "hscale" gives the horizontal scale of labels for `gap=1`, and "depth" adjusts the height of the labels with respect to the horizontal axis.

2.3   Other Functions

In addition to the before-mentioned commands, other functions are defined as follows

`Average(list)`	gives the average of values in `list`
`GroupAvg(list,opt)`	gives the average of values in `list` according to `opt`
`MovingAvg(list,int)`	gives the moving average of values in `list` by pairing the number `int` (same as `MovingAverage`)

Although CindyScript does not have a function to obtain averages, they can be calculated using the following formula

```
sum(list)/length(list);
```

However, by this calculation method, the expected value cannot be obtained in the case of a list that includes blanks and strings. As in Excel, the author's function `Average` gives an average value by ignoring blanks and strings.

In this way, labor intensive work in Excel can be replaced by the addition of efficient and easy-to-use commands.

3   Practical Example

For the data on air pollution introduced earlier, examples of data processing are shown. The data "PM20160229.csv" is given in csv format and read by the following command

```
dtorg=Readcsv("PM20160229.csv");
```

to give `dtorg`. The only data needed in that section is the date and part of the measured value for PM2.5. By the following command

```
dtall=Submat(dtorg,2..Nrow(dtorg),1..2);
```

the author made a submatrix `dtall` from the second to the last row of the data, the first and second columns of `dtorg`, using the command `Submat`.

3.1   Transition of Daily Values and of Moving Average per Week

The graph in Fig. 9 shows the daily change in levels of PM2.5 as measured in ppm and the change in the moving average over the week.

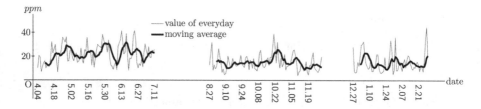

Fig. 9. Average and moving average

The graph was made using the following commands

```
dtvalue=RemoveC(dtall,1);
graphdt1=Linedata(dtvalue);
graphdt2=Movingaverage(graphdt1,7);

Setcolor("red");
Linegraph("day",graphdt1,0.05,0.05,["color->[1,0,0]"]);
Setcolor("black");
Linegraph("week",graphdt2,0.05,0.05,["dr,3"]);

ApplymatC(dtall,"Sprintf(#,2)",1);
ptnames=Linedata2(dtlabel);
Putlabel(ptnames,14,0.05,-0.5,["rot"]);
```

Here the commands `ApplymatR`, `ApplymatC` were added to modify the matrix to behave like `apply`. Without `ApplymatC`, the command

```
ApplymatC(dtall,"Sprintf(#,2)",1);
```

would be more complicated.

For the date expressed as a decimal number `Sprintf` was used, so that April 10 is displayed as "4.10" not "4.1". `Putlabel` was used to add labels. And to prevent overlap, gaps between labels were specified by skipping 14 and rotating the labels by 90° with the option `"rot"`.

3.2 Monthly Averages

To see the change in average levels of PM2.5 month by month, there was the difficulty of identifying the months consisting of different numbers of days.

To draw the graph (Fig. 10), the prepared data, `dtall`, was processed in the following way

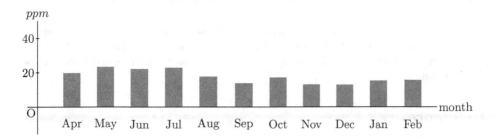

Fig. 10. Averages of each month

```
monlist=concat(4..12,1..2);
mavg=[];
forall(monlist,mon,
    mlist=select(dtall,floor(#_1)==mon);
    mavgtmp=Average(column(mlist,2));
    mavg=append(mavg,[mon,mavgtmp]);
);

graphdt=Linedata(column(mavg,2));
Setcolor([0.5,0.5,0.5]);
Bargraph("bar",graphdt,1,0.05,["dr,25"]);
Setcolor("black");

monlistE=["Apr","May","Jun","Jul","Aug","Sep","Oct","Nov",
"Dec","Jan","Feb"];
labelmon=Linedata(monlistE,["st"]);
Putlabel(labelmon,1,1,-0.5);
```

Though the list, `monlist`, is not in the natural order, it caused no problem since `forall` in CindyScript runs a temporary variable in the order listed.

4 Conclusions and Future Work

The author found that using K$_E$TCindy to process data by commands according to complicated specifications was superior to using spreadsheet software such as Excel. Also, T$_E$X documents, including accurate graphs, could be created more efficiently using K$_E$TCindy.

Furthermore, there is no need to buy expensive software to improve the functionality of spreadsheet software, which is already expensive enough, because all related software is freely accessible, making K$_E$TCindy especially valuable for education.

Finally, there is room to improve the ease of use, processing speed and modifiability of commands and functions introduced. In addition, the author would like to integrate similar commands that are still confusing.

Acknowledgments. I am deeply grateful to Professor Setsuo Takato of Toho University for supporting and advising me in this research. I am also grateful to Mr. Akira Iritani, representative of Cinderella Japan, for advice on Cinderella and CindyScript input manners.

References

1. Takato, S.: What is and how to use KeTCindy – linkage between dynamic geometry software and KeTCindy graphics capabilities. In: Greuel, G.-M., Koch, T., Paule, P., Sommese, A. (eds.) ICMS 2016. LNCS, vol. 9725, pp. 371–379. Springer, Cham (2016). doi:10.1007/978-3-319-42432-3_46
2. Moving Average. https://en.wikipedia.org/wiki/Moving_average
3. CinderellaJapan. https://sites.google.com/site/cinderellajapan/
4. Cinderella.2 Documentation. https://doc.cinderella.de/tiki-index.php
5. KETpic.com. http://ketpic.com/

Brachistochrone Problem as Teaching Material – Application of KeTCindy with Maxima

Setsuo Takato$^{(\boxtimes)}$

Toho University, Tokyo, Japan
takato@phar.toho-u.ac.jp
http://ketpic.com

Abstract. KeTCindy, which we have been developing in collaboration with Cinderella, can produce mathematics and physics teaching materials of various types such as printed materials, screen presentations, and interactive materials. These materials are more effective when mutually combined and arranged properly. As described in this paper, we use the brachistochrone problem as an example to show what materials are produced and how they might be used in classes at the collegiate level.

Keywords: KeTCindy · Cinderella · LaTeX · Maxima · Teaching materials

1 Introduction

Johann Bernoulli postulated the well-known brachistochrone problem at the end of 17th century [5]. It can be stated simply as follows:

> Given two points A and B in a vertical plane, what is the curve traced out by a point acted on only by gravity, which starts at A and reaches B in the shortest time.

In fact, the problem attracted the interest of many contemporary mathematicians, who gave the solution in their own ways. Nowadays, educators often use it as a teaching material for calculus of variations in their mathematics and physics classes. As described herein, we present a series of teaching materials using KeTCindy which we developed and which anyone can download freely [1]. KeTCindy is a macro package of Cinderella [2], which is dynamic geometry system, and Scilab [3], a numerically oriented programming language, to produce and to insert finely detailed figures into LaTeX documents not only easily but also interactively. Moreover, KeTCindy has extended functionalities to call other mathematical software packages, for example, Maxima, to use its results in KeTCindy. The following Table 1 shows what KeTCindy can do for now.

© Springer International Publishing AG 2017
O. Gervasi et al. (Eds.): ICCSA 2017, Part IV, LNCS 10407, pp. 251–261, 2017.
DOI: 10.1007/978-3-319-62401-3_19

Table 1. Can-do table of KₑTCindy

s1	Geometric figure	s6	Animation	s11	Calling Asir
s2	Graph of function	s7	Presentation	s12	Calling Fricas
s3	Making table	s8	Calling R	s13	Calling Mesthlab
s4	Bézier curve	s9	Surface	s14	Data processing
s5	3D figure	s10	Calling maxima	s15	TₑX style files

We present an example to produce figures with KₑTCindy. These figures will be used in our materials.

For simplicity, we put point A on origin O. Then we set the coordinates of point B as (5, −5). Figure 1 presents screens of Cinderella, Cindy Screen at the left, Script Editor at the upper right and Console at the lower right.

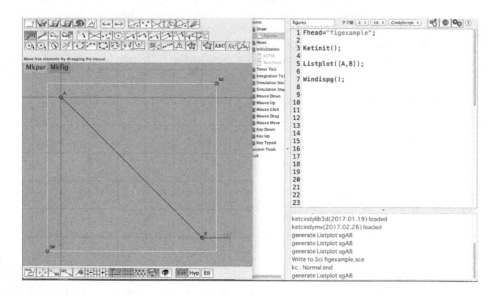

Fig. 1. Cinderella screens

The process to produce a figure is the following.

1. Add geometric points such as C and D on Cindy Screen, which are movable at any position by dragging.
2. Write scripts of KₑTCindy on Script Editor. We remark here that Cinderella has the "Cindy Script" programming language, which is easy to use and which distinguishes Cinderella from other dynamic geometry software. For example, these scripts are

```
Ketinit();  // Initialization of KeTCindy.
Bezier("1",[A,B],[C,D],["Num=50"]); //Draw a Bezier curve.
PutonCurve("P","bz1");  //Put a point P on the curve.
    //The name of the figure is appeared on the Console.
Pointdata("1",P,["Size=4"]); //Display P also as TeX figure.
Letter([P,"ne","P",B,"e","B"]);
    //Display letters also as TeX figure.
Windispg(); //Display on Cindy Screen.
```

3. Move points C, D, and P if necessary.
4. Press Mkfig button, then one can obtain data from the figure. A pdf will be displayed for checking.
5. Modify the scripts or geometric points. Then press the Mkfig button until one is satisfied.
6. Insert the figure into TEX documents using the \input command.

We show the Cindy Screen and the figure to be input in the TEX document.

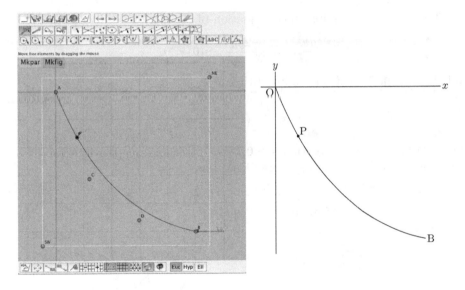

Fig. 2. Cindy screen and the TEX figure

From Sect. 2, we describe a series of teaching materials.

2   Finding Equations of Motion and Total Time

The contents of this section will be used to produce printed material to be distributed during the first class session. It is noteworthy that these figures are produced with KETCindy.

Let a curve C from O to B be represented by $r = (x(u), y(u))$ $(0 \le u \le U)$, a point P start O with the velocity $v = 0$, and the value u at time t be $u(t)$. Assume that the motion is frictionless, so the energy conservation law is satisfied. Let g represent the acceleration of gravity.

Then, from $\frac{1}{2}mv^2 = mgh = -mgy$,

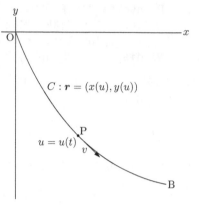

$$v = \sqrt{-2gy}. \tag{1}$$

Let s be the length of the curve C from O to P, then

$$\frac{ds}{du} = \sqrt{\dot{x}^2 + \dot{y}^2}$$

where $\dot{x} = \dfrac{dx}{du}$, $\dot{y} = \dfrac{dy}{du}$.

Using $v = \dfrac{ds}{dt}$ and (1),

$$v = \frac{ds}{du}\frac{du}{dt} = \sqrt{\dot{x}^2 + \dot{y}^2}\,\frac{du}{dt}. \tag{2}$$

Thereby, we get the differential equation of the motion

$$\frac{du}{dt} = \sqrt{\frac{-2gy}{\dot{x}^2 + \dot{y}^2}}, \quad u(0) = 0, \tag{3}$$

and the formula for calculating total time T as

$$T = \int_0^U \sqrt{\frac{\dot{x}^2 + \dot{y}^2}{-2gy}}\,du. \tag{4}$$

Here, (3) has a singular solution $u = 0$. Also, (4) is an improper integral.

We give a simple example where C is a line.

Example 1. Line $r = (au, -bu)$ $(0 \le u \le U)$

Because $\dot{x}^2 + \dot{y}^2 = a^2 + b^2$, we have the equation from (3),

$$\frac{du}{dt} = \sqrt{\frac{2gbu}{a^2 + b^2}}, \quad u(0) = 0.$$

Solving this equation, we obtain

$$u = \frac{bgt^2}{2(a^2 + b^2)},$$

and from (4),

$$T = \sqrt{\frac{2(a^2 + b^2)U}{bg}}.$$

Especially, line OB is represented as $r = (u, -u)$ $(0 \le u \le 5)$. Therefore,

$$T = 1.42857 \text{ where } g = 9.8 \text{ is used.}$$

3   Use of K$_E$TCindy with Maxima

Finding the equation for curves other than a line (Example 1) is not so easy. Therefore, we use Maxima in K$_E$TCindy. Contents of this section might be used for preparing teaching materials, not for materials itself.

Here we explain how to use K$_E$TCindy with Maxima when curve C is an inverted cycloid, a circle, and a parabola.

3.1   The Case of an Inverted Cycloid

An inverted cycloid from O is represented as

$$r = (a(u - \sin u), \ -a(1 - \cos u)) \quad (0 < u < U).$$

To simplify Eq. (3), we need only write the following scripts on Scripts Editor of Cinderella.

```
cmdL=[
  "assume",["g>0"],
  "fxy:[a*(u-sin(u)),-a*(1-cos(u))]",[],
   "d2:diff(fxy[1],u)^2+diff(fxy[2],u)^2",[],
   "d2:trigsimp",["d2"],
  "n2:2*g*(-fxy[2])",[],
   "so1:ratsimp",["n2/d2"],
   "so2:ratsimp(sqrt(so1))",[],
   "so2",[]
  ];
CalcbyM("cyc",cmdL);
```

Here cmdL is the list of Maxima commands, where each command is given as a pair of the name and arguments, and where CalcbyM is the command of K$_E$TCindy to call Maxima. The results are assigned to a variable cyc as a string or a list of strings. Actually

$$\mathtt{cyc="sqrt(g)/sqrt(a)"}$$

Therefore, Eq. (3) has a simple form. Moreover, it is easily solvable as

$$\frac{du}{dt} = \sqrt{\frac{g}{a}}, \ u = \sqrt{\frac{g}{a}}t.$$

Scripts to decide the inverted cycloid through B$(5, -5)$ are shown below.

```
cmdL=[
  "assume",["a>0"],
  "fxy:[a*(u-sin(u)),-a*(1-cos(u))]",[],
   "eq:ratsimp",["(fxy[1]+fxy[2])/a"],
   "so1:find_root",["eq","u","
  "eqr:ev",["fxy[1]-5","u=so1"],
```

```
"so2:find_root",["eqr","a",0,5],
"so1::so2",[]
];
CalcbyM("coeff",cmdL);println(coeff);
```

The results are $U = 2.412011143913525$, $a = 2.864585187658752$. From these, the total time is obtained.

$$T = \sqrt{\frac{a}{g}}\, U = 1.30406$$

3.2   The Case of a Circle

In the same way as an inverted cycloid, the equation for a circle

$$r = \left(5(1 - \cos u),\ -5 \sin u\right)\ \left(0 \le u \le \frac{\pi}{2}\right)$$

can be obtained.

```
cir="(sqrt(2)*sqrt(g)*sqrt(sin(u)))/sqrt(5)"
```

Therefore,

$$\frac{du}{dt} = \sqrt{\frac{2g}{5}}\,\sqrt{\sin u}.$$

However, we cannot find the exact solution of the equation above. The total time (4) is obtainable with

```
Mxfun("tt","integrate",["sqrt(5/(2*g*sin(u)))"]);
```

Mxfun is a command of KETCindy to execute a single command of Maxima. The results are

$$\frac{\sqrt{5}\,\beta\left(\frac{1}{4}, \frac{1}{2}\right)}{2\sqrt{2}\sqrt{g}} = 1.32434.$$

To obtain the numerical solution of the equation, we use deqplot, a command KETCindy provided to calculate the numerical solution of a differential equation using Runge-Kutta method. Then we display the integral curve. Here, because the equation has a singular solution $u = 0$, the process requires a little ingenuity as shown below.

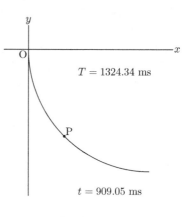

$T = 1324.34$ ms

P

$t = 909.05$ ms

1. Take u_0 close to zero, for example, $u_0 = 0.001$, and approximate the solution from 0 to u_0 by a straight line. Using Example 1, we have the time at which u becomes u_0

$$t_0 = \sqrt{\frac{2(a^2 + b^2)u_0}{bg}} \qquad (5)$$

where $(a, b) = \left(x(u_0),\ y(u_0)\right)$.

2. Use `deqplot` from t_0 to $T = 1.32434$.

```
equ="u'=(sqrt(2*9.8/5*sin(u)))";
range="t="+textformat([t0,T],6);
Deqplot("cir",equ,range,t0,u0);
```

Then $u = u(t)$ is obtained numerically.

Here we consider the case of a circle which has the same length of the inverted cycloid. KETCindy with Maxima can find the length exactly or numerically.

$$L = 7.3705338507$$

Let C be a circle through points O and B with the equation

$$\boldsymbol{r} = (5 + s - r \cos u, \ s - r \sin u).$$

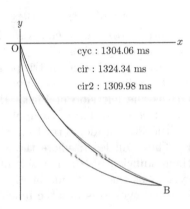

cyc : 1304.06 ms

cir : 1324.34 ms

cir2 : 1309.98 ms

Using KETCindy with Maxima again, we can determine s and r so that the arc length equals to L

$$s = 2.11125, \ r = 7.41803,$$

and obtain the total time

$$T = 1.30998.$$

3.3   The Case of a Parabola

Let a parabola be represented as

$$\boldsymbol{r} = \left(u, \ \frac{1}{5}(u^2 - 10u)\right) \ (0 \le u \le 5).$$

We can neither solve Eq. (3) nor obtain the total time (4) exactly. Therefore, the process should be numerical as follows.

1. Take a slightly large value t_1 such as $t_1 = 1.5$, and use `deqplot` from t_0 to t_1.
2. Let `dtpara` be the returned list of plotdata
   ```
   dtpara=[[t0,u0],...,[t1,u1]];
   ```
   Execute the following scripts:

   ```
   n=max(select(1..(length(dtpara)),dtpara_#_2<5));
   p1=dtpara_(n); p2=dtpara_(n+1);
   T=p1_1+(5-p1_2)*(p2_1-p1_1)/(p2_2-p1_2);
   ```

Then we have total time $T = 1.33099$.

4   Examples of Interactive Materials

In this section, we introduce two examples that are expected to be useful immediately after the first lecture, of which the contents are of Sect. 1.

4.1   Using a Bézier Curve

The Bézier curve from O(0, 0) to B(5, −5) with control points C(c_1, c_2) and D(d_1, d_2) is defined as

$$r = 3C(1-u)^2 u + 3D(1-u)u^2 + Bu^3 \quad (0 \le u \le 1).$$

We get the Eq. (3) with Maxima, although it is extremely complicated. Actually, the string returned from Maxima is

```
sqrt(((6*g*d2-6*g*c2+10*g)*u^3+(12*g*c2-6*g*d2)*u^2-6*g*c2*u)/..,
```

which has 370 characters. Also the total time is obtainable in the same way as the case of a parabola.

Put C and D as geometric points on Cindy Screen, then, moving these points, we can change the Bézier curve shape. The initial position might be on the line OB as the left side of Fig. 3. Here, the total time T(1428 ms in this case), almost equal to that of Example 1, is displayed. In accordance with the teacher's instructions, students try to minimize the total time T by moving points C and D. They will learn where these points should be put. When value T satisfies them sufficiently (the left side of Fig. 4), instruct them to display the inverted cycloid as the right side of Fig. 4. Then they will understand clearly that the inverted cycloid is just the brachistochrone curve.

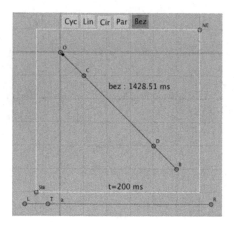 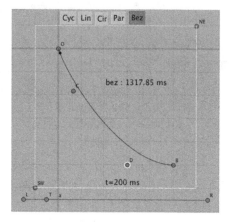

Fig. 3. Bézier curves and control points

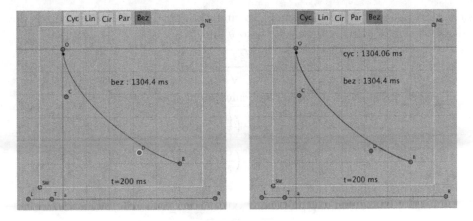

Fig. 4. Fitting the Bézier curve to the inverted cycolid

4.2 Moving the Point with a Slider

We can make a slider on Cindy Screen, putting two points L, R, and T on the segment LR. Let $t = T - L$ represent the time from the initial time. Because the motion of the point is solvable exactly or numerically, we can display the position of the point at time t as Fig. 5.

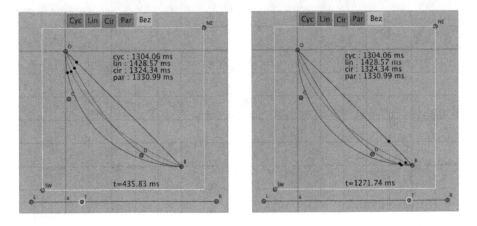

Fig. 5. Cindy screens with a slider

5 Derivation of the Brachistochrone Curve

After using interactive materials of previous section, it would be better for teachers to explain why an inverted cycloid is the brachistochrone curve. We describe the derivation briefly, although one can find many reports in the literature about it. The problem is to find the function which minimizes the left-hand side of (4). Here, we set $-y$ to y and

$$f = \frac{\sqrt{\dot{x}^2 + \dot{y}^2}}{\sqrt{y}}.$$

The Euler equations in variational calculus in this case are

$$\begin{cases} \dfrac{\partial f}{\partial x} - \dfrac{d}{du}\left(\dfrac{\partial f}{\partial \dot{x}}\right) = 0 \\ \dfrac{\partial f}{\partial y} - \dfrac{d}{du}\left(\dfrac{\partial f}{\partial \dot{y}}\right) = 0 \end{cases}.$$

Using the first equation, we have

$$\frac{\partial f}{\partial \dot{x}} = \frac{\dot{x}}{\sqrt{y(\dot{x}^2 + \dot{y}^2)}} = \sqrt{c}.$$

Therefore, we have

$$\dot{x}^2 = cy(\dot{x}^2 + \dot{y}^2)$$

$$\frac{\dot{x}}{\dot{y}} = \sqrt{\frac{cy}{1 - cy}} = \sqrt{\frac{y}{2r - y}} \quad \left(r = \frac{1}{2c}\right).$$

Put $y = 2r \sin^2 \dfrac{u}{2} = r(1 - \cos u)$. From

$$2r - y = 2r \cos^2 \frac{u}{2}, \quad \dot{y} = 2r \sin \frac{u}{2} \cos \frac{u}{2},$$

we have the following:

$$\dot{x} = \frac{\sin \dfrac{u}{2}}{\cos \dfrac{u}{2}} \cdot 2r \sin \frac{u}{2} \cos \frac{u}{2} = 2r \sin^2 \frac{u}{2} = r(1 - \cos u).$$

Solving the equation above, we get

$$\begin{cases} x = r(u - \sin u) \\ y = r(1 - \cos u) \end{cases},$$

which is the equation of a cycloid.

6 Conclusions

We have been developing KETCindy in collaboration with Cinderella to produce teaching materials of various types. We showed an example, the brachistochrone problem, as a series of materials, It would be more effective when we mutually associate these materials and arrange them properly. Teachers will give other applicable examples, similar to the brachistochrone problem and which are expected to enhance a learning effect in their class.

Acknowledgments. This work was supported by JSPS KAKENHI Grant Numbers 15K01037, 15K00944, and 16K01152.

References

1. KeTpic.com. http://ketpic.com
2. Cinderella. http://www.cinderella.de/tiki-index.php
3. Scilab. http://www.scilab.org
4. Maxima. http://maxima.sourceforge.net
5. MacTutor History of Mathematics archive. http://www-history.mcs.st-and.ac.uk/HistTopics/Brachistochrone.html
6. Takato, S., McAndrew, A., Vallejo, J.A., Kaneko, M.: Collaborative Use of KeTCindy and free computer algebra systems. In: Mathematics in Computer Science, pp. 1–12 (2017). 10.1007/s11786-017-0303-7
7. Takato, S.: What is and how to use KeTCindy - linkage between dynamic geometry software and collaborative use of KeTCindy and free computer algebra systems and LATEX graphics capabilities. In: Greuel, G.-M., Koch, T., Paule, P., Sommese, A. (eds.) ICMS 2016. LNCS, vol. 9725. Springer, Cham (2016)
8. Kobayashi, S., Takato, S.: Cooperation of KeTCindy and computer algebra system. In: Greuel, G.-M., Koch, T., Paule, P., Sommese, A. (eds.) ICMS 2016. LNCS, vol. 9725, pp. 351–358. Springer, Cham (2016). doi:10.1007/978-3-319-42432-3_43
9. Kaneko, M., Yamashita, S., Kitahara, K., Maeda, Y., Nakamura, Y., Kortenkamp, U., Takato, S.: KETCindy - collaboration of Cinderella and KETpic, reports on CADGME 2014 conference working group. Int. J. Technol. Math. Educ. **22**(4), 179–185 (2015)

Producing Teaching Materials for Spatial Figures with KeTCindy and the Educational Benefits of Combining Materials

Naoki Hamaguchi[1](✉) and Setsuo Takato[2]

[1] National Institute of Technology, Nagano College, Nagano, Japan
hama@nagano-nct.ac.jp
[2] Toho University, Chiba, Japan

Abstract. KeTpic is a macro package which generates graphical code that can be used in LaTeX. KeTCindy is the collaboration of KeTpic and Cinderella. In mathematical classes at the collegiate level, teachers often use materials for 3D figures such as graphs of two-variable functions and spatial figures. The current version of KeTCindy enables teachers to make interactive slides in pdf format, and, at the same time, efficiently provides the data to make handouts, figures for tablets, and physical models. We conducted an experimental class to research the effect of combining these materials. In this paper, we provide survey results of the above-mentioned experimental class and also show some examples of teaching materials.

1   Introduction

In mathematical classes at the collegiate level, teachers often use materials for 3D figures such as graphs of two-variable functions and spatial figures. Recently, these are presented in various ways.

1. Handouts to be distributed.
2. Slides to be presented on the screen.
3. Figures to be manipulated by students on their tablets.
4. Physical models to be displayed or passed around.

Many teachers at the collegiate level in Japan make handouts using LaTeX. However, there are few handouts with appropriate figures—in particular, ones including spatial figures. This is because it is difficult to put figures in LaTeX documents and, as for spatial figures, it is also difficult to make them in the first place. So, we have developed KETpic and KETCindy to easily put mathematical figures in handouts.

KETpic is a macro package of mathematical software such as Scilab [Sc1], which generates graphical code that can be used in LaTeX. Tpic specials and macros of pict2e are used as the graphical code.

KETCindy [KT1] is the collaboration of KETpic and Cinderella [Ci1]. Cinderella is dynamic geometry software developed by Gebert and Kortenkamp.

© Springer International Publishing AG 2017
O. Gervasi et al. (Eds.): ICCSA 2017, Part IV, LNCS 10407, pp. 262–272, 2017.
DOI: 10.1007/978-3-319-62401-3_20

The first version of KₑTCindy was released in September, 2014. Using Cinderella as the graphical user interface of KₑTpic, we can make figures more interactively. The following two figures demonstrate one example of this.

It is necessary and effective to use handouts with figures like Fig. 1 in classes about repeated integrals.

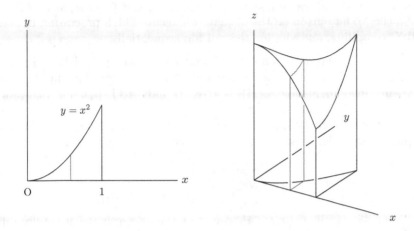

Fig. 1. Figures in LATEX documents

Figure 2 shows Cinderella screens, the Cindy Screen at the left, the Script Editor at the right. Note that Cindy Script is the programming language of Cinderella.

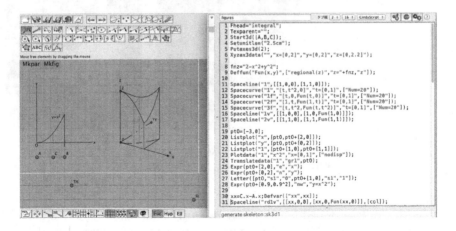

Fig. 2. Cinderella screen and script

The process to produce Fig. 1 with K_ETCindy is as follows:

1. Put segment AB and point C on the segment on the display.
2. Describe scripts for drawing a figure and generating LATEX graphic codes. For example, use `Spacecurve` to draw a spatial curve.
3. Determine projection angles θ and φ by moving points TH and FI on the Cindy screen.
4. Determine the position of a section by moving point C on segment AB.
5. Press the Mkfig button on the display to execute batch processing in Scilab, LATEX compiling, and viewing the pdf file sequentially.

Files in obj format are often used to produce figures for tablets and to make physical models. In recent years, commands for generating data in obj format have been added to K_ETpic [TH1] and K_ETCindy [HT1]. Using 3D viewing software such as Meshlab [Me1], we can display 3D figures on computer or tablet screens. Moreover, obj format data can be converted to stl format, with which 3D printers can make physical models. For example, the function

$$f(x,\,y) = \begin{cases} \dfrac{xy}{\sqrt{x^2 + y^2}} & ((x,\,y) \neq (0,\,0)) \\ 0 & ((x,\,y) = (0,\,0)) \end{cases}$$

is continuous at $(x,\,y) = (0,\,0)$. However, at the origin, it is not totally differentiable but partially differentiable. This property is made clear with the figure of the graph. In Fig. 3, the middle is a screen shot of the figure on the Meshlab screen, the right is a photo of the physical model made by a 3D printer, and the left is the figure for a handout. It is noteworthy that axes and symbols x, y, z can be generated and displayed with K_ETCindy.

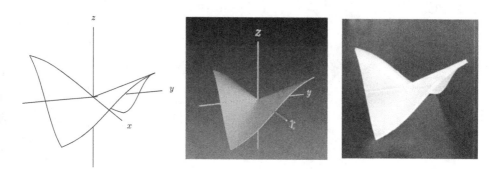

Fig. 3. The graph of $z = \dfrac{xy}{\sqrt{x^2 + y^2}}$

Recently, we have added functionality to easily make slides. Slides are useful in class plans when combined with handouts, tablets, and physical models. In this paper, double integrals transformed by polar coordinates are given as an example. We outline a teaching plan in Sect. 2, and describe the experimental class with the results of the subsequent questionnaire in Sect. 3.

2   Making a Plan for a Calculus Class

The theme is double integrals transformed by polar coordinates. We treat the function

$$z = e^{-(x^2+y^2)} + 1 \tag{1}$$

with the domain

$$D = \{ (x, y) \mid x^2 + y^2 \leqq 1,\ x \geqq 0,\ y \geqq 0 \} \tag{2}$$

as an example. The following subsections detail the plan sequence.

2.1   Explanation of Polar Coordinates and Practices

First, we explain polar coordinates with slides like Fig. 4.

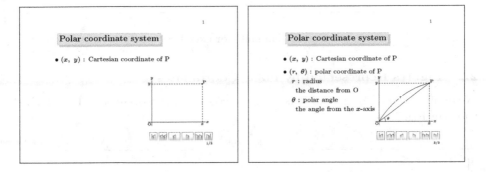

Fig. 4. Interactive slides for definition

Next, we present the left slide in Fig. 5. Distributing handouts, like Fig. 6, we have students answer the polar coordinates of a point on the screen. Once they have mostly answered, we present the right slide of Fig. 5, which includes the answer, and we have students check their work.

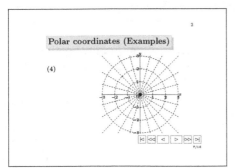
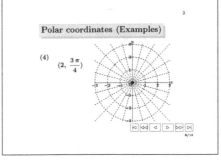

Fig. 5. Interactive slides for exercises

Figures in slides and in handouts are the same, and, needless to say, they are made with KETCindy.

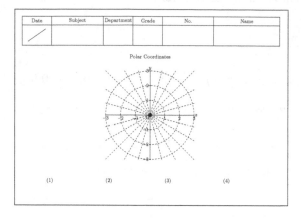

Fig. 6. Handouts for exercises

2.2   Figures Represented by Polar Coordinates

We explain what figure equations by polar coordinates represent with slides like those in Fig. 7.

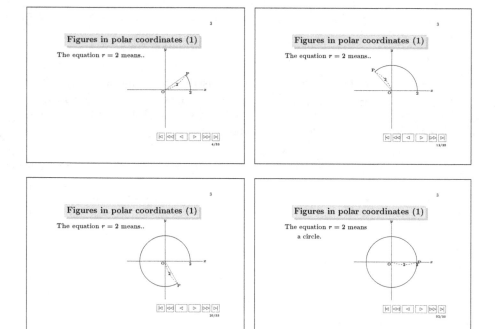

Fig. 7. Interactive slides for example figures (Color figure online)

Using the slides in Fig. 7, figures can be presented as animation by pressing the arrow keys on the keyboard. This important functionality has been added to the current version of KETCindy. Blue buttons on the slide screen have also been added for the same functionality when these pdf slides are presented on tablets.

2.3 Double Integrals Transformed by Polar Coordinates

Using slides like those in Fig. 8, we explain that the function (1) and the domain (2) are represented as follows with transformation by polar coordinates.

$$z = e^{-r^2} + 1, \quad D = \{ (r, \theta) \mid 0 \leqq r \leqq 1, 0 \leqq \theta \leqq \frac{\pi}{2} \}$$

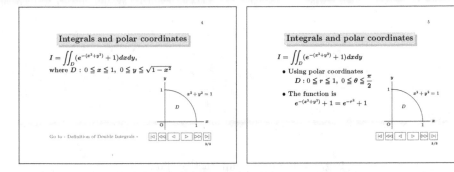

Fig. 8. Interactive slides for integrals

Next, we explain how to find a volume that is the value of a double integral by sectional mensuration with polar coordinates. Until now, we have explained this using handouts like Fig. 9, and blackboards, but, in this plan, we use slides, tablets, and physical models.

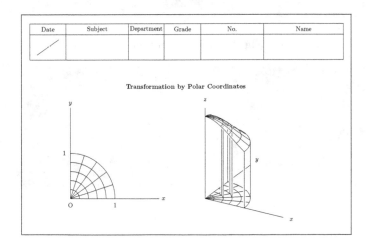

Fig. 9. Exercise for double integrals

Specifically, we do as follows:

1. Handouts, like Fig. 9, are distributed, and slides, like those in Fig. 10, are presented. These slides can also be presented as animation, such as in Fig. 7.
2. We lend one tablet per group of 4 to 6 students, and we let them manipulate figures, like Fig. 11, on the tablets.

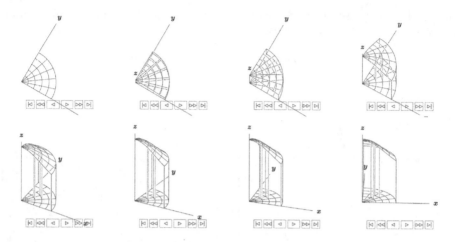

Fig. 10. Figures on interactive slides

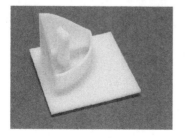

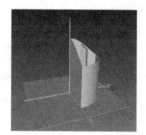
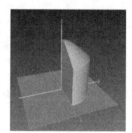

Fig. 11. Figures on tablets

Fig. 12. Physical models

3. Two physical models, like those in Fig. 12, are made. We let students pass around and handle these physical models. In this case, in consideration of the stability and durability of the physical models, we treat the function $z = \exp(-(x^2 + y^2))$, by which the height is lowered.

2.4   Explanation of Formulas of Double Integrals

Lastly, we return to the slides, like those in Fig. 13, and explain the formula for calculation.

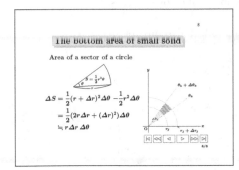
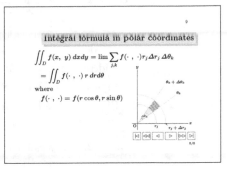

Fig. 13. Interactive slides for integral formulas

3   Our Experimental Class and Survey Results

We carried out an experimental class following the plan in the previous section.

- Date: January 11, 2017
- Students: 1st grade of college
- Subject: Calculus
- Time: 40 min

At the end of the class, we carried out the following survey:

Q1. Please indicate, on a scale of 1–4

    1: Very easily understandable
    2: Understandable
    3: Neither easy nor difficult to understand
    4: Difficult to understand

how useful each presentation style ("Handouts," "Slides," "Figures on tablets," and "Physical models," respectively) was to your understanding of the following concepts from (a) to (e).

(a) The shape of the graph of function $z = e^{-(x^2+y^2)} + 1$ (Table 1).
(b) The spatial figure the volume of which results from the double integral (Table 2).
(c) Inequalities which express the domain when using the polar coordinates system (Table 3).
(d) How to calculate the volume of minute solid shapes (Table 4).
(e) The integral formula for polar coordinates transformation (Table 5).

Table 1. Answers for (a) in number of students

	1	2	3	4	No answer
Handouts	4	12	8	0	0
Slides	10	11	3	0	0
Figures on tablets	8	9	6	1	0
Physical models	5	7	8	3	1

Table 2. Answers for (b) in number of students

	1	2	3	4	No answer
Handouts	4	13	7	0	0
Slides	10	12	2	0	0
Figures on tablets	12	8	4	0	0
Physical models	9	9	5	0	1

Table 3. Answers for (c) in number of students

	1	2	3	4	No answer
Handouts	5	13	6	0	0
Slides	10	11	3	0	0
Figures on tablets	5	10	6	1	2
Physical models	4	7	8	3	2

Table 4. Answers for (d) in number of students

	1	2	3	4	No answer
Handouts	5	11	6	1	1
Slides	10	11	3	0	0
Figures on tablets	7	9	7	0	1
Physical models	5	9	4	4	2

Table 5. Answers for (e) in number of students

	1	2	3	4	No answer
Handouts	4	12	5	1	2
Slides	11	10	3	0	0
Figures on tablets	5	7	7	3	2
Physical models	6	7	6	4	1

Q2. Choose materials that were effective in combination.

The answers (and the number of students) are as follows:
– "Handouts," "Slides," and "Figures on tablets" (8 students)
– "All materials" (4)
– "Handouts" and "Slides" (4)
– "Slides" and "Figures on tablets" (3)
– "Handouts," "Slides," and "Physical models" (2)
– "Figures on tablets" and "Physical models" (1)

Q3. Write some comments about today's class.

Their comments (and the number of those commenting) are as follows:
– I enjoyed class with new materials such as tablets and solid models. (6)
– Slide speed was too fast. (6)
– It was easy to understand because we could manipulate figures on tablets. (4)
– Understandable. (3)
– Solid models were understandable. (3)
– The transparent surface of the solid model made the part where the volume should be found clear to us. (1)
– Interactive slides were very understandable. (1)
– I could find the shapes of figures with only tablets. (1)
– Slides were the best. (1)
– Physical models are needed. (1)
– I would like to use analog materials. (1)

4   Conclusion

Overall, slides, depending on their quality, were evaluated highly in our survey, and this high evaluation was stable across all of our content types. As long as the slides are of good quality, it seems they would make an effective presentation method for any type of content.

On the other hand, it is also clear that tablets and physical models are effective when explaining the shapes of figures—with students expressing different preferences between these two. We found that there were also students whose understanding fell short with only the use of slides. For some students, tablets and physical models were most effective when it came time to explain the shapes of figures. Our goal was that students come away with a clearer understanding of the integral formula when transformed by polar coordinates than would otherwise have been possible. The survey indicates that, while slides were effective, the addition of physical models, and the manipulation of figures on tablets, also proved to be useful in understanding. For example, as survey question (e) indicates, the students credited their understanding of the slides in Fig. 13 (ranked "Understandable" or "Very easily understandable" by 21 out of 24 students) partly to the tablet work and the physical models (favorably ranked by 12 and 13 out of 24 students, respectively) that they were shown beforehand.

For this class, only two physical models were prepared, which weren't enough. In general, it's a good idea to have on hand a number of the most commonly explained shapes. Ours were solid on a 5-square-centimeter plane, and so they were about half as large as we would have liked.

In this class, two handouts were distributed. The first to assess students' initial understanding of polar coordinates, and the second to explain the transformation of double integrals with polar coordinates along with relevant exercises. We believe both handouts are still necessary.

In conclusion, KETCindy enables teachers to make interactive slides in pdf format, and, at the same time, efficiently provides the data to make handouts with exercises, figures for tablets, and/or physical models.

With good contents, and with the help of KETCindy, more interesting and more understandable lessons will be easier to create.

Acknowledgment. This work was supported by JSPS KAKENHI Grant Number 15K00944.

References

[HT1] Hamaguchi, N., Takato, S.: Generating data for 3D models. In: Greuel, G.-M., Koch, T., Paule, P., Sommese, A. (eds.) ICMS 2016. LNCS, vol. 9725, pp. 335–341. Springer, Cham (2016). doi:10.1007/978-3-319-42432-3_41

[KT1] Kaneko, M., Yamashita, S., Kitahara, K., Maeda, Y., Nakamura, Y., Kortenkamp, U., Takato, S.: KETCindy – collaboration of Cinderella and KETpic. Reports on CADGME 2014 conference working group. Int. J. Technol. Math. Educ. **22**(4), 179–185 (2015)

[TH1] Takato, S., Hamaguchi, N., Sarafian, H.: Generating data of mathematical figures for 3D printers with KETpic and educational impact of the printed models. In: Hong, H., Yap, C. (eds.) ICMS 2014. LNCS, vol. 8592, pp. 629–634. Springer, Heidelberg (2014). doi:10.1007/978-3-662-44199-2_94

[Ci1] http://cinderella.de

[Sc1] http://www.scilab.org

[Me1] http://meshlab.sourceforge.net

Authoring Quizzes with Interactive Content on the Mathematics e-Learning System STACK

Yasuyuki Nakamura[1]($\boxtimes$), Takahiro Nakahara[2], Masataka Kaneko[3], and Setsuo Takato[3]

[1] Nagoya University, Nagoya 464-8601, Japan
nakamura@nagoya-u.jp
[2] Sangensha LLC., Chitose 066-0054, Japan
[3] Toho University, Funabashi 274-8510, Japan

Abstract. The mathematics e-Learning system STACK is a quiz system where students do not select answers from options provided by teachers but instead submit mathematical expressions. This kind of e-Learning system is especially useful for mathematical science subjects. STACK is usually used for drill practices of mathematical sciences. In this paper, we propose its usage for self-learning. In order to realize self-learning using STACK, we developed interactive content using the CindyJS framework of Cinderella, a type of dynamic geometry software, and embedded it in questions for students to investigate and interact with by themselves.

1 Introduction

In the last few decades, information and communication technology (ICT) infrastructure has developed greatly in schools and universities thereby boosting the popularity of e-Learning worldwide. Online learning content can be distributed through learning management systems (LMSs) from which students can download and learn material. Online assessment systems, in other words, computer-aided assessment (CAA) systems are also an important feature of the e-Learning system as they can automatically assess whether students' answers are correct or incorrect. Students can use the system as drill practice while their level of understanding can be evaluated by it. One of the most common types of question in online assessment systems are multiple-choice questions (MCQs), in which potential options are provided by the teacher and students select a single response as their answer.

While online assessment systems can be used in scientific subjects, MCQs are not sufficient to evaluate the level of students' understanding of the subjects. For example, in a test on calculation, students can, by guesswork, simply "choose" an option from the list of potential answers, which may be the correct answer. In order to avoid this kind of problem, it is preferable to adopt other question types in which students provide mathematical expressions as answers by calculation, or what we call the "Mathematics e-Learning system." STACK [1] is one such system, while there are some others such as Maple T.A. [2], MATH ON WEB [3,4], Numbas [5], WeBWorK [6], and so on.

© Springer International Publishing AG 2017
O. Gervasi et al. (Eds.): ICCSA 2017, Part IV, LNCS 10407, pp. 273–284, 2017.
DOI: 10.1007/978-3-319-62401-3_21

Mathematics e-Learning systems are useful in drill practices for calculation because students receive instant feedback on whether their answers are true or false. Furthermore, STACK can be used for self-learning through its mechanism of sending feedback according to students' answers, in what is known as a "Potential Response Tree (PRT)." A simple example of feedback for the correct answer to a question on differentiation $\frac{d}{dx}\cos(2x)$ is shown in Fig. 1. This is a common feature, even in other mathematics e-Learning systems. In STACK, if a student inputs the answer $-\sin(2x)$, he or she may forget the rule of differentiation of the composite function, for which suitable feedback is given as shown in Fig. 2. When a student inputs the answer $2\sin(2x)$, he or she may know the rule of differentiation of composite function but may calculate the differentiation of trigonometric function carelessly. In this case, suitable feedback is given to the student as shown in Fig. 3.

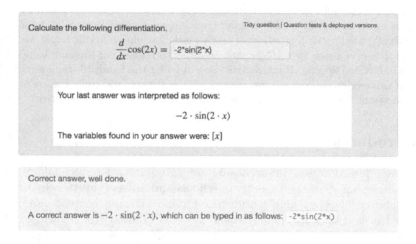

Fig. 1. An example of feedback for a correct answer in STACK.

With the help of PRT, students can recognize their misunderstandings when they input incorrect answers. However, they have to find a trigger to solve problems when they look at the questions. For example, let us consider the question related to geometric figures displayed in Fig. 4. In order to solve the question, students must draw the circle $x^2 + y^2 = 9$ and point A in their notebook, and then guesstimate the trace of point P, which is a point that is midway between A and Q that moves on the circle.

It is important for students to be provided with a trigger to solve questions by themselves, but doing so is sometimes difficult. In this paper, we would like to suggest some solutions to this problem. One of the solutions is to embed interactive content into questions to help students consider about the questions. This will eventually boost self-learning in students.

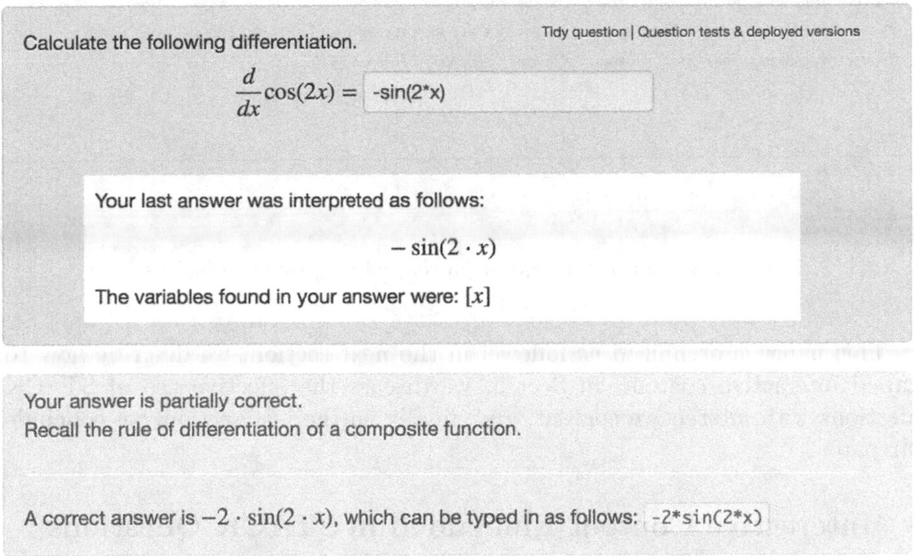

Calculate the following differentiation.

Tidy question | Question tests & deployed versions

$$\frac{d}{dx}\cos(2x) = \boxed{\text{-sin(2*x)}}$$

Your last answer was interpreted as follows:

$$- \sin(2 \cdot x)$$

The variables found in your answer were: $[x]$

Your answer is partially correct.
Recall the rule of differentiation of a composite function.

A correct answer is $-2 \cdot \sin(2 \cdot x)$, which can be typed in as follows: `-2*sin(2*x)`

Fig. 2. An example of feedback for a partially correct answer in which a student may have forgotten the rule of differentiation of a composite function.

Calculate the following differentiation.

Tidy question | Question tests & deployed versions

$$\frac{d}{dx}\cos(2x) = \boxed{\text{2*sin(2*x)}}$$

Your last answer was interpreted as follows:

$$2 \cdot \sin(2 \cdot x)$$

The variables found in your answer were: $[x]$

Your answer is partially correct.
Check the rule of differentiation of a trigonometric function.

A correct answer is $-2 \cdot \sin(2 \cdot x)$, which can be typed in as follows: `-2*sin(2*x)`

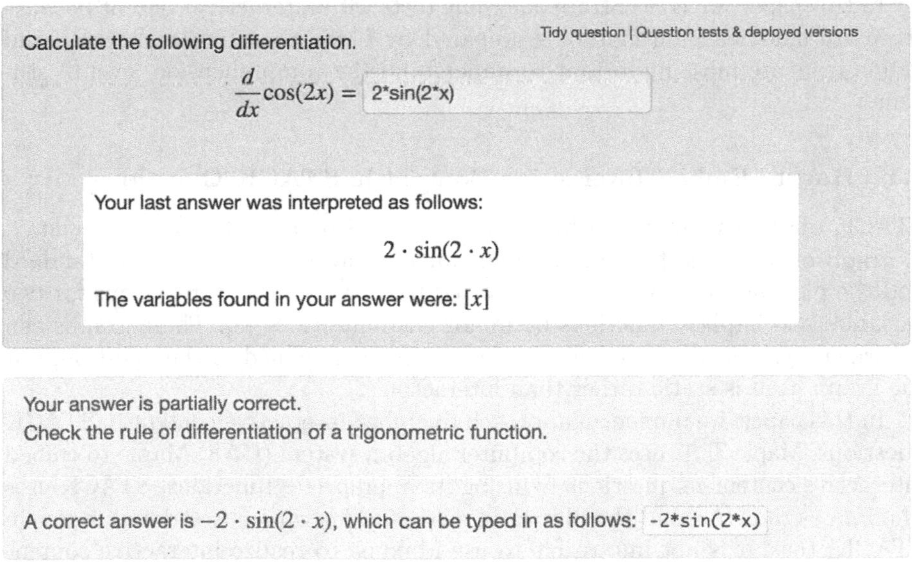

Fig. 3. An example of feedback for a partially correct answer in which a student may have miscalculated a differentiation of a trigonometric function.

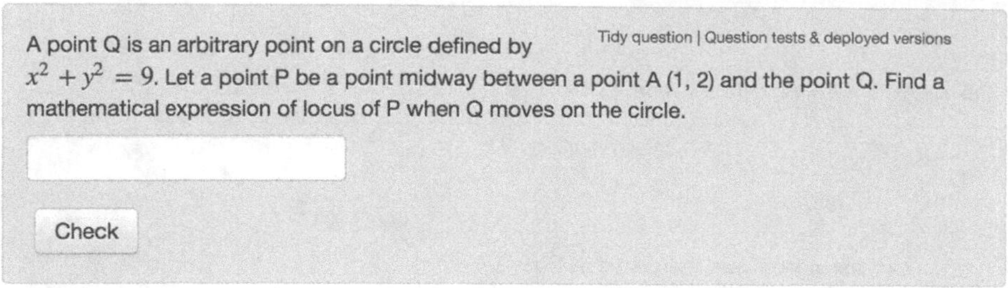

A point Q is an arbitrary point on a circle defined by   Tidy question | Question tests & deployed versions
$x^2 + y^2 = 9$. Let a point P be a point midway between a point A (1, 2) and the point Q. Find a
mathematical expression of locus of P when Q moves on the circle.

Check

Fig. 4. An example of a question related to geometric figures.

This paper is organized as follows: in the next section, we describe how to embed interactive content; in Sect. 3, we discuss the effective use of STACK questions with interactive content; and, finally, in the last section, we conclude our paper.

2   Interactive Content Embedded in STACK Questions

Embedding interactive content such as animations, movies, applications, and quizzes in learning materials to help students learn their subjects is relatively popular, particularly in e-textbooks. Some quizzes that are connected with an LMS's are prepared in e-textbooks so that teachers can grasp how much students have learned using e-textbooks by viewing their learning logs [7].

In this paper, we concentrate on online tests with interactive content because there are more learning materials prepared by LMSs than by e-textbooks, and online tests are most important to understand the comprehension level of students.

2.1   How to Embed Interactive Content in STACK Questions

STACK questions can be authored using normal texts including TeX syntax. A graph of functions for one variable can be drawn in questions as standard and the plotting function can be enhanced to draw a graph of functions for two variables and implicit functions by minor customizations [8]. These graphs can be drawn dynamically according to the parameters defined in the question, but the graph itself is static rather than interactive.

In this paper, we pursue an approach to embed interactive content in STACK questions. Maple T.A. uses the computer algebra system (CAS) Maple to embed interactive content in questions by using its appropriate functions. STACK uses Maxima as the CAS and the plotting function of Maxima is restricted to use in STACK; thus, it is not impossible to use Maxima to realize interactive content in STACK.

STACK question texts are basically written in HTML format. Therefore, one possibility is to develop JavaScript applications using libraries such as JSX-Graph [9,10], through which rich interactive content can be developed. However, a certain level of programming skill is required for this. One of the advantages of authoring questions with STACK is that it does not require advanced programming skills. The algorithms of evaluating students' answers are automatically built by the PRT. Another way to develop JavaScript content is by utilizing dynamic geometry software (DGS) such as GeoGebra [11] and Cinderella [12]. GeoGebra offers JavaScript API to interact with the GeoGebra applet. Cinderella's CindyJS [13] framework exports the JavaScript code to be embedded in the web. We adopted this framework to develop STACK questions with interactive content because it is simpler.

Although we do not explain how to prepare STACK questions in much detail here, let us briefly show how to prepare the question of Fig. 7 that we will see later as an example. The documents [14] can be referred to, to further understand the procedure.

Creating a Cinderella Content. We first developed an interactive content by using Cinderella, as shown in Fig. 5.

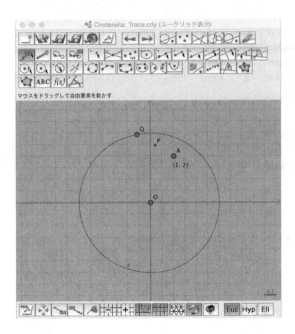

Fig. 5. An example of interactive content created by Cinderella.

Exporting to CindyJS. We can then export the created Cinderella content to CindyJS. The following exported code (with modification for display) is HTML text with JavaScript (CindyJS).

```
<!DOCTYPE html>
<html>
<head>
   <meta charset="UTF-8">
   <title>Trace.cdy</title>
   <style type="text/css">

(snip)

</style>
   <link rel="stylesheet" href="http://cindyjs.org/dist/v0.8/CindyJS.css">
   <script type="text/javascript"
   src="http://cindyjs.org/dist/v0.8/Cindy.js">
   </script>
   <script type="text/javascript">
      var cdy = CindyJS({
          scripts: "cs*",
          defaultAppearance: {
(snip)
          },
          angleUnit: "°",
          geometry: [
              {name: "O", type: "Free", pos: [0.0, -0.0, 4.0], (snip)
              {name: "A", type: "Free", pos: [-2.0, -4.0, -2.0], (snip)
(snip)
          ],
          ports: [{
              id: "CSCanvas",
              width: 556,
              height: 435,
(snip)
          }],
          csconsole: false,
          use: ["katex"],
          cinderella: {build: 1898, version: [2, 9, 1898]}
      });
   </script>
   </head>
   <body>
      <div id="CSCanvas"></div>
   </body>
</html>
```

Embedding CindyJS to STACK Question. Once we have exported the HTML file (CindyJS) exported, we simply copy and paste it to the "Question text" area in an authoring interface of STACK question (Fig. 6). The copied and pasted part is indicated with a red line in Fig. 6.

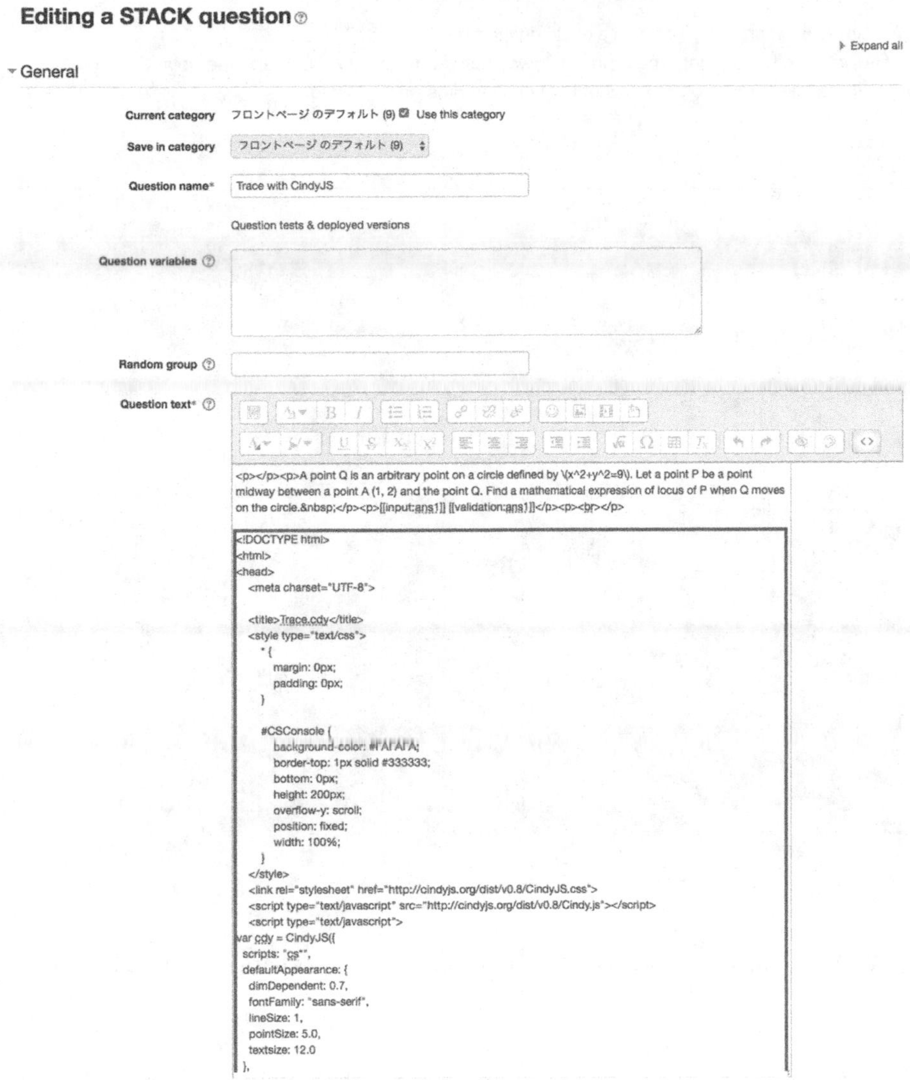

Editing a STACK questionⓘ

▸ Expand all

▾ General

Current category	フロントページ のデフォルト (9) ☑ Use this category
Save in category	フロントページ のデフォルト (9) ⬍
Question name*	Trace with CindyJS
	Question tests & deployed versions
Question variables ⑦	
Random group ⑦	
Question text* ⑦	

<p></p><p>A point Q is an arbitrary point on a circle defined by \(x^2+y^2=9\). Let a point P be a point midway between a point A (1, 2) and the point Q. Find a mathematical expression of locus of P when Q moves on the circle. </p><p>[[input:ans1]] [[validation:ans1]]</p><p>
</p>

```
<!DOCTYPE html>
<html>
<head>
  <meta charset="UTF-8">

  <title>Trace.cdy</title>
  <style type="text/css">
  * {
      margin: 0px;
      padding: 0px;
  }

  #CSConsole {
      background-color: #FAFAFA;
      border-top: 1px solid #333333;
      bottom: 0px;
      height: 200px;
      overflow-y: scroll;
      position: fixed;
      width: 100%;
  }
  </style>
  <link rel="stylesheet" href="http://cindyjs.org/dist/v0.8/CindyJS.css">
  <script type="text/javascript" src="http://cindyjs.org/dist/v0.8/Cindy.js"></script>
  <script type="text/javascript">
var cdy = CindyJS({
  scripts: "cs*",
  defaultAppearance: {
    dimDependent: 0.7,
    fontFamily: "sans-serif",
    lineSize: 1,
    pointSize: 5.0,
    textsize: 12.0
  },
```

Fig. 6. Authoring STACK question with CindyJS copied and pasted.

2.2   Examples of STACK Questions with Interactive Content

In this subsection, we will provide some examples of STACK questions with interactive content.

Calculation of Mathematical Expression of a Trace of a Point. An example of a question related to geometric figures was shown in Fig. 4 in the previous section, in which students are required to calculate the trace of the

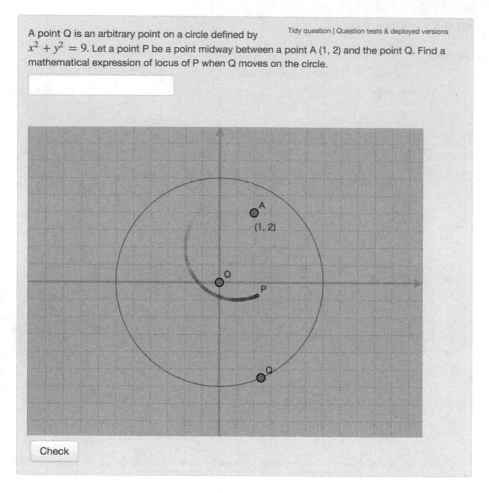

A point Q is an arbitrary point on a circle defined by   Tidy question | Question tests & deployed versions
$x^2 + y^2 = 9$. Let a point P be a point midway between a point A (1, 2) and the point Q. Find a
mathematical expression of locus of P when Q moves on the circle.

Check

Fig. 7. An example of a question related to geometric figures with embedded interactive content.

point P that is midway between A and Q and that moves on the circle. The first step in solving the question is to sketch the trace on a paper. However, this is a difficult task for some students. In order to help these students, one of the solutions is to provide interactive content in the question as shown in Fig. 7.

Students can grab the point Q and move it on the circle, thereby drawing the trace. This could act as a trigger for students who were unable to solve the question in Fig. 4.

Evaluation of Stability of Fixed Points of a System of Ordinary Differential Equations. In order to evaluate the stability of fixed points of a system of ordinary differential equations, students mainly go through mainly three steps: the calculation of fixed points, the linearization of a system of ordinary

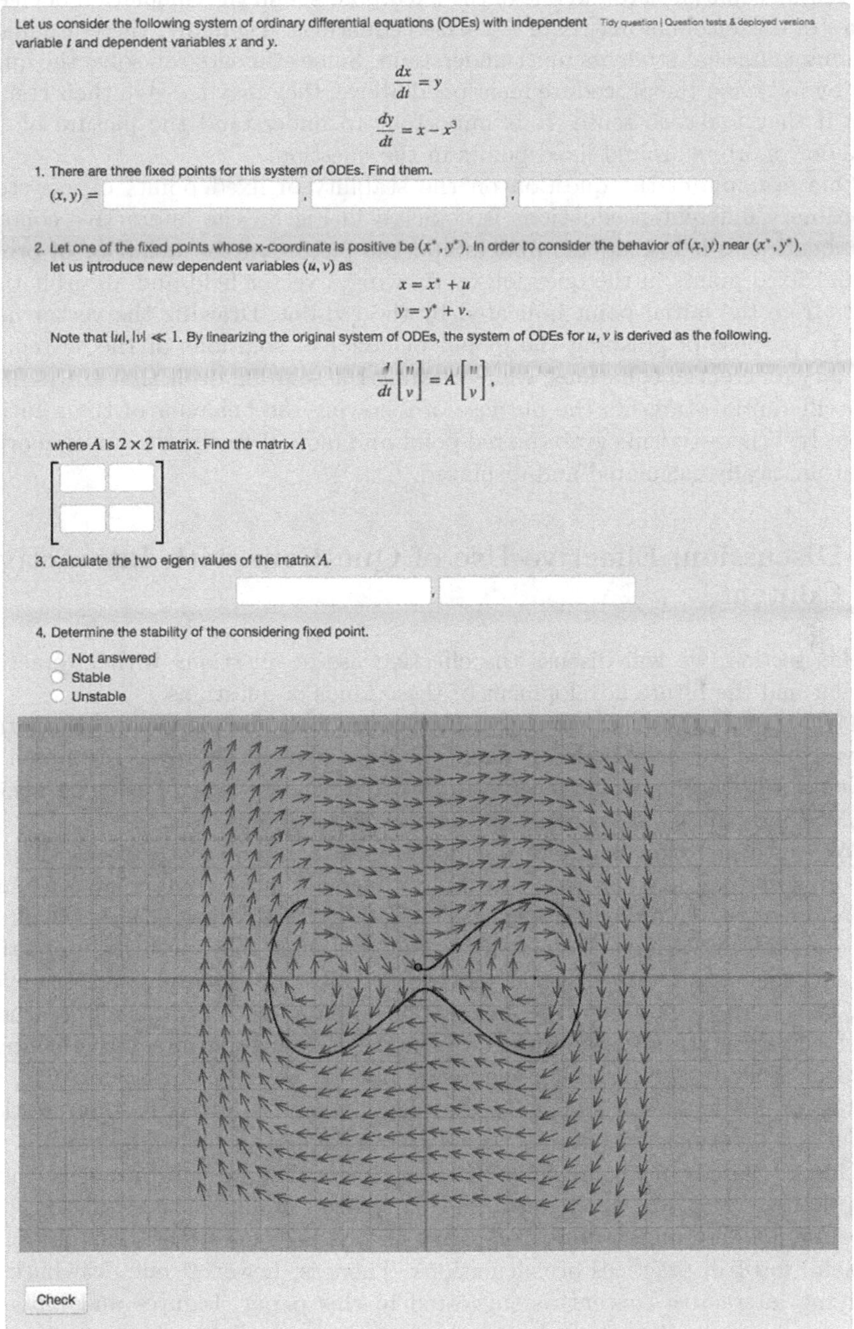

Let us consider the following system of ordinary differential equations (ODEs) with independent variable t and dependent variables x and y. Tidy question | Question tests & deployed versions

$$\frac{dx}{dt} = y$$

$$\frac{dy}{dt} = x - x^3$$

1. There are three fixed points for this system of ODEs. Find them.

$(x, y) = $ [_____] , [_____] , [_____]

2. Let one of the fixed points whose x-coordinate is positive be (x^*, y^*). In order to consider the behavior of (x, y) near (x^*, y^*), let us introduce new dependent variables (u, v) as

$$x = x^* + u$$
$$y = y^* + v.$$

Note that $|u|, |v| \ll 1$. By linearizing the original system of ODEs, the system of ODEs for u, v is derived as the following.

$$\frac{d}{dt}\begin{bmatrix} u \\ v \end{bmatrix} = A \begin{bmatrix} u \\ v \end{bmatrix},$$

where A is 2×2 matrix. Find the matrix A

$$\begin{bmatrix} \square & \square \\ \square & \square \end{bmatrix}$$

3. Calculate the two eigen values of the matrix A.

[_____] , [_____]

4. Determine the stability of the considering fixed point.

○ Not answered
○ Stable
○ Unstable

Check

Fig. 8. Question on the stability of fixed points of a system of ordinary differential equations with embedded interactive content.

differential equations around one of the fixed points, and the calculation of eigen-values of the Jacobian matrix of linearized equations. Therefore, there are many learning units that students must understand. Some students can solve the question by following the procedure mentioned above; they may leave in their results even if they make no sense. It is important to understand the picture of the behavior of orbits around fixed points in the question.

One example of the question on the stability of fixed points of a system of ordinary differential equations is depicted in Fig. 8. The interactive content is embedded to help students understand the picture of the behavior of orbits around fixed points in the question by drawing a vector field and an orbit that starts from the initial point indicated by the red dot. Drawing the vector field fits the purpose of grasping the global behavior of solutions of the system of ordinary differential equations, while drawing the solution orbit that starts from a specific initial state fits the purpose of following the behavior of the solution precisely. When students grab the red point and move it freely, the solution orbit is automatically calculated and displayed.

3   Discussion: Effective Use of Questions with Interactive Content

In this section, we will discuss the effective use of questions with interactive content and the future development of these kinds of questions.

First of all, we have considered questions that would be more suitable if interactive content were embedded in them. If these kinds of questions are posed to students, self-learning would be encouraged. This is a new way of using questions in LMSs not only for assessment but also for self-learning.

We suggested two examples of questions with interactive content (Figs. 7 and 8), but they may provide too many hints for more competent students. Therefore, it is preferable to implement a toggle switch to view or hide the interactive content. If we include a penalty to students when they view the interactive content, they will try to think as much as possible by themselves. If students view the interactive content, the action is recorded to logs in LMSs and teachers can focus their attention on those students. Alternatively, interactive content could be viewed adaptively. For the future plan of development for STACK, an interactive model is considered. In the plan, "state" is added to the question model and questions are posed to students in response to their answers [15].

One of the advantages of STACK questions is that we can formulate them with random variables, which mean that parameters of differential equations can be randomly determined every time students attempt questions. This function is useful for drill practices of calculations. There is, however, one drawback of applying interactive content as suggested in this paper. Figures and plots in interactive content do not work directly with randomly determined parameters in questions. It is necessary to find a technical solution to this loophole in the future.

4   Conclusion

We have suggested the use of interactive content in online tests. Such content was developed using the CindyJS framework of Cinderella, a type of DGS. Interactive content can be embedded in STACK, a mathematics e-Learning system. Two examples were provided: one was the question of calculation of the mathematical expression of a trace of a point and the other was the question of evaluation of the stability of fixed points of a system of ordinary differential equations. In these examples, students could use interactive content by grabbing and moving the points. This operation helps them receive a trigger to solve questions, which eventually enhances self-learning.

However, it is preferable to use interactive content adaptively, for example, by toggling a switch to view or hide the content or by displaying such content in response to the students' answers. Furthermore, there is one drawback in the use of interactive content as suggested in this paper: figures and plots do not work directly with randomly determined parameters in questions. A technical solution needs to be found for this drawback in the future.

Acknowledgement. This work was supported by JSPS KAKENHI Grant Numbers JP26282033, JP15K12377.

References

1. Sangwin, C.: Computer Aided Assessment of Mathematics. Oxford University Press, Oxford (2013)
2. Maplesoft: Maple T.A. User Case Studies. http://www.maplesoft.com/company/casestudies/product/Maple-TA/. Accessed 28 Mar 2017
3. Math, O.: Learning College Mathematics by webMathematica. http://www.las.osakafu-u.ac.jp/lecture/math/MathOnWeb/. Accessed 28 Mar 2017
4. Kawazoe, M., Yoshitomi, K.: E-learning/e-assessment systems based on webMathematica for university mathematics education. MSOR Connections **15**, 17–24 (2016)
5. Numbas at mathcentre.ac.uk. https://numbas.mathcentre.ac.uk/. Accessed 28 Mar 2017
6. WeBWork. http://webwork.maa.org/. Accessed 31 Mar 2017
7. Soga, T., Nakahara, T., Kawana, N., Fuse, I., Nakamura, Y.: Interactive learning using e-books connected with Moodle and development of Sharing environments for teaching materials. In: Proceedings of World Conference on e-Learning, pp. 1002–1011 (2015)
8. Fukazawa, K., Nakamura, Y.: Enhancement of plotting environment of STACK with Gnuplot. In: Proceedings of 21st Asian Technology Conference in Mathematics (2016). http://atcm.mathandtech.org/EP2016/contributed/4052016_21205.pdf. Accessed 30 Mar 2017
9. Gerhuser, M., Valentin, B., Wassermann, A., Wilfahrt, P.: JSXGraph dynamic mathematics running on (nearly) every device. Electron. J. Math. Technol. **5**, 26–36 (2011)
10. JSXGraph. https://jsxgraph.uni-bayreuth.de/wp/index.html. Accessed 30 Mar 2017

11. GeoGebra. https://www.geogebra.org/. Accessed 30 Mar 2017
12. Cinderella. https://cinderella.de/. Accessed 30 Mar 2017
13. CindyJS. https://cindyjs.org/. Accessed 30 Mar 2017
14. https://github.com/maths/moodle-qtype_stack/blob/master/doc/en/Authoring/index.md. Accessed 30 Mar 2017
15. Harjula, M., Malinen, J., Rasila, A.: STACK with state. MSOR Connections **15**, 60–69 (2016)

PDF Slide Teaching Materials Created Using KETCindy

Satoshi Yamashita[1]([✉]), Shigeki Kobayashi[2], Hideyo Makishita[3],
and Setsuo Takato[4]

[1] National Institute of Technology, Kisarazu College,
2-11-1, Kiyomidai-Higashi, Kisarazu 292-0041, Japan
yamashita@kisarazu.ac.jp
[2] National Institute of Technology, Nagano College,
716, Tokuma, Nagano 381-8550, Japan
[3] Shibaura Institute of Technology, 307, Fukasaku, Minuma-ku,
Saitama 337-8570, Japan
[4] Toho University, 2-2-1, Miyama, Funabashi 274-8510, Japan

Abstract. KeTCindy, a plugin for the dynamic geometry software Cinderella, enables accurate insertion of beautiful figures into a LaTeX document. KeTCindy can create not only printed teaching materials but also PDF slide teaching materials. As described in this paper, the authors explain the method of producing PDF slide teaching materials using KeTCindy and the usage of these slide materials in mathematics classes. One of the authors performed a fundamental statistics class using a PDF slide teaching material created using KeTCindy. This paper presents results of a questionnaire administered to students of the statistics course and proposes future work for PDF slide teaching materials created using KeTCindy.

1 Introduction

Collegiate mathematics comprises basic mathematics learned from high school to college, including calculus, linear algebra, and so on. Almost all collegiate mathematics teachers use LaTeX to create their original teaching materials because they can beautifully typeset sentences with mathematical expressions [1,2]. The materials are printed materials and slide materials used with a projector. Actually, is difficult for teachers to insert figures into a LaTeX document. For that reason, they often prepare teaching materials without figures. To break through this limitation, since 2006 the authors have been developing KETpic as a plugin for a mathematical software. In 2010, they completed KETpic as a plugin for Scilab [3], which is numerical computation software. Since 2014, they have been developing KETCindy as a collaboration of KETpic and Cinderella [4], which is dynamic geometry software because KETCindy can be equipped with Graphic User Interface (GUI) of KETpic [5,6]. KETCindy has the following main characteristics (Fig. 1):

© Springer International Publishing AG 2017
O. Gervasi et al. (Eds.): ICCSA 2017, Part IV, LNCS 10407, pp. 285–300, 2017.
DOI: 10.1007/978-3-319-62401-3_22

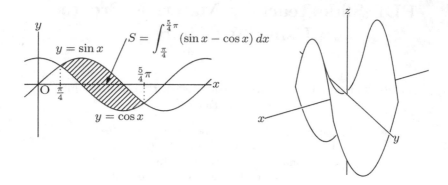

Fig. 1. Figures produced using K$_E$TCindy.

- K$_E$TCindy uses the Script Editor of Cinderella as Console User Interface (CUI) for K$_E$TCindy programming. The programming language is called *Cindy Script*.
- K$_E$TCindy uses the main screen of Cinderella as the GUI for the total image of a figure.
- K$_E$TCindy produces 2D/3D figures from line drawings.
- K$_E$TCindy uses the same font of characters and mathematical expressions as those of LATEX.
- K$_E$TCindy can slightly adjust various accessories that set the axes, line types, tickmarks, character positions, mathematical expressions, and so on.
- The figure LATEX file generated by K$_E$TCindy has extremely small capacity because it is a text file.
- The K$_E$TCindy system has two style files called *ketpic.sty* and *ketlayer.sty*. The former defines three distance variables using K$_E$Tpic. The latter defines the page layout environment called the *layer environment*.

In Sect. 2, the authors introduce the K$_E$TCindy system and explain the latest installation method.

As described in this paper, they introduce how to create PDF slide teaching materials using K$_E$TCindy and the usage of PDF slide materials. LATEX users usually use the beamer package of LATEX for creating PDF slide materials. The beamer package is loaded by calling the beamer class in the document class. Each frame environment specifies the contents to be put on one page slide. It is possible to make items appear on a slide using \pause or <a-b> like animations. The slide package of K$_E$TCindy is equipped with the same functions as the beamer package. It is possible to insert correct and beautiful figures, as shown in Fig. 1, in the position you desire. In Sect. 3, the authors explain the use of the K$_E$TCindy slide package.

Collegiate mathematics teachers require effective PDF slide teaching materials to presents lectures clearly in their classes. In Sect. 4, the authors classify the features of effective PDF slide teaching materials and show student questionnaire

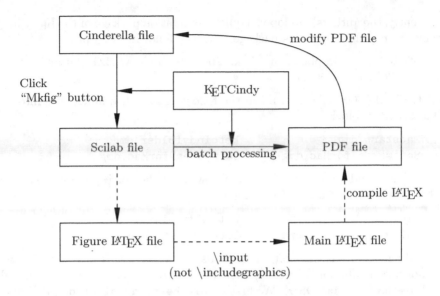

Fig. 2. Flow of the KETCindy system.

results for such a PDF slide teaching material. Finally, in Sect. 5, the authors summarize methods to create PDF slide teaching materials using KETCindy and how to use them effectively in your classes. Then the authors propose future works for additional development.

2 KETCindy System

In this section, the authors introduce the KETCindy system, which is able to insert figures into a LATEX document with the aid of Scilab numerical calculation software and a dynamic geometry software Cinderella. The KETCindy system generates a PDF file of figures using the following procedures (see Fig. 2). First, we draw geometric objects, which are points, segments, circles, and so on, on the main screen of Cinderella, and write Cindy Script, which is the programming language of Cinderella containing KETCindy commands, into Script Editor to generate the graphical data of these geometric objects. Then we execute the Cindy Script. Geometric objects are manipulated interactively on the main screen of Cinderella. Then we decide the positions of these geometric objects. When a user clicks the "Mkfig" button in the main screen, KETCindy converts the graphical data and associated commands into the Scilab commands and subsequently generates the figure LATEX file, which are formatted into LATEX graphical codes. The figure LATEX file is inserted into the main LATEX file by LATEX command \input (not \includegraphics). The compilation of the main LATEX file generates a high-quality PDF file. To simplify the whole procedure, we can use batch processing procedures displayed with dashed arrows in Fig. 2.

Recently, the authors developed a quick installation package of the KETCindy system. We can download this package from the following web page

https://www.dropbox.com/sh/kzt2bgaz07n7dr0/AABZRvOrqqCp5Tn1J ZYpnvSQa?dl=0

If our OS is Mac OS X, we download the following four disk image files into the `InstallforMac` folder:

`Macstart.dmg,`	`ketcindyfolder.dmg,`
`Softwares1forMac.dmg,`	`Softwares2forMac.dmg.`

If our OS is Windows (after ver. 7), we download the corresponding four executable files into the `InstallforWin` folder:

`Winstart.exe,`	`ketcindyfolder.exe,`
`Softwares1forWin.exe,`	`Softwares2forWin.exe.`

KETCindy system has installation methods of two types: "quick installation" and "normal installation". In this paper, the authors explain the "quick installation" method for Mac OS X. We first defrost `ketcindyfolder.dmg` and open the file `howtoinstallquickMacE.txt`. When we work according to the following procedures written on this text file, we can easily install KETCindy system using batch processing:

1. Copy `Macstart.dmg`, `ketcindyfolder.dmg` to Desktop and double click both. we obtain two folders `Macstart` and `ketcindyfolder` on the Desktop.
2. Open the folder `ketconfig` in `ketcindyfolder` and select the file `ketconfigdesktopE.sh`.
   (a) Select "get info" of this file and set "Open with" to "Terminal".
   (b) Double click the file `ketconfigdesktopE.sh`.
3. Select the file `template.cdy` in the ketcindy folder and select "get info" of this file. Set "Open with" to (copied) "Cinderella2".
4. Push the "Mkfig" button on the main screen of Cinderella. After Scilab and LATEX are executed successively, the final PDF output is displayed.
5. If you use `TeXworks` as an editor of TEX,
   (a) Launch `TeXworks`, and choose `Edit>Preference>Typeset`.
   (b) Set it as follows: Push the "+" button and write the following.
   ```
   name : texworkslatex
    program : find the following:
      /Applications/kettex/ketbin/texworkslatex.sh
    Argument : $fullname
   ```
6. Install other software
   (a) Use `Softwares1.dmg` for Cinderella and Scilab if necessary.
   (b) Use `Softwares2.dmg` for Maxima, R, etc.

Table 1. KETCindy can do the following

s01	Geometric figure	s08	Calling R
s02	Graph of function	s09	Surface
s03	MAking table	s10	Calling Maxima
s04	Bézier curve	s11	Calling Asir
s05	3D figure	s12	Calling Fricas
s06	Animation	s13	Calling Mesthlab
s07	Slide for presentation	s14	Data processing

When we carry out Item 5 above, the following seven files are generated in the folder `ketcindy/ketwork`:

```
kc.sh,
template.sce,           template.tex,
templatemain.tex,       templatemain.aux,       templatemain.log,
templatemain.pdf.
```

`kc.sh` is the batch processing file, `template.sce` is a Scilab file, `template.tex` is a figure LATEX file, and `templatemain.pdf` is a main LATEX file. `templatemain.pdf` is shown to the final PDF output (see Fig. 2).

The `ketcindy/ketsample/samples` folder holds many sample Cinderella files that can be created using the KETCindy system. As shown in Table 1, there are 14 sample folders. Some sample Cinderella files exist in each folder. The web page "Producing Teaching Materials with Drawings Using KETCindy" [7] provides additional information.

3 PDF Slide Teaching Materials

In this section, the authors introduce how to create PDF slide teaching materials using the KETCindy system. They explain it using the sample folder `s07slides` (see Table 1). First, we produce the new working folder `mywork` on Desktop and make the folder `fig` in `mywork` to save figure files which we insert into a PDF slide teaching material.

3.1 Basic Production Method

We copy two files `s07sample1.cdy` and `s07sample1.txt` from `s07slides` to `mywork`. When opening `s07sample1.cdy` using a double-click, Cinderella is started. The main screen is opened as shown on the left side of Fig. 3. When choosing **Scripting>Edit Scripts** at the upper toolbar, Script Editor is opened. The following program is written using Cindy Script (see the right side of Fig. 3):

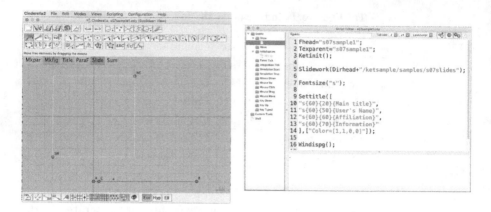

Fig. 3. Cinderella file for slides created using KᴇTCindy.

```
1.  Fhead="s07sample1";
2.  Texparent="s07sample1";
3.  Ketinit();
4.
5.  Slidework(Dirhead+"/ketsample/samples/s07slides");
6.
7.  Fontsize("s");
8.
9.  Settitle([
10. "s{60}{20}{Main title}",
11. "s{60}{50}{Name}",
12. "s{60}{60}{Affiliation}",
13. "s{60}{70}{Information}"
14. ],["Color=[1,1,0,0]"]);
15.
16. Windispg();
```

Line 1 designates a figure LATEX file's name. Line 2 designates a main text file's name that is s07sample1.txt. Line 3 shows initialization of the KᴇTCindy system. Because Line 5 means the path of the working folder, we rewrite Line 5 as follows:

Slidework(gethome()+"/Desktop/mywork");,

where gethome() means the home path /Users/<User's Name>. Line 7 means that the font size is \small in the figure LATEX file. By the program from Line 9 to Line 14, we generate the title slide. At Line 10, s{60}{20} represents the position where the characters "Main Title" are written, which is the south side (the lower) of the coordinate (60, 20) on the right side of Fig. 3. Similarly, the program from Line 11 to Line 13 is written. Line 14 means that the color of characters in the title slide is blue, which has CMYK code [1,1,0,0].

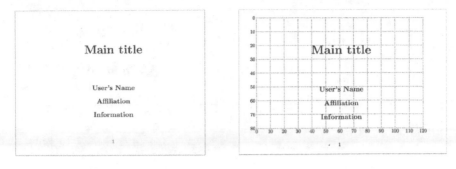

Fig. 4. Title slide created using KETCindy.

After clicking the gear mark at the end of the upper right in Script Editor, the program shown above is executed. Batch processing file `kc.sh` is generated in `mywork`. The main screen of Cinderella has six special buttons named "Mkpar", "Mkfig", "Title", "ParaF", "Slide", and "Sum" at the upper left (see the left side of Fig. 3). After clicking the "Title" button in the main screen, the PDF output of the title slide is displayed (see the left side of Fig. 4).

We can create the whole slide using the main text file `s07sample1.txt`. When we open this text file, the following program is shown:

```
 1. %Title::slide0::background//
 2. Title::slide0//
 3.
 4. %%%%%%%%%%%%%%%%//
 5. main::Main slide 1//
 6.
 7. %%%%%%%%%%%%%%%%//
 8. new::Itemize environment//
 9.
10. itemize//
11. item::content//
12. item::conclusion//
13. end//
14.
15. %%%%%%%%%%%%%%%%//
16. new::Enumerate environment//
17.
18. enumerate::[(1)]//
19. item::When the number is changed, we set the option [(1)].//
20. item::It follows that the number is changed in turn.//
21. end//
```

In fact, the mark `//` put at the end in each line generates a new paragraph of the LaTeX file for slides. In Line 5, `main::` denotes the slide for a section title;

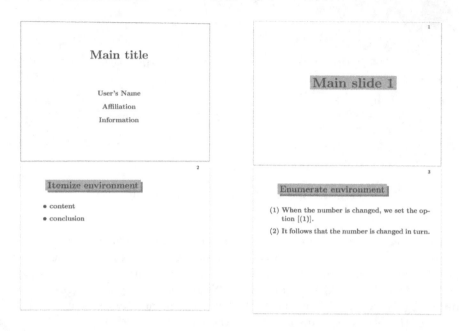

Fig. 5. Four slides created using K_ETCindy.

Main slide 1 is written as the section title. In Line 8, `new::` denotes the new slide; **Itemize environment** is written as the slide title. From Line 10 to Line 13, we can generate the itemized environment of the L^AT_EX file for slides. From Line 18 to Line 21, we can generate the enumerate environment of the L^AT_EX file for slides. In fact, `[(1)]` in Line 18 presents the option of the enumerate environment.

After returning to Script Editor of Cinderella and clicking the gear mark, one can load the text file `s07sample1.txt` by the following line:

```
2. Texparent="s07sample1";
```

At the main screen of Cinderella and clicking the "Slide" button, the PDF output of four slides is displayed (see Fig. 5). We produce the figure L^AT_EX file `background.tex` and write the following program.

```
 1. {\color[cmyk]{0.3,0.1,0.4,0}\huge\rm\normalsize
 2.
 3. \newpage
 4.
 5. \begin{layer}{120}{0}
 6. \putnotese{2}{0}{\ketpic\hspace{2mm}\ketcindy}\hspace{2mm}%
 7. \ketpic\hspace{2mm}\ketcindy\hspace{2mm}%
 8. \ketpic\hspace{2mm}\ketcindy\hspace{2mm}%
 9. \ketpic\hspace{2mm}\ketcindy\hspace{2mm}%
10. }
```

```
11. \putnotese{2}{80}{\ketcindy\ \ketpic\hspace{2mm}%
12. \ketcindy\hspace{2mm}\ketpic\hspace{2mm}%
13. \ketcindy\hspace{2mm}\ketpic\hspace{2mm}%
14. \ketcindy\hspace{2mm}\ketpic
15. }
16. \lineseg{0}{4}{125}{0}
17. \lineseg{0}{84}{125}{0}
18. \putnotese{2}{86}{sample}
19. \putnotesw{120}{86}{27/12/2016}
20.
21. \end{layer}
22.
23. }
```

This program generates the background pictures of respective slides. From Line 5 to Line 21, the layer environment is used. We can put characters or figures at the accurate position by \putnotese or \putnotesw.

We rewrite the program from Line 1 to Line 2 in s07sample1.txt in the following program:

```
1. Title::slide0::background//
2. %Title::slide0//
```

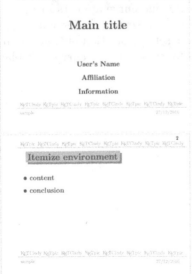
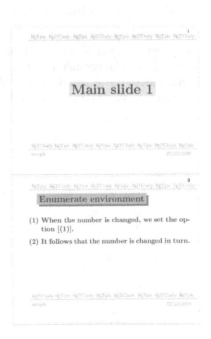

Fig. 6. Four slides with the background picture.

When clicking the gear mark in Script Editor and click the "Slide" button in the main screen, the PDF output of four slides is displayed with the background picture, as shown in Fig. 6.

3.2   Using Item Animations

The beamer package of LaTeX is equipped with item animations. The slide package of KETCindy is also equipped with them. The authors explain the use of item animations using KETCindy.

We copy two files s07sample3.cdy and s07sample3.txt from s07slides to mywork. When we open s07sample3.cdy and Script Editor, the following program is written using Cindy Script.

```
 1. Fhead="sinecurve";
 2. Texparent="s07sample3";
 3. Ketinit();
        ...
14. Setslidebody("black");
15. Setslidepage(["black"]);
16.
17. Ch=[1];
18. if(contains(Ch,1),
19.   Plotdata("1","sin(x-C.x)","x");
20. );
```

After clicking the gear mark in Script Editor, a sine curve appears in the main screen. We move the geometric point C in the main screen. A sine curve moves C.x in parallel in the x axis direction. When we set the position of C in the main screen and click the "Mkfig" button, the PDF output of a sine curve is displayed (see Fig. 7).

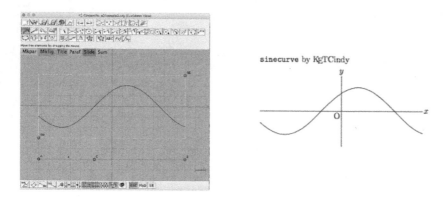

Fig. 7. Sine curve generated using KETCindy.

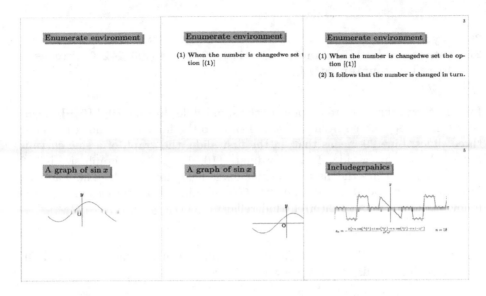

Fig. 8. PDF slide teaching materials created using KETCindy.

We open the text file s07sample3.txt. The following program is written in the text file:

```
      . . .
15. %%%%%%%%%%%%%%%//
16. new::Enumerate environment//
17. %repeat-3//
18.
19. %[2,-]::enumerate::[(1)]//
20. %[2,-]::item::When the number is changed, we set the option
    [(1)]//
21. %[3,-]::item::It follows that the number is changed in turn.//
22. %[2,-]::end//
23.
24. %%%%%%%%%%%%%%%//
25. new::A graph of $\bm{\sin x}$//
26. %repeat=2//
27.
28. layer::{100}{0}//
29. %[1]::putnote::se{10}{15}::sinecurve,0.8//
30. %[2]::putnote::se{60}{25}::sinecurve,0.8//
31. end//
32.
33. %%%%%%%%%%%%%%%//
34. new::Includegrpahics//
```

```
35.
36. layer::{100}{0}//
37. putnote::s{60}{5}::include[bb=0.00 0.00 549.00 242.00,width=
    100mm] ::fourier.pdf//
38. end//
```

Line 17 shows the three repetitions of the same slide. In Line 19, %[2,-] means that Line 19 is denoted from the second slide to the final slide among the same three slides. Line 29 means that, in the first slide, the graph of a sine curve is put at the southeast side of the coordinate (10, 15) and the graph size is 0.8 times. Line 37 means the insertion of the image file **Fourier.pdf**. The bounding box option bb=0.00 0.00 549.00 242.00 is obtained from the execution of the following line in Script Editor of Cinderella:

```
BBdata("Fourier.pdf");
```

After clicking the "Slides" button in the main screen of Cinderella, the PDF output of slides is displayed as shown in Fig. 8.

3.3   Using Flip Animations

The slide package of KᴇTCindy is also equipped with flip animations. The beamer package of LᴬTᴇX is not equipped with them. The authors explain the use of flip animations.

We copy two files s07sample4.cdy and s07sample4.txt from s07slides to mywork. When we open s07sample4.cdy and Script Editor, the following program is written by Cindy Script:

```
        . . .
14. Setslidehyper();
15.
16. Fontsize("s");
17.
18. Circledata("1",[[0,0],[2,0]]);
19. Expr([2,0],"se","2");
20. B.x=2*pi;
21.
22. mf(s):=(
23.    regional(p0,p1,tmp);
24.    p0=[0,0];
25.    p1=2*[cos(s),sin(s)];
26.    Setcolor("red");
27.    Listplot("1",[p0,p1]);
28.    Setcolor("black");
29.    Pointdata("1", p1);
30.    Bowdata("1",[p0,p1],[1,0.3,"Expr=2"]);
31.    tmp=1.1*p1;
```

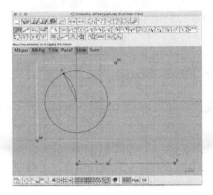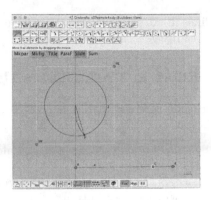

Fig. 9. Point on the circle with the slider.

```
32.   Expr(tmp,"c","\mathrm{P}");
33. );
34.
35. Setpara("pointoncircle","mf(s)","s=[0,2*pi]",["m","Div=30"]);
36. mf(C.x-A.x);
37.
38. Windispg();
```

Line 14 presents the definition of the flip advance/playback button in PDF slides using the hyperref environment of LaTeX. Line 18 shows the definition of the circle with center $(0, 0)$ and radius 2, and Line 20 presents the definition of the slider AB with a slide point C that C.x is the angle of deviation at point P (see Fig. 9). At Line 22 to Line 33, we define point P on the circle where s is equal to the angle of deviation at P. Line 35 shows the definition of 30 flip animations in the folder pointoncircle. After clicking the "ParaF" button in the main screen, we can generate 30 flip animations in the folder pointoncircle.

We open the text file s07sample4.txt. The following program is written in the text file:

```
      ...
17. %%%%%%%%%%%%%%%%//
18. new::Polar coordinates//
19. %repeat=,para=pointoncircle:{0}:s{85}{10}:input:1.2//
20.
21. \begin{minipage}{50mm}//
22. What is a track of the point P which meets $r=2$ ?\\//
23. %[31]::\hspace*{20mm}It is a circle//
24. \end{minipage}//
```

Line 19 shows that we generate the figure LaTeX files for flip animations in the folder pointoncircle and put 1.2 times of each figure at the south of the coordinate (85, 10) in the main LaTeX file s07sample4.tex. If we write only

24 lines in `s07sample4.txt`, then we generate 775 lines in `s07sample4.tex`. We can readily generate flip animations.

4   Effect in Math Classes Using PDF Slides

PDF slide teaching materials created by KₑTCindy have the following characteristics:

- Sentences are shown sequentially along with the teacher's explanation using item animations.
- Teachers can freely move the flip where they would like to show using the flip advance/playback button.
- Teachers can put the same figure in the print teaching material just as a figure in the PDF slide teaching material.

After one of the authors taught a fundamental statistics class using a PDF slide teaching material and a printed teaching material, he asked the class about it, obtaining the following responses.

1. Did you understand how to calculate an unbiased estimate of population variance?
     Yes   27/27,   No   0/27
2. Did you understand the simulation of the chi-square distribution?
     Yes   24/27,   No   3/27
3. Did you understand the chi-square test process?
     Yes   27/27,   No   0/27
4. Did you understand the method of setting the critical region using the F distribution table?
     Yes   26/27,   No   1/27
5. Did you understand the F test process?
     Yes   27/27,   No   0/27
6. Which explanation would you like? One using a blackboard or one using a PDF slide teaching material?
     A blackboard   3/27,   a PDF slide   9/27,   Both   15/27

The following opinions were obtained from students who remarked that a PDF slide teaching material was preferred.

- The teacher took sufficient time to take notes using item animations.
- The flip animations were helpful to understand the contents.
- It was possible to concentrate and hear the explanation.
- It was possible to solve a problem while confirming the solution.
- The explanation was detailed.
- It was easy to understand how to use the distribution table.

From the opinions presented above, the authors knew that item animations and flip animations were helpful for students to understand the contents. Furthermore, the authors knew the following about PDF slide teaching materials:

- Using item animations, students can have sufficient time to take notes and to confirm the solution to a problem.
- Teachers can never show a simulation using the blackboard, but they can show the simulation using flip animations.
- Teachers can provide a detailed explanation in a short time. Thereby, they can assign time to make students practice much.

5   Conclusion and Future Works

The authors have developed the KETCindy system as a plug-in for Cinderella to create teaching materials with figures using LATEX. In Sect. 2, the authors explained the process flow of KETCindy system and the usage of the quick installation package that they developed recently.

KETCindy has 14 sample folders, as shown in Table 1. In Sect. 3, the authors introduced the seventh folder s07slides that created PDF slide teaching materials using KETCindy system. The beamer package of LATEX is famous for creating PDF slide teaching materials, but it cannot create a simulation. KETCindy system enables us to create a simulation using flip animations. It is equipped with the same item animations as those of the beamer package.

One author taught a fundamental statistics class using a PDF slide teaching material and a printed teaching material created by KETCindy. In Sect. 4, they showed the results obtained from the questionnaire administered to students in the class: most students were able to understand the contents by a PDF slide teaching material, not a blackboard. When using PDF slide teaching materials, teachers devote attention to the matters described below:

- Before moving to the next slide, teachers give sufficient time to take notes to all students.
- Teachers present a procedure of the solution in turn using item animations.
- Teachers present a simulation using flip animations.
- Teachers briefly explain the contents in detail so that students can take sufficient time to practice problems by active learning.

At the end of this section, the authors propose future works related to PDF slide teaching materials created by KETCindy:

- The authors will teach collegiate mathematics in their active learning classes using PDF slide teaching materials. Then they will ask students about the class.
- Based on results of the questionnaires presented above, the authors will investigate the active learning class design using PDF slide teaching materials. Then they will investigate the efficient usage of PDF slide teaching materials by which students promote mathematical understanding.
- The authors will improve the KETCindy system so that it will become easy for teachers to use PDF slide teaching materials in their class efficiently.

Acknowledgement. This research is supported by a Japan Society for the Promotion of Science (JSPS) Grant-in-Aid for Scientific Research (C) Grant Number 16K01152.

References

1. Lamport, L.: LaTeX: A Document Preparation System. Addison-Wesley, Boston (1994)
2. Goossens, F., Braams, M., Carlisle, J., Rowley, D., Mittelbach, C.: The LaTeX Companion, 2nd edn. Addison-Wesley, Boston (2004)
3. Nagar, S.: Introduction to Scilab (2016). Independently published
4. Kortenkamp, U., Gebert, J.R.: The Cinderella. 2 Manual. Springer, Heidelberg (2012)
5. Kaneko, M., Yamashita, S., Kitahara, K., Maeda, Y., Nakamura, Y., Kortenkamp, U., Takato, S.: KETCindy - collaboration of Cinderella and KETpic reports on CADGME 2014 conference working group. IJTME **22**, 179–185 (2015)
6. Kaneko, M., Yamashita, S., Makishita, H., Nishiura, K., Takato, S.: Collaborative use of KETCindywith other mathematical tools. eJMT (To appear)
7. CASTEX Research Organization: Producing Teaching Materials with Drawings Using KETCindy (2016). https://www65.atwiki.jp/ketcindy-eng

KETpic-Matlab Toolbox for LaTeX High-Quality Graphical Artwork in Educational Materials on Bézier Curve Algorithms at a Master Level

Akemi Gálvez[1,2]([⊠]), Setsuo Takato[1], Masataka Kaneko[3], Javier Del Ser[4,5,6], and Andrés Iglesias[1,2]

[1] Department of Information Science, Faculty of Sciences, Toho University,
2-2-1 Miyama, Funabashi 274-8510, Japan
[2] Department of Applied Mathematics and Computational Sciences,
University of Cantabria, Avda. de los Castros, s/n, 39005 Santander, Spain
galveza@unican.es
[3] Faculty of Pharmaceutical Sciences, Toho University,
2-2-1 Miyama, Funabashi 274-8510, Japan
[4] Tecnalia Research & Innovation, 48160 Derio, Bizkaia, Spain
[5] University of the Basque Country UPV/EHU, Bilbao, Bizkaia, Spain
[6] Basque Center for Applied Mathematics (BCAM), Bilbao, Bizkaia, Spain

Abstract. This paper introduces a new KETpic-Matlab toolbox to generate LaTeX-embedded high-quality graphical artwork about the main algorithms for Bézier curves and related topics. The package has been implemented by the authors as a supporting middleware tool to generate educational materials for a computer-aided geometric design (CAGD) course at an advanced level (typically a Master/PhD course; even a senior course in some engineering degrees). Its primary goal is to instill geometric intuition in our students and help them develop critical thinking based on geometric reasoning for problem solving. We also aim at providing the instructors of such courses with a computer library to produce high-quality graphics for educational materials with a seamless integration into LaTeX. In this regard, all graphical objects are encoded as plain LaTeX-readable source code that yields nice pictures after standard LaTeX compilation. The application of this package to generate educational materials is discussed through six illustrative examples of interesting properties of the Bézier curves. They show that our package is very easy to use, supports many different graphical options, and fosters students' creative geometric thinking with very little effort.

Keywords: Bézier curve · De Casteljau's algorithm · Educational materials · Graphical artwork · Matlab toolbox

1 Introduction

During the last few years, the authors have been deeply involved in the development of high-quality educational materials for teaching and learning at various University levels. Among them, a course about CAGD (the acronym for

© Springer International Publishing AG 2017
O. Gervasi et al. (Eds.): ICCSA 2017, Part IV, LNCS 10407, pp. 301–316, 2017.
DOI: 10.1007/978-3-319-62401-3_23

Computer-Aided Geometric Design) is currently taught in the Master of Mathematics and Computer Science of the University of Cantabria. Similar courses are also delivered in many other Master and PhD programs, even in advanced senior year of some engineering degrees (e.g., mechanical engineering, aerospace engineering, ship building engineering). Although it also explores some remarkable applications in many fields (such as computer-aided design and manufacturing - CAD/CAM, and geometric modeling and processing for medical imaging in computer tomography (CT) and magnetic resonance imaging (MRI), to mention just two of them), the course is mainly focused on the mathematical and geometrical aspects of curves and surfaces and their properties.

In our experience, the biggest challenge of this course is how to instill a geometric intuition about the CAGD algorithms [1] in our students so that they can properly apply geometric reasoning to problem solving. Very often, we find that our students do solve problems by following an strictly algebraic approach: they focus exclusively on the equations and perform algebraic manipulations on them to get a proper solution to a given problem. However, they fail to provide a geometric interpretation to this process and typically do not related the obtained solution to any particular geometric configuration or whatever. This is a critical indication that they are operating on a purely algebraic basis, without any mental relationship with the real geometry of the problem. Clearly, there is a need for a less mechanical, "automatic-pilot" approach for this kind of courses.

In addition to other issues, part of the problem is related to the classroom materials our students typically use. Many textbooks and other materials rely on equations and algebraic manipulations more often than advisable, and usually skip the geometric interpretation. This approach, albeit undesirable, can somehow be justified: producing good graphical materials is cumbersome and time-consuming, and requires some expertise about computer tools for graphical editing, which are also usually expensive and difficult to use. In this context, the geometric flavor of our course poses a particularly challenging question:

How to provide our students with an affordable set of classroom materials with high-quality graphical artwork?

In our opinion, such materials must fulfill the following conditions:

- *they must have a strong focus on geometrical intuition:* in this regard, they should allow our students to grasp the subtle details of the most common algorithms in CAGD in a geometrical fashion rather than the (most standard but less effective) equation-based approach.
- *they must be accurate:* accuracy is essential in many CAGD geometric algorithms; otherwise, they do not work properly and students will find troubles in understanding them at full extent.
- *they must have a high visual quality:* classroom materials must include all elements required to fully understand the algorithms. Generally, they include axis labels and ticks, text annotations, legends, colors, varying types of lines (solid, dashed, dotted) with varying sizes for line thickness, and many other

graphical and text elements playing the role of visual clues for better understanding.

- *they must be affordable to produce:* this means that materials must be not only meaningful in terms of contents but also somehow optimized regarding the time and effort required to produce them. Instructors time is limited, so issues such as a long learning curve for the programs or applications used to generate the classroom materials or a large production time should be avoided. Typically, such programs should provide a number of valuable features on a user-friendly ready-to-use approach.
- *they must be easy to deploy:* this implies that the storage size of the graphical elements must be kept to the minimum. Typically, high-resolution artwork demands large file sizes, thus preventing the materials to be smoothly deployed over the web or attached to email messages. Vector graphics can be the solution for this problem, but most vector-graphics programs are intended for professional use in printing and publishing business; as a result, they tend to be quite expensive and difficult to use. A good solution should ideally overcome these drawbacks.
- *they must be LATEX-compatible:* LATEX is a standard de facto tool for high-quality scientific publishing and editing. Therefore, it is advisable for the tools used to generate educational materials to have a seamless integration into LATEX for optimal quality and performance.

Unfortunately, it is not easy to find computer tools providing all the features mentioned above. A pioneering effort in this regard was launched a few years ago under the KETpic project (see Sect. 2 for details). In this paper, we propose to tackle the issue by using a KETpic toolbox for Bézier curves developed by the authors on the popular scientific computer program *Matlab* [8].

The structure of this paper is as follows: in Sect. 2 we describe the main features of our KETpic-Matlab toolbox for Bézier curves. The application of this toolbox to generate educational materials is discussed in Sect. 3 through six illustrative examples of interesting properties of the Bézier curves. This section also illustrates the potential of our toolbox as an educational supporting tool for scientific visualization and critical geometric thinking. The paper closes with the main conclusions and some ideas for future work in the field.

2   KETpic-Matlab Toolbox for Bézier Curve Algorithms

This section describes the main features of our KETpic toolbox on Matlab. For the sake of completeness, we also present briefly KETpic to those readers not familiar with this interesting software.

2.1   About KETpic

KETpic (an acronym for *K*isarazu *E*ducational *Tpic*) is a middleware software released in 2006 for high-quality mathematical drawing in LATEX [9]. The software, conceived at the "Kisarazu National College of Technology" for educational purposes, has roots in *Tpic* system, a terminal driver that supports the LaTeX `picture` environment. Originally developed for the computer algebra system *Maple* in April 2006, it was designed to provide LaTeX end-users with extensive support for visualization and printing of high-quality graphical objects. As such, it is an ideal package to generate printed materials (books, slides, reports, etc.) with graphical content for educational purposes and professional printing. See [3–5, 7, 10, 11] for several examples and additional information about this software.

Briefly speaking, KETpic is a library of macros and scripts to generate LaTeX-readable source code for high-quality scientific artwork. Such macros can be implemented on different computer algebra systems and other scientific programs, thus yielding different versions of the package (used as plug-ins or add-ons). Depending on the scientific system they are based on, these plug-ins might typically run internally in a quite different way, but the process is usually transparent to end-users, thus minimizing the time required to get accustomed to the program. Once KETpic is loaded, users are simply requested to execute commands in the system of their choice to plot graphical data. Specialized embedded KETpic commands generate additional LaTeX source code and files, which are subsequently compiled in LaTeX in the usual manner. As a result, accurate graphical figures are readily obtained from small plain text files, an optimal solution for efficient data storage and file transfer. A first KETpic version for standard mathematical curves in Matlab is described in [2], then extended in [6].

2.2 KETpic-Matlab Toolbox Pipeline

To use the KETpic-Matlab toolbox, we have to proceed according to the following pipeline. The process starts up by opening Matlab for a new session and loading the KETpic toolbox through the following command:

```
>> Ketinit
```

Generation of figures in LaTeX from the original pictures created in *Matlab* requires to carry out some steps. As mentioned above, any graphical object is encoded as a plain text file to be compiled in LaTeX. The following script executes this process:

```
1    >> Openfile('filename.tex');
2    Beginpicture('');
3           graphical functions here (see Sect. 3 for details)
4    Endpicture(#picture);
5    Closefile();
```

This script stores all data associated with the graphical object into the file *filename.tex* for subsequent use in LaTeX. Line 1 of this script opens such a file in the folder indicated in the namepath. Second line defines the units of length for the final picture (with default value 1 cm). The command `Beginpicture` is also used to create the `\begin{picture}`...`\end{picture}` environment in

LATEX. The graphical functions in line 3 convert the data points into a sequence of LATEX-readable commands to be inserted into the `picture` environment created in line 2 for standard compilation. The command `Endpicture()` in line 4 performs two different actions: on one hand, it closes the `picture` environment in the TEX file. On the other hand, it allows us to set up the display of cartesian axes, according to its value: 1 (empty value is also feasible) if axes are to be displayed and 0 otherwise. Finally, Line 5 closes the file.

The final output of this process is the file *filename.tex* in our workspace folder. It contains a description of the graphical objects created in *Matlab* in terms of LATEX and *Tpic* commands. The file can be embedded into a standard LATEX file for compilation. The following code will yield a printout of the graphical objects within the file:

```
\documentclass[11pt]{article}
    ...
\newlength{\Width}
\newlength{\Height}
\newlength{\Depth}
    ...
\begin{document}
    ...
\input{ filename.tex }
    ...
\end{document}
```

It is the typical LATEX code with a `documentclass` declaration and the `document` environment. The only difference are three lines in the preamble (between the start of the file and the `\begin{document}` command) that specify new directives for the length units, and the `\input` command in the main body of source code that causes the indicated file to be read and processed, exactly as if its contents had been inserted in the current file at that point. Compilation of the code above generates the graphical objects described in *filename.tex* in the form of a DVI file.

3   Illustrative Examples

In this section, some illustrative examples about the application of the KETpic-Matlab toolbox described in previous section to different algorithms for Bézier curves are described. In what it follows, we assume that the reader is familiar with the main concepts about free-form parametric curves [1]. A *free-form parametric Bézier curve* $\mathbf{C}(t)$ *of degree* n is defined as:

$$\mathbf{C}(t) = \sum_{j=0}^{n} \mathbf{P}_j B_j^n(t) \tag{1}$$

where $\mathbf{P}_j$ are vector coefficients (usually referred to as the *control points*), $B_j^n(t)$ are the *Bernstein polynomials of index j and degree n*, given by:

$$B_j^n(t) = \binom{n}{j} t^j (1-t)^{n-j} \tag{2}$$

and t is the *curve parameter*, defined on the finite interval $[0,1]$. Note that in this paper vectors are denoted in bold. By convention, $0! = 1$.

3.1 Example 1: De Casteljau's Algorithm for Evaluation

The *De Casteljau's algorithm* is a recursive algorithm developed by French mathematician Paul de Casteljau in 1959 (while working for automotive company Citroën) to evaluate a Bézier curve at a point given by the parameter value $t = t_0$. Such a point $\mathbf{C}(t_0)$ can be obtained by the recurrence relation:

$$\begin{cases} \mathbf{P}_j^{(0)} = \mathbf{P}_j & j = 0, \ldots, n \\ \mathbf{P}_j^{(k)} = \mathbf{P}_j^{(k-1)}(1-t_0) + \mathbf{P}_{j+1}^{(k-1)}t_0 & j = 0, \ldots, n-k\,;\, k = 0, \ldots, n \end{cases} \tag{3}$$

In this case, $\mathbf{C}(t_0)$ is evaluated in n steps of this algorithm as: $\mathbf{C}(t_0) = \mathbf{P}_0^{(n)}$.

A very exciting feature about the De Casteljau's algorithm is the fact that it has a straightforward and appealing geometric interpretation. The process is shown graphically in Fig. 1. We start with an initial Bézier curve with 8 control points, displayed in Fig. 1 (top-left). As the reader can see, the control points are connected by a control polygon comprised of linear segments between consecutive control points. Then, we subdivide each line segment of the control polygon according to the ratio $t_0 : (1 - t_0)$ and connect the resulting points to get a new control polygon with one fewer control point (and hence, one fewer segment) for each recursion step, until eventually reaching a single point. The different steps of this process are shown in Fig. 1: the figure in top-right corresponds to the first step, where seven control points (displayed in red) are obtained. Next step is shown in the second row for six control points (displayed in green on the left) and five control points (in blue on the right). The process ends after seven steps, with a final point corresponding to the value $t = 0.4$ (displayed in brown in Fig. 1 (bottom-right)).

It is important to remark that the pictures in Fig. 1 (and actually all pictures in this paper) do not come from files in any graphical format, such as EPS, JPG, GIF, or the like. Instead, they are a simple collection of LaTeX-readable instructions from a plain text file, generated as described in previous section. As remarked above, this has the clear advantage of a very small file size (about only a few KB). In addition, no graphical editor is needed to produce or manipulate our artwork; just a few simple functions from our KETpic-Matlab toolbox are required. In this particular example, the function `DeCasteljauAlgorithm` is invoked. Its syntax is as follows:

`DeCasteljauAlgorithm(`*cp, t_0, th, iter, lgopts*`)`

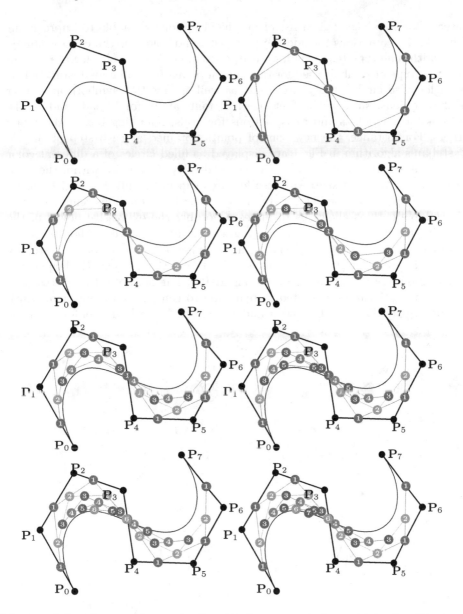

Fig. 1. (left-right, top-bottom) Graphical representation obtained with our KETpic-Matlab toolbox of all steps of the De Casteljau's algorithm for evaluation of a Bézier curve at the parametric value $t_0 = 0.4$. (Color figure online)

where *cp* indicates the list of control points for the Bézier curve, t_0 is the parameter value at which the curve is evaluated, *th* means the line thickness for the curve, *iter* means the number of steps for the De Castellau's algorithm (by default, this number is the degree of the curve, but it can be changed to any lower value), and *lgopts* is a list of graphical options available to improve our artwork. These options include the point size and color for the control points, line width, line type (e.g., solid, dashed, dotted, etc.), and color for the control polygon, type of symbols used for the control points (e.g., diamond, star, bullet, triangle, filled circle, empty circle, etc. as well as any TEX symbol), and other related options, such as the font size and font family for legends and labels, options for axis labels and ticks, options for grids, bounding boxes, and many others. For instance, the new control points obtained at each step of the De Casteljau's algorithm in Fig. 1 are displayed as filled circles of a different color for each step. Also, the iteration number is displayed in white within the filled circle for a given font size. All these features can be modified at will by using the list of options of the `DeCasteljauAlgorithm` function. This remarkable set of available options allows us to increase notably the expressive power of the resulting figures. Our students can now grasp all the details about how does this algorithm actually work, and what is the meaning of each control point step by step. As a result, the students' focus is shifted from the mathematical equations to the geometric intuition about the algorithm. Furthermore, the process displayed in Fig. 1 can be executed in real time to generate an animation, which can be displayed on a web browser and/or exported to a PDF file, for instance.

Fig. 2. Two examples of Bézier curves generated with our KETpic-Matlab toolbox.

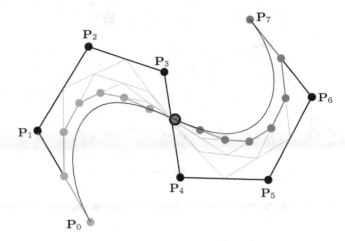

Fig. 3. Application of the De Casteljau's algorithm for curve subdivision: the original Bézier curve with 8 control points in Fig. 1 (top-left) is subdivided at the parametric value $t_s = 0.5$. As a result, the curve is subdivided into two new Bézier curves with 8 control points each (displayed in red and blue color, respectively). (Color figure online)

Figure 2 shows two examples of artistic shapes generated with our KₑTpic-Matlab toolbox and corresponding to the silhouette of a crane and a giraffe, respectively. In this case, the function BezierCurve(cp, *lgopts*) is used.

3.2 Example 2: De Casteljau's Algorithm for Subdivision

The De Casteljau's algorithm can also be applied without any modification to curve subdivision, i.e., to split a Bézier curve of degree n into two Bézier curves of the same degree n joined together at an arbitrary parameter value $t = t_s$. To this aim, it is enough to apply the recursive process described in Sect. 3.1 and then consider the two Bézier curves of degree n and control points:

$$\left\{\mathbf{P}_0^{(0)}, \mathbf{P}_0^{(1)}, \ldots, \mathbf{P}_0^{(n)}\right\} \text{ and } \left\{\mathbf{P}_0^{(n)}, \mathbf{P}_1^{(n-1)}, \ldots, \mathbf{P}_n^{(0)}\right\} \qquad (4)$$

respectively.

The geometric interpretation of this process is graphically shown in Fig. 3. The subdivision process of the original Bézier curve with 8 control points in Fig. 1 (top-left) at the parametric value $t_s = 0.5$ yields two new Bézier curves with 8 control points each. The first one, displayed in red in Fig. 3, is obtained by taking the initial control point of the control polygon for each step of the De Casteljau's algorithm, displayed in each picture of Fig. 1 (i.e., first control point $\mathbf{P}_0$ (top-left), then first control point with label 1 (top-right), then first one with label 2 (second row-left) and so on). The second curve, displayed in blue, corresponds to a similar process but taking the last control point at each step instead. The SubdivideCurve(cp, t_s, *options*) function in our toolbox returns this graphical output in one step.

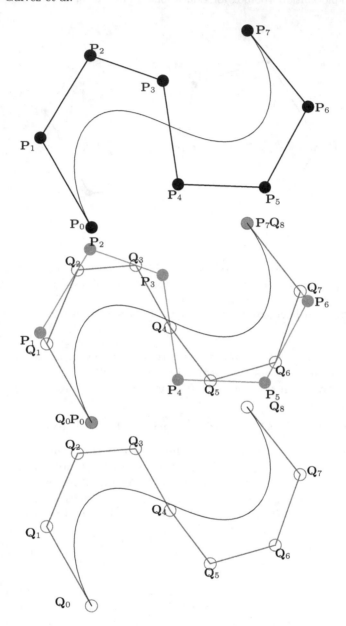

Fig. 4. Modified De Casteljau's algorithm for degree raising: (top): original Bézier curve of degree 7; (middle) original (in gray) and new control polygon (in blue) for degree raising; (bottom) resulting Bézier curve of degree 8. (Color figure online)

3.3   Example 3: Modified Algorithm for Degree Raising

From Eqs. (1)–(2), it is evident that the degree of curve $\mathbf{C}(t)$ depends on the number of control points. In general, increasing the degree makes the curve more complex and requires longer computation time, but it also gives the curve higher flexibility and increases the curve ability to design more complicated shapes. Because of this reason, it might be very helpful to be able to increase the degree of a Bézier curve without changing its shape. This process, usually called degree raising (also degree elevation), can be performed with a procedure that is not exactly the De Casteljau's algorithm, but quite similar to it.

Suppose a Bézier curve of degree n with control points $\{P_0, P_1, \ldots, P_n\}$ defined as above. We want to increase the degree of the curve to $n+1$ while still preserving the same shape of the curve. The problem is now how to compute the new control points $\{Q_0, Q_1, \ldots, Q_{n+1}\}$. Since the Bézier curve always interpolate the end control points, we can take $Q_0 = P_0$ and $Q_{n+1} = P_n$. The remaining control points can be computed as:

$$Q_j = \frac{j}{n+1}P_{j-1} + \left(1 - \frac{j}{n+1}\right)P_j \quad ; \quad j = 1, \ldots, n \qquad (5)$$

The geometric interpretation of this process is shown in Fig. 4. Starting with a Bézier curve of degree 7 (top), for each segment of the control polygon connecting the points P_{j-1} and P_j we consider the point Q_j on that segment that divides it in a ratio $\left(1 - \frac{j}{n+1}\right) : \frac{j}{n+1}$. In this particular example, we have $n+1 = 8$ and obtain the new control polygon in blue in Fig. 4 (middle). Note that the original curve is now displayed in gray to emphasize visually the new control polygon. The resulting Bézier curve of degree 8 is shown in Fig. 4 (bottom). Note that this curve and the original one have identical shape. They are obtained by using the `DegreeRaising`(*cp, options*) function in our toolbox.

3.4   Example 4: Variation Diminishing Property

An interesting feature of the Bézier curves is the variation diminishing property, which in short states that the curve is smoother than its control polygon. Geometrically, this means that if a line is drawn through the curve, the number of intersections with the curve will be less than or equal to the number of intersections with the control polygon. In our Master course on CAGD, we challenge our students to put this property in practice by using some educational materials generated with the KETpic-Matlab toolbox described in this paper. Figure 5 shows an illustrative example. Top picture displays a geometric configuration of a control polygon defined by the sequence of 5 control points in the picture and the three lines depicted in the figure. Then, we ask the students to:

- draw the control polygon
- determine the maximum number of times that the curve can intersect each of those lines
- draw the Bézier curve
- determine how many times the curve does really intersect each of those lines
- explain the results.

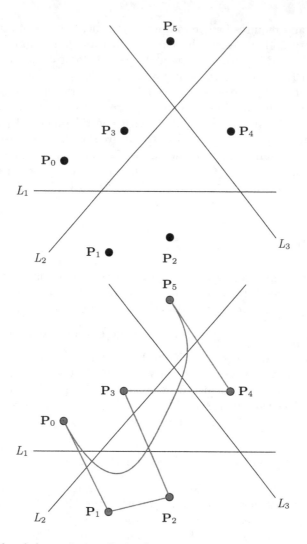

Fig. 5. Example of the variation diminishing property of Bézier curves: (top) initial configuration of control points and lines; (bottom) graphical solution to the problem.

Then, the students can check their results by using our toolbox to yield the solution to this problem, shown in bottom picture of Fig. 5. We found that many students were surprised by this graphical result, as they did expect the curve to replicate more faithfully the shape of the control polygon. Of course, any other geometric configuration for the control points and lines can readily be arranged with our toolbox, so even more intriguing situations can be discussed and analyzed. This shows the potential of our toolbox as a learning tool, as it encourages the student to think twice about this property and the expected behavior of the Bézier curve.

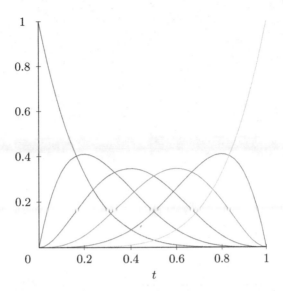

Fig. 6. Graphical representation of the Bernstein polynomials given by Eq. (2).

3.5 Example 5: Basis Functions and Partition of Unity Property

An interesting feature of the basis functions of a Bézier curve is the so-called partition of unity property, which says that:

$$\sum_{j=0}^{n} B_j^n(t) = 1 \quad ; \quad \forall t \in [0, 1] \tag{6}$$

In this example, we show the basis functions in Fig. 6 associated with a Bézier curve and ask our students to:

- determine the number of control points of the curve
- determine the degree of the curve
- check the partition of unity property for different parametric values.

While the first two questions can easily be answered from the figure, the last one is more difficult to check. A remarkable feature of our toolbox in this regard is the fact that all figures generated with it are *metric*, which means that all distances are referred to a certain unit length, so the students can actually measure distances on the figures. For instance, the reader can easily check that the unit length in the vertical and horizontal axes is exactly the same, as opposed to many other graphical representations where a golden ratio or other non-unit value is applied to the axes ratio. In fact, our students were surprised to see the basis functions displayed with equal sizes in both axes, as all textbooks show a "more stylized" version. Owing to this feature, the students can check the partition of unity directly on the figure without any size distortion.

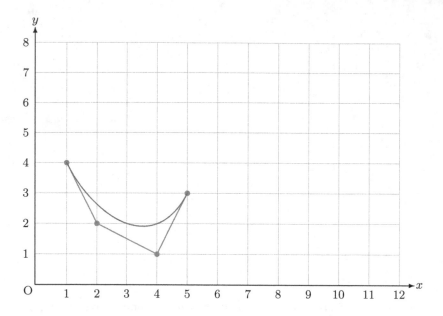

Fig. 7. Our readers are challenged to solve the problem described in Sect. 3.6 by using this figure and their geometrical reasoning.

3.6   Example 6: Connecting Bézier Curves with a Given Continuity

A very interesting (and useful) property of the control polygon of a Bézier curve is that not only the curve does interpolate the first and last control points but also the end segments of the control polygon determine the tangency of the curve at such control points. In particular, the tangent vector of the curve at the first (respectively, last) control point is given by the first (resp., last) segment of the control polygon. This property is very useful in order to connect several Bézier curves with a certain order of continuity.

To emphasize this, we give Fig. 7 to our students and ask them to determine (without using the mathematical equation of the displayed Bézier curve) some feasible control points for a second Bézier curve of the same degree as the curve shown in the figure so that:

– they are not connected at any point
– they are connected at the leftmost control point with C^0-continuity
– they are connected at the rightmost control point with C^0-continuity
– they are connected at the leftmost control point with C^1-continuity
– they are connected at the rightmost control point with C^1-continuity

After reading all paper contents so far, we think that you, our reader, are ready to solve this problem by using solely your geometrical reasoning, similar to our students. And hopefully, you will also have the same feeling of satisfaction as our own students when you realize that you grasped the main concepts about

Bézier curves with little effort taking advantage of the toolbox described here. We strongly encourage you to try. *Good luck and let's go!*.

4 Conclusions and Future Work

In this paper we introduced a new KETpic-Matlab toolbox to generate LaTeX-embedded high-quality graphical artwork about the main algorithms for Bézier curves and related topics. The package was implemented by the authors as a supporting middleware tool to generate educational materials for a computer-aided geometric design (CAGD) course at an advanced level. Its primary goal is to instill geometric intuition in our students and help them develop critical thinking based on geometric reasoning for problem solving. We also aim at providing the instructors of such courses with a computer library to produce high-quality graphics for educational materials with a seamless integration into LaTeX. In this regard, all graphical objects are encoded as plain LaTeX-readable source code that yields nice pictures after standard LaTeX compilation. The application of this package to generate educational materials is discussed through six illustrative examples of interesting properties of the Bézier curves. They show that our package is very easy to use, supports many different graphical options, and fosters students' creative geometric thinking with very little effort.

Our KETpic-Matlab toolbox has already been applied during the last academic year for two Master courses on CAGD with very encouraging results. The feedback from our students has been very positive; they praised the strong geometric orientation of the teaching materials generated with this software, its ease of use, and its smooth integration into LaTeX. However, a deeper and more formal analysis is still needed to determine its advantages and limitations at full extent. This process will require larger groups of students and a more rigorous statistical analysis based on questionnaires designed with the support of pedagogy and education sciences experts. We also plan to extend our package to the (more difficult) case of Bézier surfaces. A user's manual and some support material for teachers and instructors would also be needed for wider dissemination of this software and its adoption as a standard tool in CAGD courses worldwide. All these tasks will be part of our plans for future work in this field.

Acknowledgments. This work was kindly supported by Japanese Society for Promotion of Science (JSPS) KAKENHI Grant Numbers 15K01037, 15K00944, and 16K01152, the Computer Science National Program of the Spanish Ministry of Economy and Competitiveness, Project Ref. #TIN2012-30768, Toho University, the University of Cantabria, Tecnalia Research & Innovation, the University of the Basque Country, and the Basque Center for Applied Mathematics (BCAM).

References

1. Farin, G.: Curves and Surfaces for CAGD, 5th edn. Morgan Kaufmann, San Francisco (2002)
2. Gálvez, A., Iglesias, A., Takato, S.: New Matlab-based KETpic plug-in for high-quality drawing of curves. In: International Conference on Computational Science and its Applications-ICCSA 2009, CA, pp. 123–131. IEEE Computer Society Press, Los Alamitos (2009)
3. Gálvez, A., Iglesias, A., Takato, S.: Matlab-based KETpic add-on for generating and rendering IFS fractals. Commun. Netw. **56**, 334–341 (2009)
4. Gálvez, A., Iglesias, A., Takato, S.: KETpic Matlab binding for efficient handling of fractal images. Int. J. Future Gener. Commun. Netw. **3**, 1–14 (2010)
5. Gálvez, A., Kitahara, K., Kaneko, M.: *IFSGen4LATEX* : interactive graphical user interface for generation and visualization of iterated function systems in LATEX. In: Hong, H., Yap, C. (eds.) ICMS 2014. LNCS, vol. 8592, pp. 554–561. Springer, Heidelberg (2014). doi:10.1007/978-3-662-44199-2_84
6. Iglesias, A., Gálvez, A.: Computer software program for representation and visualization of free-form curves through bio-inspired optimization techniques. In: Hong, H., Yap, C. (eds.) ICMS 2014. LNCS, vol. 8592, pp. 570–577. Springer, Heidelberg (2014). doi:10.1007/978-3-662-44199-2_86
7. Kaneko, M., Izumi, H., Kitahara, K., Abe, T., Fukazawa, K., Sekiguchi, M., Tadokoro, Y., Yamashita, S., Takato, S.: A simple method of the TeX surface drawing suitable for teaching materials with the aid of CAS. In: Bubak, M., Albada, G.D., Dongarra, J., Sloot, P.M.A. (eds.) ICCS 2008. LNCS, vol. 5102, pp. 35–45. Springer, Heidelberg (2008). doi:10.1007/978-3-540-69387-1_5
8. The Mathworks Inc: Using Matlab, Natick, MA (1999)
9. Sekiguchi, M., Yamashita, S., Takato, S.: Development of a maple macro package suitable for drawing fine TeX pictures. In: Iglesias, A., Takayama, N. (eds.) ICMS 2006. LNCS, vol. 4151, pp. 24–34. Springer, Heidelberg (2006). doi:10.1007/11832225_3
10. Takato, S., Gálvez, A., Iglesias, A.: Use of ImplicitPlot in drawing surfaces embedded into LaTeX documents. In: International Conference on Computational Science and its Applications-ICCSA 2009, CA, pp. 115–122. IEEE Computer Society Press, Los Alamitos (2009)
11. Yamashita, S., Abe, T., Izumi, H., Kaneko, M., Kitahara, K., Sekiguchi, M., Fukazawa, K., Takato, S.: Monochrome line drawings of 3D objects due to the programmability of KETpic. In: International Conference on Computational Science and its Applications-ICCSA 2008, CA, pp. 277–283. IEEE Computer Society Press, Los Alamitos (2008)

Identification of High-Risk Hotspots Along Railway Lines

Paolino Di Felice[1]([⊠]) [iD], Antonello Di Felice[2], Mauro Evangelista[2],
Antonio Fraticelli[2], and Lorenzo Venturoni[2]

[1] Department of Industrial and Information Engineering and Economics,
University of L'Aquila, L'Aquila, Italy
paolino.difelice@univaq.it
[2] Master Students in Information Engineering,
University of L'Aquila, L'Aquila, Italy
antonello81@gmail.com, mauro.evangelista@gmail.com,
antonio.fraticelli@gmail.com,
lorenzo.venturoni@gmail.com

Abstract. Safety is a relevant issue in many context of the real life. The paper proposes a scientifically robust method for the identification of the top-N list of railway hotspots that can be used as input for the definition of a strategy of selective monitoring of the state of safety the railway network of an administrative unit (namely, a province, a region, a country, etc.), with respect to the exposure to the landslide hazard. The knowledge of the hotspots, as meant in this paper, is a conceptual tool for providing a rigorous analytical basis for narrowing down a global problem – train derailments – to smaller, highest risk, geographic areas where the management of the disaster risk is most crucial. To be applied, the method needs data about the railway lines to be kept under control and data about the geomorphology of the underlying terrain.

Keywords: Railway · Landslide · Hotspot · Topological relation · 9-intersection model · Exposure

1 Preliminary Considerations

This study proposes a method that consists of two steps. The first step identifies the portions of railway lines (hereinafter called *hotspots*) where the danger to have variations in the altitude of the terrain is high, because of the geomorphology of the underlying soil. If the ground where the tracks are leaned, or that in their immediate vicinity, undergoes only a slight altitude variation (for example due to prolonged rains), then that can determine modifications in the bed of the tracks and this, in turn, becomes a motivating factor of railway derailments. The second step returns the identified hotspots in order of decreasing propensity to the aforementioned altitude fluctuations. This output allows the scheduling of selective inspections of stretches of railway lines limiting, thus, the use of resources without lowering their level of safety.

Many methods have been developed to predict, prevent, and mitigate accidents in the railway context. He et al. [8], for example, resort to the *Principal Component*

© Springer International Publishing AG 2017
O. Gervasi et al. (Eds.): ICCSA 2017, Part IV, LNCS 10407, pp. 317–331, 2017.
DOI: 10.1007/978-3-319-62401-3_24

Analysis to identify a limited number of factors to be taken into account in order to study the rock slope stability. Theoretical studies like that just mentioned are very interesting because they help to understand the complexity of the problem by providing global information about the variables that come into play and how they are related each other, but they have the limitation of not being directly translatable into a monitoring work plan to be carried out by those who have the responsibility to ensure the safety of railway networks.

In our paper we adopt a different approach based on methods proposed in the field of *Geographical Information Science* to study the topological relationships between geographic features. The method we are going to describe enables the identification of the hotspots along a train line which are most affected by terrain instability and, therefore, a source of high potential danger of derailments. These hotspots are those that, primarily, require periodic inspections. Such a strategy exceeds the limits of the periodic checks on the entire railway path which are long and, consequently, expensive and not always useful as stressed by Sadler et al. [14]. They developed a *Geospatial Safety Risk Model*, which can help to identify "low-risk locations or routes and areas where control measures can be safely reduced, offering the potential for the railway industry to achieve significant cost and efficiency savings through the removal of unnecessary/disproportionate control measures."

The aim of our method is identical to that of Sadler et al. [14]. In fact, by returning the location of the portions of railway lines where the exposure to the landslide hazard is highest, actually it drives the responsible for the railway safety in the definition of monitoring plans and, consequently, the portions where such supervision can be thinned without lowering the level of safety for the people and for the transported assets. In summary, the goal of the study described in this paper is to develop a scientifically robust methodology for the identification of the railway hotspots which, in turn, is the input for the definition of a strategy of selective monitoring of the safety status of a category of assets strategic for a country, that is its railway network, with respect to the exposure to landslides. The exposure we refer to in this paper is called "spatial" exposure in [15].

The paper is structured as follows. Sect. 2 (Materials and methods): (a) presents the basic notations used throughout the paper (Sect. 2.1); (b) introduces the equation for the identification of the railway lines' hotspots and computation of their exposure (Sect. 2.2); (c) describes how it is possible to take advantage from the hotspots' ranking to implement a selective monitoring of those portions of the railway lines (Sect. 2.3.); (d) reports about a Case Study where the proposed method is applied to the railway network of the Abruzzo region, central Italy (Sect. 2.4). Results are summarized and discussed in Sect. 3; while brief conclusions are given in Sect. 4.

2   Materials and Methods

2.1   Notations

Hereinafter we use the following notations:

$\mathcal{G}\text{eo}\mathcal{A}\text{rea}$ is the portion of land of interest for the study. $\mathcal{G}\text{eo}\mathcal{A}\text{rea}$ is defined as the pair $<description, geometry\ of\ the\ boundary\ of\ \mathcal{G}\text{eo}\mathcal{A}\text{rea}>$, where $description$ is a string.

$\mathcal{Z} = \{z_k\ (k = 1, 2, \ldots)\}$ where z_k is a "zone". According to the existing literature, (e.g., [6, 7]), by $zone$ we mean a portion of land characterized by a set of ground conditions. The generic element of $\mathcal{Z}$ can be modelled as a "simple polygon". According to the OpenGIS Abstract Specification [12], a $simple\ polygon$ consists of a "single patch" that is associated with 1 exterior boundary and 0 or more interior boundaries. Each interior boundary defines a hole in the polygon. The boundary of a simple polygon is the set of closed curves corresponding to its exterior and interior boundaries. $card(\mathcal{Z})$ denotes the cardinality of set $\mathcal{Z}$, i.e., the number of its elements. Δz_k denotes the boundary of zone z_k, while z_k° denotes its interior.

The elements in $\mathcal{Z}$ make a full partition of $\mathcal{G}\text{eo}\mathcal{A}\text{rea}$. The generic element of $\mathcal{Z}$ (i.e., z_k) is defined as the tuple $<ID, Sz_k, boundary\ of\ z_k>$, being ID an identifying code. Sz_k is a numerical value that quantifies the $(spatial)\ probability$ that z_k produces landslides. The value of Sz_k ranges from 0 to 1. Brabb [2] introduced the term $susceptibility$ to denote such a quantitative estimate. Assessing and mapping landslide susceptibility has been a relevant issue, e.g., [6, 7, 10]. In the paper, z_k is an overloaded notation since it represents the ID of a zone ad its $geometry$ as well. The context will suggest the correct interpretation.

$\mathcal{RL} = \{l_i\ (i = 1, 2, \ldots)\}$ where l_i denotes a railway line that crosses the $\mathcal{G}\text{eo}\mathcal{A}\text{rea}$. Each line is delimited by two end points that are identified with the railway stations of departure and arrival. Each train line in $\mathcal{RL}$ is defined as the tuple $<ID, name, geometry\ of\ l_i>$, being ID an identifying code and $geometry$ of l_i the set of pairs of coordinates describing the shape of l_i. $card(\mathcal{RL})$ denotes the cardinality of set $\mathcal{RL}$, that is the number of train lines crossing the $\mathcal{G}\text{eo}\mathcal{A}\text{rea}$. A train line may be modelled as a $simple$ line, that is, as a curve with two disconnected boundaries, that does not pass through the same point more than once [12]. Δl_i denotes the boundary of line l_i, namely both its end points; while l_i° denotes the interior of l_i. Hereafter, l_i is an overloaded notation since it represents the ID of a railway line ad its $geometry$ as well. The context will suggest the correct interpretation.

$h_{ik,j}$ ($j = 1, 2, \ldots$) denotes a $hotspot$, i.e., the n-th component of the $geometry\ collection$ result of the intersection between the railway line l_i (of $\mathcal{RL}$) and the zone z_k (in $\mathcal{Z}$). Hotspot $h_{ik,j}$ is fully defined by the tuple $<ID, geometry\ of\ h_{ik,j}, Exp\_h_{ik,j}>$, being ID an identifying code, $geometry$ of $h_{ik,j}$ the geometry of the location of hotspot $h_{ik,j}$ and $Exp\_h_{ik,j}$ a positive numeric value denoting the degree of (spatial) exposure of $h_{ik,j}$ to the landslide hazard. Hereafter, $h_{ik,j}$ is an overloaded notation since it represents the ID of a hotspot ad its $geometry$ as well. The context will suggest the correct interpretation.

2.2 Identification of the Railway Lines' Hotspots, Computation of Their Exposure

In order to implement a policy of selective monitoring about the state of health of the land on which are leaned the tracks of the railway lines that cross the $\mathcal{G}\text{eo}\mathcal{A}\text{rea}$, it is required that for each l_i in $\mathcal{RL}$ the geometry of the hotspots ($h_{ik,j}$) internal to the line is returned, together with the value of their exposure (i.e., $Exp\_h_{ik,j}$). The higher is the value of parameter $Exp\_h_{ik,j}$ and bigger is the landslide hazard faced by the ground underneath the stretch of the railway line which coincides with the hotspot $h_{ik,j}$ and, in the final analysis, the greater is the risk of derailment of the train when it crosses such a portion of territory.

The value of the exposure of a generic hotspot $(h_{ik,j})$ along the railway line l_i is given by Eq. 1

$$Exp\_h_{ik,j} = Size \times Sz_k \tag{1}$$

where $Size$ is given by Eq. 2, being $N = card(Z)$.

$$Size = \frac{\text{area of } zk}{\left(\sum_{j=1}^{N} area\ of\ zj\right)/N} \tag{2}$$

Both equations come from a method proposed by Di Felice et al. [3] to compute the ranking of buildings according to their exposure to the landslide hazard.

To identify the hotspots in the railway line l_i (belonging to RL) it is necessary to calculate the intersection of l_i with the zones in Z. Given the pair (l_i, z_k), two cases are possible: $l_i \cap z_k \neq \emptyset$ (*Case* 1) or $l_i \cap z_k = \emptyset$ (*Case* 2).

Below only the *Case* 1 is investigated, since it can give rise to hotspots. The goal is to introduce a way to refine the "base" value of the exposure attached by Eq. 1 to the hotspots located along the railway lines. The method that we propose makes use of results about the *topological relations* between a pair of geographic features. In our paper, the geographic features taken into account are pairs (l_i, z_k), that is a line and an area.

Topological relations between a pair of geographic features are characterized by the *topological invariants* of the so-called 9-*intersection model*, [4], which is concisely represented as a matrix (Eq. 3), where $°$, Δ, and $^-$ denote, in order, the interior, the boundary and the exterior of a geographic feature.

$$\begin{pmatrix} l_i° \cap z_k° & l_i° \cap \Delta z_k & l_i° \cap z_k - \\ \Delta l_i \cap z_k° & \Delta l_i \cap \Delta z_k & \Delta l_i \cap z_k - \\ l_i^- \cap z_k - & l_i^- \cap \Delta z_k & l_i^- \cap z_k - \end{pmatrix} \tag{3}$$

Relevant topological invariants applicable to the 9-intersection model are the *content* (i.e., emptiness or non-emptiness) of a set, the *number of separations* in the intersection (i.e., the number of disconnected components), and the *dimension* of each "separation". By separation it is meant the geometry returned by each of the nine intersections of Eq. 3. Hereafter, $(l_i \cap z_k)$ denotes the geometry collection result of the intersection between l_i and z_k, while $\#(l_i \cap z_k)$ denotes the number of separations of such an intersection. In our study, the dimension of an intersection may be either 0 or 1.

Case 1 will be treated by taking into account the three invariants mentioned above between l_i and z_k. In addition, when possible, we will take into account the Inner Area Splitting (*IAS*) and the ENtrance Splitting (*ENS*) (introduced by Egenhofer and Shariff in [5]), to capture relevant geometric details from the topological relations between l_i and z_k.

The Content Invariant. The relations/configurations between a simple line and a simple polygon without holes are 19, [4], see Fig. 1. But since a zone can have holes (Sect. 2.1), then it is immediate to draw as many configurations starting from those of Fig. 1 simply by introducing (at least) a hole inside the polygon.

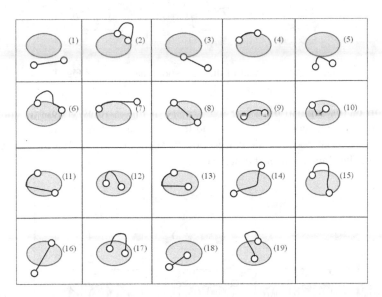

Fig. 1. The geometric configurations realizable in 2D between a simple line and a simple polygon without holes according to the 9-intersection model.

However, in the problem at hand, the meaningful configurations between l_i and z_k are a restricted subset because the area of z_k is modest when compared to the extension of l_i that, conversely, is several tens of kilometers. It follows that it is impossible that a railway line is wholly contained inside a zone (therefore configurations 8, 9, 10, 11, 12, and 13 of Fig. 1 are to be excluded), or that it has both end points in the same zone (which excludes configurations 2, 4, 6, 15, 17, and 19 of Fig. 1). Therefore, when we examine the content invariant, the configurations of Fig. 1 that are significant for our study are: 3, 5, 7, 14, 16, and 18. Configuration 1 must be ignored because it does not determine hotspots.

Number of separations. The configurations of Fig. 2 are characterized by the same content invariant (Eq. 3) of the corresponding scenes of Fig. 1, but they have a different number of disconnected components. Note that the scenes of Fig. 2 are not the only one possible, in fact the number of components can be as large as desired.

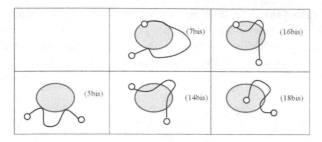

Fig. 2. A refinement of the corresponding scenes of Fig. 1.

Dimension of the separations. The five scenes of Fig. 3 show geometric configurations having the same content invariant and the same number of separations according to the 9-intersection model of the correspondent scenes of Fig. 2, but they differ from the latter for the dimension of the partitions.

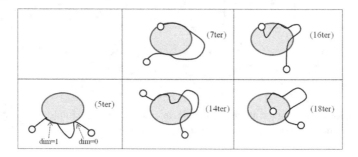

Fig. 3. Geometric variants of the scenes of Fig. 2.

Among the six configurations of Fig. 1 taken into account in this study (i.e.: 3, 5, 7, 14, 16, and 18), 14, 16, and 18 meet, in order, the three patterns of Eq. 4.

$$\begin{pmatrix} °\cap° = \neg\phi & °\cap\Delta = ? \\ \Delta\cap° = \phi & \Delta\cap\Delta = \phi \end{pmatrix} \begin{pmatrix} °\cap° = \neg\phi & °\cap\Delta = \neg\phi \\ \Delta\cap° = \phi & \Delta\cap\Delta = \neg\phi \end{pmatrix} \begin{pmatrix} °\cap° = \neg\phi & °\cap\Delta = \neg\phi \\ \Delta\cap° = \neg\phi & \Delta\cap\Delta = \phi \end{pmatrix} \quad (4)$$

Therefore, it is possible to operate a close examination about those geometric scenes by calculating the value of the *IAS* metric, whose definition is as follows:

$$IAS = \frac{\min(\text{area}(\text{leftSeparation}(l_i^° \cap z_k^°)), \ \text{area}(\text{rightSeparation}(l_i^° \cap z_k^°)))}{\text{area}(z_k)} \quad (5)$$

IAS describes how the railway line's interior divides the interior of a zone. With this separation, line l_i splits area z_k into two or more parts such that parts of the area's interior are on one side of the line, and others are located on the opposite side of the line. From Eq. 5 it follows that $0 < IAS \leq 0.5$. In the general case in which l_i splits area

z_k in several parts (Fig. 4 shows an example), each intersection identifies a hotspot. To assign them an appropriate value of exposure, it is necessary to attach to them a value of the *IAS* metric. This is achieved by applying Eq. 5 to each portion of land identified by the intersection between l_i and z_k, whose area has to be compared to the total area of region z_k. With regard to the example of Fig. 4, we have four values of *IAS*, as many as are the hotspots. Note that Eq. 5 may not be applicable to some hotspots result of the intersection between a railway line and a zone with holes. This is the case of hotspots $h_{ik,2}$ and $h_{ik,3}$ of Fig. 4 to which we assign, conventionally, $IAS = 0$.

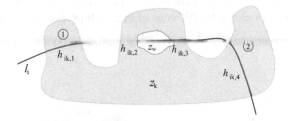

Fig. 4. A zone (z_k) with a hole (the white region). $IAS_{ik,1}$ and $IAS_{ik,4}$ are greater than zero, while $IAS_{ik,2} = IAS_{ik,3} = 0$.

Downstream of the calculation of the value of the metric *IAS*, the correction to be made to the basic value of the exposure of the corresponding hotspot is expressed by Eq. 6. Such an equation retains the value of parameter $Exp\_h_{ik,j}$ if $IAS_{ik,j} = 0.5$, while such a value is decreased up to the 50% if $IAS_{ik,j}$ tends to zero.

$$Exp\_h_{ik,j} = Exp\_h_{ikj} \times \left[1 - \left(0.5 - IAS_{ik,j}\right)\right] \tag{6}$$

For configurations 14, 16, and 18 we can operate a further close examination of the geometry of the scene by calculating the value of metric *ENS*, whose definition is given by Eq. 7.

$$ENS = \frac{length(l_i^\circ \cap z_k^\circ)}{length(\Delta z_k)} \tag{7}$$

ENS applies to relations in which the line's interior crosses the region's interior. The presence of holes inside a zone does not make Eq. 7 inapplicable to the resulting hotspots. Therefore, for example, $ENS > 0$ for the four hotspots in Fig. 4. Equation 7 normalizes the common interiors of the line and the area with respect to the length of the region's boundary. $ENS > 0$, while the upper bound is undefined from a theoretical point of view. However, for a given case study (i.e., given the sets $\mathcal{RL}$ and $\mathcal{Z}$), it is possible to compute the value of the upper bound by applying Eq. 7 to all the pairs (l_i, z_k).

For the problem at hand, it is correct to assume that $0 < ENS < 0.5$. It easy to verify that the limit value of 0.5 is reachable for zones with long and narrow shape (i.e., zones similar to a rectangle with a side much longer than the other one).

Downstream of the computation of the value of *ENS*, the correction to be made to the value of the exposure of the corresponding hotspot is expressed by Eq. 8. It retains the value of parameter $Exp\_h_{ik,j}$ if $ENS_{ik,j} = 0.5$, while it decreases such a value up to the 50% if $ENS_{ik,j}$ tends to zero.

$$Exp\_h_{ik,j} = Exp\_h_{ik,j} \times \left[1 - \left(0.5 - ENS_{ik,j}\right)\right] \tag{8}$$

The use of *ENS* captures metric information sufficient to distinguish geometric configurations that, on the opposite, are identical with respect to the three topological invariants taken into account in this study as well as with respect to the value of metric *IAS*. Let us consider, for example, the scene of Fig. 5. It proposes a railway line (l_i) that intersects in the middle two zones (z_1 and z_2).

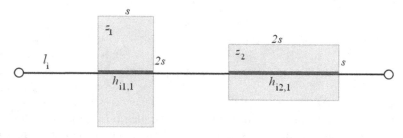

Fig. 5. Two possible instances of configuration 14 of Fig. 1.

The assumptions that describe the scene of Fig. 5 are the following: zones z_1 and z_2 have identical value of probability of triggering landslides (i.e., $Sz_1 = Sz_2$), moreover "area of z_1 = area di z_2 = $2 \times s^2$". The intersection between the railway line l_i and the zones z_1 and z_2 gives rise to two hotspots ($h_{i1,1}$ and $h_{i2,1}$). It is easy to verify that those two hotspots have the same exposure value according to Eq. 1 and the same *IAS* value, but they have different *ENS* value.

Equation 9 merges Eqs. 6 and 8.

$$Exp\_h_{ik,j} = Exp\_h_{ik,j} \times \left[1 - \left(0.5 - IAS_{ik,j}\right)\right] \times \left[1 - \left(0.5 - ENS_{ik,j}\right)\right] \tag{9}$$

2.3   From the Ranking of the Hotspots to the Selective Monitoring of Railway Lines

The intersection the railway lines in $\mathcal{RL}$ and the zones in $\mathcal{Z}$ returns $card(\mathcal{RL}) \times card(\mathcal{Z})$ hotspots. Usually, this number is very high. To identify the hotspots that primarily require monitoring it is necessary to build the $2 + card(\mathcal{RL})$ tables described in this section.

The values of the exposure assigned to the hotspots by Eq. 9 oscillate between a maximum and a minimum, the latter being close to zero. These values can be aggregated into an arbitrary number of ranges in order to structure the first of the $2 + card$ ($\mathcal{RL}$) tables. We call it "frame of reference" table. This name originates from the fact that to decide, for a given railway line in $\mathcal{RL}$, the top-N list of hotspots to be monitored with the highest priority it is necessary to refer to this table. We will return to this point shortly. The data in the frame of reference table also allow to gain an idea about the overall situation of the bed of the railway lines that cross the GeoArea.

Our proposal is to adopt five ranges of hazard (*Very High, High, Moderate, Low, and Null*) as defined in Table 1. In it, `AVG(total exposure)` denotes the arithmetic mean of the exposure values of the $card(\mathcal{RL}) \times card(\mathcal{Z})$ identified hotspots; while #hotspots denotes the total number of hotspots whose exposure value (v_i, $i = 1, ..., 5$) falls in the corresponding five ranges.

Table 1. The *frame of reference* table.

Hazard	Values of exposure	#hotspots
Very high	$Exp > 3 \times$ AVG (total exposure)	v_1
High	$1.5 \times$ AVG (total exposure) $< Exp \leq 3 \times$ AVG (total exposure)	v_2
Moderate	$0.5 \times$ AVG (total exposure) $< Exp \leq 1.5 \times$ AVG (total exposure)	v_3
Low	$0.25 \times$ AVG (total exposure) $< Exp \leq 0.5 \times$ AVG (total exposure)	v_4
Null	$Exp \leq 0.25 \times$ AVG (total exposure)	v_5

The second table to be constructed consists of $card(\mathcal{RL})$ rows and 6 columns (Table 2). The i-th row of such a table shows, in order, the total number of hotspots located along railway line l_i and, to follow, the total number of hotspots whose exposure value falls in each of the five ranges of Table 1.

Table 2. The distribution of the hotspots within the five ranges of the frame of reference table for the railway lines in $\mathcal{RL}$.

Railway lines	#hotspots	#hotspots in the very high range	#hotspots in the high range	#hotspots in the moderate range	#hotspots in the low range	#hotspots in the Null range
l_1	v_{11}	$v_{11,1}$	$v_{11,2}$	$v_{11,3}$	$v_{11,4}$	$v_{11,5}$
l_2	v_{12}	$v_{12,1}$	$v_{12,2}$	$v_{12,3}$	$v_{12,4}$	$v_{12,5}$
...	...	...	...	...	...	...
$l_{card(\mathcal{RL})}$	$v_{lcard(\mathcal{RL})}$	$v_{lcard(\mathcal{RL}),1}$	$v_{lcard(\mathcal{RL}),2}$	$v_{lcard(\mathcal{RL}),3}$	$v_{lcard(\mathcal{RL}),4}$	$v_{lcard(\mathcal{RL}),5}$

The remaining $card(\mathcal{RL})$ tables have all the same structure. The i-th of them is composed of v_{li} rows and 4 columns (Table 3). These latter denote, in sequence: the ID of the hotspot, its exposure value (according to Eq. 9), and the coordinates of its two end points (called *End Point A* and *End Point B* in the table). The coordinates are fundamental to locate on the field the hotspots to be monitored.

Table 3. The structure of the table about *all* the hotspots along line l_i.

Hotspot's ID	Hotspot's exposure	End point A	End point B
1		Latitude longitude	Latitude longitude
...	...	...	...
v_{li}		Latitude longitude	Latitude longitude

A crucial issue is *how* to identify the top-*N* hotspots (along the railway line l_i in $\mathcal{RL}$) to be flagged as priorities for mitigating the risks of derailments. Since, the value of "*N*" is not known in advance, nor it is constant for all the railway lines, to decide whether a hotspot is to be monitored or not we suggest that it is ascertained in which of the five ranges of Table 1 drops its value of the exposure. In this way there is an objective assessment of the level of hazard which weighs on the hotspot under consideration based on the comparison of its exposure value with *all* the computed values.

The value of *N* is defined as follows:

N is equal to the number of hotspots along line l_i such that $Exp\_h_{ik,j}$ falls either in the *Very High* range or in the *High* range (Table 1).

Referring to the notations in Table 2, we can write that, for line l_i, $N = v_{li,1} + v_{li,2}$. Definition above emphasizes the centrality of Table 1 as a frame of reference.

Because Eq. 9 does not take into account the elevation of the terrain inside the GeoArea, the proposed method may return *false positives*. In other words, we can say that each of the hotspots in the top-*N* list may be a false positive until it is ascertained the opposite. The easiest and fastest way to detect the false positive hotspots (belonging to a given railway line) and remove them from the top-*N* list consists in looking at each of them against the DEM of the underlying terrain by making recourse to a geo-viewer.

2.4   A Case Study

Input Datasets

GeoArea. It coincides with the boundary of the Abruzzo region; an area of about 11,000 km^2, structured as four provinces, 305 municipalities and a population of about 1,330,000.

Set Z. For the Abruzzo region, it is not available a dataset with the characteristics of set Z. What we have found was a shapefile about the *landslide inventory* of the region (a *landslide inventory* is a detailed register of the distribution and characteristics of past landslides, [9]. Landslide inventories are often used by scholars. For instance, Mandal and Maiti, [11], used landslide inventory statistics to investigate the relationship between rainfall and landslip events.). The limit of this dataset is that it does not achieve a complete partition of the region. This (real) dataset coincides with the "theoretical one" by setting $Sz_k = 0$ for the portions of land not surveyed.

Within the landslide inventory, landslides are classified according to the type of movement, the estimated age, the state of activity, the depth of failure surface, and the velocity. The categories of landslides making part of the inventory are fall/topple, rotational/translational slide, slow earth flow, rapid debris flow, sinkhole, complex landslide. Moreover, landslides are classified as *active*, *quiescent/dormant*, and *inactive*.

The elements contained in the Abruzzo landslide inventory are grouped into three susceptibility *classes* called *S1* (*low* susceptibility), *S2* (*high* susceptibility), and *S3* (*very high* susceptibility). Overall, the inventory is composed of 4,425 elements in *S1*, 8,886 elements in *S2* and 3,959 elements in *S3*. With few exceptions, it can be said the following: *S3* includes *active* landslides, *quiescent* landslides are in *S2*, while *inactive* landslides are in $S1$. The area of the landslides in Z ranges from 161 m^2 to 6,302,190 m^2. The average area measures 93,653 m^2.

As just said, the case study partitions the set of zones Z into three classes each characterized by a single value for Sz_k for all the z_k belonging to it. This is a simplification of the general case (Sect. 2.1), which does not exclude that each z_k has a specific value of Sz_k. In order to carry out the experiments, we have associated to the zones in the aforementioned three classes the probability values 0.25, 0.5 and 1, respectively. Obviously, those values may be changed, but the following constraint must be fulfilled: the value of Sz_k must be positive (remember that it expresses a probability value) and such that Sz_k (class $S1$) < Sz_k (class $S2$) < Sz_k (class $S3$).

Set $\mathcal{Rl}$. Abruzzo is crossed by nine railway lines. They all together add up to 685 km.

2.5   The Geographical DataBase

We implemented a PostgreSQL/PostGIS Geographical DataBase (shortly, Geo-DB) to store the records of the input shapefiles (namely sets $\mathcal{GeoArea}$, Z, and $\mathcal{Rl}$) and the results of the experiments to be carried out. The relevance of Geo-DBs as a tool for the management of natural hazards is well-known in the literature, see for instance [1, 13]. The Geo-DB has been enriched with a large number of PL/pgSQL User Defined Functions and SQL views through which it was possible to carry out complex processing by writing simple SQL queries.

3   Results and Discussion

This section reports about the results of the experiments we carried out, at two different levels of analysis. The first level concerns the construction of Tables 1 and 2 of Sect. 2.3, while the second level is about the top-N list of the hotspots along one of the railway lines of the Abruzzo region. The section is closed by mentioned the relevant phase of results validation.

3.1   First Level of Analysis

The intersection between the 9 Abruzzo railway lines and the 17,312 zones in Z returned 210 hotspots with exposure value greater than zero. They add up to 63.7 km. Hotspots with exposure value equal to zero are ignored because they are not to be monitored as not exposed to the landslide danger. The exposure value assigned to each hotspot by Eq. 9 ranges between 4.76 and 0. The exposure is null when $Sz_k = 0$ (see Sect. 2.4).

Table 4 shows the frame of reference table for the Case Study. Compared to Table 1 (Sect. 2.3), Table 4 also shows, for each range, the percentage of the totality of the hotspots belonging to it (forth column); the total length (in km) of all the hotspots that are part of the same range (column *length*) and the percentage value of their extension (% *Length column*) referred to the total length of the 9 railway lines of the Abruzzo region.

Table 4. An enhanced version of the frame of reference table for the case study.

Hazard	Exposure	# of hotspots	% of the hotspots	Length (km)	% Length
Very high	[1.83...4.76]	19	9.05	14.9	2.17
High	[0.88...1.83)	23	10.95	9.6	1.4
Moderate	[0.32...0.88)	53	25.24	20.5	3.0
Low	[0.15...0.32)	47	22.38	10.8	1.58
Null	(0...0.15)	68	32.38	7.9	1.15
		210		63.7	

Table 5 shows the distribution of the hotspots within the five ranges of the frame of reference table for the railway lines of the Abruzzo region. Two railway lines (namely, "Teramo – Giulianova" and "Avezzano – Roccasecca") do not appear because they do not give rise to any hotspot with exposure value greater than zero.

Table 5. The distribution of the hotspots within the ranges of the frame of reference table for the railway lines in $\mathcal{R}l_{\mathfrak{d}}$.

Railway lines	#hotspots	#hotspots in the very high range	#hotspots in the high range	#hotspots in the moderate range	#hotspots in the low range	#hotspots in the null range
1	5	0	0	0	1	4
2	38	2	1	7	10	18
3	77	9	5	24	16	23
4	3	1	0	2	0	0
5	12	0	0	2	3	7
6	27	1	7	11	2	6
7	48	5	9	8	12	14

Tables 4 and 5 show that, in the Case Study, the majority of the hotspots have a low or null level of exposure to the landslide risk, while 42 of them (the 20% of the totality of the hotspots with value of exposure greater than zero) present levels of exposure that bring out the need of more frequent controls (*Very High* and *High* exposure level). The total extent of the just mentioned 42 hotspots (24.5 km) is equal to just the 3.57% of the total length of 9 railway lines of the Abruzzo region and to the 38.46% of the total extension of the 210 hotspots. These numbers describe a state of the land on which run the tracks of the 9 railway lines that cross the Abruzzo region broadly stable, and this results in the conclusion that the monitoring actions to be taken on the field are numerically limited.

3.2   Second Level of Analysis

Table 6 shows the top-N hotspots along the railway line "Marina di San Vito – Castel di Sangro" (it has code 3 in Table 5). Such a line is long 103 km and has 77 hotspots.

For such a railway line $N = 14$, where (according to Table 5) the first 9 hotspots belong to the *Very High* range. The value of N is determined by linking the data in the second column of Table 6 to those in the second column of Table 4 that, as mentioned, acts as a frame of reference (Sect. 2.3). The top-N list of the hotspots for the remaining lines can be determined similarly.

Table 6. The top-N hotspots along line "Marina di San Vito – Castel di Sangro".

Hotspot	Exposure	Point A	Point B
1	4.76	42°11′24.598″N 14°21′23.816″E	42°11′46.928″N 14°20′58.002″E
2	3.73	41°55′23.097″N 14°17′22.451″E	41°55′6.691″N 14°17′22.150″E
3	3.56	41°52′57.975″N 14°14′39.255″E	41°52′39.796″N 14°13′48.324″E
4	3.47	41°54′44.714″N 14°17′11.585″E	41°54′39.120″N 14°17′0.727″E
5	3.41	42°2′27.055″N 14°20′52.980″E	42°1′51.642″N 14°20′54.252″E
6	2.75	41°58′50.261″N 14°22′18.812″E	41°58′43.730″N 14°22′18.515″E
7	2.73	42°1′20.307″N 14°21′17.746″E	42°0′58.483″N 14°21′34.270″E
8	2.62	41°58′55.655″N 14°22′18.294″E	41°58′52.316″N 14°22′18.410″E
9	2.48	41°58′10.316″N 14°22′14.014″E	41°57′54.260″N 14°22′2.956″E
10	1.11	41°55′52.901″N 14°18′49.777″E	41°55′58.620″N 14°18′32.945″E
11	1.10	42°11′32.235″N 14°19′47.938″E	42°11′16.294″N 14°19′56.344″E
12	0.99	42°12′39.863″N 14°23′2.996″E	42°12′38.618″N 14°23′2.477″E
13	0.96	42°1′43.719″N 14°21′5.255″E	42°1′35.123″N 14°21′8.763″E
14	0.94	41°56′46.294″N 14°21′25.414″E	41°56′40.327″N 14°21′21.419″E

3.3 Results Validation

Some of the hotspots in the top-N list of a given railway line may be a *false positive* because Eq. 9 does not take into account the terrain elevation inside the GeoArea. Through *QuantumGIS*, we found rapidly, for the Case Study, 9 false positives out of 40 top-N hotspots present in the 9 railway lines crossing the Abruzzo region (Table 5). 3 false positives fall in the *Very High* range while the remaining 6 fall in the *High* range. For all the 9 false positives, *QuantumGIS* has shown that the terrain around such hotspots is flat, so it is correct to exclude that they may be give rise to landslides even in the case of long periods of rain.

4 Conclusions and Future Work

This paper gave two contributions. Firstly, we proposed a scientifically robust method for the identification of the top-N list of railway hotspots with respect to their exposure to soil mass movements. Then, we sketched a strategy for implementing a selective monitoring of the soil under the identified hotspots, thus reducing the maintenance costs, without lowering the railway safety level, with respect to the case where the full length of the railway line has to be inspected.

The method proposed for the identification of the hotspots has its basis in con-solidated results in the *Geographic Information Science* domain. To our knowledge, this is the first time that such a point of view is adopted for the problem at hand.

The identification of the hotspots along railway lines besides allowing the imple-mentation of a selective monitoring of the lines, moreover allows the quantification of the risk which the railway lines are exposed, considering as "elements at risk" not the whole lines but just the top-N hotspots along them.

The results returned by Eq. 9 (for a given case study) usually remain stable over periods of several years, unless either it does not change the geometry of some stretch of the railway lines or updates of the data set $\mathcal{Z}$ are made available. Both these cir-cumstances are not very frequent in the reality.

In summary, we can say the following about the proposed method. Despite it is simple to be understood and implemented, it provides useful information to limit the inspection of the whole railway lines to a limited number of stretches along them.

The current proposal is the preliminary step towards the release of a software tool to be meant for the people responsible of the control of the safety of the railway beds within a given territory. The next step in our agenda will be devoted to devise an algorithm that takes into account the terrain elevation in the study area in order to eliminate the possibility of detecting false positives.

References

1. Blahut, J., Poretti, I., De Amicis, M., Sterlacchini, S.: Database of geo-hydrological disasters for civil protection purposes. Nat. Hazards **60**, 1065–1083 (2012)
2. Brabb, E.E., Harrod, B.L. (eds.): Landslides: Extent and Economic Significance, 385 pp. Balkema Publisher, Rotterdam (1989)
3. Di Felice, P., et al.: Ranking the buildings over a developed large geographic area according to their exposure to the landslide hazard. Eur. J. Geogr. **7**(3), 6–24 (2016)
4. Egenhofer, M., Herring, J.: Categorizing binary topological relations between regions, lines, and points in geographic databases. Technical report, Department of Surveying Engineering, University of Maine (1991) (revised versions in NCGIA Technical report 91-7 and NCGIA Technical report 94-1). http://www.spatial.maine.edu/~max/9intReport.pdf. Accessed Feb 2016
5. Egenhofer, M., Shariff, A.R.: Metric details for natural-language spatial relations. ACM Trans. Inf. Syst. **16**(4), 295–321 (1998)
6. Fell, R., et al.: Guidelines for landslide susceptibility, hazard and risk zoning for land-use planning. Eng. Geol. **102**, 99–111 (2008)
7. Guzzetti, F., Reichenbach, P., Ardizzone, F., Cardinali, M., Galli, M.: Estimating the quality of landslide susceptibility models. Geomorphology **81**, 166–184 (2006)
8. He, H., Li, S., Sun, H.: Environmental factors of road slope stability in mountain area using principal component analysis and hierarchy cluster. Environ. Earth Sci. **62**(1), 55–59 (2011)
9. Hervás, J.: Encyclopedia of natural hazards. In: Bobrowsky, P.T. (eds.) Encyclopedia of Earth Sciences Series, pp. 610–611 (2013). http://link.springer.com/referenceworkentry/10.1007%2F978-1-4020-4399-4_214
10. Magliulo, P., Di Lisio, A., Russo, F.: Comparison of GIS-based methodologies for the landslide susceptibility assessment. GeoInformatica **13**, 253–265 (2009)

11. Mandal, S., Maiti, R.: Assessing the triggering rainfall-induced landslip events in the Shivkhola watershed of Darjiling, Himalaya, West Bengal. Eur. J. Geogr. **4**(3), 21–37 (2013)
12. Open GISs Implementation Specification: Open GISs Implementation Specification for Geographic information – Simple Feature Access – Part2: SQL Option. Keith Ryden (ed.), Document: OGC05-134, 74 pp. (2005)
13. Rawat, P.K., Tiwari, P.C., Pant, C.C.: Geo-hydrological database modeling for integrated multiple hazards and risk assessment in Lesser Himalaya: a GIS-based case study. Nat. Hazards **62**, 1233–1260 (2012). doi:10.1007/s11069-012-0144-2
14. Sadler, J., et al.: GeoSRM – Online geospatial safety risk model for the GB rail network. IET Intel. Transport Syst. **10**(1), 17–24 (2016). doi:10.1049/iet-its.2015.0038
15. SafeLand: Guidelines for landslide susceptibility, hazard and risk assessment and zoning. Deliverable D2.4 of the Safe Land research project, 7th EU Framework Programme (2011). http://www.safeland-fp7.eu/Pages/SafeLand.aspx

Workshop on Geographical Analysis, Urban Modeling, Spatial statistics (Geo-An-Mod 2017) 32

Investigation of Social Networking Mechanisms and Their Geospatial Allocation Effects – An Agent-Based Simulation Approach

Andreas Koch[✉]

University of Salzburg, Salzburg, Austria
andreas.koch@sbg.ac.at

Abstract. The size and composition of social networks rely on the characteristics of the nodes and the (in)tangible infrastructure. The networking mechanisms themselves, however, depend on circumstances such as meeting or team collaboration opportunities. A set of determinants of networking mechanisms will be discussed in this paper, and in particular the number of events over a certain period is highlighted. This aim will be implemented by an agent-based simulation approach and empirically verified with network data from an Austrian regional project. The simulation results will finally be used to draw some conclusions on a place-based geography derived from the network-based geography.

Keywords: Team assembly mechanisms · Event dependency · Geo-social networks

1 Introduction

There are many reasons why networks emerge among people. Sometimes it is a utilitarian motivation, because they believe it is beneficial or profitable for them to collaborate. Sometimes an altruistic incitement might be the predominant cause for why they get connected, and again in other cases it could be an exogenous (and involuntary) impetus that enforces cooperation. Thus, one's willingness and ability to connect with others appear to be a crucial issue in network creation.

Beside this issue there are further conditions that influence or even determine successful social networking. One of these that is thought to be relevant in this article is the number of events (workshops, meetings, etc.) offered to potential collaborators. Based on a theoretical reference model of team assembly mechanisms, an agent-based simulation model has been developed that helps analyse determinants of social networking mechanisms. Node- and edge-based characteristics are correlated with an event-driven parameter and investigated within a certain time span. With the simulation results obtained through a comprehensive parameter space analysis we are looking for patterns that allow us to draw conclusions from the relational network geography towards a place-based geo-spatial geography. The analysis is validated with empirical data obtained from two Austrian regions using a questionnaire conducted among team leaders of a social project. Besides this we aim to develop a model that can be used as

© Springer International Publishing AG 2017
O. Gervasi et al. (Eds.): ICCSA 2017, Part IV, LNCS 10407, pp. 335–349, 2017.
DOI: 10.1007/978-3-319-62401-3_25

some kind of a toolbox in order to investigate the emergence of social network structures that rely on similar conditions as the introduced model. The use of empirical network data can be easily adapted to the respective model purposes.

2   The Simulation of Networking Mechanisms

The size and composition of social networks rely to a large part on the characteristics of the actors involved, i.e., their capabilities, needs, and aspirations to collaborate with others. It also depends on the reasons for cooperation, the kind of problems, and the (in)tangible infrastructure necessary to communicate via different channels. An important additional issue, however, comes with the nature of network mechanisms themselves, the process of how relations between actors emerge structurally, and which determinants are thought of as relevant. This latter issue considerably affects the evolution of a large network that arises from initially small teams and, by this, contributes to overcoming isolated and fragmented efforts towards a common goal. Achieving synergies through effective trans-local knowledge transfer is a goal that has been investigated in (social) network analysis for some time [2, 3, 10]. In this respect agent-based simulation is an appropriate method to explore the underlying processes that lead to these networking mechanisms [9].

As a first step of this investigation a theoretical reference model, developed by Guimera et al. [6] and made available as a NetLogo model by Bakshy and Wilensky [1], has been selected and adapted to our own needs. The question raised by Guimera et al. [6, p. 699] remains evident to some degree in our context too: "Is there a large connected cluster comprising most of the agents or is the network composed of numerous smaller clusters?" The ideal size is not necessarily given with exactly one all-encompassing network: "Successful teams evolve toward a size that is large enough to enable specialization and effective division of labor among teammates but small enough to avoid overwhelming costs of group coordination" (ibid., p. 697). Concerning our empirical research we are less interested in economic costs but in the creation of sustaining social interactions (for example, by taking the production of social capital into consideration).

In this article, these assumptions are taken as relevant premises for networking mechanisms. In so doing, our focus shifts to the parameters that influence or determine the construction of large(r) social networks that are initially small and more or less isolated due to the design of the social project. These parameters can be divided into three general domains: (i) actor-based parameters, (ii) linkage-based parameters, and (iii) place-based parameters. Chapters 5 and 6 present some selected results. Another to this contribution closely related paper of the author [7] points to the meaning of social capital as a resource for social networking.

3   The Empirical Case Studies

The empirical case studies for which an agent-based simulation model has been constructed which relies theoretically on the prototype model of Guimera et al. (2005), derive from an Austrian social project entitled "Keep the Ball Rolling". This project aims to enhance social well-being at a regional level by encouraging the local population to put ideas into practice that they are convinced are relevant. Individuals or small teams are called to submit project proposals that help reduce social injustice and promote social cohesion. Successful teams will be awarded a grant to fund their project, and in addition they will be organisationally supported. The project started in the Lungau region (Salzburg) in 2011 followed by the Steirische Eisenstrasse (Styria), the Mühlviertler Alm (Upper Austria), and the Mostviertel Mitte regions (Lower Austria) [4, 5]. The empirical data used for the following simulation models is from the Styrian and Upper Austrian regions.

The project proposals are presented by the teams at three jury meetings, and after the jury has evaluated them as successful candidates they should be implemented within a time frame of a year and a half. Every jury session is followed by a public celebration where successful projects are presented, and, due to the fact that the project implementation is scientifically accompanied by a team of researchers for the whole project period, several further meetings, ranging from small informal meetings to larger stakeholder workshops, are offered. Every team leader has been invited to participate in a semi-standardised questionnaire designed to gain knowledge about the project team in terms of their size and composition. These questionnaire results are used in the following analysis.

The analysis presented here is concerned with how the number of such meetings (i) determines the team assembly mechanisms, (ii) correlates with other determinants, and (iii) correlates with a place-based geography. This will be discussed in the next chapters.

4 The Model Design

In order to analyse the development of collaborative socio-spatial network structures of initially small(er) and unconnected teams in two Austrian regions a simulation model has been constructed that includes the general ideas of the original model proposed by Guimera et al. [6] which was introduced in Sect. 2. Bakshy and Wilensky [1] have made available a NetLogo version of the original model. This model serves as a reference model in that it helps explore and understand the fundamental mechanisms of why and how project teams assemble over time. Hence, its first function is to provide a theoretical benchmark model that enables us to categorise the empirical regional models. This has been done by the author by a first and preliminary statistical analysis [8], but will not be considered here.

Indeed, the reference model itself has been derived from the original "team assembly mechanisms" model and adapted to our own needs. Major differences of the reference model compared to the original model are: (i) the number of teams is initialised at three time steps and not stepwise; with this adaptation we represent the selection process of successful teams. (ii) teams can vary in size and (iii) in network structure; while the original model only allows the implementation of teams of three actors that are fully connected, the "Keep-The-Ball-Rolling" project does not have such restrictions. (iv) individual agents (and not only teams of three agents) are inserted as new potential collaborators; this criterion will play a crucial role in the future modelling process when data sets are available that will be collected approximately two years after the official social project's end (data of the Mühlviertler Alm region is still missing while data of the Steirische Eisenstrasse is not yet completely edited). We thus do not refer to this criterion in this paper. (v) initial teams can merge either by a team leader (who is a leader of a project team) or by a team member who is selected stochastically for a new connection; this adaptation has been implemented due to the nature of events that are realised during the project meetings and consist of stakeholder workshops, project presentations, informal meetings as well as *ad hoc* assistance from the staff of the regional offices. Although we do not consider these different event properties explicitly, they remain important to justify the "connecting role" of both agent types. The original model takes only team leaders as connectors into account. Thus, the second function of the reference model is to serve as a prototype model from which tailored empirical models can be derived.

The construction of the two regional socio-spatial network models is based on standardised questionnaires that have been conducted at the beginning of the festival project in either region. Every team leader of a project who was awarded a grant to participate with her/his project and who took part in the survey was asked about her/his team collaborators. We also know the team leader's home address (but not that of the collaborators, which affects the analysis). The numbers of actors and network ties are listed in Table 1.

Table 1. Number of registered team leaders, team members, and network ties among and between them in the Steirische Eisenstrasse (Styrian region) and the Mühlviertler Alm (Upper Austrian region)

Number of ...	Team leaders	Team members	Network ties
Styrian region	79	396	441
Upper Austrian region	59	418	655

The two models are initialised with these settings of nodes and edges. In the style of the reference model a six-dimensional parameter space is used to analyse the networking mechanisms among team leaders, team members, and between them. The aim of this procedure is to detect common patterns of relevance of and relationship between the six parameters that seem to determine the behaviour of social networks in terms of their structure and dynamic. Table 2 gives an overview of the parameters and the ranges of values within which the further simulation results have been analysed.

The parameter *selAgents* determines the likelihood that agents attending an event are willing to collaborate; for example, *selAgents* = 50% means that 50% of all attendees of a workshop are willing to collaborate. The parameter *selAgentType* specifies which agent type – the team leader or the team member – is more likely to be willing to collaborate. If *selAgentType* = 50% both agent groups are equally likely to be willing to collaborate, if *selAgentType* < 50% more team leaders are likely to be willing to collaborate. The interval of both parameters varies largely to detect network differences because of asymmetric probabilities. The maximum number of agents who are likely to collaborate, *maxSelAgents*, is a conservative estimation based on our experience of events we have organised in both regions. These three parameters affect the behaviour of the agents, while the following two affect the relationship between them. The *conTeamLeader* and *conTeamMember* parameter determine stochastically how agents connect among themselves. If, for example, *conTeamLeader* = 10%, then in 10% of all cases team leaders connect with other team leaders, and in 90% of all cases they connect with team members. The same rule applies to *conTeamMember*. The last parameter, *numEvents*, determines the number of events that take place during a simulation run. The range of values varies between one event and 160 events.

Table 2. Description of parameters used in the simulation models.

Parameter	Description	Interval of analysis
selAgents	Probability of selecting agents per event, willing to collaborate	[20, (30)[a], 80]%
selAgentType	Probability of selecting team leaders or team members per event, willing to collaborate	[20, (30), 80]%
maxSelAgents	Potential maximum number of agents per event, willing to collaborate	[4, (4), 12] abs.
conTeamLeader	Probability of team leaders actually connecting with other agents	[5, (15), 35]%
conTeamMember	Probability of team members actually connecting with other agents	[0, (10), 30]%
numEvents	Number of events that enables the establishment of new ties over a complete simulation run	[1, 2, 4, 8, 16, 32, 40, 80, 160] abs.

[a]Values in brackets indicate the increment value; for example: the interval for *selAgents* is 20, 50, and 80.

Taking into account that one simulation run takes 160 steps, which represents a time period of 160 weeks or almost three years (i.e., the project time of approx. 80 weeks and the post-project time of another 80 weeks when a *posteriori* questionnaires are conducted to evaluate the sustainability of the projects) then the number of events varies between only one meeting during and after the social festival and meetings on a weekly basis.

The social network simulation models have been created with NetLogo 6.0 [11]. The analysis of modelling results has two components: first, a statistical analysis composed of a multivariate linear regression analysis and a cluster analysis has been conducted. Second, a simulation analysis consisting of representative simulation runs investigates the behaviour of the social networks by considering the network parameters closeness centrality and betweenness centrality. The model together with a comprehensive description of the procedures implemented is available at OpenABM (https://www.openabm.org/model/5583/version/1).

5   Some Selected Model Results

With the NetLogo extension of "BehaviorSpace" all possible combinations of values (that is 3,888 in this case) within the intervals of the six variables have been computed, which led to 3,888 mean values across all variations. Each mean value is the result of eleven simulation runs using the same initial values of the variables, i.e. the internal variance is reduced to the average value. These mean values have then been used to compute average bivariate correlations and measurements of determination for the variables "number of connections among team leaders", "number of connections among team members", and "number of connections between team leaders and team members". The aim is to detect the strength and direction of relationships of the six independent variables with the emergence of network structures, which consist of both the initial network relations of the original teams (empirical data) and the newly created network relations during the simulation (modelled data). The focus – compared with the original team assembly model – is only on the development of links since no new agents were introduced.

The method to create multiple regressions is "stepwise selection" which avoids multicollinearity to some degree. Table 3 reveals that *numEvents* is the most relevant independent variable for all three dependent variables. The measurement of determination (R^2) confirms this statement. The parameter *numEvents* is, however, more relevant to explain the variation of the distribution of the links among team leaders than among team members. Team leaders benefit more, on average, from an increase of workshops and meetings than team members. This is partially due to an implicit bias, occurring because there are fewer team leaders than team members, which quickly leads to a higher number of linkages. This assessment is confirmed by the contrary fact of there being only a few events (1 to 8): under this condition team leaders are far more involved in creating a large connected social network than team members. This fact has to be taken into account to avoid lock-in effects of a well-informed stakeholder group.

Table 3. Regression patterns of the three dependent edge-related variables for the Steirische Eisenstrasse (Styria, S) and the Mühlviertler Alm (Upper Austria, UA). Source: own data

Dependent variable	Most relevant independent variable (iv)	R^2 of most relevant iv	R^2 of all included iv
Number of connections among team leaders (S)	Number of events r = 0.785	0.617	0.759
Number of connections among team leaders (UA)	Number of events r = 0.779	0.606	0.751
Number of connections among team members (S)	Number of events r = 0.633	0.401	0.525
Number of connections among team members (UA)	Number of events r = 0.623	0.388	0.505
Number of connections among all actors (S)	Number of events r = 0.756	0.572	0.687
Number of connections among all actors (UA)	Number of events r = 0.735	0.540	0.652

The statistical influence of the remaining five parameters is significantly less relevant in explaining the variation of ties among and between the two groups when compared with *numEvents*, as is illustrated in the last column of Table 3. The least relevant parameter in terms of correlation is *conTeamMember* for the team leaders and *conTeam-Leader* for the team members. One conclusion might be that even a low chance of getting actually connected is sufficient if a high number of opportunities to meet each other occurs.

The cluster analysis aims at further exploring structures that have been unknown so far. The cluster algorithm used here is the "Ward method" that yields more or less evenly distributed clusters. A variation of four to six clusters has been applied, the solution with five clusters provided good results with respect to a good discrimination of the values and interpretation of the results. As Tables 4 and 5 illustrate for both regions in a very similar way, the highest numbers of connected agents (cluster 5 in both cases) are achieved when *numEvents* is highest (which is not surprising), the likelihood of selected agents is relatively high, the share of team leaders is higher than that of team members, the maximum number of potentially selectable agents is relatively high, and the likelihood that agents will be tied together is high. If more team members are likely to be selected (*selAgentType* > 50%) then a considerable decrease of realised linkages follows. Again, the least relevant parameters are *conTeamLeader* and *conTeamMember* (though they cause the relevant discrimination between cluster 4 and cluster 5 in the Upper Austrian case study).

Table 4. Cluster analysis results for the Styrian case study region. Values represent mean values. Source: own data

Dependent variables	Cluster 1	Cluster 2	Cluster 3	Cluster 4	Cluster 5
Number of ties among team leaders	700	1,041	156	1,263	1,415
Number of ties among team Members	805	2,075	83	3,402	9,074
Number of all ties	2,132	4,248	497	7,824	10,423
Independent variables					
numEvents	73	118	18	141	160
selAgents	58	58	47	70	73
selAgentType	52	50	51	40	32
maxSelAgents	7	7	6	8	8
conTeamLeader/ conTeamMember	20/15	20/15	20/15	19/13	20/25

Although *numEvents* appears to be a highly relevant determinant in the development of large network compositions it is also highlighted in the cluster analysis results that team members benefit significantly from an increase of events. A comparison of cluster 1 and cluster 2 for the Steirische Eisenstrasse outlines that an almost doubling of *numEvents* leads to a considerably higher increase of tied team members (approx. 2,100 compared with 800) than of tied team leaders (approx. 1,500 compared with 700).

A simple concentration measurement that takes the relative development of linkages into account reveals another considerable difference between team leaders and team members. For team members the highest decile comprises 5% to 100% of all realised connections with other agents, i.e., 90% of cases represent only up to 4% of all connections. For team leaders, however, the highest decile comprises a minimum of 57% of all realised connections. These ratios of concentrations are true for both case study regions.

Table 5. Cluster analysis results for the Upper Austrian case study region. Values represent mean values. Source: own data

Dependent variables	Cluster 1	Cluster 2	Cluster 3	Cluster 4	Cluster 5
Number of ties among team leaders	184	932	1,004	1,299	1,364
Number of ties among team Members	141	1,458	5,293	2,682	10,459
Number of all ties	817	4,056	7,229	12,152	12,844
Independent variables					
numEvents	22	104	133	155	160
selAgents	47	60	66	70	72
selAgentType	51	51	38	34	34
maxSelAgents	6	7	7	9	9
conTeamLeader/ conTeamMember	20/15	20/13	20/22	20/4	21/25

Apart from the statistical analysis a simulation analysis has been performed in order to investigate the course of the network creation. In doing so, two common centrality measures have been used namely the closeness centrality and the betweenness centrality. Both centrality measures characterise an agent's position or role in the entire network. In NetLogo closeness centrality is defined "[...] as the inverse of the average of an [agent's] distances to all other [agents]" [11]. Distances are defined as shortest paths. Betweenness centrality in contrast refers to the mediator function of an agent (for example, mediating communication flows). To calculate the betweenness centrality of an agent "[...] you take every other possible pairs of [agents] and, for each pair, you calculate the proportion of shortest paths between members of the pair that passes through the current [agent]. The betweenness centrality of an [agent] is the sum of these" [11].

Based on typical and representative simulation runs of the above mentioned behaviour space analysis in NetLogo a data subset with 32 cases has been condensed (this means that extreme values have been excluded; for example, *numEvents* is equal to 80 in one case and eight in another). Figure 1 illustrates exemplarily the results of agents that possess a high closeness centrality ("high" defined as above the threshold value of 0.5) for the Steirische Eisenstrasse region. The two maps differ in the number of events during the simulation run.

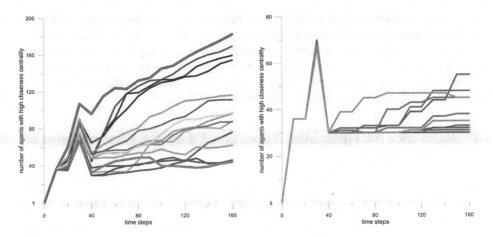

Fig. 1. Distribution of high closeness centrality agents with *numEvents* = 80 (left) and *numEvents* = 8 (right) in the Styrian case study region. (Color figure online)

16 out of the 32 simulation runs have been executed with a high number of meeting events (left map) while the other half of simulation runs used a low number of events (right map). Most obviously, the variation of results with *numEvents* = 80 is considerably larger than with a low number of events. The case with the lowest number of agents gaining a high closeness centrality (green graph, left map) is characterised by a high number of selected team leaders (because *selAgents* is high and *selAgentType* is significantly below 50% threshold value) and high linkage percentages for both types (see Table 6).

Table 6. Parameter settings that lead to the "highest number" and "lowest number" of agents with a high closeness centrality if *numEvents* = 80 and *numEvents* = 8, respectively. Values are from the Styrian case study region.

numEvents = 80	selAgents	selAgentType	conTeamLeader	conTeamMember
Highest number	80	20	35	30
Lowest number	20	80	35	30
numEvents = 8	*selAgents*	*selAgentType*	*conTeamLeader*	*conTeamMember*
Highest number	80	20	35	1
Lowest number	20	20	35	30

Compared with this case the one with the highest number of agents gaining a high closeness centrality (red graph, left map) differs in the relationship of *selAgents* and *selAgentType* which is now exactly the opposite. These results highlight the outstanding contribution of team leaders in two ways: (i) they themselves are important as central nodes within the social network; (ii) they also act as multipliers for team members to achieve a central position in the network.

The low-event cases (right map of Fig. 1) fluctuation is far less significant, here values range from 30 (blue graph) to 55 (red graph) (there are six different combinations of parameter values that lead to 30 agents gaining high closeness centrality). The most relevant determinants to explain the differences are *selAgents* and *conTeamMember*, thus one node-related and one linkage-related parameter. A comparison of the two maps convincingly shows that even a high number of supplied events does not guarantee a sufficiently high number of agents that are tightly linked together if the other parameter values do not "support" successful collaboration efforts.

6 Relevance for Geospatial Allocation Effects: A First Attempt of Interpretation

The statistical and simulation analyses reveal that the construction and (sustainable) consolidation of social networks is influenced by a high number of determinants whose interrelationships are quite complicated in terms of generating a large(r) connected network. A high number of offered events does not automatically ensure a high proportion of agents that gain a high centrality in order to provide for efficient knowledge transfer between them. In fact, even a few events can result in a reliable number of durable linkages among agents. The results emphasise that agents' willingness and opportunities to collaborate can have both a cushioning and amplifying effect.

One must take the specific sequence of the three jury meetings into account here. These jury meetings represent a particular type of events which can be replaced by other types of events with different team allocation or assembly conditions, however. In general, the nature of events must be defined according to the model purpose, which has been done in this case in close relationship to the number of events. The model as a toolbox is flexible enough to incorporate further parameters and/or changing the behaviour of agents through the entire networking process.

Due to the inclusion of new team leaders and team members at predefined time steps a temporary decline of agents with high betweenness and/or closeness centrality can arise. Fluctuations are large(r) if the number of supplied events is high, because then meetings between jury session are like to happen.

Therefore the organisation of events to foster collaboration is a challenging enterprise as social network analysis has shown. The supply of opportunities to meet each other aiming to exchange knowledge and experience has, besides its qualitative component (obligatory stakeholder meeting vs. informal team meeting), also a quantitative direction. Against all network-based determinants mentioned one should not forget, however, the geographical domain, i.e., the geospatial distribution of relevant actors. In other words, a translation from a space-of-flows geography to a space-of-places geography appears to appropriate.

The following figures (see Figs. 2, 3, 4 and 5) illustrate representative extracts of the spatial distribution of agents with high betweenness centrality (yellow), high closeness centrality (violet), and remaining team leaders (red) for a high (*numEvents* = 80) and a low (*numEvents* = 8) number of events (other parameter values are close to the values in Table 6; linkages are hidden). The scale of resolution of the agents' locations is the municipal level (distribution within the municipalities is for visualisation reasons only).

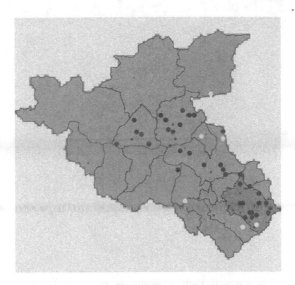

Fig. 2. Distribution of agents with high betweenness centrality (yellow) and high closeness centrality (violet) for *numEvents* = 80 in the Steirische Eisenstrasse region. Source: own data. Colours of municipalities indicate less than 2% of all projects (light green); between 2% and 20% (green); more than 20% (dark green). (Color figure online)

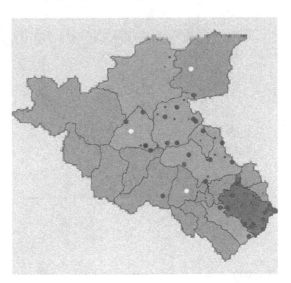

Fig. 3. Distribution of agents with high betweenness centrality (yellow) and high closeness centrality (violet) for *numEvents* = 8 in the Steirische Eisenstrasse region. Source: own data. Colours of municipalities indicate less than 2% of all projects (light green); between 2% and 20% (green); more than 20% (dark green). (Color figure online)

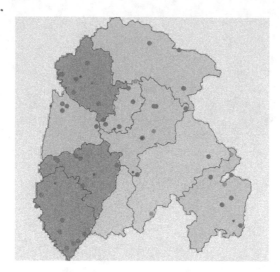

Fig. 4. Distribution of agents with high betweenness centrality (yellow) and high closeness centrality (violet) for *numEvents* = 80 in the Mühlviertler Alm region. Source: own data. Colours of municipalities indicate less than 5% of all projects (light green); between 5% and 15% (green); more than 15% (dark green). (Color figure online)

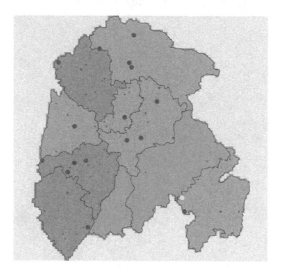

Fig. 5. Distribution of agents with high betweenness centrality (yellow) and high closeness centrality (violet) for *numEvents* = 8 in the Mühlviertler Alm region. Source: own data. Colours of municipalities indicate less than 5% of all projects (light green); between 5% and 15% (green); more than 15% (dark green). (Color figure online)

One important conclusion that can be drawn from the patterns of distribution is that the vertical structures of the social networks do not completely coincide with the structure of the places where the team leaders reside and the projects had been implemented,

respectively. Agents with high closeness and/or betweenness centrality are dispropor-
tionately more often located in municipalities with comparatively fewer implemented
projects (light green and green coloured areas compared with dark green coloured areas).
This is true for both situations of a high and a low number of events.

Although the settlement structure of the two study areas differs to some extent – in
the Styrian region there is one larger city (Leoben) while in the Upper Austrian region
a couple of smaller towns are distributed more or less evenly over the whole region –
our original assumption generally was that a centre-periphery pattern will influence the
distribution of submitted project proposals and thus the distribution of agents' locations
(team leaders as well as team members). This uneven distribution in turn would determine the structure of the social networks, namely the size of the network as well as their
levels and qualities of connections. This assumption confirmed our course of action to
spatially widely distribute locations of meetings (those meetings we were responsible
for, such as jury and stakeholder meetings. All other meeting locations had been selected
by team leaders, team members or regional office staff). The conclusion we want to draw
with the simulation model presented here is that the number of events influences the
vertical and horizontal structure of the networks in both regions though differently.
These conditions must be taken into account when using the model as a toolbox for
different purposes within this general frame.

If a high number of meetings were to be offered (Figs. 2 and 3) then the distribution
of agents with high betweenness centrality (= important communicators) is more evenly
distributed than the distribution of the projects. The result is true for the Styrian as well
as the Upper Austrian study area. In fact, this statement can be extended to the situation
of a low number of offered meetings if the closeness centrality (= important strong ties
between agents) is taken into consideration, as can be seen in Figs. 4 and 5. The peculiar
relationship between the two geographies immediately prompts the conclusion that the
decision about adequate venues for meetings should be made by taking the whole project
region into account and not concentrating mostly on the regions' larger towns.

Ultimately, personal engagement in one's own local social environment also needs
to be appreciated by rotating meeting locations across the entire region, because then
"peripherally located" agents can act as hosts and can proudly present their project work
in immediately visible form.

7 Conclusion

The purpose of the proposed simulation model is twofold: on the one hand we aimed to
analyse the impact of the quantity of events on the creation of a large(r) social network.
With the introduction of a different number of events we explicitly included the assumed
positive correlation between the number of meeting opportunities and the likelihood of
tighter connected networks, and we implicitly included different types of events (from
few formal stakeholder meetings to many informal project meetings). On the other hand
we aimed to create a model that can be used as a (kind of a) toolbox that enables representations of network creation processes by taking agent behaviour and quality of relation into account. As has been illustrated this can be easily achieved.

The theoretical and empirical relationship between a network-based and a place-based geography could have been analysed with a more thorough (geo-)statistical approach. We decided to abstain from this step at the current status of the simulation model because of two reasons: (i) Data availability is currently restricted to team leaders only; it would be necessary to know more about actual or potential connections of the team members of the small initial project teams. (ii) The selection process of project teams is weakly biased by attempts of the jury to avoid spatial concentration; the project "Keep The Ball Rolling" is anxious to allocate successful team projects as geographically wide as possible. If these restrictions would be surmounted a Point Pattern Analysis (PPA) technique could be applied in order to detect differences of empirical point distributions compared with randomly distributed points. PPA can result in the detection of clustered or even point patterns.

At the moment we only use coarse qualitative assessments as evaluation criteria. With these assessments we can, however, conclude that the models provide satisfying results. On average, we offer approx. eight official events during and after the project phase. Moreover, we know from these meetings that a high proportion of project leaders met more often though not every second week. If, based on this knowledge, the models are correctly calibrated we obtain model results that are similar to our empirical experience.

Besides the analytical justification for evenly distributed event locations it is also a deliberate decision from a normative point of view, because then the aim of making social engagement visible will be achieved more sustainable and just.

References

1. Bakshy, E., Wilensky, U.: NetLogo Team Assembly model. Center for Connected Learning and Computer-Based Modeling, Northwestern University, Evanston, IL (2007). http://ccl.north-western.edu/netlogo/models/TeamAssembly
2. Batagelj, V., Doreian, P., Ferligoj, A., Kejžar, N.: Understanding Large Temporal Networks and Spatial Networks. Wiley, Chichester (2014)
3. De Nooy, W., Mrvar, A., Batagelj, V.: Exploratory Social Network Analysis with Pajek. Cambridge University Press, Cambridge (2005)
4. Gstach, I., Kapferer, E., Koch, A., Sedmak, C. (eds.): Sozialatlas Mühlviertler Alm. Mandelbaum Verlag, Wien (2015)
5. Gstach, I., Kapferer, E., Koch, A., Sedmak, C. (eds.): Sozialatlas Steirische Eisenstraße. Mandelbaum Verlag, Wien (2013)
6. Guimera, R., Uzzi, B., Spiro, J., Amaral, L.A.N.: Team assembly mechanisms determine collaboration network structure and team performance. Science **308**, 697–702 (2005)
7. Koch, A.: Determinants of social networking mechanisms and their potential effects on a place-based geography: an agent-based simulation approach. GI_Forum J. Geogr. Inf. Sci. **3** (2017, in print)
8. Koch, A.: The impact of event determinants on team assembly mechanisms of social networks. In: ESSA Proceedings 2016, Rome (2016)
9. Namatame, A., Chen, S.-H.: Agent-Based Modeling and Network Dynamics. Oxford University Press, Oxford (2016)

10. Robins, G., Pattison, P.: Interdependencies and social processes: dependence graphs and generalized dependence structures. In: Carrington, P.J., Scott, J., Wasserman, S. (eds.) Models and Methods in Social Network Analysis. Cambridge University Press, Cambridge (2005)
11. Wilensky, U.: NetLogo. Center for Connected Learning and Computer-Based Modeling, Northwestern University, Evanston, IL (1999). http://ccl.northwestern.edu/netlogo/

Geostatistical Analysis of Settlements Induced by Groundwater Extraction

Rose Line Spacagna[✉], Alessandro Rasulo, and Giuseppe Modoni

University of Cassino and Southern Lazio, Cassino, Italy
{rlspacagna,a.rasulo,modoni}@unicas.it

Abstract. One of the most important effects induced by the over-exploitation of aquifers is the land subsidence. This dangerous situation may reduce in relatively short time the functionality and safety of structures and infrastructures present on a territory and impair their efficiency and stability. The city of Bologna is one of the most sensational cases of Italy, especially for the amount of recorded settlements and the great historical and cultural value of exposed assets. This article analyses the spatial and temporal distribution of settlements over an area of about $270\,km^2$ including the centre of the city. The topographical measurements, carried out starting from 1943 with a progressively increasing detail, highlight an articulated framework of settlements with maximum values exceeding 4 m. After a brief introduction of the phenomenon and its causes, a geostatistical analysis has been performed on a Geographical Information System. In order to validate the results, the potential damage on buildings present in the area has been evaluated. To this end, data were collected regarding the geometrical characteristics and the structural types of the buildings. The strain levels from the current configuration of the ground surface have been calculated for each of them. Finally, the expected damage levels have been assessed, following the classifications proposed in the literature that allow to assign a severity level for each building. These results were compared with damage observed by previous studies. This approach is a prerequisite to the planning of any vulnerability mitigation strategy.

Keywords: Subsidence · Settlements · Building damages · Geostatistics · GIS

1 Introduction

The principal consequence of the rapid evolution of the population, intensive urbanization and industrialization is the increase of the water supply demand. This activity can produce important changes in the territory.

In particular, the water request often leads to withdrawing of large quantities of water in concentrated portions of the subsurface and this, under certain circumstances, can generate deformations of the ground surfaces. The incidence of these factors become particularly problematic when the modifications occur in a relatively short time, such as to interact with human activities. The subsidence induced intensive extraction of groundwater is one of the most troublesome phenomena that can affect flood plains. The importance of this phenomenon in densely populated areas has been demonstrated by

© Springer International Publishing AG 2017
O. Gervasi et al. (Eds.): ICCSA 2017, Part IV, LNCS 10407, pp. 350–364, 2017.
DOI: 10.1007/978-3-319-62401-3_26

many examples that have become well known case studies. The Mexico City [19, 33], Santa Clara valley [24], Houston [18], London [31], Japan [32], China [13] and Spain [30] are only a few examples.

In this work, the attention has been focused on the city of Bologna, which is subject to an important subsidence phenomenon, since the end of World War II, due to water extraction of the underground water table. Several studies have shown the effects on the buildings of the town, especially at the historic center of the city [1, 11]. The first part of this work concerns the updating of a previous study of the spatial and temporal evolution of the subsidence phenomenon [20]. Based on information provided by Arpae Emilia Romagna [3], it was possible to update the settlements database. The high level of quality of the new dataset allow to perform analysis at different scale, by means of a Geographical Information System. In particular, the local spatial analysis has been validated by evaluating the effects of subsidence on the buildings of the old town, using the database of the National Geoportal [17] and comparing the values of the deformations with the limits suggested by the literature.

Starting from the available data, the aim of this work is the definition of the procedure, useful in order to planning possible actions for mitigating risk by reducing the vulnerability of buildings.

2 Settlements in the Area of Bologna

As shown by the literature [1, 5, 11, 15, 20, 22, 23, 28], the subsidence observed in recent decades in the Emilia Romagna region and in particular in the city of Bologna has been extensively studied from many points of view. Since its first settlement, the city has been affected by long-term deformation phenomena of the soil, due to consolidation induced by the own weight of the large alluvial deposits. These phenomena, extended to the entire Po Valley, have experienced acceleration in the decades since the 1950s, similarly to what happened to other northern Italian cities such as Milan, Venice and Ravenna. The ground deformations occurring in these cities and surrounding areas have produced significant settlements, which reached, in the most relevant cases, strain rate of several tens of centimetres per year [12].

A recent study [20] analysed the spatial distribution of subsidence in the area of Bologna and its temporal evolution (1943–2005). It covered an area of approximately 272.25 km^2 (Fig. 1), between the Reno River and the Savena River and including the whole city. The spatial and temporal analysis, carried out with the support of a geographic information system, showed a progressive development of total and differential settlement, consistent with the characteristics of the subsoil, the pumping activity and the effects found on buildings.

The study carried out for a large-scale interpretation includes qualitative and quantitative, spatial and temporal data regarding the properties of the soil, groundwater levels and subsidence.

The basic steps for the analysis were the processing of data using geostatistical methods [14]. When the studied phenomenon is described by several variables, from the sampling data, it is possible to represent such phenomenon over the whole area by

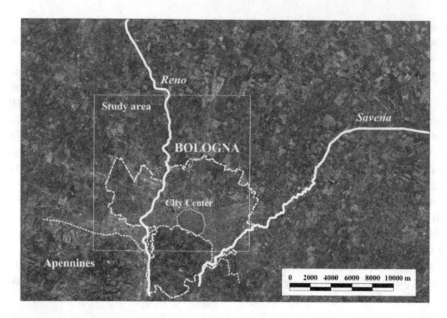

Fig. 1. Study area affected by subsidence induced by groundwater withdrawals [20].

interpolating information, exploiting the structure of the data distribution. The value assumed by the variable in a point is not independent from the value measured in another location. In particular, values measured in neighbouring points are more related than values measured at distant points. This spatial correlation is analysed by means of the variogram, calculated as half of the average of the standard deviation between two values z at distance of h:

$$\gamma(h) = \frac{1}{2}E\left\{[Z(x + h) - Z(x)]^2\right\} \tag{1}$$

The variogram γ (h) is modelled by a function who describes the link between two values of the variable measured at a distance equal to h. In general, the function grows with h, indicating that the variability increases with distance, until reaching at a certain distance, called "range", a limit value $\gamma(\infty)$ called "sill". Two values Z(x) and Z(x + h) are related if the length of the vector h is less than the "range". The range translates the notion of "distance of influence" of a value. The variogram model is use for the estimation of the variables in unsampled points. In geostatistical analysis, the linear interpolator is called "Kriging".

Among the various aspect, the previous study [20] focused on the spatial and temporal analysis of the settlements within the study area. For this purpose, different topographical campaigns promoted by different agencies were considered. From this information, six time intervals have been examined: 1943–1973, 1973–1983, 1983–1987, 1987–1992, 1992–1999 and 1999–2005. Even though the first periods the data points were very weak, with the evolution of the geometric levelling network, the number of data available increases considerably. Moreover, the spatial data configuration was not the same for each period, making complicated the study of time evolution of the phenomenon in the whole are. Therefore, for each interval, the settlements have been estimated by ordinary kriging. The results allowed to evaluate the cumulated settlements within the study area for entire period of 1943-2005 by mean of ordinary kriging (Fig. 2).

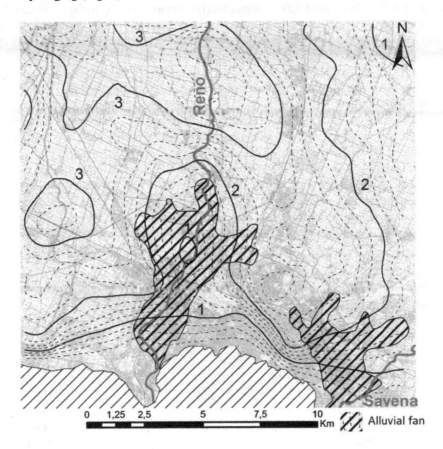

Fig. 2. Cumulated settlements (in metres) in time span 1943–2005 [20].

The cumulative settlements vary from a minimum of 0.7 m to a maximum of 4 m, with a maximum velocity in the 1970–1980 period comprised between 2.5 and 20 cm/year. The highest values fortunately occur in the area surrounding the center, being regulated by lowering the aquifer and the thickness of the compressible deposits.

Since 1999, the Arpae, the Regional Agency for Prevention, Environment and Energy of Emilia-Romagna, developed a study commissioned by Emilia Romagna Region, in collaboration with the DICAM (University of Bologna). The study aimed to update the geodetic knowledge of the subsidence through geometric levelling of high accuracy and interferometric analysis of satellite radar data. In particular, several maps were developed showing isokinetic curves of the entire territory of the Emilia Romagna region [4]. The first of those maps, is the result of the processing of data from satellites (ERS1 and ERS2) of the European Space Agency (ESA) on the period 1992–2000, and is based on the velocity of movement related to around 160000 points. The second map, as the product of the analysis of data obtained from satellites Envisat (ESA) and Radarsat (Canadian Space Agency), for the period 2002–2006, and is based on the velocity of movement relative to about 140000 points. The third map, referring to the period 2006–2011, has been realized on the basis of analysis carried out by interferometric radar performed by T.R.E. s.r.l. (Tele-Rilevamento Europa s.r.l.) through the technique of Permanent Scatterers (PSInSARTM) developed and patented by Polytechnic University of Milan (POLIMI). Compared to the previous maps, it was possible to count on, thanks to the new algorithm used for the interferometric analysis of a number of considerably more measuring points: 315371 against 142000 the previous points.

The technological evolution of the monitoring system of the subsidence phenomenon of the Emilia Romagna region allows to update the previous study [20]. In particular, it is possible to complete the study of the distribution of the settlements in the area of Bologna, updating it to 2011. For this purpose, from the maps of the isokinetic curves provided by Arpae [4], the settlements for the reference period were computed and the cumulate settlements for the period 1943–2011 were calculated. The Fig. 3 shows the map of cumulated settlements obtain by mean of ordinary kriging.

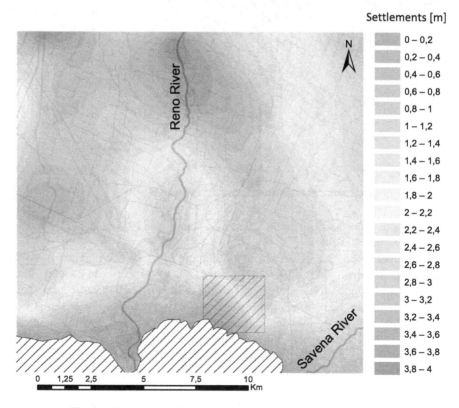

Fig. 3. Cumulated settlements (in metres) in time span 1943–2011

Comparing the Fig. 3 with previous analyses (Fig. 2), the maps of cumulated settlements do not exhibit significant variation in spatial distribution or in maximum value. In fact, the phenomenon of subsidence, in the last period 2005–2011, presents a general reduction, with an average rate of about 2 cm/year [4].

3   Old City Centre of Bologna

At the end of the 70's, as a consequence of observation of damages over several buildings in the city center, the local government institutions and agencies have undertaken a number of surveys to assess the causes of this unexpected phenomenon. The focus was on Zamboni street buildings, the main artery located in the north-eastern part of the center.

Several studies permitted to collect information regarding damage on buildings and, in particular, the area most affected by these phenomena is the Zamboni street [1, 11] an artery which runs radially in the direction of NE, from the center to the outskirts of town. In Fig. 4, the buildings with significant damage are indicated: the "*torre degli asinelli*" (Ravegnana square), the church of San Giacomo, some buildings near the Conservatory and several buildings of the University, up to the San Donato square.

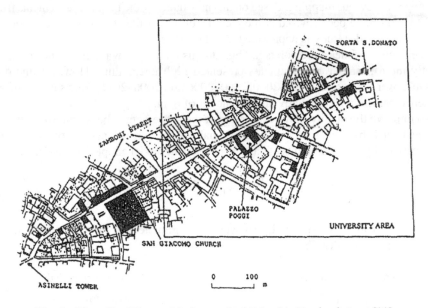

Fig. 4. Map of buildings with damage highlighted in Zamboni street [11].

Many studies have been promoted in order to detect deformations of the soil in the area, by means of geometric levelling networks ever more precise (Fig. 5). Studies conducted by Pieri and Russo [21–23], Alessi [1], Arca and Beretta [2], Folloni et al. [16], Crapa and Folloni [11] and e Bondesan et al. [7] are some examples.

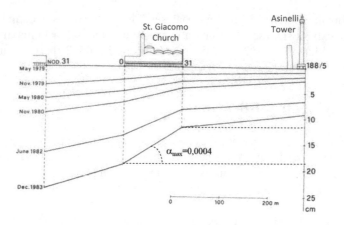

Fig. 5. Profile of the settlement in Zamboni street during the period 1943 [1].

The use of satellite method has allowed us to acquire information much more wide-spread than a topographic survey (levelling lines): a number of points as much as two orders of magnitude higher than the number of levelling benchmark on which could counting the previous mapping. Based on this new data set, the maps of settlements from 1943 to 2011 have been revised at the local level, i.e. at the center of the city. In this case, the area under study is approximately 7 km^2 (Fig. 6).

The number of measured points falling into this local zone was very reduced, consequently the estimation of settlements presented high uncertainty. However, the data available over the periods 1992–2000, 2000–2006 and 2006–2011, from satellite measurements, present a significantly higher amount of data.

To improve the quality of the estimation of the settlements, the spatial structure has been analyzed, by means of variografical analysis, in correspondence of the periods characterized by larger amounts of data. The theorical model adopted in this analysis is:

$$\gamma(h) = c\left[1 - \exp\left(-\frac{h}{R}\right)^p\right] \tag{2}$$

Where R (range), c (sill) and p (power) are parameters to be calibrated with the experimental values (Table 1).

Table 1. Parameter of variogram model of settlements for recent periods

Parameter model	1992–2000	2000–2006	2006–2011
Power	1.63	1.53	1.55
Range [m]	2435	2670	2852
Partial sill [m^2]	0.0074	0.0044	0.0011

This spatial structure has been used in order to estimate, using ordinary kriging, the settlements from 1943 to 2011. Figure 6 shows the map of cumulated estimates settlements from 1943 to 2011 at the historical center of the city. The cumulated settlements present high variability from a minimum of 0.5 m to a maximum of 2.5 m along a distance of about 2 km.

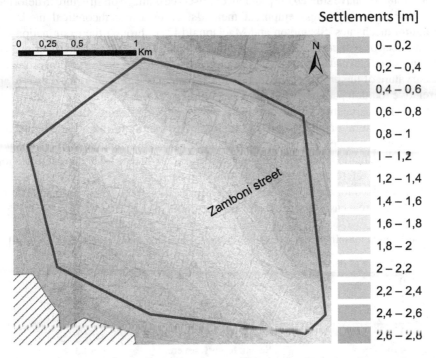

Fig. 6. Observed settlements in the time span 1943–2011 (in meters) within the historic center

4   Prevision of the Damage on Buildings

The damage on buildings, from the formation of small cracks up the structure collapses, can be related to the development of angular distortions [27] or tensile strains [8]. The

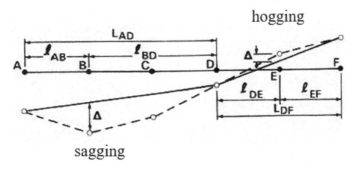

Fig. 7. Definition of relative deflection Δ and deflection ratio Δ/L – sagging e hogging [8].

limit values depend on the type of structure and the deformation mode (sagging or hogging) (Fig. 7).

Many authors have studied the problem of observed damage on structure in deformed configuration, both through empirical methods, or by using theoretical models of continuum mechanics. Skempton and MacDonald [27], through the examination of a large number of real cases, provide some design guidelines on maximum permissible deflections that can cause damage to the architectural elements and structural problems. The curvature of the profile of the foundation settlements is related to the damage, and the relative rotation parameter β is used as an indicator of damage on the building.

Another classification of the damage consist in distinguishing the aesthetic, functional and structural damage [9]. These main classes can be further divided into categories, creating a scale of severity of the damage. This classification of the damage is based on the evaluation of the limiting tensile strain ε_{lim}, which is related to each category of damage with reference to a particular building material.

The ε_{lim} values for each category, reported in Table 2, have been obtained from the examination of real cases and model of masonry buildings [6, 10].

Table 2. Relationship between category of damage and limiting tensile strain ε_{lim} [6, 10].

Category of damage	Normal degree of severity	ε_{lim} [%]
0	Negligible	0–0.05
1	Very slight	0.05–0.075
2	Slight	0.075–0.15
3	Moderate	0.15–0.3
4 to 5	Severe to very severe	>0.3

Based on the Timoshenko beam theory [29], a semi-empirical method has been developed that correlates the foundation settlements with the occurrence of visible cracking in the building [8].

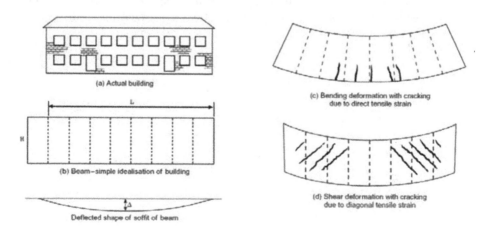

(a) Actual building

(b) Beam–simple idealisation of building

Deflected shape of soffit of beam

(c) Bending deformation with cracking due to direct tensile strain

(d) Shear deformation with cracking due to diagonal tensile strain

Fig. 8. Cracking of a simple beam in bending and shear [8].

The building is idealized as an isotropic, linear elastic beam of length L and height H (Fig. 8). By imposing an inflection (hogging), it is possible to develop different configuration of deformation: bending, deformation diagonal and the combination of the two. In bending deformation, the maximum tensile value is ε_{bmax}. And in shear deformation the maximum tensile value is ε_{dmax}.

Considering a concentrated load in the middle of the beam, the expression of relative deflection (2), in the case of deformation due to both bending and shear configuration, is given by the Timoshenko beam theory [29]:

$$\Delta = \frac{PL^3}{48EI}\left[1 + \frac{18EI}{L^2HG}\right] \tag{3}$$

Where E is the Young's modulus, G is the shear modulus, I is the second moment of area and P is the punctual load.

Considering the neutral axis of the beam on the lower edge, a Poisson's ratio equal to 0.3 and a ratio E/G equal to 2.6, the Eq. (2) can be reformulated in terms of inflection ratio Δ/L:

$$\frac{\Delta}{L} = \left[0.083\frac{L}{H} + 1.3\frac{H}{L}\right]\varepsilon_{bmax} \quad \text{(bending strain)} \tag{4}$$

$$\frac{\Delta}{L} = \left[0.064\frac{L^2}{H^2} + 1\right]\varepsilon_{dmax} \quad \text{(diagonal strain)} \tag{5}$$

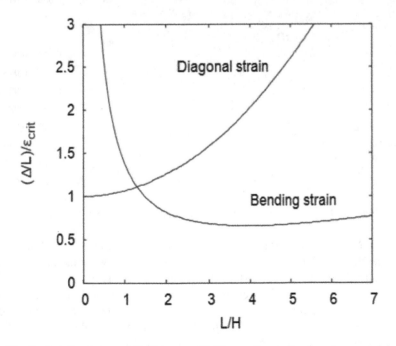

Fig. 9. Relation between $(\Delta/L)/\varepsilon_{lim}$ and L/H according to the deep beam model.

The diagram of the inflection ratio in function of the ratio L/H, is presented in Fig. 9. For a ratio L/H > 1.5, the failure mechanism is governed by bending strain, however, if L/H < 1.5 is governed by diagonal strain.

5   Analysis of the Damage of the Historical Center of the City

From the estimate value of cumulated settlements throughout the observation period (1943–2011), the relative inflection values Δ has been calculated in correspondence of a regular grid points spaced by 50 m. The calculation has been performed for each point, considering the relative inflection value along the different principal directions and taking into account the maximum value.

The map of the estimated of the relative inflection Δ (Fig. 10) shows that the area of greatest interest for this phenomenon is close to San Donato square.

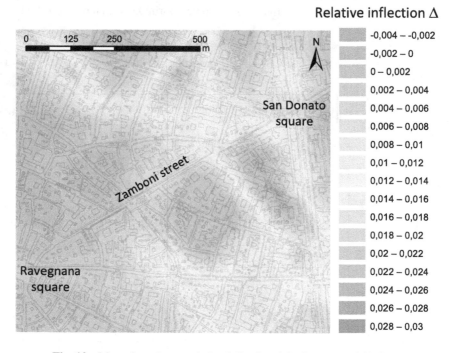

Fig. 10. Map of maximum relative inflection Δ in time span 1943–2011

From the National Geoportal [17] it was possible to get the main building charac-teristics (height, size, location, etc.) for the whole city, following methodologically a procedure already attempted with ISTAT data by [25, 26]. In particular, in the database, "Buildings of the provincial main cities", the geometric information (area, perimeter and height) for each building are available. In case of irregular shapes, the plan of the building has been assimilated to a rectangular ones. Therefore, if the height is known it is possible to obtain the characteristic length of the buildings.

In order to perform specific analysis, all the information have been managed inside a Geographical Information System (GIS). In particular, the input information concerns two main parts: the phenomenon of subsidence and urban heritage (historical, industrial,...). In both cases the data are available to the public through web portal [3, 17].

Implementing within the GIS the equations for the classification of damage on buildings proposed by the literature, it is possible to assess the effects of settlements on the structures of the historical center of the city of Bologna.

The maximum value of relative inflection obtained from the estimated map (Fig. 10) has been assigned to the centroid of the building. Then the values of ε_{bmax} and ε_{dmax} have been calculated using the Eqs. (4) and (5), and assessed the ε_{lim} value in function of the ratio L/H.

According to the limit values shown in Table 2, the colour classes have been defined in order to distinguish the different levels of damage. Based on the assessments carried out in this work, the buildings with different criticality level have been identified. The Fig. 11 focus on the area of San Donato square.

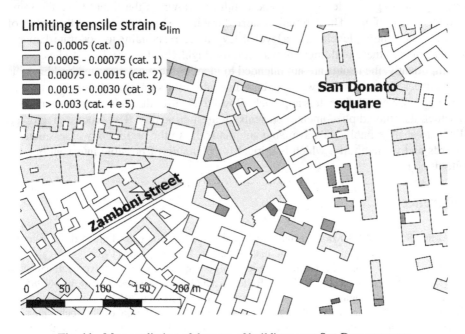

Fig. 11. Map prediction of damage of buildings near San Donato square

6   Conclusions

Based on new data available (Arpae Emila Romagna [3]), it was possible to complete the previous study about ground settlements in the city of Bologna, for the 1943–2011 period. The subsidence phenomenon has a minor effect, in the most recent period (2005–2011), and the new data confirm the trend previously observed.

However, the variation of settlements are significant in correspondence of the historic city center, the area most affected by the presence of historical buildings. The quality and quantity of information available for the last period have enabled local study of the phenomenon. This aspect was essential to move from a smaller scale analysis. The lack of data at small distances limits the quality of the geostatistical interpolation. In particular, in correspondence with the center of the city, the geostatistical analysis made it possible to estimate the settlements based on a considerably greater number of data.

Subsequently, the effects of these settlements on the buildings of the historic center of the city have been evaluated. From the information in the database of the "Buildings of the provincial main cities" of the National Geoportal [17] and with the help of analytical reports, the strain levels from the current configuration of the ground level has been calculated for each building. Finally, the expected damage levels has been assessed the expected damage levels, based on classifications proposed in the literature.

It should be noted that the limit values defined in Table 2 have been obtained for masonry buildings, while not all of the buildings shown in the figure have the same architectural typology. The estimation carried out have shown an area, in the center of old city, where the ε_{lim} levels reach a level of severity corresponding to moderate damage. In fact, some of these buildings are part of those highlighted in previous studies.

Importantly, the results are not intended to identify the most damaged buildings, as the feedback obtained in this work are based on various assumptions (geometry, type of building,…). Nevertheless, this approach allows to identify the areas in correspondence of which the studied phenomenon presents greatest criticality. The processed adopted allows to analyse public data available automatically to the preliminary assessment of hazards and vulnerability, which is critical for planning of possible interventions for mitigating risk.

References

1. Alessi, R.: La subsidenza nel centro storico della città di Bologna. Il grado di dissesto dei fabbricati nella zona di via Zamboni. Inarcos, n. 456. Bologna, Italy (1985)
2. Arca, S., Beretta, G.P.: Prima sintesi geodetico-geologica sui movimenti verticali del suolo nell'Italia Settentrionale (1897–1957). Bollettino di Geodesia e scienze affini, n. 2 (1985)
3. Arpae Emilia Romagna. https://www.arpae.it/. Accessed 31 Mar 2017
4. Bitelli, G., Bonsignore, F., Pellegrino, I., Vittuari, L.: Evolution of the techniques for subsidence monitoring at regional scale: the case of Emilia-Romagna region (Italy). Proc. IAHS **372**, 315–321 (2015)
5. Bonsignore, F., Chahoud, A., Cristofori, D., Farina, M., Martinelli, G., Villani, B.: Subsidence and groundwater in Emilia-Romagna region: a comparison between subsidence rate and piezometric levels. In: Proceedings of 4th European Congress on Regional Geoscientific Cartography and Information Systems, Bologna, pp. 604–605, 17–20 June 2003
6. Boscardin, M.D., Cording, E.G.: Building response to excavation-induced settlement. Jnl Geo Engrg, ASCE **115**(1), 1–21 (1989)
7. Bondesan, M., Gatti, M., Russo, P.: Movimenti verticali del suolo nella Pianura Padana orientale desumibili dai dati I.G.M. fino a tutto il 1990. Bollettino di Geodesia e scienze affini, n. 2 (1997)

8. Burland, J.B., Wroth, C.P.: Settlement of buildings and associated damage. In: Proceedigns of Conference on Settlement of Structures, Cambridge, UK, pp. 611–654 (1974)
9. Burland, J.B., Broms, B.B., de Mello, V.F.B.: Behaviour of foundations and structures – SOA report, session 2. In: Proceedings of 9th International Conference SMFE, Tokyo, vol. 2, pp. 495–546 (1977)
10. Burland, J. B.: Assessment of risk of damage to buildings due to tunnelling and excavation, Invited special lecture. In: Proceedings 1st International Conference on Earthquake Geotechnology and Engineering - IS-Tokyo, vol. 95 (1995)
11. Capra, A., Folloni, G.: Subsidence controls in the Town of Bologna. In: Proceedings of the Fourth International Symposium on Land Subsidence, IAHS Publication no. 200 (1991)
12. Carminati, E., Martinelli, G.: Subsidence rates in the Po Plain, northern Italy: the relative impact of natural and anthropogenic causation. Eng. Geol. **66**, 241–255 (2002)
13. Chen, M., Tomás, R., Li, Z., Motagh, M., Tao Li, T., Hu, L., Gong, H., Li, X., Yu, J. e Gong, X.: Imaging land subsidence induced by groundwater extraction in Beijing (China) using satellite radar interferometry. Remote Sens., **8**(6), 468 (2016)
14. Chilès, J.P., Delfiner, P.: Geostatistics: Modeling Spatial Uncertainty. Wiley, New York (1999)
15. Croce, A.: Subsidence et mécanique des sols dans la vallée du Po. Annales de l'Institut Technique du Batiment et des Travaux Publics, no 328, Paris (1975)
16. Folloni, G., Radiconi, F., Russo, P.: La subsidenza del territorio bolognese dal 1983 al 1983. Inarcos, n. 571. Bologna, Italy (1996)
17. Geoportale Nationale. http://www.pcn.minambiente.it/mattm/. Accessed 31 Mar 2017
18. Lockwood, M.G.: Ground subsides in Houston areas. Civ. Eng. **24**(6), 48–50 (1954)
19. Marsal, R.J., Mazari, M.: El subsuelo de la Ciudad de Mexico, The subsoil of Mexico city. Universidad Autonoma de Mexico, Facultad de Ingenieria, 2nd ed. 614 p. (1962)
20. Modoni, G., Darini, G., Spacagna, R.L., Saroli, M., Russo, G., Croce, P.: Spatial analysis of land subsidence induced by groundwater withdrawal. Eng. Geol. **167**, 59–71 (2013)
21. Pieri, L., e Russo, P.: Studio del fenomeno di abbassamento del suolo in atto nella zona di Bologna. Bollettino di Geodesia e scienze affini, n. 3 (1977)
22. Pieri, L., Russo, P.: The survey of soil vertical movements in the region of Bologna. In: Proceedings of the Third International Symposium on Land Subsidence, Venezia, Italy (1984)
23. Pieri, L., Russo P.: Situazione attuale delle ricerche sull'abbassamento del suolo nel territorio bolognese. Inarcos, p. 456 (1985
24. Poland, J.F.: Land subsidence due to groundwater development. ASCE J. Irrig. Drainage Div. **84**, 11 (1958). Paper 1774
25. Rasulo, A., Testa, C., Borzi, B.: Seismic Risk analysis at urban scale in Italy. In: Gervasi, O., Murgante, B., Misra, S., Gavrilova, Marina L., Rocha, A.M.A.C., Torre, C., Taniar, D., Apduhan, Bernady O. (eds.) ICCSA 2015. LNCS, vol. 9157, pp. 403–414. Springer, Cham (2015). doi:10.1007/978-3-319-21470-2_29
26. Rasulo, A., Fortuna, M.A., Borzi, B.: A seismic risk model for Italy. In: Gervasi, O., Murgante, B., Misra, S., Rocha, A.M.A.C., Torre, C., Taniar, D., Apduhan, Bernady O., Stankova, E., Wang, S. (eds.) ICCSA 2016. LNCS, vol. 9788, pp. 198–213. Springer, Cham (2016). doi: 10.1007/978-3-319-42111-7_16
27. Skempton, A.W., Mac Donald, D.H.: The allowable settlements of buildings. In: ICE Proceedings: Engineering Divisions, vol. 5, issue 6, pp. 727–768 (1956)
28. Stramondo, S., Saroli, M., Tolomei, C., Moro, M., Doumaz, F., Pesci, A., Loddo, F., Baldi, P., Boschi, E.: Surface movements in Bologna (Po Plain- Italy) detected by multitemporal DInSAR. Remote Sens. Environ. **110**, 304–316 (2007)
29. Timoshenko, S.: Strength of Materials – Part 1. D van Nostrand Co. In., London (1957)

30. Tessitore, S., Fernández-Merodo, J.A., Herrera, G., Tomás, R., Ramondini, M., Sanabria, M., Duro, J., Mulas, J., Calcaterra, D.: Comparison of water-level, extensometric, DInSAR and simulation data for quantification of subsidence in Murcia City (SE Spain). Hydrogeol. J. **24**(3), 1–21 (2016)
31. Wilson, G., Grace, H.: The settlement of London due to underdrainage of the London clay. J. Inst. Civil Eng. London **19**, 100–127 (1942)
32. Yamamoto, S.: Recent trend of land subsidence in Japan. In: Barends, F.B.J., Brouwer, F.J.J., Schroder, F.H. (eds.) Land Subsidence, Publication n. 234, pp. 487–492. IAHS (1995)
33. Zeevaert, L.: Foundation Engineering for Difficult Subsoil Conditions. Van Nostrand Reinhold Company Inc., New York (1983)

Decomposing and Recomposing Urban Fabric: The City from the Pedestrian Point of View

Alessandro Araldi$^{(\boxtimes)}$ and Giovanni Fusco$^{(\boxtimes)}$

Université Côte-Azur, CNRS, ESPACE, Nice, France
{alessandro.araldi,giovanni.fusco}@unice.fr

Abstract Urban fabric is a fundamental small-scale component of urban form with important relations to social, economic or environmental phenomena. It is the result of interplay between buildings, parcels and street segments. Quantitative analysis of urban fabric on a large scale has often privileged selected morphological aspects, linked to micro-climatic or energy consumption issues. The planning approach has privileged aerial rather than pedestrian point of view. This paper proposes a methodology for the recognition and characterization of urban fabric taking a different stance. After the definition of a new network-based partition of urban space based on the pedestrian point of view, we describe an innovative computational method: firstly, urban fabric is broken down in its components, and shape-perception indicators are computed through geoprocessing techniques. Secondly, spatial patterns on the street network are identified with geostatistical analysis. Finally, Bayesian clustering is carried out for the re-composition, identification of urban fabric types and qualification of sub-spaces within the city.

Keywords: Urban form · Urban fabric · Network constrained local indicators of spatial association · Bayesian clustering

1 Introduction

Characterizing urban form is an essential task for the study, modeling and simulation of urban systems; it contributes to the understanding of how phenomena take place in space and are possibly influenced by urban form. The form of the urban built-up environment is related to the development of human activities as well as their spatial distribution: *"we shape our buildings, thereafter they shape us,"* Winston Churchill's famous quotation has been developed by different theories and empirical studies, showing how the layout of physical components of the city can influence distribution, concentration and value taken by several socio-economical phenomena [1]. Relations between physical and socioeconomic components of urban spaces are still a major research issue in the absence of comprehensive measures of physical appearance [2] together with a misconceived and incomplete approach to the analysis.

When analyzing urban form within a quantitative approach, built-up density coverage is the traditional parameter used to describe cities and used to distinguish central areas from peripheries and rural spaces; this indicator is not adapted to describe the complexity of the contemporary metropolitan cities. Berghauser Pont et al. [3]

© Springer International Publishing AG 2017
O. Gervasi et al. (Eds.): ICCSA 2017, Part IV, LNCS 10407, pp. 365–376, 2017.
DOI: 10.1007/978-3-319-62401-3_27

suggested an alternative approach declining the concept of density in four variables expressing intensity, compactness, open space ratio and building height. This approach however still falls short of a comprehensive view of urban form at a micro-scale, beyond the issue of built-up elements. Surface distribution of built up elements is also the sole concern of fractal analysis of urban form [4]. When the focus of the analysis of urban form is on the street network, modelled either with a primal [5] or dual approach [1], configurational analyses identify multi scalar properties of the network under the free movement assumption, but do not consider other elements composing urban form.

The concept of urban fabric, proposed by the traditional school of urban morphology [6, 7] offers a more comprehensive view of urban form at the micro-scale. Urban fabric is the overall pattern emerging from the interplay between buildings, parcels, streets and site. In their qualitative study of the historical processes beyond the observable urban fabrics of traditional European cities, urban morphologists always privilege a well-defined spatial unit: the urban block enclosed by street segments. These works are nevertheless limited to relatively small scales (neighbourhoods, old cities). Urban blocks have also been used as base spatial units by more recent geoprocessing analyses [8–10]. The pertinence of city blocks as basic units in the analysis of urban fabrics is nevertheless challenged by more recent suburban developments [11] and seems to correspond more to the planner's aerial view of the city than to the perception of pedestrian moving in urban space [12].

This paper proposes a new geo-processing based methodology, Multiple Fabric Assessment, to identify and characterize urban fabrics in a whole metropolitan area, integrating their different components and privileging the pedestrian point of view.

The paper is structured as follows. Section 2 specifies the objectives of the analysis. Section 3 presents the methodology: definition of a new spatial unit, identification of a set of urban form descriptors, geo-statistical protocol to calculate spatial patterns of urban features and classification method identifying the different urban fabrics. Preliminary results are discussed in Sect. 4, mentioning perspectives of future work.

2   Objectives

The introduction highlighted the need of new methodological protocols to identify and characterize urban fabrics in their complexity. Different objectives can of course lead to different methodological choices. The precise objectives that we define for our analysis of urban form are to move: (i) from manual calculations to a systematic geoprocessing method; (ii) from the planner's aerial point of view to the pedestrian point of view; (iii) from an expert-based recognition of urban fabric types to a bottom-up inferential procedure; (iv) from small scale-analysis of neighborhoods to the analysis of a whole metropolitan area. Some of these goals are related: only an automated and bottom-up geoprocessing protocol allows analyzing a vast metropolitan area.

In order to evaluate the new methodological protocol, we tested it on a real-world case study: the French Riviera metropolitan area, in Southern France (Fig. 1). Once the independent Principality of Monaco is included, this area has a population of more than one million inhabitants over 1500 km^2. This space is a unique conjunction of natural and urban landscapes: firstly, the topography, with elevation ranging from the sea level up to 1700 m of the pre-Alps (passing through hills and valleys differently sloped). Secondly the socio-political and historical influences on the urban planning. Traditional villages and suburban developments are spread around three high density urban areas. From east to west, we find: Monaco and its skyscrapers, the most densely populated sovereign nation in the world; the urban agglomeration of Nice with a regular meshed core inspired by the Turin model [13], surrounded by hilly and less tightly planned areas. And finally the urban agglomeration of Cannes-Grasse-Antibes characterized by land irregularity together with the car-centered sprawl development of the lasts 50 years [14]. The combination of all these elements produces a sequence of urban centers and peripheral areas of different size and different morphology. This study area will give us the opportunity to test our method and to identify in a bottom-up approach different urban fabrics. Within a wider research agenda, urban fabric recognition and characterization on the French Riviera is a preliminary phase of future modelling of the relationship between perceived urban forms and urban functioning.

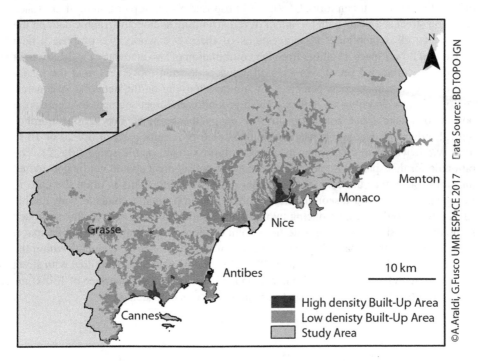

Fig. 1. Definition of the base spatial units of the analysis.

3   Methodology

Multiple Fabric Assessment is a three-step protocol for the analysis of urban fabrics. After defining appropriate goal-specific spatial units, it can be summed up as follows:

1. geoprocessing protocols to calculate a matrix of morphological indicators for urban fabrics;

2. identification of spatial associations of indicator values (local patterns) on a network constrained space;
3. clustering of local patterns through Bayesian methods in order to identify and characterize urban fabrics.

3.1   A New Spatial Unit Partition of Urban Space: The Pedestrian Point of View

As introduced earlier, when analysing urban fabrics through geo-processing, we first need to define the base spatial unit. Several approaches have been proposed in the literature: grid [15], parcel system, urban blocks [8–10], administrative boundaries [14], etc. Hamaina et al. [16] proposes for the first time a particular urban space partition based on a generalized Thiessen polygon starting from the built-up footprint. Studying different issues than urban form, Okabe [17] proposed a similar partition of urban space based on street segments with the intent of redistributing sociodemographic data on the street network. Combining the suggestions of these two works, we propose a new division of urban space, resulting from the combination of two elements: the urban street network, a connected set of segments allowing pedestrian movement, and the planar extension of urban space as perceived by humans moving on the network. A generalization of Thyssen polygons is thus created around each street segment to identify the portion of planar space conventionally served by the segment. For several morphological indicators, we only consider a double-sided proximity band of 50, 20 or 10 m total width within this polygon, in order to approximate visible space (Fig. 2). The rationale for this spatial unit definition is that a street segment should not be considered the limit, but rather the core of a fragment of urban fabric. This is often the case in European cities where discontinuities in urban fabric normally coincide with double carriageway boulevards, producing two different spatial units. Moreover, this approach is the most consistent with the pedestrian point of view: when standing in public space, people perceive the urban fabric on both sides of the street, not the elements within the four sides of a block. In our study area, 99.562 elements were thus identified with street segment length between 4 and 300 m and an average conventional surface of 13000 m^2 (but only 1670 m^2 when 20 m band of visible space is considered).

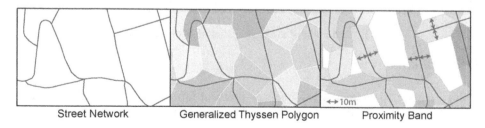

Fig. 2. Definition of the base spatial units of the analysis.

3.2   Decomposing Urban Fabric Components

The street network morphology and the built up forms are the main components of urban fabric considered in this research. Twenty-one indicators, obtained through geoprocessing in GIS, were calculated for each spatial unit: selection criteria of indicators are the relevance and complementarity of the information carried by each of them when describing urban fabrics following the theory of urban morphology analysis [18] reinterpreted through the pedestrian point of view.

Network morphology is analyzed through the street segment *Length,* its *Linearity* (or inversely, its *Windingness*), together with three indicators representing the *Local Connectivity* of the street network. **Built-up morphology** is characterized by the traditional building *Coverage Ratio* index implemented on our spatial unit; surface density information is then enriched by information about *Built-up Type prevalence* of size based categorization of buildings: 0–125 m^2 (independent small houses), 125–250 m^2 (big villas and small traditional multi-family buildings which are particularly frequent in our study area), 250–1000 m^2 (row-houses and medium-sized blocks of flats), 1000–4000 m^2 (modern large blocks of flats, commercial, industrial or service buildings), larger than 4000 m^2 (mainly functionally specialized big buildings). By considering the presence/absence of ordinary dwellings, we calculate the *Specialization of Building Types. Building Contiguity* informs whether the urban fabric is characterized by adjoining buildings, linked to the compactness of the urban environment at a very fine grain. **Site Morphology** measures the presence of high sloped surfaces in the proximity band.

As introduced earlier, our indicators aim at describing the main physical aspects influencing pedestrian movement and perception; they are obtained by measuring a single component of urban fabric as well as their combinations [19]:

Network-Building Relationship indicators describe the building geometry analyzed and perceived in relation to the street segment. For this reason, they are computed only on the narrower proximity bands of 10 or 20 m around the street segment, hence respecting the pedestrian perspective assumption. The *Street Corridor Effect,* measuring the façades alignment to the street segment, the *Proximity Band Building Height,* the *Open Space Width* and the *Height/Width Ratio.* The *Building frequency along the street network* informs us on the serial vision of different buildings along street segment. Following the same approach, *Land ownership fragmentation along the street network* is used as an indicator of **Network-Parcels Relationship**. Finally, the relation between street **Network and Site Morphology** is analyzed through *Street Acclivity.* Parcel morphology in itself, although being central in the study of the morphogenetic processes [6, 7] is considered less relevant for pedestrian movement and perception. The operational definition of each indicator is given in Table 1.

3.3   Spatial Patterns on Networks: ILINCS

The punctual/hyper-local value of an indicator for each spatial unit is not adapted to describe the wider spatial patterns of urban fabrics. Urban fabrics are characterized by the arrangement in space of urban components with consistent morphological values;

Table 1. The 21 indicators matrix for urban fabric morphology.

Urban fabric component	Indicator	Definition
Network Morphology	Street length	Network length of the street segments between two intersections [m]
	Linearity/Windingness	Ratio between Euclidean distance and segment length
	Local connectivity	Average presence nodes of degree 1
		Average presence nodes of degree 4
		Average presence nodes of degree 3, 5 or more
Built-up Morphology	Prevalence of Building types	Ratio between 0–125 m^2 building surf. and total built-up surf. in 50 m PB
		Ratio between 125–250 m^2 building surf. and total built-up surf. in 50 m PB
		Ratio between 250–1000 m^2 building surf. and total built-up surf. in 50 m PB
		Ratio between 1000–4000 m^2 building surf. and total built-up surf. in 50 m PB
		Ratio between > 4000 m^2 building surf. and total built-up surf. in 50 m PB
	Proximity band coverage ratio	Building coverage ratio on the 50 m proximity band
	Building Contiguity	Weighted average of buildings frequency on built-up units
	Specialization of Building Types	Ratio between specialized building footprint and 50 m PB surf.
Network-Building Relationship	Street corridor effect	Ratio between parallel façades and street length in 10 m PB
	Proximity band building height	Ratio between building vol. and surf. inside 20 m proximity band
	Open Space Width	Ratio between open space within 20 m PB and street length
	Height/Width Ratio	Ration between average building height and average open space width within the 20 m PB
	Building frequency along the street network	Ratio between number of buildings in 20 m PB and street length
Network-Parcels Relationship	Land ownership fragmentation along the street network	Ratio between number of parcels in 20 m PB and street length
Site Morphology	Surface slope	Ratio between high sloped (S > 30°) and total space-unit in 50 m PB
Network-Site Relationship	Street acclivity	Computed as segment average of arctan (slope)

spatial continuity and aggregation is a key-factor for their significance, even more if we adopt the pedestrian point of view. Several authors have suggested clustering spatial units using the raw values of morphological indicators: Gionnopoulou et al. [10] use hierarchical clustering, Diday [20], Gil et al. [21] and Bernabé et al. [9] use k-means. By so doing, spatial relations among adjoining spatial units are overlooked and the clustering of spatial units does not necessarily lead to the identification of urban fabrics. Through Geo-SOM, Hamaina et al. [16] introduce spatial constrains in clustering, but their use of Euclidean distance between buildings is not coherent with our pedestrian street-network viewpoint. We thus propose a preliminary phase of detection of spatial patterns for each morphological indicator. Local Indicators of Spatial Association (LISA, [22]) are a well-established approach to detect statistically significant spatial patterns; we apply its network-constrained version (ILINCS, [23]) considering contiguity on the street network. [24] showed the difference between LISA and ILINCS in the particular case of the analysis of urban morphology and how ILINCS are best fitted when analyzing patterns from the pedestrian point of view. In another work [25] the same authors also highlight the need to analyze the statistical distribution of the indicator values, in order to select between Getis-Ord's G or Moran's I local statistics, and to apply an empirical Bayesian correction, if needed, in order to take into account heteroscedasticity of morphological rates [26].

Through these network-constrained geostatistical analyses we pass from a collection of morphological values for each spatial unit to statistically significant spatial patterns which correspond to hot- and cold-spots of given morphological characteristics, using the usual categories of LISA analysis (High-High, Low-Low, Low-High, High-Low and Not-Significant), as illustrated in Fig. 3. These geostatistical classifications are the result of the analysis of the values of each spatial unit (street segment proximity band) considered in association with its neighbors on the street network, using a neighborhood topological depth value of 3 units.

3.4 Recomposing and Characterizing Urban Fabrics: Bayesian Classification

In order to identify urban fabrics, we still have to combine the results of the 21 geostatistical analyses. Urban fabrics from the pedestrian point of view are precisely the perception of persistent combinations and co-occurrences of different morphological characteristics. At the same time, a few key characteristics could identify a given urban fabric even in the presence of a certain variability on other morphological aspects. A particular compact and dense traditional urban fabric could for example be characterized by consistently high building coverage ratio, high street corridor effect, building contiguity and height/width ratio, but some heterogeneity of building types and network connectivity (low share of degree 1 nodes but high share of either degree 4 or degree 3 nodes). Clustering approaches aiming at achieving high intra-cluster homogeneity based on variance minimization on the values of all the indicators (like k-means in [9, 20, 21], SOM in [27], and geo-SOM in [16]) are not well fitted for this task.

Fusco [14] proposes Bayesian clustering precisely to identify groups of individuals sharing a few key characteristics, which could vary from one group to the other.

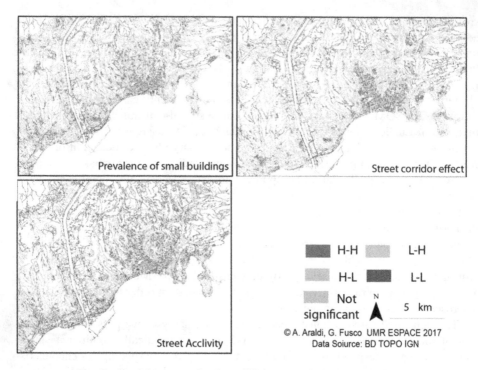

Fig. 3. Spatial patterns for three different morphological indicators.

Unlike his application, we will not require a multi-step procedure to identify latent factors. The careful theory-driven feature selection of our analysis justifies the use of a naïf Bayesian classifier on the 21 morphological indicators. Another crucial difference from the aforementioned work is the use of the results of the geostatistical analyses of the indicators, instead of the raw indicator values. We will thus perform Bayesian clustering of categorical values (HH, LL, HL, LH, NS) which, in their turn, summarize the statistical significance of spatial patterns defined on a street network.

4 Results and Discussion

Using 8 different random seeds, 1000-step random walks explored the solution space to obtain optimal Bayesian clustering of our spatial units. The search constraints were a minimum cluster content of 1% of the spatial units, a minimum average probability of assignment of units to each cluster of 0.9 and a maximum of 20 clusters. The optimal score (combining log-likelihood of the clustering solution given the data and a penalization for the increasing number of clusters) was always found for the 9 cluster solution. A successive refining phase of the 9 cluster solution was carried out by imposing this fixed number of clusters to the 8 random walks. The obtained results were almost identical, the best one showing a contingency table fit score of 59.4%.

The projection of the 21 variables (i.e. the results of the 21 geostatistical analyses) in mutual information space (Fig. 4a) shows little redundancy among morphological indicators (variables are well separated), justifying *ex post* our feature selection. Even more clearly, the projection of the clustering solution (Fig. 4b) shows 9 well defined, and once again well separated, clusters. Their interpretation in terms of urban fabric characteristics (which are given by the Bayesian network in terms of probabilities) goes beyond the scope of this methodological paper. We will briefly say that clusters 3, 5 and 2 correspond to traditional urban fabrics, cluster 4 to modern discontinuous urban fabrics, clusters 7 and 8 to suburban fabrics, clusters 0 and 1 to non-urbanized areas with sparse buildings, and cluster 6 to very peculiar connective artificial fabrics, with sparse specialized buildings, bonding together modern and suburban fabrics to the traditional urban fabrics. Above all, when projected in geographic space (Fig. 5a) the clusters identify well defined spatial patterns of connected spatial units defining the spatial extent of a given urban fabric type. The image represents the area around the city of Antibes. The old city center is clearly distinguishable on the right, in brown color (cluster 3), surrounded by traditional urban fabric of the late XIX and early XX (cluster 5). More peripheral urban sectors belong to clusters 2 and 6, whereas vast suburban areas (cluster 7) border the city to the north and to the south, corresponding to the Antibes Cape. The traditional fabrics of smaller cities (here Vallauris) are islands within suburbia. Finally, connective artificial fabrics correspond to retail developments around extra-urban roads and to the technical space around the port of Antibes. Similar results are found for the cities of Nice, Cannes, Cagnes-sur-Mer, Monaco and Menton, and are consistent with expert knowledge on the study area (as in [13]). The contrast is striking with the 9 cluster solution obtained with the raw values of morphological indicators (Fig. 5b). Lacking any spatial constraint, the clustering procedure produces a mere typology of spatial units and fails to recognize that peculiar spatial arrangements of these typologies could be characterized as a unique urban fabric.

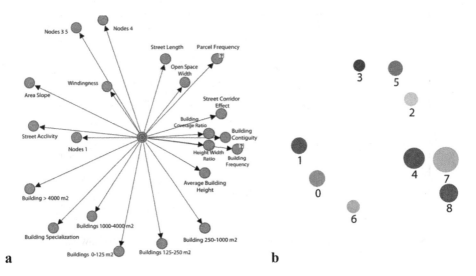

Fig. 4. Projections in mutual information space: variables (a) and clusters (b).

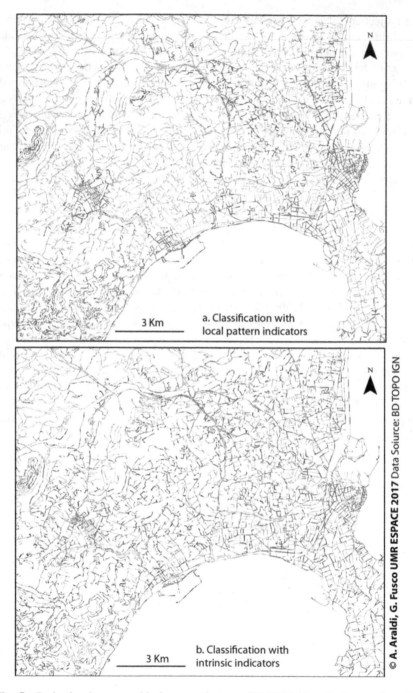

a. Classification with
local pattern indicators

3 Km

b. Classification with
intrinsic indicators

3 Km

© A. Araldi, G. Fusco UMR ESPACE 2017 Data Soiurce: BD TOPO IGN

Fig. 5. Projection in geographical space: clusters of ILINCS (a) and of raw values (b).

As we already mentioned in Sect. 2, different objectives lead to different methodological choices in the analysis of urban fabric. We assess the results obtained for the cities of the French Riviera as particularly satisfactory with respect to the objective of identifying different urban fabrics as potentially perceived by pedestrians moving on a street network, at the scale of a whole metropolitan area. Morphological indicators of street corridor effect, of open space width around the movement path, of presence of building types within a given proximity band, of street acclivity or of network connectivity are particularly informative from the pedestrian's point of view and can more easily be related to relevant human phenomena like retail activity, quality of life, crime or health in the city. Clearly enough, if the analysis of urban fabric focuses on micro-climatic or energy-consumption issues as in [15], aspects like city surface roughness, taking into account non-visible parts of the city block, could be more important and result in the identification of different families of urban fabrics.

5 Conclusions and Perspectives

We proposed a multi-step geoprocessing approach to identify urban fabrics in a vast metropolitan area. It integrates a matrix of morphological indicators taking into account the pedestrian point of view, network-constrained geo-statistics and Bayesian clustering. The method proved successful in identifying urban fabrics and their spatial arrangements in the real-world case of the French Riviera metropolitan area, even if the clustering results deserve a more attentive geographical analysis from an urban morphology perspective. The proposed methodology is clearly linked to the pedestrian point of view on urban fabrics and its result can differ considerably from analysis focused on micro-climatic or energy-consumption issues. At the same time, by privileging the pedestrian point of view, our approach should be privileged for other human-related phenomena. As already mentioned, this is the main research perspective of our work. Other interesting perspectives can also be highlighted. The first one is the study of the link between the identified urban fabrics and the historical processes behind the observed morphologies. From a more methodological point of view, the probabilistic content of the Bayesian clustering should be better exploited to identify uncertainties in the knowledge of urban form.

Acknowledgements. This research was carried out thanks to a research grant of the Nice-Côte d'Azur Chamber of Commerce and Industry (CIFRE agreement with UMR ESPACE).

References

1. Hillier, B.: Space is the Machine. Cambridge University Press, Cambridge (1998)
2. Naik, N., et al.: Do people shape cities, or do cities shape people? The co-evolution of physical, social and economic change in five major cities. NBER Working Paper No. 21620 (2015)
3. Berghauser Pont, M.Y., Haupt, P.: SPACEMATRIX, Space, Density and Urban Form. NAi Publishers, Rotterdam (2010)

4. Thomas, I., et al.: Fractal dimension versus density of built-up surfaces in the periphery of Brussels. Papers Reg. Sci. **86**, 287–308 (2007)
5. Porta, S., et al.: The network analysis of urban streets: a primal approach. Environ. Plann. B Plann. Des. **33**(5), 705–725 (2006)
6. Conzen, M.R.G.: Alnwick, Northumberland: A Study in Town-Plan Analysis, vol. 27. Institute of British Geographers Publication, George Philip, London (1960)
7. Caniggia, G., Maffei, G.: Lettura dell'edilizia di base. Firenze, Alinea (1979)
8. Puissant, A., et al.: Classification des tissus urbains à partir de données vectorielles – Application à Strasbourg. In: SAGEO 2010 Proceedings, Toulouse, pp. 198–211 (2010)
9. Bernabé, A., et al.: Classification automatique des tissus urbains par la méthode des nuées dynamiques. 31e Rencontres AUGC, Cachan, France (2013). http://augc2013.ens-cachan.fr/Data/Articles/Contribution1150.pdf
10. Giannopoulou, M., et al.: Using GIS to record and analyse historical urban areas. J. Land Use Mob. Environ. **4**, 43–47 (2014). Tema
11. Panerai, P., et al.: Forms urbains: de l'îlot à la barre, Ed. Parenthèses, Marseilles (1977)
12. Lynch, K.: The Image of the City. MIT Press, Cambridge (1960)
13. Graff, P.: Une ville d'exception. Nice dans l'effervescence du 20e siècle. Serre, Nice (2013)
14. Fusco, G.: Beyond the built-up form/ mobility relationship: spatial affordance and lifestyles. Comput. Environ. Urban Syst. **60**, 50–66 (2016)
15. Long, N., Kergomard, C.: Classification morphologique du tissu urbain pour des applications climatologiques. Le cas de Marseille. Revue Int. de Géomatique **15**(14), 487–512 (2005)
16. Hamaina, R., Leduc, T., Moreau, G.: A new method to characterize density adapted to a coarse city model. In: Popovich, V., Claramunt, C., Schrenk, M., Korolenko, K. (eds.) Information Fusion and Geographic Information Systems (IF AND GIS 2013). LNGC, pp. 249–263. Springer, Heidelberg (2014). doi:10.1007/978-3-642-31833-7_16
17. Okabe, A., Sugihara, K.: Spatial Analysis along Networks: Statistical and Computational Methods. John Wiley & Sons, Ltd., Chichester (2012)
18. Borie, A., Denieul, F.: Methode d'analyse morphologique des tissus urbains traditionnels, UNESCO (1984). http://unesdoc.unesco.org/images/0006/000623/062310fb.pdf
19. Lévy, A.: Urban morphology and the problem of the modern urban fabric: some questions for research. Urban Morphol. **3**(2), 79–85 (1999)
20. Diday, E.: Une nouvelle méthode en classification automatique et reconnaissance des formes la méthode des nuées dynamiques. Revue de Stat. Appliquée **19**(2), 19–33 (1971)
21. Gil, J., Beirão, J.N., Montenegro, N., Duarte, J.: On the discovery of urban typologies: data mining the many dimensions of urban form. Urban Morphol. **16**(1), 27–40 (2012)
22. Anselin, L.: Local indicators of spatial association. Geog. Anal. **27**(2), 93–115 (1995)
23. Yamada, I., Thill, J.C.: Local indicators of network-constrained clusters in spatial patterns represented by a link attribute. Ann. Ass. Am. Geog. **100**(2), 269–285 (2010)
24. Araldi, A., Fusco, G.: Urban form from the pedestrian point of view: spatial patterns on a street network. In: Proceedings of INPUT 2016, INPUT 2016, Turin, Italy, 14th–15th September 2016, pp. 32–37 (2016)
25. Fusco, G., Araldi, A.: Urban fabric with Bayesian LINCS: empirical evidences from the French Riviera. In: SAGEO 2016, Nice, France, 7th–8th December 2016
26. Assunção, R.M., Reis, E.A.: A new proposal to adjust Moran's I for population density. Stat. Med. **18**, 2147–2162 (1999)
27. Fusco, G., Perez, J.: Spatial analysis of the Indian subcontinent: the complexity investigated through neural networks. In: Proceedings of CUPUM 2015, CUPUM 2015, Cambridge, MA, United States, July 2015, vol. 287, pp. 1–20 (2015)

A GIS Tool to Estimate Flow at Ungaged Basins Using the Map Correlation Method

Duygu Ocal[1]([✉]) and Elcin Kentel[2]

[1] Department of Geodetic and Geographic Information Technologies,
Middle East Technical University, 06800 Ankara, Turkey
ocal.duygu@metu.edu.tr
[2] Water Resources Laboratory, Department of Civil Engineering,
Middle East Technical University, 06800 Ankara, Turkey
ekentel@metu.edu.tr

Abstract. Water resources management has been a critical component of sustainable resources planning. One of the most commonly used data in water resources management is streamflow measurements. Daily streamflow time series collected at a stream gage provide information on the temporal variation in water quantity where the gage is located. However, streamflow information is often needed at ungaged catchments especially when the stream gage network is not dense. One conventional approach to estimate streamflow at an ungaged catchment is to transfer streamflow measurements from the spatially closest stream gage, commonly referred to as the donor or reference gage using the drainage-area ratio method. Recently, the correlation between daily streamflow time series is proposed as an alternative to distance for reference stream gage selection. The Map Correlation Method (MCM) enables development of a map that demonstrates the spatial distribution of correlation coefficients between daily streamflow time series at a selected stream gage and all other locations within a selected study area. Although utility of the map correlation method has been demonstrated in various studies, due to its geostatistical analysis procedure it is time-consuming and hard to implement for practical purposes such as installed capacity selection of run-of-river hydropower plants during their feasibility studies. In this study, an easy-to-use GIS-based tool, called MCM_GIS is developed to apply the MCM in estimating daily time series of streamflow. MCM_GIS provides a user-friendly working environment and flexibility in choosing between two types of interpolation models, kriging and inverse distance weighting. The main motivation of this study is to increase practical application of the MCM by integrating it to the GIS environment. MCM_GIS can also carry out the leave-one-out cross-validation scheme to monitor the overall performance of the estimation. The tool is demonstrated on a case study carried out in Western Black Sea Region, Turkey. ESRI's ArcGIS for Desktop product along with a Python script is utilized. The outcomes of inverse distance weighting and ordinary kriging are compared. Results of GIS-based MCM are in good agreement with the observed hydrographs.

Keywords: GIS · Map Correlation Method · Ordinary kriging · Spatial statistics

© Springer International Publishing AG 2017
O. Gervasi et al. (Eds.): ICCSA 2017, Part IV, LNCS 10407, pp. 377–391, 2017.
DOI: 10.1007/978-3-319-62401-3_28

1 Introduction

The population and level of urbanization are growing at a high rate in the world. These developments result in greater demands of energy and water. Therefore, planning and management of water resources is an important issue, especially for regions like Turkey, which have high hydropower potentials. The design and implementation of hydraulic structures require streamflow time series. Estimation of this important data at locations where no observation exists, directly affect the design of hydraulic structure and, effective and sustainable planning and utilization of water resources. Especially in developing countries, available hydrologic data, in this case the streamflow data is very limited. Thus, accurate and practical estimation methods are needed. Despite the extensive literature on this topic, there is not a single, commonly accepted method to estimate streamflow at ungaged catchments [25, 27]. Hydrological models or transfer of streamflow data from gaged catchments can be used to estimate streamflow at ungaged catchments [8, 32]. Hydrological models require site-specific data and expertise, and for some applications, it is not necessary to know the causal relationship between rainfall and runoff [18]. For example, during the feasibility studies of run-of-river hydropower plants, the flow duration curves are used to identify installed capacities. For such applications, streamflow time series from observed time series of neighboring catchments can be transferred to the ungagged site.

Currently one of the most widely used methods to transfer streamflow time series from a gaged catchment to an ungagged one is the drainage-area ratio method (DAR) [19]:

$$Qu_t = \frac{A_u}{A_g} Qg_t \qquad (1)$$

Where Qu_t is the streamflow on day t at the ungaged site, Qg_t is the streamflow on day t at the reference stream gage, A_u is the drainage area of the ungaged catchment, and A_g is the drainage area of the reference stream gage. As can be seen in Eq. (1), selection of a reference stream gage is crucial in estimating streamflow data at an ungaged catchment. Traditionally, the reference stream gage is selected as the spatially closest station to the ungaged location [7, 13, 14, 23, 26]. Estimation of the streamflow data at ungaged catchments rely on the assumption that spatially close locations generate similar hydrologic responses. However, there are other approaches suggested for the selection of the reference stream gage [5, 30]. Archfield and Vogel [3] introduced a new method, called the Map Correlation Method (MCM) that implements a reference stream gage selection strategy based on correlations between daily streamflow time series. Other studies were conducted using their framework [4, 11, 13] and demonstrated the utility of the MCM.

The MCM estimates the daily streamflow data by transferring the attributes of the most correlated stream gage to the ungaged location. A spatial interpolation technique, ordinary kriging, is used to estimate the correlations between daily streamflow time series observed at stream gages within the study area with those at the ungaged catchment. Archfield and Vogel [3] applied this method to a study area located around New England, USA with 28 stream gages. Their findings showed that, the MCM generally provided improved estimates of daily streamflow data compared to those obtained using the closest stream gage as the donor. In addition, Ergen [11] concluded that the MCM is applicable to other study regions, such as Western Blacksea Basin, and determined the most correlated stream gage correctly in one third of ungagged locations within the study area.

Spatial statistics, also referred to as geostatistics, was first discussed in the 1950's (Kolmogorov and Wiener) and it continues to draw attention from different disciplines, especially earth sciences. The spatial components of the MCM, such as relative positions of streamflow observations and ordinary kriging algorithm creates great opportunity of its integration with GIS. The MCM is a geostatistical approach that requires completion of multiple steps (see [3, 11]) that involve time-consuming numerical calculations. Moreover, modifications, such as increasing the extent of the study area (i.e. including data from additional stream gages or removing stream gages from the analysis) requires application of the whole procedure from the beginning. This complexity may hinder utilization of the MCM in practical applications. Moreover, a map showing the spatial distribution of the correlation coefficient between daily streamflow time series at an ungaged location and all other locations in the study area is generated as the output of the MCM and representation of this map in the GIS environment together with other relevant spatial information may be useful for decision makers [1, 2, 6, 10]. Thus, a GIS tool will facilitate visualization of the results as well.

The goal of this study is to develop a GIS tool, MCM_GIS, to carry out the MCM to increase its utilization in practice by minimizing the computation time and complexity. The original MCM [3] used ordinary kriging (OK) for spatial interpolation of correlations. In this study, inverse distance weighting (IDW) is used in addition to OK and the results are compared. The MCM_GIS allowed easy and quick implementation of IDW within the MCM algorithm. Utilization of MCM_GIS is demonstrated at a study area in the Western Blacksea Basin, Turkey.

2 Study Area

Western Blacksea Basin is used as the study area (see Fig. 1). First, all the stream gages with common observation periods within the study area are identified. List and characteristics of 13 stream gages with 10-year streamflow data from 1995 to 2014 is summarized in Table 1. Table 1 is inserted into GIS as a point layer with a projected coordinate system, European Datum 1950 UTM zone 36 N. It is important to mention that stream gages 1307, 1330 and 1332 are not connected to other stream gages although the remaining stream gages are grouped within two separate sub-basins.

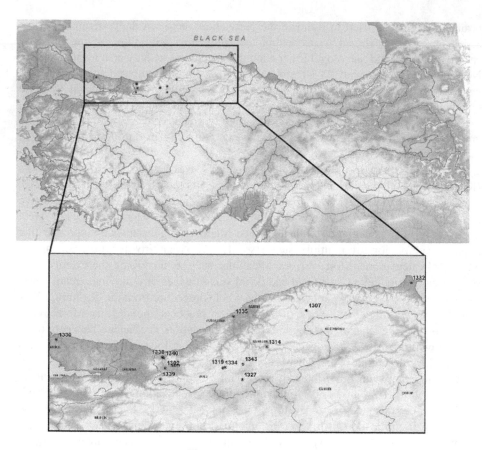

Fig. 1. The study area

Table 1. The summary of the stream gages located in the study area

No	Catchment location	Drainage area (km²)	Elevation (m)	Observation period (years)
1302	Buyukmelen	1988.00	115	1952–2012 (excluding 1963, 1971, 1972, 1992, 2008)
1307	Devrekani Cayi	1097.60	815	1953–2012 (excluding 1955, 2005)
1314	Soganli Cayi	5086.80	271	1962–2012
1319	Mengen Cayi	766.40	507	1964–2012 (excluding 1981, 1998, 2008)
1327	Ulusu	953.60	1142	1966–2012
1330	Yeniciftlik D.	23.10	39	1966–2012 (excluding 1990,1991)
1332	Karasu	340.00	20	1968–2012

(*continued*)

Table 1. (*continued*)

No	Catchment location	Drainage area (km²)	Elevation (m)	Observation period (years)
1334	Bolu Cayi	1095.30	541	1966–2012 (excluding 1994)
1335	Filyos Cayi	13300.40	2	1963–2012
1338	Lahana Deresi	104.80	16	1979–2012 (excluding 1980, 1985, 1986)
1339	Aksu Deresi	105.20	634	1980–2012
1340	Buyukmelen	2174.00	23	1980–2012 (excluding 2006)
1343	Korubasi Deresi	125.00	780	1991–2012

3 Method

3.1 Spatial Interpolation Methods

Inverse Distance Weighting. IDW interpolation assumes that things that are spatially close to each another are more alike than those that are farther apart. To predict a value for any unmeasured location, IDW uses the measured values surrounding the prediction location. The measured values closest to the prediction location have more influence on the predicted value than those farther away. The general formula for IDW is formed as a weighted sum of the data [12]:

$$\hat{Z}(s_o) = \sum_{i=1}^{N} \lambda_i Z(s_i) \tag{2}$$

where $Z(s_i)$ is the measured value at the location s_i, λ_i are the weights assigned to each measured point at the ith location, s_o is the prediction location, $\hat{Z}(s_o)$ is the value that is being predicted and N is the number of measured values surrounding the prediction location that will be used in the prediction.

The formula to determine the weights is the following with the assumption that the sum of the weights assigned to each measured point is equal to 1 [12]:

$$\lambda_i = d_{i0}^{-p} / \sum_{i=1}^{N} d_{i0}^{-p} \quad and \quad \sum_{i=1}^{N} \lambda_i = 1 \tag{3}$$

As the distance becomes larger, the weight is reduced by a factor of p. The quantity d_{i0} is the distance between the prediction location, s_0, and each of the measured locations, s_i.

The rate at which the weights decrease is dependent on the value of p. The optimal p value is determined by minimizing the root-mean-square prediction error (RMSPE) [17]. The IDW algorithm provided in GIS is used in this study.

Kriging. Kriging uses geostatistical features of input data and it is widely used for hydrologic data predictions such as precipitation, underground water distribution and drought analysis [20, 29]. It creates prediction surfaces by incorporating the statistical properties of the measured data [16]. Kriging produce, not only a prediction surface, but also uncertainty (error) surfaces that provide an indication of the performance of the predictions as well [9]. The Kriging tool in GIS fits a mathematical function to a specified number of points, or all points within a specified radius (i.e. neighbourhood) to determine the output value for each location.

Kriging is similar to IDW in that it weights the surrounding measured values to derive a prediction for an unmeasured location. The general formula for both interpolators is formed as a weighted sum of the data as given in Eq. (2). Details of ordinary kriging and its utilization in the MCM algorithm can be found in [16] and [13], respectively.

3.2   The Map Correlation Method

Archfield and Vogel [3] proposed this method to estimate daily streamflow data at ungaged basins using correlation coefficients between daily streamflow data collected at a number of stream gages within a study area. Later on, Ergen and Kentel [18] integrated the MCM with the multiple-source sites DAR method and investigated the applicability of the MCM in the Western Black Sea Basin, Turkey. The MCM assumes that the correlation between their daily streamflow measurements of two catchments is an indicator of hydrologic similarities. All of these spatial aspects represent an opportunity for easy implementation of the method by GIS tools. The procedure for the MCM is given in Fig. 2. Four main steps of the MCM to estimate the streamflow time series at an ungagged location are provided below.

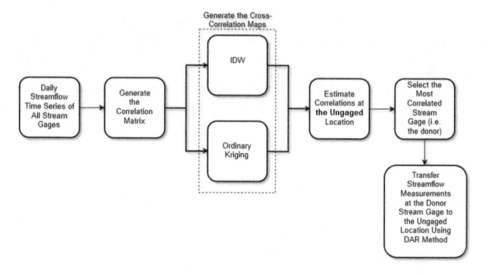

Fig. 2. General framework of the revised MCM

Table 2. Correlation matrix for 13 stream gages located in Western Black Sea Basin, Turkey

Gage number	1302	1307	1314	1319	1327	1330	1332	1334	1335	1338	1339	1340	1343
1302	1.00	0.84	0.79	0.80	0.82	0.70	0.78	0.84	0.91	0.77	0.85	0.99	0.80
1307	0.84	1.00	0.85	0.86	0.85	0.67	0.77	0.89	0.91	0.62	0.75	0.84	0.85
1314	0.79	0.85	1.00	0.93	0.93	0.58	0.65	0.91	0.91	0.48	0.78	0.77	0.91
1319	0.80	0.86	0.93	1.00	0.88	0.55	0.63	0.94	0.91	0.47	0.76	0.79	0.93
1327	0.82	0.85	0.93	0.88	1.00	0.65	0.71	0.87	0.89	0.56	0.81	0.81	0.87
1330	0.70	0.67	0.58	0.55	0.65	1.00	0.70	0.59	0.66	0.75	0.57	0.73	0.55
1332	0.78	0.77	0.65	0.63	0.71	0.70	1.00	0.68	0.75	0.68	0.67	0.79	0.64
1334	0.84	0.89	0.91	0.94	0.87	0.59	0.68	1.00	0.93	0.53	0.80	0.83	0.91
1335	0.91	0.91	0.91	0.91	0.89	0.66	0.75	0.93	1.00	0.65	0.81	0.90	0.90
1338	0.77	0.62	0.48	0.47	0.56	0.75	0.68	0.53	0.65	1.00	0.63	0.80	0.48
1339	0.85	0.75	0.78	0.76	0.81	0.57	0.67	0.80	0.81	0.63	1.00	0.83	0.75
1340	0.99	0.84	0.77	0.79	0.81	0.73	0.79	0.83	0.90	0.80	0.83	1.00	0.78
1343	0.80	0.85	0.91	0.93	0.87	0.55	0.64	0.91	0.90	0.48	0.75	0.78	1.00

1. *Creating the Correlation Matrix*

   Using the daily streamflow time series data with long observation periods, the correlation matrix is prepared between gaged locations. Streamflow data of all the stream gages with common observation period (i.e. potential donor/reference stream gages) located in the selected study area are used to generate the correlation matrix. Larger number of potential reference stream gages will result in better correlation maps. As an example, the correlation matrix derived for the case study (see Fig. 1) is given in Table 2 (see Fig. 3 for relative locations of 13 stream gages).

2. *Creating Cross-Correlation Maps*

   This step is the main motivation for the GIS integration to the MCM method. The correlation between each gaged location and the ungaged point is estimated using spatial interpolation algorithms (OK or IDW) of GIS. For example, when 1314 is assumed as ungagged, a spatial interpolation map is generated using the remaining 12 stream gages. The cross-correlation map generated using correlations of streamflow data of 1302 with those of remaining stream gages located within the study area is given in Fig. 3. The details of this procedure is given in the Appendix of Ergen and Kentel [18].

3. *Selection of a Reference Stream Gage*

   Each of the cross-correlation maps will be used to estimate a correlation between the ungaged point and corresponding gaged point. For example, the correlation between 1302 and 1314 is 0.83 from Fig. 3. Spatial queries can be done effortlessly with the involvement of GIS technologies. The third step of the MCM is to select the most correlated stream gage based on the cross-correlation maps obtained in the previous step. Thus, the donor gage is identified as the gage that has the highest correlation with the ungaged location.

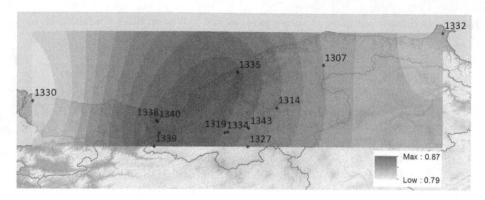

Fig. 3. Cross-Correlation Map generated by ordinary kriging with the correlations of stream gage 1302 when stream gage 1314 was assumed as ungagged

4. *Transferring the Attributes of the Donor/Reference Stream Gage*
   The last step of the method is transferring streamflow data from the most correlated stream gage (i.e. donor) to the ungagged location using the DAR method (Eq. (1)).

3.3 The GIS Tool: MCM_GIS

In the GIS tool, Python is used as the scripting language since it is available in many GIS softwares and has many applications on open source GIS studies [31]. The tool is ready to be used in ArcGIS products with the help of Arcpy library, however, the tool can be shared on different GIS platforms that supports Python with minor changes as well.

First, a study area around the ungaged location and stream gages with common observation periods within this study area need to be identified. Then the correlation matrix is calculated and the coordinates of all the stream gages and the ungaged point are determined and input to MCM_GIS. These inputs are converted into spatial layers by MCM_GIS. A point layer containing the correlation coefficient data for every column of the correlation matrix (i.e. one point layer for each stream gage) is formed. The conversion process is performed by MCM_GIS using Arcpy, Os and Pandas libraries in Python. At the end of these steps, inputs for spatial interpolation are ready.

MCM_GIS allows utilization of either OK or IDW for spatial interpolation. OK model parameters are determined through a trial-and-error procedure. Parameters resulting in the lowest RMSE value are selected and used in the model. Common model parameters for OK and IDW are output raster cell-size, search radius (i.e. neighborhood circle) and minimum number of observation points. In addition, IDW requires the power value p, while OK requires the semi-variogram type (e.g. circular, spherical, exponential, Gaussian and linear), lag size, major range, partial sill and nugget values. These parameters can be adjusted based on trends and distributions of available data. Upon completion of the interpolation, correlation coefficient estimations are obtained from the cross-correlation maps and the most correlated stream gage is selected as the donor/reference stream gage. An example calculation is shown in Fig. 4. In this figure,

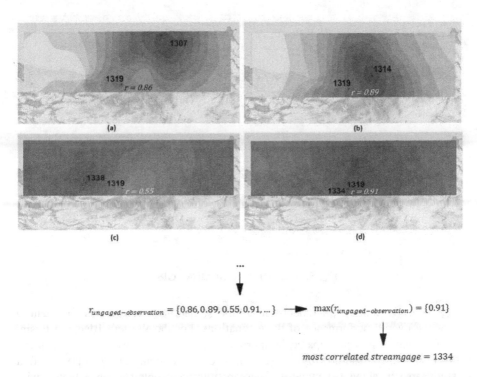

$$r_{ungaged-observation} = \{0.86, 0.89, 0.55, 0.91, ...\} \longrightarrow max(r_{ungaged-observation}) = \{0.91\}$$

most correlated streamgage = 1334

Fig. 4. Selection process of the most correlated stream gage (i.e. the donor/reference).

1319 is assumed to be ungaged and the correlation maps are created. For example, Fig. 4(a) is the correlation map generated using correlations between 1307 and all other stream gages in the study area. One such correlation map is generated for each of the stream gages found in the study area. Three of the remaining correlation maps, those of 1314, 1338 and 1334 are given in Fig. 4(b), (c) and (d), respectively. The correlation maps are used to determine the correlation coefficient between the ungaged location (i.e. 1319 in this example) and each of the other stream gages found in the study area. For example, the correlation coefficient between 1319 and 1307 is determined as 0.86 from Fig. 4(a). Similarly, correlation coefficients between 1319 and 1314, 1338 and 1339 are determined as 0.89, 0.55, and 0.91 from Fig. 4(b), (c) and (d), respectively. Then the stream gage having the largest correlation with the ungaged location is selected as the reference/donor. The GIS tool has an easy to use interface as shown in Fig. 5. As the last step, daily streamflow time series at the ungaged location is calculated using the DAR method (Eq. (1)) and the identified donor/reference stream gage.

MCM_GIS is designed to perform computations of a leave-one-out cross-validation procedure for each of the stream gages used in the study area as well. This computation provides a performance report for the MCM that summarizes observed and estimated correlation values within the study area. Based on this performance report, suitability of the MCM, the number of stream gages, the length of the observation period, and selection of the interpolation method can be assessed. Spatial distribution, observation

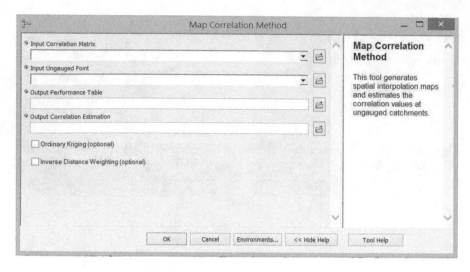

Fig. 5. User interface of MCM_GIS

period, connectivity of the catchments affect this estimation, therefore, it is important to monitor the overall performance of the estimations. For the Western Blacksea Basin, the performance report is prepared in approximately one hour. After receiving satisfactory results, the streamflow time series can be obtained at any ungaged point within the study area in about ten minutes. These results were obtained on a laptop with Windows 10 operating system, 8 GB RAM, 7th Generation Intel Core processor. The working environment is represented in Fig. 6. Overview of the layers used in the analysis are on the left side and Python window can be seen on the right side of the screen where the scripts are loaded to perform geoprocessing.

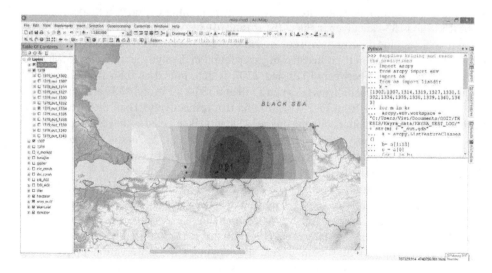

Fig. 6. The working environment of MCM_GIS

4 Results

The Nash-Sutcliffe Efficiency, NSE values are determined in order to evaluate the goodness of fit of the estimation performed in GIS. NSE is a commonly used performance indicator in hydrological estimations [3, 17, 28, 31]. NSE values are calculated using the following equation [24]:

$$NSE = 1 - \left[\frac{\sum_{i=1}^{n} (X_i^{obs} - X_i^{est})^2}{\sum_{i=1}^{n} (X_i^{obs} - \overline{X^{obs}})^2} \right] \tag{4}$$

Where X_i^{obs} is the i-th observed value, X_i^{est} is the i-th estimated data and $\overline{X^{obs}}$ is the averaged value of all observed data. NSE values that are lower than zero indicates that the average of the observed data is a better estimator than the model applied.

In this study, to evaluate the performance of the MCM at the Western Blacksea Basin, a leave-one-out cross-validation procedure is carried out and the results are discussed here. Donor/reference stream gages are identified using both IDW and OK, and the results are compared with those obtained using the closest stream gage as the reference stream gage. Performances of these three approaches are compared in Table 3. The performance of the estimations improved when the donor is selected using the MCM instead of the nearest stream gage. As can be seen in Table 3, out of 13 stream gages, results are obtained only at 11 of them since IDW and OK were not able to carry out spatial interpolation for remaining two stream gages (i.e. 1330 and 1332). There are certain studies stating kriging is a better interpolator than IDW, while estimating geographical data [15, 21, 22]. Even though the overall performance of two different interpolation methods are very similar in our study, for one of the stream gages (i.e. 1343) IDW performed better. Leave one-out cross-validation procedure with OK and IDW are performed relatively easily with the help of MCM_GIS.

Table 3. Nash-Sutcliffe efficiency values identified using different reference gage selection criteria

Ungaged	Nearest stream gage	The most correlated stream gage using MCM with OK	The most correlated stream gage using MCM with IDW
1302	0.89	0.89	0.89
1307	0.47	0.60	0.60
1314	−1.23	0.52	0.52
1319	0.74	0.82	0.74
1327	0.50	0.61	0.50
1334	0.44	0.71	0.44
1335	0.70	0.80	0.80
1338	0.29	0.29	0.29
1339	0.31	0.39	0.31
1340	−1.44	−1.44	−1.44
1343	0.59	0.42	0.75

As an example, comparison of hydrographs for the stream gage 1307 for the year 2003 are given in Fig. 7. It can be seen that streamflow estimation obtained using the most correlated stream gage is in better agreement than those obtained from the spatially closest stream gage. Generation of the hydrograph for any year within the observation period at any of the stream gages when it is assumed as ungaged is relatively easy using the outputs of MCM_GIS.

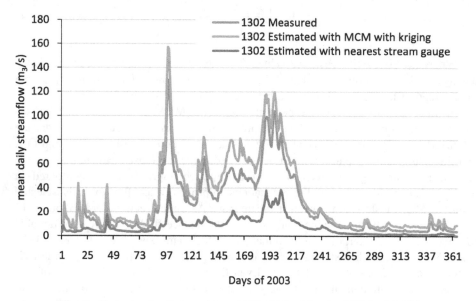

Fig. 7. Hydrograph of stream gage 1302 obtained by the MCM with OK

5   Conclusions

A GIS-based streamflow estimation tool to automatize the MCM procedure is developed in this study. MCM_GIS, minimizing the time and effort spent to estimate daily streamflow data at an ungaged location, will be useful for water resources planning and management problems such as feasibility studies of small hydropower plants. The GIS-based tool utilizes the Map Correlation Method to estimate streamflow time series at ungaged locations. MCM_GIS allows utilization of IDW in addition to OK for spatial interpolation. The performance of MCM_GIS is tested at the Western Blacksea Basin and satisfactory results are obtained with the advantage of ease of use and less computational time requirement.

The most important contribution of the tool is to partially automate the multi-step procedure of the MCM into a single GIS-based tool. While saving time, prediction accuracy is not compromised. Another important point is the distribution of the MCM_GIS. As stated earlier, the tool is written in Python and it is directly compatible with ESRI products. With minor modifications, MCM_GIS can be accustomed for other GIS softwares as well.

Lack of a dense stream gage network and unavailability of common long-enough observation period represent limitations in the estimation process. Thus, it is important to evaluate the performance of MCM_GIS in estimating daily streamflow time series at a selected site. To achieve this goal, a tool to carry out the leave-one-out cross-validation approach is also embedded into MCM_GIS. The performance report generated by the leave-one-out cross-validation tool is useful in identifying the boundaries of the study area and the period of the stream flow time series to be used in the model.

Through fast and partially automatic calculation, MCM_GIS simplifies application of the MCM and facilitates evaluation of the results through better visualization for decision makers. We believe that MCM_GIS will increase utilization of the MCM in practice.

6 Future Work

Future work can focus on the applications of the GIS tool to other study areas with different characteristics. The performance of the estimation can be investigated for different observation periods as well.

As future work, utility of MCM_GIS in predicting other hydrological features such as precipitation at ungagged location can be investigated. Other variations, such as utilization of multiple reference gages instead of a single one as originally suggested in the MCM, seasonal analysis, and such are topics for future studies as well.

References

1. Aydin, N.Y.: GIS-based site selection approach for wind and solar energy systems: a case study from Western Turkey. Doctoral dissertation, Middle East Technical University (2009)
2. Aydin, N.Y., Kentel, E., Duzgun, H.S.: GIS-based site selection methodology for hybrid renewable energy systems: a case study from western Turkey. Energy Convers. Manag. **70**, 90–106 (2013)
3. Archfield, S.A., Vogel, R.M.: Map correlation method: selection of a reference streamgage to estimate daily streamflow at ungaged catchments. Water Resour. Res. **46**(10) (2010)
4. Archfield, S.A., Vogel, R.M., Wagener, T.: Rainfall-runoff model calibration at an ungauged catchment using the map-correlation method. AGU Fall Meeting Abstracts (2009)
5. Arsenault, R., Brissette, F.P.: Continuous streamflow prediction in ungauged basins: the effects of equifinality and parameter set selection on uncertainty in regionalization approaches. Water Resour. Res. **50**(7), 6135–6153 (2014)
6. Asadi, S.S., Vuppala, P., Reddy, M.A.: Remote sensing and GIS techniques for evaluation of groundwater quality in Municipal Corporation of Hyderabad (Zone-V), India. Int. J. Environ. Res. Public Health **4**, 45–52 (2007)
7. Asquith, W.H., Roussel, M.C., Vrabel, J.: Statewide analysis of the drainage-area ratio method for 34 streamflow percentile ranges in Texas, U.S. Geological Survey, Scientific Investigations Report, 2006-5286 (2006)
8. Bardossy, A.: Calibration of hydrological model parameters for ungauged catchment. Hydrol. Earth Syst. Sci. **11**, 703–710 (2007)

9. Bailey, T.C., Gatrell, A.C.: Interactive Spatial Data Analysis, vol. 413. Longman Scientific & Technical, Essex (1995)
10. Campbell, M.H., Apparicio, P., Day, P.: Geographic analysis of infant mortality in New Zealand. Aust. N. Z. J. Public Health **28**(3), 221–226 (2014)
11. Ergen, K.: Application of the map correlation method to the Western Blacksea Basin. Master's Thesis, Middle East Technical University (2012)
12. ESRI Development Team: Geostatistical Analyst Tutorial (2010)
13. Esralew, R.A., Smith, S.J.: Methods for estimating flow-duration and annual mean-flow statistics for ungaged streams in geological survey, Scientific Investigations Report, 2009-5267 (2009)
14. Emerson, D.G., Vecchia, A.V., Dahl, A.L.: Evaluation of drainage area ratio method used to estimate streamflow for the Red River of the North Basin, North Dakota and Minnesota. U. S. Geological Survey, Scientific Investigations Report, 2005-5017 (2005)
15. Gong, G., Mattevada, S., O'Bryant, S.E.: Comparison of the accuracy of kriging and IDW interpolations in estimating groundwater arsenic concentrations in Texas. Environ. Res. **130**, 59–69 (2013)
16. Isaaks, E.H., Srivastava, R.M.: Applied Geostatistics. Oxford University Press, Oxford (1989)
17. Johnston, K., Ver-Hoef, J.M., Krivoruchko, K., Lucas, N.: Using ArcGIS Geostatistical Analyst. ESRI, Redlands (2001)
18. Kentel, E., Ergen, K.: An integrated map correlation method and multiple-source sites drainage-area ratio method for estimating streamflows at ungauged catchments: a case study of the Western Black Sea Region. Turkey. J. Environ. Manag. **15**, 309–320 (2016)
19. Korleski, C., Strickland, T.: Biological and water quality study of Grand River Basin, State of Ohio Environmental Protection Agency, EPA Technical Report EAS/2009-6-5 (2009)
20. Kuzucu, A.: Seyhan Havzasi'nda Kurakliğin Zamansal Ve Alansal Değişiminin İncelenmesi. Master's Thesis, 9 Eylul University (2016)
21. Luo, W., Taylor, M.C., Parker, S.R.: A comparison of spatial interpolation methods to estimate continuous wind speed surfaces using irregularly distributed data from England and Wales. Int. J. Climatol. **28**, 947–959 (2007)
22. Mbilinyi, B.P., Tumbo, S.D., Mahoo, H.F., Mkiramwinyi, F.O.: GIS-based decision support system for identifying potential sites for rainwater harvesting. Phys. Chem. Earth Parts A/B/C **32**, 1074–1081 (2007)
23. Mohamoud, Y., Parmar, R.: A Regionalized flow duration curve method to predict streamflow for ungaged basins: a case study of the Rappahannock Watershed in Virginia, USA. In: 8th IAHS Scientific Assembly and 37th IAH Congress, Hyderabad, India (2009)
24. Nash, J.E., Sutcliffe, J.V.: River flow forecasting through conceptual models part I - a discussion of principles. J. Hydrol. **10**(3), 282–290 (1970)
25. Parajka, J., Viglione, A., Rogger, M., Salinas, J.L., Sivapalan, M., Bloschl, G.: Comparative assessment of predictions in ungauged basins - part 1: runoff hydrograph studies. Hydrol. Earth Syst. Sci. **17**, 1783–1795 (2013)
26. Patil, S., Stieglits, M.: Controls on hydrologic similarity: role of nearby gauged catchments for prediction at an ungauged catchment. In: 8th Hydrology and Earth System Sciences Discussions (2011)
27. Ravazi, T., Coulibaly, P.: Streamflow prediction in ungauged basins: review of regionalization methods. J. Hydrol. Eng. **18**(8), 958–975 (2013)
28. Shu, C., Ouarda, T.B.M.J.: Improved methods for streamflow estimates at ungauged sites. Water Resour. Res. **48**, W02523 (2012)
29. Theodossiou, N., Latinopoulos, P.: Evaluation and optimisation of groundwater observation networks using the Kriging methodology (2007)

30. Yuan, L.L.: Using correlation of daily flows to identify index gauges for ungauged streams. Water Resour. Res. **49**, 604–613 (2013)
31. Zambelli, P., Gebbert, S., Ciolli, M.: Pygrass: an object oriented Python Application Programming Interface (API) for Geographic Resources Analysis Support System (GRASS) Geographic Information System (GIS) (2013)
32. Zelelew, M.B., Alfredsen, K.: Transferability of hydrological model parameter spaces in the estimation of runoff in ungauged catchments. Hydrol. Sci. J. **59**(8), 1470–1490 (2014)

Multiple Bayesian Models for the Sustainable City: The Case of Urban Sprawl

Giovanni Fusco[1(✉)] and Andrea Tettamanzi[2]

[1] CNRS, ESPACE, Université Côte-Azur, Nice, France
giovanni.fusco@unice.fr
[2] CNRS, Inria, I3S, Université Côte-Azur, Sophia Antipolis, France
andrea.tettamanzi@unice.fr

Abstract. Several possible models of urban sprawl are developed as Bayesian networks and evaluated in the light of available evidence, also considering the possibility that further, yet unknown models could offer better explanations. A simple heuristic is proposed in order to attribute a likelihood value for the unknown models. The case study of Grenoble (France) is then used to review beliefs in the different model options. The multiple models framework proves particularly interesting for geographers and planners having little available evidence and heavily relying on prior beliefs. This last condition is very frequent in research on sustainable cities. Further options of multiple models evaluations are finally proposed.

Keywords: Urban sprawl · Uncertainty · Model selection · Belief revision · Bayesian networks · Grenoble

1 Introduction

Practitioners and policy-makers assume that attaining sustainable urban development is essentially a question of data monitoring, decision making and policy implementation in a context of well-established scientific theories and positive knowledge of the urban realm. On the contrary, understanding, measuring and managing urban sustainability is a complex task and uncertainty is omnipresent in the kind of knowledge we have on the sustainable city. Urban sustainability is in fact a multi-dimensional issue, involving socioeconomic, environmental, urban design and governance aspects. Cities are complex systems, whose knowledge is always partial, incomplete, if not contradictory (when different points of view are taken into account). Even more, when dealing with sustainable development, researchers and practitioners have to foresight alternative possible futures, whose knowledge is by definition uncertain.

This paper will focus on the case of the possible effects of policies aimed at limiting urban sprawl. Urban sprawl is a central issue for the sustainable city. Letting the city grow through low-density, functionally specialized new suburban developments produces direct consequences (over-consumption of natural and agricultural land) and indirect ones (longer trips, car-dependence, increased greenhouse gas emissions, need for new expensive road infrastructures and/or high level of road congestion) which challenge the goals of sustainable urban development [1, 2]. The spatial interaction between the city and its suburbs also

© Springer International Publishing AG 2017
O. Gervasi et al. (Eds.): ICCSA 2017, Part IV, LNCS 10407, pp. 392–407, 2017.
DOI: 10.1007/978-3-319-62401-3_29

plays an important role. Camagni, Capello and Nijkamp [3] highlight that the city/suburbs opposition poses a social dilemma: households want to take advantage of economy of agglomeration offered by the city (in terms of job opportunities, services, etc.) but try individually to avoid the diseconomies of agglomeration of living in the dense city (congestion, poor environmental quality). By moving to the suburbs they obtain better environmental amenities and are still capable of profiting of jobs and services offered by the city thanks to increased car-mobility. By so doing, they increase congestion and pollution in the city, worsening quality of life for city dwellers and pushing more households to opt for a suburban residence. Densification strategies, both in the inner city and in its suburbs have thus been proposed [4–6] in order to limit and eventually revert urban sprawl. These strategies make nevertheless strong assumptions on the impacts and even on the acceptability of densification by resident populations [7]. Conflicting hypothesis can thus be identified in an extremely rich literature on the ability of planning policies to curb urban sprawl, namely through densification strategies [8–11]. In North America, authors like Gordon and Richardson [12, 13] have challenged both the feasibility and the opportunity of sprawl containment, seeing suburbanization as the most efficient market-driven allocation of land respecting consumer preferences. Consensus is wider in Europe on the impossibility of accommodating uncontrolled sprawl in much more constrained geographical settings. Negative consequences on the traditional city centers (often observed in North America) are also seen as a major challenge for European cities, given the economic, heritage and symbolic value of traditional urban cores.

But even within this consensus, different assumptions can lead to different models of the interplay between population growth, congestion, city/suburbs relations, densification policies, resident perceptions and urban sprawl. These underlying assumptions also reflect different beliefs in the most plausible outcomes of observed trends of urban sprawl and of the capacity of densification policies to have a real impact on these trends. We think that modelers accompanying decision-making and policy formulation should integrate and not ignore this multiplicity of possible models. We follow in this the principle of multiple explanations first formulated by the ancient Greek philosopher Epicurus: if several theories are consistent with the observed phenomena, retain them all.

Within this paper we will thus propose in Sect. 2 two extremely simplified alternative models of the interplay between densification policies and urban sprawl. These models reflect two particularly prominent views in the debate on urban densification that can be found in Europe and, more specifically, in France. We will formalize the models as Bayesian networks (BN) organizing expert knowledge in the form of probabilistic relations. At the same time the two BN should not be considered as the only possible explanatory models. An expert within a decision-making context could be more or less confident in each of the two models, but should also allow some skepticism in the ability of either of them to capture reality. Some plausibility should thus be given to the fact that both models fail to explain urban sprawl and that a third, unknown model or even no model at all links urban sprawl to underlying trends and to densification policies. In Sect. 3, we will assess how new evidence could be used to review beliefs in models through a Bayesian framework and how beliefs in model and elements of evidence could be combined to calculate beliefs in outcomes of urban sprawl. The final section will explore how different theoretical frameworks could be used instead of Bayesian probabilities to integrate uncertainties linked to multiple possible models of urban sprawl.

2   Two Alternative Models of Urban Sprawl

2.1   Bayesian Networks to Model Uncertain Relations Behind Urban Sprawl

Two alternative models for the relation between densification policies and urban sprawl have thus been formalized as Bayesian Networks [14, 15]. Bayesian Networks (BN) are systems of probabilistic relations implemented on a directed a-cyclical graph which can be used to model uncertain causal knowledge among stochastic variables. BN have already been proposed as models of spatial systems [16, 17] once appropriate expert knowledge is elicited in terms of probabilities. Marcot et al. [18] give guidelines for BN development and update/revision, combining expert knowledge and empirical evidence, in the field of ecological modelling and conservation.

Figure 1 shows the causal graph of the two models that we developed. Both models include the same fifteen variables, seven of which correspond to the city sub-model and seven to the suburbia sub-model while the last variable, the demographic growth of the whole study area, is considered external to the system. To simplify domain knowledge, variables are either binary (yes/no, stable/increase, preserved/endangered, etc.) or ternary (stable/decrease/increase, stopped/limited/accelerated, etc.). Within each sub-system, decision variables are identified. Densification is a policy applicable both to the city and to the suburbs. Within the city, it can correspond to urban infill, to brownfield development or to replacement of smaller buildings with bigger ones. In the suburbs soft densification (infill of single-family houses) is often opposed to hard densification (where bigger buildings are mixed to single-family houses). A common urban policy in France is also city renovation, which includes the development of modern transit (usually light-rail transit), requalification of public space and public-funded renovation of old buildings. A contested policy is the development of employment in suburbs: some see it as a way of containing daily mobility of suburbanites, other see it as an encouragement to further urban sprawl. Many internal variables are perceptions by resident households: perception of city quality of life, perception of suburban amenities (mainly environmental amenities linked to low-density urbanization) and perception of suburban quality of life (combining environmental amenities with presence of jobs and services). These are often non-observable variables, unless expensive ad hoc surveys are carried out. The four decision variables and the external one are the independent variables of the model.

Even by adhering to a given set of theoretical assumptions, BN are particularly well-suited tools to model the kind of knowledge experts have on the phenomena under study. Cause-to-effect relations between geographic and sociodemographic variables are relatively "dirty", uncertain: the same causes can produce different effects and several additional variables are missing in the model. Causal probabilistic relations are thus a good option to model uncertain causal knowledge. But even with binary and ternary variables, the number of probabilistic parameters in the BN is daunting.

The ten dependent variables are governed by almost 300 probabilistic parameters in Model 2 (almost 250 in Model 1), which are clearly impossible to elicit from experts. Noisy logical gates NoisyOr, NoisyAnd and NoisyMax [19, 20] have thus been used to model in a simplified way, under the assumption of independence of causal impact, the sufficient/necessary causal links among the variables. Leak parameters can also be used

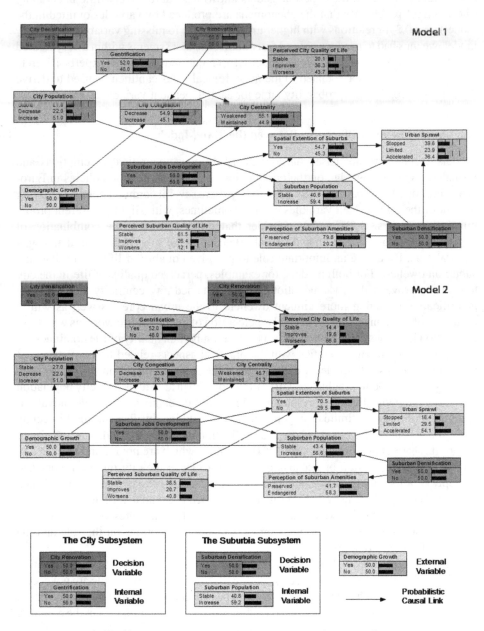

Fig. 1. Two Bayesian network models for urban sprawl.

to take into the account the effect of additional variables which are missing in the models. Model 1 thus required the elicitation of only 38 non-null parameters, Model 2 required 42. These parameters are judgments on the probabilistic force of the relations within a limited number of possible values (0.4, 0.5, 0.6, 0.7, 0.8 and 0.9, the value 1 being reserved to deterministic relations). Two possible leak parameters were also considered: 0.1 for relations, which the expert considers knowing with relatively little uncertainty (there is a 0.1 probability that the phenomena are produced by variables omitted in the model), and 0.2 for relations with higher uncertainty due to missing variables. For every model, we thus had to produce around forty numerical assessments within a very limited number of possible values. This is a realistic effort requested on domain experts. Discrete probabilistic functions associated to the noisy logical gates can then be used to derive the complete conditional probability table for each dependent variable of the models.

2.2   Analogies and Differences Between the Two Models

Models 1 and 2 are not based on completely different theoretical assumptions and formalize expert knowledge on the possible impacts of densification policies in European cities on a time span of 10–20 years. They share several common points, justifying the use of the same fifteen variables even if, sometimes, with slightly different probabilistic parameters. Both models consider that urban sprawl is the combination of increased suburban population and spatial extension of the suburbs in natural and agricultural land. Both give an important role to perceived quality of life from urban and suburban dwellers. For both models, for examples, perceived quality of life in the city tends to improve with city renovation, with maintained city centrality and with city gentrification (bringing more affluent dwellers to the urban core) as well as with a reduction of city congestion (conversely, perception of quality of life worsens when city congestion increases). For both models, perceived suburban quality of life combines the perception of suburban amenities with the practical aspects related to the presence of jobs and services. Both models finally agree on the demographic connections between city and suburbs. Demographic growth of the whole urban area fuels both city population and suburban population. Gentrification (which is often catalyzed by city renovation) tends nevertheless to diminish city population (wealthier dwellers normally occupy more space than poorer ones), whereas densification increases the ability of the city to absorb its share of demographic growth. Households which are not retained by the city (because of gentrification or because of a desire to leave the city due to a worsened perception of its quality of life) increase the demographic pressure on suburbs. When perceived quality of life in the suburbs worsens, households tend to migrate further away and this produces a spatial extension of suburbs and finally contributes to the acceleration of urban sprawl. But the two models make opposite assumptions on the role and the impacts of densification policies.

On the whole, Model 1 is relatively neutral on the direct impact of densification policies on household perceptions, considering that the majority of people are not necessarily hostile to densification, though recognizing an important role to city renovation on city congestion and on the perceived quality of life of its inhabitants. On the contrary, it assumes that densification can produce positive indirect effects: it allows the city and the suburbs to accommodate demographic growth within the present urban boundaries and, above all, it limits the risks that population growth in the suburbs endangers the perceived quality of life of their residents (densification policies aim at controlling the quality of urban and suburban infills). For Model 1, suburban jobs development weakens the traditional city-center and both directly and indirectly (by diminishing the perceived quality of life in the city), it favors further suburbanization, spatial extent of suburbs and ultimately accelerates urban sprawl. Model 1 corresponds to the majority view of European urban planners and to the recommendations of official documents from the French ministry and the EU Commission [4].

Model 2 assumes a positive role of suburban jobs development in reducing city congestion, an assumption that was traditionally underlying many urban plans by local authorities in France and in Europe, even if it has been later put in question by authors like Wiel [21]. Above all, Model 2 assumes that densification policies, both in the city and in the suburbs, will be negatively perceived by a majority of households and will have negative effects on city congestion, even more if they are not accompanied by city renovation policies. On the whole, even without accepting the extreme positions found in the American literature [12, 13], the assumptions behind this model are more pessimistic on the ability of urban planning to stop urban sprawl and suggest more limited goals of sprawl containment.

2.3 Using BN Models to Revise Beliefs

Once elements of evidence are entered in the models, the BN can propagate this information and revise the beliefs on non-observed variables. Bayesian belief revision, based on Bayes' theorem (1) and on its generalization given by Jeffrey's rule (2), can thus be used to propagate both elements of certain and uncertain evidence [22, 23].

$$p(H_i|E) = \frac{p(E|H_i)p(H_i)}{\sum_i p(E|H_i)p(H_i)} \tag{1}$$

Where H_i are the different hypotheses for which beliefs have to be revised given evidence E.

$$q(H_i|E) = \sum_j q_j p(H_i|E_j) \tag{2}$$

Where beliefs q_j are distributed over several possible outcomes for E and each $p(H_i|E_j)$ is calculated according to (1).

To be more precise, Bayesian belief revision within a BN is done by considering the probabilities of a child variable for a given configuration of the values of its parent variables as a multinomial distribution (binomial distribution for binary variables). The distributions are defined a priori by expert elicited parameters and can be used to revise beliefs on the marginal probabilities of variables of interest once elements of evidence are entered in the model. Following a thorough Bayesian approach, the probabilistic parameters can also be updated through the use of the corresponding conjugate prior distributions (Dirichelet and Beta distributions) if an incremental learning of model parameters is sought for, like in [24]. Within our research, we are not interested in parameter updating (see discussion further).

We can thus suppose we implement a given set of policies and calculate the new beliefs on the variable "urban sprawl" given by the two models (Fig. 2). Model 1 suggests that the densification of city and suburbs, together with city renovation and a policy aiming at hindering job developments in the suburbs will very probably stop urban sprawl (p = 0.78) or possibly limit it (p = 0.14). These beliefs are particularly insensitive to the demographic growth scenario.

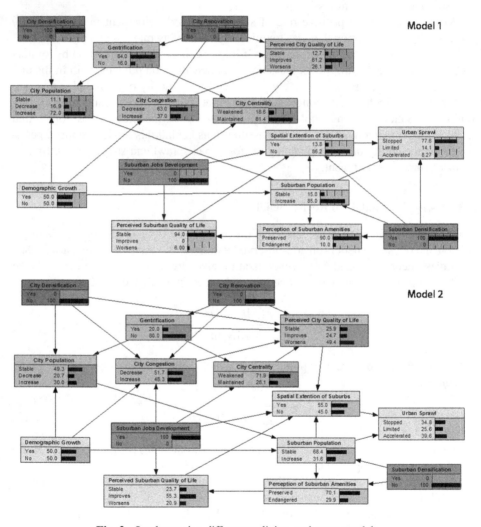

Fig. 2. Implementing different policies on the two models.

Model 2, on the contrary, favors the implementation of a completely opposite set of policies: no densification, whether in the city or in the suburbs, no city renovation but development of jobs in the suburbs. The final impact on urban sprawl is relatively uncertain (even if it is clearly better than any other set of policies implementing densi-fication): sprawl could be stopped (p = 0.35), limited (p = 0.26) but also accelerate (p = 0.39). These beliefs are very sensitive to the demographic growth scenarios, though remaining relatively uncertain: by increasing population, urban sprawl should probably accelerate (p = 0.47, with probability of stop falling to 0.25); in the absence of population growth, urban sprawl should be probably stopped (p = 0.45, with probability of accel-eration falling to 0.32). Uncertain evidence could also be propagated, as for example if we consider population growth very probable (p = 0.8) but not certain.

3   Belief Revision Between Alternative Models

3.1   Problem Statement

The central point in our paper is not belief propagation within a BN. A much more crucial goal is to make the best use of available evidence from case studies (which are always relatively rare) in order to reassess our beliefs in models. Subsequently, revised beliefs in models and belief propagation within each model could be combined to derive new beliefs on a few variables of interest, given the available evidence.

The main characteristic of our epistemic framework is considering Models 1 and 2 as two alternative plausible explanations of urban sprawl, together with a more uncertain option considering urban sprawl as the consequence of an unknown third model (which could also be a model of stochastic independence from any other domain variable). Raftery [25, 26] has already proposed Bayesian frameworks for model selection in the social sciences, an indication subsequently made by Withers [27] within the geographical science. The core of model selection lies in the identification of the best model between Model 1 (M1) and Model 2 (M2), knowing some empirical evidence E and revising some prior belief on model plausibility (p(M1), p(M2)). Using Bayes' theorem (1), one can evaluate the posterior odds of the two models, given the evidence:

$$\frac{p(M1|E)}{p(M2|E)} = \frac{p(E|M1)}{p(E|M2)} \frac{p(M1)}{p(M2)} \tag{3}$$

The first term of the right side of the equation is known as Bayes factor, defined as the ratio of the likelihoods of the evidence given each model. When the parameter space of each model is considered, likelihoods must be calculated as a complete integral on all parameter space, which is often intractable. Bayesian Information Criterion (BIC) is then used as an approximation of Bayes factor. If, as we will do here, we consider model parameters as fixed, Bayes factor can be directly calculated through belief propagation in the two Baye-sian networks.

At the same time, as already anticipated, our frame of discernment of possible models is significantly richer:

$$\Theta_{Models} = \{M1, M2, \ldots, Other\}$$

Where Mi are the possible models considered and $Other$ stands for any other possible model not yet formulated. The modeler can have prior beliefs on these possible options (including the option *Other*) and can calculate likelihoods from available models. It cannot however calculate the likelihood p(E|Other), which is necessary in order to apply Bayes theorem for revising the beliefs on the possible models. We thus propose an approach to estimate the likelihood of the option *Other* given the evidence E respecting the following principles:

1. p(E|Other) = 0 if at least one of the formulated explanatory models Mi is completely plausible (for at least one i, likelihood $Mi = 1$);
2. p(E|Other) = 1 if no other formulated explanatory models is minimally plausible (for all i, likelihood $Mi = 0$).
3. p(E|Other) should grow as the likelihood of the formulated explanatory models diminishes.

These principles correspond to the human quest of explanation for observed phenomena, considering the current accepted explanatory knowledge and its ability to explain the new phenomena. If, among several currently accepted models, at least one of them is a plausible explanation of newly observed phenomena, no push for new models is felt, and the newly acquired empirical evidence is used to arbitrate between available models. The plausibility of new, yet to be formulated models is high when newly observed phenomena cannot plausibly be accounted for by any of the available models. History of science often witnessed this course of events. We could then write:

$$p(E|Other) = 1 - f(Max\ (p(E|Mi))) \tag{4}$$

Where f is a suitable monotonic decreasing function varying between 0 (when Max(p(E|Mi)) = 0) and 1 (when Max(p(E|Mi)) = 1). One possible operationalization of (4) is:

$$p(E|Other) = 1 - Max\ (p(E|Mi))^\alpha \tag{5}$$

if $\alpha < 1$ the push to look for new models is sublinear with the lack of plausibility of the best available model, if $\alpha > 1$ it is super-linear. Once an appropriate α is chosen, reflecting the attitude to lack of plausibility of the best available model, we can calculate thanks to (5) likelihoods for all model options given observed evidence E and, through Bayes' theorem (1), we can revise our beliefs in the different model options. If, instead of certain evidence E, we have uncertain evidence $p(E_i)$, Jeffrey's rule (2) can be used to revise beliefs.

3.2   Application to the Possible Models of Urban Sprawl

Let us imagine that an urban geographer is relatively confident in Models 1 and 2 as possible explanations of urban sprawl and its relations to densification policies in French cities. He does not want to commit to any of the two models in particular and he does not want to bar the possibility that other models, not yet formulated, could explain urban sprawl in French cities. He could thus assign prior probabilities 0.45, 0.45 and 0.1 to Model 1, Model 2 and Other within Θ. How should he revise these beliefs with newly acquired knowledge on a case study to which the models could be applied?

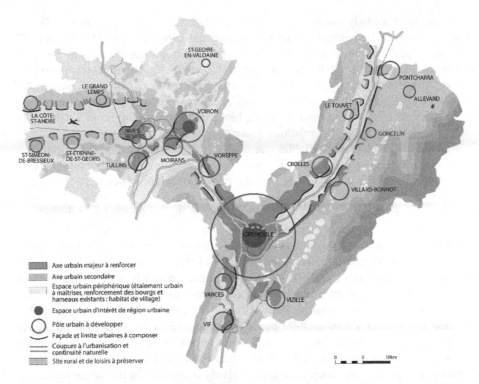

Fig. 3. Densification policies in Grenoble regional master plan of 2000. Source: [27]

The metropolitan area of Grenoble, in the alpine region of southern France, offers a good feedback on densification policies in French cities (Fig. 3). At its core lies the city of Grenoble, a mid-sized city of 155 000 inhabitants. Around the central city, a vast peripheral area hosts a population three times more important. The periphery develops along three main axes going south, north-east and north-west and following three main alpine valleys. Most of these peripheral areas are made of residential suburbs, surrounding a few historical villages and industrial or commercial surfaces. We will focus our attention on this study area for a period stretching from 1999 to 2013.

Over this period, Grenoble and its surrounding municipalities have implemented one of the most coherent densification policies in France, both in the central city and in the suburban areas, promoted by the adoption of the development and town planning master plan of 2000 [28, 29] and of several local town plans. The central city has also implemented important policies of city renovation, as the Urban Renovation Program of 2005 [30], the extension of the LRT lines A and B and the opening of two new LRT lines in 2006 and 2007. The same coherence cannot be found in terms of suburban jobs development. The master plan in 2000 foresaw the development of industrial, service and retail jobs in a few key areas of the suburbs. Indeed, jobs have steadily grown between 1999 and 2013 both in the central city (passing from 85 000 to 93 000) and in the rest of the metropolitan area (passing from 136 000 to 207 000 within a much larger geographic perimeter, see further).

We could thus easily assess that, for the Grenoble study area, variables *City Densification*, *Suburban Densification*, *City Renovation* and *Suburban Jobs Development* all have value "yes" over the period 1999–2013. As for the population growth of the study area, it passed from 631 000 inhabitants to 684 000, with an 8.4% increase, which is in line with the general steady demographic growth of France during the same period. We will thus assign value "increase" to variable *Demographic Growth*. These five values define a scenario of policies and demographic growth for our study area, which are independent of the probability relations of our two models.

A few easily measurable variables can also be used to introduce observed evidence in this scenario and evaluate model likelihood given the scenario and the evidence. City population was thus relatively stable over the period, oscillating between 153 000 and 156 000 inhabitants. Suburban population, on the other hand, rose from 478 000 to 528 000, a 10.5% increase over the 15 years. We can thus assign values "stable" and "increase" to variables *City Population* and *Suburban Population*, respectively.

Finally, the spatial extension of the suburbs within the metropolitan area was particularly important. Metropolitan areas are defined in France by the National Institute of Statistics and Economics (INSEE) as functional urban areas where more than 40% of the active population in each municipality commutes to the central city or to other municipalities in the metro area. Thus defined, the metropolitan area of Grenoble included 119 municipalities in 1999 but as many as 197 in 2013. Even if the newly incorporated municipalities were already well developed in 1999, their population increase strongly depended on household migration from the central city and other central municipalities and they were progressively integrated in the urban functional area. We can thus assign the value "yes" to the variable *Spatial Extension of Suburbs* between 1999 and 2013.

When these new findings are entered in the BNs, we can calculate marginal joint probabilities of 0.0636 for Model 1 and of 0.0992 for Model 2. These values correspond to the likelihoods of the two models given the scenario (defined by independent variables) and the observed findings (i.e. the three further empirically determined variables). We can thus revise our beliefs in the different model options using Eq. (5).

Table 1 shows the results of the belief revision assuming two different attitudes to lack of plausibility of the best available model: linear ($\alpha = 1$) and sublinear ($\alpha = 0.25$). The case study of Grenoble is clearly a counter-example for the two acknowledged models of urban sprawl. The most conflicting element of evidence of the case study with the models is the relatively stable city population in spite of overall demographic growth and the city densification policies (for both models city gentrification becomes then the most plausible cause of the observed phenomena). Overall, the likelihood value is relatively low for both models (even if it is higher for Model 2 than for Model 1). Equation (5) thus produces relatively high likelihoods for other possible models, compatible with the observed evidence: 0.4388 in the sublinear case, 0.9008 in the linear case. Bayesian belief revision (Eq. 1) thus results in much more uncertainty within our frame of discernment of possible models. In the sublinear case, belief in Model 2 is almost the same as the one in other possible models (0.38 and 0.37, respectively) and slightly higher than for Model 1. In the linear case, the most plausible model is the one yet to be discovered (posterior belief = 0.55), highlighting the weaknesses of available models.

Table 1. Belief revision for model options given the case study of Grenoble.

	Model 1	Model 2	Other
			Sublinear ($\alpha = 0.25$)
prior belief	0.45	0.45	0.1
likelihood	0.0636	0.0992	0.4388
posterior belief	0.24	0.38	0.37
			Linear ($\alpha = 1$)
prior belief	0.45	0.45	0.1
likelihood	0.0636	0.0992	0.9008
posterior belief	0.18	0.27	0.55

3.3 Discussion

The interpretation of the Grenoble case study in terms of hard evidence could be challenged. Even if this example was selected for its paradigmatic role and for the ease of interpretation of the available evidence, a soft/virtual evidence approach could be more appropriate [22, 23]. In the absence of an unambiguous protocol allowing the interpretation of available evidence, expert-based interpretation of evidence could be used. This could possibly result in soft or virtual evidence, assigning probabilities or likelihoods (respectively) to the fact that city or suburban densification has really taken place in the study area during the 1999–2013 period. Equation (2) would then be used to propagate evidence in the Bayesian networks. By so doing, the likelihoods of the two models would increase accordingly (reducing as a consequence the likelihood of other models), but the main conclusion would be the same: belief in Model 2 increases slightly compared to belief in Model 1, but belief in other models, which was particularly low a priori, becomes much higher now, considerably increasing uncertainty among model options.

Should Models 1 and 2 be discarded altogether in the analysis of urban sprawl in French metropolitan areas during the last decades? Our Bayesian belief revision doesn't reach this conclusion, as a unique counter-example is not sufficient to invalidate our models, given our prior beliefs. France has around 50 metropolitan areas of more than 200 000 inhabitants, having applied more or less coherent policies of densification to counter sprawl. The proposition to be evaluated is indeed the ability of our two models to cover this domain, and only a more thorough analysis of this set could possibly arrive to such a conclusion. If such analysis were to produce a very low value of posterior belief for one of the two models, this could indeed be disqualified as a pertinent model for our domain. If both models were characterized by very low posterior beliefs, the geographer's conclusion should be the need to look for alternative models, based on different theoretical assumptions and possibly more attentive to specific dynamics observed in French metropolitan areas. As often in the social sciences, we remain within a falsification approach with is much weaker than Popper's [31]: evidence concurs to make theoretical explanations incrementally more or less plausible, up to the point where the scientific community decides that a given model is no longer acceptable.

From this point of view, we are not interested in Bayesian updating of model parameters. Posterior expected values of parameters could indeed be calculated through conjugate priors of the multivariate distributions in the Bayesian Networks. Parameters in the conditional probability tables would then be allowed to drift considerably from the values derived from the elicited knowledge modelled through the noisy logical gates. Sophisticated parameter updating schemes could also be used, by assigning experience equivalents to the prior knowledge incorporated in the models. Prior knowledge could then be possibly swamped by data, as new case studies are presented to the models. But the resulting models would be less and less linked to precise theoretical assumptions, and finally harder to falsify, given their ability to adaptively incorporate newly acquired evidence.

It is also worth highlighting how our problem differs from more classical robust Bayesian modelling as presented by Bolstad [32]. When modelling binomial or multi-nomial stochastic processes, Beta and Dirichelet priors are normally linearly combined with a flat prior, to which the modeler assigns a very low prior belief. By doing so, the modeler makes sure that possible miss-specifications of the priors don't result in a wrong posterior distribution: when data contradict the prior, the posterior depends more on the data than on the prior. An important theoretical assumption underpins these operations: the observed phenomena are governed by a simple binomial or multinomial distribution whose parameters can possibly be wrong, but the posterior model will always have the same functional structure. In our problem, the possible models are Bayesian Networks, which are complex combinations of binomial and multinomial distributions. It is impossible to find appropriate conjugate distributions to combine with a flat prior. Moreover, the models have different structures (and not just different parameters) and possible other models are not just the "flat equivalent" of the available ones. They are yet to be developed models with particular structure and parameters, which are presently unknown. Our approach is thus more a belief revision heuristic among available and unavailable models backed by Bayesian calculus, than a precise Bayesian calculus of posterior model parameters within a given model structure.

4   Conclusions: Further Frameworks for Multiple Models of Urban Sprawl

This paper showed how Bayesian belief revision together with a particular framework assigning likelihood to unknown models can be used in order to assess prior beliefs on multiple models. This approach seems particularly interesting whenever the modeler is able to express his beliefs in terms of additive probabilities and when the amount of available evidence is relatively small, giving thus great importance to prior probabilities. This last condition is very frequent in research on sustainable cities: a few case studies are the empirical evidence of broadly formulated, alternative models of sustainable urban development. The case of urban sprawl in the metropolitan area of Grenoble also highlighted issues of knowledge elicitation and domain definition for the models. It was finally shown how a single counter-example is not sufficient to invalidate the two proposed models, given our prior beliefs.

However, Bayesian networks and Bayesian calculi are by no means the only tool that can be employed to reason about alternative hypotheses in the light of the available evidence. Artificial intelligence, in particular, has dedicated much effort to devising formal and computational frameworks for representing and managing uncertainty, on the one hand, of which Bayesian networks are but one offshoot, and belief revision on the other hand.

When it comes to representing and managing uncertainty, it is important to underline that two aspects of uncertainty must be distinguished: (i) stochastic uncertainty, resulting from a system behaving in a random way, and (ii) epistemic uncertainty (or ignorance), resulting from a lack of knowledge about a system.

Dempster-Shafer theory of evidence [33], and Phil Smets' transferable beliefs model [34], which is an interpretation thereof, is a theory of uncertainty whose aim is to give a mathematical account for epistemic uncertainty, besides stochastic uncertainty. The theory of evidence is rooted in probability theory, but it innovates in allowing for the allocation of a probability mass to events, rather than just elementary events or individual sample points.

The basic ingredients of the Dempster-Shafer theory of evidence are:

- a basic belief assignment, in the form of a probability mass distribution m over (sets of elementary) events A included in Ω, such that the mass of the empty set is null and the mass of all events sums up to one.
- a belief function Bel, determined by the basic belief assignment: Bel(A) is the sum of the masses of all events included in A.
- a plausibility function Pl, also determined by the basic belief assignment and dual to the belief function: Pl(A) is the sum of the masses of all events that have a non-null intersection with A; thus Bel(A) = 1 − Pl(complement of A).

The process of changing beliefs when new evidence becomes available is central to the evidence theory. The intuition behind it is that a basic belief assignment m represents an epistemic (or credal) state of an agent and, if further evidence becomes available to the agent, in the form of a proposition φ, the agent should change m to reflect this new evidence. In particular, the agent should rule out all worlds where φ does not hold and transfer their previous belief mass to worlds where φ holds. It should be noticed that this is essentially a conditioning process, whereby $m(\cdot)$ is conditioned by φ to yield $m(\cdot|\varphi)$. One possible way to perform such a belief transfer is by means of the so-called Dempster rule of conditioning.

Possibility theory [35] is another mathematical theory of uncertainty based on fuzzy set theory, alternative to probability theory. It differs from this latter by the use of a pair of dual set-functions (possibility and necessity measures) instead of only one. This feature makes it easier to capture partial ignorance. Besides, it is not additive and makes sense on ordinal structures. Possibility theory has a strong relation with the theory of evidence, not only because the two share basically the same objective, but also because both theories use monotonic (or non-additive) measures to represent beliefs.

The advantage offered by these two theories, with respect to Bayesian probabilities, is their capability of representing epistemic uncertainty in an explicit fashion. The theory of evidence, in addition, may represent stochastic uncertainty as well in a way that is fully compatible with probability theory, while the relationship between possibility theory and probability is subtler; nevertheless, transformations from possibilities to probabilities and *vice versa* have been proposed and studied in the literature [36]. How these two theories might be applied to our problem of model selection is left for future work. The main issue that would have to be addressed to this purpose is a suitable definition of the "sample space" Ω underlying the model selection problem, given which, the uncertainty associated with the models might be represented, respectively, as a probability mass distribution over the power set of Ω or a possibility distribution over Ω. It should finally by assessed how these more sophisticated AI theories of uncertain knowledge could be integrated in decision making in the field of sustainable urban development.

References

1. Foley, J., et al.: Global consequences of land use. Science **309**, 570–573 (2005)
2. Mcdonald, R., Kareiva, P., Forman, R.: The implications of current and future urbanization for the global protected areas. Biolog. Conserv. **141**, 1695–1703 (2008)
3. Camagni, R., Capello, R., Nijkamp, P.: Towards sustainable city policy: an economy-environment-technology nexus. Ecol. Econ. **24**, 103–118 (1998)
4. European Commission: European Sustainable Cities: Report of the Expert Group on the Urban Environment, Sustainable City Project. European Commission, Brussels (1996)
5. Calthorpe, P., Fulton, W.: The Regional City: Planning for the End of Sprawl. Island Press, New York (2001)
6. Duany, A., Plater-Zyberk, E., Speck, J.: Suburban Nation: The Rise of Sprawl and the Decline of the American Dream. North Point Press, New York (2000)
7. Breheny, M.: Urban compaction: feasible and acceptable? Cities **14**(4), 209–217 (1997)
8. Fouchier, V., Merlin, P. (eds.): High Urban Densities – A Solution for our Cities? Consulate General of France in Hong Kong (1994)
9. Charmes, E. (ed.): La densification en débat. Etudes foncières, special issue, 145 (2010)
10. PUCA: Vers des politiques publiques de densification et d'intensification douces? In: Workshop Proceedings (2014). http://www.urbanisme-puca.gouv.fr/IMG/pdf/S2-politiques-publiques-de-densification-douces-2.pdf
11. Laugier, R.: L'étalement urbain en France. Synthèse documentaire. Centre de Ressources Documentaires Aménagement Logement Nature. Ministère de l'Ecologie, du Développement Durable, des Transports et du Logement, Paris (2012)
12. Gordon, P., Richardson, H.: Beyond polycentricity: the dispersed metropolis, Los Angeles 1970–1990. J. Am. Plann. Assoc. **62**(3), 289–295 (1996)
13. Gordon, P., Richardson, H.: Are compact cities a desirable planning goal? J. Am. Plann. Assoc. **63**(1), 95–106 (1997)
14. Jensen, F.: Bayesian Networks and Decision Graphs. Springer, Berlin (2001)
15. Korb, K., Nicholson, A.: Bayesian Artificial Intelligence. Chapman & Hall/CRC, Boca Raton (2004)
16. Fusco, G.: Démarche géo-prospective et modélisation causale probabiliste. Cybergéo, 613 (2012). http://cybergeo.revues.org/25423
17. Scarella, F.: La ségrégation résidentielle dans l'espace-temps métropolitain. Ph.D. thesis, University of Nice Sophia Antipolis (2014)
18. Marcot, B., Steventon, J., Sutherland, G., McCann, R.: Guidelines for developing and updating Bayesian belief networks applied to ecological modeling and conservation. Can. J. Forest Res. **36**, 3063–3074 (2006)

19. Henrion, M.: Some practical issues in constructing belief networks. In: Kanal, L., Levitt, T., Lemmer, J. (eds.) Uncertainty in Artificial Intelligence, vol. 3, pp. 161–173 (1989). Elsevier
20. Diez, F., Drudzel, M.: Canonical probabilistic models for knowledge engineering. Technical report CISIAD-06-01 (2007)
21. Wiel, M.: La transition urbaine ou le passage de la ville pédestre à la ville motorisée. Mardaga, Liège (1999)
22. Bilmes, J.: On virtual evidence and soft evidence in Bayesian networks. UWEE Technical report 2004-0016. University of Washington (2004)
23. Pan, R., Peng, Y., Ding, Z.: Belief update in Bayesian networks using uncertain evidence. In: Proceedings of the 18th IEEE International Conference on Tools with Artificial Intelligence, ICTAI 2006, pp. 441–444. IEEE (2006)
24. Josang, A., Haller, J.: Dirichelet reputation systems. In: Proceedings of the 2nd International Conference on Availability, Reliability and Security, ARES 2007 (2007)
25. Raftery, A.: Bayesian model selection in social research. Sociol. Methodol. 25, 111–163 (1995)
26. Raftery, A.: Rejoinder: model selection in unavoidable in social research. Sociol. Methodol. 25, 185–195 (1995)
27. Withers, S.: Quantitative methods: Bayesian inference. Bayesian Thinking Prog. Hum. Geogr. 26(4), 553–566 (2002)
28. DDT Isère: Comment favoriser la densification? Direction Départementale du Territoire 38, Grenoble (2015)
29. AURG: Schéma Directeur de la Région Grenobloise. Agence d'Urbanisme de la Région Grenobloise, Grenoble (2000)
30. GRA: Programme de Rénovation Urbaine de l'agglomération grenobloise. Grenoble Alpes-Métropole, Grenoble (2005)
31. Fusco, G., et al.: Faire science avec l'incertitude : réflexions sur la production des connaissances en Sciences Humaines et Sociales. In: Proceedings of Incertitude et connaissances en SHS: production, diffusion, transfert, MSHS Sud-Est, Nice, halshs-01166287 (2015)
32. Bolstad, W.: Introduction to Bayesian Statistics, 2nd edn. John Wiley, New York (2007)
33. Shafer, G.: A Mathematical Theory of Evidence. Princeton University Press, Princeton (1976)
34. Smets, P., Kennes, R.: The transferable belief model. Artif. Intell. 66, 191–234 (1994)
35. Dubois, D., Prade, H.: Possibility Theory. Plenum, New York (1988)
36. Dubois, D., Prade, H., Sandri, S.: On possibility/probability transformations. In: Lowen, R., Roubens, M. (eds.) Fuzzy Logic, pp. 103–112. Kluwer, London (1993)

Developing Spatial Indicators Using a Uniform Tessellation to Measure Urban Transformation

Johan Maritz[✉], Alize le Roux, and Gerbrand Mans

Council for Scientific and Industrial Research, Pretoria, Gauteng, South Africa
{jmaritz,alerouxl,gmans}@csir.co.za

Abstract. South Africa's largest cities are subjected to high rates of urbanization with a projected 8 million people migrating to these urban spaces by 2030 [1]. Managing and guiding this growth is made more difficult due to the countries 'apartheid city' past - a segregated city form inherited from the pre-democratic order in 1994 where towns and cities were spatially engineered along racial divides. With the advent of a democratic order in South Africa in 1994 a number of policy frameworks have seen the light all of which have indicated the need to spatially transform cities and settlements – to break from the pre-1994 apartheid city. Measuring the progress made in spatial and socio-economic transformation has proven difficult as some information have only been provided at city or Local Municipal scale. To measure spatial outcomes, city performance, quality of life etc. a series of local and international city scale indicators has been developed. These however are only useful when comparing cities; it does not convey sub-city scale change or transformation. This paper profiles an approach that uses a single-sized uniform tessellation to create demographic and economic indicators for nine cities and explores the utilisation of this tessellated framework to analyse and depict demographic and economic change over time.

Keywords: Spatial framework · Tessellation · Transformation of cities · City indicators · South-Africa

1   Introduction

Presently, South Africa like many other African countries is experiencing high levels of urbanization with The Presidency [1] projecting that nearly 8 Million people will migrate to these urban spaces by 2030. The United Nations [2] estimates that in 2030, 71% of South Africa's population will be living in urban areas, reaching nearly 80% by 2050. Cities have to track this growth and change in order to adequately respond to and guide (infrastructure) investment decisions. In the past, cities would develop this data for their own use; however, this makes comparison between cities difficult, if not impossible. Developing consistent comparable data allows cities to learn from the experience of other cities and efficiently use their resources to build sustainable cities. An additional and uniquely South African challenge relates to South Africa's Apartheid past which resulted in segregated cities. Apartheid city design, especially the fact that many township areas were placed on the periphery of cities, left a legacy of sprawled, low density,

© Springer International Publishing AG 2017
O. Gervasi et al. (Eds.): ICCSA 2017, Part IV, LNCS 10407, pp. 408–421, 2017.
DOI: 10.1007/978-3-319-62401-3_30

two-tier cities that resulted in inefficiencies and unequal access to economic and service opportunities affecting the livelihoods of many South African citizens([3–5]). Since the change to a democratic government in 1994, the need to address the resulting socio-economic inequalities, racially divided cities and to spatially transform cities to provide equal opportunities and sustainable means of living for all citizens has been placed high on the political and planning agenda (See [6–11]).

The term 'spatial transformation' is often used more broadly to refer to far-reaching urban change or urban restructuring. It is also a descriptive term to encapsulate the idea that cities have changed greatly over time due to urbanization (See [12, 13]). However within the South African context, Oranje [14] indicates that spatial transformation relates mostly to those efforts aimed at *addressing the physical manifestations of Apartheid planning*. Exploring and tracking place-specific progress and spatial transformation is, however, a major challenge, not only in South Africa but in many other fast growing cities in the world and especially in the Global South [15]. Challenges to adequately measure (detect) changes and explore implications thereof include not only identifying and developing relevant spatial-specific indicators or measures, but also issues related to data availability, exploration, temporal and place-based comparisons, resources and the capacity to track change [16]. Spatially-specific indicators are critical, not only in: (1) investigating how the landscape has changed and how much progress has been made with spatial transformation in South African cities during the last 20 years, but also to; (2) contribute towards driving and monitoring just and sustainable spatial outcomes in cities moving forward.

This article showcases the results and methodologies used in developing particular explorative, standardised and replicable sub-city level spatial indicators which were developed to track spatial change and progress with spatial transformation at sub-city scale over the last 20 years in South African cities. It reflects work undertaken to support the 2016 State of Cities Report[1], published by the South African Cities Network.

2 Developing Indicators to Track Spatial Change in South Africa

In 2014, a 'Spatial Transformation of Cities' Conference was held in Johannesburg and the event reaffirmed that in order to gauge if actions to transform cities are manifesting in actual change, evidence needs to be tracked. There is thus a need to identify and develop a suite of suitable indicators to measures and track transformation. Kusek and Rist [17, p. 65] define indicators as "the quantitative or qualitative variables that provide a simple and reliable means to measure achievement, to reflect the changes connected to an intervention, or to help assess the performance of an organization against the stated outcome". Before creating any indicator it is important to know what objective needs to be achieved. Indicators are only appropriate "when they are measured against an objective" [17, p. 57].

The starting point in the development was to consider the existing data sources, from which spatial specific indicators can be developed, to determine their use and viability.

---

[1] http://www.socr.co.za/.

Currently most locally relevant spatial data sources for metropolitan cities are presented using the local municipal demarcation. Some items do goto a finer grain using statistical spatial units such as Wards, Sub-places or even Small Area Units (units used in South Africa by the local census bureau, Statistics South Africa). These items allow for not only city-to-city comparison, but also intra-city comparisons. However, these demarcations vary from one census to the next which does not allow comparability over time.

3 Objectives

One of the key objectives of the research project was to develop indicators to explore spatial change, levels of growth and spatial transformation on an intra-city level over time. In other words, particular indicators relating to bridging the data gap and **exploring sub-city level changes were the focus**. The intention was to identify spatial patterns and concentrations of people and activities, growth areas and linked changes in urban structure, resource allocation and effectiveness of public services provision (e.g. public transport). It should be acknowledged that spatial change can be depicted innumerous ways and that no single indicator can provide a clear indication of spatial transformation as it relates to the subjective experiences of people within cities. It can however be utilised to provide an objective overview of major socio-economic shifts. Spatial indicators can, however, add value in providing some indication of embedded spatial patterns and the areas undergoing the biggest changes within cities (in terms of population density, concentration of economic activity), and also in addressing questions related to the spatial relationships between such changes. The intent was to spatio-temporally track aligned data to identify:

- spatial specific patterns of population concentration and growth;
- spatially embedded formal economic concentration, agglomeration and growth patterns; and
- enable comparative analyses of fine-grained spatial patterns and changes in spatial patterns within cities – comparing place specific spatial change, as well as comparing spatial change and growth patterns between cities.

4 Developing Spatial Specific Indicators – Challenges and Principles

4.1 Challenges When Developing Spatial Indicators

There are a number of challenges associated with the development of spatial indicators. Some of the most noticeable challenges include the unavailability or incompleteness of data, difficulties collecting source data, methodological changes in the capturing of source data, incomplete time series data and inconsistent statistical methods used in the indicator-development phase. The spatial unit used when capturing data poses additional constraints, such as, (1) size variation, creating a statistical bias also known as the modifiable areal unit problem (MAUP) and (2) significant boundary changes between data collection periods (e.g. census years).

The scalability of data (e.g. South African voting districts which do not align to units such as sub-place or main place or even small area layers) also adds additional constraints in indicator development. It is also the objective to have indicators that are more spatially-specific or of a sufficiently fine resolution to allow the observation of localised changes in the data. This overcomes some of the generalisation that occurs when using larger administrative units such as local municipal boundaries.

4.2 Challenges of Scale

It is important to note that although some of the information collected by various metros, departments and institutions might be collected at local sub-city level, the information presented in the various indicators are regularly aggregated and aimed at a broader scale and intended for a comparison of cities. The reporting units being used for city-level indicators are administrative units (mostly local municipal unit) which do not reflect the true spatial grain of features such as population distribution, land-use patterns, etc. [18]. Metropolitan areas, such as Gauteng, stretch across local municipal boundaries, yet are mostly reported within a particular local municipality (the seat of Metropolitan area). The measurement of items is influenced by the scale that is used, when aggregating information, a measure of generalization occurs [18]. This is particularly relevant when considering an item that is scale-dependant where the geographic extent is sensitive to the spatial arrangement [20, p. 200]. This begs the question – what is its usefulness in measuring spatial transformation? To enable sufficient pattern detection of spatial features it is necessary that the scale be sufficiently fine (for purposes of detecting spatial transformation for example). When the size of measurement unit decreases the spatial variance or heterogeneity also decreases [21]. Appropriate finer-grained information is more useful to grasp the spatially explicit realities which in turn can contribute more to policy–relevant information. A constraint can, however, be in the computational complexity required if a completely new or unaligned fine spatial unit is used.

4.3 Grain of the Tessellation

The resolution of the spatial unit used to present the information can impact on what is portrayed. Using different units to group information can create different statistical and visual results. This is the result of group aggregation and inferencing underlying (continuous) data into different sized zones and is more problematic when larger zones are used [22]. MAUP (a term coined by Openshaw and Taylor in the late 70's) is a well know spatial statistical bias problem when analysing and representing spatial data with varying spatial scale and resolution. This is a particular and noticeable problem when representing quantity mapping (e.g. population densities) [23].

This problem is clearly observed in Fig. 1 showing population changes from 1996 to 2011 using two zone types: map a reflects sub-place units where as map b reflects information using a fine grained uniform hexagon tessellation. The result of what is reflected in terms of growth and decline appears substantially different – aggregation

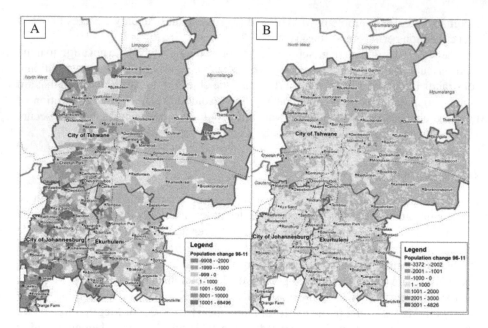

Fig. 1. Change in total population per sub-place 1996–2011 compared to hexagon tessellation for the Tshwane, Johannesburg and Ekurhuleni metros [24].

using the coarser sub-places unit reflects what appears to be substantial increases in quite large areas (and the opposite in cases of decline) whereas, when looking at the same change in a finer grained map (using the same density increments for the thematic map categories), the changes are much more isolated or focused making the areas of change appear less dramatic. This does however allow much more focused analysis of the causes with a high probability that the casual deductions will be more accurate due to less generalisation in the area of influence being considered or then help with a more focused intervention.

5   Research Approach and Methodology

The development and exploration of sub-city indicators required several steps which included; basic research into each item, data extraction (or update if already available), preparation, and calculation of the indicator, as well as considering and reflecting on the standards with respect to developing indicators. However, it also required the development of a separate new uniform tessellation to correct for the spatial bias introduced by the sub-place boundaries.

To improve the spatial resolution of information at sub-city level, a single fine grained uniform hexagon tessellation (using 1 sqkm hexagons) was created for each city. Total population and economic information was assigned to this hexagon tessellation using a dasymetric mapping process, which is defined generally as the use of an ancillary data set to disaggregate coarse resolution data to a finer resolution [25]. This was done for both population and total economic production (process explained later in this section).

5.1 Creation of Tessellation

To accommodate for the statistical bias introduced by size and scale variation (discussed in the previous section) we propose that a 1 sqkm hexagon be used as the basic spatial analysis unit. The unit was considered to be of a fine enough resolution maximising spatial granularity while preserving computational processing time. In order to ensure that the indicators were comparable between cities the hexagons had to nest with the main administrative boundaries of the cities. The process followed to derive the 1 sqkm hexagons included; (1) Selecting all administrative boundaries of participating cities and (2) Subdividing the administrative boundaries of the cities into a fine equal-sized resolution. Various iterations were run to ensure that the finest grain resolution were chosen that still allowed for optimal computational processing time when aggregating the disaggregated data layers.

The administrative city areas were systematically divided into 1 sqkm equally sized hexagons using the 'Repeated shapes for ArcGIS' tool developed by Jenness [26]. Each one of the hexagons derived had a unique assigned spatial ID to serve as the primary key. This basic analysis unit (1 sqkm Hexagon) corrects visual distortions and statistical bias and allows a fine enough resolution to make comparisons of quantities (how much is located were) feasible and statistically significant. Such a unit proves particularly useful for spatial analysis and visualisation due to its equal size and fine resolution.

5.2 Dasymetric Assignment

The population data was assigned to the analysis units (hexagon tessellation) based on an algorithm developed by the CSIR and which is based on the principles of dasymetric mapping. A dasymetric map is the result of a procedure applied to a spatial dataset for which the underlying statistical surface is unknown, but for which the aggregate data already exists. The aggregate dataset's demarcation is however not based on variation in the underlying statistical surface but rather the result of convenience of enumeration [25, 27]. The production of a dasymetric map involves transforming data from the arbitrary zones of the aggregate dataset to recover (or try to recover) and depict the underlying statistical surface. This transformation process incorporates the use of an ancillary dataset that is separate from, but related to, the variation in the statistical surface [25]. Dasymetric mapping therefore has a close relationship with areal interpolation – the transformation of data from a set of source zones to a set of target zones with different geometry [26, 29, 30]. Areal interpolation is mostly an aerial weighting procedure and does not take ancillary sources into consideration when the spatial distribution of data is refined. Many areal interpolation methods can be incorporated into dasymetric mapping methods to improve the detail of a choropleth map below the level of the enumeration unit [29, 31]. As can be deduced from the principles of dasymetric mapping as a method of areal interpolation, the accuracy of the depiction of the data is heavily dependent on the quality of the ancillary data used to predict the variation in the spatial distribution of the variable in question. Another consideration is also that the ancillary data used must be updated regularly (at least yearly) to ensure consistency for future updates [32].

The ancillary data set used in this specific instance was a reclassified version of the SPOT Building count [31], of which ESKOM the national electricity provider, is the custodian. This is a spatial dataset consisting of about 14,000,000 points. Each point representing a building structure in the country. CSIR then went through an incremental process of classifying these points according to the underlying land cover. Then, based on the underlying land cover and amount of people according to the census within the area the point is based in, an approximate number of people – potentially residing in this structure – was assigned to the point. The result is that each point has a potential weight (number of persons residing there) relative to all other points in the country. The points therefore represent, or try to represent, the underlying statistical surface of the census data. As a result of assigning these potential population weights per point a flexible data frame was created to allow the transference of any socio-economic census data (household based data) from any of the census demarcations to a demarcation of choice by the user. This allocation and re-allocation procedure is represented by following inputs and processing steps [32]:

Input variables:

1. Population total per origin unit
2. Points that represent houses for the whole country
3. Weight per point representing potential household size

Process Steps:

4. Link points to origin units
5. Sum the weights of the points belonging to each origin unit
6. Per origin unit divide the weight of each point belonging to that origin unit by the sum of the weights as calculated in (5) above (thus proportional contribution of each point per origin unit)
7. Multiply the proportional contribution of each point with the population of the origin unit that point belongs to (thus redistribute the population per origin unit proportionally to the points inside that origin unit based on the relative weight of the point, getting the population per point)
8. Link points to destination unit
9. Sum the population per point (7 above) for the destination unit a group of points belong to.

5.3   Visualization

There has been large uptake of 3D information through applications such as virtual earth, Google Earth and second life and it is proving very useful for urban planning [34]. Through technology advancement, more application of 3D is becoming available to the mainstream public user. The advantage of presenting spatial information in 3D is that complex information can be provided to audiences with little or no cartographical or GIS experience [35]. In this project the spatial information created in 2D was converted to 3D using ArcGIS Pro. A 3D scene was created using both background layers as well as online maps. Values such as population or economic production numbers were used to create the elevation item. The landscape was titled to portray the 3D extruded values of the hexagon values for the relevant cities. The hexagon information was not only used in 3D map form, the data was also further analysed using transects and is arithmic maps.

An added advantage of using a fine grained uniform hexagon tessellation to portray and analyse the data is that it allows for more aesthetic maps without any MAUP effect. The regular sized grid also contributed to easy and accurate communication of the transect data as each value unit is equal in distance when portrayed on a graph which eliminates any distortions and leads to easy interpretation and communication.

6   Application

Using this fine grained uniform hexagon tessellation enables users to see a less distorted picture of the information because the information is sufficiently fine grained. It can also be displayed in different ways, primarily aimed at the identification and comparison of:

- Spatial patterns of concentration and growth of a particular trend i.e. population density within a city, and also across boundaries – highly useful in discussions regarding nodes, corridors, identification of growth areas in and on border areas, etc. (See Figs. 2 and 3);

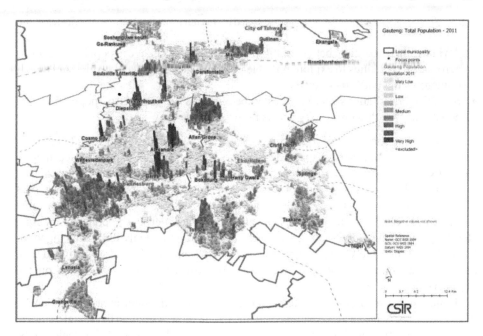

Fig. 2. Spatial patterns of population concentration reflected for the three metropolitan areas in Gauteng for 2011 [24].

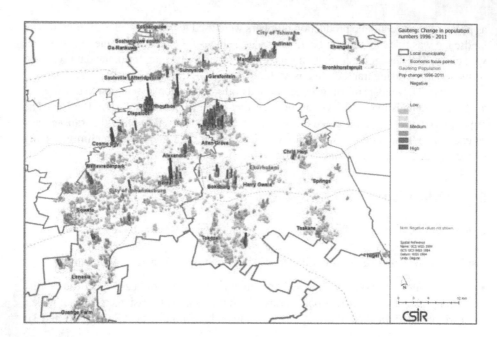

Fig. 3. Spatial patterns of population growth reflected for the three metropolitan areas in Gauteng [24].

- An indicator across time between cities, i.e. increase and change in population density across different cities to explore possible patterns, i.e. increased densities and development on the outskirts of cities;
- Spatial concentrations and changes/embeddedness of patterns of population and economic growth within a city across time (See Fig. 4).

Using a fine grained uniform hexagon tessellation as depicted in Fig. 2 enables a comparable depiction across space. Using GIS software a 3D-bar landscape map is created with the extruded values representing the value of the attribute (population or total economic production). Looking at the 3D tessellation of population further assists in 'reading' the values. The advantage is that the areas of largest growth or highest value can be easily observed more clearly. Dense versus less-densely populated areas are clearly visible. Taking the same spatial surface but comparing only the change in population (Fig. 3) helps to visualize whether the growth that materialised was aligned with development objectives such as 'not developing township type settlements on the periphery of cities', etc.

Using this approach, different items can be depicted for the same area – Fig. 4 depicts the change in population as well as in economic production. Although the actual numbers cannot be compared one-to-one, the change when reflected along a relative scale can be useful when comparing change in population versus economic production.

Considering the locational and strategic planning context it then becomes easier to judge the result of policies such as densification, corridor development or economic development growth points. Comparing planned with actual development can assist in informing planners and city managers whether their efforts in transforming cities, in line

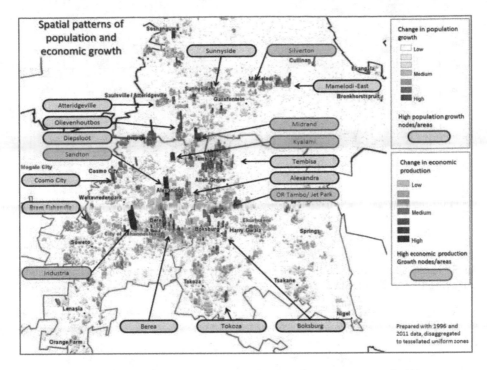

Fig. 4. Comparing spatial patterns of population and economic growth [24].

with their spatial plans, are succeeding or not. The contribution of the spatial concentration and growth indicator is, however, not merely in the identification of patterns as illustrated above, but even more so in enabling advanced spatial analyses related to comparison of patterns across distance bands and over time. An example of comparison of areas across different distance bands is done by developing line transects. Figure 5 uses uniform distance intervals, drawn from this newly developed socio-economic sub-city indicator dataset, where the values are truer when considering distribution and distance than datasets that vary in size. A buffer distance of 5 km is applied along the transect. A more statistically unbiased representation is created because the units along the transect are regular.

In the same vein, comparison of areas across different time scales can be done by developing 'heat contour' maps (see Fig. 6) that also use uniform intervals, where this newly developed socio-economic sub-city indicator dataset enables comparison across time scales whilst data gathering and sub-place area boundaries have shifted.

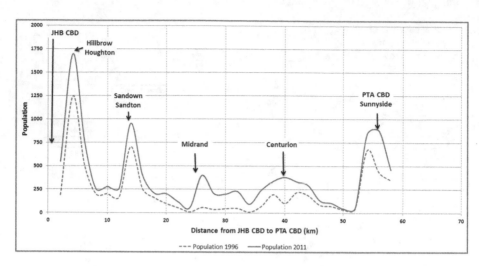

Fig. 5. Linear transect from the JHB CBD to the PTA CBD reflecting the change in population comparing 1996 to 2011 [36].

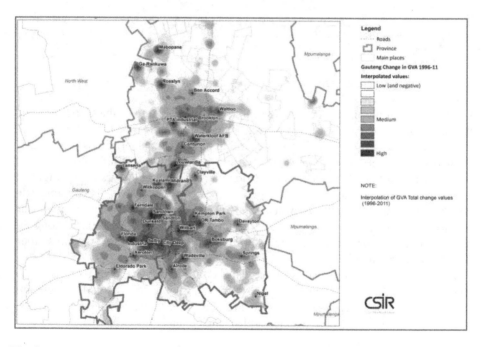

Fig. 6. Highest values reflecting economic nodes in the Gauteng city region, reflecting embedded patterns of economic concentration between the time periods 1996 to 2011 [24].

This paper presented an approach which uses a fine-grained uniform spatial unit to present change and trend data. Given the importance of measuring change and reporting on spatial planning outcomes, the value of finer-grained information becomes obvious.

Considering the examples used it is clear that this is useful in judging the extent of spatial transformation in our cities. Much work still needs to be done to test its application with city authorities and to expand information variables.

7 Reflections and Conclusion

To contribute towards achieving spatial transformation objectives, and tracking progress in this regard, the need for the development, extension and use of spatially and temporally aligned sub-city level indicators is evident. Although there are currently numerous indicators aimed at measuring city performance in South Africa, most utilise only city-level information. This does not reflect the spatial realities underlying change, development or even decay. Such information allows planners and researchers to investigate whether their policies/strategies are having the intended effect. Also critical is that when change is reflected, this also requires that spatial units remain constant (or alternatively it would require an adjustment process where spatial extent has changed). As indicated it is unlikely that a single indicator can measure spatial transformation.

It is crucial to support the wide range of ongoing indicator initiatives in South Africa and internationally, and to strive for the use of trustworthy official data. However, there is also a need to explore the benefits and improvement of spatially refined and aligned sub-city indicators that can provide spatially-specific views on place-specific progress and challenges in the endeavour towards spatial transformation. The innovative approach and findings of the endeavour to develop spatio-temporally aligned sub-city level indicators does not only provide a solid baseline to track change in cities in South Africa, but also provides a basis to explore and improve the development and value of such spatial-specific indicators within the context of developing countries and fast growing cities. In reflecting on the research and development process, a number of key considerations regarding the development, value and use of such indicators can be summarised:

- The value of place-specific views on population increase and decline in specific parts of cities, and especially in city regions (moving beyond the metropolitan/city borders). An indicator built on a finer spatial granularity is more useful to grasp the spatial realities. It can provide a view of population change in the broader area, and not as an aggregate value.
- In order to create fine-grained socio-economic data it is critical to maintain proxy data sets that are used to assign values to such fine-grained spatial units with confidence, in order to create a representative picture.
- It enables spatial analyses and presentation of change in different ways to make comparative analyses possible. It allows for additional analysis - such as creating transects across city space. Keeping the unit type a constant size also makes for better comparison between cities. Should such tessellations be extended beyond the city boundary it will also indicate cross-border change.
- Indicators are often the result of contained data combination or processing, as such it does not represent all realities. For example, depicting economic activity does not include the informal economy.

References

1. The Presidency N.P.C.: National Development Plan: Vision for 2030 (2011). http://www.nationalplanningcommission.org.za/Documents/devplan_ch8_0.pdf. Accessed 20 Oct 2016
2. United Nations: World Urbanization Prospects: The 2014 Revision. Department of Economic and Social Affairs, Population Division (2014) (ST/ESA/SER.A/352)
3. Bertaud, A.: The cost of Utopia: Brasilia, Johannesburg and Moscow (2001). https://www.researchgate.net/publication/237378682_The_costs_of_Utopia_Brasilia_Johannesburg_and_Moscow. Accessed 20 Oct 2016
4. Du Plessis, D.: A critical reflection on urban spatial planning practices and outcomes in post-apartheid South Africa. Urban Forum (2014) **25**(1), 69–88 (2013)
5. Le Roux, A., Augustijn, P.W.M.: Quantifying the spatial implications of future land use policies in South Africa. S. Afr. Geogr. J. **99**(1), 29–51 (2015)
6. Oranje, M., Harrison, P., Van Huyssteen, E., et al.: A Policy Paper on Integrated Development Planning, 63 p. (2000)
7. Oranje, M., Van Huyssteen, E.: Nestling national 'transformation' imperatives in local 'servicing' space: critical reflections on an intergovernmental planning and implementation project. Town Reg. Plann. **58**, 6–16 (2011)
8. SA Cities Network: SPLUMA as a tool for spatial transformation. Johannesburg (2015)
9. National Planning Commission: National Development Plan, Pretoria, SA Cities Network, 70 p. (2012)
10. Todes, A.: Urban growth and strategic spatial planning in Johannesburg. S. Afr. Cities **29**(3), 158–165 (2012)
11. UNDP: The impacts of social and economic inequality on economic development in South Africa. Prepared by TIPS for UNDP, New York (2014)
12. Turok, I.: Settlement planning and urban transformation. In: Spatial Transformation of Cities Conference, Pretoria, 4–6 March 2014
13. Harrison, P., Todes, A.: Spatial transformation in a "loosening state": South Africa in a comparative perspective. Geoforum **61**, 148–162 (2015)
14. Oranje, M.: Spatial transformation and urban restructuring: lessons for the 20-year old post-apartheid south African city? In: Spatial Transformation of Cities, Pretoria, 4–6 March 2014
15. Amindarbari, R., Sevtsuk, A.: Measuring growth and change. In: Metropolitan Form (working paper), City Form Lab, Cambridge 30 p. (2013)
16. Bickford, G.: Transit oriented development: an appropriate tool to drive improved mobility and accessibility in South African cities? In: Spatial Transformation of Cities, Pretoria, 4–6 March 2014
17. Kusek, J.Z., Rist, R.C.: Ten steps to a results based monitoring and evaluation system. In: A Handbook for Development Practitioners, 268 p. The World Bank, Washington, DC (2004)
18. Hagenlocher, M., Kienberger, S., Lang, S. et al.: Implications of spatial scales and reporting units for the spatial modelling of vulnerability to vector-borne diseases. In: GI Forum 2014 - Geospatial Innovation for Society, pp. 197–206. OAW Verlag, Wien (2014)
19. Fotheringham, A.S.: Scale-dependant spatial analysi. In: Goodchild, M., Gopal, S. (eds.) Accuracy of Spatial Databases, pp. 221–228. Taylor and Francis, London (1989)
20. Blaschke, T.: The role of the spatial dimention within the framework of sustainable landscapes and natural capital. Landscape Urban Plann. **75**(3–4), 198–226 (2005)
21. McGarigal, K.: UMass Landscape Ecology Lab (2013). http://www.umass.edu/landeco/teaching/landscape_ecology/schedule/landeco_schedule.html. Accessed 22 Oct 2016
22. Jelinski, D., Wu, J.: The modifiable areal unit problem and implications for landscape ecology. Landscape Ecol. **11**(3), 129–140 (1996)

23. Wong, D.W.S.: The Modifiable Areal Unit Problem (MAUP). In: Janelle, D.G., Warf, B., Hansen, K. (eds.) WorldMinds: Geographical Perspectives on 100 Problems: Commemorating the 100th Anniversary of the Association of American Geographers 1904–2004, p. 638. Dordrecht, Netherlands (2004)
24. Maritz, J.: Selected indicators for SACN SOCR2015 (SET 2). CSIR, Pretoria (2015)
25. Eicher, C.L., Brewer, C.A.: Dasymetric mapping and areal interpolation: implementation and evaluation. Cartography Geogr. Inf. Sci. **28**(2), 125–138 (2001)
26. Jenness, J.: Jeff Jenness - ArcGIS repeating shapes (2012). http://www.jennessent.com/arcgis/repeat_shapes.htm. Accessed 18 Oct 2016
27. Mennis, J., Hultgren, T.: Dasymetric mapping for disaggregating coarse resolution population data. In: Proceedings of the 22nd Annual International Cartographic Conference, Coruna, Spain, 6–9 July 2005
28. Bloom, L.M., Pedler, P.J., Wragg, G.E.: Implementation of enhanced areal interpolation using MapInfo. Comput. Geosci. **22**(5), 459–466 (1996)
29. Fisher, P.F., Langford, M.: Modelling the errors in areal interpolation between zonal systems by Monte Carlo simulation. Environ. Plann. **27**(2), 211–244 (1995)
30. Goodchild, M.F., Lam, N.S.: Areal Interpolation: a variant of the traditional spatial problem. Geo-processing **1**, 297–312 (1980)
31. Hay, S.I., Noor, A.M., Nelson, A., et al.: The accuracy of human population maps for public health application. Trop. Med. Int. Health **10**(10), 1073–1086 (2005)
32. Mans, G.: Developing a geo-data frame using dasymetric mapping principles to facilitate data integration. In: AfriGEO Conference: Developing Geomatics for Africa, Cape Town, May–June (2011)
33. De La Rey, A.: Enabling decision making with the SPOT5 building count. Position IT, Pretoria, June 2008 (2008)
34. Ki, J.: Developing a GIS based web-GIS system for landscape and urban planning. Int. J. Dig. Earth **6**(6), 580–588 (2013)
35. Voženílek, V.: Cartography for GIS: Geovisualization and Map Communication. Palacký University, Olomouc (2005)
36. Napier, M., Le Roux, A., Van Heerden, J.L.: Seeing spatial inequality: analysing density and value gradients in South African cities to test commonly held assumptions and inform future action (working paper). CSIR, Pretoria (2016)

The Impact of Land-Use Changes
on Accessibility to Forests and Potential
for Leisure Time Physical Activity

A Scenario Based Approach

Henning Sten Hansen[(✉)]

Aalborg University Copenhagen,
A.C. Meyers Vaenge 15, 2450 Copenhagen, Denmark
hsh@plan.aau.dk

Abstract. Land-use changes is an ongoing process where particularly the urban expansion is taking place at a steadily increasing rate. Sometime spontaneous and in other occasions planned. Often the urban growth takes place on former forest or agriculture land. However, with the increasing awareness of nature protection, climate change, and human health, some regions plan for a more sustainable use of land by nature restauration and afforestation programmes. Through a scenario based approach the current paper analyses how land-use changes exemplified through the Danish afforestation programme can contribute to increasing accessibility to forest areas and create enhanced possibilities for a more physical active leisure time, which is important to avoid several life style related diseases like obesity, type 2 diabetes, and circulatory disturbances.

Keywords: Land-use changes · Urban growth · Afforestation · Physical activity · Public health · GIS modelling

1 Introduction

Land-use changes are complex interactions between the human society and the bio-physical environment. Land-use change has several important drivers, where the increasing demand for living space per person is a leading driver in urban growth and infrastructure expansion. Thus, the Danish built-up land has increased from 6% in 1995 to 7% in 2015 land cover, and this expansion has mainly taken place on farmland, which has been reduced from 66% in 1995 to 61% in 2015[1].

Currently about 14.5% of the Danish surface are covered with forest, but since 1989 the official Danish policy has been to double the Danish forest area before the end of the 21th century [1, 2]. According to Statistics Denmark the forest area has increased from 445,391 ha in 1990 to 615,254 ha in 2013 (see Footnote 1). While the objective of doubling the forest area was originally triggered by agricultural over production, the focus is now on nature values and opportunities for outdoor recreation. The experiences have shown that economic incentives are a prerequisite for afforestation on privately

---

[1] http://www.statistikbanken.dk/statbank5a/selectvarval/saveselections.asp.

© Springer International Publishing AG 2017
O. Gervasi et al. (Eds.): ICCSA 2017, Part IV, LNCS 10407, pp. 422–436, 2017.
DOI: 10.1007/978-3-319-62401-3_31

owned land. Possible financial sources may include CO_2 sequestration, groundwater protection measures, air quality improvement and achieving recreational values. Therefore, the subsidised afforestation will prioritise size, continuity to existing forests, landscape considerations, drinking water interests, and proximity to urban areas. According to these principles, the Danish area is subdivided into three major groups: (a) positive areas with enhanced subsidies for private afforestation, (b) negative areas where afforestation is prohibited, and (c) other areas where afforestation is allowed but without public subsidies.

During the last 10–15 years there has been enhanced focus on the health effects of prolonged sitting during leisure time – e.g. TV watching, computer use, or driving a car. Studies have demonstrated that sedentary leisure time behaviour is a risk factor for type 2 diabetes, cardiovascular diseases, and colon cancer, which shortens life expectancy [3]. Several studies have focused on the role of the surrounding environment, since sedentary behaviour may be influenced by the physical context we live in [4]. Thus, many studies have found, that accessibility to green space to be associated with leisure time physical activity [5].

Therefore, the aim of the current research has been to analyse how the future land-use development with parallel urban expansion and increased forest area will impact the citizen's accessibility to forests - and the potential for increased physical activity. After the current introduction follows a chapter on the theories applied. Next, the implementation of the modelling framework is described and the results presented and discussed. The paper ends with a conclusion and outlines for further research within the topic.

2 Theory

Land-use modelling at detailed level is a challenging task, and several methods have been developed during the last nearly 20 years. Below, we describe the method applied in the current paper. In addition, we describe current research on the relationship between accessibility to green spaces – e.g., forests – and leisure time physical activity.

2.1 Land-Use Modelling

The projections of future land-use are based on the LUCIA (Land Use Change Impact Analysis) modelling framework [6–10]. Basically, LUCIA simulates future land-use patterns based on socio-economic drivers at two distinct levels – a regional level represented by counties or municipalities and a local level represented by cells in a regular lattice. LUCIA is a traditional multi-criteria evaluation system with factors and constraints, where the spatial dynamics are modelled through constrained cellular automata (CA). Cellular automata is an obvious way to take spatial interaction into account and CA based models have been a very popular way of implementing dynamic land-use models. Basically, cellular automata models determine the number of cells to be changed in the next time step endogenously based on the transition rules defined. However, the pure CA approach is not appropriate for land-use simulation, and like other recent CA based models [11]. LUCIA is based on constraint cellular automata being driven by external forces. LUCIA has a multi-level structure, where the upper regional level represents the drivers, whereas the detailed lower level represents the land-use.

The amount of land is in practice fixed, and therefore a competition for land between the different land-use classes exists. Land is devoted to the use that generates the highest potential profitability, although this principle is modified by legal constraints like designation of protected areas. These principles lead to a land-use competition hierarchy, where protected areas take the primary position, followed by urban land-use, cropland, grassland, and forest [12].

The cells are divided into three main categories: The active land-use types, which are forced by demands generated externally; the passive land-use types, which enter into the calculations by being transformed into an active land-use, and finally the static land-uses types, which cannot be transformed, but may affect the land-use simulation by attracting or repelling land-use transformation in their vicinity. Thus, the cells needed for urban development are first allocated from the passive or the secondary/tertiary active land-use classes. Next, the secondary active land-use class takes it share, from the passive or tertiary classes etc. The passive land-use classes are mainly represented by different kinds of natural vegetation, but most often crop and grassland serves as a passive class for urban expansion. The static classes remain unchanged during the simulation.

The driving forces for the quantity of rural-urban change are population growth and economic development. These drivers represent what we call macro-level drivers, and they are modelled externally to our model in various sector models, and thus define the demand for land from each active land-use type. Many national statistical offices make every year national level projections for population, and these national figures are afterwards distributed to the local level (municipalities).

At the micro level, we deal with factors often used in various land-use modelling efforts. The first factor involved in the model is the neighbouring effect, which represents the attractive or repulsive effects of various land-uses within the neighbourhood. It is generally well known that some land-use types for example private service (shopping) tends to cluster, whereas others – e.g. recreation and industry tend to repel each other. However, cells, which are more remote, will have a smaller effect. Within the model, we refer to this effect by the term proximity. Often the proximity effect has been estimated through the calibration phase, but we have developed a new method to quantify and analyse neighbour effect in land-use modelling [13]. Through access to urban land-use maps for several consecutive years, we can easily identify the neighbouring land-uses for new urban cells. The empirically derived neighbourhood functions confirm the expected positive attraction between existing residential areas and new cells with residential land-use. Similarly, our expectations regarding the repellent effect between existing industrial land-use and new residential cells are confirmed. Besides proximity, LUCIA can handle up to 5 additional factors. The second of the factors is the suitability of each grid cell – i.e. how the specific characteristics of each cell can support a given land-use. The third factor is accessibility – i.e. access to the transportation network. Some activities like shopping require better accessibility than for example recreational activities. Often the latter activity even feels attracted to areas with low accessibility due to for example lower noise levels in such areas. These three

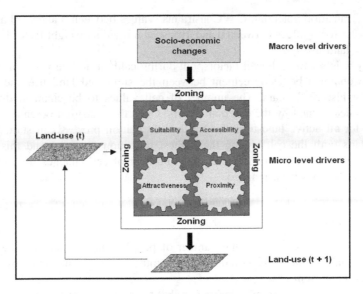

Fig. 1. The LUCIA modelling framework

headline factors – proximity, suitability and accessibility define the basic preconditions for the cells ability to support a given urban land-use, and are in some degree fixed, although the accessibility can be changed by for example improving the infrastructure. Currently, we have used land values and accessibility motorway junctions as optional factors. Finally, we have added a random raster to support spontaneous growth. The strength of the random element can be managed by a factor weight. The overall modelling concept is illustrated in Fig. 1.

Policy making at national and local level have a strong influence on land-use – particularly policies that have a spatial manifestation like creation of conservation areas or designation of areas for subsidised development [14]. However, more general legislation like the EU Common Agricultural Policy has a strong indirect influence on the spatial development in the rural areas. However, the current version of the model does only involve policies and legislation with an explicit spatial aim under the headline Zoning.

The factors have dimensionless values between 0.0 and 1.0, whereas the constraints (Zoning) most often have binary values – 0 or 1. However, if needed, continuous constraints are supported. By combining the factors and constraints for each active land-use type (L), we can estimate for each cell the transition potential (P) for changing the land-use from one type to another. Additionally, we need to incorporate the spatial distribution of the socio-economic drivers.

The potential for each cell to change land-use type at the next time step is given by the function below

$$PL(t+1) = CL1(t) * CL2 * \ldots CLn * \sum (wLi * FLi)$$

where P = Transition potential, C = Constraints (values between 0 and 1 – but often 0 or 10), F = Factors (values between 0 and 10), w = individual weight factor between 0 and 10, L = land-use type.

Initially w is set to 10 for all factors, but during calibration, the value of w can be lowered to obtain a better agreement between the simulated land use and the real land-use for historical years. The number of cell values to be changed during the iterations is determined by the external drivers. Once the transition potential has been calculated for all active land-uses the cell transformation process can start. The cell changes starts with the cell having the highest transition potential and this process proceeds downwards until the predetermined number of cell changes for each active land-use category has been reached.

2.2   Population Density

Population density is defined as the number of people within a specific spatial unit. Thus, we can talk about population density in countries, cities, municipalities, and grid cells - as in the current case.

When you have point based information about each person in the study area it is a straight forward process to calculate the population density unit by just counting the number of persons within each spatial unit. However, in most cases this is not the situation, and even if we had access to data on every single person for historical years, the density for each spatial unit will change over time. The approach applied in the current project is based on the assumption, that each residential-cell within a munici-pality for example will have the same population density. Population projections for each of the simulation years are the main driver for urban development in the LUCIA model, and accordingly available for each spatial unit at the macro level. The popu-lation density for each cell in a macro level spatial unit can then be calculated by dividing the population within that spatial unit with the number of residential cells within the spatial unit. This calculation is repeated for all macro level spatial unit, and for all simulation years. This approach supports the possibility to have different pop-ulation densities between highly urbanised areas compared to less urbanised areas.

2.3   Physical Activity and Accessibility to Green Space

The accessibility to green space is one of the environmental factors that is most often related to levels of physical activity, and many studies have shown that there is a distance decay in the use of recreational facilities. Accessibility is here defined as the ability of city dwellers to reach green space. Thus, Nielsen and Hansen [15] found a highly significant association between distance and use for all types of green areas – summer time as well as winter time. The distance decay found was in all instances characterised by a rather steep decline in use frequency with increasing distance. This was particularly evident after the first 100–300 m distance [15].

In another study, Neuvonen et al. [16] found that the shorter the distance to green space areas, the more frequently the citizens will visit and use them. In their study from Helsinki they analysed two different types of areas – one type with 30% green space and another type with 60% green space. The highest degree of participation in recreation was found in neighbourhoods adjacent to areas with 60% green space, and the lowest degree of participation was found in neighbourhoods with only 30% green space coverage within 2 km distance from the neighbourhood.

A third study by Toftager et al. [17] confirmed the importance of distance and concluded that citizens living more than 1 km from green space had lower use of green space than citizens living closer than 300 m to green space. Schipperijn et al. [18] brought another aspect of green space into the accessibility to green space discourse by introducing the 'quality' aspect. He found that the 'quality' of the green space has an impact in the attractiveness for walking, running, playing, etc., and for example wooded areas has a significant effect.

The studies presented here all shows that the distance to green areas is an important factor to explain visits to recreation areas defined as forests and green parks.

3 Implementation

3.1 The Study Area

The research is carried out in Region North Jutland, which is one of the five Danish regions, and Aalborg University is located within this region. The region corresponds to the dark green area in Fig. 2. The area of Region North Jutland is 7881 km^2, and the population was 587,335 by January 2017. The largest municipality Aalborg had 211,937 inhabitants by January 2017[2]. Region North Jutland is generally considered as a region lacking behind in economic development, and the annual average income is 37,500€, which is clearly below the national average income of 41,360€ per person[2].

The Danish regions carried out detailed surveys on public health among the adult population in 2010 and 2013[3]. The aim of the survey was to analyse quality of life, health behaviour, and sickliness in the adult population for health planning purposes and to identify regional differences. Physical activity was one of the variable being analysed, and the distribution can be seen at Fig. 3. Among the five Danish regions Region Northern Jutland had the highest degree of self-reported sedentary lifestyle with 18.3% in 2010. The Copenhagen Metropolitan Region the similar value was 14.2%. The situation in Region Northern Jutland was a little improved in 2013, where the share of adults with sedentary lifestyle dropped to 17%.

According to the same surveys about two thirds of the adult population aims at increasing their level of leisure time physical activity, and therefore we have chosen Region Northern Jutland as case area in the current paper. The total sample in both surveys included 35,700 individuals, which were invited by mail to participate in the health survey by filling out an enclosed paper questionnaire or complete the questionnaire online. The response rate was 65.5% in 2010 but lowered to 56.6% in 2013 [19]. When assessing the results you need to be careful about the representativeness of the answers, when only about half of the population actually responded to the questionnaire.

---

[2] https://www.statistikbanken.dk/statbank5a/default.asp?w=2560.

[3] http://www.danskernessundhed.dk.

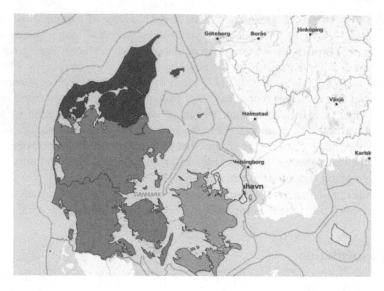

Fig. 2. The regional distribution of self-reported sedentary leisure time 2010. Region Northern Jutland is the dark green area in the north-west. (Color figure online)

3.2   Drivers for Land-Use Change

The socio-economic drivers at the macro level (here municipality level) comprise factors such as: population change, industrial structure, economic development, technological change, policies and legislation. These conceptual drivers must be converted into demand for land for all the active land-use types, and this process is not straightforward at all. Generally, we will expect that a growing population will increase the demand for residential purposes, and this is usually correct, but what about static and even declining population. This situation could free cells from residential to other purposes, but this is seldom the case. Within Region Northern Jutland the number of people rose marginally from 580,190 to 582,168 – corresponding to just 0.003% - during the calibration period from 2000 to 2015. Some municipalities have even experienced declining population – and at the same time an enlarged residential area! This reflects the so-called thinning out effect, where each dwelling unit houses fewer and fewer people [20, 21]. The subsidisation for afforestation is reflected in the model by assigning a factor grid with the value 10 for the positive areas, the value 4 for the areas without subsidisation, and the value 0 for the negative areas.

3.3   Data

Land-use simulation involves a wide range of data, and providing the data needed as well as the pre-processing is a rather time consuming effort. The data set used in the current project is land-use data, soil type data, road network, land values, spatial planning regulations, population development, and regional economic growth index. The basic source for land-use information in the model is CORINE land-cover for the years 2000, 2006, and 2012. Unfortunately, the level of thematic detail in CORINE land-cover does not satisfy our requirements for the built-up areas and protected nature. Therefore, we introduced two auxiliary data sets. The Danish Building and Housing register, which contains detailed information about each building in Denmark and facilitates the construction of spatio-temporal database for urban land-use [22]. Currently we were only interested in the following urban land-use categories: residential, industry, service, and summer cottages. Using the Danish national 100×100 m grid we summarised the built-up area for each use category within each grid cell and assigned the use having the biggest area to the cell. A further criterion is that the number of urban cells within a 3×3 Moore neighbourhood must be greater than 1—otherwise it is not considered built-up. The next step was to merge the new detailed urban land-use data sets with CORINE, in order to produce the final and improved land-use layers. Thus 16 new land-use grids for each of the years 2000–2015 were produced.

The land-use types are divided into three categories (Table 1). The most important category is active land-use types, which are forced by the demands generated externally. Another category is passive land-use types, which are not driven by an external demand, but on the other hand enter into the calculations, because cells can disappear by being transformed into one of the active land-uses. The final category is the static land-uses, which cannot be transformed into one of the active land-uses, but will nevertheless affect the land-use simulation by attracting or repelling land-use transformation within their vicinity.

Remark, that forest is listed under as well the active as the passive land-use classes. Forest is a secondary active land-use meaning that urban development can take place on forestland, but at the same time forest can expand on for example agriculture land.

3.4 Scenarios

Scenarios have often been used to facilitate discussions on a wide range of challenging topics like climate change [23, 24], but contrary to assessing the impact of current activities, the future can only be imagined vaguely and beyond our immediate time horizon. Thus, the economic development, demographic change, introduction of new technologies, and adopting new regulations and policies – all influence the future land-use. Therefore, scenarios are fictional - being impossible to verify; scenarios are predictive describing what *could* happen but not what *will* happen [25].

Currently, we have developed two different policy scenarios describing the possible development paths for the future land-use in Northern Jutland.

Baseline scenario: This scenario is a 'simple' projection based on model parameters, which are calibrated using the period 2000–2015. This scenario is only described as a reference scenario, but is not used for any land-use projections in the further impact analysis. The future demands for land needed for housing, industry and service use are based on existing official population projections at municipality level until 2040. The expected demand for new summer cottages is basically dependent on the economic growth, and – of-course - no official projections are available. Therefore, we assume the future yearly growth to be equal to observed average demand for the period 2000–2015. The constraints represented by the Danish spatial planning regulations are

Table 1. Land-use divided into dynamic categories

Active classes	Passive classes	Static classes
Residential areas	Grass and arable land	Harbours
Industrial areas	Forest	Airports
Service areas	Semi-nature	Waste & extraction
Summer cottages	Wetlands	Lakes
Forest	Recreational areas	Sea

crisp (values 0 or 1). The afforestation is as expected in the policy of doubling the Danish forest area before the end of the century.

Scenario A: This scenario is nearly like a 'simple' projection of the current situation, but it represents a more sustainable societal development. As mentioned earlier we have already very strict spatial planning rules, limiting urban sprawl, and during the last ten years the bigger cities in Denmark with a wider supply of jobs and services have experienced a rapid growth, while the smaller villages in the periphery of the country have suffered under a declining population. Medium sized towns with frequent and fast public transport connections to the larger cities are also attractive locations for living.

This development is reflected in the modelling by expecting a decrease of 10% in per-capita land consumption and by introducing into the model an urban density factor. Urban density is here defined as the focal sum of the number of urban cells within a 3500-metre circular radius. The afforestation programme is following the original ambitions on doubling the forest area within a 100-years period in accordance with the focus on sustainable development in this scenario.

Scenario B: Generally, we have very strong and binding spatial planning regulations, but in during the last 2–3 years we can observe a deregulation of the national planning acts. Therefore, we have changed the spatial planning constraints, so it is partly legal to create new settlements in areas, which is prohibited today and in scenario A. The 0 and 1 constraint values in the scenario A are replaced by 0.4 and 0.6 respectively in scenario A to represent the effect of weaker spatial planning regulations. Furthermore, the weight associated with the proximity factor is reduced with 50% compared to scenario A in order to impede edge growth. Finally, the effect of the random factor is doubled compared to scenario A to support spontaneous growth. The population drivers are similar to the baseline scenario, but the estimated demands for land are increased by 10% to reflect the expected higher per-capita land consumption as expected in A. In addition, it is expected that rapidly decreasing fuel prices will encourage the citizens to settle outside the larger cities, where the house prices are too high for many citizens. The afforestation project is reduced to 25% of the original ambitions is expected due to the less focus on environment in policy scenario A.

4   Results and Discussion

The simulation period was limited to 25 years from 2015 to 2040 for each of the two scenarios. This is a rather long-term planning horizon, and beyond such a time span uncertainty will increase dramatically. The cell size applied is 100×100 m, and the model contains $1905 \times 1370 = 2,609,850$ grid cells. Calibration of the factor weights was carried out using a fifteen-year period from 2000 to 2015.

For the A scenario, the built-up areas increase from 28579 ha to 29541 ha, the forest areas increase from 78609 ha to 95602 ha, while the agricultural areas are being reduced from 408271 ha to 397184 ha within the same 25-years simulation period. For the B scenario, the built-up areas expand to 29975 ha, the forest area to 82890 ha, and the agriculture areas are reduced to 404355 ha.

The results of the two simulations can be seen in Figs. 3 and 4, where we have zoomed into an area around Aalborg – the capital city in Northern Jutland. The lighter red areas represent the residential areas, whereas the forests are shown in darker green. The differences in residential areas are not so obvious, but a closer inspection shows that the smaller settlements are growing more in scenario B compared to scenario A, where the urban expansion is more compact. The expansion of forest areas is – as expected - much more visible between the two scenarios, where scenario A shows much larger forest areas than scenario B.

In order to find the residential areas within walking distance from the nearest forests, two buffer zones of 300 m and 600 m respectively were created using the Expand tool in LUCIA. Euclidian distances were used in the calculation of buffer zones. The black areas refer to residential areas within 300 m from forest areas, whereas the grey areas refer to residential areas within 600 m from forests.

Next step, was to estimate the number of people living within each buffer zone applying the method described above in paragraph 2.2. The population density for all residential cells were calculated for each of the three years and for both scenarios. Then, the number of people living within 300 m and 600 m from forests is estimated (Fig. 5).

For scenario A with centralised urban development the number of hectare residential area within the 300-metre buffer zone increased from 2908 in 2015 to 3598 in 2040 corresponding to 24%, and the number of people living that distance from forests increased from 54399 to 65668, which is nearly 21%. The reason behind the little lower percentage increase in population compared to the expansion of residential area is due to the differences in population density across the region. The 600-metre buffer zone generates similar results when comparing the years 2015 and 2040. The residential area within 600 m from forests increased with 25% (from 5883 ha to 7381 ha) and the number of people with 23% (from 108402 to 132826). Thus, even for a centralised urban development scenario, the afforestation programme can increase the number of people living within reasonable distance from forests with more than 20%.

For the B scenario with more decentralised urban development but with slower afforestation rate, the residential area within the 300-metre buffer zone increases from 2908 ha in 2015 to 3285 ha in 2040. This a growth of about 13%. The number of people living within this zone increases from 54399 to 59532 corresponding to 9%.

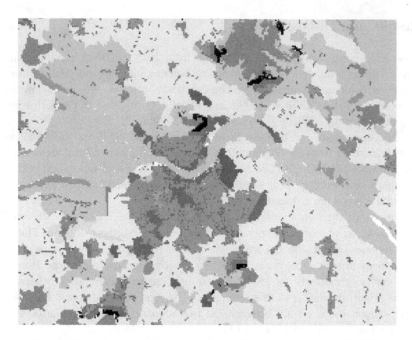

Fig. 3. Land-use simulation result 2040 - Scenario A. Scale 1:250,000.

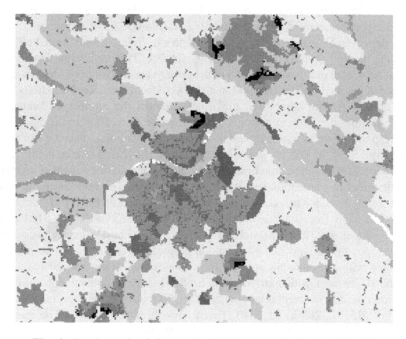

Fig. 4. Land-use simulation result 2040–Scenario B. Scale 1:250,000.

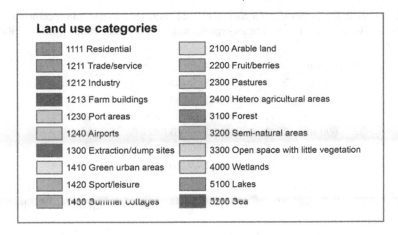

Land use categories

1111 Residential		2100 Arable land	
1211 Trade/service		2200 Fruit/berries	
1212 Industry		2300 Pastures	
1213 Farm buildings		2400 Hetero agricultural areas	
1230 Port areas		3100 Forest	
1240 Airports		3200 Semi-natural areas	
1300 Extraction/dump sites		3300 Open space with little vegetation	
1410 Green urban areas		4000 Wetlands	
1420 Sport/leisure		5100 Lakes	
1430 Summer cottages		5200 Sea	

Fig. 5. Legend for the land-use maps

Within the 600-metre buffer zone, the residential area increases with 19% from 5883 ha in 2015 to 7004 ha in 2040, and the number of people within this zone increases with 15% from 108,402 to 124,632. This is clearly lower than in scenario A, but still not so low as expected from the large reduction in afforestation. The reason for this is that the decentralised urban development will expand smaller villages compared with scenario A.

An overall comparison between the two scenarios shows that the rate of afforestation has the largest effect on accessibility to forests than a centralised versus decentralised urban development strategy. Thus, in 2040 there will be 8000 more people living within the neighbourhood of forests in scenario A than in B. The population figures, for Region North Jutland was 582,168 in 2015 and is estimated to be 591,295 in 2040. Following scenario A this means that the number of people living within less than 600 m from forest increase from 19% of the region's population to 23% in 2040 (Table 2).

At the end, we will add some critical points to our research. First, the Euclidian accessibility measure applied din the current paper can be questioned although walking and running people do not necessary need to follow roads, footpaths, and biking paths. However, if you want to use your bike, or walking with a baby carriage, it is off-course important that you can follow a road or path to your destination, but using a raster based modelling approach with a 100-metre cell size, we have to rely on Euclidian distances.

Population density is not straight forward to estimate on 100-metre grid cells. The population density is partly related to the value of land. Higher land values in the larger cities generally result in higher population density, whereas lower land values in smaller towns and villages provide possibilities for larger parcels and therefore lower population densities. This challenge is only partly addressed in the current research. Aalborg is the only larger city on Region Northern Jutland, and it has overall a higher population density than the other municipalities, but the density varies a lot from very high in the centre of Aalborg City to much lower density in the Western part of the city

Table 2. Accessibility to forest as number of hectare residential area within specified distances from forests. The numbers in parentheses representing people living within specified distances from forest.

Distance	Year	Scenario A	Scenario B
300 m	2000	2796 ha/(53585)	
	2015	2908 ha/(54399)	
	2040	3598 ha/(65668)	3285 ha/(59532)
600 m	2000	5522 ha/(105206)	
	2015	5883 ha/(108402)	
	2040	7381 ha (132826)	7004 ha (124632)

with very large and expensive villas, and in Eastern Aalborg with a lot of multi-storeys residential buildings.

Healthy lifestyle is not only about having easy access to forest and nature areas for doing physical activity. Socio-economic status is also a determining factor, but several studies have shown that regardless of socio-economic status good conditions there is a significant relationship between accessibility to green space and leisure time physical activity [4, 15, 17]. However, there is no linear relationship between accessibility green space and leisure time physical activity. Thus, a 20% increase in accessibility to green space does not imply that the number of people actually being physical active in their leisure time with 20%, but there is a potential for more people to forget the sedentary life style.

5   Conclusion

Land-use changes takes place every day, and where the most important changes are related to urban growth, and most often taking place on former agriculture land but in some occasions even forests [26]. Denmark has rather little forest area, and the increasing awareness of nature protection, climate change, and human health, some regions plan for a more sustainable use of land by nature restauration and afforestation programmes. For the land-use simulation we used the LUCIA model, which has been used in several other land-use related projects

Human health has received more attention during the last 10–15 years, where there has been enhanced focus on the sedentary life style, which implies obesity, diabetes 2, and different cardiovascular diseases. Parallel to this several studies have shown, that easy accessibility to green space like forests has a positive effect on people's physical activity level during leisure time.

Through a scenario based approach the current paper has analysed how land-use changes can contribute to increasing accessibility to forest areas and create enhanced possibilities for a more physical active leisure time. The LUCIA land-use simulation model is applied and the future land-use until 2040 is calculated for two different scenarios is created. Scenario A assumes a centralised urban development together with an afforestation programme aiming at doubling the Danish forest areas before the end of the century. The other scenario B assumes a more growth oriented development with decentralised urban development and with a 50% lower afforestation rate compared with scenario A. Both scenarios exhibit as expected an increased accessibility to forest measured as the number of people living within 300 m and 600 m from forest respectively. For scenario A the number of people living within 600 m from forest increased with 23% and for scenario B the number of people living within the 600 m buffer zone increased with 15%. Thus, it can be concluded that a decentralised urbanisation facilitates people's accessibility to green space and accordingly potential for people being more physical active in their leisure time.

The next step will be to extend the current study to cover the whole Danish territory and further developing the population density algorithm to avoid the disadvantages using the current method.

References

1. Danish Forest and Nature Agency: The Danish National Forest Programme in an International Perspective. Ministry of the Environment, Copenhagen (2004)
2. Madsen, L.M.: The Danish afforestation programme and spatial planning: new challenges. Landscape Urban Plan. **58**, 241–254 (2012)
3. Lee, I.M., Shiroma, E.J., Lobelo, F., Puska, P., Blair, S.N., Katzmarzyk, P.T.: Effect of physical inactivity on major non-communicable diseases worldwide: an analysis of burden of disease and life expectancy. The Lancet **380**, 219–229 (2012)
4. Storgaard, R.L., Hansen, H.S., Aadahl, M., Glümer, C.: Association between neighbourhood green space and sedentary lifestyle time in a Danish population. Scand. J. Public Health **41**, 846–852 (2013)
5. Coombes, E., Jones, A.P., Hillsdon, M.: The relationship of physical activity and overweight to objectively measured green space accessibility and use. Soc. Sci. Med. **70**, 816–822 (2010)
6. Hansen, H.S.: An adaptive land-use simulation model for integrated coastal zone planning. In: The European Information Society. Lecture Notes in Geoinformation and Cartography, pp. 35–53 (2007)
7. Hansen, H.S.: LUCIA - a tool for analysing the environmental impact by land-use changes. Kart og Plan **68**, 20–28 (2008)
8. Hansen, H.S.: Modelling the future coastal zone urban development as implied by the IPCC SRES and assessing the impact from sea level rise. Landscape Urban Plan. **98**, 141–149 (2010)
9. Fuglsang, M., Münier, B., Hansen, H.S.: Modelling land-use effects of future urbanization using cellular automata: an Eastern Danish case. Environ. Model Softw. **50**, 1–11 (2013)
10. Hallin-Pihlatie, L., Rintala, J., AndeHasnen, H.S.: Integration of climate change land-use scenarios in nutrient leaching assessment. Int. J. Clim. Change Strat. Manage. **5**, 285–303 (2013)
11. Barredo, J.I., Kasanko, M., McCormick, N., Lavalle, C.: Modelling dynamic spatial processes: simulation of urban future scenarios through cellular automata. Landscape Urban Plan. **64**, 145–160 (2003)
12. Rounsevell, M.D.A., Reginster, I., Araújo, M.B., Carter, T.R., Dendoncker, N., Ewert, F., House, J.I., Kankaanpää, S., Leemans, R., Metzger, M.J., Schmit, C., Smith, P., Tuck, G.: A coherent set of future land use change scenarios for Europe. Agr. Ecosyst. Environ. **114**, 57–68 (2006)

13. Hansen, H.S.: Empirically derived neighbourhood rules for urban land-use modelling. Environ. Plan. **39**, 213–228 (2012)
14. Verburg, P.H., Schot, P., Dijst, M.J., Veldkamp, A.: Land use changes modelling: current practice and research priorities. GeoJournal **61**, 309–324 (2004)
15. Nielsen, T.S., Hansen, K.B.: Do green areas affect health? Results from a Danish survey on the use of green areas and health indicators. Health Place **13**, 839–850 (2007)
16. Neuvonen, M., Sievanen, T., Tönnes, S., Koskela, T.: Access to green areas and the frequency of visits – a case stydy in Helsinki. Urban Forestry Urban Greening **6**, 235–247 (2007)
17. Toftager, M., Ekholm, O., Schipperijn, J., Stigsdotter, U., Bentsen, P., Groenbaek, M., Randrup, T.B., Kamper-Joergernsen, F.: Distance to green space and physical activity: a Danish national representative survey. J. Phys. Act. Health **8**, 741–749 (2011)
18. Schipperijn, J., Bentsen, P., Troelsen, J., Toftager, M., Stigsdotter, U.: Associations between physical activity and characteristics of urban green space. Urban Forestry Urban Greening **12**, 109–116 (2013)
19. Region Northern Jutland. Health Profile 2013 – Well-being, Health and Illness in Northern Jutland. Region Northern Jutland, 264 pages (2014). In Danish. http://www.rn.dk/Sundhed/Til-sundhedsfaglige-og-samarbejdspartnere/Folkesundhed/Publikationer
20. Romano, B., Zullo, F., Fiorine, L., Ciabo, S., Marucci, A.: Sprinkling: an approach to describe urbanization dynamics in Italy. Sustainability **9**, 1–17 (2017)
21. Scheider, A., Mertes, C.M.: Expansion and growth in Chinese cities, 1978–2010. Environ. Res. Lett. **9**, 1–11 (2014)
22. Hansen, H.S.: A quasi-four dimensional database for the built environment. In: Westort, Caroline Y. (ed.) DEM 2001. LNCS, vol. 2181, pp. 48–59. Springer, Heidelberg (2001). doi:10.1007/3-540-44818-7_9
23. Arnell, N.W., Livermore, M.J.L., Kovats, S., Levy, P.E., Nicholls, R., Parry, M.L., Gaffin, S. R.: Climate and socio-economic scenarios for global-scale climate change impacts assessments: characterising the SRES storylines. Glob. Environ. Change **14**, 3–20 (2004)
24. Eickhout, B., van Meijl, H., Tabeau, A., van Rheenen, T.: Economic and ecological consequences of four European land use scenarios. Land Use Policy **24**, 562–575 (2007)
25. Shearer, A.W.: Scenario-based studies for landscape planning. In: Shearer, A.W., Mouat, D. A., Basset, S.D., Binford, M.W., Johnson, C.W., Saarinen, J.A., Gertler, A.W., Kahyaoglu-Koracin, J. (eds.) Land Use Scenarios – Environmental Consequences of Development, pp. 1–15. CRC Press, Florida (2009)
26. Romano, B., Zullo, F.: Models of urban land use in Europe: assessment tools and criticalities. Int. J. Agric. Environ. Inf. Syst. **4**, 80–97 (2013)

Spatial Methods to Measure Natura 2000 Sites Insularization in Italy

Alessandro Marucci[1] , Francesco Zullo[1] , Elisa Morri[2] ,
Lorena Fiorini[1] , Serena Ciabò[1] , Riccardo Santolini[2] ,
and Bernardino Romano[1(✉)]

[1] University of L'Aquila, Via G. Gronchi 18, 67100 L'Aquila, Italy
bernardino.romano@univaq.it
[2] University "Carlo Bo" Urbino, Via A. Saffi 22, 61029 Urbino, Italy

Abstract. It is interesting to notice how Nature 2000 is described as an instrument of "widespread ecological network throughout the EU territories", insisting in a definitional imprecision that has been dragging on for more than twenty years, and that was often, also authoritatively, criticized by many. Undoubtedly, many of these elements constitute the focal point of local ecological networks for species conservation importance, but their functionality depends on equally undoubtedly by the presence of ecologically permeable matrices that enable the biotic flows dynamics. The Italian Regions are the subjects of this study, as an expression of homogeneous forms of territorial government and as a reference on the administrative level for the implementation of Community policies for Nature 2000 network. The method followed in the work refers to an evaluate spatial fragmentation conditions methodology and the SCIs are the evaluated patches, which have a high dispersion on the national territory. This research has been conducted to show how the central issue of habitat and species conservation is still currently the fragmentation provoked by mobility infrastructures and urban growth.

Keywords: Environmental fragmentation · Landscape planning · Ecological network

1 Introduction

On the Italian Ministry of Environment, Land and Sea webpage (http://www.minambiente.it/pagina/rete-natura-2000) are described, using didactic language, the aims and goals of Natura 2000 project:

"Natura 2000 is the main European Union policy's instrument for biodiversity conservation. It is a widespread ecological network throughout the EU territory, established according to the Council Directive 92/43/EEC called "Habitat", to protect in the long term the conservation of natural habitats and wild flora and fauna species in danger of disappearance or rare on at the Community level. Natura 2000 network is constituted by the Sites of Community Importance (SCIs), identified by the Member States according to the Habitat Directive, which are subsequently designated as Special Area of Conservation (SAC)".

© Springer International Publishing AG 2017
O. Gervasi et al. (Eds.): ICCSA 2017, Part IV, LNCS 10407, pp. 437–450, 2017.
DOI: 10.1007/978-3-319-62401-3_32

It is interesting to notice how Nature 2000 is described as an instrument of "widespread ecological network throughout the EU territories", insisting in a definitional imprecision that has been dragging on for more than twenty years, and that was often, also authoritatively, criticized by many (Battisti 2011).

Here, we are not going to explain again the constitutional details of ecological networks, referring to a multitude of much quoted scientific works (Linehan et al. 1995; Forman 1995; Jongman 1995; Bennett 1999; Romano 1999; Fahrig 2003; Battisti 2003; Crooks and Sanjayan 2006; Boitani et al. 2007; Gibelli and Santolini 2015). However, it should be emphasized, solely for introductory purposes of this work, the conceptual unstitching between the shared model of ecological network and geographical configuration of Nature 2000 sites, particularly to the ones belonging to the Sites of Community Importance (SCIs). Italy has almost 2.000 sites (Table 1), with an average size of about 1600 ha, placed at widely varying distances between them: from a few hundred meters to tens of kilometers. Undoubtedly, many of these elements constitute the focal point of local ecological networks for species conservation importance, but their functionality depends on equally undoubtedly by the presence of ecologically permeable matrices that enable the biotic flows dynamics. The scientific knowledge on Nature 2000 sites has been scrupulously examined during the last decade, thanks to a substantial provision of economic resources from the Regions. On the contrary, the knowledge on territories eco-functional prerogatives, which contain the sites themselves, is very limited. On these territories there have been carried out a settlement and transformative pressure, without special precautions, responding to the same economical-political-social criteria that have always driven it, well before "Habitat" Directive was enacted and effective.

Table 1. Terrestrial SCIs and SCAs (Special Conservation Areas) distribution and consistency by region (data processed by http://www.minambiente.it/pagina/sic-zsc-e-zps-italia - January 2016)

REGION	Regional Area (ha)	Terrestrial SCIs/SCZ			
		Number	Area (ha)	% region	Mean Area (ha)
Abruzzo	1082699,34	53	232707,00	21,5%	4390,70
Basilicata	1007279,56	41	38672,00	3,8%	943,22
Calabria	1522338,44	178	70197,00	4,6%	394,37
Campania	1360917,22	93	321391,00	23,6%	3455,82
Emilia-Romagna	2218436,81	71	78064,00	3,5%	1099,49
Friuli-Venezia Giulia	785992,83	55	75302,00	9,6%	1369,13
Lazio	1722149,03	161	98526,00	5,7%	611,96
Liguria	540594,93	126	138067,00	25,5%	1095,77
Lombardy	2386118,81	175	204430,00	8,6%	1168,17
Marche	974954,49	68	94488,00	9,7%	1389,53
Molise	446103,32	76	65607,00	14,7%	863,25
Piedmont	2538879,38	95	119548,00	4,7%	1258,40
Puglia	1953385,64	73	232618,00	11,9%	3186,55
Sardinia	2392007,60	87	269333,00	11,3%	3095,78
Sicily	2555398,17	208	360735,00	14,1%	1734,30
Tuscany	2268095,74	90	207770,00	9,2%	2308,56
Trentino-Alto Adige	1360076,94	146	158679,00	11,7%	1086,84
Umbria	846107,82	97	103212,00	12,2%	1064,04
Valle d'Aosta	326092,95	25	25926,00	8,0%	1037,04
Veneto	1842399,67	63	198871,00	10,8%	3156,68
Total	30130028,68	1981	3094143,00	10,3%	1561,91

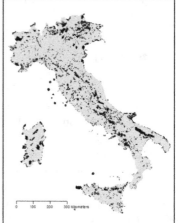

Even if it is possible to see multiple signals for approach variations from European bodies, currently much more careful to improve the ecological coherence of Nature 2000 network, taking actions directed on the agricultural picture and on the settlement diffusion (Bonnin et al. 2007; EEA 2010; CE 2012; CE 2016), it still remains an unsolved issue the Italian terrestrial SCIs' objective ecological fragmentation. These last ones are distributed with a 10 ha/km^2 ratio (Table 1), inside an area where the settlement presents the same average density (about 7% urbanized surface and 3% suburban road surface) and an high population density (almost 200 inhabitants/km^2), with multiple disturbance effects now well explained by a vast scientific production on this subject (Bierwagen 2005; Girvetz et al. 2008; EEA 2011; Romano et al. 2014; Fiorini et al. 2016; Zullo et al. 2016). SCIs' eco-functional solution has to be provided by the ecological networks, considered as Regional institutional layers. The Italian Regions where a local "designed" ecological network has become part of ordinary regulations regarding the urban transformations supervision, are very few (Umbria, Lombardy, Emilia Romagna, Tuscany and Marche). On the rest of the Italian territory, the environmental matrices that contain Nature 2000 sites continue to face settlement evolutions, solely driven by the municipal urban planning tools, which, not even rarely, show sensibility toward the ecological connections subject, but that are still episodic and random (Montanari et al. 2010; Lombardi et al. 2014; Frontoni et al. 2014; Ragni 2009; Malcevschi and Lazzarini 2013).

What have been just stated is shown in Fig. 1: in the SCIs' immediate adjacency mileage range, during the 50s, there were 84.000 ha of urbanized areas; later on, after 2000, they became more than 300.000 ha, with an average increase of 260%, therefore, there was an important emphasis on the habitat isolation of these strategic habitats.

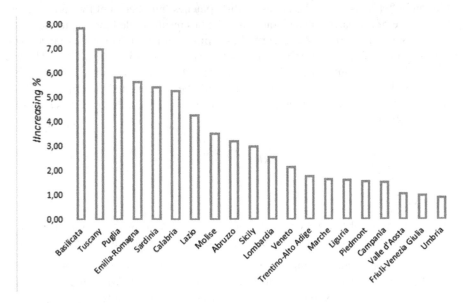

Fig. 1. Urbanized surfaces increase within 1 km buffer from Italian Nature 2000 sites.

For the reasons given, jointly with the progress of Nature 2000 sites settling phases, that are management plans approval, SCAs conversion, PAF (Prioritizing Action Frame) implementation, today it appears essential to explore the subject of their spatial and ecological fragmentation, to avoid further transformative behaviors that may seriously affect the role of biodiversity conservation that the European Directives give to Nature 2000 system.

2 Materials and Methodologies

The Italian Regions are the subjects of this study, as an expression of homogeneous forms of territorial government and as a reference on the administrative level for the implementation of Community policies for Nature 2000 network; while the processed information come from the ministerial SCIs dataset, updated at January 2016 (Table 1). The method followed in the work refers to an evaluate spatial fragmentation conditions methodology, already implemented and tested in 2012, however, applying it to the Italian "bio-permeable" areas and forests, whose definitions are referred to the general guidelines (Romano and Zullo 2012). In this research the SCIs are the evaluated patches, they have a high dispersion on the national territory, and their buffer radial step is equal to 500 m; therefore, the considered distances were: 500, 1000, 1500, 2000, 2500 m (Fig. 2). Buffer's depth, intended as the radial segment of the patch edges, it is always constant. The buffer generation surrounding the patches generates the reduction of the distances among them till the overlapping of the created buffers, that, thanks to the aggregative effect, weld together. As a result, a new configuration is formed, where the number of the resulting patches decreased. This new configuration allows us to put in relation buffer's distances and corresponding patches' numbers, until we arrive at the extreme value of n.1 patch when all the original ones result welded the one to the other. Hence, it is possible to elaborate curves that put in relation buffer's distances and patches' number (fragmentation reduction curves) as shown in Fig. 2 about Umbria Region. Afterward, from this data, fragmentation reduction curves were implemented, carrying the buffer's distance in the x-axis, and the Fragmentation Reduction Rate (FRR) in the y-axis. Given that there is order 1 buffer and the following ones are order $1 + i$, the FRR value is:

$$FRR = \frac{Np_{(1+i)}}{Np_{(1)}} \tag{1}$$

Where:

$Np_{(1)}$ = number of patches deriving from the aggregation with order 1 buffer
$Np_{(1+i)}$ = number of patches deriving from the aggregation with order $1 + i$ buffer

Fragmentation reduction curve shows that the greater the distance between the buffer, the more compact are the patches, with an increase of environmental continuity. From the functions that express the fragmentation curves (generally third grade polynomial), it is possible to calculate reduction distances of the fragmentation itself (FRDx). Where there is fragmentation reduction distances the patches partition

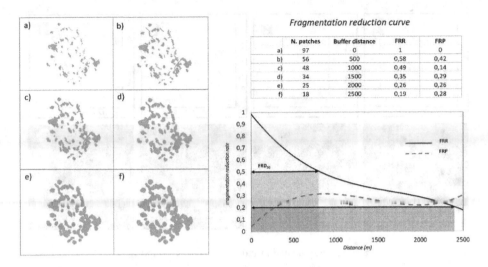

	N. patches	Buffer distance	FRR	FRP
a)	97	0	1	0
b)	56	500	0,58	0,42
c)	48	1000	0,49	0,14
d)	34	1500	0,35	0,29
e)	25	2000	0,26	0,26
f)	18	2500	0,19	0,28

Fig. 2. FRD indexes calculation method: buffer aggregative graphic framework with constant radial segment (500 m), following the Umbria region example.

decreases for a certain ratio: for example, FRD show the aggregation distance corresponding to a measured fragmentation reduction of 50–80%.

Fragmentation reduction curves geometry (Fig. 3) allows to classify four sampling models. A and D are the extreme cases. In the A example, it is sufficient to work on short distances to connect the patches together because they are already quite aggregated. Instead, D case is about greatly scattered patches, and it is necessary to work on long distances. B and C are the intermediate cases. In the B case there is a group of patches very close one to the other and some other one is more distant. In the C example there is a group of patches quite close between them (environmental matrices few disaggregated) and other residual patches more isolated.

Simultaneously with the FRR and FRD, it was created another index called Fragmentation Reduction Performance (FRP), which corresponds to the aggregate patches reduction ration, while moving from one buffer to another. Given that there is order m buffer and the following ones are $m + 1$, the FRP value is:

$$FRP = 1 - \frac{Np_{(m+1)}}{Np_{(m)}} \tag{2}$$

Where:

$Np_{(m)}$ = number of patches deriving from the aggregation with order m buffer
$Np_{(m+1)}$ = number of patches deriving from the aggregation with order $m + i$ buffer

This index shows buffer's welding distance where there is the higher level of aggregation. It appears to be a more convenient distance where to invest plan and project resources, to obtain as a result continuity among the Nature 2000 sites.

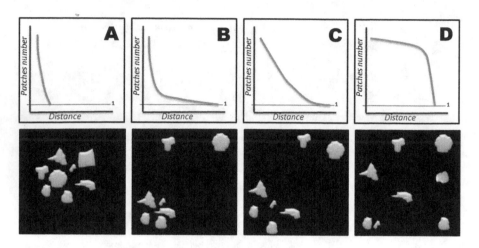

Fig. 3. Fragmentation reduction curves sampling

3 Results

In the last half century, one of the major effects on the urban conversion was the spatial and ecological habitat isolation of the most important Italian natural areas for the bio-diversity conservation. Figure 4 highlights the drastic reduction of territorial sections, happened in 2000 (organized on a 5×5 km plot), with low urban density (UD < 2%) compared to the existing situation during the '50s. It is not clear that exists a link between the latitudinal belts and the phenomenon analysed in this work, which it appears to be mainly related to local dynamics. However, developing this information separately for each of the three Italian geographic areas, it is evident how the parameter doubled in the Northern Italian regions and more than tripled in the Centre and Southern Italy.

With the Italian SCIs' habitat isolation study, conducted following the previously stated method, we can see that (Fig. 5) more than a half of the Regions (11 out of 20) show a situation close to the Fig. 3 C model, with slightly concentrated and rather far sites, with very progressive patches welding and very high FRD_{50} (exceeding 1 km).

Only in Molise and Campania are found similar situations close to B model, being most of the SCIs very concentrated and having a very high FRD_{50} (within a 500 m range). Hybrid C and D models concern most of the Regions including Marche, Umbria, and Sicily, with a part of the SCIs' highly concentrated and the other part very scattered, with an FRD_{50} included between 500 m and 1 km, but with an FRD_{80} far superior to 2 km. The only case which appears to be clearly belonging to the D model is the Abruzzo's one, while Sardinia is the Region with more distant and more scattered sites, which generate the highest FRD_{50} and FRD_{80} values, both far superior to 2 km (Fig. 6). According to Figs. 5 and 6 indications, it appears quite clear that suppose an, even partial (up to 50%), Italian SCIs' welding it is an extremely hard operation because it should be considered that the implementation of conservation and protection norms and regulations should cover average distances that are too long for a territory

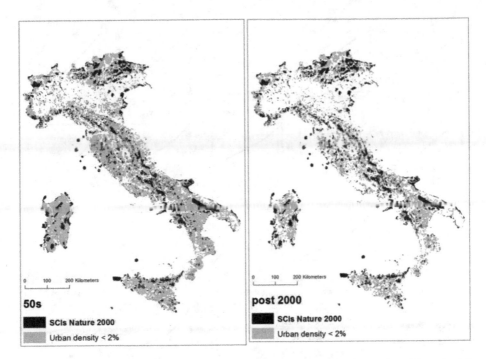

Fig. 4. Last 50 years' reduction of low urban density territorial Sections (5 × 5 km plots) in Italy.

with a very high level of urban sprawl. As already pointed out, national average urbanization density is equal to 7%, with Regional peaks of 14%; without including the very dense infrastructure network, whose spatial incidence is calculable to be in a 3% incremental. In most of the Regions, not even a reduction of 20% would be readily achievable, considering that FRD_{20} sometimes are inferior to 200–300 m (Fig. 6). Regarding efficiency (performance), it has to be noticed that 15 out of 20 Regions show maximum values (FRP_{max}) around 1000 m (Fig. 5). For six Regions, (Lombardy, Marche, Umbria, Lazio, Calabria and Sicily) FRP_{max} also coincide with FRD_{50}, meaning that the most convenient intervention on 1000 m produce also the aggregation of half of Nature 2000 sites surfaces.

Only in the case of Molise and Campania, the most efficient intervention on 1000 m would produce aggregation results superior to 50%. In this sense, it could be assumed that a few hundred meters fragmentations can be mitigated within the urban projects setting, therefore taking actions for the design and the organization of the residential complexes, local road networks and private and public green areas. Instead, in order to restore ecological continuity lines on average distances superior to 1 km, which seems to be the average distance for almost all the regions, it will be necessary to resort to planning and territorial rules instruments, incurring in far more complex issues like removing and lightening the barriers, which in any case, will last for many years.

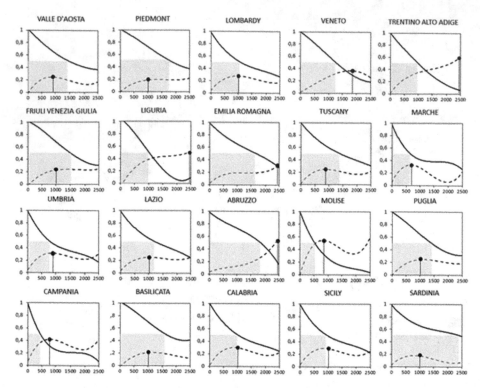

Fig. 5. SCIs' fragmentation reductions curves in the Italian regions (on the y-axis FRR values, on the x-axis buffers' distances. FRD$_{50}$ values are in grey, while FRP$_{max}$ (Fragmentation Reduction Performance) curve is dashed).

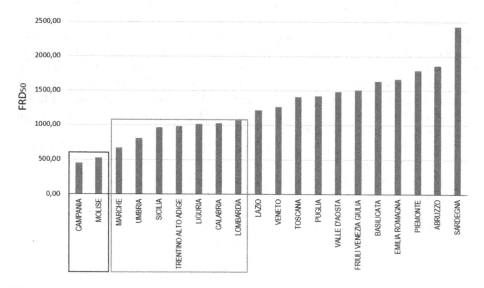

Fig. 6. FRD$_{50}$ values for the Italian regions with group of regions with an index lower to 500 m and 1 km.

Thus, considering SCIs' separation pattern, expressed by calculated FRD_x indexes, it results clearly the second stated condition. However, SCIs' are partially absorbed by semi-natural matrices that are infiltrated in urbanized contexts and maintain high environmental quality residual grades. These are the already defined bio-permeable spaces, which would allow reaching higher connectivity grades, surpassing very close separation distances.

In fact, Romano and Zullo (2012) shows how, calculated on bio-permeable matrices, FDR_{50} values sharply contract for all the Regions with values always below 600 m, and that only in two cases, for the FRD_{80} (Lombardy and Puglia) they exceed one kilometer. These are spatial dimensions that are more feasible for urban projects and plans, for whose application, with a general role of ecologic connection, it could be sufficient implement norms of protection, also limited, compatible with many productive ordinary human activities. The problem lies in the progressive erosion of bio-permeable surfaces, caused by settlement activities, which are carried out with inadequate controls on the environmental consequences, outside the highly controlled perimeters. For this purpose, it has been conducted an analysis on the Italian SCIs' habitat isolation by region (Fig. 7), that well point out the high pressure on the hinterlands, provoked by the increase of urban surfaces in the surrounding areas, either close than far.

Fig. 7. Habitat insularization curves processing method framework

The method here applied is always based on the spatial gradient expressed by progressive buffers with a 1 km pace (from 1 to 5) consecutive to the single SCI. The urbanization density is calculated within the buffers using artificial surfaces deriving from the local database, and based on these data, through tendency lines, variation curves, that describes the previously stated densities, are constructed. As showed in Fig. 8 this methodology allows us to obtain a clear indication of the major or minor presence of urban surfaces within the kilometric rings that surround Nature 2000 sites, and therefore, where and how far from these locations there are more pronounced disorders linked to land use and intensive anthropic attendance. If the available data allow it, habitat isolation curves can also be calculated for different time sections, in this way it is possible to notice the changes occurred over time, or also considering the local urban tools (PRG) expansive contents, highlight PRG full execution potentially expressible pressures. In the following case, regarding Umbria region, these data were indeed available, so there have been drawn diachronic curves for all the SCAs.

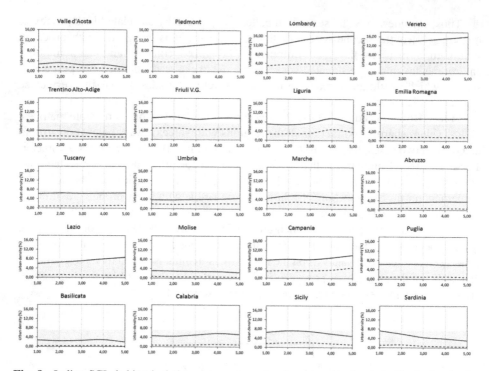

Fig. 8. Italian SCIs habitat isolation curves on regional aggregation level: in black, density in 2000; in dashed, density in the '50s and in grey average national density (7%). On the x-axis there are the buffer distances evaluated.

A weak spot of this methodology is that calculated settlement pressures do not take into account urban densification directionality and thus the possible presence of sectors totally free from any disturbs, which are more suitable for biotic transitions. In this sense, a methodological integration is under development.

The difference between calculated habitat isolation curves in the '50s and after 2000 (Fig. 8) shows clearly where and in what region the fragmentations, due to high settlement densification, were more evident. In Piedmont, Lombardy, Veneto, Friuli, Liguria, Emilia Romagna, Lazio, Campania, Puglia, Sicily and also Sardinia the values that emerge are quite high for the urban densities either within the proximity buffers (1–2 km), or in the medium distances buffers, similar to the national average 7%. Certainly, the index is much higher in the Northern Italy big industrialized regions (up to 10–15% of the value of immediate proximity within the first kilometric buffer in Piedmont, Lombardy, Veneto, and Friuli). However, in 12 out of 20 regions the SCIs' matrices are highly urbanized (exceeding the 7%) is a significant data that shows, statistically, the fragmentation condition that Italian habitats endure, and of which we have already discussed above. In these circumstances, it is extremely hard to create those ecological networks that, despite being considered by the European Community and most of the regions, should provide a decisive contribution to national bio-diversity conservation. If the situation is evaluated on a regional scale, it could appear better for those regions morphologically more articulated and with mountain or hilly agricultural economies, such as Valle d'Aosta, Trentino, A.A., Marche, Umbria, Abruzzo, Molise and Basilicata. On the average regional scale these phenomena look much less uninformed, but, considering singularly every SCAs, they appear to be more pronounced. In Fig. 9 there is an analysis of Umbria SCAs' habitat isolation that also used the local urban tools in force (PRG) dataset which made possible to have a typological classification of 5 models that covers the entire regional 97 SCAs records.

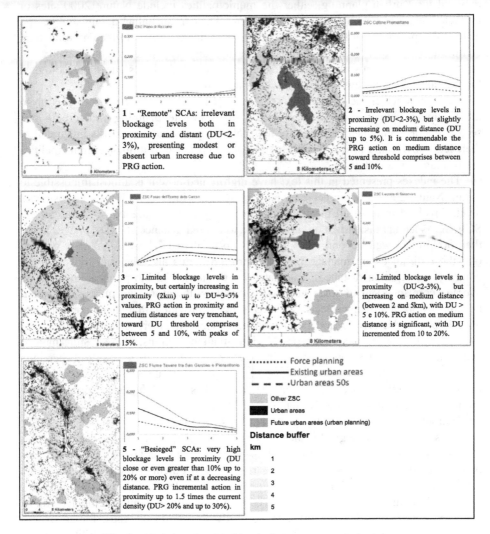

Fig. 9. Umbria SCAs' habitat isolation curves prototypes.

4 Conclusions

This research has been conducted to show how the central issue of habitat and species conservation is still currently the fragmentation provoked by mobility infrastructures and urban growth. As advanced and sophisticated the Nature 2000 sites management and protection measures could be, the results of biodiversity conservation will never be stabilized over time if there will not be enforced extended matrices transformations control policies. It is indeed a very complex issue because it has to involve the entire regional local urban planning, either the municipalities include Nature 2000 sites or protected areas, or they are very far from them. The current Italian administrative and technical capacity is not sensible, except for some dozens cases, to the environmental continuity issue. Or at least it not sensible to such an extent that one municipality can influences the decisions made by its PRG for reasons linked to some sites ecological functionality, located few kilometers within its borders.

Connect together the whole territory, from an environmental perspective, is up to the Ecologic Networks, considered as the superordinate planning structure in this sector; but, as mentioned before, only few Italian regions have networks integrated in their legislative frameworks, having the actual competence to influence municipalities urban planning activities.

The indexes presented in this text have highlighted how it is almost impossible to obtain Nature 2000 sites connectivity efficient results without get all the administrative levels involved in it. In all the Italian regions (Fig. 6) to reduce by 50% the current SCIs/SCAs habitat insularization, it is needed to exceed distances (FRD_{50}) never lower than 500 m and well beyond one kilometer (up to almost 3 km). As already pointed out, these distances are manageable only through norms and planning tools. On the contrary, aggregation distances, calculated on the territorial bio-permeability, are on average correspondent to some hundreds of meters, therefore, are quite easily manageable by local urban projects planning offices, provided that there are adequate guidelines for the private and public workers. Thus, it emerges the importance of implementation of ecological networks designs in all the regions. These designs have to evaluate every soil section connectivity quality, especially in a country where the settlements main feature is the extreme dispersion, penetrating every area, even the most remote, following a quite peculiar pattern that has been defined as "sprinkling" by the recent scientific literature (Romano et al. 2017).

Undoubtedly, there are many gaps that must be filled in the fragmentation field, which is becoming strategic for the conservation of global biological values species that are in Italy. Further researches and specific interventions are needed on the "efficient" ecological networks, to consider real gaps to potential biotic fluxes through infrastructural lines and urban plots, conducting large scale maps studies. For example, these kind of studies conducted in Umbria have shown how alongside the 134 km of the E45 route (Valle del Tevere) there are only 17 significant gaps, for an overall development lower than 4 km, with the arterial road transversal permeability equal to 2,6%. Numbers and situations of this entity are verifiable all over the national road network, even though the majority of those are not acknowledged due to lack of investigations on ecological occlusion of the infrastructures (Henle et al. 1997; Jaeger et al. 2007; Romano et al. 2012), which there are only in very few regional cases.

The present work is now redirecting toward a methodological approach of habitat insularization curves (Figs. 7 and 8), to implement directional evaluation techniques of occlusions caused by urbanization and the road network, in order to provide support to network ecological corridors and stepping stones identification studies.

Acknowledgements. The methodology presented has been implemented in the research project and monitoring supported by Umbria Region, that we want to thank for the resources given. The indicators used have been developed within the SUNLIFE project (LIFE 13/NAT/IT/000371 - Strategy for the Natura 2000 Network of the Umbria Region).

References

Battisti, C.: Habitat fragmentation, fauna and ecological network planning: toward a theoretical conceptual framework. Ital. J. Zool. **70**, 241–247 (2003)

Battisti, C.: Ecological network planning – from paradigms to design and back: a cautionary note. J. Land Use Sci. (2011). doi:10.1080/1747423X.2011.639098

Bennett, A.F.: Linkages in the landscapes. The role of corridors and connectivity in wildlife conservation. IUCN, Gland, Switzerland and Cambridge, UK, 254 p. (1999)

Bierwagen, B.G.: Predicting ecological connectivity in urbanizing landscapes. Environm. Plann. B: Plann. Des. **32**, 763–776 (2005)

Boitani, L., Falcucci, A., Maiorano, L., Rondinini, C.. Ecological networks as conceptual frameworks or operational tools in conservation. Conserv. Biol. **21**(6), 1414–1422 (2007)

Bonnin, M., Bruszik, A., Delbaere, B., Lethier, H., Richard, D., Rientjes, S., van Uden, G., Terry, A.: The Pan-European ecological network: taking stock. Council of Europe, Nature and Environment, N. 146 (2007)

Commissione Europea: Orientamenti in materia di buone pratiche per limitare, mitigare e compensare l'impermeabilizzazione del suolo. CE, p. 62 (2012). doi:10.2779/81286

Commissione Europea: Future brief: no net land take by 2050?. CE 14, 62 (2016). doi:10.2779/537195

Crooks, K.R., Sanjayan, M.: Connectivity Conservation, Conservation Biology, vol. 14. Cambridge University Press, Cambridge (2006)

EEA: Assessing biodiversity in Europe — the 2010 report. EEA, p. 64 (2010). ISSN 1725-9177

EEA: Landscape fragmentation in Europe. EEA-FOEN, p. 92 (2011)

Fahrig, L.: Effects of habitat fragmentation on biodiversity. Ann. Rev Ecol. Syst. **34**, 487–515 (2003)

Fiorini, L., Zullo, F., Romano, B.: Urban development of the coastal system of the Italian largest Island: Sicily and Sardinia. Ocean Coast. Manag. (2016). doi:10.1016/j.ocecoaman.2016.12.008

Forman, R.T.: Land Mosaics: The Ecology of Landscapes and Regions. Cambridge University Press, New York (1995)

Frontoni, E., Mancino, A., Zingaretti, P., Malinverni, E.S., Pesaresi, S., Biondi, E., Pandolfi, M., Marseglia, M., Sturari, M., Zabaglia, C.: SIT-REM: an interoperable and interactive web geographic information system for fauna, flora and plant landscape data management. Int. J. Geo-Inf. **3**(2), 853–867 (2014)

Gibelli, G., Santolini, R.: Ecological functions, biodiversity and landscape conservation. In: Gambino, R., Peano, A. (eds.) Nature Policies and Landscape Policies, pp. 59–67. Springer, Cham (2015)

Girvetz, E.H., Thorne, J.H., Berry, A.M., Jaeger, J.A.G.: Integration of landscape fragmentation analysis into regional planning: a statewide multi-scale case study from California. USA. Landscape Urban Plann. **86**, 205–218 (2008)

Henle, K., Alard, D., Clitherow, J., Cobb, P., Firbank, L., Kull, T., McCracken, D., Moritz, R.F.A., Niemelä, J., Rebane, M., Jaarsma, C.F.: Approaches for the planning of rural road networks according to sustainable land use planning. Landscape Urban Plann. **39**(1), 47–54 (1997)

Jaeger, J.A.G., Schwarz-von Raumer, H.G., Esswein, H., Müller, M., Schmidt-Lüttmann, M.: Time series of landscape fragmentation caused by transportation infrastructure and urban development: a case study from Baden-Württemberg Germany. Ecol. Soc. **12**(1), 22 (2007)

Jongman, R.H.G.: Nature conservation planning in Europe, developing ecological networks. Landscape Urban Plann. **32**, 169–183 (1995)

Linehan, J., Gross, M., Finn, J.: Greenway planning: developing a landscape ecological network approach. Landscape Urban Plann. **33**(1–3), 179–193 (1995)

Lombardi, M., Giunti, M., Castelli, C.: La rete ecologica toscana: aspetti metodologici e applicativi. Ri-Vista **XXII**(1), 90–101 (2014)

Malcevschi, S., Lazzarini, M.: Tecniche e metodi per la realizzazione della Rete Ecologica Regionale. Regione Lombardia, p. 240 (2013)

Montanari, I., Carati, M., Costantino, R., Santolini, R.: Qualità ecologica, l'approccio emiliano-romagnolo. Ecoscienza **3**, 56–59 (2010)

Ragni, B. (ed.): RERU, Rete Ecologica Regionale dell'Umbria. Petruzzi ed., p. 241 (2009)

Romano, B.: La continuità ambientale nella pianificazione. Urbanistica **112**, 156–160 (1999). INU

Romano, B., Zullo, F.: Landscape fragmentation in Italy. Indices implementation to support territorial policies. In: Campagna, M., De Montis, A., Isola, F., Lai, S., Pira, C., Zoppi, C. (eds.) Planning Support Tools: Policy analysis, Implementation and Evaluation, pp. 399–414. Franco Angeli Ed. (2012). ISBN 9788856875973

Romano, B., Zullo, F., Fiorini, L.: Dati sulla urbanizzazione italiana: verso la terza generazione. Ri-Vista 00, 30–43 (2014). ISSN 1724-6768

Romano, B., Zullo, F., Fiorini, L., Ciabò, S., Marucci, A.: Sprinkling: an approach to describe urbanization dynamics in Italy. Sustainability **9**(97) (2017). doi:10.3390/su9010097

Romano, B., Ciabò, S., Fabrizio, M.: Infrastructure obstruction profiling: a method to analyse ecological barriers formed by transport infrastructure. In: Wagner, P.J., Nelson, D., Murray, E. (eds.) Proceedings of the 2011 International Conference on Ecology and Transportation. Center for Transportation and the Environment, pp. 110–120. North Carolina State University, Raleigh (2012)

Zullo, F., Marucci, A., Fiorini, L., Ciabò, S., Romano, B.: New techniques for land surveying, monitoring and environmental diagnosis: a comparative analysis. In: Proceedings XIV International Forum World Heritage and Degradation, Napoli, 16–18 June 2016 (2016)

Spatial Multicriteria Analysis Approach for Evaluation of Mobility Demand in Urban Areas

Mauro Mazzei[✉] and Armando Luigi Palma

National Research Council, Istituto di Analisi dei Sistemi ed Informatica
"Antonio Ruberti", Via dei Taurini, 19, 00185 Rome, Italy
mauro.mazzei@iasi.cnr.it, palma@arpal.it

Abstract. This work describes the municipalities of the province of Rome in terms of ISTAT economic data relating to the industry and to industrial production, employment, demographics and the demand for mobility as measured by the displacement flows. This matrix the rows of which are municipalities of a given province and columns the aforementioned variables, it applies factor analysis to identify the socio-economic profile of the territories from the distribution of the territories distributed in homogeneous areas identified on each factorial axis (municipal ranking of each factor), and no longer agglomerated by town. The result identifies homogenous areas within an assigned geographic region, regardless of the breakdown in municipality of the province.

Keywords. GIS · Spatial data analysis · Multivariate statistical analysis

1 Introduction

Objective of this analysis is the research for variations of the settlement phenomenon in the province of Rome, a phenomenon that between the two censuses of 2001 and 2011 has revealed a significant urban population dispersal, which has gradually moved to the suburbs of the city and, frequently, even in the neighboring municipalities, determining needs for mobility, towards the main pole attractor constituted from the city center, which inevitably led, in the morning rush hour, traffic congestion that can be seen now, in all quadrants also periphery of the city.

The causes of population dispersal are probably attributable to the high housing costs in the city center, high costs that have been produced by the high and growing demand for settlements of the tertiary industry, costs that have led to the forced displacement of the residences, given the consequent staffing operating costs for workers and students from outlying areas and surrounding municipalities. The higher payroll operating costs are obviously due to the higher time required for access to places of work and study, and to the services of the service sector.

As a result, they increased the average distances of systematic trips home-work and home-studio, resulting in amplification of the congestion on the lines of penetration to the city of Rome. In addition, it should be noted the phenomenon of large shopping malls, with their impact on congestion levels, which especially on weekends are the

© Springer International Publishing AG 2017
O. Gervasi et al. (Eds.): ICCSA 2017, Part IV, LNCS 10407, pp. 451–468, 2017.
DOI: 10.1007/978-3-319-62401-3_33

main nodes attractors of journeys in the city. A recent survey of the Mobility Agency on the five largest shopping centers in Rome, found in the day on Saturday over 170,000 visitors in total of which only 5.9% have used the local public transport, while the remaining 88% used the private car.

In the period from 2001 to the Istat census of 2011, the population has suffered a slight increase of around 100,000 units (+3.5%), reaching 2.913 million residents. You can highlight two major macro areas: the innermost where the population tends to be stable, and the outer bands, those formed by the border municipalities of the province, where instead dominated by a substantial increase in population. But simultaneously, there is, compared to 2001, a higher incidence of high average age, i.e. an aging population, which translates into a lower propensity to displacement.

The population has changed over time an increasingly important place in the resident population in Rome. If we consider the relationship between the population of the provincial belt, made up of 120 municipalities, and the City of Rome, the debt ratio increased in six years, from 2006 to 2012 of 6%, from 48.3% to 53.1%. But if we consider the population of the 120 municipalities of the province, except Rome, relative to the sum of the provincial population, the demographic weight of the metropolitan belt increases of 2%, from 32.6% in 2006 to 34.7% in 2012.

From 2006 to 2012, the population of Rome has increased by about 85,000 residents, while that of the provincial Belt has increased by 175,000 residents, with an average annual growth rate of just over 2%, this rate that is four times greater the average annual population growth rate of resident Rome. Today, just over 65% of the entire population of the province is located in Rome, and the seven municipalities of Guidonia, Fiumicino, Pomezia, Tivoli, Velletri, Civitavecchia and Anzio not comprise 30% of the provincial population belt, excluding Rome. Among these municipalities, the largest, Guidonia, does not exceed 85 thousand residents, which has a population size comparable to one of the districts, and even among the most populous of Rome. To this we must add that some municipalities in the province, Fiano Romano, Ardea and Fonte Nova, have been affected in recent years by a significant growth of the population in the ratio between 2006 and 2011 reached 20%.

In the provincial scenario, most of the terms of trade between the centers of the territory, converge towards the main center; so that the regional road transport system can be radiocentric considered. All municipalities have a strong attraction to Rome, while less important are the transversal relations.

Like many other Italian metropolitan areas, Rome live for years a demographic stagnation, and it is already clear the phenomenon of the relocation of the population towards the periphery and towards the satellite towns of the province where they are definitely more advantageous conditions of the real estate and housing market.

The economic system is composed, according to the last available ISTAT data, from 1.192 million employees, and records with respect to the ISTAT 2001 census, an increase of about 100,000 employees, or 9.1%. On the other hand, in the decade between 2001 and 2011, there was evidence of an outsourcing process due, primarily, to the affirmation of the advanced tertiary activities (IT, financial intermediation, etc.), and more generally, entrepreneurial, to the expense of workers employed in industry and commerce, while the institutions of the sector has kept constant the consistency of its employees.

According to mobility forecasts that flow from that scenario, in the short and medium term it is conceivable a weakened radiocentric model since the poles settlement attractors and moving generators are intended for an increase to the detriment of the most central areas of the city that tend to losing residents. In particular, Acilia and Ostia show a marked tendency to increasing population in the medium to long term.

Recent analyzes have predicted a reduction of 7,000 employees in the central areas of the city, compared with an increase of 165 thousand people speculated in the peripheral bands of Rome.

The comparison of the census data of 2001 and the full implementation scenery of PRG predictions, highlights an increasing population settled around 150 thousand residents, an increase of staff in the various economic sectors of 250 thousand units.

1.1 Vehicles and Characteristics of Mobility

A mobility related phenomenon, in the scenario described above settlement, is the continued growth of the vehicle fleet that in the year 2012, according to ACI (Automobile Club d'Italia), reached as a whole the share of 2.5 million vehicles, with a motorization rate 856 vehicles per 1000 residents. This figure is the highest among the main Italian towns. The rate of specific engine for motor vehicles is instead of 641 cars per 1000 residents.

In line with the evolution of the territorial and socio-economic structure of the metropolitan area of Rome, in recent years there have been significant changes in qualitative and quantitative variations of mobility [1, 2]. These changes are attributable to the centrifugal tendencies of the residences and businesses that have shifted the center of gravity attractive and generative traffic out of the city, thereby changing the distribution of mobility characteristics [13, 14].

In the city of Rome alone, between 2004 and 2013, there has been a reduction in overall mobility which in percentage terms is around 23%. This is a decrease of about 1.4 million displacements in the day type, a result of which the total displacements are today 4.7 million units.

To complete the picture that emerges of mobility, for example, by studies in Rome for the preparation of the General Urban Traffic Plan (PGTU), with 4.7 million journeys generated only by residents in the city of Rome, we must add the more than 800 thousand of residents traveling in the province who daily go to Rome for work or study.

This component attractiveness of Rome with respect to the province appears to be growing, compared to 2001, about 250 thousand units, confirming the trend, which is already underway for several years, a gradual shift of population quotas from the center towards the periphery and towards the municipality belt [5–7].

The City of Rome covers an area of 1,287 km^2 of which 290 km^2 are the urban area of the city. For compiling the data on commuting convenience, measured by ISTAT during the last census of the year 2011 and published in 2016, it was taken as a territorial reference unit for topografical sections. That reference has allowed to carry out a more in-depth analysis of census data on the demand for mobility which takes account of even short-distance commuting [8].

2 Processing Method and Results

Census data processing was performed with a specific developed software using a
database that ISTAT collected during the last census of 2011 and published in 2016.

This database is structured in tables whose content refers to the moves of each
censored source section to a censored destination section [3, 4]. In this commute data
base between the source-destination censored sections, modal breakdown parameters
and displacement duration parameters were not indicated (see Table 1) [9].

Table 1. Census variables considered for processing – ISTAT 2016

Description of variable	Value
Region of origin	List of Italian region January 1, 2011 - ISTAT
Province of origin	List of Italian province January 1, 2011 - ISTAT
Municipality of origin	List of Italian municipality January 1, 2011 - ISTAT
Place of origin	List of Italian place January 1, 2011 - ISTAT
Section source of origin	List of Italian section January 1, 2011 – ISTAT
Region of destination	List of Italian region January 1, 2011 – ISTAT
Province of destination	List of Italian province January 1, 2011 - ISTAT
Municipality of destination	List of Italian municipality January 1, 2011 - ISTAT
Place of destination	List of Italian place January 1, 2011 - ISTAT
Section source of destination	List of Italian section January 1, 2011 - ISTAT
Total student	Count variable
Total workers	Count variable
Total of individuals	Count variable

The other database we used for all municipalities in the province of Rome is the
O-D matrix detected by ISTAT. The Origin-Destination matrix of travel for work or
study refers to the population living in family or cohabitation detected at the 15th
General Census of Population (reference date: October 9, 2011). The file contains data
on the number of people moving between areas or within the same municipality -
classified, as well as the reasons for traveling, for sex, the means of transport used, the
time of departure and the journey time.

The O-D matrix is stuctured in a methodological document that, in addition to
describing the structure of data, provides guidance for the use of the matrix, with
particular reference to the variables obtained with sampling method of transport, time
slot of departure and travel time [10–12].

In Fig. 1 shows the processing results commuter flows between the various census
sections of the City of Rome, which shows that the displacements for study is 438.111,
while for business purposes are 846.883, for a total of 1.284.994 movements. In Fig. 2
are deduced commuter flows that target Rome and Fig. 3 its flow graph total of shifts
for study and work that is 218.000.

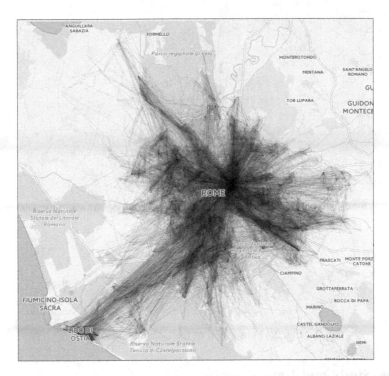

Fig. 1. The example refers to the calculation of commuting within Rome (Rome to Rome), between the various census tracts.

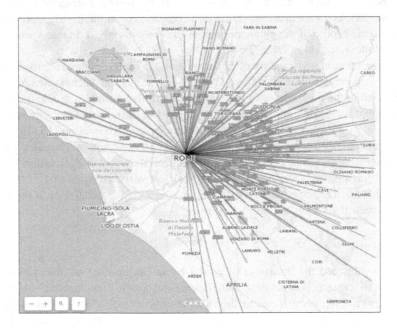

Fig. 2. Processing result commuter flows from all municipalities in the province of Rome to Rome.

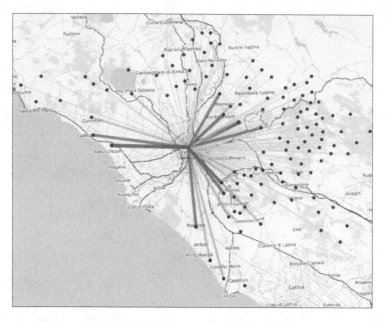

Fig. 3. Flow graph of total displacement.

3   Case Study and Data

Each of the 121 municipalities of the province of Rome has been described in terms of 43 census ISTAT variables in 2011 and considered suitable to represent the socio-economic profile of the municipalities of the test province. Of these variables is a list in the following table (Table 2):

It was then considered a matrix of 121 rows and 43 columns, where the rows contain the objects (municipalities) to which you want to investigate the latent structure, and the columns contain the coordinates of the chosen descriptive variables. Since the units of these coordinates are not homogeneous, it proceeded, at the outset of being standardized by calculating, for each variable, the mean and the standard deviation [15, 16].

They are obtained as well from the original Xi, descriptive variables j of the phenomenon under examination, the new standardized variables Zi, j which have the property of having, each, on average, equal to 0 and variance equal to 1.

From this matrix Z standardized data was subsequently calculated the R correlation matrix between the variables considered, being:

$$R = 1/m \, Z' \, Z$$

where Z' is indicated the transpose of Z and by m the number of observed objects. Obviously the R matrix is symmetric with the elements of the main diagonal are all equal to 1. And from this matrix R the method of the main components (or Hotelling) was applied for the description of which reference should be made to the literature [17–21].

Table 2. Data 2014 ISTAT – Province of Rome

N° of variables	Numeric indicator
1	Students (domestic travel to the City)
2	Employees (domestic travel to the City)
3	Total displacement (internal to the City)
4	Students (originally directed by the City of Rome)
5	Workers (originally directed by the City of Rome)
6	Total displacement (originally directed by the City of Rome)
7	Municipal area (sq km)
8	Resident population 2001
9	Resident population 2011
10	Density of popolaz. to 2011
11	Sup. soil consumatoal 2012 (ha)
12	Sup. cover artific. (has)
13	% area. location live and producers. (2011)
14	Area. loc. live and productive (sq km)
15	Variat rate. annual average popol. resident
16	Variat rate. popol ten-year average. resident
17	Change. potential user buildings
18	Change. index underuse homes
19	Change. abitaz potential use. Inhabited in the centers
20	Change. % Average compraven price. homes
21	Change. unemployment rate
22	Change. economic dynamism index
23	Pop./kmq (Pop.res.+Balance pendol.)/Superf.Comunale.
24	% Pop.res. settlements+houses scattered/Pop.res.
25	% houses scattered/Tot. Abitaz
26	% Resid. commuters by private/Resid. pend.
27	% Abit. occup. low affollam./Tot. ab. oc
28	Rapp. U.L. Trade detail s.f./sup. inhabited areas and prod.
29	% secon school pupils. Grade II at risk abandonment.
30	% of early exit from the education and training system
31	Unemployment rate
32	Rate of Unemployment. youth
33	Incidence of young people out of work and training market
34	Incidence families with potential economic hardship
35	Incidence elderly alone
36	Suicides × 100 000 ab
37	Crowding of housing index
38	Exchange inutilizzaz. (Use potential) buildings
39	Exchange inutilizzaz. (Use potential) appartment
40	housing exclusion index (accidents. Impr accommodation.)

(continued)

Table 2. (*continued*)

N° of variables	Numeric indicator
41	Incidence resid buildings. dilapidated storage box
42	Index of availability of services in the home
43	Average age of the recent housing

The principal component analysis is a multivariate statistical technique that allows to explain the variability of a statistical variable in k dimensions Z = (Z1, Z2, ..., Zk) in terms of k variables Y1, Y2, ...,Yk, linear combinations of the Zj. It has:

$$Y_i = \sum_j b_{ij} Z_j (i = 1, 2, \ldots, k) \tag{1}$$

Where b_{ij} are constants to be determined. Y_i are called the main components of the variable Z and assuming are not related to each other ordered by importance, in the explanation of the variability of Z we have that:

$$\text{cov}(Y_i, Y_j) = 0 \, (i \neq j) \tag{2}$$

$$V(Y_1) \geq V(Y_2) \geq \ldots \geq V(Y_k) \tag{3}$$

where *cov* is covariance and *V* is variance. Without loss of generality we can assume that the variables Z_i are standardized, with mean equal to 0 and variance equal to 1, so as to eliminate the influence of the origin and the unit of measurement data. So that it results the following expression:

$$Z_j = (X_j - \mu_j)/\sigma_j \tag{4}$$

Also impose the condition that the overall variance of Z_j is equal to that of Y_i, i.e.:

$$\sum_i V(Y_i) = \sum_i V(Z_i) = k \tag{5}$$

At last, suppose that the vectors

$$b_i = (b_{i,1}, b_{i,2}, \ldots, b_{i,k}) \tag{6}$$

have unit length, i.e., they fulfill the condition:

$$\sum_j b_{ij}^2 = 1 (i = 1, 2, \ldots, k) \tag{7}$$

On account of this, the vectors b_i that maximize then the variance of Y_1, of Y_2, ..., to Y_k with the constraints (3) and (4), are the eigenvectors of the matrix C of the coefficients of correlation between the variables Z_j, which correspond to the eigenvalues $\lambda_1, \lambda_2, \ldots, \lambda_k$ of C, sorted by non-increasing value. We have that:

$$|C - \lambda I| = 0 \tag{8}$$

$$b_i(C - \lambda_i I) = 0 \tag{9}$$

where I is the unit matrix. The matrix C is symmetric and positive definite for which the solutions λ_i of the (8) are non-negative and such that their sum (trace of the matrix C) is equal to k. We have that:

$$\sum_i \lambda_i = k \ (i = 1, 2, \ldots, k) \tag{10}$$

The variance of the i-th component is:

$$V(Y_i) = \lambda_i \tag{11}$$

And the contribution of Y_i to the overall variance is:

$$P_i = V(Y_{i)}/k = \lambda_i/k \tag{12}$$

Following are the salient processing results by the method of the main components, which describe the latent structure of the 121 municipalities of the Province of Rome. In Table 3 shows the cumulative percentages of the first 6 eigenvalues of the matrix R that indicate the overall share of the explained variance of the system with the first 6 main components, while the eigenvalues residues have indicated each contribution to the variance below the 4% and therefore, they have been neglected. Also reported are the coefficients of correlation between the input variables and factors emerged (see Table 4), while in Tables 5, 6 and 7 are listed the municipalities with the respective coordinates, in descending order, in tables only the first six and the last six values are reported and calculated in the space of the first 6 main components, which explain a total of 64% of the overall variance of the system [22, 23].

In Table 4 shows the correlation coefficients of the variables divided into the first 6 principal components of the first six eigenvalues.

Below are the Tables 3, 4 and 5 of the factor coordinates in descending order on the axes of the first six and the last six results.

Table 3. Principal components

I	II	III	IV	V	VI
.25	.42	.50	.55	.60	.64

Table 4. Factor loading

Factor	N°. of variable	Factor loading
I	1	1.0
	2	1.0
	3	1.0
	7	0.97
	8	1.0
	9	1.0
	11	0.99
	12	0.99
	14	0.99
	36	1.0
II	4	0.94
	5	0.96
	6	0.96
	10	0.67
	13	0.57
III	15	0.63
	16	0.65
	20	0.71
	26	0.69
	34	0.70
	39	−0.71
	43	−0.57
IV	30	0.77
	33	0.69
	35	0.55
V	18	−0.58
	27	0.46
	37	−0.75
VI	21	0.80
	31	0.62
	32	0.68

From the reading of the numerical calculation results made you can be seen as follows where the color intensity is higher on positive data (See Figs. 4, 5, 6, 7, 8 and 9).

The main Factor is maximally correlated with variables that define high prevalence in the population size of the municipalities in question.

The second Factor is characterized by the variables that denote a positive economic dynamics and settlement, favored by a significant generation of movements, for study and work, towards the center of Rome.

Table 5. I–II factor

I factor scores		II factor scores	
Roma	112.01	Guidonia Montecelio	20.64
Ciampino	4.40	Ciampino	17.67
Fiumicino	4.02	Fiumicino	15.04
Guidonia Montecelio	3.16	Marino	12.71
Pomezia	3.03	Fonte Nuova	11.79
Anzio	3.01	Pomezia	10.92
Ciciliano	−2.71	Saracinesco	−6.27
Saracinesco	−2.72	Capranica Prenestina	−6.62
Vallinfreda	−2.75	Jenne	−6.89
Capranica Prenestina	−2.88	Rocca Canterano	−7.04
Vivaro Romano	−2.97	Cervara di Roma	−7.06
Cervara di Roma	−3.12	Vivaro Romano	−8.24

Table 6. III–IV factor

III factor scores		IV factor scores	
Ardea	9.85	Vivaro Romano	10.12
Fiano Romano	9.11	Saracinesco	9.89
Fonte Nuova	8.78	Poli	6.43
Sant'Angelo Romano	7.77	Rocca Canterano	5.65
Fiumicino	7.67	Licenza	5.42
Labico	7.56	Casape	5.30
Cineto Romano	−8.25	Sacrofano	−3.30
Roviano	−9.72	Guidonia Montecelio	−3.56
Rocca Canterano	−10.60	Monte Porzio Catone	−3.91
Jenne	−10.66	Grottaferrata	−3.99
Vivaro Romano	−11.47	Ciampino	−4.32
Vallepietra	−13.79	Roma	−4.43

The third Factor is the size of the demographic and urban growth of the municipalities of the belt, resulting in significant increase in mobility by private car to the attractor pole consists of the Rome. The demographic dynamics supported by good accessibility to the Rome resulted in the rise in house prices, which are generally newly built, with a significant rate without use due to the compression of demand in the face of unsustainable prices from families with a potential discomfort economic.

Table 7. V–VI factor

V factor scores		VI factor scores	
Saracinesco	6.10	Vallinfreda	7.18
Rocca Canterano	4.87	Vivaro Romano	5.95
Vallepietra	4.85	Percile	5.56
Filacciano	3.77	Affile	5.07
Nerola	3.17	Licenza	4.92
Vallinfreda	2.98	Saracinesco	4.91
Vicovaro	−2.68	Gavignano	−3.31
Capranica Prenestina	−3.01	Trevignano Romano	−3.43
Rocca Santo Stefano	−3.38	Marano Equo	−3.84
Arcinazzo Romano	−3.45	San Gregorio da Sassola	−3.95
Castel San Pietro Roma	−4.81	Sant'Oreste	−4.04
Percile	−5.10	Torrita Tiberina	−4.26

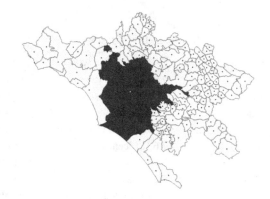

Fig. 4. I factor scores

Fig. 5. II factor scores

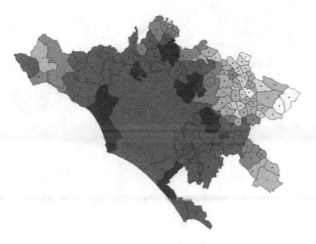

Fig. 6. III factor scores

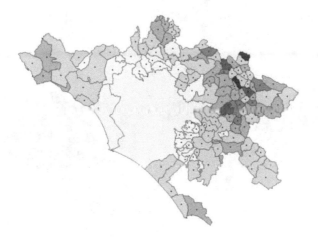

Fig. 7. IV factor scores

The fourth Factor realizes the existing social unrest in the towns of the belt, social distress manifested by significant rates of people living alone compared to the resident population, and with the young people coming out prematurely from education and training system, forming so that layer of young people excluded from the labor market and vocational training.

The fifth Factor characterizes the size of the housing situation in the municipalities, housing situation in general is marked by a significant low rate of housing overcrowding.

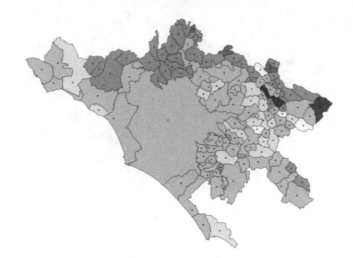

Fig. 8. V factor scores

Fig. 9. VI Factor scores

The sixth Factor is oriented in the direction of youth problems related to a high unemployment rate which varies over time is increasing.

Table 8. Groups

Gr		Gr		Gr		Gr	
1	Artena	9	Licenza	12	Anguillara Sabazia	12	Monte Compatri
2	Cave		Marano Equo		Anzio		Monte Porzio Catone
3	Magliano Romano		Marcellina		Ariccia		Monterotondo
4	Montelibretti		Monteflavio		Bracciano		Morlupo
5	Nemi		Montelanico		Campagnano di Roma		Nazzano
6	Ponzano Romano		Montorio Romano		Canale Monterano		Nerola
7	Roma		Moricone		Capena		Nettuno
8	Genazzano		Olevano Romano		Castel Gandolfo		Palestrina
	Santa Marinella		Percile		Castelnuovo di Porto		Palombara Sabina
9	Affile		Pisoniano		Castel S. Pietro R.		Pomezia
	Agosta		Poli		Cerveteri		Riano
	Allumiere		Riofreddo		Civitavecchia		Rignano Flaminio
	Anticoli Corrado		Rocca Canterano		Civitella San Paolo		Rocca di Papa
	Arcinazzo Romano		Rocca di Cave		Colleferro		Rocca Priora
	Arsoli		Roccagiovine		Colonna		Sacrofano
	Bellegra		Rocca Santo Stefano		Fiano Romano		San Polo dei Cavalieri
	Camerata Nuova		Roiate		Formello		Sant'Angelo Romano
	Canterano		Roviano		Frascati		Segni
	Capranica Prenestina		Sambuci		Gallicano nel Lazio		Tivoli
	Carpineto Romano		San Gregorio da Sassola		Gavignano		Torrita Tiberina
	Casape		Sant'Oreste		Genzano di Roma		Trevignano Romano
	Castel Madama		San Vito Romano		Grottaferrata		Valmontone
	Cerreto Laziale		Subiaco		Guidonia Montecelio		Velletri
	Cervara di Roma		Vallepietra		Labico		Zagarolo
	Ciciliano		Vallinfreda		Lanuvio		Lariano
	Cineto Romano		Vicovaro		Mandela		Ladispoli
	Filacciano		Vivaro Romano		Manziana		Ardea
	Gerano	10	Saracinesco		Marino		Ciampino
	Gorga	11	Tolfa		Mazzano Romano		San Cesareo
	Jenne	12	Albano Laziale		Mentana		Fiumicino
							Fonte Nuova

Fig. 10. Aggregate map

4 Conclusions

Given the 121 municipalities of the province of Rome, we have described them in terms of 43 variables on the demand for mobility within and towards Rome, as well as other various specific socio-economic and territorial characteristics.

Factorial analysis has demonstrated eleven major components can explain 78% of the overall variance of the system. The representative points of the municipalities 121 were distributed on each of the components emerged, in descending order of coordinated, from the largest to the smallest on the positive semi-axis on the negative semi-axis (larger absolute value).

This reduces the system of municipalitys by a space 43 to a size 11 to size (using factor analysis). I wanted to see if this new space in 11 sizes, the representative points of municipalitys grouped in the same groups that, with a good cluster likeness [24, 25].

The similarity coefficient T between two municipalities can vary between 0 and 1. In this process I used a threshold T = 0.77 after sampling some producing or few (low threshold) or too many (high threshold) groups. The method used and that of the similarity matrix which is a square symmetric matrix whose elements i, j are 1 if the municipalities i and j are similar (that is, have their similarity coefficient > T), 0 otherwise. The similarity matrix has been interpreted as the adjacency matrix associated to a digraph. In particular, being a symmetric matrix, it can be interpreted as the matrix of an undirected graph [26].

To determine the similarity coefficient s (i, j) between two municipality i and j, i calculated the modules of the i-th representative vectors and the j-th municipality, that is, D_i and D_j, having:

$$s(i, j) = \sum_k \left(D_{i,k} * D_{j,k}\right) / \left(D_i * D_j\right)$$

with $D_{i,k}$ the components of the vector D_i where $D_i = \sqrt{\Sigma D_{i,k}^2}$. Thus the 121 municipalities are aggregated according to their inherent and objective "similarity" arising from the peculiarities of the descriptive variables (see Table 8 and Fig. 10).

The first three main components explain each, respectively, 25%, 17% and 8%, for a total of 50% of the overall variability of the system. After optimizing by rotating the axes, having obtained a total explained variance greater than 0.30, the first two main components are characterized by maximum load factors (coefficients of correlation between variables and factors) or close to the unit. These variables describe the current state of the system, mainly regarding aspects related to the demographic size of municipalities.

The third major component, which alone explains 8% of the overall variance of the system, is characterized by the descriptive variables of the demographic dynamics of the municipalities in question. (Average annual and ten-year variation rate of the resident population, rate of change in average house purchase price, study or work mobility demand by private means of transport, households with potential economic disadvantages, etc.).

It should be noted that all clusters corresponding to cluster analysis assigned to cluster 12 are located on the positive half of the third major component. This explains that municipalities in Group 12 are those in the province of Rome who most need public accompanying measures for their socio-economic growth.

From the cluster analysis emerged 12 groups in which the first 7 are composed of only one municipality, group 8 is composed of two municipalities. Group 9 is made up of 49 municipalities which would seem less dependent on Rome's economic activities as they are municipality where agricultural activities prevail with reduced industrial and tertiary activity, which is less propitious to mobility.

Group 12 is made up of 61 municipalities and is thus the largest in the belt of the main pole made up of the city of Rome gravitating on this from an economic point of view with intense radio-centric mobility.

The remaining groups are made up of individual municipalities with individual socio-economic and geographical features.

A data mining method is being processed for automated extraction of profiles of each group.

References

1. Batty, M.: An activity allocation model for the Notts/Derby sub-region. Regional Stud. **4**(3) (1970)
2. Broadbent, T.A.: Zone size and spatial interaction. Centre for Environmental Studies, Working Note 106 (1969)

3. Carroll, J.D., Bevis, H.W.: Predicting local travel in urban regions. In: Papers and Proceedings of Regional Science Association, vol. 3 (1957)
4. Hayes, C.: Retail location models. Centre for Environmental Studies, Working Paper 16 (1968)
5. Cripps, E.L. Limitations of the Gravity Concept, in Styles (1968)
6. Cripps, E.L., Carter, E. The empirical development of a disaggregated residential location model: some preliminary results. Urban Systems Research Unit, University of Reading, Working Paper 9 (1971)
7. Freeman, F.: Wilbur Smith and Association: London Traffic Survey, vol. II. Greater London Council (1966)
8. Hansen, W.G. How accessibility shapes land use. J. Am. Inst. Planners (1959). Maggio
9. Isard, W.: Methods of Regional Anaiysis. MIT Press, Cambridge (1960)
10. Lakshmanan, T.R., Hansen, W.G.: A retail market potential model. J. Am. Inst. Planners (1965). Maggio
11. Lewis, J.P.: The invasion of planning. J. Town Plan. Inst. (1970). Maggio
12. McLaughlin, J.B. et al.: Regional Shopping Centres in North West Englattd, Part 11. University of Manchester (1966)
13. Shcneider, M.: Gravity models and trip distribution theory. In: Papers and Proceeding of the Regional Science Asso.ciution, vol. 5 (1959)
14. Styles, B.J. (ed.): Gravity Models in Town Planning. Lanchester Polytechnic (1968)
15. Tanner, J.C.: Some factors affecting the amount of travel. Road Research Laboratory Paper No. 58 (1961)
16. Wilson, A.G.: The use of entropy maximising methods in the theory of trip distribution. J. Transp. Econ. Policy **3**(1) (1969)
17. Hotelling, H.: Analysis of a complex of statistical variables into principal components. J. Educ. Pasychol. (1933)
18. Girshick, M.A.: Principal components. J. Am. Stat. Assoc. (1936)
19. Hotelling, H.: Simplified calculation of principal components. Psychometrika (1936)
20. Cusimano, G.: La metodologia statistica condizionata dell'analisi di più variabili. DELF-Palermo (1955)
21. Saddocchi, S.: Manuale di analisi statistica multivariata, F. Angeli (1980)
22. Wilson, A.G.: Disaggregating elementary residential models. Centre for Environmental Studies, Working Paper 37 (1969)
23. Wilson, A.G.: Entropy in urban and regional modelling. Centre for environmental studies, Working Paper 26 (1969)
24. Johnson, M.P.: A spatial decision support system prototype for housing mobility program planning. J. Geog. Syst. **3**(1), 49–67 (2001)
25. Johnson, M.P.: Spatial decision support for assisted housing mobility counseling. Dec. Support Syst. **41**(1), 296–312 (2005)
26. Mazzei, M., Palma, A.: Comparative analysis of models of location and spatial interaction. ICCSA **4**, 253–267 (2014)

Analyzing Effective Factors on Urban Growth Management Focusing on Remote Sensing Indices in Karaj, Iran

Mohamad Molaei Qelichi[1], Beniamino Murgante[2],
Rahmatollah Farhoudi[1], Saeed Zanganeh Shahraki[1(✉)],
Keramatollah Ziari[1], and Ahmad Pourahmad[1]

[1] Faculty of Geography, University of Tehran, Tehran, Iran
Saeed.zanganeh@ut.ac.ir
[2] School of Engineering, University of Basilicata, Potenza, Italy

Abstract. Although the growth of cities is a positive phenomenon, but the problem is an uncontrolled and unbalanced growth of cities. In order to control this growth, different policies in different countries have suggested. These policies don't always have the same content and they can have different effects on the city and its surroundings. Like many developing countries, Iranian cities rapidly growing in terms of population and physically expanding at a high rate. This research investigates the factors that account for urban growth management in Iranian cities. Karaj metropolis has been studied as a case. Karaj has been experiencing significantly higher rates in the total area of urban environments mostly due to its socioeconomic attractions over four decades ago. To evaluate the dimensions of urban growth management in Karaj city, Factor analysis was used in form of classified sampling. Furthermore, in order to describe the variables in the districts of Karaj city, the COPRAS method is used. Finally, differences between urban area and indices of built-up area were analyzed. Results show that five factors effect on urban growth management in Iranian cities; policies and rules factor, physical, economic, social and environmental factors.

Keywords: Urban growth management · Factor analysis · Built-up indices · COPRAS · Karaj city

1 Introduction

The rapid growth of cities around the world is due to the cities' inability to provide services for their rapidly growing populations. Since the 1960s, urban sprawl has become a global problem in relation to metropolitan growth, not only in North America and Western Europe but also in some cities in developing countries (Keiner et al. 2005).

This paper is based on the Ph.D dissertation under the title "Explanation and presentation of optimal pattern to urban growth management in Karaj city, Iran", presented in Faculty of Geography, University of Tehran.

© Springer International Publishing AG 2017
O. Gervasi et al. (Eds.): ICCSA 2017, Part IV, LNCS 10407, pp. 469–484, 2017.
DOI: 10.1007/978-3-319-62401-3_34

Like many developing countries, Iranian cities are growing in population and physically growing at a high rate.

One of the towns faced with the problem of uncontrolled horizontal growth, is the city of Karaj. It was a garden city until 1960s, but with immigration growth; destruction of green areas and transfer of agricultural water to Tehran, the new Karaj has been emerged. Its physical development is one of the main challenges of the city, which has caused the loss of orchards and agricultural lands and increased the cost of municipal services. Other problems include the scattered construction, traffic congestion, loss of identity and social characteristics of neighborhoods, pollution, loss of natural landscapes, poor quality of life and etc.

"A variety of attitudes to control growth have been cultivated ever since. These have been captured through the notion of growth management" (Pallagst 2007). However, 'growth management' and 'growth control' are used interchangeably. The term of urban growth management refers to managing restrictions on growth or on those who are under the influence of growth or its management (Cho 2005). Contemporary urban systems are affected by two dominant paradigms in the field of urban growth. The first one is the European notion which follows the 'Growth Management' through 'Urban Growth Boundary' (make restrictions on suburban expansion through limiting or defining the contours of the Green Belt). Also ideas such as Urban Service Area, Urban Limit Line, Urbanized Tier and Designated Growth Area are derived from this paradigm (Caves 2005). Another one (US), is mainly based on the idea of 'New Urbanism', and in particular 'Smart Growth' that has accepted the suburban sprawl as an inherent and fundamental reality of the contemporary city. American model tries to face the sprawl and decentralization of cities relying on a strategy of 'Compactness' and 'transit-oriented development (TOD)' and maintain the proportionality of permanent conflict between exterior and interior cities (Trancik 1986; Duany et al. 2000; Walters and Brown 2004; Loeb 2008).

In Iran urban growth management policies have been proposed for rapid and irregular growth of suburbs and deal with challenges such as sprawl and connection of the suburban to the capital city (Ismaeilpour et al. 2014). The tools include: master plan, zoning, subdivision regulations, taxes, development costs, investments on infrastructure and other policy instruments, affecting the development of land and construction. This research tries to improve the modern urban growth management by experiment global urban growth management. It can also provide the necessary conditions for improving the quality of urban life by helping to establish a systematic process.

2 Methodology

2.1 Study Area

Karaj is capital of Alborz Province in Iran spanning between latitudes 35°67′–36°14′N and longitudes 50°56′–51°42′E and covers total area of 141 km^2 (Iranian Statistics Center 2012). Karaj has been experiencing a significantly growing in total area of urban environments mostly due to its socioeconomic attractions over the last four decades ago.

Past developments and current challenges has led to some instability in various aspects of environmental, socio-cultural, political-security, economic, spatial and etc. in this range that makes the Karaj boundary into a local and national issue (Sakieh et al. 2014). Figure 1 shows the geographical location of Karaj city.

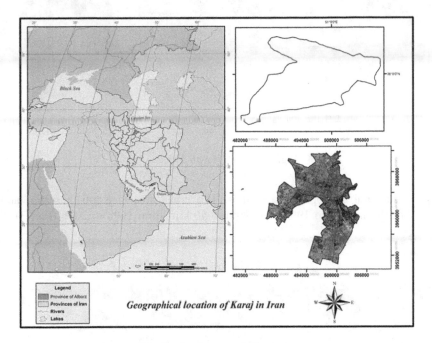

Fig. 1. Study area of Karaj city

2.2   Data Collection

Through reviewing the related literature, variables were extracted and using questionnaire was analyzed in SPSS 22 software. To evaluate the dimensions of urban growth management in Karaj city, Factor analysis has been used in form of classified sampling. Also to describe the present situation in terms of urban growth management variables in the districts of Karaj city, COPRAS method was used. Finally using satellite images and indices of NDBI and BRBA the urban growth was analyzed. These indices use combinations of bands in order to extract a particular land cover.

3   Results and Discussion

3.1   Urban Growth in Karaj

In the first stage of our analysis, the urban growth process in the study area was investigated. In Fig. 2 the urban expansion has shown for the years 1984, 1998 and 2016. As Figure shown, unbalanced growth of urban population in Karaj effected on

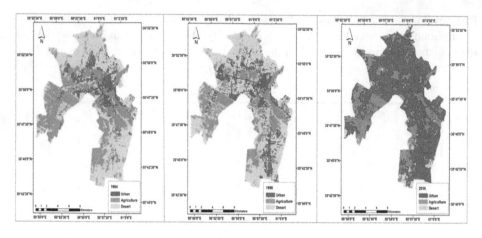

Fig. 2. Urban growth in Karaj

losing agricultural and open space lands. The urban area in Karaj increased about 13.695 km^2 from 1984 to 1998, and about 5.56 km^2 from 1998 to 2016 (Fig. 3).

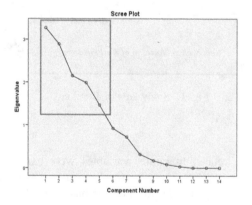

Fig. 3. Scree plot of Eigenvalues

3.2 Dimensions of the Urban Growth Management Using Factor Analysis

Factor analysis is a technique to identify emergent multistability within the phase space of a system of responses to a set of measures. The Five factor model of personality is an inductive model (Friedman and Schustack 2012) which identified the emergent multistable factors (e.g., Openness, Conscientiousness, Extraversion, Agreeableness, Neuroticism) from repeated factor analyses of behavioral-affective measures (Digman 1990).

Factor analysis results in which used to identify and study factors affecting urban growth management (Severine 2007) in study area of Karaj. Results of KMO test have shown that with 0.722 and more than 0.6 acceptable for factor analysis. Factor analysis is based on the correlation matrix of the variables. Table 1 indicates variables and relationship between variables with initial and extraction communalities.

Table 1. Correlation between variables

Communalities	Initial	Extraction
Sprawl problem	1	0.905
Municipal zoning	1	0.73
Provide housing opportunities	1	0.778
Restrain population growth	1	0.895
Improve urban vitality	1	0.867
Regulating physical development	1	0.621
Improve quality of life	1	0.932
Containing urban development	1	0.899
Financial healthy	1	0.673
Increase neighborhood quality	1	0.943
Improvements of urban infrastructures	1	0.827
Sustainable income of municipality	1	0.82
Farmland and open space preservation	1	0.924
Environmental healthy	1	0.951

Extraction Method: Principal Component Analysis.

Communalities is the proportion of each variable's variance that can be explained by the factors (Rietveld and Hout 1993). Variables with low values are not well represented (Kaur 2015). As shown in Table 1, extraction for all of variables is the greater than 0.5.

In the following, in order to define the optimal number of factors, Scree plot has used. The eigenvalues associated with each factor is shown in Fig. 3 the five factors indicated 84.029% of the total variance in the data. The remaining urban growth management dimensions did not explain any significant amount of variances in growth management satisfaction from the city. Therefore it could be significantly reduced the complexity of variable systems using these five factors with losing just 15.970% of variables (Table 2).

Table 2. Extraction factors before the rotation

Component	Extraction sums of squared loadings		
	Total	% of variance	Cumulative %
1	3.27	23.357	23.357
2	2.89	20.644	44.002
3	2.15	15.358	59.36
4	1.988	14.198	73.558
5	1.466	10.471	84.029

Extraction Method: Principal Component Analysis.

One of the most important concepts in factor analysis is rotation of factors (Osborne 2015). Factors are rotated for better interpretation since unrotated factors are ambiguous. The goal of rotation is to achieve an optimal simple structure which attempts to have each variable load on as few factors as possible, but maximizes the number of high loadings on each variable (Rumme 1970; Yong and Pearce 2013). Rotation methods are either orthogonal or oblique. Simply put, orthogonal rotation methods suppose that the factors in the analysis are uncorrelated (Dean 2009). Orthogonal rotation is when the factors are rotated 90° from each other, and it is supposed that the factors are uncorrelated (Yong and Pearce 2013). On the other hand, Oblique rotation, which allows the factors to be statistically related (Tabachnick 1996). oblique rotation produces a pattern matrix that contains the factor or item loadings and factor correlation matrix that includes the correlations between the factors (Yong and Pearce 2013). The decision between orthogonal and oblique or varimax rotation was conducted on each scale using data (Rummel 1970; Pirasteh et al. 2008). "Varimax minimizes the number of variables that have high loadings on each factor and works to make small loadings even smaller" (Yong and Pearce 2013). As you can see in Table 3 rotation sums of squared loadings for each factor is calculated.

Table 3. Rotationsums of squared loadings and percent of explained variance for each factor

Component	Rotation sums of squared loadings		
	Total	% of variance	Cumulative %
1	2.548	18.201	18.201
2	2.415	17.250	35.452
3	2.407	17.193	52.645
4	2.398	17.125	69.770
5	1.996	14.259	84.029

Extraction Method: Principal Component Analysis.

In rotated component matrix, columns indicate derived factors and rows indicate input variables. Loadings represent degree to which each of the variables "correlates" with each of the factors and their range are from −1 to 1 (Yong and Pearce 2013) (Table 4).

In this research, the five factors identify the dimensions of urban growth management as follows:

First Factor

As shown in Table 3, the mean value of this factor is 2.548 that accounts for 18.201% of variance and is the most important factor. This factor can be labeled as "policies and rules"; since it shows high loadings on the attributes of municipal zoning, restrain population growth and containing urban development.

Second Factor

This factor shows about 17.25% of the data set's common variance. Therefore this factor could be called as "physical" factor, since it shows high loadings on the attributes of sprawl problem and regulating physical development.

Table 4. Rotated component matrix[a]

	Component				
	1	2	3	4	5
Sprawl problem	.083	.870	−.366	−.086	.014
Municipal zoning	.698	−.221	.103	.425	−.039
Provide housing opportunities	.329	.501	.552	−.124	−.314
Restrain population growth	.931	.159	−.045	−.023	.009
Improve urban vitality	.139	−.002	.010	.920	.014
Regulating physical development	.034	.766	.040	.175	.020
Improve quality of life	.021	.569	.404	.577	.333
Containing urban development	−.942	−.106	.024	−.017	−.015
Financial healthy	.269	.151	−.527	−.404	.370
Increase neighborhood quality	−.033	−.210	.430	−.830	.153
Improvements of urban infrastructures	.144	.317	−.754	.355	−.104
Sustainable income of municipality	.110	.047	.838	.017	−.320
Farmland and open space preservation	.159	−.283	−.212	−.015	.879
Environmental healthy	−.198	.401	−.107	−.050	.859

Extraction Method: Principal Component Analysis.
Rotation Method: Varimax with Kaiser Normalization.
[a]Rotation converged in 6 iterations.

Table 5. The weight of criteria in entropy

Criteria	Weight	Criteria	Weight
Sprawl problem	0.044	Containing urban development	0.021
Municipal zoning	0.049	Financial healthy	0.047
Provide housing opportunities	0.112	Increase neighborhood quality	0.014
Restrain population growth	0.107	Improvements of urban infrastructures	0.087
Improve urban vitality	0.094	Sustainable income of municipality	0.083
Regulating physical development	0.129	Farmland and open space preservation	0.104
Improve quality of life	0.017	Environmental healthy	0.092

Third Factor
This factor indicates about 17.193% of the data set's common variance. The eigenvalue for this factor is 2.407. This factor can be labeled as "economic" factor, and links provide housing opportunities, financial healthy, improvements of urban infrastructures and sustainable income of municipality.

Fourth Factor
The eigenvalue for the fourth factor is 2.398. This factor accounts for about 17.125% of the data set's common variance. The fourth factor consists of three variables: improve urban vitality, improve quality of life and increase neighborhood quality. This factor can be labeled as "social" factor.

Fifth Factor

The eigenvalue for the fifth factor is 1.996. This Factor indicates about 14.259% of the data set's common variance and including farmland and open space preservation and environmental healthy. Therefore, this factor can be labeled as "environmental" factor.

3.3 Analyzing the Urban Growth Management Indicators in Karajdistricts

COPRAS is one of the multi criteria decision making techniques and is using for the ranking of alternatives. In order to this purpose, uses the weight of criteria (Kaklauskas et al. 2006; Kanapeckiene et al. 2010; Chatterjee and Chakraborty 2012; Mulliner et al. 2013).

COPRAS was first put forward by (Zavadskas et al. 2008), is used to prioritize the alternatives on the basis of several criteria along with the associated criteria weights (Das et al. 2012). COPRAS has the ability to account for both positive (maximizing) and negative (minimizing) evaluation criteria (Mulliner et al. 2013). To execute the COPRAS model these step must be running:

At the first step, weight of each criterion must be assigned. To weighting, Entropy method is used (Table 5). Entropy is a major concept in the physical sciences, social sciences and information theory, so that reflects the uncertainty of the expected information content of a message. In other words, the Entropy is a criterion in the information theory that indicates the uncertainty expressed by a discrete probability distribution. This uncertainty can be described as follows (Sudhira et al. 2003):

$$E = -k \sum_{i=1}^{n} [p_i \times Lnp_i] \qquad (1)$$

Where K is a positive constant and it is determined as if we have:

E.0 $\leq$ E $\leq$ 1 is calculated from the probability distribution of P_i based on the statistical mechanism. Decision-making matrix of multi-attribute models contains information that Entropy can be used as a criterion for its evaluation. The information content of the matrix is calculated as P_{ij} in the following.

$$p_{ij} = \frac{r_{ij}}{\sum r_{ij}} \forall i, j \qquad (2)$$

And we will have for E_j per criteria:

$$E_j = -k \sum_{i=1}^{n} [p_i \times Lnp_{ij}]; \forall j \qquad (3)$$

So that it keeps the value of E_j between 0 and 1.

The uncertainty or deviation degree (d_j) is calculated from data stating that how much useful information does the jth criteria make available for the decision-maker? If the standardized data be closer to each other then it reflects that the competing alternatives are not significantly different in terms of those criteria. Thus, the role of that index should be reduced as much in decision-making. Therefore (Affisco and Chanin 1990):

$$d_j = 1 - E_j; \forall j \tag{4}$$

And finally, for weights (W_j) of the criteria, we have:

$$w_j = \frac{d_j}{\sum_{j=1}^{n} d_j}; \forall j \tag{5}$$

After weighting the criteria, decision-making matrix D as next step of COPRAS is forming. This matrix is an $(M \times N)$ matrix in which element a_{ij} demonstrates the performance of alternative Ai when it is evaluated in terms of decision criterion C_j (Triantaphyllou 1998) (Table 6).

Table 6. Decision matrix of criteria

Criteria	District 1	District 2	District 3	District 4	District 5	District 6	District 7	District 8	District 9	District 10	District 11	District 12
Sprawl problem	3.2	3.3	2.73	2.5	2.61	2.31	2.41	3	3.6	2.8	3.4	3.1
Municipal zoning	2.66	2.71	2.43	3.27	2.9	2.12	2.98	2.34	2.11	2.33	2.77	2.03
Provide housing opportunities	3.5	2.74	2.15	2.22	3	2.37	3.65	3.42	3.66	2.57	2.45	1.8
Restrain population growth	3.37	3.06	2.88	3.14	3.1	2.43	2.66	2.98	3.2	3.27	4.03	1.4
Improve urban vitality	3.41	3	2.89	2.29	3.08	2.87	3.65	1.83	2.17	2.45	3.77	2.8
Regulating physical development	2.95	3.15	1.36	2.72	1.8	1.69	2.54	2.73	2.68	1.9	2.55	2.9
Improve quality of life	3.43	3.23	3.11	2.88	2.81	3.06	3.78	3.19	3.27	2.99	3.65	3.22
Containing urban development	3.12	3.3	3.62	3	3.48	3.73	3.66	3.45	3.47	3.3	2.95	4.19
Financial healthy	2.84	3.2	3.28	3.11	3.65	2.2	2.94	3.57	3.2	4.1	3.46	3.42
Increase neighborhood quality	3.53	3.14	3.75	3.59	3.52	3.77	3.5	4.23	3.7	3.91	3.27	3.39
Improvements of urban infrastructures	2.59	3.9	2.47	2.05	3.4	2.26	2.52	2.29	2.6	3.12	3.53	3.03
Sustainable income of municipality	4.31	3.19	3.4	3.09	2.74	3.27	4.2	3.57	2.9	3.21	2.19	2.4
Farmland and open space preservation	2.05	1.84	2.48	3.3	2.65	2.81	2.82	2.86	2.39	3.63	4	3.17
Environmental healthy	2.67	2.93	3.26	3.16	2.09	2.37	3.43	3.81	3.22	3.61	4.13	4.29

The second step is in any multi-criteria analysis is normalization of the decision-making matrix D. Normalization translates data measured with different units – such as points, ratio and percentage – into weighted dimension- less variables, allowing their direct comparison by the following equation (Mulliner et al. 2013) (Table 7):

$$d_{ij} = \frac{q_j}{\sum_{j}^{n} = 1 x_{ij}} x_{ij} \tag{6}$$

Table 7. Weighted normalized decision matrix

Criteria	A1	A2	A3	A4	A5	A6	A7	A8	A9	A10	A11	A12
Sprawl problem	0.004	0.004	0.003	0.003	0.003	0.003	0.003	0.004	0.005	0.004	0.004	0.004
Municipal zoning	0.004	0.004	0.004	0.005	0.005	0.003	0.005	0.004	0.003	0.004	0.004	0.003
Provide housing opportunities	0.012	0.009	0.007	0.007	0.010	0.008	0.012	0.011	0.012	0.009	0.008	0.006
Restrain population growth	0.010	0.009	0.009	0.009	0.009	0.007	0.008	0.009	0.010	0.010	0.012	0.004
Improve urban vitality	0.009	0.008	0.008	0.006	0.008	0.008	0.010	0.005	0.006	0.007	0.010	0.008
Regulating physical development	0.013	0.014	0.006	0.012	0.008	0.008	0.011	0.012	0.012	0.008	0.011	0.013
Improve quality of life	0.002	0.001	0.001	0.001	0.001	0.001	0.002	0.001	0.001	0.001	0.002	0.001
Containing urban development	0.002	0.002	0.002	0.002	0.002	0.002	0.002	0.002	0.002	0.002	0.002	0.002
Financial healthy	0.003	0.004	0.004	0.004	0.004	0.003	0.004	0.004	0.004	0.005	0.004	0.004
Increase neighborhood quality	0.001	0.001	0.001	0.001	0.001	0.001	0.001	0.001	0.001	0.001	0.001	0.001
Improvements of urban infrastructures	0.007	0.010	0.006	0.005	0.009	0.006	0.006	0.006	0.007	0.008	0.009	0.008
Sustainable income of municipality	0.009	0.007	0.007	0.007	0.006	0.007	0.009	0.008	0.006	0.007	0.005	0.005
Farmland and open space preservation	0.006	0.006	0.008	0.010	0.008	0.009	0.009	0.009	0.007	0.011	0.012	0.010
Environmental healthy	0.006	0.007	0.008	0.007	0.005	0.006	0.008	0.009	0.008	0.009	0.010	0.010

In Eq. 1, q_j is the significant of i-th criterion and X_i is the value of i-th criterion in the j-th alternative of a solution (Kaklauskas et al. 2010). In the next step positive (maximizing) and negative (minimizing) of criteria are described (Mulliner et al. 2013). The formula for this estimation is obtained by following:

$$s_j^- = \sum_{z_{j=+}} d_{ij} s_j^+ = \sum_{z_{j=-}} d_{ij} \tag{7}$$

The sum of the weights for the criteria as shown in Table 8 is calculated using Eq. 7. (Konstantinos 2008). In final step, determining the relative importance of the alternatives (Q_j) by the following equation (Das et al. 2012):

$$Q_j = s_j^+ + \frac{s_{min}^- \sum_{j}^{n} = 1 s_j^-}{s_j^- \sum_{j}^{n} = 1 \frac{1 s_{min}^-}{s_j}} = s_j^+ + \frac{\sum_{j}^{n} = 1 s_j^-}{s_j^- \sum_{j}^{n} = 1 \frac{1}{s_j}} \tag{8}$$

In Eq. 8, Sj is the sums of the weighted normalized values are computed for both the beneficial attributes (s_j^+) and non-beneficial attributes (s_j^+). The value of Q indicates the priority of each alternative according to criteria. The greater value of alternatives illustrates better rank (Komardey et al. 2011).

Table 8. Results of COPRAS method

	$Sj+$	$Sj-$	Q	Nj	$Rank$
A1	0.072	0.017	0.083	90.53	6
A2	0.068	0.018	0.079	86.26	10
A3	0.065	0.009	0.086	93.51	5
A4	0.066	0.015	0.079	85.5	11
A5	0.069	0.011	0.086	93.86	4
A6	0.061	0.01	0.08	86.73	8
A7	0.075	0.014	0.089	97.14	2
A8	0.069	0.016	0.082	88.97	7
A9	0.067	0.016	0.079	86.34	9
A10	0.073	0.012	0.089	97.08	3
A11	0.079	0.016	0.092	100	1
A12	0.063	0.017	0.075	81.08	12

The results of the COPRAS model indicate that districts 10, 7 and 11 has better status than the other districts in terms of satisfaction with urban growth management. As in metropolitan area of Karaj population growth is focused in the center and this is

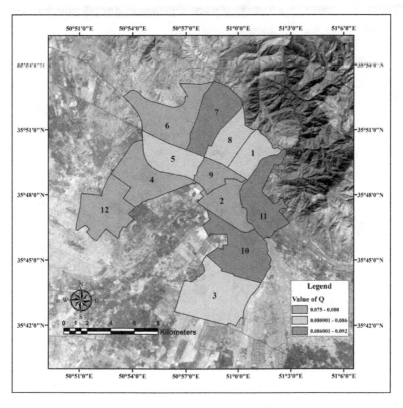

Fig. 4. Districtsranking by COPRAS

due to the centripetal forces such as concentration of economic activities, infrastructure and culture (Fig. 4).

3.4   Remote Sensing Indices in Karaj

The remote sensing data was used in study area. Normalized Difference Built-Up Index (NDBI) and Band Ratio for Built-Up Area index (BRBA) has been devised from Landsat Thematic Mapper (TM) in 1984 and Sentinel 2 in 2017. The NDBI is a method presented by (Zha et al. 2003), which determines the urban area as following equation: (Table 9).

Table 9. Equation of NDBI

Index	Satellite image
$\mathbf{NDBI_{L5}} = (\mathrm{Band_5} - \mathrm{Band_4})/(\mathrm{Band_5} + \mathrm{Band_4})$	Landsat 5 TM
$\mathbf{NDBI_{S2}} = (\mathrm{Band_{11}} - \mathrm{Band_8})/(\mathrm{Band_{11}} + \mathrm{Band_8})$	Sentinel 2 MSI

Results of the analysis showed the index value of $-1 \sim 1$ which indicates total built-up area. An index value less than 1 refers to more built-up lands. As shown in Fig. 5, built-up areas are increased in Karaj city.

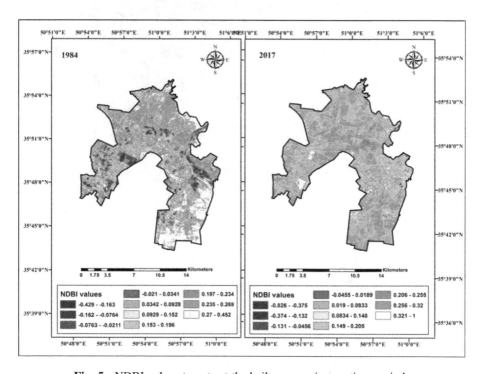

Fig. 5. NDBI values to extract the built-up area in two time periods

In this research, the built-up areas have also been measured from BRBA. The BRBA proposed by (Waqar et al. 2012) was applied in the Landsat TM image using bands. The BRBA is as (Bouzekri et al. 2015): (Table 10).

Table 10. Equation of BRBA

Index	Satellite image
$BRBA_{L5} = (Band_3)/(Band_5)$	Landsat 5 TM
$BRBA_{S2} = (Band_4)/(Band_{11})$	Sentinel 2 MSI

BRBA index results indicated that there is a development in north and southeast of city similar to the NDBI results (Fig. 6).

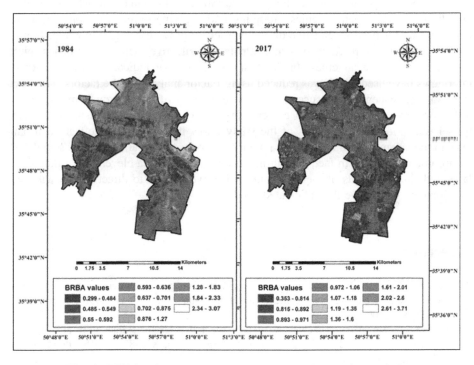

Fig. 6. BRBA values to extract the built-up area in two time periods

With the advance of remote sensing technology, it is possible to study urban land use environments using satellite remote sensing data (Zhang et al. 2016). As a whole, outputs from our investigations will clearly highlight of the environmental monitoring, and detect the changes between the indices of the both areas to observe and quantify urban and land use changes.

4   Conclusions

Although urbanization is a global event, this event is very dynamic in Iran (Seifolddini and Mansourian 2014). The rapid development of urbanization in Iran has been causing problems in different areas and urban environments incapability of responding to the problems led to uneven development of cities. In Iran urban growth management policies including concentrated-deconcentrated growth management policies, zoning, growth management by concentration balance, growth management using the transfer of the development right and the urban growth boundary. In relation to these issues, Karaj metropolis's periphery is faced with numerous challenges which affects the national territory. Past developments and current challenges has led to some instability in various aspects of environmental, socio-cultural, political-security, economic, spatial and etc. in this range that makes the Karaj boundary to a local and national issue. From urban land policy and legislation, we realized this important point that the use of any kind of politics and law, at any time has certain tangible effects which shaped the growth and development of cities. Adopting and applying different policies of urban land in Iran, has been so effective on the way cities grow, especially in Karaj, Iran.

The aim of this research was to evaluate the effective factors on urban growth management in Iranian cities. In the first step, effective indicators through expert interviews have used which was reduced using Factor analysis to five factors. The next step was assessment of the success rate and efficiency of urban growth management indicators from the viewpoint of citizens, the districts of Karaj city using COPRAS model was prioritized. Findings of the study show that five factors effect on urban growth management in Iranian cities; policies and rules, physical, economic, social and environmental factors. In fact, growth management could be a clever use of planning, laws and financial tools of the state and local governments to direct the growth and development to achieve the anticipated needs.

References

Affisco, J.F., Chanin, M.N.: An empirical investigation of integrated multicriteria group decision models in a simulation/gaming context. Simul. Gaming 21(1), 27–47 (1990). doi:10.1177/1046878190211003

Bouzekri, S., Lasbet, A.A., Lachehab, A.: A new spectral index for extraction of built-up area using Landsat-8 data. J. Indian Soc. Remote Sens. 43(4), 867–873 (2015). doi:10.1007/s12524-015-0460-6

Caves, W.: Encyclopedia of the City. Routledge, NewYork, London (2005)

Chandra Das, M., Sarkar, B., Ray, S.: A framework to measure relative performance of Indian technical institutions using integrated fuzzy AHP and COPRAS methodology. Socio-Econ. Plann. Sci. 46(2012), 230–241 (2012)

Chatterjee, P., Chakraborty, S.: Material selection using preferential ranking methods. Mater. Des. 35, 384–393 (2012). doi:10.1016/j.matdes.2011.09.027

Cho, J.: Urban planning and urban Sprawl in Korea. Urban Pol. Res. 23(2), 203–218 (2005)

Das, M.C., Sarkar, B., Ray, S.: A framework to measure relative performance of Indian technical institutions using integrated fuzzy AHP and COPRAS methodology. Socio-Econ. Plann. Sci. **46**(3), 230–241 (2012). doi:10.1016/j.seps.2011.12.001

Dean, J.: Choosing the right type of rotation in PCA and EFA. Shiken JALT Test. Eval. SIG Newsl. **13**, 20–25 (2009)

Digman, J.M.: Personality structure: emergence of the five-factor model. Annu. Rev. Psychol. **41**, 417–440 (1990). doi:10.1146/annurev.ps.41.020190.002221

Duany, A.A., Plater-Zyberk, E., Speck, J.: The inner city. In: Carmona, M., Tiesdell, S. (eds.) Urban Design Readers. Architectural Press, Oxford (2000)

Friedman, H.S., Schustack, M.W.: Personality: Classic Theories and Modern Research, 5th edn. Allyn & Bacon, Boston (2012). ISBN 0-205-05017-4

Yong, A.G., Pearce, S.: A beginner's guide to factor analysis: focusing on exploratory factor analysis. Tutor. Quant. Methods Psychol. **9**(2), 79–94 (2013)

Ismaeilpour, N., Zare, M., Nasrian, Z.: Urban growth management tools emphasizing to controlling sprawl. National Conference on Geography, Urban Planning and Sustainble Development. University Aviation Industry, Tehran (2014)

Kaklauskas, A., Zavadskas, E.K., Naimaviciene, J., Krutinis, M., Plakys, V., Venskus, D.: Model for a complex analysis of intelligent built environment. Autom. Constr. **19**(3), 326–340 (2010). doi:10.1016/j.autcon.2009.12.006

Kaklauskas, A., Zavadskas, E.K., Raslanas, S., Ginevicius, R., Komka, A., Malinauskas, P.: Selection of low-e windows in retrofit of public buildings by applying multiple criteria method COPRAS: a Lithuanian case. Energ. Build. **38**(5), 454–462 (2006). doi:10.1016/j.enbuild.2005.08.005

Kanapeckiene, L., Kaklauskas, A., Zavadskas, E.K., Seniut, M.: Integrated knowledge management model and system for construction projects. Eng. Appl. Artif. Intell. **23**(7), 1200–1215 (2010). doi:10.1016/j.engappai.2010.01.030

Kaur, P.: An empirical study on factors affecting faculty retention in Indian business schools, pp. 63–73. Springer, New Delhi (2015). https://doi.org/10.1007/978-81-322-1979-8_5

Konstantinos, D., Patlitzianas, A.P., Psarras, J.: An information decision support system towards the companies' environment formulation of a modern energy. Renew. Sustain. Energ. Rev. **12** (2008), 780–790 (2008)

Kumar Dey, P., Nath Ghosh, D., Chand Mondal, A.: A MCDM approach for evaluating bowlers performance in IPL. J. Emerg. Trends Comput. Inf. Sci. **2**, 563–573 (2011)

Keiner, M., Koll-Schretzenmayr, M., Schmid, W.A.: Managing Urban Futures: Sustainability and Urban Growth in Developing Countries. Ashgate, Aldershot (2005)

Loeb, D.: Urban voids: grounds for change reimagining Philadelphia's vacant lands. Archit. Des. **78**(1–2), 68–73 (2008)

Mulliner, E., Smallbone, K., Maliene, V.: An assessment of sustainable housing affordability using a multiple criteria decision making method. Omega **41**(2), 270–279 (2013). doi:10.1016/j.omega.2012.05.002

Osborne, J.W.: What is rotating in exploratory factor analysis? Pract. Assess. Res. Eval **20**(2) (2015). http://pareonline.net/getvn.asp?v=20&n=2

Pallagst, K.M.: Growth Management in the US, Between Theory and Practice. Ashgate Publishing Limited, England (2007)

Pirasteh, A., Hidarnia, A., Asghari, A., Faghihzadeh, S., Ghofranipour, F.: Development and validation of psychosocial determinants measures of physical activity among Iranian adolescent girls. BMC Pub. Health **8**, 150 (2008). doi:10.1186/1471-2458-8-150

Rietveld, T., van Hout, R.: Statistical Techniques for the Study of Language and Language Behaviour. De Gruyter Mouton, Berlin, Boston (1993). doi:10.1515/9783110871609

Rummel, R.J.: Applied Factor Analysis. Northwestern University Press, Evanston (1970)

Sakieh, Y., Amiri, B.J., Danekar, A., Feghhi, J., Dezhkam, S.: Simulating urban expansion and scenario prediction using a cellular automata urban growth model, SLEUTH, through a case study of Karaj City. Iran. J. Hous. Built Environ. 30(4), 591–611 (2014). doi:10.1007/s10901-014-9432-3

Severine, M.: The Influence of Local Political Coalitions on the Effectiveness of Urban Containment Policies: Empirical Evidence from Six U.S. States. Florida State University, New York (2007)

Seifolddini, F., Mansourian, H.: Spatial-temporal pattern of urban growth in Tehran Megapole. J. Geogr. Geol. 6(1), 70–80 (2014). doi:10.5539/jgg.v6n1p70

Sudhira, H.S., Ramachandra, T.V., Raj, K.S., Jagadish, K.S.: Urban growth analysis using spatial and temporal data. J. Indian Soc. Remote Sens. 31(4), 299–311 (2003). doi:10.1007/BF03007350

Tabachnick, B.G., Fidell, L.S.: Using Multivariate Statistics, 3rd edn. Harper Collins, New York (1996)

Triantaphyllou, E.: Encyclopedia of Electrical and Electronics Engineering, vol. 15, pp. 175–186. Wiley, New York (1998). Webster, J.G. (ed.)

Trancik, R.: What is lost space? In: Urban Design Readers. Architectural Press, Oxford (1986)

Waqar, M.M., Mirza, J.F., Mumtaz, R., Hussain, E.: Development of new indices for extraction of built-up area & bare soil from landsat data, vol. 1, p. 136 (2012). doi:10.4172/scientificreports.136

Walters, D., Luise Brown, L.: Design First: Design-based Planning for Communities. Architectural Press, Oxford (2004)

Zavadskas, E.K., Kaklauskas, A., Turskis, Z., Tamošaitienė, J.: Selection of the effective dwelling house walls by applying attributes values determined at intervals (2008). https://doi.org/10.3846/1392-3730.2008.14.3

Zha, Y., Gao, J., Ni, S.: Use of normalized difference built-up index in automatically mapping urban areas from TM imagery. Int. J. Remote Sens. 24(3), 583–594 (2003)

Zhang, Y., Balzter, H., Liu, B., Chen, Y.: Analyzing the impacts of urbanization and seasonal variation on land surface temperature based on subpixel fractional covers using landsat images, vol. 10(4), pp. 1–13 (2016)

Iranian Statistics Center: Karaj statistical yearbook 2012. Tehran, Iran (2012)

A Comparative Study Employing CIA Methods in Knowledge-Based Urban Development with Emphasis on Affordable Housing in Iranian Cities (Case: Tabriz)

Behzad Ranjbar nia[1], Beniamino Murgante[2(✉)],
Mohamad Molaei Qelichi[3], and Shahrivar Rustaei[1]

[1] Faculty of Geography and Planning, University of Tabriz, Tabriz, Iran
beniamino.murgante@unibas.it
[2] School of Engineering, University of Basilicata, Potenza, Italy
[3] Faculty of Geography, University of Tehran, Tehran, Iran

Abstract. The majority of this research has been situated in the methods of crisp Micmac and Fuzzy Linguistic Micmac as systematic modeling tools under CIA method. In the current study, both Micmac and Fuzzy linguistic Micmac methods are applied and also compared to analyze the interrelationships between the KBUD and affordable housing variables in Tabriz city, Iran. The obtained results and the rankings taken from both crisp Micmac and FL Micmac are almost the same but few cases, which indicates accuracy of the employed methods. This little variation happens due to the using fuzzy values in FL Micmac that is more precise. One of the advantages of the fuzzy linguistic Micmac is its capability in employing heat maps. The heat maps show whether the system's variables has great influence/dependence on each other or has not. In other words, these maps enable the decision maker to look the strength of the system in a glance, from the existing relations between the factors. The other advantageous of the heat maps is, clustering the factors in an optical mode, because the factors with the same range of influence/dependence may have same role in the system. In our analyzed system, despite of being superior of some variables, the strength of the whole system is in the middle and lower.

Keywords: Knowledge-based · Urban development · Affordable housing · CIA methods · Tabriz

1 Introduction

The growing complication and uncertainty of various developments in future of towns as well as the broad span of key variables from local stages to worldwide levels enforce planners and practitioners adapting a recent approach besides engaging new theories and paradigms in urban planning. The intended paradigm, named knowledge-based urban development (or KBUD), has been presented at the end years of 20th century regarding the effectiveness of knowledge economy on urban communities (Yigitcanlar et al. 2008a). In this regard, KBUD, is considered as a strategic management policy or

© Springer International Publishing AG 2017
O. Gervasi et al. (Eds.): ICCSA 2017, Part IV, LNCS 10407, pp. 485–501, 2017.
DOI: 10.1007/978-3-319-62401-3_35

approach applicable to human dwellings, has reached renown as a strong strategy for sustainable social, urban and economic growth, and for the post-modern development of urban areas and also for competition in all levels (Yigitcanlar et al. 2008a). In this case, in addition to employing new paradigms for coming future of cities, planners or city authorities need future-based methods to utilize the intended theories in proper manner and select best options to plan for coming age.

Futures studies are a knowledge which is able to illustrate the coming events including opportunities and different conditions. It calms concerns, doubts and ambiguity and enables the community to make clear where we can or should go by employing conscious and smart choices, and likely the possibilities appear. In other words, futures-based methods and studies should be noticed as an attempt in forming the future in a dynamic and conscious way (Alizadeh et al. 2008). According to Bell 2003 Futures studies means taking some steps for: "(1) interpreting the past; (2) understanding the present; (3) making decisions and taking action at present; and (4) balancing present and future use of resources" (Bell 2003). It could be concluded the most important aims of such studies that are supported by most researchers are recognition, evaluation, experiment, and recommendation of feasible, possible, and desired futures. Nowadays an increasing number of authority centers are employed in future studies and reinforce this scope of profession. This is due to that making scenarios and future studies are related to creating inspiring perspectives and discovering unknown strategies to perform them.

In this manner, city planners are not exceptions and increasingly apply the futures-based methods in long term urban planning. The various options for the future of the city are formed based on different set of factors/variables from local to global levels in terms of knowledge-based urban development (One of those variables is affordable housing which itself, has 13 sub-criteria that will be indicated in the following). Therefore, planning for the future affordable housing within KBUD framework can be seen as an important challenge especially in Iran with growing rate of urbanization. In the recent 30 years, the population of urban areas has increased from 25 million people to 59 million. The mentioned condition has resulted the scarcity of lands in urban scales for new developments. Shortage of land in urban areas moved cities toward adopting excessive density policies to respond the growing demand of housing especially in big urban areas. In this research, we have chosen Tabriz city as one of the big cities of Iran. In addition to what was mentioned about big towns of Iran, we should add creation of slum areas in city borders of such cities. In this case Tabriz city is not an exception. According to Tabriz municipality estimates, close to 500000 residents of Tabriz (of 1600000 populations), are living in slum areas with ill-conditioned houses. In the other hand, according to future perspective document of Tabriz development (2025), Tabriz city in order to compete in all scales (local, national and global) should be moved toward knowledge-based urban development concept. To achieve the mentioned goal, researchers must have a basis. In the research, in addition to use 32 knowledge-based urban development variables driven by Yigitcanlar and Lönnqvist (2013) theory, researchers employ 13 sub-variables regarding affordable housing within a system framework (45 variables) to analyze impacts which both KBUD and affordable housing variables may have on each other. In other words, one of the objectives of the research is prediction of knowledge-based urban development impact on affordable housing to make clear vision for policy makers of urban authorities from future urban development of Tabriz city by employing two new methods.

Accordingly, it is broadly comprehended as a group of methods to be applied by various authorities predict coming futures by motivating innovation to observe a wide range of possibilities and scenarios (Amer et al. 2013, p. 25). Such scenarios are regarded as logical definitions of alternative hypothesized futures which indicated various perspectives on different periods of past, present or future developments, that can be considered as an important basis for accomplishing actions (Van Notten 2005), in each scale or stage especially in city developments. Scenario systems are employed in making of various feasible models of the coming future; and their target is to produce a figure of oriented knowledge that can be served as a powerful guidance for lines (Kosow and Gabner 2008). Among the most popular methods in terms of qualitative methods TIA[1], FCM[2] (Jetter and Schweinfort 2011) Interpretive Cross Impact Simulation (Enzer 1980) and CIA[3] are considered as the most effective methods. In the current research, we focus on two CIA methods within category of structural analysis. One popular method which was introduced by Godet is Micmac (Godet 2000; Dupperin and Godet 1973). This method has gained much notion. Many researches have been accomplished on it and hence, most of them have developed the method to be more applicable (Duperrin and Godet 1975; Helmer 1977). It should be stated, the prosperity of employing cross-impact analysis is related to systematic analysis of interrelated functions between feasible future developments. Godet recommends employing the mentioned method as the first step in the process of Scenario Planning. In this stage, the specialists define the group of variables related to the subject and afterward, they determine interactions among the variables to recognize the role of different variables in the system. As MODO (2014) describes: "MICMAC analyses the importance of a given set of variables through a matrix that contains the influence that each variable has on the others". The global influence is indicated by using values between 0 and 3. The main characteristic of the process depends on its capability to discover both direct/indirect influence/dependence between factors. This method has been applied in many fields successfully.

Despite being very successful tool, it is not lack of defect. The given values are ambiguous due to the subjective characteristic of these data, impreciseness on the given ideas, not compatible opinions among the experts and so on. In this regard, the existed vagueness is not well-addressed when using these methods, because they employ integer numbers in modeling and also aggregating specialists' opinions. Another disadvantage is low possibility of interpretation of the obtained outcomes, which due to being valued numerically, it does not present proper meaningfulness answers and etc. (MODO 2014). In this manner, to resolve these stated problems and reach a more powerful approach besides compare the obtained results from two methods (Micmac and fuzzy linguistic Micmac), researchers are intended to use Computing with Words (CW) techniques which was proposed by MODO (2014). This technique is called Fuzzy Linguistic Micmac.

---

[1] Trend Impact Analysis.

[2] Fuzzy Cognitive Maps.

[3] Cross Impact Analysis.

Researchers to choose a robust and optimum method in terms of selection of key variables of the knowledge-based urban development which have more impacts on the affordable housing variables need to compare these methods in Tabriz city.

In the current study, both Micmac and Fuzzy linguistic Micmac methods are applied and also compared to analyze the interrelationships of the KBUD and affordable housing variables in Tabriz city. Here we should answer the following questions?

1. What future-based method is more proper to use for city development plans?
2. What variables of knowledge-based urban development play key role in making better future for building affordable houses in Tabriz city?

2   Methodology

The objective of this research is to employing two future-based methods and also comparing the obtained results by them. Our motivation is necessity of using such methods in urban studies to predict the future condition of cities. As mentioned before, Tabriz city in order to be well-located in the knowledge-based urban development path needs to utilize new future-based methods to clarify its development priorities. In this regard, we have used both Micmac and Fuzzy linguistic Micmac in terms of structural analysis to reach a logical way to be applied in Iranian cities to assess most influential/dependent variables.

2.1   Study Area

City of Tabriz is one of the big cities in Iran and capital of east Azerbaijan province. The latitude and longitude are respectively 38°8′N and 46°15′E. Tabriz is the biggest city in the northwest side of the Iran and it is known as culture, politics, commerce, official pole of the country. Due to the accommodating many industrial factories and companies (and also 600 manufactures company), Tabriz is regarded as the second big industrial city following the capital city Tehran. University of Tabriz located in east part of the town is established as the 2nd university after Tehran University. Additionally this town is celebrated as "City of initials" and "safest city of Iran". After Tehran, this town is known as the second in building towers, therefore it is regarded as the skyscrapers city in the Iran. Population rate of Tabriz city is estimated 1,700,000 persons.

According to studies by the United Nations about different cities across the world published in an online magazine, Tabriz is the most beautiful and developed Iranian. This should be noted that, World Health Organization named Tabriz as the healthiest and most hygienic city in Iran two years ago. Tabriz has also been identified as an Iranian city at the forefront of private investment and the most successful in fulfilling the provisions of Article 44 of the Constitution [which deals with privatization of state companies]. The provincial capital of East Azerbaijan was also named as the World's Carpet Capital in 2015 by UNESCO and the World Crafts Council. Only 11 cities have been designated as a World Crafts City. As the representative of Muslim cities on that list Tabriz is in the lead. Additionally, this city has been selected as the tourism capital of Islamic nations in 2018 (Fig. 1).

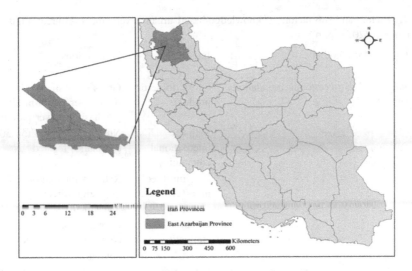

Fig. 1. Study area

3   Results

3.1   Structural Analysis

In this method (structural analysis) we move from the description of the system's indicators and also their interrelations, that both of them are given by specialists. In MICMAC method, three types of relations or influence are described (0 = no influence, 1 = weak influence, 2 = medium and 3 = strong). From our data, the global dependence and influence (direct/indirect) for any indicators are computed by sum the columns and rows. The obtained results of numerical values taken from experts are then employed to rank the indicators and to make the dependence/influence map by drawing the pair influence/dependence for each variable. This resulted map categorizes the indicators in 4 classes that each side has its own interpretation. The quadrants permit the recognition of the various aspects of the system including: inputs, linkage, excluded and resultant indicators of the global systems (Castellanos et al. 2013).

The aim of intended method is determining the key factors, among set of factors distinguished by specialists. Basically, crisp Micmac has three stages:

- **Defining** set of factors
- **Specifying** the various relationships among the factors.
- **Identifying** the most important (key) factors between all the factors.
- **Defining set of factors**. The factors in complicated systems are determined

With the idea of several specialists, literature review and brain storming. An unarranged factor is indicated as an output in this phase. In the current study, we uses a set of KBUD variables derived by (Yigitcanlar and Lönnqvist 2013) and affordable housing factors extracted by researchers from relevant literature review which is known as the main source of knowledge-based urban development (Table 1).

Table 1. Factors and sub-factors of knowledge-based urban development. Source: Yigitcanlar and Lönnqvist (2013, p. 6.)

Indicator categories	Indicator sets	Indicators	Descriptions
Economic development	Macro-economic foundations	Gross domestic product	Gross domestic product (GDP) per capita in USD purchasing power parities
		Major international companies	Number of global top 500 companies located
		Foreign direct investment	Ratio of international share in foreign direct investments
		Urban competitiveness	Global urban competitiveness index ranking
	Knowledge economy foundations	Innovation economy	International city ranking in innovation economy
		Research and development	Ratio of research and development expenditure in GDP
		Patent applications	Patent cooperation treaty patent applications per million inhabitants
		Knowledge worker pool	Ratio between professionals and managers and all workers
Socio-cultural development	Human and social capitals	Education investment	Ration between public spending on education and GDP
		Professional skill base	Ratio of residents over 18 years with tertiary degree
		University reputation	World university rankings
		Broadband access	Ratio of access to fixed broadband subscribers per capita
	Diversity and Independency	Cultural diversity	Ratio of people born abroad
		Social tolerance	International country tolerance ranking
		Socio-economic dependency	Ratio between the elderly population and the working age
		Unemployment level	Ratio of unemployment

(continued)

Table 1. (*continued*)

Indicator categories	Indicator sets	Indicators	Descriptions
Enviro-urban development	Sustainable Urban development	Eco-city formation	International city ranking in eco-city
		Sustainable transport use	Ratio of sustainable transport mode use for commuting
		Environmental impact	CO_2 emissions in metric tons per capita
		Urban form and density	Population density in persons per sq.km
	Quality of life and place	Quality of life	International city ranking in quality of life
		Cost of living	International city ranking in cost of living
		Housing affordability	Ratio between GPD per capita and median dwelling price
		Personal safety	International city ranking in e-government
Institutional development	Governance and planning	Government effectiveness	Level of government effectiveness
		Electronic governance	International city ranking in e-government
		Strategic planning	Level of KBUD strategies in strategic regional and local development plans
		City branding	International city ranking in city branding
	Leadership and support level of institutional and managerial leadership in overseeing KBUD	Effective leadership	Level of institutional and managerial leadership in overseeing KBUD
		Strategic partnership and networking	Level of triple-helix and PPPs and global networking global city ranking
		Community engagement	Level of institutional mechanisms for community building and public participation
		Social cohesion and equality	Level of income inequality in Gini coefficient

Table 2. Factors and sub-factors of affordable housing

Variables of affordable housing	Source
Population density	Kontokosta 2015; Park et al. 2016
Household size	Austin et al. 2014
Energy consumption	Ren et al. 2015
Electricity consumption per capita	Yang 2010
Number of bedrooms	Davison et al. 2016
Number of bathrooms	
Land size	
Time changes for job accessibility	Zhang and Man 2015
Distance to transit stop	Park et al. 2016
Number of new housing units produced annually	Silverman 2009
Number of existing housing units rehabilitated annually	
Median household income	Schively 2008
Number of rental units managed annually	Silverman 2009

Specifying the relationships between the factors. The team of relevant specialists processes a n x n matrix that indicates the impact of factors on the others and vice versa. The mentioned matrix is known as Matrix of Direct Influence (MDI), and the main source of knowledge and expertise in determining the influence of factors are experts. Here, we have the definitions of various weights of impacts.

- 0 means no influence on variable.
- 1 means weak influence on variable.
- 2 means strong influence on variable.
- 3 means very strong influence on variable.

Based on Godet, "in real systems only about 30% of the cells of the MDI matrix have values different from 0" [4].

Identifying the key factors. It can be stated that the important step of the method is discovering the key variables. In direct method, global direct dependence and influence is directly identified based on the Matrix of Direct Influence, while the in terms of indirect global dependence and influence, it is clarified by influence of a variable through other variables of the system.

3.2   FL Micmac

In the current research, we use of linguistic factors derived from MODO (2014) to have a comparison between this method and crisp Micmac and model the interrelations. This method permits the experts to weight these interrelations by employing linguistic values instead of using numerical labels.

Initially, to employ this method, we should determine the set of linguistic values (pre-defined by triangular fuzzy numbers) which will be applied to specify the degree of influence/dependence of one factor on another (see Table 3). Afterward, the specialists utilize linguistic values to set the impact range for each pair of factors.

Ultimately, from the upper and low-order ideals a new set of linguistic value is described for the overall dependencies and influences (Fig. 2).

Table 3. Determination of global influence and dependence of each variable with numerical values (left) and linguistic labels (right) Source: (Castellanos et al. 2013).

Var	V1	V2	V3	inf
V1	0	0	1	1
V2	0	0	3	3
V3	0	1	0	1
Dep	0	1	4	0

Var	V1	V2	V3	inf
V1	Null	Null	Low	**Low**
V2	Null	Null	High	**Med**
V3	Null	Low	Null	**Low**
Dep	**Null**	**Null**	**Med**	Null

To establish the linguistic label that corresponds to each variable, an aggregation operator is applied (see Table 3 right). The information obtained from this operator allows ordering and plotting the variables in an analogous way to MICMAC. This information together with the linguistic labels associated to each variable permits to analyze the results from a relative and absolute point of view as we can see in Fig. 3.

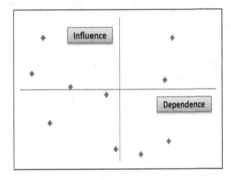

Fig. 2. Influences-dependences map in MICMAC.

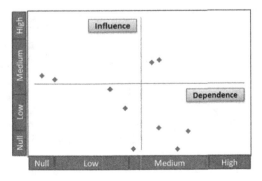

Fig. 3. Influences-dependences map with linguistic labels.

3.3   Comparison of Both Crisp and FL Micmac Methods in a Case Study

To evaluate employed methods, researchers have selected a case study to compare both methods of Micmac and fuzzy linguistic Micmac methods and also to determine the most influential factors of knowledge-based urban development on affordable housing of Tabriz. The data was obtained by using expert's opinions about the impact of various factors on each other within a system including 45 variables of both knowledge-based urban development and affordable housing. It should be noted that the focus of this part is evaluating the obtained results in terms of urban studies besides comparing the results taken from both mentioned methods. In this research the number of 50 experts firstly confirmed the 45 variables as the basis of the study, which can be observed in Tables 1 and 2.

In the fuzzy linguistic method, researchers select $N = 3$ which were defined as fuzzy triangular numbers: (Weak = [1, 1, 2], Moderate = [1, 2, 3], Strong = [2, 3, 3]}, and as it is seen, the same number engaged in the original crisp method (Micmac) by employing three values (1, 2, 3). In order to calculate the dedicated values, researchers use both crisp Micmac and fuzzy linguistic Micmac software. The summary of results are illustrated in the Table 4, that includes the factors on the first five top ranked and last five ranked of both the Micmac and FL Micmac methods.

Table 4. Top and last five positions of the global direct influence rankings, according to MICMAC and FLMICMAC

Variable (Crisp Micmac)	Micmac		Variable (Fuzzy Linguistic Micmac)	FL Micmac	
	D inf value	D inf rank		D inf value	D inf rank
27-Strategic planning	112	1	27-Strategic planning	73.5	1
25-Government effectiveness	110	2	25-Government effectiveness	71.5	2
26-Electronic government	99	3	3-Foreign direct investment	63.33	3
4-Urban competitiveness	97	4	1-Gross domestic product	62.5	4
15-Foreign direct investment	97	5	3-Urban competitiveness	62.5	5
.	.	.	.	.	.
.	.	.	.	.	.
.	.	.	.	.	.
45-Number of rental units	62	41	9-Educational investment	35.33	41
37-Number of bedrooms	61	42	14-Social tolerance	33.66	42
7-Patent applications	59	43	13-Cultural diversity	32.16	43
35-Energy consumption	58	44	11-University reputation	43.5	44
38-Number of bathrooms	42	45	36-Electricity consumption	31.83	45

Table 5. Top and last five positions of the global indirect influence rankings, according to MICMAC and FLMICMAC

Variable (Crisp Micmac)	Micmac		Variable (Fuzzy Linguistic Micmac)	FL Micmac	
	D inf value	D inf rank		D inf value	D inf rank
27-Strategic planning	4.74	1	27-Strategic planning	38.20	1
25-Government effectiveness	4.68	2	25-Government effectiveness	38.10	2
26-Electronic government	4.18	3	3-Foreign direct investment	37.77	3
4-Urban competitiveness	4.16	4	1-Gross domestic product	37.77	4
28-City branding	4.14	5	30-Strategic partnership and networking	37.75	5
.	.	.	.	.	.
.	.	.	.	.	.
.	.	.	.	.	.
7-Patent applications	2.63	41	24-Personal safety	35.96	41
45-Number of rental units	2.60	42	14-Social tolerance	35.84	42
37-Number of bedrooms	2.51	43	13-Cultural diversity	35.55	43
35-Energy consumption	2.50	44	36-Electricity consumption	35.54	44
38-Number of bathrooms	1.75	45	45-Number of rental units	35.12	45

A number of significant results have been reached after the employment of two intended versions to our case, as they are indicated in Tables 3 and 4. The obtained rankings have tremendous similarities but the FL Micmac is more accurate. This is counted as the first significant result (Table 6).

Table 6. Kendall's tau-b test

Ranking (crisp vs. FL Micmac)	Kendall's coefficient
Direct influence	0.710
Direct dependence	0.770
Indirect influence	0.823
Indirect dependence	0.810

After obtaining the results, we used a correlation Kendall's tau-b test to check the significant variations based on the methods rankings. As it is observed in Table 5, no significant variations are seen between two employed method's rankings. Additionally, a significant positive correlation is observed between both original crisp Micmac and fuzzy Micmac methods. However, Fuzzy linguistic Micmac method has more accuracy, since the obtained judgments vagueness by experts' are underlined by using fuzzy sets. Now we can focus on the top ranked variables obtained from long calculations which are shown in Tables 3 and 4. As it is seen, the obtained results of five top ranked variables from both crisp and FL Micmac methods are the same, except one variable on both direct/indirect influence results. Based on the obtained results, from five top ranked variables in terms of direct influence in both methods, four variables (government effectiveness, strategic planning, urban competitiveness, foreign direct investment) are the same. These results illustrate the important role of urban authorities and also necessity of codifying strategic plans for fulfilling knowledge-based urban development and ultimately promoting affordable housing condition in Tabriz city. Such results illustrate that, Tabriz city in order to advance in providing sustainable and affordable houses must be more proactive and conscious in terms of employing strategic plans for future of the city.

3.4   Interpretation of Distribution of Various Factors in the Influence/Dependence Chart

In order to visualize the obtained results of both linguistic and crisp values, we employ two charts obtained from the mentioned methods. The left sided chart is related to FL Micmac and the right sided is corresponded to the crisp Micmac. The definition of these charts is given in the following:

Portraying interrelationships (see Fig. 4) could be accomplished in a 4 district chart. In this manner, both axes of vertical and horizontal are measured according to the violence of dependence and influence of criteria based on the overall values they gain. Of four different districts, each zone plays various roles in the system.

Determinant Factors. In crisp Micmac, north-west part of the chart is dedicated to these factors which also are known as influent variables while, for FL Micmac, these variables are located south-east. This happens because of the design of software by producers. Due to the high impact the global system and also less dependency, these variables can direct the whole system regarding the control which we can make on them. A change in these variables may have huge impact on the overall condition of this system. For the case of Tabriz city, some determinant and also common factors in both methods are: Educational investment, socio-economic dependency, Social tolerance, Socio-economic dependency Energy consumption, Electricity Consumption Per Capita.

Excluded Factors. These variables are placed in south-west zone of the chart with little dependence and influence. Obviously, these factors are known as 'out of line' variables in the system. This is because; they can neither profit from system nor stop a significant evolution of it. Albeit, there can be big difference among the variables of this group of factors. Discharged variables are placed close to the beginning of axes and with a scale of impact; they can be removed from secondary arms, while they have capability to be used as feasible supporting measures. It should be noted that the future knowledge-based plan of affordable housing will be formed by some superior factors which mostly are related to city authorities. Nevertheless, it is considered rather influent than dependent. The lists of common factors are:

Patent applications, eco-city formations, sustainable transport use, number of bedrooms, land size, distance to transit stop.

Relay Factors. These variables locate in north-east side of the chart, In this category, factors are both known very influent and dependent. These are also called instable variables because of having 'boomerang effect'. Additionally, they are able to reinforce or prevent any primary strike in the system. In our case, we have common factors between both methods. These variables are: Gross domestic product, foreign direct investment, urban competitiveness, Innovation economy Research and development, city formation and density, quality of life, government effectiveness, electronic government, median household income. By looking the obtained results, it is revealed that, most of the located factors in north-west part of the chart in both methods are same. The only difference is related to different location of variables in this area. This is because of high accuracy of employing linguistic fuzzy techniques in fuzzy linguistic Micmac method.

Depending Factors. It is seen that, on side is left from four available sides in our charts. In crisp Micmac, the group of variables is located in south-east part of the chart, while in FL Micmac; it is visible in north-west side. These variables are identified as exit factors of the system which are also named as result factors. Their status in the system indicates high dependency and little influence. In our category, two variables are in common among the employed methods which composed of: Living environment, strategic partnership and networking, population density. In order to visualize the obtained results of both linguistic and crisp values, we employ two charts obtained from the mentioned methods. The left sided chart is related to FL Micmac and the right sided is corresponded to the crisp Micmac. The definition of these charts is given in the following:

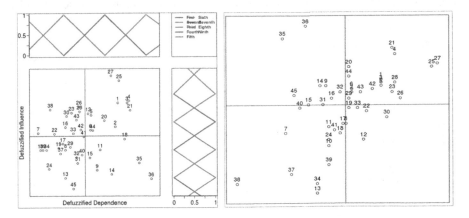

Fig. 4. Fuzzy influence/dependence planes showing the defuzzified influence-dependence pairs and the output linguistic term sets on the axes

It should be noticed that placing a variable on the top of the ranking or chart does not necessarily reflect its' high influence or dependence. In other words this means that the intended variable has higher influence within the system than others, but not necessarily high in absolute terms. This case could not be indicated in the crisp Micmac. Such matter is solved in Fuzzy Linguistic Micmac by illustrating the overall influence/dependence of variables in heat maps. It should be stated that linguistic labels are much easier to better grasp and interpretation by people.

3.5   Overall Linguistic Results Depiction in Heat Maps

Another advantage which FL Micmac can have is producing heat maps to indicate the overall influence/dependence of the variables. In this section, we have produced 2D heat maps which are shown in Fig. 5, in both direct and indirect influence/dependence. In other words, these maps are intended to indicate that despite having priority of some variables on the others; the important matter is degree of their influence/dependence overall. The Micmac method has no such capability as mentioned.

In this regard, to have a distinct map of the absolute dependence/influence of employed variables, it is feasible to brief all of the information in such maps (Fig. 5) illustrating the number of factors with each integration of absolute values of linguistic dependence/influence. In the current research, in the direct and also indirect method, these maps indicate moderate and lower than moderate linguistic terms which are visible in the obtained results. In this case, any square of the obtained map is related to a possible integration of linguistic dependence and influence, and the violence of color expresses the number of variables that have that type of integration of values at the result. Such plot can be accomplished for both methods (direct and indirect), and expresses definite information in an easy way to interpret. In addition, it gives a global perspective of how influential/dependent variables act in our system. So in this case, the overall manner of the entire system is resumed in a plot that assisting a better grasp. The detailed stage of this presentation relies on the granularity $\bar{N}$ which is set by the specialist. For our case study, we have set $\bar{N} = 9$.

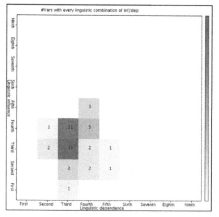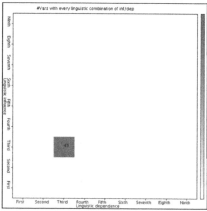

Fig. 5. Number of factors with any possible integration of linguistic influence and dependence for granularity levels at the output by researchers.

The number of various used at the result of the indirect method is small, and they are gathered around labels. This happens because of the fact that in the indirect method there is tension to decay the results after long calculations, guiding ultimately to more unified results that is a prevalent disadvantages of plenty linguistic processes. For this, the normalization accomplished here by taking the βth root tends to prevail such problem. In our case study, these plots permits the expert to check at a first look, that is, most of the factors show intermediate and lower intermediate overall dependence and influence. Additionally, heat maps also serve as a method of bunching the factors, because those with the same integration of linguistic influence and dependence can play an analogous role. In the current research, these obtained plots permits decision maker to check the whole system performance at first glance. In our plots, most of the factors are placed in a lower-intermediate district in terms of global dependence and influence. In addition, heat maps act in a way to cluster the factors, because those variables with the same integration may have a similar role.

4 Conclusions

As a result of the permanent altering of urban areas and appearing their complexity and ambiguous future, an increasing demand for various options and creative planning approaches is felt. A growing concern of practitioners and decision makers in terms of employing various types of strategies for facing the future is considered, resulting the necessity of using principled measuring the subjects corresponded to the accomplishment of future-based planning methods in regard with urban and spatial planning.

Albeit, decision-making approaches for knowledge-based urban development policies is obtaining enhanced notion and knowledge city criteria are imagined to direct decision-making for improved urban futures, the employment of knowledge-based urban development variables for policy makers is still under progress specially in terms of providing affordable housing.

The current research provides a case study of the Tabriz for examining the comparison the results obtained of two employed methods of crisp Micmac and Fuzzy Linguistic Micmac as a systematic modeling tools under CIA method. The effort can be considered a necessary, but not sufficient, condition and a first step towards future-based assessment in affordable housing within the framework of knowledge-based city assessment. The findings of this comparison are indicated in following:

- The obtained results and hence the rankings taken from both crisp Micmac and FL Micmac are almost the same but in few cases, which indicates accuracy of the employed methods. This little variation happens due to the using fuzzy values in FL Micmac that is more precise. In this manner, in both methods, of five top ranked results, we have four same variables including: government effectiveness, strategic planning, urban competitiveness, foreign direct investment. By considering the obtained results, the preference of good governance in Tabriz city to achieve knowledge-based city goals (promoting affordable housing) is hugely felt. Knowledge-based urban development and its variables like affordable housing is a complicated approach that city authorities may not have a clear background of its long terms strategies and policies. The obtained results show that, strong correlation can be existed among these four variables. Local governments can arrange strategic plans to achieve sustainability and knowledge city objectives to be considered as high qualified region with increased gross domestic product.

- One of the advantages of the fuzzy linguistic Micmac is its capability in employing heat maps. The heat maps show whether the system's variables has great influence/dependence on each other or has not. In other words, these maps enable the decision-maker to look the strength of the system in a glance, from the existing relations between the factors. The other advantageous of the heat maps is, clustering the factors in an optical mode, because the factors with the same range of influence/dependence may have same role in the system. In our system, despite of being superior of some variables, the strength of the whole system is in the middle and lower. Therefore, the systems do not reflect a strong influence among the variables.

References

Alizadeh, A., Motlagh, V.V., Nazemi, A.: Scenario Planning. Institute for International Energy Studies (IIES), Tehran (2008). (Text in Persian)

Amer, M., Daim, T.U., Jetter, A.: A review of scenario planning. Futures **46**, 23–40 (2013)

Austin, P.M., Gurran, N., Whitehead, C.M.E.: Planning and affordable housing in Australia, New Zealand and England: common culture; different mechanisms. J. Hous. Built. Environ. **29**(3), 455–472 (2014)

Bell, W.: Foundations of Futures Studies: History, Purposes and Knowledge: Human Science for a New Era, vol. 1. Transaction Publishers, New Brunswick/London (2003)

Castellanos, N.D., Masegosa Arredondo A.D., Iglesias, J.V., Novoa Hernandez, P., Pella, D.A.: Improving scenario method for technology foresight by soft computing techniques. In: The 4th International Seville Conference on Future-Oriented Technology Analysis (FTA), 12–13 May, Seville, Spain (2013)

Davison, G., Han, H., Liu, E.: The impacts of affordable housing development on host neighbourhoods: two Australian case studies. J. Hous. Built Environ. (2016). http://link. springer.com/10.1007/s10901-016-9538-x

Duperrin, J.C., Godet, M.: SMIC 74-a method for constructing and ranking scenarios. Futures **7**(4), 302–312 (1975)

Duperrin, J.C., Godet, M.: Methode de hierarchisation des elements d un sisteme, RapportEconomique du CEA R-45-51 (1973)

Enzer, S.: Interix – an interactive model for studying future business environments: part I. Technol. Forecast. Soc. **17**(2), 141–159 (1980)

Godet, M.: The art of scenarios and strategic planning: tools and pitfalls. Technol. Forecast. Soc. **65**(1), 3–22 (2000)

Helmer, O.: Problems on future research. Futures **9**, 17–31 (1977)

Jetter, A., Schweinfort, W.: Building scenarios with fuzzy cognitive maps: an exploratory study of solar energy. Futures **43**(1), 52–66 (2011)

Kontokosta, C.E.: Do inclusionary zoning policies equitably disperse affordable housing? A comparative spatial analysis. J. Hous. Built Environ. **30**(4), 569–590 (2015)

Kosow, H., Gabner, R.: Methods of Future and Scenario Analysis; Overview, Assessment, and Selection Criteria, DIE Research Project, Development Policy: Questions for the Future, Bonn (2008)

Models of Decision and Optimization Research Group (MODO): A new fuzzy linguistic approach to qualitative cross impact analysis. J. Appl. Soft Comput. **24**, 19–30 (2014)

Park, Y., Huang, S.-K., Newman, G.D.: A statistical meta-analysis of the design components of new urbanism on housing prices. J. Plann. Lit. **31**(4), 435–451 (2016)

Ren, X., Yan, D., Hong, T.: Data mining of space heating system performance in affordable housing. Build. Environ. **89**, 1–13 (2015). doi:10.1016/j.buildenv.2015.02.009

Schively, C.: Sustainable development as a policy guide: an application to affordable housing in island communities. Environ. Dev. Sustain. **10**(6), 769–786 (2008)

Silverman, R.M.: Perceptions of nonprofit funding decisions: a survey of local public administrators and executive directors of community-based housing organizations (CBHOs). Public Org. Rev. **9**(3), 235–246 (2009)

Van Notten, P.: Writing on the wall: scenario development in times of dis-continuity. Ph.D. thesis, University of Maastricht, Maastricht, The Netherlands (2005)

Yang, Y.: Sustainable Urban Transformation Driving Forces, Indicators and Processes. ETH ZURICH (2010). www.ETHZurich/ch/library/e-collection

Yigitcanlar, T., Lönnqvist, A.: Benchmarking knowledge-based urban development performance: results from the international comparison of Helsinki. Cities **31**, 357–369 (2013)

Yigitcanlar, T., O'Connor, K., Westerman, C.: The making of knowledge cities: Melbourne's knowledge-based urban development experience. Cities **25**(2), 63–72 (2008a)

Zhang, C., Man, J.: Examining job accessibility of the urban poor by urban metro and bus a case study of Beijing. Urban Rail Transit **1**(4), 183–193 (2015). http://link.springer.com/10.1007/s40864-015-0026-5

Dynamic Guidance of an Autonomous Vehicle with Spatio-Temporal GIS

Alireza Vafaeinejad[(✉)]

Faculty of Civil, Water and Environmental Engineering, Shahid Beheshti University, Tehran, Iran
a_vafaei@sbu.ac.ir

Abstract. Most of computer-vision systems for vehicle guidance are tuned for highway scenarios. Developing autonomous or driver-assistance systems for complex urban traffic pose new algorithmic and system architecture challenges. This paper introduces a novel system that uses Spatio-Temporal GIS principles and a new traffic determination algorithm. The prototype system can be used as a part of autonomous vehicles controlling structure with analytical capabilities. For these purposes, predicting vehicle motion is done through trajectories. The trajectories are generated using spatial and aspatial information in GIS environment. Then, vehicle is navigated by GPS and a fuzzy logic map matching is used to locate the vehicle position on the map. Traffic congestion algorithm, which passed through 82.5% of evaluations cases successfully, is performed by vehicle's velocity in the third step. Finally, heuristic real-time route finding algorithm is used for dynamic updating of planned vehicle trajectory. Furthermore, the system is open so that further extensions such as controlling autonomous vehicle for avoiding or leaving the banned regions are possible.

Keywords: Autonomous vehicle · Dynamic guidance · Spatio-Temporal GIS · Traffic congestion

1 Introduction

From a research point of view, autonomous vehicles for urban environment are viewed as mobile robots which execute the task of displacing efficiently and guiding themselves through the streets [1]. The modern robotic paradigm indicates that robots have to execute five basic tasks: perceiving environment, deciding reactions, guiding dynamically and planning route, implementing a service layer for managing the fleet of vehicles and responding user's requests and finally realizing them [1].

All mentioned tasks are interested subjects for active research. Traffic detection, route planning and dynamic guidance, which can be considered as parts of these tasks are under investigation in the followings. Many researchers have studied on recent cases to improve quality and capabilities of the tasks [2–6].

Nevertheless, majority of the above mentioned researches are single purposed, because they can just operate based on one proposed case. Hence, they are not cost

© Springer International Publishing AG 2017
O. Gervasi et al. (Eds.): ICCSA 2017, Part IV, LNCS 10407, pp. 502–511, 2017.
DOI: 10.1007/978-3-319-62401-3_36

effective for guiding autonomous vehicle(s) which need multiple applications and analysis in real-time. In addition, most of them use prevalent tools for detecting congestion and guiding vehicles that will cause affinity of autonomous vehicles to various tools.

For solving the mentioned challenges, it is necessary to find an algorithm for detecting congestion, which act without using conventional tools (such as surveillance cameras). In addition, a system that can be equipped with analytical capability and customization is required. GIS (Geospatial Information System) can provide these abilities [7, 8]. Then can be used for our purpose. With respect to variation of autonomous vehicle temporally & spatially, Spatio-Temporal GIS can provide our requirement.

This paper presents the steps for developing a system for guiding autonomous driving vehicles. This will be done by proposing a new algorithm for automatic vehicle detection in traffic congestion (without using conventional tools such as video camera) and Spatio-Temporal GIS (STGIS) capabilities for going out of congestion.

2   System Design and Implementation

The proposed system can be used as a part of the control structure of an autonomous vehicle, which moves in urban environments and has the ability of guiding vehicle. Figure 1 presents the system flowchart.

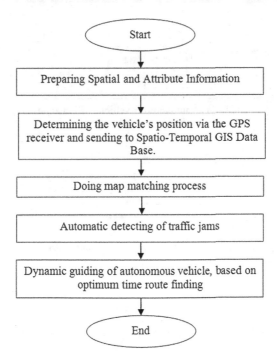

Fig. 1. Flow chart of the system

2.1 Preparing Spatial and Attribute Information

Various analyses can be carried out in Spatio-Temporal GIS. These analyses should be operated on accurate and up-to-date information. The primitive spatial information used in this research, was digital maps (1:1000) of Tehran covering vicinity of Vanak square which produced by Tehran Municipality.

The reference ellipsoid of these maps was WGS84 with UTM projection system. These maps were controlled for some errors such as (overshoot, undershoot, spike, switchback ...) to be ready for GIS analysis. Attribute information such as streets names, delay time, passing time, were also linked to the spatial information.

2.2 Integrating of GPS and STGIS

Recently, GPS (Global Positioning System) technologies are increasingly used in various applications of transportation planning and operation [9]. In order to track the autonomous vehicles, latitude, longitude and time, which are obtained by GPS, will be needed. These data will be stored in Spatio-Temporal Database (STDB).

STDB uses four-generation systems to retrieve, manipulate, represent and store spatially and temporally referenced data [10]. The third one is suitable for this study and has been used to handle data in database. Figure 2 represents a schematic view of this concept.

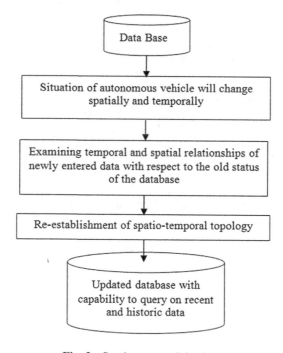

Fig. 2. Spatio-temporal database

In this study, the data is collected with the period of five second (Our GPS up-date rate). The first record of database is processed and information fields of latitude, longitude and time are populated. At this time, a point with the same coordinates will be shown as a graphical object of autonomous vehicle in STGIS. Other records are handled based on the above figure.

2.3 Map Matching Process

The proposed system must correct the positional errors introduced by GPS receiver and recognize the streets from other features in the map and be able to apply map matching process. The basic idea of conventional map matching is comparing the vehicle's trajectory against known streets close to the previous matched position. The street whose shape most closely resembles the current trajectory and previously matched street is selected as the one on which the vehicle is apparently travelling [11].

However, when a map matching based vehicle is travelling in a city area, there may be many streets patterns matching the trajectory reported by the positioning sensors at any given moment. It may be difficult to distinguish precisely on which particular street the vehicle is travelling.

Rather, the system may conclude that the vehicle is "more likely" to be on certain streets and "less likely" to be on some other streets. Therefore, techniques for dealing with qualitative terms such as likeliness are required in the map matching process. Fuzzy logic can be used as an effective method dealing with this task. Zhao (1997) has introduced an efficient algorithm for handling fuzzy logic map matching which has been applied in the system (see appendix) [11].

2.4 Detecting Congestion

Traffic engineering activities usually use wide variety of information and parameters [12]. Our new method has been proposed for modelling and detecting congestion without considering most of these criteria. It is clear that when a vehicle is located in congestion, its velocity will be reduced proportional to the congestion volume. If the vehicle is located in congestion, it can be said that the velocity of vehicle in particular time will be less than a threshold. Of course, for evaluating this hypothetical suggestion different statistical measurements and observations based on street speed limit, date time and the average velocity of vehicle with respect to congestion volume are required.

Accordingly, the congestion volume was measured for some streets near Vanak square in the September of 2006. In the streets which critical velocity was 50 km/h, the velocity average was measured 23.8 km/h. This measurement has been done during a week (excluding holidays) repeatedly between 7:30 to 9:00 AM and 6:00 to 7:30 PM (the rush hour periods). With respect to the results, following constraints were defined for detecting traffic and guiding vehicle (following thresholds are subjective and varies according to the normal traffic pattern).

- If the velocity is in the range of 20–23.8 km/h, congestion will be smooth and fluent, so vehicle can continue moving along the predefined path.

- If the velocity is in the range of 10–20 km/h, congestion is not so heavy and vehicle can leave the path or continue moving.
- If the velocity is less than 10 km/h, congestion is heavy and the vehicle should be guided to evacuate the traffic.

For this purpose, forty vehicles were recorded in three sequentially five seconds. These observations were categorized in three groups (see Fig. 3).

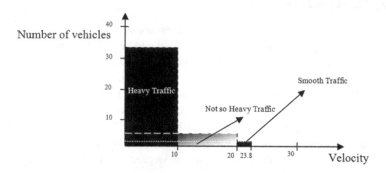

Fig. 3. Examination of the explained method for detecting traffic with forty vehicles

The first vertical bar contains thirty-three vehicles, which situated in heavy congestion. Second part includes five vehicles, which put in middle congestion and the last one is consisted of two vehicles, which located in smooth congestion.

For two recent groups reducing velocity maybe originated from another reasons such as pedestrian or drivers offends. Thus, it is concluded that these conditions are correct for 82.5% of observations in the case study.

2.5   Analytical Modeling with STGIS

STGIS is able to apply changes occurred in time to the model and update it. Based on updated model, various analyses such as finding the nearest facility (for example; gas station) with respect to the vehicle's movement can be done.

In this research, When a vehicle is located in congestion, STGIS can find the nearest available node or junction to the vehicle's position. Then, new path to destination node will be found based on minimum time or distance and the vehicle will be able to change its predefined trajectory.

Since the number of nodes in urban environment is huge, real-time route finding may not be done effectively. Therefore, it is better to consider a heuristic programming to enhance route finding efficiency.

There are different heuristic and probabilistic methods. In recent study, two heuristic shortest path algorithms, which run fastest on real road networks, have been considered. These two algorithms are graph growth algorithm implemented with two queues (TQQ) and Dijkstra algorithm implemented with double buckets (DKD) [13]. These algorithms have been introduced in Pallottino 1984 and Ahuja et al. 1993 respectively [14].

The processing time of these mentioned algorithms and some others were evaluated using real road networks. The algorithms were implemented using various nodes. Table 1 shows execution time of the algorithms.

Table 1. Execution times of algorithms with one to one condition

Number of nodes	Dijkstra	Graph growth	DKD	Genetic
500	0.38	0.42	0.41	0.92
1000	3.48	3.78	3.21	4.78
2000	12.23	11.22	10.56	14.6
3000	38.74	29.89	27.43	35.43
4000	50.23	44.65	41.23	53.34
5000	102.38	89.34	85.65	104.04

Table 1 concludes that when the number of nodes is more than 2000, DKD has better performance than others do. Therefore, this algorithm used for real-time route finding.

In order to implement the algorithm in STGIS environment, some of effective parameters in urban traffic such as volume of traffic congestion, intersection and passing delay and type of streets (e.g., major, local and Collector) which are essential for time based route finding were simulated. Based on these parameters, route-finding algorithm was performed for changing the predefined path of autonomous vehicle (Figs. 4 and 5).

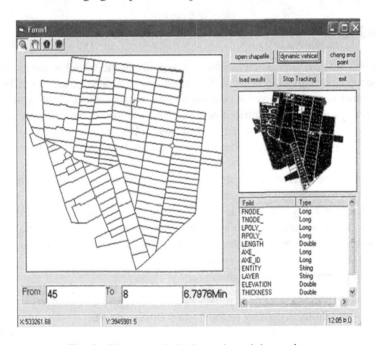

Fig. 4. Shortest path finding using minimum time

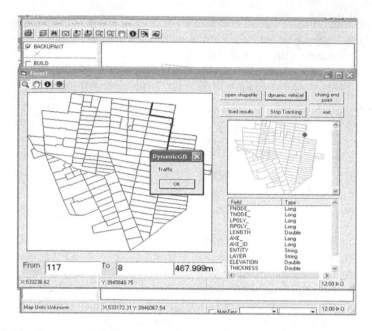

Fig. 5. Shortest path finding using minimum distance and detecting congestion

3   Conclusion

Autonomous vehicles, also called mobile robots and robotic vehicles, for use in urban environments are in their early stage of development. This paper concentrated on developing a system to be used as a part of controlling structure in urban autonomous vehicles. The proposed system has two contributions. The first is automatic recognition of location for autonomous vehicles in traffic jam and the second is introducing Spatio-Temporal GIS (STGIS) functionality for Dynamic guidance of the vehicles and going out of congestion.

Using the traffic determination algorithm will cause freedom from using conventional tools (such as surveillance cameras). In addition, using STGIS that is equipped with analytical capability will provide more facilities for guiding vehicles. For example with STGIS, further extensions such as controlling autonomous vehicle for avoiding or leaving the banned regions are doable. So using STGIS in the control structure of an autonomous vehicle can improve the efficiency.

The future researches can concentrate on:

- Evaluation of presented method to detect traffic congestion in different conditions for testing suitability according to the normal traffic pattern.
- Defining constraints to detect automatic congestion using fuzzy logic method.

Using other Spatio-Temporal functions such as not entering to inclusion and exclusion zones or finding the nearest facility to the vehicles position.

Appendix

See (Fig. 6).

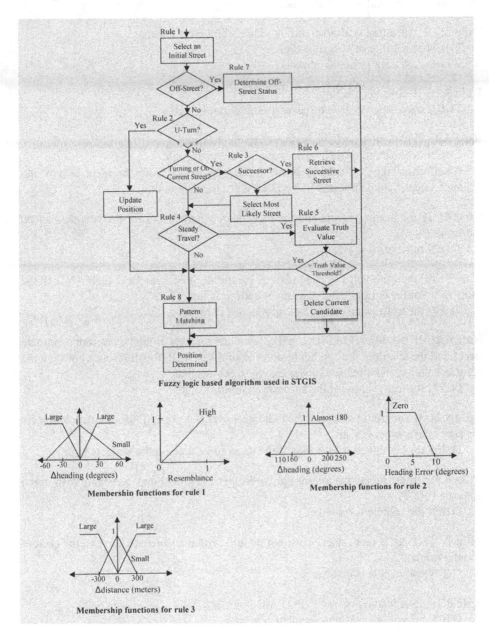

Fig. 6. The fuzzy logic map-matching algorithm and its rules [11]

Rule 1: If Δheading is small
THEN resemblance of the route is high.
Where "Δheading" is defined as the difference between the direction of the street segment and the heading of the vehicle.

Rule 2: IF Δheading is almost 180° AND heading error is zero
THEN possibility of U-turn is high.
Where AND is a minimal operator.

Rule 3.1: IF Δdistance is large
THEN necessity to retrieve successive segment is high.

Rule 3.2: IF Δheading is large and heading error is zero
THEN necessity to retrieve successive segments is high.
Where Δdistance is defined as the difference between the segment length and distance which vehicle has traveled on that particular segment.

Rule 4: IF the heading errors and the root mean square errors for the vehicle's speed are small
THEN the motion is steady.

Rule 5: IF the truth value of the previous candidate street pattern is high AND IF the truth value of the current candidate street pattern is high
THEN the truth value of the correspondence is high.

Rule 6.1: IF the difference between the distances traveled along the current candidate street and the length of the candidate street is small AND IF the difference between the vehicle heading and direction of successive street is small
THEN the truth value for the successive street is high.

Rule 6.2: IF the truth value of the candidate street is high AND IF the truth value for the successive street is high
THEN the combined truth value of the moving vehicle on the street is high.

Rule 6.3: IF no street pattern similar to the path of travel can be found with given distance
THEN the vehicle is on-street.

Rule 7: IF there is more than one street pattern within a given distance to the current vehicle motion
THEN the vehicle is on-street.

Rule 8.1: IF Δheading is small AND Δdistance is small
THEN resemblance of this segment is high.

Rule 8.2: IF resemblance of this segment is high AND resemblance path is high
THEN resemblance of the whole path is high.

References

1. Benenson, R.: Cars Perception, State of the Art. Center of Robotics, ENSMP, Paris (2005)
2. Alder, J.L., Satapathy, G., Manikonda, V., Bowles, B., Blue, V.J.: A multi-agent approach to cooperative traffic management and route guidance. Transp. Res. Part B Methodol. **39**, 297–318 (2005)
3. Al-Hasan, S., Vachtsevanos, G.: Intelligent route planning for fast autonomous vehicles operating in a large natural terrain. Robot. Autonom. Syst. **40**, 1–24 (2002)
4. Yuan, S., Chun, S.A., Spinelli, B., Liu, Y., Zhang, H., Adam, N.R.: Traffic evacuation simulation based on multi-level driving decision model. Transp. Res. Part C Emerg. Technol. **78**, 129–149 (2017)
5. Huang, W., Yan, C., Wang, J., Wang, W.: A time-delay neural network for solving time-dependent shortest path problem. Neural Netw. **90**, 21–28 (2017)
6. Fu, L.: An adaptive routing algorithm for in-vehicle route guidance systems with real-time information. Transp. Res. Part B Methodol. **35**, 749–765 (2001)
7. Vafaeinezhad, A.R., Alesheikh, A.A., Hamrah, M., Nourjou, R., Shad, R.: Using GIS to develop an efficient spatio-temporal task allocation algorithm to human groups in an entirely dynamic environment case study: earthquake rescue teams. In: Gervasi, O., Taniar, D., Murgante, B., Laganà, A., Mun, Y., Gavrilova, Marina L. (eds.) ICCSA 2009. LNCS, vol. 5592, pp. 66–78. Springer, Heidelberg (2009). doi:10.1007/978-3-642-02454-2_5
8. Vafaeinezhad, A.R., Alesheikh, A.A., Nouri, J.: Developing a spatio-temporal model of risk management for earthquake life detection rescue team. Int. J. Environ. Sci. Technol. **7**, 243–250 (2010)
9. Nadi, S., Delavar, M.R.: Spatio-Temporal modeling of dynamic phenomena in GIS. In: The 9th Scandinavian Research Conference on Geographical Information Science, ScanGIS 2003, Espoo, Finland (2003)
10. Roshannejad, A.A.: The Management of Spatio-Temporal data in a national geographic information system. Ph.D. Thesis, University of Twente (1996)
11. Zhao, Y.: Vehicle Location and Navigation System. Artech House Inc., Norwood (1997)
12. Lee, J., Lim, Y., Chi, S.: Hierarchical modeling and simulation environment for intelligent transportation systems. Sage J. **80**, 61–76 (2004)
13. Zhan, F.B.: Three fastest shortest path algorithms on real road networks: data structures and procedures. J. Geogr. Inf. Dec. Anal. **1**, 69–82 (1996)
14. Ahuja, R.K., Magnanti, T.L., Orlin, J.B.: Network Flows: Theory, Algorithms and Applications. Prentice Hall, Englewood Cliffs (1993)

Automated Web-Based Geoprocessing of Rental Prices

Harald Schernthanner[1(✉)], Sebastian Steppan[3], Christian Kuntzsch[2], Erik Borg[4], and Hartmut Asche[2]

[1] Institute of Earth and Enviromental Science, University of Potsdam,
Karl-Liebknecht-Strasse 24/25, 14476 Potsdam, Germany
hschernt@uni-potsdam.de
[2] Department of Geography, University of Potsdam,
Karl-Liebknecht-Strasse 24/25, 14476 Potsdam, Germany
{christian.kuntzsch,gislab}@uni-potsdam.de
[3] Hochschule Mainz - University of Applied Sciences,
School of Technology – Geoinformatics and Surveying,
Lucy-Hillebrand-Straße 2, 55128 Mainz, Germany
sebastian.steppan@hs-mainz.de
[4] German Aerospace Center (DLR),
German Remote Sensing Data Center National Ground Segment,
Kalkhorstweg 53, 17235 Neustrelitz, Germany
Erik.Borg@dlr.de

Abstract. Increasingly, geodata processing is being relocated to web-based services. A pioneering role was played here by the Open Geospatial Consortium(OGC) and the standardized OGC Web Processing Services (WPS). In addition to WPS, a large number of non-standardized online services and libraries, developed in the recent years, allow the web-based processing of spatial data. As geodata processing moved to web-based services, it led to an exponential increase in the availability of data with a spatial component on the World Wide Web.

Several web-based services possess the capabilities to geoprocess real estate data as rental prices. The aim of this article is to explore semi-or fully-automatedweb-based realtime geodata processing of rental data. A fully functional implementation of a nearly real-time-generated rental mapis presented. Till now, no comparable service exists.

Keywords: Geoprocessing · Automatation · Rental prices · Housing

1 Introduction

Up to date rent price maps, published on the Internet, are based on the quarterly, temporal snapshots of calculated rental price predictions. The prices are mostly modelled by the means of the non-spatial modelling approaches like hedonic regression [16]. (Semi-)automated spatial approaches don't exist yet. Based on a catalogue of conceptual requirements, we present a prototype process chain of a (semi-)automated spatial geoprocessing service of rental prices. It includes an online interpolation of rental price data, with everything from the web processing service to the web-based visualization touched upon. Based on the process chain, three prototypes are discussed in this article.

© Springer International Publishing AG 2017
O. Gervasi et al. (Eds.): ICCSA 2017, Part IV, LNCS 10407, pp. 512–524, 2017.
DOI: 10.1007/978-3-319-62401-3_37

The first is a full, running implementation of a nearly real-time-generated rental map. The second and the third are experimental geovisualization approaches.

The outline of this article is as follows. We start with an overview of the state-of-the-art of web-based geodata processing services. Next, a criteria-based request catalogue, serving as the conceptual basis for the implementation of prototypical, automated, real-time processing of rental price data, is presented. The third section depicts a proof of concept: three developed prototypes are presented. Finally, we conclude with a summary of the major results of the research presented and an outlook on the still unanswered research questions.

2   State-of-the-Art Web-Based Geodata Processing

2.1   Evolution of Geospatial Web from Standardized to Non-standardized Services

Next, milestones in the development of the geospatial web, as the building components of automated, web-based rental dataprocessing services are presented. Nowadays, the World Wide Web provides an ideal environment, not only for geodata storage and publishing, but also for the processing of spatial information. In many ways, standardization favored the fact that GIS functionalities are increasingly provided within web browsers. Standardization means the implementation of uniform standards and rules for the creation of simple interfaces. This results in tremendous advantages in compatibility between the products, the communication between the components is simplified and the development effort is reduced, resulting in time and cost savings. Undoubtedly, mainly the OGC and the International Organization for Standardization (ISO) historically pushed the development of the so-called WebGIS (Web geographic information systems). The most common OGC standards providing interfaces for geodata requests, used in traditional WebGIS, are the Web Feature Service (WFS) and the Web Map Service (WMS) [17].

Besides the OGC standards, map application programming interfaces (API) emerged with the appearance of Google Maps in 2005. The APIs, as a pillar of the historical Web 2.0, interact with other users and distribute content from websites [1]. An API has access to a web service that allows a computer program to access and manipulate data from another web service. The APIs have stimulated the growth of the Geoweb, and new communities emerged as a result on the Internet [15].

For further reading about APIs and online geoprocessing services, the two following sources are recommended: (1) A profound overview of and introduction to map APIs is given by Peterson (2014) in his textbook "Mapping in the Cloud". [12] (2) Hofer (2014) [7] did a systematic literature overview of the state of the art of online geoprocessing technology.

2.2   Overview Over up to Date Existing Services and Implementations

Basically, we distinguish between three different service architectures[4, 9]. Infrastructure as a Service (IaaS): Enables the upload of data, helps publish own web services.

Platform as a Service (PaaS): Enables creation of WebGIS applications without programming.

Software as a Service (SaaS): Enables the use of different software, thematic map services, analysis tools, as well as access to and use of data, maps, and applications already hosted within an environment.

An extended literature review revealed several services or libraries, which contributed to the development of the prototype. A strict assignment to the three basic service infrastructures isn't possible; the services overlap. For the prototype development, the services taken into account consist of programming libraries and cloud-based services. They are, with the exception of ArcGIS Online, all non-OGC-conforming services. The services considered include the following:

1. R is a statistical programming language, the RStudio Server, by self definition "a browser based interface to a version of R running on a remote Linux server". R Studio [13], can create large records, using numerous functions. This enables fast creation of maps and transfer of data, for queries and visualization.
2. ArcGIS Online is a cloud-based mapping platform [3] for data processing via the Internet.
3. CARTO is a cloud-based web service (software as a service, SaaS) for map-based data visualization, including many functions for data analysis [2].
4. MapBox (MapBox, 2017) is an open source platform with its own interface for the implementation of web maps, and geodata processing [10].
5. Turf.js is a JavaScript library. By its own definition, it does modular "advanced geospatial analysis for browsers and node" [21].
6. GDAL (Geospatial Data Abstraction Library) is an open source software library for processing raster data and is integrated into many of the above listed service; but can also be used applied as standalone command line tool [6].

3   Criteria-Based Request Catalogue

Certain defining criteria, based on Schernthanner's et al. research [16], form the conceptual basis for the implementation of prototypical, automated, real-time processing of rental price data service. The subsequent sections address the crucial building blocks and name the most relevant criteria that have to be included in a criteria-based request catalogue of an automated, real-time processing of rental price data service.

3.1   Criterion 1: Database of Geocoded Rental Data

Rental data acquisition is often carried out by using the standardized interfaces (e.g., REST/SOA). Oftentimes, the data sources are not freely available. Authentication has to be requested and access to rental data bases is limited.

The most important criterion is the availability and automated purchase of rental data. A prototype should fetch rental price in near real time via interfaces to geocoded rental data provided by e.g. real estate portals by REST APIs.

On the ProgrammableWeb website (www.programmableweb.com), which is one of the most popular directories for APIs, one finds several thousand geocoded data sources with primary or secondary metrics. In 2012, the programmable web named 40 real estate APIs (The programmable web, 2012). For a prototype, freely accessible REST APIs offering geocoded rental data should be used. Only a few services, e.g. Nestoria for European data [11] (cf. Sect. 4.1) or Zillow [22] can be used.

3.2 Criterion 2: Real Time Interpolation

Based on the acquired geocoded rental data base, the presence or absence of spatial autocorrelation should be detected automatically via common tests such as the Morans I. In case of available spatial autocorrelation, the prototype has to fit the variogram and directly derive accuracy measures such as a root mean square error (RSME) of a model. Afterward, geostatistical interpolation should be applied to spatially estimate the base rent per square meter in the area of interest. Preferably, methods from the Kriging family should be used, especially Ordinary Kriging (OK). Schernthanner et al. [16] compared several thousand model runs of OK versus the hedonic regressions. One of the fundamental discoveries of this research is that the geostatistical interpolator OK gives more accurate comparisons than hedonistic regression models. In all comparisons, OK gave more accurate results. For that reason, OK is recommended as the geostatistical interpolator of choice. For operational use, OK must therefore be an integral part of automated services. An automated implementation of variograms and tests of spatial autocorrelation provide a valuable basis for web-based processing of real estate data.

3.3 Criterion 3: Geovisualization

The last criteria is the geovisual representation of the trend surfaces as a slippy map (map that slips around when movin the mouse, zoom and pan is possible).The target audience is on the one hand the apartment seeker in the current rental market situation, and on the other hand, the professional players in the rental market who provide such services as an analytical tool for monitoring the leasing market. Depending on the target audience, the service should be either fully automatic in real time in order to create rental pricing interfaces, or semi-automated user interactions, such as displaying of the variogram or of descriptive statistics results.

The following figure (cf. Fig. 1) shows a flowchart of the proposed geoprocessing workflow.

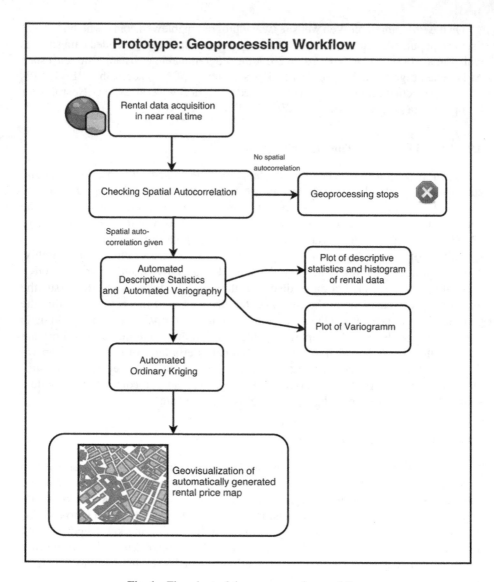

Fig. 1. Flowchart of the geoprocessing workflow.

The services discussed (c.f. Sect. 2.2) were intensively examined for the criteria set. A table of the results of the examination is given below (Table 1).

Table 1. Results of the examination. Transparent: A (available), perfectly applicable for prototype. Gray: P/A (partially available), partially applicable for prototype. Horizontal lines: N/A (not available), not applicable for prototype.

	Live Fetching of rental data	(Automated-) variography	Interpolation (Real Time using OK)	Geovisualization via slippy map
R	A: via Jsonlite/ Curl	A: via R automap	A: via R automap	A: via LeafletR
Arc GIS Online	N/A	P/A Semivariogramm is simulated	P/A: not in realtime. Bayesian empirical Kriging	A: Wide selection of webmaps and functions to interact with webmaps
Carto	A: Connects to several databases	N/A	N/A: Just heatmaps	A: Wide selection of webmaps and functions to interact with webmaps
MapBox	A: Live Integration of GeoJson	N/A	P/A: via integration of turf.js	A: Wide selection of webmaps and functions to interact with webmaps
Turf.js	N/A	N/A	P/A: No OK. Isolines, Tin, Planepoints	A: Full integration to Leaflet.js and MapBox.js
GDAL	A: via Bash-Script	N/A	P/A: No OK. invdist, invdistnn, average, nearest neighbor, linear	N/A

4   Proof of Concept: Prototypes

As proof of concept, three prototypes have been developed. The first is a prototype implemented with R (RSudio and Shiny Server). The first prototype already demonstrates the possibilities that full automation enables.

The second and third are more experimental prototypes implemented with turf.js. All three prototypes are based on data fetched by the Nestoria API, a publicly-accessible API.

4.1 Data Sources

The Nestoria API serves as a "vertical search engine" by its own definition (Nestoria 2017); Nestoria offers real estate data from the databases of several real estate portals. The relational structure of several databases is restructured to the relations of Nestoria's own data model. Therefore, they offer a homogenized data structure. The authors developed a Rscript, using the R "jsonlite" package which is a JSON parser. It fetches geocoded real estate data to "fuel" the prototype. Fetched database extracts provide 32 fields containing information relevant for renting or purchasing real-estate offers. Besides price information —prices mentioned in the Euro, with and without service costs—the listing type (rent or buy), the property type, and the size of the real estate is stored within Nestoria's database. Further information on the portfolio of real estates is kept in the database—e.g., an image URL, keywords for the offer, and the string of a summary are hosted. Moreover, the date and time of the inclusion of the offer are recorded. The database holds fields such as the bathroom number, bedroom number, and construction year of the real estates. The information is geocoded in latitudinal and longitudinal decimal degrees in world geodetic system (WGS) coordinates. The accuracy of the geocoding is indicated by a 10-point scale from 1 (best) to 10 (worst) estimated geocoding. An exemplary request of 20 offers located in Soho/London (UK) can be found by calling the example's search listing URL: https://api.nestoria.co.uk/show_example?name=search_listings_uk&syntax=1.

The Nestoria API does not require any kind of authentication (as OAuth or an API key) and delivers current real estate date from all big and some smaller German real estate portals. Downloads are limited to 20 or 50 data points per page and to 1,000 offers per request. So, for a larger area, an adaption of the geographical area of interest has to be defined. For example, a bounding box of geographical coordinates or a filter of the requested parameters, help to download information like ranges of apartment sizes. The request parameters are well-documented on the Nestorian developers' website [10]. The script loops through the pages provided by the API and puts the result into an R data frame. The R data frame easily can be exported as comma separated values (CSV) for further use in a desktop geographic information system e.g. QGIS or ArcGIS. A frequently occurring problem in fetching real estate data service are blockages by the data provider (HTTP 403 error), due to excessive usage and frequent changes in the data model that complicate the automated geoprocessing.

4.2 R-Shiny App

The first developed prototype was developed with R-Shiny and was tested with rental data of the German cities Berlin and Potsdam. Shiny is a framework for R to make interactive web applications [14]. The prototype is fully working and targets expert users, who search for an analytical instrument for real time monitoring of rental markets. The app provides a graphical user interface (GUI) with several tabs and pull-down menus:

1. Tab 1 represents a logarithmized square meter price. By means of the layer selection, the base layers of the map view can be changed.

2. Tab 2 presents the results of an automatically realized variography. Currently also a model cross-validation and the mean error of the interpolation model is integrated.

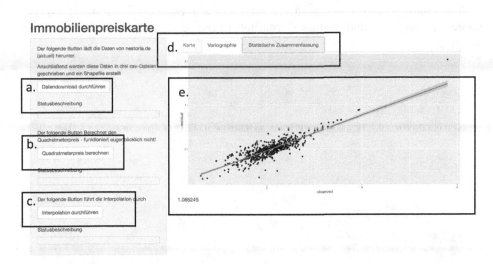

Fig. 2. GUI of the prototype: a. buttonto fetch rental data via the Nestoria API, b. button to calculate the base rent per squaremetre, c. run OK interplation, d. several tabs for showing the: 1. automatically generated rental map, 2. automatically variagrogram, 3. derived descriptive statistics, e. example for an automatically generated variagrogram

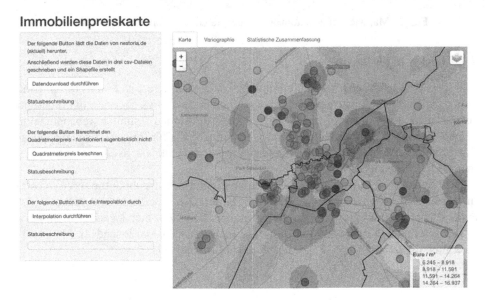

Fig. 3. GUI of the prototype and map view of an automatically generated rental price map of Potsdam. Green points represent rental offers. (Color figure online)

3. Tab 3 provides a statistical summary of the descriptive statistics of the data. In the first prototype, it presents a histogram, as is shown.
4. Tab 4 is a still empty place-holder, prototypical transformation that can be filled with further functions. The data download button and the interpolation buttons work.

The prototype can be accessed via: http://www.mietpreiskarte.de. The following figures (cf. Figs. 2, 3 and 4) show screenshots of the demonstrating the fully working prototype.

Fig. 4. Map view of an automatically generated rental price map of Berlin.

4.3   Turf.js Experiments

The second and more experimental prototype was coded in turf.js. It aims to serve the target audience of the apartment seekers, who want to get a quick overview of the current spatial distribution of rental prices. Jan Fajfr [5] developed a similar webapplication named "FlatPricer" implemented in turf.js and mapbox.js for Prague. His webapplication is based on openly available rental data provided rental data, available on the open data portal of the city of Prague.

Our application generates isolines of equal rental prices (without the service costs) in Berlin. The isolines are generated by a client-side processing and rendering of approximately 3,000 data points (from November 2016). The map legend is still a work in progress, though it can be opined that the making of custom legends in Mapbox.js should be improved (adaptive legends would preferable) (Fig. 5).

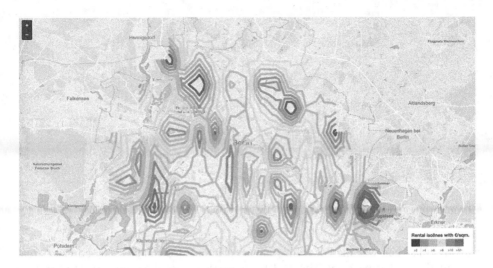

Fig. 5.   Screenshot of the turf.js isoline experiment. Rental isoline map of Berlin.

The isolines have been generated by using the turf.js isoline function. The turf.js JavaScript library and this prototype are both under development. Several problems of the prototype have to be solved as:

1. The legend, or to be specific, the class building and also the alignment of the legend on the web map are problematic.
2. Processing a huge number of data points with JavaScript on a client needs a several minutes of computational time.

The full screen web map of the isoline experiment also can be accessed via: http://hatschit.alkaid.uberspace.de/Turf_tin_3000_isolines_colors.html.

Our third experimental prototype was coded in turf.js interpolates a subset of 178 rental offers of three-room apartments from the city of Potsdam (data was downloaded at the 19th of March 2017) by an Inverse Distance Weighted interpolation algorithm and should demonstrate the interpolation capabilities of turf.js.

From an analytical viewpoint, the resulting map (cf. Fig. 6) isn't that useful and just shows a spatial trend of estimated three room apartment offers base rents in absolute € prices. Absolute prices had to be interpolated, as the apartment sizes in the fetched data were missing. IDW actually is one of the least applicable spatial interpolators for rental data, due to known effects as bull eyes; but turf.js's client side processing is in heavy development and we expect other interpolation algorithms will be integrated soon to the turf.js library. So far turf.js is capable to interpolate isolines, plane points, triangulated irregular networks and IDW.

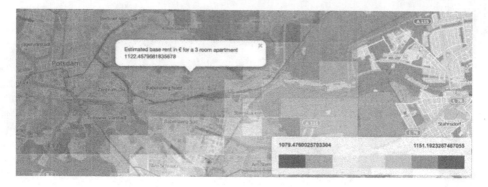

Fig. 6. Screenshot of the turf.js IDW experiment. Map extract of a three room apartment rental map of Potsdam, interpolated by IDW.

The full screen web map of the isoline experiment also can be accessed via: http://hatschit.alkaid.uberspace.de/IDW_TURF_Choropletes/Potsdam_example.html.

5   Conclusions and Discussion

This paper presents and discusses novel and innovative approaches for the automated geo-processing of real-estate rental prices. Web-based geodata processing is becoming more and more convenient; for the first time, a prototype that combines near real-time geo-processing and automatic mapping of rental data was implemented here; its concept is of a generic nature. So, though the web processing services are evolving very rapidly, the conceptual core of the presented paper serves as a basis to pave the way for similar projects that can be realized in the near future, with even simpler applications and services. The prototype relies on recent research results on the spatial analysis and geovisualization of rental prices, though other rental price maps also exist. For example, the well known Trulias US home price heat map [20] does not follow research findings (neither cartographic nor scientific findings). Our approach, unlike other approaches, follows a fully automated geoprocessing in almost real time by fetching rental data live, considers research results and tries to operationalize them. The developed prototype is strictly based on the presence or absence of spatial auto correlation, while other approaches ignore Tobler's first law of geography [19]—"Everything is related to everything, but near things are more related than distant things"—and therefore neglect real estate agents' mantra that exactly three things are important in real estates: location, location, and location [18]. In our approach, the rental market is less affected by some real characters compared to the sales market and hence this type of analysis is potentially less error-prone. The prototype clearly shows in which directions an automatically generated geoprocessed rental price map can go in order to be research-based and fully operational for several target groups. Besides the live fetching, checking of the auto-correlation of data and the live Kriging, the automatically derived semi-variogramm and descriptive statistics promise a move into the right direction.

Consideration of the location and the rental price per square meter must be seen critically. Intrinsic real estate values, such as the apartments equipment (e.g. room number or heating type), or other possible relevant parameters, such as distance to the public transport system, have not been incorporated in the model. Therefore, the model might smoothen certain effects of further secondary variables on the price. Incorporation of secondary variables could be achieved using further techniques. I.e. Geographic weighted regression as used by Manganelli et al. [8], or ordinary co-kriging might be interesting. However, the computational time compared to OK is exponentially higher [16]. Smoothening effect, as well as the exponentially higher computational time, have to be investigated.

Further issues of the prototype should be reviewed critically. Our prototype depends on the Nestoria database. Without access to such APIs, it would not be possible to develop a prototype like the suggested one. Several practical and research questions are still unanswered. The most urgent ones, from the authors' perspective, are: First, how to find solutions to overcome the dependency on only a few accessible REST APIs by research into spatial real estate data mining and real estate geodata fusion; second, how to improve the automatically generated geovisualization by automatically integrating cartographic rules into the geo-processing process. Moreover, further prototyping and target group specific tests of further development stages of prototypes have to be realized for transferring the concept into an operational environment.

References

1. Batty, M., Crooks, A., Hudson-Smith, A., Milton, R., Anand, S., Jackson, M., Morley, J.: Data Mash-ups and the Future of Mapping. JISC, Bristol (2010)
2. Carto: Predict through location (2017). https://carto.com/. Accessed 13 Mar 2017
3. ESRI: ArcGIS Online, Mapping without limits (2017). http://www.esri.com/software/arcgis/arcgisonline. Accessed 13 Mar 2017
4. ESRI: Implementing Web GIS (2013). http://www.esri.com/esri-news/arcnews/fall13articles/implementing-web-gis
5. Fajfr, J.: FlatPricer (2017). https://flatpricer.com/Home/CityStats?id=Praha. Accessed 13 Mar 2017
6. GDAL: GDAL - Geospatial Data Abstraction Library (2017). http://gdal.org/. Accessed 13 Mar 2017
7. Hofer, B.: Uses of online geoprocessing technology in analyses and case studies: a systematic analysis of literature. Int. J. Digit. Earth 8(11), 901–917 (2015)
8. Manganelli, B., Pontrandolfi, P., Azzato, A., Murgante, B.: Using geographically weighted regression for housing market segmentation. Int. J. Bus. Intell. Data Min. 13 9(2), 161–177 (2014)
9. Meier, J.D.: Software as a Service (SaaS), Platform as a Service (PaaS), and Infrastructure as a Service (IaaS) (2010). http://bit.ly/2mSr9bk. Accessed 13 Mar 2017
10. MapBox: Maps that move you (2017). https://www.mapbox.com/. Accessed 13 Mar 2017
11. Nestoria: Home - Nestoria API - Methods - Search Listing (2017). http://www.nestoria.co.uk/help/api-search-listings. Accessed 13 Mar 2017
12. Peterson, M.P.: Mapping in the Cloud. Guilford Publications, New York (2014)
13. R Studio: Download RStudio Server v1.0.136 (2017). https://www.rstudio.com/products/rstudio/download-server/. Accessed 13 Mar 2017

14. R Studio: Shiny by RStudio. A web application framework for R (2017). http://shiny.rstudio.com/. Accessed 13 Mar 2017
15. Scharl, A., Tochtermann, K. (eds.): The Geospatial Web: How Geobrowsers, Social Software and the Web 2.0 are Shaping the Network Society. Springer, London (2009)
16. Schernthanner, H., Asche, H., Gonschorek, J., Scheele, L.: Spatial modeling and geovisualization of rental prices for real estate portals. In: Gervasi, O., Murgante, B., Misra, S., Rocha, A.M.A.C., Torre, C., Taniar, D., Apduhan, Bernady O., Stankova, E., Wang, S. (eds.) ICCSA 2016. LNCS, vol. 9788, pp. 120–133. Springer, Cham (2016). doi: 10.1007/978-3-319-42111-7_11
17. Stollberg, B., Zipf, A.: Geoprocessing services for spatial decision support in the domain of housing market analyses. In: Proceedings AGILE (2008)
18. Stroisch, J.: Immobilien Bewerten Leicht Gemacht. Haufe-Lexware, Munich (2010)
19. Tobler, W.R.: A computer movie simulating urban growth in the Detroit region. Econ. Geogr. **46**(sup1), 234–240 (1970)
20. Trulia: US home prices and hear map (2017). https://www.trulia.com/home_prices/. Accessed 11 May 2017
21. Turf: Advanced geospatial analysis for browsers and node (2017). http://turfjs.org/. Accessed 13 Mar 2017
22. Zillow: Real estate and mortgage data for your site (2017). https://www.zillow.com/howto/api/APIOverview.htm. Accessed 13 Mar 2017

A GIS-Based Methodology to Estimate the Potential Demand of an Integrated Transport System

Gabriele D'Orso and Marco Migliore[✉]

Transport Research Group, Department of Civil Environmental Aerospace and Materials Engineering, University of Palermo, Viale delle Scienze Building 8, 90128 Palermo, Italy
marco.migliore@unipa.it

Abstract. In the design of a new public transport system or of an extension of an existing system, the choice of a suitable placement of stations and stops in the territory and the definition of the main axes are very important. The different choice in the number and distribution of the stops of a road transport system or of a railway transport system, in fact, makes the system more or less widespread and affects the consistency of the catchment area and the attractiveness of the system. The accessibility of a system, add to the reliability in providing the service, is the fundamental parameter influencing the modal split of the users. Therefore, the Public Administration must have tools able to evaluate different scenarios.

The GIS (Geographic Information System) is the natural environment for viewing, managing and editing of geo-referenced data, so it can be effectively used to assess the accessibility of a public transport system and its catchment area. Moreover, it allows to compare different design scenarios, determining the induced benefits and analyzing the critical aspects; GIS is therefore a useful decision support system for Public Administration, directing choices on the basis of objective evidence. The purpose of this paper is to illustrate a GIS-based methodology to estimate the potential demand, in terms of resident population and employees, of an integrated public transport system. As a case study, the integrated public transport system of the City of Palermo has been analyzed, including the tram system and the urban railway system.

Keywords: GIS · Transport demand · Accessibility · Decision support system · Integrated transport system

1 Introduction

In the last years, because of the increasingly important problem of pollution and high levels of congestion on the road network, many urban centres are affected by sustainable mobility policies and in particular policies which promotes intermodality and pedestrian mobility, undertaken by the Public Administration. It is necessary, in fact, that the public transport supply increases its level of service in order to reduce problems such as high vehicle volumes on the roads, poor attractiveness and low levels of the use of public transport system. Therefore, administrations should design interventions and implement strategies that could guide transport demand towards public transport and sustainable transport modes. Even the city of Palermo is slowly moving towards this direction.

© Springer International Publishing AG 2017
O. Gervasi et al. (Eds.): ICCSA 2017, Part IV, LNCS 10407, pp. 525–540, 2017.
DOI: 10.1007/978-3-319-62401-3_38

The determination of the accessibility and of the catchment area of the public transport system is a task of fundamental importance for understanding how the transport system will respond to the needs of the potential demand.

Accessibility is defined as "whether or not people can get to services and activities at a reasonable cost, in reasonable time and with reasonable ease" [9].

Therefore, a transport system is widespread and accessible when it is widely distributed on the territory as well as easily reachable from many users as possible, both in spatial and temporal terms. These features make the public transport system dynamic and attractive [16].

The main aim of this work is to evaluate the accessibility of the railway system and the tram system planned by the Administration of Palermo.

2   The Integrated Public Transport System of Palermo

The integrated public transport system of Palermo consists of the rail link, connecting the city to the airport "Falcone e Borsellino" and to the regional rail network, the rail ring, which will be, at the end of the work, a circular line which affects the central districts, and the tram system.

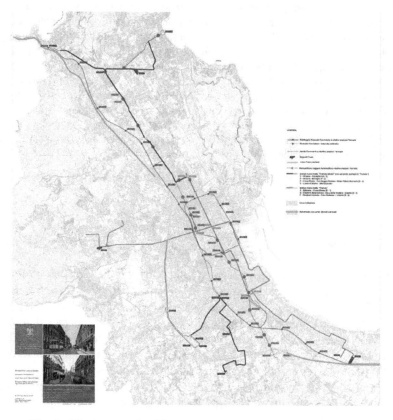

Fig. 1. The integrated public transport system of the city of Palermo

The railway link extends for 30 km, 13 within the city. Currently there are 13 active stations and trains make service with a frequency of two trains per hour and per direction. Interventions provide the doubling of the underground line, the modernization of the existing stations and the building of five new stations, with a total of 18 active stations at the end of the works.

The work on the rail ring provide, instead, its closure, which will be carried out in two stages. There are currently 4 existing stations and other 4 will be realized.

The current tram system consists of 4 lines with 44 active stops. The Administration has provided that the system will be expanded with the creation of 7 new lines, with different priorities, in order to make the transport supply more uniform and widespread in the territory and create a real connected network of trams [21] (Fig. 1).

3   Isochrones and Catchment Area

The aim of the methodology developed in this study is to assess whether the planned interventions produce a significant expansion of the catchment area.

The catchment area has been determined by reference to pedestrian accessibility at stops and as the area enclosed by isochrones, which allow you to determine the number of potential destinations that can be reached by pedestrians within a predetermined time, starting from any station.

The isochrones cover distances of 150, 300 and 500 m on foot by the user, necessary to access to the transport network.

Considering a pedestrian speed of 3.6 km per hour, the travel times which charac terize the isochrones are shown in Table 1.

Table 1. Isochrones and travel time

Isochrones	Travel time (min)	Distance (m)
1	2, 5 min	150
2	5 min	300
3	8 min	500

As shown in Fig. 2, the isochrones can be identified with reference to a topological distance (radial isochrones) or, more accurately, with reference to the metric distance from a point, calculated in reference to a network (spatialized isochrones). In this case, it was preferred to use the first type of isochrones, because we didn't have a pedestrian network but only a road network for tracing the spatialized isochrones.

The catchment area has been determined in terms of resident population and employees potentially served by the system. The data on the resident population in the various census sections provide us indications on the potential origins of the movement, while the data on employees show us the potential destinations.

Demographic data and data on the employees were provided by ISTAT, which has made them during the General Census of Population and Housing and the Census of Industry and Services, both made in 2011 [19]. It is precisely in the identification of catchment area that Geographic Information Systems can play a crucial role [17], being

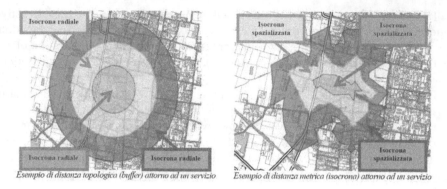

Esempio di distanza topologica (buffer) attorno ad un servizio   *Esempio di distanza metrica (isocrona) attorno ad un servizio*

Fig. 2. Radial isochrones and spatialized isochrones

tools that allow you to make spatial operations and associate geographical data with other data type, such as demographic data [2–4, 7].

4   Software

For the determination and the visualization of the catchment area, it has chosen to use QGIS, an open source geographic information system, released under a free license. This tool offers a growing number of features provided by the basic functions and numerous downloadable plug in. To create a database in which to import data, called "postgres", PostgreSQL, an object-relational database, with a free license, has been used. PostgreSQL allows you to query data using SQL. These data are collected in a series of tables with foreign keys, which serve to connect them. In addition, the spatial extension of PostgreSQL, PostGIS, which allows the management of geo-referenced data and confers to the database all the typical spatial analysis capabilities of a GIS, has been installed.

5   Determination of the Catchment Area

In order to visualize tram stops and train stations in QGIS, present and future locations were identified and marked in Google Earth. For each tramline, for the railway link and the railway ring, different place marks, placed in the exact geographical location of stops or stations, were created and were saved as kml files (Fig. 3).

The kml files were then imported as point layers into QGIS clicking "Add Vector", and the result is shown in Fig. 4.

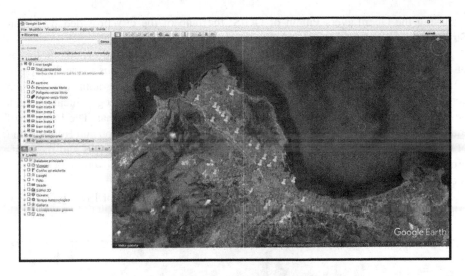

Fig. 3. Placemarks in Google Earth

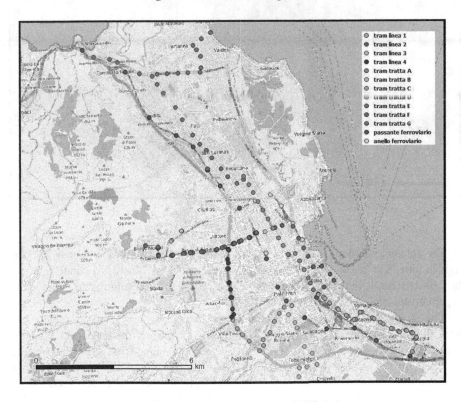

Fig. 4. Stops and stations in QGIS

Using the OpenLayers Plugin of QGIS, the map of the city provided by Open-StreetMap was imported as cartographic base map [20].

A second phase involved the visualization of the data on population and employees of the municipal area in GIS. We referred to the data on the Census made by Istat in 2011. ISTAT, on its website, publishes the territorial bases and geographic data of each census section, which is located within the municipal area; these geographical data can be viewed through a GIS software since they are given in shp format. The Institute of Statistics also provides the data of the General Censuses of Population and Housing and of the Censuses of Industry and Services in xls format; through QGIS and the PostgreSQL database, it has been possible to associate the census data to the census section [18].

The shp file of census sections, downloaded from the website of ISTAT, has been loaded as a new project layer. The result is shown in Fig. 5.

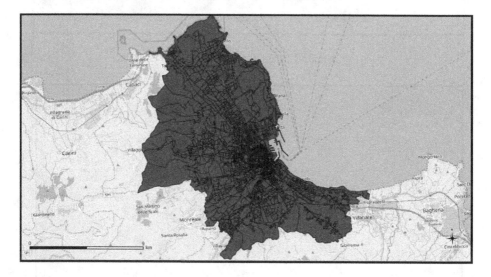

Fig. 5. Census sections

The reference system is WGS 84 UTM Zone 32 N. The municipal area has been divided into 2834 census sections, with different extensions. There is a condensation of the census sections in the central districts of the city, while the suburbs are divided into larger census sections.

The shape file was also imported into the database "postgres" as table called "r19_11_wgs84", through the application PostGIS Shapefile Import/Export Manager. Then census data, collected in an Excel file, were downloaded from ISTAT website. In the "postgres" database it was created a table, called "population", and the empty columns "sec", in order to receive the identification numbers of the census sections, and "population", in order to receive the corresponding values of the resident population, were added.

The following strings in SQL have been written:

```
ALTER TABLE population ADD COLUMN sec numeric;
ALTER TABLE population ADD COLUMN population numeric;
```

The columns were filled with data from the Excel file, relative to the census sections and values of population residing in them, saved at first as a text file in .txt format. The creation of a new table, called "census_section", in the database and the mix between the table "population" and the table "r19_11_wgs84," has made it possible to have geographic data and population data in a single vector. The query was as follows:

```
CREATE TABLE census_section AS
SELECT section, population, sec, geom
FROM population, r19_11_wgs84
WHERE section=sec;
```

This vector has been imported as a new layer in QGIS using the command "Add Vector PostGIS" and its visual style has been modified so that census sections are coloured with different shades of colour depending on the value of the population living in them (Fig. 6).

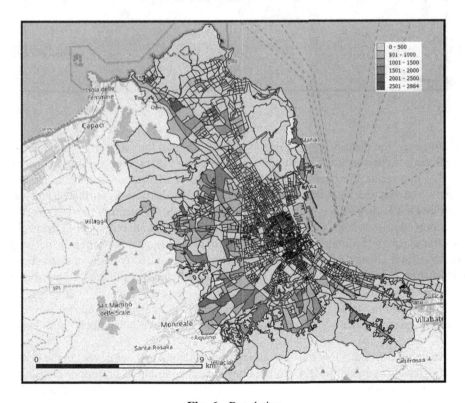

Fig. 6. Population

Similar operations have been carried out for the data on employees. ISTAT, in the realization of the Census of Industry and Services, has divided the employees, depending on the business sector, in:

- employees in the industrial sector;
- employees in public institutions;
- employees in no profit institutions.

Thanks to the QGIS plugin "mmqgis" has been possible to make buffering operations around the stations and identify the isochrones corresponding to distances of 150, 300 and 500 m walked by a pedestrian [10–12] (Fig. 7).

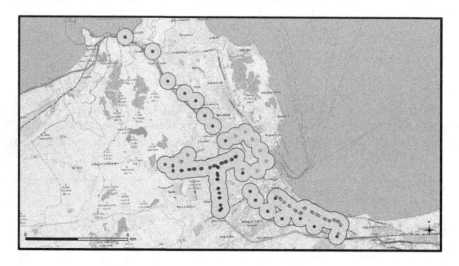

Fig. 7. Buffering

However, the identified catchment area does not give the number of residents and employees of different sectors, who are intercepted by the transport system. In order to achieve this result, the intersection between the layer of isochrones and the layer of census sections, which has the data on population and employees as attributes, has been made in QGIS, clicking on "Vector/Geoprocessing tools/Intersection".

Some census sections are partially within the catchment area. In order to determine the effective population/number of employees that is in the catchment area further steps are necessary. Using QGIS it is possible to evaluate the effective area of each census section that is within the catchment area and the effective population or number of employees that each census section owns.

In the attribute table it is possible to click on "field calculator" adding the three columns "areaeff", "perc.area" and "popeff" (or "addimpeff", "addipeff" and "addn-peff").

An approximation about the distribution of population and employees in the census sections has been made. In fact, the population was regarded as uniformly distributed within the census section. With this simplification, the effective population as a product of population of the entire census section area for the percentage of area of the census section which actually falls within the catchment area has been calculated.

These modifications have been saved and the layers have been saved with a name. For example, the layer regarding the population which falls in the catchment area of 500 m of the integrated system, is saved with the name of "pop_sistema_integrato_500", while that relating to employees in the industry with the name of "add_imp_sistema_integrato_500". The shape files, which were created for each considered scenario and for the fixed distances of buffering, have been imported into the PostgreSQL database with the application "PostGIS Shapefile Import/Export Manager".

Finally, for each scenario, the total population and the total number of employees, which fall in the catchment area generated by distances of buffering of 150, 300 and 500 m, are calculated by means of queries in SQL language similar to the following:

```
SELECT SUM (popeff)
FROM pop_sistema_integrato_500

SELECT SUM (addimpeff)
FROM pop_sistema_integrato_500
```

The next paragraph shows the results in table form (Tables 2, 3 and 4) and the display of the catchment areas in QGIS for each scenario.

Table 2. Potential demand (150 m)

Buffering 150 m	Origins (Population) [%]	Destinations (Employees) [%]	Potential demand [%]
Railway link-current tram network (Scenario 1)	7.63	7.48	0.57
Railway link-current tram network-railway ring (Scenario 2)	8.37	9.65	0.81
Railway link- railway ring- current tram network- line A	10.34	16.86	1.74
Railway link- railway ring- current tram network- lines A, B	10.53	17.50	1.84
Railway link- railway ring- current tram network- lines A, B, C	11.74	18.22	2.14
Railway link- railway ring- current tram network- lines A, B, C, D	12.95	19.28	2.50
Railway link- railway ring- current tram network- lines A, B, C, D, E	14.26	20.94	2.99
Railway link- railway ring- current tram network- lines A, B, C, D, E, F	15.01	24.28	3.64
Integrated system (Scenario 3)	15.22	24.36	3.71

Table 3. Potential demand (300 m)

Buffering 300 m	Origins (Population) [%]	Destinations (Employees) [%]	Potential demand [%]
Railway link-current tram network (Scenario 1)	20.72	19.97	4.14
Railway link-current tram network-railway ring (Scenario 2)	24.03	29.72	7.14
Railway link- railway ring- current tram network- line A	29.73	44.08	13.10
Railway link- railway ring- current tram network- lines A, B	29.90	44.57	13.33
Railway link- railway ring- current tram network- lines A, B, C	32.69	46.39	15.16
Railway link- railway ring- current tram network- lines A, B, C, D	35.55	48.10	17.10
Railway link- railway ring- current tram network- lines A, B, C, D, E	38.93	51.82	20.17
Railway link- railway ring- current tram network- lines A, B, C, D, E, F	40.17	56.02	22.50
Integrated system (Scenario 3)	64.81	56.30	36.49

Table 4. Potential demand (500 m)

Buffering 500 m	Origins (Population) [%]	Destinations (Employees) [%]	Potential demand [%]
Railway link-current tram network (Scenario 1)	39.12	38.34	15.00
Railway link-current tram network-railway ring (Scenario 2)	46.97	58.66	27.55
Railway link- railway ring- current tram network- line A	51.85	71.01	36.82
Railway link- railway ring- current tram network- lines A, B	51.85	71.01	36.82
Railway link- railway ring- current tram network- lines A, B, C	55.83	73.10	40.81
Railway link- railway ring- current tram network- lines A, B, C, D	59.55	74.56	44.40
Railway link- railway ring- current tram network- lines A, B, C, D, E	63.65	77.56	49.37
Railway link- railway ring- current tram network- lines A, B, C, D, E, F	63.97	79.13	50.62
Integrated system (Scenario 3)	64.81	79.43	51.48

6   The Decision Support System and the Design Scenarios

Three scenarios have been considered. Scenario 1 (Fig. 8) is representative of the current public transport system, because there are the stations of the railway link and the stops of the tram lines currently operating (lines 1, 2, 3 and 4). Scenario 2 (Fig. 9) takes into account the addition of the rail ring, while the scenario 3 (Fig. 10) contemplates the extension of the tram system with the addition of new lines.

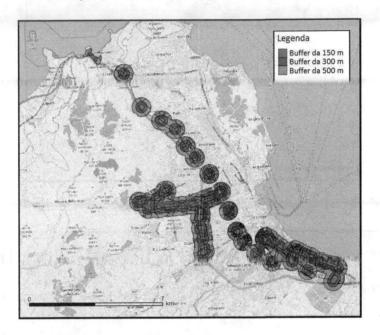

Fig. 8. Scenario 1

The mentioned analyses, which are developed in a GIS environment, allow the development of a decision support system able to calculate the potential demand for the integrated transport system, varying the axes that constitute the public transport network in the design phase. The transport demand may be computed using the joint probability that the origin-destination pair of any journey falls within the area of influence of the stations/stops of the integrated system.

As mentioned before, the resident population and the employees of individual census sections are proxy variables of the origins and destinations of the journeys for different reasons for the journeys.

This analysis allowed the identification of interventions that involve the most significant benefits and of those which had less significant effects.

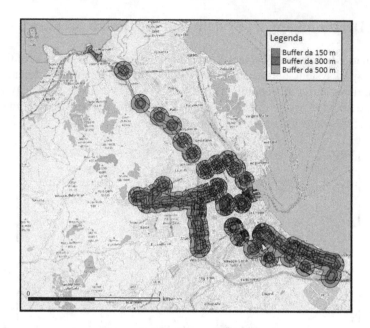

Fig. 9. Scenario 2

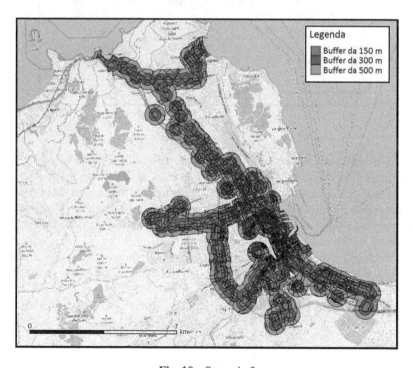

Fig. 10. Scenario 3

7   Discussion

The results show that the realization of the new tram lines could intercept a larger number of users. In fact, considering a radius of the catchment area of 300 m, which is the most frequently considered distance for this kind of analysis, around 36% of the transport demand is potentially intercepted for the scenario 3, while only 7% of the demand is potentially intercepted by the transport supply in scenario 2. Considering a radius of 500 m, the integrated system is able to potentially cover more than 50% of total O/D pairs and, in particular, the closure of the rail ring and the expansion of the tram system could be crucial in order to intercept a larger catchment.

Some tram lines are uneconomic, i.e. lines E and F, since they have high investment costs due to their length but they involve very small increments of the transport demand intercepted.

Once the potential demand will be determined, the use of an appropriate random utility model for evaluating the demand modal split will be able to support the analyst to calculate the reliable demand attracted by the integrated transport system [1, 15].

A cost-benefit and a multicriteria analysis will assess the success of individual lines within the network at the design stage, taking into account, on the one hand, of the benefit of upgrading infrastructure computed as a function of the transport demand satisfaction and of the services offered from the transport system, and, second, of the costs of the infrastructure investment and its management, as well as of the positive and negative externalities generated by the investment [5, 8, 14].

In this case study, for the evaluation of the reliable transport demand in the different scenarios, the modal split has been calculated using a multinomial logit model,

Table 5. Reliable demand (500 m)

Buffering 500 m	Potential demand [%]	Effective demand [%]
Railway link-current tram network (Scenario 1)	15.00	6.00
Railway link-current tram network-railway ring (Scenario 2)	27.55	11.02
Railway link- railway ring- current tram network- line A	36.82	14.73
Railway link- railway ring- current tram network- lines A, B	36.82	14.73
Railway link- railway ring- current tram network- lines A, B, C	40.81	16.32
Railway link- railway ring- current tram network- lines A, B, C, D	44.40	17.76
Railway link- railway ring- current tram network- lines A, B, C, D, E	49.37	19.75
Railway link- railway ring- current tram network- lines A, B, C, D, E, F	50.62	20.25
Integrated system (Scenario 3)	51.48	20.59

considering the service of the railway link, the railway ring, the tram lines and some bus lines with an high level of frequency, taking into account the introduction of the Limited Traffic Zone and the parking pricing policy [13]. The modal split, as result of this analysis, has been equal to 40% of the potential demand [6].

So, considering a radius of buffering of 500 m, the reliable demand attracted by the integrated system has been evaluated as the 40% of the potential demand and the results are shown in Table 5. Therefore the integrated transport system designed for the city of Palermo could be able to intercept the 20% of the transport demand.

8   Conclusion

The adopted methodology has been developed to evaluate the spatial accessibility and the social equity of an urban public transport system. Currently, it has been applied to the public transport network of the city of Palermo in order to analyze the spatial accessibility and the equality in the distribution of urban services and the impact that the planned transport projects will have on spatial accessibility by public transport.

Therefore, it compares the zone accessibility by public transport and can estimate the accessibility impacts by proposed transport infrastructure changes.

The methodology also provides an overview of the attractiveness of the zones in order to identify the "hotspots", which are areas of potential congestion that may require specific management approaches.

It can also identify those zones that are relatively poorly served by public transport system.

Moreover, the study was conducted to estimate the transport demand, to develop procedures that can be standardized and systematically applied, and, finally, to investigate the travel behaviour of the resident population.

The methodology has been designed and developed not only to estimate the demand within the City of Palermo, but in perspective of an application in similar territorial context or also in a different one. For an example, the methodology could be used with other design scenarios containing new distributions of population and employees in the various zones using models that predict the distribution of the residents on the territory as function of new levels of accessibility. In fact, the strength of this methodology is the ability to take into account both transport and land-use systems for accessibility analysis and for the evaluation of the transport demand.

Then this work showed how GIS is an effective decision support system for the Public Administration, allowing it to identify the most effective project proposals. Furthermore, this methodology has allowed the construction of the catchment areas and the determination of the demand potentially served by a public transport system without resorting to the construction of an O/D matrix, which is always approximate; we used accurate data such as those on the resident population and on employees.

The use of spatialized isochrones, generated on the basis of a pedestrian network, would have involved a larger accuracy in the determination of the results.

The adopted methodology allowed us to verify that the scenario designed by the Municipal Administration actually manages to ensure a significant expansion of the catchment areas and makes the integrated system of public transport rail more attractive in transport demand, compared to the current transport system.

For the realization of an integrated system of this type much time and money will have to be employed and the administration's efforts will be rewarded only through proper management of the system, especially in terms of choice of frequencies and choice of service fees. These choices will be critical to ensure that the system will attract a significant part of the transport demand from the private car.

References

1. Amoroso, S., Migliore, M., Catalano, M., Galatioto, F.: A demand-based methodology for planning the bus network of a small or medium town. Eur. Transp. - Trasporti Europei **44**, 41–56 (2010)
2. Burrough, P.A.: Principles of Geographical Information Systems for Land Resource Assessment. Clarendon Press, Oxford (1986)
3. Burrough, P.A., McDonnel, R.: Principles of Geographical Information Systems. Oxford University Press, Oxford (1998)
4. Castelluccio, F., D'Orso, G., Migliore, M., Scianna, A.: GIS infomobility for travellers. In: Gervasi, O., Murgante, B., Misra, S., Rocha, A.M.A.C., Torre, C., Taniar, D., Apduhan, Bernady O., Stankova, E., Wang, S. (eds.) ICCSA 2016. LNCS, vol. 9788, pp. 519–529. Springer, Cham (2016). doi:10.1007/978-3-319-42111-7_41
5. Catalano, M., Migliore, M.: A Stackelberg-game approach to support the design of logistic terminals. J. Transp. Geogr. **41**, 63–73 (2014)
6. Ciccarelli, M., Migliore, M.: Il Passante ferroviario di Palermo: analisi della potenzialità e possibile trasferimento modale. Thesis work, University of Palermo (2015)
7. DeMers, M.N.: Fundamentals of Geographic Information Systems. Wiley, New Jersey (2005)
8. Horner, M.W., Grubesic, T.H.: A GIS-based planning approach to locating urban rail terminals. Transportation **28**(1), 55–77 (2001)
9. Karou, S., Hull, A.: Accessibility modelling: predicting the impact of planned transport infrastructure on accessibility patterns in Edinburgh, UK. J. Transp. Geogr. **35**, 1–11 (2014)
10. Laurini, R., Thompson, D.: Fundamentals of Spatial Information Systems. Academic Press, London (1992)
11. Laurini, R.: Information Systems for Urban Planning: A Hypermedia Cooperative Approach. Taylor and Francis, London (2001)
12. Longley, P.A., Goodchild, M.F., Maguire, D.J., Rhind, D.W.: Geographic Information Systems and Science. Wiley, New York (2010)
13. Migliore, M., Burgio, A.L., Di Giovanna, M.: Parking pricing for a sustainable transport system. Transp. Res. Proced. **3**, 403–412 (2014)
14. Migliore, M., Catalano, M.: Urban public transport optimization by bus ways: a neural network-based methodology. WIT Trans. Built Environ. **96**, 347–356 (2007)
15. Migliore, M., Catalano, M., Lo Burgio, A., Maritano, L.: The analysis of urban travellers' latent preferences to explain their mode choice behavior. WIT Trans. Ecol. Environ. **162**, 193–203 (2012)
16. Migliore, M., Lo Burgio, A., Maritano, L., Catalano, M., Zangara, A.: Modelling the accessibility to public local transport to increase the efficiency and effectiveness of the service: the case study of the Roccella area in Palermo. WIT Trans. Built Environ. **130**, 163–173 (2013)

17. O'Sullivan, D., Morrison, A., Shearer, J.: Using desktop GIS for the investigation of accessibility by public transport: an isochrones approach. Int. J. Geogr. Inf. Sci. **14**(1), 85–104 (2001)
18. Worboys, M.F., Duckham, M.: GIS: A Computing Perspective, 2nd edn. CRC Press, Boca Raton (2004)
19. Istituto Nazionale di Statistica (ISTAT): 15° Censimento Generale della Popolazione e delle Abitazioni (2011). http://www.istat.it
20. OpenStreetMap. http://www.openstreetmap.org
21. Studio di Fattibilità per l'ampliamento del Sistema tranviario della Città di Palermo, Comune di Palermo - Area Tecnica della Riqualificazione urbana e delle Infrastrutture (2016)

Geospatial Database for Seamless Pedestrian Navigation in Germany: Status and Acquisition Technologies

Hartmut Asche[✉]

Hasso Plattner Institute for Software Systems Engineering,
Prof. Dr. Helmert Strasse 2 3, 14482 Potsdam, Germany
Hartmut.Asche@hpi.uni-potsdam.de

Abstract. Positioning, orientation and targeted movement in a 3D environment are fundamental human needs that facilitate a perception of the world around us. Navigation and route guidance of pedestrians require geospatial data specifically dedicated to pedestrian navigation. In a feasibility study, extant geospatial databases were investigated to study their suitability for seamless, cost-effective routing, and navigation of pedestrians in public space. This research was guided by the assumption that such dedicated databases with seamless national coverage were lacking in Germany. To validate this hypothesis, the status quo has been assessed. In addition methods and techniques have been investigated facilitating cost-effective generation and maintenance of a uniform, seamless database for pedestrian navigation. The availability of spatial objects relevant to pedestrian navigation and data acquisition concepts has been determined in two study regions; these regions are representative of urban and rural areas. This paper, therefore, deals with the geospatial data requirements for pedestrian navigation, the evaluation of existing databases, and discussions of cost-effective acquisition strategies for missing pedestrian navigation data.

Keywords: Pedestrian navigation · Routing · Orientation · Geospatial databases · Data acquisition · Seamless area coverage

1 Introduction

Positioning, orientation, and purposeful movement in real or virtual 3D surroundings are fundamental human needs. All three actions are crucial in establishing one's position in the environment not only from a geographical perspective but also in a much wider sense. Orientation, in particular, is based on the human perception of space during the course of which mental images or maps of the environment are created that facilitate targeted spatial action [1, 7, 8, 11]. This is particularly true in the case of pedestrians whose spatial actions constitute an integral (but frequently neglected) part of a multi-modal mobility environment. Graphical representations of spatial mobility information in analog or digital media (town plans, hiking maps, navigation systems, etc.) communicate this spatial knowledge in a most effective way. Expressive navigation media requires a dedicated geospatial database for the particular mobility application domain

© Springer International Publishing AG 2017
O. Gervasi et al. (Eds.): ICCSA 2017, Part IV, LNCS 10407, pp. 541–554, 2017.
DOI: 10.1007/978-3-319-62401-3_39

concerned. Pedestrian navigation (PN) and the corresponding navigation media require geospatial data matched to the specific requirements of pedestrians.

Media and applications supporting PN are currently largely based on vehicle navigation systems. These systems pioneered route finding and route guidance when they were introduced more than 30 years ago. Today a range of vehicle navigation systems is primarily available from commercial providers for individual countries (such as Germany) and continents (e.g. Europe). In accordance with their designation the geodata included in their systems as well as their functionalities largely support usage in individual car navigation. Specific data or objects relevant to PN, such as pavements, passages in blocks of houses, park lanes, and landmarks, are generally missing across vehicle navigation databases.

Hence, navigation systems and, more particularly, geospatial data that is specifically tailored to suit the needs of PN enjoy limited availability. This shortage is largely because dedicated and seamless PN databases are in short supply not only in central European countries like Germany, but also in most other regions of the world.

One reason for this might be a widely shared underestimation of the relevance and potential of this vast (but vastly important) field of geospatial research and applications in the past. This corresponds to a lack of research on the nature and requirements of geospatial data usable in PN, which, in turn, is reflected in the small number of relevant publications, both scientific and practical.

To identify the nature and the amount of data required for proper PN in-depth research calls for on the status, acquisition, and processing of specific geodata that enable true PN. This paper deals with the geospatial data requirements for pedestrian navigation, evaluates existing databases and discusses cost-effective acquisition concepts for missing pedestrian navigation data.

2   Principles of Pedestrian Navigation

It is a truism that anyone who is autonomously moving in public space is a pedestrian. The term designates a large and heterogeneous collective body composed of a variety of different groups. Regardless of the differences, pedestrian navigation in general (collective body) and in particular (specified user groups) is governed by the following principles [7, 8, 20, 22]:

- The movement of pedestrians in geographic space is unrestricted except for obstacles or barriers. Pedestrians are certainly not limited to given linear structures (i.e. paths, roads, streets, paths, water courses, slopes, building fronts, borders, etc.), however such structures do influence a pedestrian's decision on which route to take.
- Pedestrians frequently do not cover the distance between their starting position and the target location in a direct path. Spatial movement is instead the result of individual situational adaptation to the spatio-temporal environment. In addition, spontaneous changes in direction and route are possible at any time.
- Notwithstanding, pedestrians with group-specific characteristics (i.e. age, medical condition, the use of assistive means, etc.) move in space at very low speeds. This

results in specific perception and navigation patterns dominated by orientation along distinctive objects (landmarks) as well as visual stimuli and sounds.

The above factors will have to be taken into account while generating PN databases and dedicated media supporting the orientation and movement of pedestrians in public space [10, 11, 14, 15]. Regardless of the fundamental similarities of spatial movement and orientation, the information requirements of pedestrians can significantly differ from individual route finding [16, 17, 19].

Therefore, it is understood that dedicated and ancillary geographic data (i.e., objects, landmarks, names, etc.) are an indispensable prerequisite for the creation of media and systems facilitating proper PN. Such data need to provide seamless areal coverage of the reference area (of a city, such as Berlin; of a country, such as Germany, and of a continent, such as Europe). Pedestrian routing data, like any other routing data, must take the form of topological networks of nodes and edges or directed graphs. The latter constitute the mathematical basis for navigation and routing.

3   Databases for Pedestrian Navigation

For a country such as Germany, currently, geospatial data meeting the above requirements are hardly available at a national or regional scale. In addition, no proven information and communication media exist that provide pedestrians with spatial images with which they are able to safely orientate and move in the geographic space targeted. In a recent R&D feasibility study[1], we investigated existing geospatial databases in Germany with respect to their usability for PN [2, 3, 5]. The research was conducted under the hypothesis that dedicated databases and media that allow for seamless coverage as well as cost-effective routing and navigation are lacking in the country.

At present, the following geospatial databases are available that can either be directly used as the basis for PN or indirectly as an appropriate foundation to generate a dedicated database for PN: (1) vehicle navigation databases from major commercial companies, (2) topographic databases from the mapping agencies of German federal states, and (3) free crowd-sourced databases. Their suitability for a seamless database for PN has been thoroughly investigated within two study areas (urban/rural) in and around the city of Potsdam.

Vehicle navigation databases. Geospatial databases for car navigation (VNS) with a complete coverage of Germany are available from a number of largely commercial

---

[1] The research presented above is a part of the following feasibility study: *Approaches to the implementation of seamless and cost-effective pedestrian navigation in Germany* funded by the German Federal Ministry for Education and Research (BMBF). The project partners were the Institute for Social Research and Social Economy (Saarbrücken) and the Geoinformation Research Group of Potsdam University. The financial support of the BMBF is gratefully acknowledged.

providers, out of which Here (Germany) and TomTom (The Netherlands)[2] count among the most important. The usage of vehicle navigation data is charged, either with the accompanying navigation systems or as graphic-free digital datasets. Data, data attributes and data structure have been matched to the requirements of individual motorists and the respective user groups of car drivers. Geospatial objects in the databases have been acquired from existing map data, among them road maps, and data acquisition teams by on-site data collection with, in recent years, car-based multisensor instruments. PN-related geospatial objects and attributes independent of vehicle navigation are largely missing in these databases. This general situation has not fundamentally changed since the compilation of these databases began in the 1980s. Nevertheless, for some time now, all systems offer a pedestrian mode of navigation. While selecting this mode, it can be found that pedestrians are basically routed like cars due to the lack of dedicated PN data. Only travel time is calculated based on the speed of an average pedestrian. Vehicle navigation data thus do not provide an appropriate base for proper PN.

Topographic databases. Since 1989, the ATKIS geospatial database of the mapping agencies of the German federal states[3] is available in a scale range relevant to pedestrian navigation (1:25K, 1:10K). The use of these data is charged. Very recently, however, some data have been made freely available via the geoportals of the respective agencies. The ATKIS database is based on the so-called Digital Landscape Models (DLM) from which a detailed object feature catalogue (FC) has been derived. Geospatial data stored in ATKIS represent all topographic objects that can be acquired by geodetic methods and are persistent (no spatial, semantic or temporal change is witnessed on a short time-scale). Thematic data relevant to navigation and routing are not included in the database. This is why the data from ATKIS are not routable. Because of their topographic nature, the ATKIS data are characterised and noted down on the basis of their geometric precision. The ATIKS DLMs are organised in different scale models which are partly independent of each other. For PN, the relevant scale models are the so-called Basic DLM (scale 1:25K) as well as the more recent 1:10K DLM. Both, the Basic and the 1:10K DLMs incorporate objects required for PN up to a limited extent.

Owing to the federal structure of the mapping agencies, the DLMs are built and updated separately for each federal state. As a result, to this day, the database incorporates semantic and/or geometric differences that become particularly obvious at the

---

[2] Vehicle navigation companies harbour extensive proprietary databases dedicated to car navigation. The geometric and thematic quality of object data as well as the completeness and up-to-datedness of data vary from company to company, and from region to region. Precise vehicle navigation data are prerequisite for driverless cars – this sheds a light on the economic value of these data.

[3] ATKIS is the acronym used to signify the Authoritative Topographic-Cartographic Information System of the German topographic survey. Owing to the federal structure of Germany, there is no national mapping agency responsible for a seamless geospatial data coverage in the relevant scales of 1:5K to 1:25K. Content, structure, updating generation, and the use of DLMs among mapping agencies is coordinated by the Consortium of Surveying Agencies (AdV). Nevertheless, there are minor differences in the respective DLMs of the federal states. As a result a uniform official geospatial database providing seamless coverage in large scales and medium scales is lacking. ATKIS is now an integral part of the wider AAA system.

federal states' borders. This situation impedes a seamless use of the database. In principle, it seems possible to harmonise the different DLMs of one scale to allow for seamless data use. However, the required data processing overhead is so high that it almost equals the expenditure for fresh data acquisition. Making the ATKIS data routable for any navigational use is even more complex. Because of the aforementioned shortcomings, ATKIS data cannot be utilised for PN. In particular, they do not meet the requirements of seamless area coverage and cost-efficiency.

Crowd-sourced databases. OpenStreetMap (OSM)[4] is the world's largest geospatial database that is compiled and updated by legions of volunteers (so-called 'mappers'), most of whom are non-professionals [4]. It is a global open-source database created from volunteered geographic information (VGI) that covers large to small scales [6]. In Germany, the OSM data are available at scales required for PN [13]. No compulsory rulebook exists that monitors the processes of data acquisition, data processing and database inputs; rather, there exist ambiguous guidelines. Consequently, the OSM data are highly variable in quality when reaches geographic, semantic and temporal data resolution. Mappers in Germany are substantially contributing to the OSM database making it among one of the richest databases online. The OSM data are seamlessly available free of charge under a free license.

The OSM database contains a variable number of geospatial objects and attributes related to PN. Owing to the acquisition procedure, pedestrian-relevant data are, in most cases, not available possessing the required quality. Furthermore, they are not routable in their original form. Despite these shortcomings, the OSM data can be seen to constitute an appropriate, albeit slim, basis for the generation of a seamless database for PN by applying the methods of data mining.

The examination of major geospatial databases reveals that dedicated data for PN either do either not exist or can only be found with geographic, semantic or topological limitations (Table 1). Based on the evaluation of the two study areas, we have calculated that the volume of the existing geospatial data usable for PN amounts to less than 30%. More than 70% of geodata for PN need to be captured. In consequence, data collection rather than data mining is vital for the generation of a seamless geospatial database for PN. Considering the area of a country like Germany this is a massive task. Therefore, it is essential to apply and/or develop innovative methods of data acquisition, preferably, fully automated ones. A precise determination of the objects and attributes to be collected for such databases is of equal importance. This can be achieved by generating a dedicated data model for PN, from which an object feature catalogue (PN-FC) can be derived as the basis for targeted data acquisition and processing.

---

[4] OpenStreetMap (OSM) is a free editable geospatial database of the world released with an open-content license. Started in 2004 as an online project, OSM tries to overcome the restrictions on availability and use of map data still in place in many parts of the world. A collaborative mapping project, its database is being built and updated by millions of volunteers largely from scratch. OSM data are acquired by volunteers performing more or less systematic ground surveys using mapping tools such as handheld GPS units, notebooks, digital cameras, etc. OSM is the most prominent example of volunteered geographic information (VGI).

Table 1. Key characteristics of existing geospatial databases (section)

Feature	VNS	ATKIS	OSM
Seamless coverage	Yes	National: no/regional: yes	Yes
Geometric accuracy	Very high	Very high	Very high/high
Thematic focus	Vehicle navigation	Topography	Topography/themes
PN-relevant objects	Minimal/few	Minimal	Medium
Routing capability	Yes	No	No
License fee	Yes	Yes	Yes

4   Data Acquisition for Pedestrian Navigation

In the feasibility study, we established the type and the amount of geospatial objects and attributes required for PN. For that purpose, we investigated two outdoor study areas in and around Potsdam that represent typical urban and rural/urban areas. A complete empirical survey of all the objects relating to pedestrians and their movement in public space has been carried out for both of these areas. Parallel to the ground survey a data model for PN was developed. The data model was completed using a two-way adjustment process with the PN data stock determined from the study areas and vice versa.

Data model and object catalogue for pedestrian navigation. In addition to the objects determined from the study areas, we based the development of the PN data model on a study of the relevant literature as well as an in-depth analysis of a number of existing geospatial databases such as the ones discussed above. A geospatial object related to PN can be characterised by its geometric shape (position, neighbourhood, geometry type, i.e., point or line, etc.) and thematic/semantic features (traffic lights, pavements, etc.). Features can have different attributes (tarmac, paving, unsurfaced etc.). All the geospatial data directly or indirectly related to PN have been systematised in a generic data model for PN (PN-M). For operational use in data acquisition and filtering, an object feature catalogue (PN-FC) has been derived from the data model (Table 2). This FC has been used as a reference to assess the existing geospatial databases above.

Table 2. Object feature catalogue for pedestrian navigation (section)

Feature class	Feature group	Feature	Attribute	Attribute value
2000_Traffic	2100_Pedestrian traffic	2101_Walkway	KAT_GW = category	1201_Pavement
3000_Settlements	3100_Bulit-up area	3101_Industrial area	KAT_IGF = category	3102_Retail
4000_Water bodies	4100_Water area	4102_Standing waters	GST_Area status	4302_Nature reserve
5000_Vegetation	5100_Special vegetation	5101_Vegetation area	BEG_accesability	3701_Walkable
8000_POI	8000_Admin./publ. order	8101 Administration	KAT-VO = category	4601_Parliament

Applying the PN-FC to the above databases (all of which relate to Germany) has produced the following results:

(1) Geospatial objects that are essential for pedestrians' route finding and guidance are not incorporated in any of the databases investigated – particularly, in the relevant acquisition and presentation scales of 1:5K to 1:15K.

(2) Independent PN is not supported by any of the databases investigated. Either these databases are not routable (ATKIS, partly OSM) or they solely support vehicle navigation.

(3) The geospatial databases of the federal mapping agencies do not provide unified, harmonised, and seamless coverage for all of Germany.

(4) The use of geodata from official mapping agencies and vehicle navigation is subject to a charge. The seamless use for a complete territory will result in significantly large license fees. Although the pricing policies of mapping agencies are beginning to change, this falls short on cost-effectiveness.

(5) Substantial data deficits have been found in existing geospatial databases when it comes to facilitating independent PN in the broadest sense. Such geodata infrastructure does not exist in Germany. Hence, the application of data mining methods at a larger scale scenario is not an option. In consequence, the extensive acquisition of geographic objects relevant to PN is imperative.

Study areas. As previously mentioned, we have determined the kind and the amount of missing data from existing geospatial databases and the ensuing extent of data acquisition in the two study areas that are representative of the urban and the rurban/rural settings of various midsize central European cities with less than 200,000 inhabitants. The urban study area is located in the centre of Potsdam, which contains shops and historic quarters (Dutch quarter), and is much frequented by Potsdamers and tourist pedestrians visiting the city (Fig. 1).

Fig. 1. Urban study area in the Potsdam city centre (WorldView-2, section): [left] panchromatic imagery at 0.46 m resolution, [right] multispectral imagery at 1.84 m resolution

Based on the PN-FC a complete survey of each PN-related object and attribute has been conducted in the study area. All objects relevant to PN were manually mapped on the ground. The result was an ideal data stock fully usable for PN. This database was compared with the respective OSM database for that study area to determine the missing objects and/or attributes. Test criteria applied include the completeness of geospatial objects and the correctness of geometric and/or semantic attributes. It has been found that the OSM database is incomplete for the purpose of PN. Moreover, relevant PN data was not seamlessly available in the study area (Fig. 2). Data gaps relate to geometry as well as attribution, particularly pavement/path width, surface, gradient and lighting, street/road crossings, kerb lowering, tactile paving and geographic names (paths, lanes, objects). In total, we identified that less than 30% of the existing OSM data is usable to build and populate a dedicated PN database. We assume that the situation that has been detected in the study area can be considered representative of the complete area of Germany.

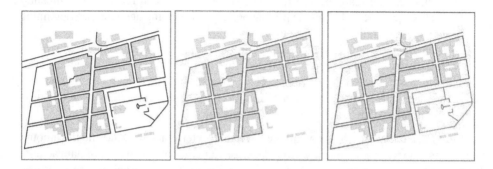

Fig. 2. Urban study area Potsdam, PN-relevant object pavement: [left] ideal dataset (8,486 m = 100%), [middle] pavements mapped (6,395 m = 75%), [right] pavements in OSM (2,126 m = 25%)

A comparison of the ideal data stock for PN with the official ATKIS or commercial vehicle navigation databases revealed that the geospatial data relating to PN were almost entirely lacking. Consequentially, they were excluded as potential data providers to generate a PN database. Overall, a detailed investigation of the study areas has shown that data mining of existing geospatial databases is of minor significance in relation to the generation and population of a dedicated PN database. Instead, data acquisition of PN-related objects is of paramount importance for that task.

Acquisition methods and technologies. It has been demonstrated that data acquisition for PN is a huge task. In this study, we have established that around 70% of all PN related data need to be collected initially. Based on data acquisition in the study areas, we calculate the expense shown in Table 3.

Table 3. Calculated expense of data acquisition based on study areas

Area of interest	Area (km²)	Mapping expense	Expense including postprocessing (h)
Study area Potsdam: urban	0.36	16 h	24 h
Study area Potsdam: rural	1.00	44 h	67 h
City area Potsdam	187	346 d	519 d
Germany (built-up area)	48,482	156 y	234 y

Considering both, the validation findings above and the necessity to collect the bulk of PN data, strategies, and processes need to be developed for building and updating a uniform geospatial database for PN. The magnitude of the task requires such a database to be generated in a cost-effective manner and to provide a seamless areal coverage. The following key points have been defined for the acquisition of PN data:

(1) Collection of PN data is based on the PN-FC that is developed in the feasibility study presented here.
(2) Data acquisition of about 70% of PN data is based on the existing OSM database.
(3) Complete and seamless data provision for large areas in a medium-term period (3 to 5 years).
(4) Definition and use of cost-effective data acquisition processes to populate the PN database.
(5) Seamless and cost-effective updating of data in the PN database.

Consequently, only geospatial data acquisition methods based on very high-resolution sensor imagery have been investigated in this study. Methods selected include data collection from operational remote sensing from space (satellite sensors) and non-operational terrestrial remote sensing (LIDAR, scanners, etc.).

Operational satellite-based remote sensing. Operational remote sensing data are globally available since 1972 (Landsat-1) with an ever-increasing spatial, spectral and radiometric resolution. Stereo images are being acquired since 1985 (Spot-1). Operational remote sensing data, available from the respective data archives, are multispectral, multi-temporal and multi-resolution. With minor exceptions, the purchase of such data is subject to a charge that is essentially a function of the resolution and processing levels offered. In this project, we examined a WorldView-2[5] data set that provides very high-resolution data (0.46 m panchromatic, 1.84 m multispectral) principally suitable for PN (WV, 2017). Objects relevant to PN can be detected either by their spectral signature or by methods of computer vision. Data pre-processing allows for the elimination of data irrelevant to PN (objects not part of PN-FC). Due to a recent breakthrough in open-source image processing software data acquisition can be cost-effective.

A detailed analysis of WorldView-2 data for the study areas including ground controls showed that, for the time being, very high-resolution operational remote sensing cannot be used as the sole data source for PN data. Limitations identified refer to geometric resolution (for example: the height of kerb), spectral resolution (for example: the ambiguous spectral signature of objects) as well as information-free areas (for example: shadows). We assume that these obstacles will be removed with the rapidly advancing improvement of image resolution. For instance, the most recent addition to the WorldView family, WorldView-4, operational since November 2016, provides panchromatic imagery of 0.31 m resolution and 4-band multispectral imagery at a

---

[5] The U.S. American WorldView-2 satellite is an operational very high resolution earth observation sensor launched in October 2009. Operating at an orbit altitude of about 770 km, WorldView-2 provides panchromatic imagery of 0.46 m resolution and 8-band multispectral imagery with 1.84 m resolution. Data products are commercially available at various processing levels [21]. Applications of WorldView-2 data include location-based services [9].

resolution of 1.24 m from an orbit altitude of about 617 km. It seems therefore feasible that in a medium-term period operational highest-resolution remote sensing data will become a suitable source for the extraction of PN data. For the time being, operational remote sensing data can readily be utilised for updating an already existing database.

Non-operational terrestrial remote sensing data. Earthbound remote sensing data are the result of acquisition campaigns limited in time with terrestrial sensors, such as terrestrial scanners, lasers or LIDAR. The latter technologies yield very high-resolution 3D point clouds of data. For the first time terrestrial sensors have been employed in a large scale for the collection of street-related data in the Google Street View project. The result is a global high-resolution database of geocoded 3D imagery. Comparable data are being acquired, for example, by the German vehicle navigation company Here or recent regional mobility projects like map4guide [18] in Berlin. Owing to a range of technologies employed, applied data acquisition and processing expenditure are extremely complex and costly. For economic as well as temporal reasons this approach is not expedient when it comes to the acquisition of seamless PN data.

Experimental terrestrial optical multi-sensor data. The *Integrated Positioning System* (IPS), an innovative optical multi-sensor system developed by the German Aerospace Center (DLR) [12], can be considered a promising alternative facilitating cost-effective and seamless data acquisition for PN (Fig. 3). Originally designed as a system for real-time navigation and 3D modelling on Mars, a miniaturised handheld prototype has been constructed for terrestrial use. Its core consists of an optical digital stereo camera for data acquisition combined with an inertial system for positioning and orientation. System control has been ported to a mobile device (smartphone) allowing for easy operation of the IPS. Initial testing has shown that objects defined in the PN-FC can automatically be acquired with a geometric resolution in the centimetre range. Location of objects is based on the measurements of the inertial system and GPS positioning is not required. That is why the IPS can be used for outdoor as well as indoor data acquisition. IPS data support both outdoor and indoor PN. Other than automatic collection of PN data, the IPS can also be used for mapping. The sensor system is able to generate maps in which every pixel is assigned a distance from the sensor. This allows the identification of objects including relative position and size.

Assessing its experimental use for the acquisition of geospatial data related to PN, we conclude that the IPS is the acquisition system of choice when it comes to a seamless and cost-effective capture of PN data. We expect that use of the IPS will significantly cut personnel, temporal and financial expenditure of PN data acquisition. Verification of this hypothesis is subject to a follow-up R&D project recently submitted.

Fig. 3. Optical 3D data for outdoor/indoor PN navigation acquired by IPS (section)

5   Implementation Strategies

One key result of the feasibility study presented here is the fact that neither seamless geospatial data for PN are available to date nor are the cost-effective acquisition procedures in place in Germany; we assume that this is the case in other central European countries as well. Taking into account the magnitude of the task, a strategy is required to allow a medium-term acquisition of a PN database. Referring to the generation of the ATKIS database by the mapping agencies of the German federal states, we propose the creation of the PN database in 3 to 4 consecutive implementation steps. Steps 1 to 3 are mandatory and Step 4 is optional. Given the necessity of seamless data collection, the

Table 4. Summary: geospatial objects related to pedestrian navigation, availability and acquisition technology (section)

Nr.	Objekt	Merkmal	Priorität	Iso	\multicolumn{3}{Verfügbarkeit im Testgebiet Potsdam}			\multicolumn{3}{Verfügbarkeit im Testgebiet Marquardt}			\multicolumn{2}{Erfassungs- verfahren}		\multicolumn{5}{Auswertung nach Punktesystem}					Kommentar
					OSM	ATKIS	DOS	OSM2	ATKIS2	DOS2	FE	CS	Summe Quellen Stadt	Summe Quellen Land	Summe Quellen Gesamt	Summe Erfassung	Summe gesamt	
1	Gehweg	GEOM	P1		◐	◐	◐	◐	◐	◐	◐	◐	3	3	6	1	15	Bügersteige fehlen in allen drei Datensätzen (in OSM & ATKIS attributiv an Straßen geknüpft); CS: erfordert Möglichkeit zur Erfassung von Linien
2	Gehweg	Geographischer Name	P2		◉	◉	◉	◉	◉	◉	◉	◉	2	4	6	2	18	
3	Gehweg	Wegbreite	P3		◉	◉	◉	◉	◐	◉	◉	◉	2	1	3	2	9	Attribut relevant für Rollstuhlfahrer und Rollatornutzer; FE: abh. Von geom. A.
4	Gehweg	Kategorie	P3		◉	◉	◉	◉	◉	◐	◉	◉	4	3	7	2	16	In Marquardt überwiegend nicht korrekt
5	Gehweg	Belag	P3		◉	◐	◉	◐	◉	◉	◐	◉	0	1	1	1	5	FE: Diff. nach "befestigt" / "unbefestigt" ist möglich. Für genauere Differenzierung bessere spektrale Auflösung als bei Testdaten notwendig
6	Gehweg	Steigung	P2	x	◉	◉	◉	◉	◉	◉	◉	◐	0	0	0	3	3	Voraussetzung FE: hochaufgelöstes DGM; CS: Neigungsmesser (wer hat sowas schon?), oder A-GPS Smartphone.
7	Gehweg	Beleuchtung	P2	x	◉	◉	◉	◉	◉	◉	◉	◉	0	0	0	2	2	Sicherheitsaspekt; FE: Laternen über Schattenwurf erkennbar, bei Verdeckungen aber nicht möglich
8	Gehweg	Nutzung	P2		◉	◉	◉	◉	◉	◉	◉	◉	0	0	0	2	2	ATKIS: Attribut (zuvor "Zuständigkeit") in DB für Auswertung nicht enthalten
9	Gehweg	Fahrradnutzung	P4		◉	◉	◉	◉	◉	◉	◉	◉	4	4	8	2	18	
10	Gehweg	Blindenleitsystem	P3		n.a.	n.a.	n.a.	◉	◉	◉	◉	◉	Mehr Infos!	0	Mehr Infos!	1	Mehr Infos!	FE: nicht aus Satellitendaten (geom. Auflösung!)
11	Gehweg	Brücke	P3		n.a.	n.a.	n.a.	◉	◉	◉	◉	◉	Mehr Infos!	0	Mehr Infos!	4	Mehr Infos!	FE: 3D
12	Gehweg	Tunnel	P3		n.a.	n.a.	n.a.	n.a.	n.a.	n.a.	◉	◉	Mehr Infos!	Mehr Infos!	Mehr Infos!	2	Mehr Infos!	FE Tunnel: Extraktion von Tunneleein-/-ausgang u.U. möglich, Verlauf jedoch nicht → bringt nichts

implementation steps define the priorities of PN-related objects and their acquisition over time (P1–P4, Table 4). Execution of each implementation step is calculated for a time span of about 1,5 years. We suggest the following implementation steps:

(1) Implementation Step 1 (Year 1 and Year 2)

- Establishment of the geometric basis for navigation and routing: acquisition of pavements, paths, their centre lines and metric lengths.

As a result, the collective body of pedestrians is provided with information about the available pedestrian routes and their metric lengths.

(2) Implementation Step 2 (Year 2 and Year 3)

- Basic semantic information related to routes (for example: use, geographic name, etc.).
- Route properties relevant to pedestrians in general (for example: gradient, lighting, etc.).
  As a result, data collected are not differentiated considering the various pedestrian subgroups.

(3) Implementation Step 3 (Year 3 and Year 4)

- Semantic information for defined subgroups (elderly pedestrians, visually impaired pedestrians, pedestrians with physical disabilities, etc.). For example: route width, tactile paving, etc.
- Route properties.
- Points of interest (POIs) relevant to pedestrians, such as bridges, tunnels, etc.

(4) Implementation Step 4 (year 4 to 5)

- All other relevant data, i.e. POIs perceived as landmarks.

To build a basic data stock for PN, the execution of Implementation Steps 1 and 2 is recommended. In Step 2, it may suffice to distinguish the attributes of paved and unpaved routes. This attribute can be further specified in Step 3. If in the initial period navigation guidance is not based on landmarks, acquisition of high-priority landmarks or POIs can be postponed. The above considerations show that it is possible to treat the complete attribution of a geospatial PN object with different priorities.

6   Conclusion

It has been shown that targeted spatial actions of pedestrians, such as orientation, route finding and movement in public space require geospatial data with high spatial and attributive resolution as well as seamless areal coverage. An investigation into the existing geospatial databases representing the relevant application domains of vehicle navigation and topographic coverage has found that such data only exist in rudimentary to basic forms to date in existing spatial databases. If data relevant to PN are available at all, they frequently lack seamless areal coverage.

This situation limits PN to consist of only general navigation instructions. Genuine progress in proper PN will only be achieved when a geospatial database dedicated to PN is created. Generation of a PN database requires a specific PN data model and a derived PN-FC defining all objects, features, and attributes essential for PN. The PN-FC is at the core of a set of rules governing the acquisition of PN-related geodata. Results of the feasibility study presented here indicate that data capture for seamless PN is a massive task in terms of effort, resources, time, and cost. Research into appropriate data collection methods has made it clear that a medium-term, nationwide, and cost-effective solution can only be based on automated data acquisition and processing. A novel 3D data capture system (IPS) has been found to be a promising option to acquire PN-related data at a reasonable cost in large areas. The validation of its potential is the subject of a follow-up R&D project.

The research presented here highlights the fact that pedestrian behaviour and PN, in particular, constitute a vast field of spatial action hitherto widely neglected, but of considerable economic and societal importance. This applies all the more strongly if PN is not looked at separately but as part of the multimodal mobility chain of from door to door (so-called 'first' and 'last mile'). Creating a dedicated geospatial database for seamless PN will undoubtedly be an important contribution to advance targeted orientation, route finding and navigation in a complex multimodal mobility environment.

Acknowledgements. Within the scope of the pedestrian navigation project, the cooperation of the following people is gratefully acknowledged: Andreas Fricke, Carolin Kucharczyk, Christian Kuntzsch and Lasse Scheele, all those belonging to the Geoinformation Research Group (Potsdam), as well as Daniel Bieber and Kathleen Schwarz of the Institute for Social Research and Social Economy (Saarbrücken). Thank you all for your valuable contributions.

References

1. Allen, G.: Spatial abilities, cognitive maps, and wayfinding: bases for individual differences in spatial cognition and behavior. In: Golledge, R. (ed.) Wayfinding Behavior – Cognitive Mapping and Other Spatial Processes, Baltimore, pp. 46–80 (1999)
2. Asche, H., Bieber, D., Schwarz, K., Kuntzsch, C.: EasyGoing – Machbarkeitsstudie. Ansaetze zur Umsetzung einer flaechendeckenden und kostenguenstigen Fussgaenger-navigation. [EasyGoing – feasibility study. Approaches to the implementation of seamless and cost-effective pedestrian navigation in Germany] Vision paper. Unpubl. Saarbrücken, Potsdam (2015)
3. Asche, H., Kuntzsch, C.: EasyGoing – Machbarkeitsstudie. Ansaetze zur Umsetzung einer flaechendeckenden und kostenguenstigen Fussgaengernavigation. [EasyGoing – Feasibility study. Approaches to the implementation of seamless and cost-effective pedestrian navigation in Germany] Final report subproject data acquisition. Unpubl. Potsdam (2016)
4. Bennett, J.: OpenStreetMap. Be your own cartographer. Birmingham (2010)
5. Bieber, D., Schwarz, K., Nock, L., Zoerkler, M.: EasyGoing – Machbarkeitsstudie. Ansaetze zur Umsetzung einer flaechendeckenden und kostenguenstigen Fussgaenger-navigation. [EasyGoing – Feasibility study. Approaches to the implementation of seamless and cost-effective pedestrian navigation in Germany] Final report subproject pedestrian groups, cognition, abilities. Unpubl. Saarbrücken (2016)

6. Coleman, D.: Potential contributions and challenges of VGI for conventional topographic base-mapping programs. In: Sui, D., Elwood, S., Goodchild, M. (eds.) Crowdsourcing Geographic Knowledge: Volunteered Geographic Information (VGI) in Theory and Practice, New York, London, pp. 245–264 (2013)

7. Cornell, E.H., Sorenson, A., Mio, T.: Human sense of direction and wayfinding. Ann. Assoc. Am. Geogr. **93**(2), 399–425 (2003)

8. Darken, R.P., Peterson, B.: Spatial orientation, wayfinding, and representation. In: Stanney, K.M. (ed.) Handbook of Virtual Environment Technology, New Jersey, pp. 493–518 (2002)

9. DG. Digital Globe (2017). https://www.digitalglobe.com/industries/location-based-services. Accessed Mar 2017

10. Egenhofer, M., Raubal, M.: Comparing the complexity of wayfinding tasks in built environments. Environ. Plann. B Plann. Des. **25**(6), 895–913 (1998)

11. Golledge, R.: Human wayfinding and cognitive maps. In: Golledge, R. (ed.) Way-finding Behavior – Cognitive Mapping and Other Spatial Processes, Baltimore, pp. 5–45 (1999)

12. Grießach, D., Baumbach, D., Börner, A., Buder, M., Ernst, I., Funk, E., Wohlfeil, J., Zuev, S.: IPS – a system for real-time navigation and 3D modeling. Int. Arch. Photogramm. Remote Sens. Spatial Inf. Sci. **XXXIX-B5**, 21–26 (2012)

13. Haklay, M.: How good is volunteered geographical information? A comparative study of OpenStreetMap and ordnance survey datasets. Environ. Plann. B Plann. Des. **37**, 682–703 (2010)

14. Karimi, H.A., Jiang, M., Zhu, R.: Pedestrian navigation services: challenges and current trends. Geomatica **67**(4), 259–271 (2013)

15. Kluge, M., Asche, H.: Validating a smartphone-based pedestrian navigation system prototype. In: Murgante, B., Gervasi, O., Misra, S., Nedjah, N., Rocha, A.M.A.C., Taniar, D., Apduhan, B.O. (eds.) ICCSA 2012. LNCS, vol. 7334, pp. 386–396. Springer, Heidelberg (2012). doi: 10.1007/978-3-642-31075-1_29

16. May, A., Ross, T., Bayer, S., Tarkiainen, M.: Pedestrian navigation aids: information requirements and design implications. Pers. Ubiquitous Comput. **7**(6), 331–338 (2003)

17. Millonig, A., Schechtner, K.: Decision loads and route qualities for pedestrians — key requirements for the design of pedestrian navigation services. In: Waldau, N., Gattermann, P., Knoflacher, H., Schreckenberg, M. (eds.) Pedestrian and Evacuation Dynamics 2005, pp. 109–118. Springer, Heidelberg (2007)

18. M4G. Map4guide (2013). http://www.m4guide.de. Accessed Mar 2017

19. Sobek, A.D., Miller, H.J.: U-access: a web-based system for routing pedestrians of differing abilities. J. Geograph. Syst. **8**(3), 269–287 (2006)

20. Wolbers, T., Hegarty, M.: What determines our navigational abilities? Trends Cogn. Sci. **14**(3), 138–146 (2010)

21. WV2. WorldView-2 (2017). http://www.satimagingcorp.com/satellite-sensors/worldview-2. Accessed Mar 2017

22. Zacharias, J.: Pedestrian behavior and perception in urban walking environments. J. Plann. Lit. **16**(1), 3–18 (2001)

A Proposal for the Spatial Planning Monitoring System in Serbia

Ljiljana Živković[(✉)]

Ministry of Construction, Transport and Infrastructure, Belgrade, Serbia
liliana.zivkovic@gmail.com

Abstract. After the adoption of the Spatial Plan of the Republic of Serbia (SPRS) in 2010, and introduction of the first set of spatial development indicators with the same, there is a need for establishment of a modern GIS-oriented monitoring system. This monitoring system should support the SPRS implementation and spatial development policy management in general in a more comprehensive, visually understandable and interactive way. At the same time, there is a growing body of knowledge on monitoring systems, followed by an increasing number of the territorial monitoring systems for spatial planning and development in Europe (like ETMS, INTERCO, KITCAPS and others). Based on this knowledge body, and including specific needs of Serbian spatial development system, this paper proposes (1) spatial development indicator definition, (2) data model for spatial development policy monitoring and (3) geovisualization model, required for the building of monitoring system for spatial planning in Serbia. In future, this monitoring system should underpin a better evaluation of spatial development trends on the national level, stimulate a greater involvement of spatial planning focus groups in the spatial planning process, as well as support the spatial development policy evidence-based decision-making on sustainable and cohesive development principles.

Keywords: Spatial development policy · Spatial planning · Spatial development indicators · Spatial planning monitoring system · Serbia

1 Introduction

After 6 years from the adoption and reporting on the Spatial Plan of the Republic of Serbia (SPRS) [1] implementation, a concept of a modern GIS-based monitoring system for the spatial development trends follow-up and the evidence-based spatial development policy decision-making is still in evolving phase. This concept must include a set of the already identified spatial development indicators by the Implementation Program for the SPRS [2], which are selected exactly for the evaluation of the development goals and targets determined by the SPRS, as well as for the analysis of sustainability and cohesive properties of the spatial development trends in Serbia.

On the other side, after the European Observation Network for Territorial Development and Cohesion (ESPON) [3] program launching in 2002, supported by the other European initiatives in domain of the data management for policy coordination (like

© Springer International Publishing AG 2017
O. Gervasi et al. (Eds.): ICCSA 2017, Part IV, LNCS 10407, pp. 555–570, 2017.
DOI: 10.1007/978-3-319-62401-3_40

INSPIRE [4]), the number, variation and specialization of the territorial monitoring systems for cohesive, smart and sustainable territorial development in Europe [5] is growing. These GIS-based territorial monitoring systems aim to support the coordination of various spatial development policies in Europe by measuring and evaluating these policies' impacts within the certain areas, securing thus reliable platforms for the evidence-based spatial development decision-making process and planning in general.

Using the experiences of these European territorial monitoring systems for spatial development, and taking into account the Serbian spatial planning system specific needs and conditions, this paper researches and presents the possible concept and approach to the building of GIS-based spatial planning monitoring system in Serbia.

Thus, in this article, firstly proposed are: (1) definition for the spatial development indicator, (2) data model for the spatial development policy monitoring, and (3) model for the spatial development indicators' values and analyzed territorial development trends geovisualization within the GIS-based monitoring system. On the end, the expected effects of the here proposed monitoring system concept and geovisualization approach on the spatial planning system and policy decision-making in Serbia would be discussed. Also, possible future steps towards the GIS-based monitoring system for spatial planning monitoring in Serbia establishment would be identified.

Innovative aspect of the here presented research refers to the methodology for (1) the establishment of the GIS-oriented monitoring system for spatial development policy management in Serbia, and (2) the adaptation and implementation of the European territorial monitoring systems' best practices within the specifics of Serbian spatial planning system domain.

In this research, Serbian spatial planning system has been chosen for a case study since the author is familiar with the same. Additionally, having status of the EU candidate country, Serbia at the moment invests significant efforts towards accession to the relevant EU initiatives, including ESPON, INSPIRE and other territorial cooperation programs.

2   Spatial Planning in Serbia

Current national spatial development plan, that is, SPRS, has been adopted in 2010 and it presents vision for the spatial development up to 2020. [1] After the period of rational comprehensive planning during socialism, with too rigid structure for responding to the fast social changes in Serbia, this SPRS has assumed the more sophisticated approach by including the sustainable and cohesive development principles and goals to lead its implementation. Therefore, Dželebdžić and Bazik [6] find this period to be reinventing one for the spatial planning in Serbia.

Additionally, SPRS has introduced an idea of spatial planning in Serbia as a continual process of integrated responding to the challenges towards achievement the national spatial development policy goals, as well as priorities of the other relevant European policies, like TA2020 [7], Europe2020 [5] and others. This approach stresses the need for a continual monitoring of the spatial development trends, and directly justifies the need for building the advanced spatial planning monitoring system in Serbia [6] (Fig. 1).

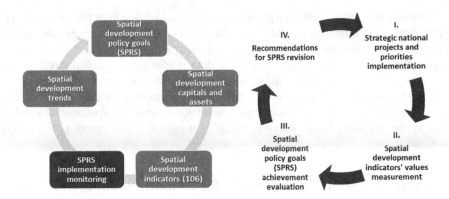

Fig. 1. Spatial development policy cycle and monitoring mechanism on national level in Serbia

Also, responding to the today's spatial dynamics and spatial planning trends, SPRS has assumed for the decision-making power and responsibility for the spatial development policy in Serbia to be transferred and/or shared with the different levels and focus groups. This new approach to the spatial development policy implementation and management has been followed by the identification of mentioned set of the spatial development indicators, which are linked directly to the spatial development goals and targets determined by the SPRS, and indirectly to the other relevant national and EU policies priorities and initiatives (Fig. 1).

In other words, responding to the need for development of the monitoring system for spatial planning in Serbia that could "properly reflect spatial planning outcomes in complexity of integrating multi-spatial levels and cross-sectoral policies" [6], two Implementation Programs for the SPRS have been adopted since 2010, for periods 2011–2015 and 2016–2020 [2]. In these documents, the set of 106 spatial development indicators have been identified as one that could in an adequate way describe and present the spatial development state in Serbia, and thus provide efficient instrument for the continual monitoring of spatial development trends and policy implementation up to 2020. Taking into account the European integration aspirations of Serbia, this set of 106 indicators for the spatial development trends monitoring includes also some indicators that are used for the monitoring of European territory within the ESPON program [3]. Dželebdžić and Bazik [6] claim that on this way it is reinforced the main strength and advantage of the ESPON initiative [3] within the Serbian spatial development indicators set, namely availability of the comparable data across the time and space relating to the ESDP process in general, and TA2020 [7] and Europe2020 [5] targets in particular.

Up till now, the monitoring of the SPRS implementation and spatial development policy in Serbia was performed as the annual activity of the reporting [8], where as major problems were identified the lack of data, available data format and/or applied methodology for data collection, different data resolutions, [9] etc. However, despite the strategic need for the modern and interactive GIS-based monitoring system for spatial planning and spatial development policy management, which would be able to connect to the other territorial monitoring systems in Serbia, region and Europe in general, building of this monitoring system is still delaying.

Therefore, this article proposes possible concept and approach to the establishment of spatial planning monitoring system in Serbia. Proposal includes the spatial development indicators definition or fact sheet, needed for the indicators' description, values interpretation and usability assessment; then, data model for the spatial development policy monitoring by collecting, processing, storing, analyzing and management of indicators values; and, finally, possible model for the geovisualization of indicators' values, needed for the analyses and better understanding of the spatial development trends as well as the efficient decision-making on spatial development policy future directions.

3   Territorial Monitoring Systems for Spatial Planning in Europe

Since the launching of the ESPON program in 2002 [3], as a tool for measuring and comparing the spatial impacts of EU policies against the ESDP objectives, number of other territorial monitoring initiatives for the policies implementation support has emerged [10]. These initiatives are differing related to their specific objectives (ATTRACT-SEE [11], KITCAPS [12], INTERCO [13], etc.), territorial scopes (AIRO [14], ETMS [15], etc.) and the other analytical elements, but common for all these monitoring systems is the support to the cohesive territorial development goal achievement by the sustainable living and working conditions development and follow up [10, 16, 17].

Spatial planning activity is deeply affected by the knowledge representation and management [18]. Therefore, the ESPON program success, as the knowledge and information platform for the territorial policies monitoring, evaluation and geovisualization in Europe, has triggered a large proliferation of the different monitoring systems or observatories for the spatial planning domain, which are perceived as the innovative planning tools, especially for the strategic level [3, 17]. Further, Soria-Lara et al. [17] research confirmed that spatial planning monitoring systems' maps are excellent tools for spatial planning, since they can improve the process of learning and understanding of the different focus groups (decisions makers, planners and the public) on present and future problems within the spatial planning process. Lindberg and Dubois [19] agree that visualization is "a key feature supporting spatial visioning and the co-production of a shared transnational understanding of the spatial planning in Europe", and additionally stress that the spatial planning monitoring systems should address the specific and strategic important themes relevant for the current political ambitions, since politicians are one of the main focus groups.

Further, Lindberg and Dubois [19] argue that selection of the appropriate set and combination of indicators is critical for the capacity of the spatial planning monitoring systems to secure the meaningful communication between the focus groups, as well as to support the key policy needs for the evidence-based development management (Fig. 2). However, besides importance of the choice and visual presentation (interactive and online) of the limited number of relevant spatial development indicators for the success and usability of each monitoring system, the authors emphasize also the need for durability of spatial planning monitoring systems [6, 12, 16, 19]. The latter demands well prepared documentation as well as traceable information on the selected spatial development indicators, like a fact sheet and metadata, which would ensure reproducibility and consistency of the analytical work over time, and provide comparability of the spatial development indicators values across time and space [13, 15, 19].

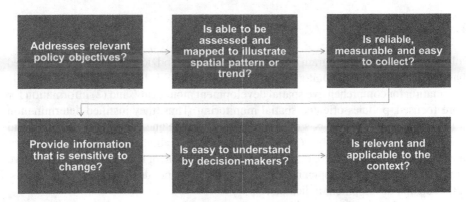

Fig. 2. Spatial development indicator: selection flow (source: KITCAPS [12])

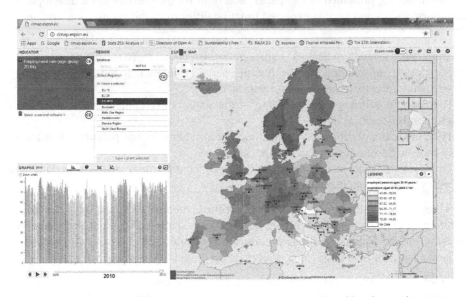

Fig. 3. ESPON online mapping tool: key ESPON indicators at regional level – employment rate (age group 20–64) (figure is for illustrative purposes only) [3, 15]

Therefore, appropriate presentation of the territorial dynamics by the spatial development indicators usually includes, but is not limited to [13, 15, 19]: (1) the fact sheet for each spatial development indicator with the indicator definition and core metadata needed for its usability, analysis and values interpretation, and (2) the spatial development indicator values geovisualization by the maps, graphs and charts for the spatial development disparities analysis and trends identification (Fig. 3). Thus, these elements for the description, interpretation and presentation of the spatial development dynamics, using the spatial development indicators' values, would be also critical for the concept and approach design, development and usability of the researched and here proposed spatial planning monitoring system for Serbia.

4 Methodology

Following the ESPON program knowledge body, Dželebdžić and Bazik [6] concluded that the spatial planning monitoring in Serbia has to provide two set of information: (1) information for comprehensive spatial development monitoring, and (2) information for more focused, policies-oriented spatial monitoring. Thus, they justified determination of the two types of indicators within the SPRS: outcome and output, respectively. And while the outcome indicators (37 of them) present qualitative targets of the spatial development in Serbia till 2020, the output indicators (106 of them) present quantitative values of the spatial development process itself. This paper deals with the later, that is, output spatial development indicators.

Based on that, methodology for creating proposal for the spatial planning monitoring system in Serbia, presented in this paper, was built for the output spatial development indicators' values and against expected functionalities from this monitoring system:

– To enable collection, storage, processing, analyses and geovisualization of the output spatial development indicators' values in consistent and reproducible way;
– To provide information for the output spatial development indicators' usability assessment and their values interpretation;
– To secure monitoring and evaluation of the spatial development states, disparities and trends in Serbia;
– To provide possibilities for connecting to the other relevant policies' monitoring systems in Serbia, region and Europe; and
– To be reliable platform for the spatial development planning decision-making and policy management in general; etc.

Thus, analyzing the already developed territorial monitoring systems for the spatial planning in Europe, as well as relying on the above identified required functionalities for the GIS-based spatial planning monitoring system in Serbia, creating proposal for the same assumed next three steps, which are described further in this chapter:

– Building definition for the spatial development indicators;
– Creating data model for the spatial planning monitoring domain; and
– Preparing model for the geovisualization of the spatial development trends.

4.1 Defining Spatial Development Indicator

Using the existing knowledge and experiences from the territorial monitoring systems in Europe, which are mentioned before in this paper, creation of the definition for the spatial development indicator has involved adaptation of the one already developed definition for the Attract-SEE project [11]. This project was implemented in the period

2012–2014 within the South East Europe Transnational Cooperation Program, and it produced as the main result the common framework for the territorial attractiveness monitoring in the South East Europe region.

Thus, here proposed definition for the spatial development indicator has included all the parameters from the Attract-SEE's territorial attractiveness indicator definition, with some smaller adjustments and additions for the specific needs of the Serbian spatial planning system, and spatial development policy monitoring domain itself.

Since the Attract-SEE project's territorial attractiveness indicator definition relied on the existing standards within the ESPON program, this means that here proposed spatial development indicator definition has also included advantages of the ESPON's indicator definition method. On this way, the spatial development indicators definition data for the Serbian spatial planning monitoring system would support also their (indicators') reuse, reproduction, consistency and comparability in future.

4.2 Modeling Spatial Planning Monitoring Domain

Complying with the previous spatial development indicator definition (Sect. 4), and extending again the Attract-SEE project's data model according to the expected functional and thematic advantages from here researched spatial planning monitoring system (Sect. 4), a conceptual data model for spatial planning monitoring domain in Serbia was built using:

– UML language advantages; and
– International and national data management standards (like INSPIRE, Serbian NSDI), where possible, as well as Serbian spatial planning monitoring system's needs.

4.3 Defining Geovisualization Model for Spatial Development Trend Monitoring

Similar to the approaches in the two previous steps (Sects. 4.1 and 4.2), defining proposal for the geovisualization within the spatial planning monitoring system, that is, for the presentation of the spatial development trends in Serbia, involved the analyses and adaptation of the already existing geovisualization models within the other spatial planning monitoring systems in Europe. In this case, especially the experiences and models of the ETMS [15] and INTERCO [13] projects have been analyzed and adapted.

That means that maps, graphs and diagrams for the geovisualization of the set of 106 output spatial development indicators should be based on the already recognized and accepted geovisualization approaches, techniques and tools, which are here just adapted to the specific needs of the GIS-based spatial planning monitoring system for Serbia.

Also, here created and presented model for the geovisualization is based on the selected sample of the spatial development indicators, which values were collected and processed for the reporting on SPRS implementation and spatial development trends in Serbia in 2013 [8].

5   Towards Monitoring System for Spatial Planning in Serbia

5.1   Spatial Development Indicator Definition

By using the same parameters for describing each indicator, below proposed fact sheet for the spatial development indicator definition (Table 1) should provide:

- Description of all indicators in the uniform way;
- Indicators core metadata, data and values to be collected in consistent and comparable manner;
- Indicators data to be reusable by the other development initiatives and policies monitoring systems, as well as the information systems in general;
- Usability assessment of the each indicator for the different spatial planning focus groups' applications; and
- Context for the interpretation of identified indicators' values and development trends.

Table 1. Fact sheet for the spatial development indicator (Employed persons by the highest education level attained) (adapted from the Attract-SEE project [11])

Parameter	Indicator definition
ID	7
Name	Employed persons by the highest education level attained
Active	Yes
Definition	Share of the employed with the high education in an area
Purpose	Information on the education level of employed within an area indicates on level of social cohesion, as well as on the effects of government policy aimed at spatially balanced education level among employed population
Determination	The percentage of the employed with the highest education in the total employed population within a certain area
Publishing frequency	Annually
Unit of measure	% of employed
Indicator type	State
Indicator category	1
Goal	More even-balanced regional development and improved social cohesion
Target	Improving social and economic cohesion – Improving spatial balance of the education among the employed

5.2   Data Model for Spatial Planning Monitoring Domain

Based on the proposed spatial development indicator definition (Sect. 5.1), here is proposed data model for the spatial planning monitoring system in Serbia. Besides that definition, this data model has taken into account also the requirements of the initiative for the development of European spatial data infrastructures for the environmental and related policies implementation support (like INSPIRE [4]), as well as the other projects for the spatial development indicators management in Europe (like ESPON [3]). Using the Unified Modeling Language (UML) (Fig. 4), the created data model should secure indicators' data harmonization and interoperability advantages, which are essential for the future linking of the Serbian spatial planning monitoring system with the other relevant information and monitoring systems in Serbia, region and Europe.

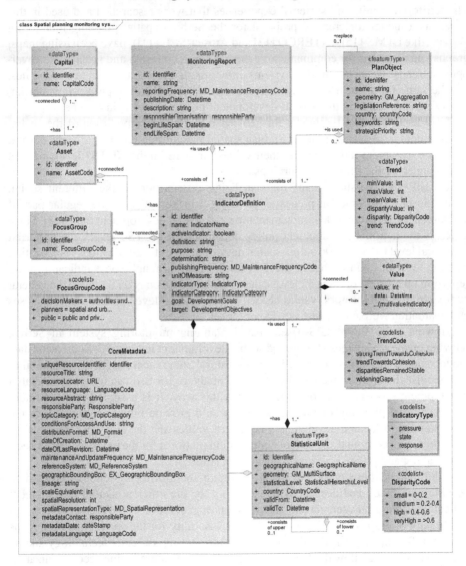

Fig. 4. Proposed data model for the spatial planning monitoring system in Serbia (adapted from the Attract-SEE project [11])

Also, proposed data model for the spatial planning monitoring domain in Serbia is the object-oriented and scalable. It consists of the core metadata and spatial development indicators data classes and code lists, and provides storage for the five indicators' dimensions: spatial, thematic, lineage, temporal and dataset.

5.3 Geovisualizing Model for Spatial Development Trends Monitoring

The territorial monitoring systems' experiences that were researched and used in this paper, as a model for creating proposal for the Serbian spatial planning monitoring system (like ETMS [15], INTERCO [13] and Attract-SEE [11]), have been using maps, graphs and diagrams for communicating the territorial cohesion and sustainable development trends. These monitoring systems differ among them in their scopes and scales, but the same for all of them is the supportive role for collecting, processing, storing, analyzing and signaling the various development policies' effects in Europe.

In order to propose the model for geovisualizing and interpretation of the spatial development dynamics within the Serbian spatial planning monitoring system, several spatial development indicators and their values for 2013 on the NUTS3 level are used in this paper for the illustrative purposes.

Up till now the static maps for visualizing distribution of the different social, economic or environmental processes or subjects in Serbia were the regular part of annual reporting on the SPRS implementation and spatial development trends [8]. Since SPRS is the national development policy document for NUTS0 level[1], the preferred analytical level for those 106 output spatial development indicators' values visualization was the level of county, that is, NUTS3 level. Also, although some indicators were reporting on NUTS1 or NUTS2 levels, due to lack of data on NUTS3 level, the general comparability of indicators' values needed for the spatial development trends analyses and evaluation were on the just satisfactory level.

However, the future GIS-based spatial planning monitoring system in Serbia, relaying on the advantages of proposed spatial development indicator definition and data model, should support the more efficient indicators' values accessibility, comparability and geovisualization, as well as the advanced analyses for two or more related spatial development processes and/or indicators. On this way, it is assumed that the future Serbian spatial planning monitoring system would provide improved context for the understanding of spatial development indicators values and development trends; also, it would secure continual and reliable information platform for the evidence-based decision-making and policy priorities management (Fig. 5).

Additionally, here proposed spatial planning monitoring system is expected to provide new functionalities, methods and tools for the efficient spatial development indicators values management and, thus, to support generation of the greater variety and complexity of graphs and diagrams with better usability for the spatial planning focus groups in Serbia (Fig. 6). Besides, this future monitoring system's technology and its interactivity should allow the focus groups to adjust indicators' values geovisualization to their needs, which would in return demand and justify further development of this

---

[1] Statistical division of Serbia made by the Statistical Office of the Republic of Serbia is not officially recognized and confirmed by the EUROSTAT.

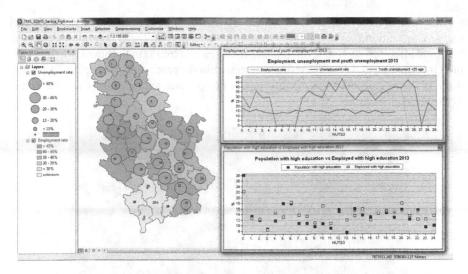

Fig. 5. Proposed analysis and geovisualization for the target "Sustainable demographic development and diversity of regional economies" (Spatial development indicators: Migratory balance, Population density and Employment by economic sectors)

spatial planning monitoring system's functionalities based on the focus groups' requirements.

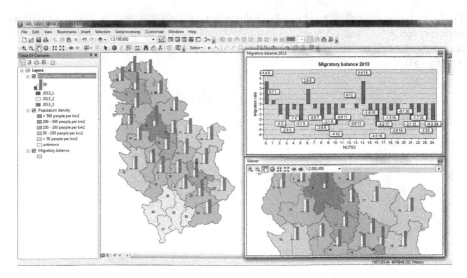

Fig. 6. Proposed analysis and geovisualization for the target "Improving social and economic cohesion" (Spatial development indicators: Employment rate, Unemployment rate, Youth unemployment <25 age, Persons with the high education and Employed with high education)

Comparing to the visualization techniques used for the reporting on SPRS implementation in period 2011–2014 [8], it is expected that additional information, like graphs and diagrams for the spatial development disparities and cohesion and sustainability trends visualization (Figs. 7 and 8), would further improve understanding of the both short- and long- run spatial development processes and trends in Serbia. Also, this additional information and new geovisualization within the proposed spatial planning monitoring system could add new quality to the projections and scenarios for the future development in Serbia.

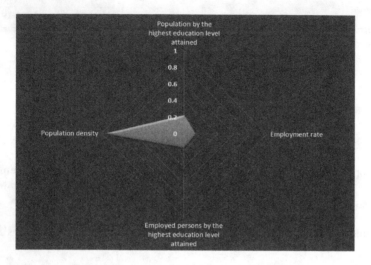

Fig. 7. Proposed disparities level graph for the target "Sustainable demographic development and improved social and economic cohesion"; Trend identification: trend towards regional cohesion with small-to-medium disparities (0–0.4), except for population density with very high disparity (>0.6)

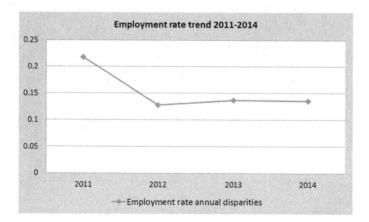

Fig. 8. Proposed disparities level graph for the target "Reducing social exclusion and poverty"; Trend identification: small annual disparities prevailing (0–0.2), trend toward cohesion

In other words, here presented monitoring system, with its broader analytical capabilities and various geovisualization potentials, should better support the policy decision-making process on side of spatial planners and the other focus groups in Serbia. Also, this new system should make already investing efforts in the spatial development in Serbia much more efficient and effective towards cohesive and sustainable development goals.

Although it was not possible to be illustrated in this paper, it should be noted that interoperability of the proposed data model for the spatial planning and development policy monitoring in Serbia, would enable connection to the other relevant monitoring systems in region and Europe. This should bring new methodological advantages, spatial development understanding as well as policy challenges to the Serbian spatial planners and society in general.

6 Discussion

Applied methodology for the building proposal of the spatial planning monitoring system in Serbia is in the accordance with the latest data management standards, which are directed to the development of knowledge and information platforms in Europe for supporting the vision of smart, inclusive and sustainable growth up to 2020 [5]. Additionally, the proposed approach to the establishment of this monitoring system responds to the latest vision within the territorial development management domain in Europe, directed to the achievement of cohesive and sustainable development principles through the participatory and integrated planning concepts and common development standards implementation.

Also, by using the spatial development indicator definition and the data model that are developed as the results during the Attract-SEE project [11], as well as implementing recommendations from the other spatial data and monitoring management programs and projects (like ESPON [3], INSPIRE [4], INTERCO [13], KITCAPS [12]; etc.), proposed concept and approach to the Serbian spatial planning monitoring system ensure the possibilities for the same to connect, compare and share the data and information with the other similar or related systems in Serbia and region.

In general, main disadvantage of presented concept and research results refers to (1) the lack of resources for the implementation of this monitoring system in Serbia today, as well as (2) the general lack of data on different NUTS and LAU levels. These data are needed both for the establishment of the proposed spatial planning monitoring system, as well as for fulfillment of the projected capabilities for the same to support the cohesive and sustainable development decision-making and national spatial development policy management.

Also, it should be noted that implementation of this monitoring system would support the mentioned reinvention of the spatial planning in Serbia, as well as the taken step-by-step approach to its evolution, modernization and adjustment to the dynamics of spatial planning domain in Europe [6].

Finally, here proposed solution for the spatial planning monitoring system in Serbia, especially its projected capability of interactivity, would support the existing spatial planning focus groups' network in Serbia and develop it further through the greater involvement, responsibility and participatory planning activities.

7 Conclusion

In order for the spatial planning process in Serbia to be continually supported and directed towards achievement of the sustainable and cohesive development policy goals, this paper proposes concept and approach to the establishment of monitoring system for the spatial planning. Started by identifying the preferred capabilities for this new system, and using the already defined set of the spatial development indicators by the SPRS as well as the experiences from the other relevant European monitoring systems, proposed and described solutions in this paper assumed three steps to be taken for building the spatial planning monitoring system in Serbia. First, standard parameters for the spatial development indicators description should be defined as the fact sheet; they are preconditions for the spatial development indicators to be collected and described in the uniform manner, to be reproducible in a long run and interpreted within the context of the particular NUTS level. Second, the interoperable data model for the spatial planning monitoring domain in Serbia should be implemented for the collection and storing spatial development indicators values and other information. Third, after indicators' values processing and analyses, proposed geovisualization model for the spatial development states, disparities and trends should be implemented for the better communication, understanding and greater usability of the monitored results in form of the maps, different graphs and diagrams.

The main advantage of the proposed concept and approach is their adoption and implementation of the European best practices in domain of the monitoring systems for spatial planning and development policy management. This should allow in future this new monitoring system to be capable to connect and compare the indicator values and spatial development trends in Serbia within region, ESPON and Europe in general. Also, assumed interactivity of proposed spatial planning monitoring system would create conditions for the participatory and integrated planning concepts further development in Serbia.

The main obstacles at the moment for the establishment of this spatial planning monitoring system refer to the lack of resources in general, as well as the lack of standardized – EUROSTAT- data and information for the indicators' values calculations.

However, in future it is expected that initiatives towards establishment of the Serbian spatial planning monitoring system would continue in certain form and pace, since the need for the same is clearly recognized and the number of activities are already running in the other sectors and spatial planning communities, which would enable its eventual establishment.

References

1. Spatial Plan of the Republic of Serbia (Abridged version in English language). http:// 195.222.96.93//media/zakoni/Spatial%20Plan%20of%20the%20Republic%20of%20Serbia _2010-2020_abridged%20(1).pdf
2. Implementation programs for the Spatial Plan of the Republic of Serbia 2011–2015 and 2016– 2020. http://mgsi.gov.rs/cir/dokumenti/dokumenti-za-sprovodjenje-prostornih-planova
3. ESPON Inspire Policy Making by Territorial Evidence. https://www.espon.eu/main/
4. INSPIRE Infrastructure for spatial information in Europe. http://inspire.ec.europa.eu/
5. EUROPE 2020 A strategy for smart, sustainable and inclusive growth. http://ec.europa.eu/ eu2020/pdf/COMPLET%20EN%20BARROSO%20%20%20007%20-%20Europe %202020%20-%20EN%20version.pdf
6. Dželebdžić, O., Dazik, D.: National indicators for evaluating the outcome of reinventing spatial planning in Serbia. SPATIUM Int. Rev. (24), 27–36 (2011). doi:10.2298/SPAT1124027D, http:// www.doiserbia.nb.rs/img/doi/1450-569X/2011/1450-569X1124027D.pdf
7. EU: Territorial Agenda of the European Union 2020 (2011). http://ec.europa.eu/regional_ policy/en/information/publications/communications/2011/territorial-agenda-of-the- european-union-2020
8. Reports on the Spatial Plan of the Republic of Serbia Implementation and spatial development state for 2011, 2012, 2013, 2014. http://mgsi.gov.rs/cir/dokumenti/dokumenti-za-sprovodjenje- prostornih-planova
9. Garau, C., Masala, F., Pinna, F.: Cagliari and smart urban mobility: analysis and comparison. Cities 56, 35–46 (2016). https://dx.doi.org/10.1016/j.cities.2016.02.012
10. Faludi, A.: The European spatial development perspective shaping the agenda. Eur. J. Spatial Dev. (21) (2006). http://www.nordregio.se/Global/EISD/Refereed%20articles/refereed21.pdf
11. Živković, L., Marani, S., Berk, S., Dežman Kete, V., Špeh, N., Trapani, F., Esposito, G., Milić, D., Živanović, T., Barborič, B.: Towards a monitoring information system for territorial attractiveness policy management in south east Europe. In: Geodetski vestnik, vol. 59, no 4, pp. 752–766, Ljubljana, Slovenia (2015). doi:10.15292/geodetski-vestnik.2015.04.752-766, http://issuu.com/mfoski/docs/gv_12015_4
12. ESPON: KITCAPS Key Indicators for Territorial Cohesion and Spatial Planning (2013). https://www.espon.eu/programme/projects/espon-2013/targeted-analyses/kitcasp-key- indicatorsterritorial-cohesion-and
13. ESPON: INTERCO Indicators of territorial cohesion – Final report (2013). https://www.espon.eu/ programme/projects/espon-2013/scientific-platform/interco-indicatorsterritorial-cohesion
14. Walsh, C., Blair, N., Hetherington, J., Gleeson, J.: Towards a Spatial Monitoring Framework for the Island of Ireland: a Scoping Study (2012). http://iclrd.org/wp-content/uploads/ 2012/04/Spatial-Monitoring-Framework-for-the-island-of-Ireland.pdf
15. ESPON: ETMS European Territorial Monitoring System (2014). http://etms.espon.eu/
16. OECD: The spatial monitoring system of the German Federal Office for building and regional planning (BBR) as a tool for political counseling (2004). http://www.oecd.org/site/worldforum/ 33846622.pdf
17. Soria-Lara, J.A., Zúñiga-Antón, M., Pérez-Campaña, R.: European spatial planning observatories and maps: merely spatial databases or also effective tools for planning? Environ. Plann. B Plann. Des. 42(5), 904–929 (2015). http://journals.sagepub.com/doi/abs/10.1068/ b130200p

18. Deplano, G., Campagna, M., De Montis, A.: Regional and local planning system monitoring: the GIS support in spatial development management. In: 4th AGILE Conference, Brno, Czech Republic   (2001)   https://www.academia.edu/1062563/Regional_and_local_planning_system_monitoring._The_GIS_as_support_in_spatial_developmen_management
19. Lindberg, G., Dubois, A.: How to Monitor Territorial Dynamics, Nordregio News Publication Issue (2014). http://www.nordregio.se/Publications/Publications-2014/Monitoring-Territorial-Dynamics/

Clustering Algorithms for Spatial Big Data

Gabriella Schoier[(✉)] and Caterina Gregorio

DEAMS – Department of Economic, Business, Mathematic and Statistical Sciences "Bruno de Finetti", University of Trieste, Tigor, 22, 34100 Trieste, Italy
gabriella.schoier@deams.units.it

Abstract. In our time people and devices constantly generate data. User activity generates data about needs and preferences as well as the quality of their experiences in different ways: i.e. streaming a video, looking at the news, searching for a restaurant or a an hotel, playing a game with others, making purchases, driving a car. Even when people put their devices in their pockets, the network is generating location and other data that keeps services running and ready to use. This rapid developments in the availability and access to data and in particular spatially referenced data in a different areas, has induced the need for better analysis techniques to understand the various phenomena. Spatial clustering algorithms, which groups similar spatial objects into classes, can be used for the identification of areas sharing common characteristics. The aim of this paper is to analyze the performance of three different clustering algorithms i.e. the *Density-Based Spatial Clustering of Applications with Noise* algorithm (DBSCAN), the *Fast Search by Density Peak* (FSDP) algorithm and the classic *K-means* algorithm (K-Means) as regards the analysis of spatial big data. We propose a modification of the FSDP algorithm in order to improve its efficiency in large databases. The applications concern both synthetic data sets and satellite images.

Keywords: Spatial data mining · Clustering algorithms · DBSCAN · FSDP · K-Means · Arbitrary shape of clusters · Handling noise · Image analysis

1 Introduction

The rapid developments in the availability and access to spatially referenced information in a variety of areas, has induced the need for better analysis techniques to understand different phenomena. Spatial clustering algorithms, which groups similar spatial objects into classes, can be used for the identification of areas sharing common characteristics.

Clustering is an unsupervised classification of patterns - observations, data items, or feature vectors - into groups or clusters [10]. Cluster analysis can be defined as the organization of a collection of patterns - usually represented as a vector of measurements, or a point in a multidimensional space - into clusters based on similarity [7].

The clustering problem has been considered in many contexts and by researchers in different disciplines. It is useful in several exploratory pattern-analysis, grouping, decision-making and machine-learning situations, including data mining (see e.g. [8]),

© Springer International Publishing AG 2017
O. Gervasi et al. (Eds.): ICCSA 2017, Part IV, LNCS 10407, pp. 571–583, 2017.
DOI: 10.1007/978-3-319-62401-3_41

spatial data mining (see e.g. [1, 4, 14]), document retrieval, image segmentation, and pattern classification.

Clustering techniques have been recognized as primary Data Mining methods for knowledge discovery in spatial databases, i.e. databases managing 2D or 3D points, polygons etc. or points in some d-dimensional feature space (see e.g. [14, 25, 26]).

The aim of this paper is to compare a classical density based algorithm i.e. *the Density-Based Spatial Clustering of Applications with Noise* algorithm (DBSCAN) (see [6, 7, 13, 22–24]) with *the Fast Search by Density Peak* (FSDP) [21] and the classic *K-means* algorithm (K-Means) for the identification of clusters in a Spatial Big Data context. As regards the FSDP algorithm a modification of this algorithm in order to improve its efficiency in the application on Big Data has been proposed. The implementation has been performed in the R language.

2   Some Observations on Spatial Big Data

Spatial data mining can be used for browsing spatial databases, understanding spatial data, discovering spatial relationships, optimizing spatial queries.

Spatial data, as other kinds of data, are becoming bigger and bigger, although since the introduction of GIS and desktop GIS in particular, GIS users and experts have become facing with the issue of managing big amount of data, even though often data were much more difficult to retrieve than today. In geographical terms, the nature of data is such that an increase of dimension of the dataset is always very possible, both in terms of the number of the records to be considered, as well as in terms of the attribute of the geographical data. Both the vector and raster data formats used in GIS analysis tend to be multidimensional, i.e., containing a quantity of elements to be considered in any form of grouping and aggregation. In any case at least two fields (if not three) are needed to store the spatial information while all the attribute data contribute to increasing the dimension of the dataset. Satellite imagery in particular represents another case, in which redundant information is also considered, as very close pixels present very little differences although weighting in the processing, storage and visualization time of the data. So compression algorithms on one side and proficient clustering tools are needed in order to extract the more precise and complete set of geographic information [15–19, 27].

In this paper, the data used for the analysis, have been bit-map images which are real examples of raster spatial analysis. In this case each image is formed by a regular grid of pixels, a color present in every cell of this grid has 24 bit (16 million of colors are possible). The units of analysis are the pixels; we consider both spatial and non-spatial attributes of these units. This analysis, called "Segmentation of images", is essential in the manipulation, recognition and object-based analysis of multimedia resources [2, 5, 28].

3 The Methodology

In this paper the performance and the computational requirements of three spatial algorithms (see e.g. [20]) are compared in the case of application to spatial Big Data: *the Density-Based Spatial Clustering of Applications with Noise* algorithm (DBSCAN), *the Fast Search by Density Peak* (FSDP) and the classic *K-means* algorithm (K-Means).

K-means and DBSCAN are two well known clustering algorithms while the FSDP clustering algorithm is a density algorithm proposed in 2014 (see [21]).

3.1 DBSCAN Algorithm

In this section we consider clustering methods based on the notion of density. These regard clusters as dense regions of units which are separated by regions of low density (representing noise); moreover they may be used to discover clusters of arbitrary shape (see e.g. [3, 4, 10–12]).

Among these the *DBSCAN* algorithm is a locality-based algorithm relying on a density based notion of clustering. Density based methods can be used to filter out noise (outliers) and discover clusters of arbitrary shape. This algorithm judges the density around the neighborhood on an unit to be sufficiently dense if the number of points within a distance *EpsCoord* of an unit is greater than *MinPts*, in this case the unit is a *core point* otherwise is a *border point*. This algorithm has been generalized in different papers.

The key idea is that for each point of a cluster the neighborhood of a given radius has to contain at least a minimum number of points, i.e. the density in the *neighborhood* has to exceed some threshold. The shape of a *neighborhood* is determined by the choice of a distance function for two points p and q, denoted by $dist(p, q)$ The *Epscoord* neighborhood of a point q is defined by

$$N_\varepsilon(q) = \{q \in D | dist(p,q) \le \varepsilon\},$$

where D is a data set of points.

A naive approach could require for each point in a cluster that there are at least a minimum number (*MinPts*) of points in an *Eps-neighborhood* of that point. However, this approach fails because there are two kinds of points in a cluster, points inside of the cluster (*core points*) and points on the border of the cluster (*border points*).

In general, an *Eps-neighborhood* of a border point contains significantly less points than an *Eps-neighborhood* of a core point. Therefore, one would have to set the minimum number of points to a relatively low value in order to include all points belonging to the same cluster. This value, however, is not characteristic for the respective cluster particularly in the presence of noise. Therefore, one has to require that for every point p in a cluster C there is a point q in C so that p is inside of the *Eps-neighborhood* of q and $N_\varepsilon(q)$ contains at least *MinPts* points.

This definition is elaborated in the following: a point p is *density reachable* from a point q if there is a chain of points $p_1, p_2, ..., p_{n-1}, p_n$ where $p_1 = p$ and $p_n = q$ such that p_i is *direct density reachable* from p_{i+1}.

Moreover a point p is *directly density reachable* from a point q if p belongs to the neighborhood of q and q is a core point.

The clustering formed from DBSCAN follows the rules written below:

1. A point can only belong to a cluster if and only if it lies within the *Epscoord-*neighborhood of some core point in the cluster.
2. A *core point o* within the *Epscoord-* neighborhood of another core point p must belong to the same cluster as p.
3. A *border point r* within the *Epscoord-* neighborhood of some core point must belong to the same cluster to at least one of the core points.
4. A border point which does not lie within the *Epscoord-* neighborhood of any core point is considered to be noise.

3.2   A Density Based Algorithm: Clustering by Search and Find of Density Peaks (FSDP)

A clustering algorithm named "Clustering by fast search and find of density peaks" (FSDP) has been proposed in 2014 by [21] this modification is for finding the centers of clusters quickly.

They propose an approach based on the idea that cluster centers are characterized by a higher density than their neighbors and by a relatively large distance from points with higher densities. This idea forms the basis of their clustering procedure in which the number of clusters arises intuitively, outliers are automatically spotted and excluded from the analysis, and clusters are recognized regardless of their shape and of the dimensionality of the space in which they are embedded.

The accuracy of their algorithm depends on the threshold, and no efficient way was given to select its suitable value, i.e., the value was suggested be estimated on the basis of empirical experience.

Our modification regards the implementation i.e. it follows the steps of the *densityClust* R package with two substantial differences: as input it takes the data matrix instead of the distance matrix in so doing the calculation of the distance between points is done during the steps of the algorithm. This avoids saving a large distance matrix that requires a huge memory usage.

3.3   K-means Algorithm

The K-means algorithm is very well known (see e.g. [7]). The algorithm allocates the data points (objects) into clusters, so as to minimize the sum of the squared distances between the data points and the center of the clusters.

The centers of the clusters are initialized by randomly selecting from the data or by fixing particular data points, then the data set is clustered in the process of assigning each point to the nearest center. When the data set has been identified, the average position of the data points within each cluster is calculated and the cluster center then moved to the average position. This process is repeated until a condition of stopping is reached, in other words the algorithm has these steps:

Step 1: Place K points into the space represented by the objects that are being clustered. These points represent initial group centroids.

Step 2: Assign each object to the group that has the closest centroid.

Step 3: When all objects have been assigned, recalculate the positions of the K centroids.

Step 4: Repeat Steps 2 and 3 until the centroids no longer move or another stopping rule is achieved. This produces a separation of the objects into groups from which the metric to be minimized can be calculated.

The K-means algorithm requires three user-specified parameters: number of clusters K, cluster initialization, and distance metric. The most critical choice is K.

K-means is typically used with the Euclidean metric for computing the distance between points and cluster centers. As a result, K-means finds spherical or ball-shaped clusters in data. K-means with Mahalanobis distance metric has been used to detect hyperellipsoidal clusters (see [9]), but this comes at the expense of higher computational cost. In certain cases it is possible to improve the results of algorithm using the standardization of the variables.

3.4   The Implementation of the Three Algorithms Using the R Language

The datasets used were formed by 250 000 observations and 5 variables: two spatial, the x and y coordinates of the pixel, and three non-spatial, the 3 RGB color bands (red, green and blue) of the point. Before applying the algorithm, a standardization of the variables has been performed, this standardization avoid problems in the results of the implementation of both the FSDP and K-means algorithms.

As written before the *R* language has been used for the analysis. The *dbscan*, *stats* and the *densityClust R* packages have been used for analyzing the data, whereas the *raster* and *rgdal* packages have been used for managing the raster objects and the visualization of the results.

To apply the "Fast search by density peak" algorithm on big data we have created a new R implementation of the algorithm. Our implementation follows the steps of that of the *densityClust R* package with two substantial differences: as input it takes the data matrix instead of the distance matrix, so the calculation of the distance between points is done during the steps of the algorithm. This avoids saving a large distance matrix that requires a huge memory usage.

The metric used is the Euclidian one this is the same used in the classical DBSCAN and the K-means algorithms. In order to reduce computational time some of the functions have been written in C++ language, hence we used the *Rcpp* package to integrate R and C++.

The three algorithms require different parameters: number of clusters for the K-means, threshold value for the radius of the epsilon neighborhood (eps) and minimum number of points of the epsilon neighborhood (minpts) for the DBSCAN and local density (ρ) and minimum distance to higher density points (σ) thresholds for the FSDP. To choose the values of the parameters for the density-based algorithms two plots were used: the K-NN distance plot for the DBSCAN(see Fig. 1(a)) and a decision graph for the FSDP (see Fig. 1(b)). The K-NN distance plot represents the k-nearest neighbor distances. Once set the *minpts*, which can be the dimensionality of the dataset plus one or higher, eps is the first knee in the *minpts*-NN distance plot (see Fig. 1(a)).

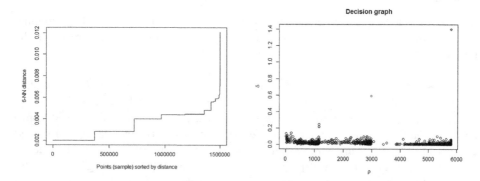

Fig. 1. (a) K-NN distance plot (b) Decision graph

In the decision graph we can see the distribution of the points relatively to the parameters ρ and σ.

The points with high σ and high ρ will be clusters centers, hence by looking at the graph we can decide which is the threshold values of ρ and σ above which the cluster centers are identified. In the figure they are the two points colored in red and green.

4   Computational Aspects

In the analysis of Big Data computational aspects are fundamental in considering which method has to be used; in particular CPU time and RAM usage have to be taking into account. As regards the choice of one of the three algorithms that have been considered, comparing the CPU times, we verified that the K-means algorithm is the most performing as in the DBSCAN and the FSDP time increases very quickly as the number of points gets larger (see Fig. 2).

An implementation of the DBSCAN has been proposed which drastically reduces the computational time needed by using the Lagrange distance instead of the Euclidian one has been proposed [23].

The use of the distance matrix instead of the data matrix in the FSDP algorithm leads to other computational aspects as regards the RAM usage: whereas the K-means and the DBSCAN require few mega-bites to perform the analysis even on very big dataset, to calculate and save the distance matrix needed to apply the FSDP algorithm

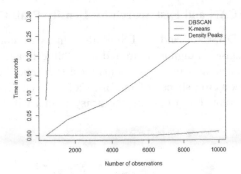

Fig. 2. CPU time

an enormous amount of RAM is required. This made it impossible to apply the FSDP algorithm to spatial Big Data. As an example, for the data set that we considered of 250 000 units demanded more than 200 Gb of RAM.

This is why we propose an R implementation of the "Fast Search by Density Peaks" (FSDP) that takes as input the data matrix and therefore allows to apply the algorithm to Big Data. Our version of the FSDP for Big Data calculates the distance between points only when is needed avoiding to save a complete distance matrix that would have more than 10 billion elements to save.

5   The Application Results and Discussion

5.1   R Implementation from *"densityclust"* Package and the New Big Data Implementation

First of all, we verify that the performance of our new Big Data implementation of FSDP in R is the same as the one of the *densityClust* R package. A dataset of 10 000 pixels has been used for this scope. The results are shown in Fig. 2. As one can see the result is the same (Fig. 3).

Fig. 3. Comparison of original R implementation and Big Data implementation in R

5.2 K-means, DBSCAN and Fast Search by Density Peak Clustering

To test the K-means, DBSCAN and the FSDP algorithms we consider some applications to a synthetic dataset, a digital photo and to satellite images.

In the data set presented in Fig. 4 we consider a synthetic dataset consisting in a partition in regular geometric shapes of uniform color. Each cluster has been represented by a different color. From now on the noisy points will be always colored in black.

Fig. 4. A synthetic data set

Even in this simple synthetic dataset, the DBSCAN outstands the other two algorithms. As one can see the FSDP algorithm shows the poorest results (see Fig. 5).

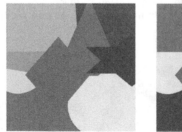  

Fig. 5. Results of k-means, DBSCAN and Density Peak respectively

Next, we have applied the algorithms to a digital picture (Fig. 6).

This is a good example of how the k-means algorithms is not able to detect clusters of irregular shapes and on the contrary the DBSCAN is very good at it. The DBSCAN in this dataset produces a result extremely precise, i.e. the cluster representing the

Fig. 6. Digital photo

shadow of the pony. The FSDP algorithm performs slightly better than the k-means but still the result is completely satisfactory (see Fig. 7).

Fig. 7. Results of k-means, DBSCAN and FSDP respectively

Next applications regard data sets of satellite images. The former is a LANDSAT 8 Satellite image of the gulf of Trieste (see Fig. 8) the latter a LANDSAT 8 Satellite of the Alps (see Fig. 10).

The results of the K-means and the FSDP algorithm don't seem to differ very much, they perform very well. In this case, even though the separation line between the "sea cluster" and the "land cluster" is irregular the K-means is able to distinguish between the two areas and so do the SFDP. However even in this case, the DBSCAN performance is the most convincing because it is the only one what recognizes as noise the clouds in the right upper corner (see Fig. 9).

This is a much more challenging satellite image than the previous one so it is not surprising that the k-means fails to recognize clusters of so irregular shape. In this last example also the results of the DBSCAN algorithm are not perfect, but still better than the FSDP and the k-means algorithms (see Figs. 10 and 11).

Fig. 8. LANDSAT 8 Satellite image -Trieste gulf http://landsatlook.usgs.gov/viewer.html

Fig. 9. Results of k-means, DBSCAN and Density Peaks respectively

Fig. 10. Image LANDSAT 8 Satellite – Alps http://landsatlook.usgs.gov/viewer.html

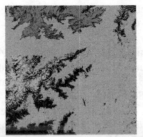

Fig. 11. Results of k-means, DBSCAN and Density Peak respectively

6 Conclusions

In this paper three way of clustering methods applied to identify homogeneous areas in a Spatial Big Data context are compared: *the Density-Based Spatial Clustering of Applications with Noise* algorithm (DBSCAN), *the Fast Search by Density Peak* (FSDP) and the classic *K-means* algorithm (K-Means).

As regards the FSDP algorithm a modification of this algorithm, in order to improve its efficiency in the application on Big Data, has been proposed. The implementation has been performed using the R language.

The applications regards both synthetic and real datasets. The spatial clustering analysis allowed to obtained good bit-map images and good representation of satellite images.

The main advantage of K-means algorithm is its simplicity and speed which allows it to run on large datasets. One problem of the application of the K-means is the necessity of knowing *a prori* the number of clusters. Other problem regard the identification of noise (outliers) and the discovering of clusters of arbitrary shape.

DBSCAN is robust enough to identify clusters in noisy data, requires just a few parameters and is mostly insensitive to the ordering of the points in the database. This algorithm is efficient even for very large spatial databases, discovers clusters of arbitrary shape and does not need to know the number of clusters in the data a priori, as opposed to K-means. Our modification of the FSDP algorithm regards the implementation with two substantial differences: as input it takes the data matrix instead of the distance matrix; this avoids saving a large distance matrix that requires a huge memory usage.

References

1. Bailey, T.C., Gatrell, A.C.: Interactive Spatial Data Analysis. Addison Wesley Longman, Edinburgh (1996)
2. Bedard, Y.: Beyond GIS: Spatial On-line Analytical Processing and Big Data. University of Maine (2014). http://umaine.edu/scis/files/2014/09/Beyond-GIS-Spatial-On-Line-Analytical-Processing-and-Big-Data-Yvan-Bedard.pdf

3. Chen, Y., Suel, T., Markowetz, A.: Efficient query processing in geographic web search engines. In: SIGMOD 2006, Chicago, Illinois, USA, 27–29 June 2006 (2006). http://cis. poly.edu/suel/papers/geoquery.pdf
4. Cressie, N.: Statistics for Spatial Data. Wiley, London (1993)
5. Cugler, D.C., Dev, O., Evans, M.R., Shekhar, S., Medeiros, C.B.: Spatial Big Data: Platforms, Analytics, and Science. http://www.spatial.cs.umn.edu/geojournal/2013/ geojournal.pdf. Accessed 22 Sept 2016
6. El-Sonbaty, Y., Ismail, M.A., Farouk, M.: An Efficient density-based clustering algorithm for large databases. In: Proceedings of the 16th IEEE International Conference on Tods with Artificial Intelligence (ICTAI) (2004)
7. Ester, M., Kriegel, H.P., Sander, J., Xiaowei, X.: A density-based algorithm for discovering clusters in large spatial databases with noise. In: Proceeding of the 2nd International Conference on Knowledge Discovery and Data Mining, pp. 94–99 (1996)
8. Fayyad, U., Piatesky–Shapiro, G., Smyth, P.: From Data Mining to Knowledge Discovery in Databases (1996). http://www.kdnuggets.com/gpspubs/aimag-kdd-overview-1996-Fayyad. pdf
9. Fahad, A., Alshatri, N., Tari, Z., Alamri, A., Khalil, I., Zomaya, A.Y., Foufou, S., Bouras, A.: A survey of clustering algorithms for big data: taxonomy and empirical analysis. IEEE Trans. Emerg. Topics Comput. **2**(3), 267–279 (2014)
10. Han, J., Kamber, M., Tung, A.K.H.: Spatial Clutering Methods in Data Mining: A Survey (2001). ftp://ftp.fas.sfu.ca/pub/cs/han/pdf/gkdbk01.pdf
11. Hemalatha, M., Naga Saranya, N.: A recent survey on knowledge discovery in spatial data mining. Int. J. Comput. Sci. Issues **8**(3), 473–479 (2011)
12. Jan, A.K.: Data clustering. 50 years beyond K-means. Pattern Recogn. Lett. **31**(8), 651–666 (2010)
13. Khan, K., Rehman, S.U., Fong, S., Sarasvady, S.: DBSCAN: past, present and future. In: The Fifth International Conference on the Applications of Digital Information and Web Technologies, February 2014, pp. 232–238 (2014)
14. Koperski, K., Han, J., Adhikary, J.: Mining Knowledge in Geographical Data (1998). ftp:// ftp.fas.sfu.ca/pubcs/han/pdf/geo_survey98.pdf.
15. Lee, J., Kang, M.: Geospatial big data: challenges and opportunities. Big Data Res. **2**(2), 74–78 (2015)
16. Liu, J., Li, J., Li, W., Wu, J.: Rethinking Big Data: a review on the data quality and usage issues. PRS J. Photogrammetry Remote Sens. **115**, 134–142 (2016)
17. Mao, J., Jain, A.K.: A self-organizing network for hyper-ellipsoidal clustering (HEC). IEEE Trans. Neural Netw. **7**(1), 16–29 (1996)
18. Mennis, J., Guo, D.: Spatial Computing. "Spatial Data Mining". https://www.youtube.com/ watch?v=sZeb93O_z2w&list=PLN5UPhO05nn8WE4ZbzUwUhzq_p2XChK6r&index=3. Accessed 22 May 2016
19. Mohebi, A., Aghabozorgi, S., Wah, T.Y., Herawan, T., Yahyapour, R.: Iterative Big Data clustering algorithms: a review. Soft. Pract. Exp. **46**(1), 107–129 (2016)
20. Pragati, S., Hitech, G.: A review of density-based clustering in spatial data. Int. J. Adv. Comput. Res. **2**(5), 210–213 (2012)
21. Rodriguez, A., Laio, A.: Clustering by fast search and find of density peaks. Science **344** (6191), 1492–1496 (2014)
22. Sander, J., Ester, M., Kriegel, H.P., Xiaowei, X.: Density-based clustering in spatial databases: the algorithm GDBSCAN and its applications (1999). http://www.dbs.informatik. uni-muenchen.de/Publikationen/

23. Schoier, G., Bato, B.: A modification of the DBSCAN algorithm in a spatial data mining approach. In: Meeting of the Classification and Data Analysis Group of the SIS, CLADAG 2007, Macerata, 12–14 September 2007, pp. 395–398. EUM, Macerata (2007)
24. Schoier, G., Borruso, G.: A methodology for dealing with spatial big data. Int. J. Bus. Intel. Data Min. **12**(1), 1–13 (2017)
25. Steinbach, M., Ertöz, L., Kumar V.: The Challenges of Clustering High Dimensional Data (2003). http://www-users.cs.umn.edu/ ~ kumar/papers/high_dim_clustering_19.pdf
26. Xu, R., Wunsch II, D.: Survey of Clustering Algorithms (2005). http://ieeexplore.ieee.org/iel5/72/30822/01427769.pdf
27. Wang, S., Yuan, H.: Spatial data mining in the context of big data. In: 2013 International Conference on Parallel and Distributed Systems, December 2013, pp. 486–491 (2013)
28. Ye, Q., Gao, W., Zeng, W.: Color image segmentation using density-based clustering. In: 2003 IEEE International Conference on Acoustics, Speech, and Signal Processing, vol. 3, p. III 345 (2003)

Interoperable Sharing and Visualization of Geological Data and Instruments: A Proof of Concept

Simone Lanucara[1,2] , Alessandro Oggioni[1] ,
Giuseppe Modica[2(✉)] , and Paola Carrara[1]

[1] Istituto per il Rilevamento Elettromagnetico dell'Ambiente, Consiglio
Nazionale delle Ricerche (IREA-CNR), Via Bassini 15, 20133 Milan, Italy
{lanucara.s,oggioni.a,carrara.p}@irea.cnr.it
[2] Dipartimento di Agraria, Università degli Studi Mediterranea di Reggio
Calabria, Località Feo di Vito, 89122 Reggio Calabria, Italy
giuseppe.modica@unirc.it

Abstract. Traditionally, maps and data were analyzed and created by desktop
software tools. Today, thanks to World Wide Web, open source software tools
and international standards, practitioners and researchers can share maps, data,
and measures. Sharing can be done with different software tools, proprietary or
open source, and with varying degrees of interoperability. Most geological maps
and data collected by instruments are produced by governmental organizations
and they are encoded in official languages and data schemas of their producers.
Linguistic barrier, different visual representations and data schemas hinder the
usefulness of online maps and data, obtained from different sources. In the
present paper, we report a research aiming to overcome these aforementioned
barriers. To this end, after having described their main characteristics, we
exploited and summarized the main findings of using geoscience thesauri,
international standards for web sharing, visual and data harmonization. We used
GeoScience Markup Language (GeoSciML-Portayal) to harmonize geological
maps collected in the context of a multidisciplinary study focused on a coastal
area located in Southern Italy, (Costa Viola); Sensor Metadata Language
(SensorML) to describe geological instruments; Observations and Measurements (O&M) to harmonize geological data collected by instruments. We used
geoscience thesauri based on Simple Knowledge Organization System (SKOS)
to enrich semantically the aforementioned geological maps, data and instruments. A distributed Spatial Data Infrastructure (SDI), implemented using free
and open source software for geospatial (FOSS4G), was provided taking
advantage on Open Geospatial Consortium (OGC) standards to share data and
information in an interoperable, harmonized and semantically enriched way.

Keywords: Geoscience thesauri · Free and Open Source Software for
Geospatial (FOSS4G) · Spatial Data Infrastructures (SDIs) · Semantic
enrichment · Sensor Metadata Language (SensorML) · GeoScience Markup
Language (GeoSciML) · WebGIS

© Springer International Publishing AG 2017
O. Gervasi et al. (Eds.): ICCSA 2017, Part IV, LNCS 10407, pp. 584–599, 2017.
DOI: 10.1007/978-3-319-62401-3_42

1 Introduction

On a global scale, different research institutions and governmental agencies publish geological maps, datasets and metadata on web geoportals [1]. Among these, at international level, it is worth citing the United States Geological Survey (USGS) (http://www.usgs.gov) and the Geoscience Australia (http://www.geoscience.gov.au) geoportals. At national level, interesting examples are geoportals of the Geological Survey of Italy (http://sgi.isprambiente.it), ARPA Piemonte (http://webgis.arpa. piemonte.it/geoportale) and Emilia Romagna Region (http://geoportale.regione. emilia-romagna.it/it). In most cases, geoportals use different types of visual and textual representation of the information, while geological data of each authority are structured in a different way. Moreover, geoportals usually miss information on geological instruments and, often, the data collected directly from these instruments.

Like other geospatial data, to enable an interoperable sharing of geological maps and data, international and national geoportals mainly adopt the Open Geospatial Consortium (OGC) standards and their recommended services [2]: Web Map Service (WMS) for the distribution of maps, Styled Layer Descriptor (SLD) for the definitions of graphic styles and legends, Web Feature Service (WFS) for sharing vector data, Web Coverage Service (WCS) for sharing multi-dimensional coverage data and Catalog Service for the Web (CSW) for sharing metadata catalogs.

The overabundance of information produced by new technologies can be considered as a knowledge enrichment in supporting decision-making [3]. However, the level of interoperability, is still lacking in the harmonization of data model and visualization and in the semantic inclusion [4, 5], a gap which makes difficult to discover, compare and analyze data attained from different sources. For geological maps and data, this gap has been removed developing two models:

- GeoSciML [6] (http://www.geosciml.org), a Unified Modeling Language (UML) data model and a Geography Markup Language (GML) based on the WFS standards, allowing a harmonized data modeling;
- GeoSciML-Portrayal [7], a GML simple-feature application schema based on a small, highly simplified core of GeoSciML, allowing an interoperable and harmonized sharing of visual representation, based on WMS and SLD standards.

When coupled with thesauri, both models also allow a semantic enrichment of data and maps [8]. They enabled to develop the OneGeology project [9] and OneGeology-Europe [10] that targeted the interoperable and harmonized sharing on the web of geological data and maps at a Global and European level respectively.

Nevertheless, description and sharing of measuring instruments is still missing in GeoSciML and GeoSciML-Portrayal, while this capability is given by adopting the Sensor Web Enablement (SWE) [11] OGC framework. In particular, SensorML [12] provides means of defining any sensor or measuring device, so that information on sensors can be "understood" by machines and utilized automatically in complex workflows. Moreover, Sensor Observations Service (SOS) interfaces enable the interoperable web sharing [13] of measuring devices defined by SensorML.

Generally, data surveyed by means of geological instruments are shared as Hypertext Markup Language (HTML) tables, log viewers using Scalable Vector Graphics (SVGs) and JavaScript language. As a matter of fact, these different data formats can constitute another barrier in the integration of data from different sources. To overcome this specific obstacle, a chance is given by the OGC Observations and Measurements standard (O&Ms) [14], that defines eXtensible Markup Language (XML) schemas for observations, for features involved in sampling and use SOS interfaces for interoperable web sharing. It is worth noticing that links between O&M and GeoSciML are widely recognized in relation to delivery of geological sampling and analytical data such as geochemistry and geochronology [7].

In the present paper, we describe a methodology developed with the aim to share in an interoperable, semantically enriched and harmonized way geological instrument descriptions, measures and geological maps collected in the context of a multidisciplinary study [15]. The proposed methodology accomplishes with international standards for web sharing and has been developed using SKOS-based geoscience thesauri and FOSS4G tools.

The paper is organized as follows: the next Sect. (2.1) briefly presents the geological maps, instruments and data collected in the multidisciplinary study; Sect. 2.2 describes the software architecture designed for the distribution of data, maps and information on instruments. Sections from 2.3 to 2.6 describe methodology for sharing on the web geological maps, data and instrument metadata. The last Sect. 3 describes the results obtained in the test, the current issues, future works and it concludes the paper.

2 Materials and Methods

The following sections describe the methodology adopted for the sharing of geological instruments, data and maps.

2.1 Context: Data

The geological data, maps, instruments and related metadata on which we tested the methodology for interoperable, semantically enriched and harmonized sharing were collected in the context of a multidisciplinary study aimed at the dynamic characterization of the historical terraced landscape of Costa Viola, a coastal region in Southern Italy, in view of its sustainable management [16]:

- geological maps for the area of interest were obtained from the Geological Map of Calabria, scale 1:25,000 [17] by means of traditional operations of vectorization. These data were stored in a single table in a PostgreSQL-PostGIS (http://postgis.net) geospatial database;

- geological instrument descriptions and coring data have been obtained by public and private agencies in paper format.

2.2 Software Architecture Adopted in the Test

To enable an interoperable, harmonized and semantically enriched sharing, based on OGC standards, we developed a distributed SDI. From a technological perspective, SDIs are Information Technology platforms for management, discovery, publication and use of geospatial data and relative metadata [18]. Different and widespread are the solutions adopted to design and implement SDI architectures [19]. The solutions can be proprietary, e.g. Esri vendor [20], or free and open source; in particular, the development of applications in FOSS4G environment is supported by the wide availability of software suites [21], which make possible to share and publish maps, data and metadata.

The distributed SDI, we developed, is composed by two nodes. The first node, installed at CNR IREA of Milano, acts as a repository and shares information on geological instruments and relative collected data; the second node, installed at the Mediterranea University of Reggio Calabria acts as a repository and distributes information of geological maps. We also, designed and implemented a WebGIS client that has direct access to the OGC services shared by the two nodes and provides a graphical user interface (GUI) with data and maps. These two nodes were chose taking an advantage from previous research projects and experiences of the research group [18, 22, 23]. In addition, we chose the two nodes approach to test and prove interoperability capabilities of the architecture and to let each providing organization its complete autonomy in data distribution.

We developed the first node of the infrastructure using the free and open-source software suite *Geoinformation Enabling Toolkit StarterKit®* (GET-IT - http://www.get-it.it). Developed by a joint research group of CNR-IREA & CNR-ISMAR under the flagship project RITMARE (www.ritmare.it), GET-IT is completely free and open-source and has among its objectives to facilitate the creation of data infrastructures for the observational network, allowing users to share on the web (OGC standard) their sensors, data and metadata. The GET-IT suite has been developed starting from the software GeoNode (http://geonode.org), a widely known geospatial content management system [24, 25]. GeoNode, lacking sensor sharing facilities and semantic enrichment, has been edited and new facilities have been added, both client and server side, for the creation, semantically enabled, and the management of measures and metadata of instruments [22].

The second node of the infrastructure was built taking advantage of using FOSS4G software. The implemented node has a multi-tier architecture composed by three layers with different functions: (1) a data repository to store data and metadata in a geospatial database developed in PostgreSQL with PostGIS extension; (2) a server, developed in

GeoServer (http://geoserver.org) and GeoNetwork opensource (http://geonetwork-opensource.org), to manage data and metadata stored and publish them on the web using OGC standard interfaces; (3) a front-end client (i.e., the WebGIS client) developed in the GeoExt (http://geoext.org) framework, to provide a graphical user interface to view and analyze data. All above components are implemented in a virtual environment, (i.e., a virtual machine), based on the Ubuntu operating system, and managed by Microsoft Server Datacenter with Hyper-V enabled.

2.3 Geological Instruments

For uploading, publishing and sharing on the web of the descriptions of the geological instruments, i.e. coring tools (driller and coring equipment), and their relative data, the first node of the infrastructure exploits the usage of OGC standards in the SWE framework. This framework, thanks to its high level of abstraction and associated use of schemes such SensorML, O&M and standard service such SOS, allows to create, store and share on the web instruments metadata and measures [13].

We modeled information on the geological instruments, originally printed and distributed on paper, according to the scheme SensorML and in XML format. For each instrument, this modeling phase was carried out by the definition of the identification code, sensor type, manufacturer, operator, classification, input/output, parameters, and additional characteristics. This has been also performed by GET-IT that includes a metadata editor, called EDI [26], which allows an easy and friendly instrument registration (SensorML editing) through GUI and auto completion facilities.

We harmonized and semantically enriched SensorML descriptions exploiting geoscience thesauri, basic elements for representing geoscience knowledge in the context of the Semantic Web [27]. In details:

- Sensor type definition have been borrowed from the terms present in the Natural Environment Research Council (NERC) vocabulary [28]. The NERC vocabulary server (http://vocab.nerc.ac.uk/) provides a web access to lists of standardized terms that cover a broad spectrum of disciplines;
- Outputs parameters definition have been borrowed from the terms present in the GeoSciML vocabulary (http://resource.geosciml.org/), developed by the Commission for the Management and Application of Geoscience Information (CGI). The GeoSciML vocabulary service provides a web access to lists of standardized descriptions of geological features (http://def.seegrid.csiro.au/sissvoc/cgi201211/collection).

Below an example of a rock corer sensor type (1) and of a lithology output parameter (2), in SensorML schema and XML format, exploiting the NERC and GeoSciML vocabularies:

```
(1)<sml:classifier name: "SensorType" >
  <sml:Term
    definition:"http://vocab.nerc.ac.uk/collec-
tion/L05/current/53/">
    <sml:label>SensorType</sml:label>
    <sml:value>Rock corers</sml:value>
  </sml:Term>
</sml:classifier>
(2)<sml:output name="Lithology">
  <swe:Quantity
    definition="http://resource.geosciml.org/classi-
fier/cgi/lithology/">
  </swe:Quantity>
</sml:output>
```

```
<swes:DescribeSensorResponse xsi:schemaLocation="http://www.opengis.net/swes/2.0
http://schemas.opengis.net/swes/2.0/swesDescribeSensor.xsd http://www.opengis.net/gml/3.2
http://schemas.opengis.net/gml/3.2.1/gml.xsd http://www.opengis.net/gml
http://schemas.opengis.net/gml/3.1.1/base/gml.xsd http://www.opengis.net/sensorML/1.0.1
http://schemas.opengis.net/sensorML/1.0.1/sensorML.xsd http://www.opengis.net/swe/1.0.1
http://schemas.opengis.net/sweCommon/1.0.1/swe.xsd">
    <swes:procedureDescriptionFormat>http://www.opengis.net/sensorML/1.0.1
  </swes:procedureDescriptionFormat>
  <swes:description>
    <swes:SensorDescription>
      <swes:validTime>
        <gml:TimePeriod gml:id="tp_9DF28C47D29298DAC56D5B15EC92324CF1F97C01">
          <gml:beginPosition>2017-03-10T14:36:27.745Z</gml:beginPosition>
          <gml:endPosition indeterminatePosition="unknown"/>
        </gml:TimePeriod>
      </swes:validTime>
      <swes:data>
        <sml:SensorML version="1.0.1">
          <sml:member>
            <sml:System gml:id="Double_core_barrel_T2">
              <gml:description>This double core barrel, in quality steel N80,
              gives an high penetration because of the small cutting surface.
              The inner non-rotating tube preserves the sample from the
              torsional stress of the rods and prevents from washing out the
              core. It gives an high penetration in hard rocks because of the
              small cuttingsurface with all the consequent benefits as high
              coring percentage, less bending and wear on the equipment.
              </gml:description>
              <gml:name>Double core barrel T2</gml:name>
              <sml:keywords>
                <sml:KeywordList>
                  <sml:keyword>
                  http://resource.geosciml.org/classifier/cgi/lithology/
                  </sml:keyword>
                  <sml:keyword>
                  http://vocab.nerc.ac.uk/collection/P02/current/MBAN/
```

Fig. 1. SOS DescribeSensorResponse, in XML format, for metadata of a double core barrel.

Besides defining sensors by SensorML; we used the SOS services provided by GET-IT to enable their interoperable sharing; the operation performed was SOS InsertSensor that registers the instruments in the repository, and shares the information in the form of interoperable SOS services, so that it is possible to retrieve it in XML format through the SOS operation DescribeSensor. The following Fig. 1 shows an example of SOS DescribeSensor response for a geological instrument (double core barrel).

By GET-IT it is possible to view information on the instrument also in the more friendly form of a HTML page. The following Fig. 2 shows the same description of double core barrel of Fig. 1 in the user friendly way provided by GET-IT: information is the same but the presentation is deeply changed.

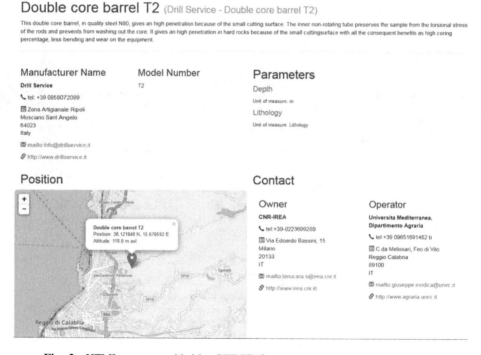

Fig. 2. HTML page, provided by GET-IT, for metadata of a double core barrel.

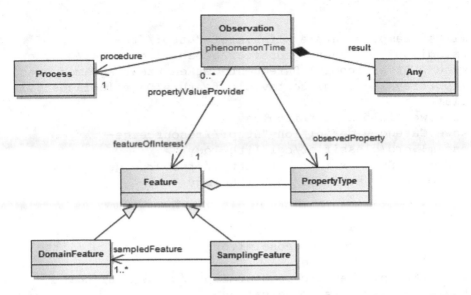

Fig. 3. Unified modeling language (UML) for basic O&M observation model (source: Bröring et al. 2011).

2.4 Geological Measures

In the same way, we modeled the geological measures collected by instruments, originally printed and distributed on paper, according to the O&M schema. In this schema, each observation is composed by the following elements (Fig. 3):

- Feature Of Interest (FOI): a representation of a real-world object that is under study;
- Phenomenon time: time of sampling;
- Result time: time when the observation's result has been created. It is possible to sample in a determinate time (phenomenon time) and insert the observation in O&M in another time;
- Procedure: instance of a process that has performed the observation.
- Observed property: label of the property which is observed (parameter).
- Result: the result value of the observation.

The FOI was modeled as web link to the WFS of the geological feature interested by measurement while the definition of the measured parameters (observed property in O&M) was borrowed from the terms present in the GeoSciML vocabulary.

Below an example of a core drilling result in O&M with: geological feature interested by measurement exploiting WFS link (1), observed property (lithology) (2) and value of the measurement (3) exploiting GeoSciML vocabulary:

```
(1)<sf:sampledFeature xlink:href="http://ru-
ralsdi.unirc.it:8080/geoserver/geoscimlportrayal/ows?ser-
vice=WFS&version=1.1.0&request=GetFeature&typeName=geosci
mlportrayal:geologiacostaviola&featureID=geologiacostavi-
ola.3"/>
(2)<swe:field name="Lithology">
<swe:Category definition="http://resource.ge-
osciml.org/classifier/cgi/lithology/">
<swe:codeSpace xlink:href="http://resource.ge-
osciml.org/classifier/cgi/lithology/"/>
</swe:Category>
</swe:field>
(3)<swe:values>
0@46@http://resource.geosciml.org/classifier/cgi/lithol-
ogy/clastic_sandstone
46@140@http://resource.geosciml.org/classifier/cgi/li-
thology/mica_schist</swe:values>
```

Once modeled data following O&M, we used the SOS services provided by GET-IT to store them and enable their interoperable distribution. The operation performed was SOS InsertObservation to register data in the Milano node repository, and to provide them in the form of interoperable SOS services, so that it is possible to retrieve them in XML format through the SOS operation GetObservation. The following Fig. 4 shows an example of SOS GetObservation response for geological data collected by a double core barrel.

2.5 Geological Maps

For publishing and sharing on the web the geological maps, the node of Dipartimento di Agraria of the Università degli Studi di Reggio Calabria (DA-UniRC) use WMS OGC standard and GeoSciML-Portrayal schema. This schema was developed to provide a harmonized visualization of geological maps in WMS standard. For geological maps the schema contemplate three classes (Fig. 4): GeologicUnitView for geological map units, ContactView for contacts between geological units, and shear Displacement StructureView for shear displacement structures (i.e., fault and shear zones). In this work, we harmonized the Geological Map of Calabria (nominal scale 1:25,000), thanks to schema mapping from the existing data model to the data model of the class GeologicUnitView.

```xml
<?xml version="1.0" encoding="UTF-8"?>
<sos:GetObservationResponse xmlns:sos="http://www.opengis.net/sos/2.0" xmlns:xsi="
http://www.w3.org/2001/XMLSchema-instance" xmlns:om="http://www.opengis.net/om/2.0" xmlns:gml
="http://www.opengis.net/gml/3.2" xmlns:xlink="http://www.w3.org/1999/xlink"
xsi:schemaLocation="http://www.opengis.net/swes/2.0
http://schemas.opengis.net/swes/2.0/swes.xsd http://www.opengis.net/sos/2.0
http://schemas.opengis.net/sos/2.0/sosGetObservation.xsd http://www.opengis.net/gml/3.2
http://schemas.opengis.net/gml/3.2.1/gml.xsd http://www.opengis.net/om/2.0
http://schemas.opengis.net/om/2.0/observation.xsd">
    <sos:observationData>
        <om:procedure xlink:href="
        http://sp7.irea.cnr.it/sensors/heavy_getgit_it/procedure/T2/double_core_barrel/T2/
        2016050214009863"/>
        <om:observedProperty xlink:href="
        http://resource.geosciml.org/classifier/cgi/lithology/"/>
        <om:featureOfInterest xlink:href="
        http://ruralsdi.unirc.it:8080/geoserver/geoscimlportrayal/ows?service=WFS_version=
        1.1.0_request=DescribeFeatureType" xlink:title="BAGNARA COUNTRY GEOLOGY"/>
        <om:result xmlns:ns="http://www.opengis.net/swe/2.0" xsi:type=
        "ns:DataArrayPropertyType">
            <swe:DataArray xmlns:swes="http://www.opengis.net/swes/2.0" xmlns:swe="
            http://www.opengis.net/swe/2.0" xmlns:sml="
            http://www.opengis.net/sensorML/1.0.1" xmlns:sams="
            http://www.opengis.net/samplingSpatial/2.0" xmlns:sf="
            http://www.opengis.net/sampling/2.0" xmlns:xs="
            http://www.w3.org/2001/XMLSchema">
                <swe:DataRecord>
                    </swe:field>
                    <swe:field name="Litology">
                        <swe:Category definition="
                        http://resource.geosciml.org/classifier/cgi/lithology/">
                            <swe:codeSpace xlink:href="
                            http://resource.geosciml.org/classifier/cgi/lithology/"/>
                        </swe:Category>
                    </swe:field>
                </swe:DataRecord>
            </swe:elementType>
            <swe:values>0@15@
            http://resource.geosciml.org/classifier/cgi/lithology/clastic_sandstone
                15@75@
                http://resource.geosciml.org/classifier/cgi/lithology/mica_schist
                15@102@
                http://resource.geosciml.org/classifier/cgi/lithology/mica_schist
                </swe:values>
            </swe:DataArray>
        </om:result>
    </sos:observationData>
</sos:GetObservationResponse>
```

Fig. 4. SOS GetObservationResponse response in XML format for data collected by a double core barrel.

The mapping was executed by extract, transform and load (ETL) procedure [29]. The ETL procedure extracts spatial data from source to target, transform the source data model to a new output and enable the users to request the new output in a different format (Fig. 5).

GeoSciML-Portrayal provides semantic harmonization of data by the usage of GeoSciML vocabulary. We exploited this chance implementing the vocabulary for the description of the type of geological units, lithology, and age (as defined by the International Commission on Stratigraphy, http://www.stratigraphy.org/).

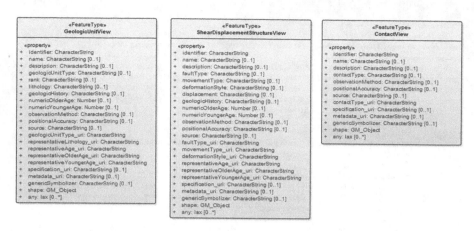

Fig. 5. UML   GeoSciML-Portrayal   classes   (http://www.geosciml.org/geosciml/4.0/documentation/html).

Below, an example of a geological unit type (1), clastic conglomerate lithology (2) of Miocene age (3) exploiting GeoSciML-Portrayal and GeoSciML vocabulary:

```
(1)<geoscimlportrayal:geologicunittype_uri>
http://resource.geosciml.org/classifier/cgi/geologicunit-
type/geologic_unit
</geoscimlportrayal:geologicunittype_uri>
(2)<geoscimlportrayal:representativelithology_uri>
http://resource.geosciml.org/classifier/cgi/lithol-
ogy/clastic_conglomerate
</geoscimlportrayal:representativelithology_uri>
(3)<geoscimlportrayal:representativeage_uri>
http://resource.geosciml.org/classifier/ics/ischart/Mio-
cene
</geoscimlportrayal:representativeage_uri>
```

Furthermore, geological maps, already harmonized with the GeoSciML-Portrayal schema and semantically enabled using vocabularies, have been visually harmonized with the use of SLD: this schema establishes naming conventions for attributes commonly used to symbolize geological maps. The use of standard vocabularies with these attributes for geological age and lithology enables map symbolization using shared legends to achieve visual harmonization of provided maps.

2.6   WebGIS Client

The geological maps produced in the framework, semantically enhanced and tied, and integrated with geological core data and description of geological instrument, are able to show geological settings of the test area. Showing, querying and consulting the geospatial information in a friendly way, from a unique access point, implies the development of a WebGIS client. Indeed, capabilities of WebGIS to show geospatial-temporal patterns and geospatial relations are widely recognized [30, 31]: they allow users to view and query geospatial information in an easy way [32].

To implement the present WebGIS we have adopted the FOSS4G environment offered by the GeoExt framework [33]. It is a powerful toolkit that combines the web-mapping library OpenLayers (https://openlayers.org/) with the user interface of Ext JS (https://www.sencha.com/products/extjs/). OpenLayers is an open source JavaScript library, used to visualize interactive maps in web browsers [19]: it provides the application programming interface (API) allowing the access to various sources of geospatial information on the Web, i.e. OGC interfaces, commercial satellite base maps (i.e., Google Maps, Bing Maps, DigitalGlobe, etc.), OpenStreetMap images (OSM), etc. Ext JS is a JavaScript framework for building feature-rich, cross-platform web applications for desktops, tablets, and smartphones.

The adopted solution allows to get the OGC standards service and relative data published by the distributed SDI developed (e.g. WMS, WFS, SLD services provided by the Mediterranea University node and the SOS services provided by CNR IREA node) and from other geospatial information in the web (e.g. DigitalGlobe satellite and OSM images). The WebGIS client developed allows browsing, zooming, and querying the semantically enhanced geological maps (Fig. 6) of the test area, the instruments information and the coring data.

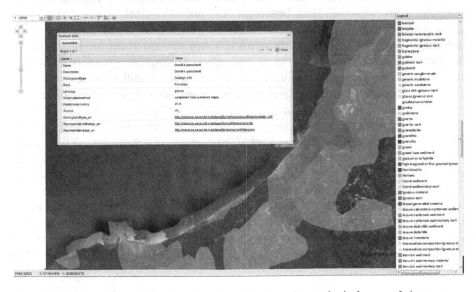

Fig. 6. Snapshot of WebGIS client interface showing: the geological map of the test area overlaid on a Digital Globe satellite image, legend of the geological map, query (feature info) on a single geologic feature.

3 Results, Conclusions and Future Work

Geological data provide several information about the surface and subsurface geological features. This data can be used in exploration of natural resources, in the resolution of environmental problems [34] and can constitute a backbone in monitoring systems within Strategic Environmental Assessment (SEA) [35]. Integration of existing geological maps with borehole data, collected by coring tools, give a complete picture of the geological feature of an area, but, as seen in paragraph 1, face different interoperability issues: syntactic, schematic and semantic.

To faces this issues we developed a distributed SDI composed by two nodes for sharing geological maps, instrument and related data, in a syntactic interoperable way, exploiting OGC standards. As discussed in paragraph 2.2, the first node acts as a repository and shares information on geological instruments and relative collected data, the second node, acts as a repository and distributes information of geological maps. For enabling schematic interoperability we modeled geological coring tools (paragraph 2.3), core drilling results (paragraph 2.4) and maps (paragraph 2.5) exploiting SensorML metadata language and O&M and GeoSciML-Portrayal data schemas. Moreover, semantic interoperability and harmonization is obtained exploiting GeoSciML geoscience thesaurus. We also, designed and implemented a WebGIS client that has direct access to the OGC services shared by the two nodes and provides a GUI for semantically enhanced maps, instruments information and coring data as discussed in paragraph 2.6. Standardized common interfaces, schema, and syntax for information encoding is a fundamental requirement for interoperable SDI.

As discussed, GeoSciML and GeoSciML-Portrayal meet these requirements for geological maps. Moreover, link between O&M and GeoSciML allows adding geological sampling and analytical data such as geochemistry and geochronology. Exploiting GeoSciML geoscience thesaurus is a step forward in the full realization of interoperability at the semantic level and alleviate linguistic barriers. Anyway, description and sharing geological instruments information is still missing, though this additional information can enable quality control procedures, improve data comparison so that geological data can be used in a more effective way.

In the present research, we stress the capacity of SensorML in modeling and sharing information provided by geological instruments (e.g. coring tools), in a distributed SDI. To this end, SensorML has proven to have good capabilities. Moreover, it can be also semantically enriched by exploiting terms from thesauri. We also tested as coring tools, observations and geological maps can be linked exploiting the CGI geoscience vocabularies. In particular we adopted a linking approach in order to automatically and run-time fill the content of some terms of SensorML, O&M and GeoSciML; in this way they are automatically updated whenever the authority that maintains each vocabulary update it and they result to be machine readable. The created links are:

- the output parameter (swe:Quantity definition) of SensorML and observed property (swe:Category definition) of O&M are linked to the common definition http://resource.geosciml.org/classifier/cgi/lithology/ (see paragraph 2.3);

- by the use of the same GeoSciML vocabulary term in the result value of the O&M observation (swe:Value) and in the representative lithology uniform resource identifier (geoscimlportrayal:representativelithology_uri) of GeoSciML-Portrayal property a link is established between O&M and GeoSciML-Portrayal (see paragraph 2.5);
- a further link between O&M and GeoSciML is obtained by inserting in O&M, as value of sampled feature (sf:sampledFeature), the Uniform Resource Locator of the corresponding GeoSciML geological feature (provided by the service WFS) (see paragraph 2.4).

It is worth noticing the need for the development of GUI for editing SensorML for geological survey instruments, and to this aim, EDI metadata editor offers a solution. The same need concerns geological O&M and currently no suitable tool can be found in literature. Further research issues will focus on exploring in more detail how other types of geological instruments (e.g. geophysical and geotechnical) and measures can be described by SensorML and O&M as well as how their descriptions can be linked to GeoSciML. In particular, we consider important to provide a user interface for share, in a standard and semantic enriched way, data of geological cores. Finally, other developments will deal with sustainable models of land management pursuing the right balance between economic development and ecological quality [36, 37].

Acknowledgements. This research has been funded by projects: PONa3_00016-RI-SAF@MED (Research Infrastructure for Sustainable Agriculture and Food in Mediterranean area) and PON03PE_00090_3, in the framework of National Operational Programme (NOP) for Research and Competitiveness 2007–2013 of the Italian Ministry of Education, University and Research (MIUR) and Ministry of Economic Development (MiSE), and co-funded by the European Regional Development Fund (ERDF); Flagship Project RITMARE-Italian Research for the Sea coordinated by the Italian National Research Council and funded by the Italian Ministry of Education, University and Research within the National Research Program 2011–2013.

References

1. Maguire, D.J., Longley, P.A.: The emergence of geoportals and their role in spatial data infrastructures. Comput. Environ. Urban Syst. **29**, 3–14 (2005)
2. Balestro, G., Piana, F., Fioraso, G., Perrone, G., Tallone, S.: Sharing data and interpretations of geological maps via standardised metadata and geoportals. Ital. J. Geosci. **132**, 254–262 (2013)
3. Murgante, B., Garramone, V.: Web 3.0 and knowledge management: opportunities for spatial planning and decision making. In: Murgante, B., et al. (eds.) ICCSA 2013. LNCS, vol. 7973, pp. 606–621. Springer, Heidelberg (2013). doi:10.1007/978-3-642-39646-5_44
4. Lanucara, S., Carrara, P., Oggioni, A., Modica, G.: Interoperable sharing and visualization of geological data and instruments: preliminary results. Rend. Online della Soc. Geol. Ital. **40**, 574 (2016)
5. Agresta, A., Fattoruso, G., Pollino, M., Pasanisi, F., Tebano, C., De Vito, S., Di Francia, G.: An ontology framework for flooding forecasting. In: Murgante, B., et al. (eds.) Computational Science and Its Applications – ICCSA 2014. LNCS, vol. 8582, pp. 417–428. Springer, Cham (2014)

6. Sen, M., Duffy, T.: GeoSciML: development of a generic geoscience markup language. Comput. Geosci. **31**, 1095–1103 (2005)
7. Richard, S.M.: GeoSciML portrayal—an intermediate path to interoperable web map services. In: 34th International Geological Congress, Australian Geosciences Council (2012)
8. Ebner, M., Schiegl, M., Stöckl, W., Heger, H.: From printed geological maps to web-based service oriented data products – strategies, foundations and problems. In: EGU General Assembly Conference Abstracts, p. 7374 (2012)
9. Jackson, I.: OneGeology - making geological map data for the earth accessible. Episodes **30**, 60–61 (2007)
10. Cipolloni, C., Tellez-arenas, A., Serrano, J., Tomas, R.: OneGeology-Europe: architettura, geoportale e servizi web per rendere accessibile la Carta Geologica d'Europa. In: Atti 14a Conferenza Nazionale ASITA 2010, Brescia, pp. 609–613 (2010)
11. Botts, M., Robin, A.: OpenGIS® sensor model language (SensorML) implementation specification. In: Design, vol. 180 (2007)
12. Botts, M., Percivall, G., Reed, C., Davidson, J.: OGC® sensor web enablement: overview and high level architecture. In: Nittel, S., Labrinidis, A., Stefanidis, A. (eds.) International conference on GeoSensor Networks, pp. 175–190. Springer, Heidelberg (2008)
13. Oggioni, A., Bastianini, M., Carrara, P., Minuzzo, T., Pavesi, F.: Sensing real-time observatories in marine sites - a proof-of-concept. In: Proceedings of the 3rd International Conference on Sensor Networks, pp. 111–118. SCITEPRESS - Science and and Technology Publications (2014)
14. Cox, S.: CSIRO research publications repository - observations and measurements - XML implementation. In: Open Geospatial Consortium/Implementation Standard OGC 10-025r1, p. ix, 63 p. (2011)
15. Modica, G., Praticò, S., Pollino, M., Di Fazio, S.: Geomatics in analysing the evolution of agricultural terraced landscapes. In: Murgante, B., et al. (eds.) Computational Science and Its Applications – ICCSA 2014. LNCS, vol. 8582, pp. 479–494. Springer International Publishing, Cham (2014). doi:10.1007/978-3-319-09147-1_35
16. Modica, G., Praticò, S., Pollino, M., Di Fazio, S.: Geomatics in Analysing the Evolution of Agricultural Terraced Landscapes. Springer, Cham (2014)
17. Casmez: Carta Geologica della Calabria (1969)
18. Modica, G., Pollino, M., Lanucara, S., La Porta, L., Pellicone, G., Di Fazio, S., Fichera, C.R.: Land suitability evaluation for agro-forestry: definition of a web-based multi-criteria spatial decision support system (MC-SDSS): preliminary results. In: Gervasi, O., et al. (eds.) Computational Science and Its Applications - ICCSA 2016. LNCS, vol. 9788, pp. 399–413. Springer International Publishing, Cham (2016)
19. Steiniger, S., Hunter, A.J.S.: The 2012 free and open source GIS software map – a guide to facilitate research, development, and adoption. Comput. Environ. Urban Syst. **39**, 136–150 (2013)
20. Maguire, D.J.: ArcGIS: general purpose GIS software system. In: Encyclopedia of GIS, pp. 25–31. Springer, Boston (2008)
21. Brovelli, M.A., Minghini, M., Moreno-Sanchez, R., Oliveira, R.: Free and open source software for geospatial applications (FOSS4G) to support future earth. Int. J. Digit. Earth., 1–19 (2016)
22. Fugazza, C., Menegon, S., Pepe, M., Oggioni, A., Carrara, P.: The RITMARE starter kit - bottom-up capacity building for geospatial data providers. In: Proceedings of the 9th International Conference on Software Paradigm Trends, pp. 169–176. SCITEPRESS - Science and and Technology Publications (2014)

23. Pollino, M., Modica, G.: Free web mapping tools to characterise landscape dynamics and to favour e-participation. In: Murgante, B., Misra, S., Carlini, M., Torre, C.M., Nguyen, H.-Q., Taniar, D., Apduhan, B.O., Gervasi, O. (eds.) Computational Science and Its Applications – ICCSA 2013. LNCS, vol. 7973, pp. 566–581. Springer, Berlin, Heidelberg (2013)

24. Benthall, B., Gill, S.: SDI best practices with GeoNode. In: Proceedings of Free and Open Source Software for Geospatial Conference (2010)

25. Winslow, D.: GeoNode Architecture: wrangling $100 million worth of open source software to make SDI building a walk in the park. In: Proceedings of Free and Open Source Software for Geospatial Conference (FOSS4G 2010) (2010)

26. Pavesi, F., Basoni, A., Fugazza, C., Menegon, S., Oggioni, A., Pepe, M., Tagliolato, P., Carrara, P.: SOFTWARE METAPAPER EDI – a template-driven metadata editor for research data. J. Open Res. Softw. **4**, 1–10 (2016)

27. Ma, X., Carranza, E.J.M., Wu, C., van der Meer, F.D., Liu, G.: A SKOS-based multilingual thesaurus of geological time scale for interoperability of online geological maps. Comput. Geosci. **37**, 1602–1615 (2011)

28. Leadbetter, A., Lowry, R., Clements, O.: The NERC vocabulary server: version 2.0. In: EGU General Assembly Conference, pp. 1–34 (2012)

29. Vassiliadis, P.: A survey of extract–transform–load technology. Int. J. Data Warehous. Min. **5**, 1–27 (2009)

30. Kraak, M.-J.: The role of the map in a Web-GIS environment. J. Geogr. Syst. **6**, 83–93 (2004)

31. Pollino, M., Caiaffa, E., Carillo, A., Porta, L., Sannino, G.: Wave energy potential in the mediterranean sea: design and development of DSS-WebGIS "waves energy". In: Gervasi, O., et al. (eds.) ICCSA 2015. LNCS, vol. 9157, pp. 495–510. Springer, Cham (2015). doi:10.1007/978-3-319-21470-2_36

32. Oliveira, A., Jesus, G., Gomes, J.L., Rogeiro, J., Azevedo, A., Rodrigues, M., Fortunato, A.B., Dias, J.M., Tomas, L.M., Vaz, L., Oliveira, E.R., Alves, F.L., Boer, S.D.: An interactive WebGIS observatory platform for enhanced support of integrated coastal management. J. Coast. Res. **70**, 507–512 (2014)

33. Mishra, S., Sharma, N.: WebGIS based decision support system for disseminating NOWCAST based alerts: OpenGIS approach. Glob. J. Comput. Sci. Technol. **16** (2016). No. 7-E

34. Chang, Y.-S., Park, H.-D.: Development of a web-based geographic information system for the management of borehole and geological data. Comput. Geosci. **30**, 887–897 (2004)

35. Selicato, M., Torre, C.M., La Trofa, G.: Prospect of integrate monitoring: a multidimensional approach. In: Murgante, B., et al. (eds.) ICCSA 2012. LNCS, vol. 7334, pp. 144–156. Springer, Heidelberg (2012). doi:10.1007/978-3-642-31075-1_11

36. Torre, C., Morano, P., Tajani, F.: Saving soil for sustainable land use. Sustainability **9**, 350 (2017)

37. Balena, P., Sannicandro, V., Torre, C.M.: spatial multicrierial evaluation of soil consumption as a tool for SEA. In: Murgante, B., et al. (eds.) ICCSA 2014. LNCS, vol. 8581, pp. 446–458. Springer, Cham (2014). doi:10.1007/978-3-319-09150-1_32

A GIS-Based Model for the Analysis of Ecological Connectivity

Andrea Fiduccia[1]([⊠]) 🆔, Francesca Pagliaro[1] 🆔,
Luca Gugliermetti[1] 🆔, and Leonardo Filesi[2] 🆔

[1] Department of Astronautical, Electrical and Energy Engineering (DIAEE),
Sapienza, University of Rome, Via Eudossiana 18, 00184 Rome, Italy
andrea.fiduccia@uniroma1.it
[2] Department of Design and Planning in Complex Environments,
IUAV University, Santa Croce 1957, Ca' Tron, 30135 Venice, Italy

Abstract. A model for the calculation of Potential Ecological Network at regional level has been presented in this paper. Through the use of GIS techniques and Natural Protected Areas and Land Use Map GIS datasets, the proposed model links two Ecological Network approaches (Species-Specific and Land Units) using the Least - Cost Path (LCP) algorithm. The nodes of the Ecological Potential Network have been analyzed using the Graph Theory. Specific GIS workflows have been set up to model the ecological connectivity in problematic mapping conditions, such as under road bridges and on the riverbanks. The main workflow requires a rasterization of the input datasets to allow the LCP algorithm application. The variations of the pixel resolution have been analyzed in terms of accuracy of the output and computation time of the model. The results underline an emerging property of Potential Ecological Networks, the Secondary Nodes, which are a set of nodes at the intersection of Linkages built by the LCP algorithm.

Keywords: Potential Ecological Networks · Ecology · GIS · Spatial analysis

1 The Ecological Network Paradigm

The concept of network is widely used in the ecology field [1] and the Ecological Networks have been developed and used in the context of Landscape Ecology [2–4]. The Ecological Network is a system of natural and semi-natural landscape elements, which aims to preserve the biodiversity against landscape fragmentation and decrease environmental depletion. Subpopulations who live in isolated patch of habitat can not survive for a long time if the landscape is fragmented. In fact, the flow of organisms among patches of habitat are the key to population survival, according to the theory of equilibrium of island biogeography [5] and metapopulation theory [6]. Thus, Ecological Network considers natural environments not as closed units, but as interconnected parts of a wider system [7]. Natural and semi-natural units ensure the connectivity between habitats, which is an essential condition to preserve species. In fact, even a wide protected area can not preserve its ecological structure if left isolated from other ecological patterns.

© Springer International Publishing AG 2017
O. Gervasi et al. (Eds.): ICCSA 2017, Part IV, LNCS 10407, pp. 600–612, 2017.
DOI: 10.1007/978-3-319-62401-3_43

According to the model developed by Bennett [8], Ecological Network are composed by the following six elements:

- Core Areas, which are the main component of Ecological Networks, supporting communities with a wide number of biodiversity types and individuals. Core Areas are characterized by biotopes, natural and semi-natural habitats, land and sea ecosystems and need to be protected.
- Buffer Zones, adjacent to Core Areas, are the link between society and nature.
- Wildlife Ecological Corridors, which are landscape structures used for maintain and recover the connections between ecosystems and biotopes, supporting the conservation of species and habitats.
- Stepping Stones, which are smaller natural areas where organisms can temporarily stop during their journey on ideal routes.
- Restoration Areas, which are natural areas created through renaturation interventions made to complete the structural gaps in the Ecological Network.
- Sustainable Use Areas, characterized by complex interrelationship between sustainable use of natural resources and maintenance of ecosystem services.

The Ecological Network is a theoretical paradigm applied at European and Global levels [9]. In the context of the Pan-European Biological and Landscape Diversity Strategy (PEBLDS), Pan-European Ecological Networks (PEEN) are one of the main aspects in the biodiversity conservation [10].

In Italy, Ecological Networks has been included in programs and projects at region, province, district and municipal levels [11]. The authorities recognize the Italian Regional Land Planning and Province Land Planning as the optimal level for ecological network planning. The application of ecological networking in the south of Italy, including Sicily and Sardinia, is one of the main aims of the Regional Operational Planning (POR) [12, 13]. Furthermore, Ecological Networks are also included in the environmental objectives of the New Italian General Plan for Transportation [14], that is comprehensive of the Road Ecology Planning paradigm, which aims at highlighting and explaining the connections between infrastructural and ecological networks [15–18].

GIS platform is the most appropriate tool for the Ecological Networks identification [19], using Remote Sensing as valuable source of updated information [20, 21]. However, these tools require a large amount of geo-referenced and updated data to calculate the ecosystems fragmentation and connectivity. Such datasets can be archived and analyzed in different formats, projections, scales and semantic models. Therefore, GIS platform should be designed to solve data harmonization and interoperability problems.

In this work, a conceptual model of Potential Ecological Network has been proposed and its identification and calculation has been made through GIS procedures. The outputs of the proposed model are ready-to-use GIS datasets for land planners, that can be easily implemented using open source GIS tools and open data.

The aim of the model is to create an effective tool for land planning able to close the gap between two existing Ecological Networks approaches: the Species-Specific and the Land Ecological Networks. Moreover, the model employs Networks Metrics in the Potential Ecological Network to focus the critical areas that should be investigated using ecological analysis and carefully planned.

2   GIS Analyses for Ecological Connectivity

2.1   The Main Workflow

The structure of the proposed Ecological Network is based on the Bennett model [8] integrated with two additional hypotheses:

- The Nodes (Core Areas and Stepping Stones) are the barycenter of natural protected areas (Parks and Natura 2000 Sites).
- The Linkages (Corridors) are calculated using the mathematical ecological behavioral model (LCP analysis).

Since the Ecological Network proposed in this paper is the output of a mathematical model, we call it "Potential Ecological Network".

Currently, Potential Ecological Networks do not evaluate Sustainable-Use Areas. Furthermore, they should be integrated with further ecological analyses from a land planning perspective.

The model of Potential Ecological Network developed in this work can simulate the behavior of little mammals and amphibious basing on the hypothesis that animals move in a certain ecosystem only when this action is perceived as safe from predators. For this reason, it is possible to identify different "safety" levels in the land use map of a certain ecosystem. When the Potential Ecological Network is identified in a GIS GRID environment, the accessibility between two locations can be modeled as "least cost-path" (LCP) problem. Thus, the best route is the one where the sum of the values of each cell of the route is the minimum [22]. Another possible interpretation of the land use classification model is based on "impedance" equivalence; the safer movement is the one with lower impedance values. On the contrary, high impedance values indicate a dangerous movement. Zoologists define a matrix of land use based on impedance levels for every Target Species X (where X is the species number) [23].

To create a model suitable for an Italian Region, classifiable as Administrative EU NUTS Level 2 Area, the operative steps are the following (see Fig. 1):

- Step 1. Collection of official GIS datasets, which are available as Open Data nowadays:
  - Parks and Natura 2000 Sites.
  - Land Cover.
  - Census coverage and database.
  - Hydrological network.
  - Transportation Network.
- Step 2. Selection of a number n of Target Species through ecological and zoological analyses.
- Step 3. Vector GIS workflow to produce Biopermeability-oriented Land Use maps.
- Step 4. Definition of Impedance Matrixes for the Target Species through ecological and zoological analyses.
- Step 5. Connection of the Biopermeability-oriented Land Use map to the Impedance Matrix for the Target Species X.

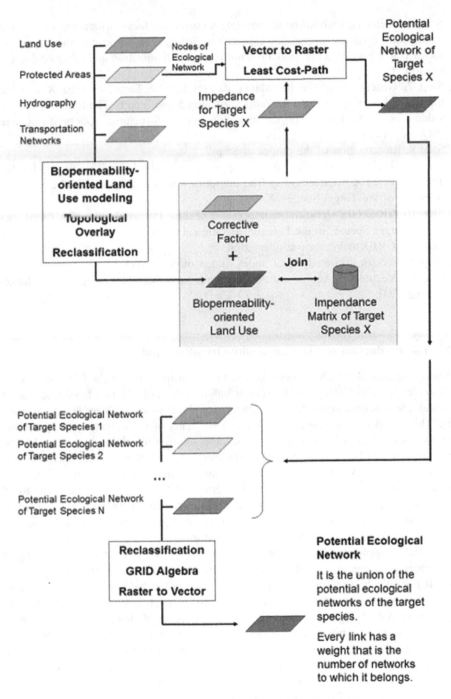

Fig. 1. Main GIS workflow for the Potential Ecological Network.

- Step 6. Vector GIS workflow to calculate a correction factor which must be added to impedance values (Impedance Correction Factor). The purpose of the correction factor is to consider in the model the influence of urbanization and other ecological constraints.
- Step 7. Generation of the Impedance dataset for the Target Species X using a topological overlay between the outputs of Step 5 and Step 6. The final Impedance value for each feature is calculated using a Structured Query Language (SQL) operator.
- Step 8. Rasterization of the output of Step 7.
- Step 9. GRID GIS workflow for the application of the behavioral model for the Target Species X (LCP analysis). The output of this step is the Potential Ecological Network of the Target Species X.
- Step 10. GRID GIS workflow of integration of the n Potential Ecological Networks of the Target Species in the Potential Ecological Network.
- Step 11. GRID to Vector transformation.
- Step 12. Vector GIS analysis of nodes (index of centrality).
- Step 13. Vector GIS Analysis of eco-mosaic around the nodes using fragmentation indexes [24].

2.2 The Production of Biopermeability-Oriented Land Use

A Land Use map at a scale 1:10000 is a suitable starting point in the GIS process for the calculation of an Ecological Network at Italian regional level. In a Land Use map at that scale, features narrower than the dimension related to the scaleare not be mapped [25]. This could be a problem for structural elements of the biopermeability model, such as a secondary road or a creek. A possible solution to this problem could be to enhance the Land Use map using linear features datasets, such as road networks and hydrography networks. The linear features of the two networks will be transformed to their real average dimension using a buffer operator. A thematic attribute (i.e. the Road Class or the Hierarchy) can be easily joined to numeric information about the average width of the features. The buffered road and hydrography network will integrate the land use map using a topological overlay operator.

Another mapping problem occurs when there are two overlapped objects, i.e. a river under a bridge, since only the one on the top is represented in the Land Use map. If the objects on the top are less important than the hidden ones, they must be removed from the representation. For an instance, vegetation under a bridge is more important than the bridge itself from biopermeability point of view, since the vegetation works as connector in the model. This problem requires more complex GIS workflows. The workflow for two modelling examples in this way have been shown: vegetation on the roadside of a road under a bridge; rivers and vegetation along riverbanks.

In the first case, the scenario can be implemented with a road on a bridge over another road. The input datasets are a Land Use map (polygonal features) and a road network (linear features). Bridges must be explicitly modeled in the road network. The operative steps are the following (see Fig. 2):

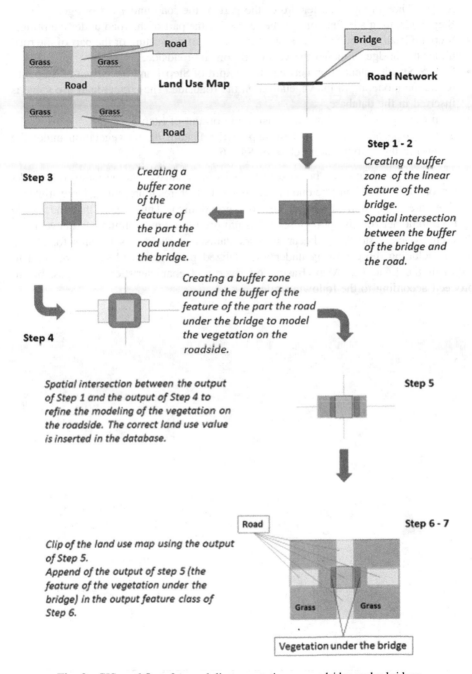

Fig. 2. GIS workflow for modeling vegetation on roadsides under bridges.

- Step 1. Creating a buffer zone of the linear feature of the bridge.
- Step 2. Spatial intersection between the buffer of the bridge and the road under the bridge. The output is the feature of the part of the road under the bridge.
- Step 3. Creating a buffer zone of the feature of the part of the road under the bridge.
- Step 4. Creating a buffer zone around the buffer of the feature of the part of the road under the bridge to model the vegetation on the roadside.
- Step 5. Spatial intersection between the output of Step 1 and the output of Step 4 to refine the modeling of the vegetation on the roadside. The correct land use value is inserted in the database.
- Step 6. Clip of the land use map using the output of Step 5.
- Step 7. Append of the output of step 5 (the feature of the vegetation under the bridge) in the output feature class of Step 6.

The same workflow can be used to model rivers and vegetation along riverbanks under road bridges. It must be underlined that only features representing large stretches of river are mapped in the Land Use polygonal map. This means that the whole hydrographic network is not represented as required to grant continuously between the different zones. Instead, the linear network dataset of rivers has features for all the rivers including those flowing under artificialized pavements and should be used to augment the Land Use Map. Basing on river real characteristics, it is possible to proceed according to the following rules:

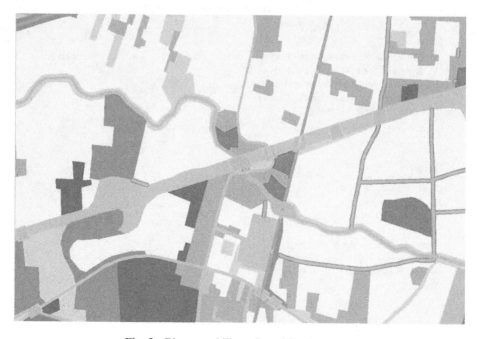

Fig. 3. Biopermeability-oriented land use map.

1. If a river linear feature overlaps a river polygonal feature, the correct land use is river polygonal feature.
2. If a river linear feature overlaps a not-urbanized land use feature, the correct land use is the buffer of river linear feature.
3. If a river linear feature overlaps an urbanized land use feature, the correct land use is the urbanized land use feature.

An example of the Biopermeability-oriented Land Use Map output of the GIS workflow is shown in Fig. 3.

3 Discussion

3.1 The Impedance Correction Factor

The first possible approach implemented in the Ecological Network focuses on animal and plant species (Species-Specific Ecological Network [26]). Animal and plant species are taxonomic units with specific intrinsic characteristics on evolutionary, ecological, and behavioral perspectives. Therefore, they may be affected by landscape pattern changes because of habitat fragmentation due to an anthropogenic origin. Species-Specific Ecological Networks provide information on the distribution pattern of species, which may be used as basis for the design of species-specific action plans assuming that the land transformation processes have effects on specific biological targets.

The second possible approach to Ecological Networks focuses on an integrated analysis of phytoclimatology, geology and vegetation aimed to identify homogeneous land units [27]. This approach – called Land Ecological Networks [27] - is based on a comparison between the real heterogeneity generated by human activities and the potential heterogeneity under natural conditions of the entire spatial mosaic.

The model of Potential Ecological Network proposed in this work combines these two approaches. The area of presence of the Target Species is calculated through the Impedance Correction Factor. By this methodology the algorithm builds an Ecological Network only where the Target Species lives [28].

The model has been tested at regional level, locating it in Veneto, a North Italian Region (see Fig. 4). In this case, the Settlement Risk Index (SIx) [29] has been used as Impedance Correction Factor. SIx measures the land sensibility to ongoing urbanization processes, analyzing urbanization phenomena through morphological factors (altimetry, slope, exposure) and urbanistic factors (accessibility to urban centers, proximity to the road network).

3.2 Primary Nodes and Secondary Nodes of the Ecological Network

In the proposed Potential Ecological Networks, the Primary Nodes are the set of centroids of natural protected areas; they "origins" and "destinations" in the LCP algorithm. The Linkages are defined as polylines by the LCP algorithm. The Linkages can cross each other and the Secondary Nodes are identified at the intersection among linkages. Therefore, Secondary Nodes are an output of LCP algorithm and characterize the Potential Ecological Network.

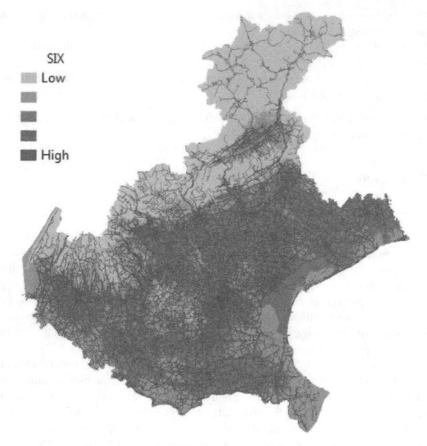

Fig. 4. The settlement risk index for region Veneto (Italy).

In the context of Graph Theory, Potential Ecological Network are planar multigraphs, which means that some Nodes are connected by more than one Linkage. Each linkage is characterized by a Degree of Relevance, which measures the number of Ecological Network it belongs to. In other words, the Degree of Relevance is the number of Target Species using the Linkage.

The Nodes have been analyzed using the Degree of Incidence, which measures the number of Linkage incident to the Node. In other words, the Degree of Incidence measures the importance of a Node in the species flow through the landscape [4].

The calculation of the Degree of Incidence highlights a characteristic of Potential Ecological Networks: the existence of a subset of nodes with a very high degree of incidence belonging to Secondary Nodes. They point out situations that will be subject to subsequent analysis and insights in the planning phase of the ecological net-work management.

3.3 Spatial Resolution of the Impedance GRID Dataset

The Impedance dataset must be rasterized in order to make it a suitable input for the LCP algorithm ("vector to GRID transformation" - Step 8 of the main workflow). The "vector to GRID transformation" uses an attribute value of the vector feature class. The operator averages the value of the attribute for the features covered by the pixel and assign the averaged value to the pixel. Thus, the increment of the raster resolution increases the fidelity of the attribute values (in the pixel values) of the vector features. However, the higher the resolution of the pixels, the longer the processing time of rasterization and the LCP algorithm [30]. As for big databases, the increase of the processing time is highly not-linear.

Table 1. Comparative tests of the LCP algorithm

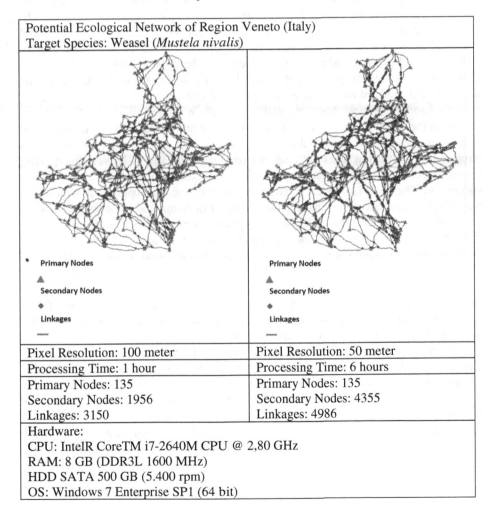

Potential Ecological Network of Region Veneto (Italy) Target Species: Weasel (*Mustela nivalis*)	
Pixel Resolution: 100 meter	Pixel Resolution: 50 meter
Processing Time: 1 hour	Processing Time: 6 hours
Primary Nodes: 135 Secondary Nodes: 1956 Linkages: 3150	Primary Nodes: 135 Secondary Nodes: 4355 Linkages: 4986
Hardware: CPU: IntelR CoreTM i7-2640M CPU @ 2,80 GHz RAM: 8 GB (DDR3L 1600 MHz) HDD SATA 500 GB (5.400 rpm) OS: Windows 7 Enterprise SP1 (64 bit)	

Different resolutions in the rasterization process could produce different spatial configurations of the Potential Ecological Network even if the Land Use feature class is the same. For this reason, a compromise between spatial resolution of the analysis and processing time is needed.

The results of the test on the territory of Veneto (Italy) are shown in Table 1.

4   Conclusions

The Potential Ecological Network proposed in this paper has been developed from a conceptual model and then applied on an Italian region through an operative GIS workflow.

From a conceptual viewpoint, the Potential Ecological Network closes the gap between the Species-Specific and the Land Ecological Networks obtaining a unified model of Ecological Networks in the perspective of Ecological Land Planning. The Potential Ecological Network proposed in this paper supplies approximated spatial shapes of the Ecological Network, but it can be already considered as a useful tool for ecological land planning. More detailed results can be obtained involving traditional techniques of ecological planning at design level (scale 1:5000 or 1:2000) based on feedback and needs of communities, stakeholders, and experts.

The Land Ecological Network arises from the need to enhance the ecological quality of the territory even with regard to plants. For this reason, it is based on maps of vegetation series, in which the vegetation is not represented solely on a physiognomy-structural basis but also in terms of potentiality. The vegetation series brings together all those vegetation typologies connected by relationships of biological succession. The Land Ecological Network is based on the assumption that widespread naturalness is, however, positive for the dispersal of fauna and does not address the problems related to the needs of the various species. A method such as that proposed in this article, primarily designed for moving organisms (animals) if applied to a vegetation series map, would provide very comprehensive information for both fauna and plants.

The GIS workflow is widely applicable using Open Source GIS Tools and Open Data. This workflow faces the problem of the integration of polygonal Datasets (Land Use Maps) with linear datasets (Transportation Networks and Hydrographic Networks) to correctly model the biopermeability of a land.

The main problematic aspect found in the model lies in the location of Primary Nodes, which have been identified as barycenter of the polygons of Natural Protected Areas. However, they can be generated in other locations using other criteria, such as environmental ones. In fact, a Multicriteria Analysis on Fragmentation Index and Settlement Risk Index could be used for this purpose.

Finally, a future development of this work could be the application of Network Analysis to Ecological Networks. This analysis could show more properties of the network allowing to explore and evaluate the potentiality of Secondary Nodes.

References

1. Borret, S.R., Moody, J., Edelmann, A.: The rise of network ecology: maps of the topic diversity and scientific collaboration. Ecol. Model. **293**, 111–127 (2014)
2. Calabrese, J.M., Fagan, W.F.: A comparison-shopper's guide to connectivity metrics. Front Ecol. Environ. **2**(10), 529–536 (2004)
3. Forman, R.T.T., Godron, M.: Landscape Ecology. Wiley, New York (1986)
4. Farina, A.: Principles and Methods in Landscape Ecology. Chapman and Hall, London (1998)
5. MacArthur, R.H., Wilson, E.O.: The Theory of Island Biogeography. Princeton University Press, Princeton (1967)
6. Levins, R.: Extinction. In: Gertenshaubert, M. (ed.) Some Mathematical Question in Biology. Lectures in mathematics in the Life Science. American Mathematical Society, Providence (1970)
7. Turner, M.G., Gardner, R.H.: Quantitative Methods in Landscape Ecology. The Analysis and Interpretation of Landscape Heterogeneity. Springer, New York (1994)
8. Bennett, G.: Integrating Biodiversity Conservation and Sustainable Use: Lessons Learned From Ecological Networks. Gland, Cambridge (2004)
9. Bennett, G., Mulongoy, K.J.: Review of experience with ecological networks, corridors and buffer zones. Secretariat of the Convention on Biological Diversity, Montreal, Technical Series No. 23 (2006)
10. Jones-Walters, L., Snethlage, M., Civic, K., Çil, A., Smit, I.: Making the Connection! Guidelines for Involving Stakeholders in the Implementation of Ecological Networks. ECNC, Tilburg (2009)
11. Filpa, A., Romano, B. (eds.): Pianificazione e reti ecologiche, Planeco - Planning in ecological network. Gangemi Editore, Roma (2003)
12. Rete Nazionale delle Autorità Ambientali e delle Autorità della Programmazione dei fondi strutturali comunitari 2000–2006 Unità di Coordinamento Gruppo di Lavoro Rete Ecologica: La Rete Ecologica ed i Fondi Strutturali nelle Regioni Obiettivo 1. Stato di attuazione, problematiche e proposte di intervento. Report Giugno (2003)
13. Rete Nazionale delle Autorità Ambientali e delle Autorità della Programmazione dei fondi strutturali comunitari 2000–2006 Unità di Coordinamento Gruppo di Lavoro Rete Ecologica: La Rete Ecologica e la riprogrammazione del QCS – Aggiornamento del Report sulle Relazioni regionali previste dal QCS Ob.1 2000- 2006 post Mid term Review (paragrafo 3.2 Asse I- Criteri e indirizzi per l'attuazione – 6 Rete Ecologica), XI Comitato di Sorveglianza del QCS Ob.1 2000–2006. Roma, 10 maggio (2006)
14. Italian Ministry for Infrastructures: General Plan for Transportation and Logistics. Gazzetta Ufficiale n. 163 16-07-2001
15. Bennett, A.F.: Roads, roadsides and wildlife conservation: a review. In: Saundersand, D.A., Hobbs, R.J. (eds.) Nature Conservation 2: The Role of Corridors, pp. 99–118. Surry Beatty & Sons, Chipping Norton (1989)
16. Forman, R.T.T.: Road ecology: a solution for the giant embracing us. Landscape Ecol. **13**, iii–v (1998)
17. Forman, R.T.T.: Horizontal processes, roads, suburbs, societal objectives, and landscape ecology. In: Klopatek, J.M., Gardner, R.H. (eds.) Landscape Ecological Analysis: Issues and Applications, pp. 35–53. Springer, New York (1999)
18. Forman, R.T.T.: Estimate of the area affected ecologically by the road system in the United States. Conserv. Biol. **14**, 31–35 (2000)

19. Jongman, R.H.G., Pungetti, G. (ed.) Ecological Networks and Greenways: Concept, Design, Implementation. Cambridge University Press, Cambridge (2004)
20. Gillespie, T.W., Foody, G.M., Rocchini, D., Giorgi, A.P., Saatchi, S.: Measuring and modeling biodiversity from space. Prog. Phys. Geogr. **32**(2), 203–221 (2008)
21. Wright, C.: Spatiotemporal dynamics of complex ecological networks: power-law scaling and implications for conservation planning. In: Nature Precedings (2008)
22. Longley, P.A., Goodchild, M.F., Maguire, D.J., Rhind, D.W. (eds.): Geographical Information Systems: Principles, Techniques, Applications and Management. Wiley, New York (1999)
23. Kool, J.T., Moilanen, A., Treml, E.A.: Population connectivity: recent advances and new perspectives. Landscape Ecol. **28**, 165–185 (2013)
24. Uuemaa, E.M., Antrop, J., Roosaare, R.M., Mander, Ü.: Landscape metrics and indices: an overview of their use in landscape research. Living Rev. Land. Res. **3**, 1 (2009)
25. European Environment Agency: CLC2006 technical guidelines (2007)
26. Fall, A., Fortin, M.-J., Manseau, M., O'Brien, D.: Spatial graphs: principles and applications for habitat connectivity. Ecosystems **10**, 448–461 (2007)
27. Blasi, C., Zavattero, L., Marignani, M., Smiraglia, D., Copiz, R., Rosati, L., Del Vico, E.: The concept of land ecological network and its design using a land unit approach. Plant Biosyst. **142**(3), 540–549 (2008)
28. Fiduccia, A., Fonti, L., Leone, H.: Reti ecologiche e pianificazione territoriale: il caso della Regione Basilicata. Atti XXVI Conferenza Nazionale A.I.S.Re., Napoli (2005)
29. Romano, B., Ciabò, S., De Santis, E., Fabrizio, M., Zullo, F.: Urban settlement sensibility assessment. Morphological-based analysis in italian case studies. Planum. J. Urbanism **2** (2013). No. 27
30. Laurini, R., Thompson, D.: Fundamentals of Spatial Information Systems. Academic Press, London (1992)

Simulation of Hydrograph Response to Land Use Scenarios for a Southern Chile Watershed

Vladimir J. Alarcon[✉], Jose P. Hernandez A., and Hernan Alcayaga

Civil Engineering School, Universidad Diego Portales, 441 Ejercito Ave., Santiago, Chile
{vladimir.alarcon,hernan.alcayaga}@udp.cl,
jose.hernandez@mail.udp.cl

Abstract. In this research, the hydrological response to changes in land use for the Quilmo River watershed (Southern Chile) is assessed. The assessment is performed using the Hydrological Simulation Program-Fortran code (HSPF). The hydrological response to predominant land uses of non-native planted forests, agricultural lands, grasslands, and native forests was sequentially simulated. The hydrological model was initially calibrated for stream flow at the exit of the watershed ($R^2 = 0.66$, $P < 0.001$). The calibrated model was used for simulating the hydrological responses under two flood events: a peak flood (August 24, 2002), and a moderate flood of (October 14, 2002). The simulated land use scenarios were sequentially and independently input to the model. Results showed that for both flood-events the hydrological response to non-native forests or agricultural lands was very similar to the baseline hydrograph corresponding to 2002 land use. The hydrological response to predominant grasslands and native forests was significantly different. For the August 24 flood, the model calculates that extreme minimum flows and low base flows take place when native forest is the predominant land use. When the watershed is covered by grasslands the most balanced hydrograph (moderate droughts and moderate peak flows) is produced. For the moderate flood event of October 14, the highest values of peak flows and base flows were produced when the watershed is predominantly covered by grasslands. However, the hydrograph for grasslands still showed the most balanced response (moderate droughts and moderate peak flows). For native forests, the response hydrograph shows low base flows but also low peak flows. Therefore, combining grasslands with native forests may provide a balanced hydrograph not only with respect to magnitudes of flow (high base flows and moderated peak flows) but also on their timing. Both conditions are favorable for flood control and drought mitigation.

Keywords: Land use · Hydrological modeling · Quilmo River · Chile

1 Introduction

Besides being the element of greater abundance on earth, water is also a key factor for the preservation of biodiversity in our planet. The increase of the world population and economic growth have led to a growing demand for this resource and calculations show that if the current water overuse trend does not change, the world will face a 40% water

© Springer International Publishing AG 2017
O. Gervasi et al. (Eds.): ICCSA 2017, Part IV, LNCS 10407, pp. 613–625, 2017.
DOI: 10.1007/978-3-319-62401-3_44

supply deficit by the end of 2030 [1]. Chile has a great diversity of climates and geographies; therefore watersheds with different hydrological regimes are located throughout its territory. However, Chile is not safe from those anticipated risks.

According to [2], land use and its dynamics are among the factors that most affect the components of the hydrological cycle: evapotranspiration, surface runoff, groundwater recharge and infiltration. The dynamics of change in land cover depend on seasonal variations in the characteristics of the soil coverage and the natural growth/decay of the forest. It can also be the result of human activities such as urbanization, deforestation and the conversion of land use from one use to another. An example of this is the change currently taking place in native forests in South-Central Chile. Human activities (agriculture) and fires and the absence of management practices [2] have produced substantial changes in the water balance of several watersheds. Vast areas of native forests have been eliminated and converted to agricultural lands and, in recent decades, to non-native fast-growing forests [3, 4] cited by [2].

Recent studies [5] have shown the negative effects of the conversion of native forests to non-native forests on ground water reserves and water yield in Southern Chile [6–8]. These studies found that forest cover produces less run-off and increased evapotranspiration, when compared with other types of land covers such as agriculture, scrublands and prairies. The presence of vegetation, mainly of forests, causes large amounts of rainfall interception [9, 10]. It is reasonable to say that the runoff generation capacity is not only dependent of the type of vegetation but also of plant species: pine vs. eucalyptus or Acacia; (alfalfa vs. oats or wheat). However, is somewhat more difficult to guess the impact of change in land use on resources of groundwater and subsurface water because of the complex relationship between evapotranspiration, infiltration, inter-flow and coverage of soils.

In ungauged watersheds (or watersheds with limited monitoring) characterization of the impact of changes in the soil coverage is very important. Given that the vegetation plays an important role in the water balance of a watershed [11], in basins predominantly covered by different types of vegetation, quantifying changes in plant covers may allow qualitatively estimate the effects on surface water flow. In Chile, many rural watersheds are not monitored or are monitored sparingly. Also, the predominant land cover categories in rural watersheds are: forests, grasslands, shrubs, non-native forests and agriculture (vegetative covers). Generating a methodology that uses limited hydrological and land use information and, via simulation, could be used to infer the behavior of the surface water flow could be a way of alleviating the absence of data that characterize the surface hydrology of these basins.

In this research, the hydrological response to changes in land use for the Quilmo River watershed is assessed. The watershed drains a forest/agricultural basin located in Southern Chile. The assessment is performed through hydrological modeling. The Hydrological Simulation Program-Fortran code [12] is used for modeling the hydrology of the watershed for the period June–August 2002. The hydrological response to the following predominant land uses was simulated: non-native planted forests, agricultural lands, grasslands, and native forests. The simulation of the hydrological response to the four land use scenarios was performed for two flood events: a peak flood (August 24,

2002) and a moderate flood of (October 14, 2002). The simulated land use scenarios were sequentially and independently run.

2   Methods

2.1   Study Area

The Quilmo River watershed is located in Southern Chile (Fig. 1) in the Province of Ñuble, (Bio Bio Region). The Quilmo River watershed is a sub-basin of the Chillan River, a tributary of the Itata River that drains to the Pacific Ocean.

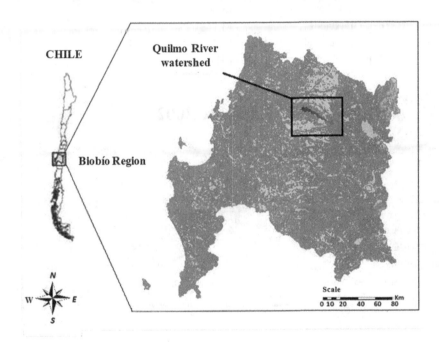

Fig. 1. Study area. The Quilmo River watershed is located in Southern Chile.

The watershed has an approximate area of 106.6 km² characterized by soft slopes, with topographical elevations ranging from the 87 m to 728 m above sea level. The average slope of the basin of the Quilmo watershed is approximately 5%. Its climate is temperate-mediterranean, with mild and rainy winters and dry and hot summers. The Quilmo River is fed mainly by rain and the minimum flows occur between the months of January and April.

Table 1 and Fig. 2 present the spatial distribution and percent area covered by predominant land use categories, for year 2002. As shown, the main land use categories are: native forest, non-native forest plantations, grasslands/shrublands, and agricultural crops (mostly wheat crops).

Table 1. Table captions should be placed above the tables.

ID	Land use 2002	Area (Km²)	% Watershed
1	Non-native forest (Mature)	25.7	24.1
2	Non-native forest (Young)	15.9	14.9
3	Non-native forest (Intermediate)	6.7	6.3
4	Native forest	14.5	13.6
5	Shrub lands	13.6	12.7
6	Grasslands	13.1	12.3
7	Agricultural land	17.2	16.1
Total		106.6	100.0

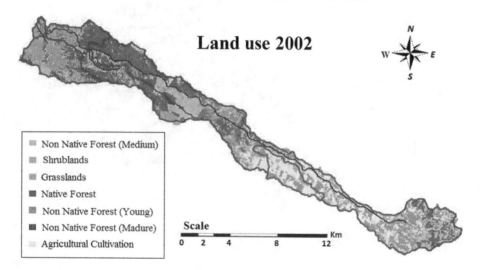

Fig. 2. Land use/Land cover in Quilmo River watershed in year 2002.

2.2 Meteorological and Stream Flow Data

The average annual precipitation in the region ranges between 1076 mm to 2000 mm [13], generally increasing from North to South directions. The watershed soils are primarily loamy clays which cover 57.2% of the basin (mostly associated with forests) and loams (associated with agricultural activities) [14]. Between 1964 and 1983 the annual average stream flow at the exit of the Quilmo River watershed was 2.21 m³/s, with a minimum value of 0.01 m³/s (04/02/1969) and maximum value of 48.30 (m³/s) (20/06/1974) [15].

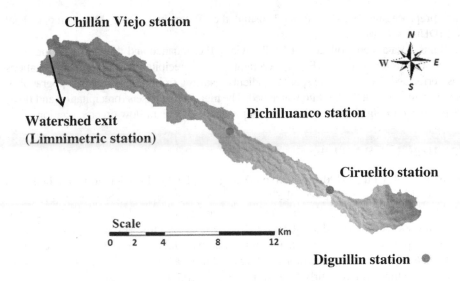

Fig. 3. Meteorological and stream flow stations in the study area.

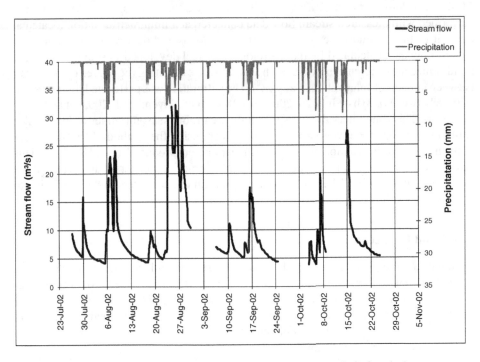

Fig. 4. Precipitation and stream flow data during the period of analysis.

Precipitation and flow data were obtained from [14]. Precipitation data were reported at an hourly time scale (mm/hour). Stream flow data were also collected at an hourly temporal scale for year 2002, at the exit of the watershed (Fig. 3). All meteorological and stream flow data preprocessing was performed using the Watershed Data Management Tool (WMDUtil) software.

Rainfall data were collected at Chillán viejo, Pichilluanco and the Ciruelillo meteorological stations for year 2002 (Fig. 3). Averaging of the precipitation data from those stations was performed to compensate spatial gradients resulting from differences in topographical elevation throughout the Quilmo watershed. The measured datasets (precipitation and flow) are presented in Fig. 4. Notice the strong dependence of stream flow on precipitation.

2.3   Hydrological Modeling

Hydrological Code. Hydrological modeling of the Quilmo River watershed was performed using the Hydrological Simulation Program Fortran, HSPF (Donigian et al. 1983). The HSPF software is designed for modeling and simulating non-point-source and point-source watershed hydrology and water quality. Time-series of meteorological data (precipitation and evapo-transpiration), land use and topographical data were used to estimate stream flow hydrographs at the exit of the watershed. Simulation results were produced in the form of hourly time-series of streamflow.

Model Development and Calibration. In this research, hydrological calibration was performed with measured stream flow data collected at a limnimetric station located at the exit of the Quilmo River watershed (Fig. 3). Measured data were compared with stream flow data calculated by the hydrological model developed in study. We sought to minimize the difference between both sets of data, evaluating the degree of similarity between numerical values statistically (R^2). The calibration was performed for the period of time between 0:00 h of July 26, 2002, and 18:00 h of November 1, 2002, at an hourly time-step. This time interval covers the study area rainy season (winter of 2002). The calibration of the model was carried out iteratively using the method of trial-and-error until an optimal combination of hydrological parameters produced a good R^2 value. This process was performed in two parts: (i) modification of parameters that directly affect the hydrological cycle of the basin, (ii) configuration of parameters in direct relation to agro-forestry soils coverage.

2.4   Land Use Scenarios

With the calibrated model, several different scenarios of land use were generated using as meteorological forcing the 2002 precipitation dataset. These scenarios were implemented so that the model predicts the hydrological response of the watershed to extreme changes in the land use coverage. Predominant land uses (as quantified and shown in Table 1) were selected for these simulations.

The scenarios were as follows:

Scenario 1, watershed covered by non-native forests: pine and eucalyptus
Scenario 2, watershed covered by grasslands: natural land use of Southern Chile.
Scenario 3, watershed by native forests: natural land use of Southern Chile.
Scenario 4, watershed covered completely by farmland: agricultural crops (wheat).

3   Results

3.1   Hydrological Calibration

The results of the hydrological calibration performed at hourly time scale are shown in Figs. 5 and 6. The resulting calibration followed sequential adjustment of model parameters related to the hydrological cycle.

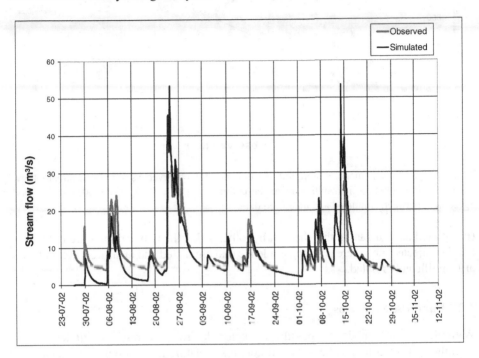

Fig. 5. Hydrological model calibration. Hourly hydrographs for observed and simulated stream flow.

Figure 5 shows hydrographs at hourly time scale for measured and simulated stream flow values for the calibration period: July 27 to October 24, 2002. The figure shows that observed and simulated values have similar temporal trends. The model slightly underestimates stream flow values especially at the beginning of the simulation (until August 20, 2002). However, once the model has passed that warming-up initial phase, the underestimation of flow is less evident. The model also tends to slightly overestimate peak flows; however the simulation results for most of the simulation period are good, as statistical indicators attest it (Fig. 6).

The statistical indicators of fit used in this research were the correlation coefficient R^2 and the Pearson P value. As shown in Fig. 6, the hydrological calibration process shows good agreement between simulated and observed stream flow values ($R^2 = 0.66$). This R^2 value is within acceptable values according to the literature [16]. The statistical significance of this correlation analysis resulted in a Pearson's P value smaller than 0.001

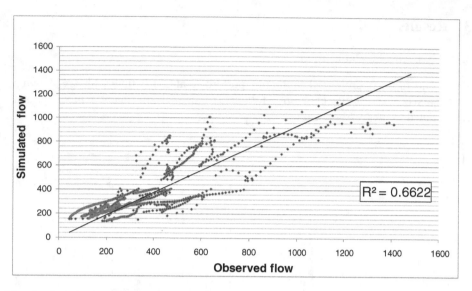

Fig. 6. Hydrological model calibration. Scatter-plot for observed vs simulated stream flow. Statistical indicators of fit resulting from the calibration (R^2 = 0.66, P < 0.001) show good agreement between simulated and measured data.

(two-tailed test), meaning that the null hypothesis that the two variables are not correlated is rejected, i.e., there is strong evidence that simulated and measured stream flows are significantly related.

3.2   Land Use Scenarios

With the calibrated model it is possible to explore hydrological responses under various hypothetical conditions of land use. Although simulating the hydrological response to any arbitrary combination of land use is possible, in this research we simulated extreme land use conditions. Knowing the response of the watershed to drastic changes in land cover could be used to infer the hydrological response to partial combinations of those conditions. The scenarios explored correspond to those described in Sect. 2.4. These analyses were carried out for the most significant floods that occurred in August 24 and October 14, 2002.

August 24, 2002 Flood (Peak Flood). The model calculates that the maximum values of stream flow rate occur when the watershed is fully covered by native forest (Fig. 7). In addition, the peak flow for this coverage is slightly delayed when compared to the occurrence of the peak flow in the baseline hydrograph. This could due to the greater storage capacity of the native forest canopy which would produce more effective interception and consequently less rapid runoff during strong precipitation events.

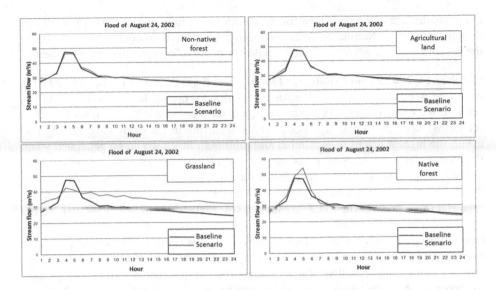

Fig. 7. Hydrological response for the flood of August 24, 2002 (peak flood). Land use scenarios: non-native forest, agricultural land, grassland, native forest. The baseline hydrograph corresponds to actual 2002 land use (Table 1).

Figure 7 also shows that agricultural lands and non-native forests produce a hydrograph response very similar to that produced for land cover in year 2002 (base line). This could be due to the fact that the watershed in 2002 is primarily covered by agricultural lands and planted non-native forests, i.e., the hydrographs are not affected by the expansion of those land use coverages. Table 2 shows representative values of stream flow for the scenarios simulated in this research.

Table 2. Representative stream flows for simulated land use scenarios during August 24 flood.

	2002 (baseline)	Grassland	Native forest	Non-native forest	Agric. lands
Maximum flow	47.57	42.48	54.09	46.44	48.14
Minimum flow	24.15	32.00	23.45	25.17	23.84
Average flow	30.05	35.60	29.76	30.41	29.82

Table 2 further demonstrates that the largest peak flows would be when the watershed is covered by native forests. The most extreme minimum flows also occur for this scenario. Hence, this type of land use coverage is not appropriate if flood or drought management measures are being implemented. The land use scenario that appears to be the most optimal to obtain a balanced hydrograph (without extreme flood events or drought) is produced when the watershed is predominantly covered by grasslands. Combining grasslands and native forests (which delays peak flows) may provide a balanced hydrograph not only with respect to magnitudes of flow but also with respect to the occurrence of the peak flow. Both conditions are favorable for flood control and drought mitigation. Non-native forests and agricultural lands do not produce changes to the baseline hydrograph and therefore could not be used for watershed management.

October 14, 2002 Flood (Moderate Flood). The flood event of October 14 (2002) is moderate when compared with the August 24 flood. This moderate flood was chosen because we wanted to explore the hydrological response of the basin (under the same scenarios) to the most common flood events occurring in the study area. During this event, the highest values of maximum and minimum flows would be generated when the basin is fully covered with grasslands (Fig. 8). However, the magnitude of the peak flows would be much smaller than any of the peak flows that occurred in August 24, 2002; i.e., small to moderate peak flows. The native forest coverage also generates important peak flows but of lesser magnitude as those corresponding to grassland. Native forest generates smaller flows than the baseline hydrograph. If the basin were completely covered by grasslands, the hydrological response of the watershed to a moderate flood event (such as the October 14 flood) would be to generate greater base flows than those corresponding to the baseline. If agricultural crops or non-native forests would cover the entire basin, the resulting hydrograph would be very similar to the baseline (Table 3).

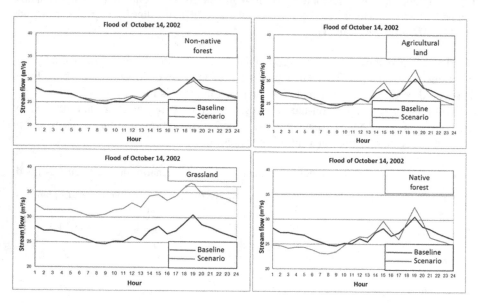

Fig. 8. Hydrological response for the flood of October 14, 2002 (moderate flood). Land use scenarios: non-native forest, agricultural land, grassland, native forest. The baseline hydrograph corresponds to actual 2002 land use (Table 1).

The hydrographs shown in Fig. 8 and the stream flow values shown in Table 3 (corresponding to the flood event of October 14, 2002) confirm the hypothesis that was established for the flood event of August 24: land use that would combine grasslands with native forest may be appropriate for flood control or drought mitigation because a

Table 3. Representative stream flows for simulated land use scenarios during October 14 flood.

	2002 (base-line)	Grassland	Native forest	Non-native forest	Agric. lands
Maximum flow	30.58	36.81	32.56	29.73	32.56
Minimum flow	24.66	30.30	23.02	25.34	24.01
Average flow	26.87	32.84	26.00	26.93	26.64

balanced hydrograph will be produced (low peak flows and high base flows). Also, non-native forests and agricultural lands do not significantly change the baseline hydrograph and therefore may not be used for watershed management.

4   Conclusions

The hydrological model developed in this study was successfully calibrated for stream flow at the exit of the Quilmo River watershed. Simulated versus measured stream flow hourly time-series were statistically compared through the calculation of the correlation coefficient (R^2). A numerical value of $R^2 = 0.66$ was achieved, indicating good fit, considering that the time-series were composed by hourly stream flow data. An additional Pearson´s significance test was performed resulting in $P < 0.001$, indicating that the correlation is evident.

The calibrated model was used for simulation of four land use scenarios for two flood events: a peak flood that took place in August 24, 2002; and a moderate flood that occurred in October 14, 2002. The simulated land use/land cover scenarios considered the watershed being covered predominantly by: non-native planted forests, agricultural lands, grasslands, and native forests. The scenarios were run sequentially and independently from each other.

Results showed that for both flood events the hydrological response of the Quilmo River watershed to predominant non-native forests land use, or predominant agricultural land use, was very similar to the hydrological response to the actual land use in 2002 (comparison baseline). In fact, in 2002, 40% of the watershed was covered by those land use categories, and this would explain the results achieved for non-native forests and agricultural lands.

The hydrological response to grasslands and native forests, however, was significantly different to the baseline hydrological response to 2002 land use conditions. For the August 24 flood, the model calculates that a delayed largest peak flow occurs when the basin is predominantly covered by native forest. Also, for these conditions, the most extreme droughts (minimum flows) and low base flow conditions take place. When the watershed is covered by grasslands, the most balanced hydrograph (moderate droughts and moderate peak flows) is produced. This would lead to conclude that combining grasslands with native forests (which delays peak flows) may provide a balanced hydrograph not only with respect to magnitudes of flow (high base flows and moderated peak flows) but also on its timing. Both conditions are favorable for flood control and drought mitigation.

The moderate flood event of October, 2002, allowed the exploration of the hydrological response (under the same land use scenarios) for the most frequent events in the Quilmo River watershed. The highest values of peak flows and base flows were generated when the basin is predominantly covered by grasslands. However, the hydrograph for grasslands still shows the most balanced response (moderate droughts and moderate peak flows). If the watershed would be predominantly covered by native forests, the response hydrograph shows low base flows but also low peak flows. These results confirm the hypothesis that was established for the August 24 flood event: the combination of grasslands with native forests would provide a balanced hydrological response with respect to magnitudes of flow and timing of peak flows. This conclusion is consistent with research in other watersheds [17–19] with similar characteristics to Quilmo River watershed.

Acknowledgements. This study was supported by a grant of CONICYT REDES 140045. The authors thank the editor and two anonymous reviewers for their useful suggestions and comments.

References

1. UNESCO: Informe de las naciones unidas sobre los recursos hídricos en el mundo 2015. Secretaria del programamundial de evolución de losrecursoshídricos. División de las cienciasdelagua. Perugia, Italia (2015)
2. Oyarzun, C., Fréne, C., Lacrampe, G., Huber, A., Hervé, P.: Propiedadeshidrológicas del suelo y exportación de sedimentosen dos microcuencas de la Cordillera de la Costa en el sur de Chile con diferentecobertura vegetal. BOSQUE **32**(1), 10–19 (2011)
3. Oyarzún, C.E.: A Huber: water balance in young plantations of Eucalyptus globulus and Pinusradiata in Southern Chile. Terra **17**, 35–44 (1999)
4. Lara, A., Donoso, C., Aravena, J.C.: La conservacióndelbosquenativo de Chile: problemas y desafíos. In Armesto J, C Villagrán, M Arroyo eds. Ecología de losbosquesnativos de Chile. Santiago, Chile. Editorial Universitaria, pp. 335–361 (1996)
5. Armesto, J., Manuschevich, D., Mora, A., Smith-Ramírez, C., Rozzi, R., Abarzúa, A., Marquet, P.: From the Holocene to the Anthropocene: a historical framework for land covers change in Southwestern South America in the past 15.000 years. Land Use Policy **27**, 148–160 (2010)
6. Huber, A., Ioumé, A., Bathurst, J.: Effect of Pinusradiata plantations on water balance in Chile. Hydrol. Process. **22**, 142–148 (2008)
7. Lara, A., Little, C., Urrutia, R., McPhee, J., Alvarez-Garreton, C., Oyarzun, C., Soto, D., Donoso, P., Nahuelhual, L., Pinto, M., Arismendi, I.: Assessment if ecosystem services as an opportunity for the conservation and management of native forest in Chile. Forest Ecol. Manag. **258**, 415–424 (2009)
8. Little, C., Lara, A., McPhee, J., Urrutia, R.: Revealing the impact of forest exotic plantations on water yield in large scale watersheds in South-Central Chile. J. Hydrol. **374**, 162–170 (2009)
9. Huber, A.C.: Oyarzún: Factoresreguladores de la intercepciónenunbosqueadulto de Pinusradiata D Don. Bosque **23**(2), 43–49 (1984)

10. Oyarzun, C., Huber, A., Vásquez, S.: Balance hídricoentresplantaciones de Pinusradiata, I: Redistribución de las precipitaciones. BOSQUE **6**(1), 3–13 (1985)
11. López, F.:Restauraciónhidrológicaforestal y control de la erosión. Ingenieríaambiental, Ministeriodel Medio Ambiente, Madrid, España, Edn. Mundi-Prensa, 902 p. (1998)
12. Donigian Jr., A.S.B., Haith, D.A., Walter, M.F.: HSPF parameter adjustments to evaluate the effects of agricultural best management practices, U.S. EPA Environmental Research Laboratory, Athens, GA, PB-83-247171 (1983)
13. Debels, P., Link, O., Brevis, W.: A rainfall-runoff and pesticide export model for a South-Central Chilean watershed with forestry and agricultural land use. In: Proceedings Scientific and Technological Cooperation between Flanders and Chile Workshop, 17–19 September, Ghent, Belgium (2001)
14. Alcayaga, H.:Modelación de la exportación de Simazinadesdeunacuencaagroforestalusando un SIG. Memoria para optar al título de Ingeniero Civil. Facultad de ingeniería, U. de Concepción, Concepción, Chile (2003)
15. MOP: Estudio de ProcesosHidrológicosen la Cuenca Hidrográfica del Estero QuilmoOctavaRegión. Thesis, Facultad de ingeniería, Universidad de Concepción, Chile (2004)
16. Moriasi, D., Arnold, J., Van Liew, M., Bingner, R., Harmel, R., Veith, T.: Model evaluation guidelines for systematic quantification of accuracy in watershed simulations. Trans. ASABE **50**(3), 885–900 (2007)
17. Dons, A.: Hydrology and sediment regime of a pasture, native forest, and pine forest catchment in the Central North Island, New Zealand. J. Forest. Sci. **17**(2/3), 161–178 (1987)
18. Recha, J.W., Lehmann, J., Walter, M.T., Pell, A., Verchot, L., Johnson, M.: Stream discharge in tropical headwater catchments as a result of forest clearing and soil degradation. Earth Interact. **16**(13), 1–18 (2012)
19. Grant, G.E., Lewis, S.L., Swanson, F.J., Cissel, J.H., McDonnell, J.J.: Effects of forest practices on peak flows and consequent channel response: a state of science report for western Oregon and Washington. USDA For. Serv. Gen. Tech. Rep. PNW-GTR **760**, 1–82 (2008)

Geospatial Visualization of Automotive Sensor Data: A Conceptual and Implementational Framework for Environment and Traffic-Related Applications

Patrick Voland[✉] and Hartmut Asche[✉]

Geoinformation Research Group, Department of Geography,
University of Potsdam, Karl-Liebknecht-Straße 24/25, 14476 Potsdam, Germany
{patrick.voland,hartmut.asche}@uni-potsdam.de

Abstract. In the era of Big Data and the Internet of Things modern automotive vehicles have become complex mobile computational systems on wheels. The sensors included in these systems record a multitude of car- and traffic-related data, as well as environmental parameters outside the vehicle. The data recorded can be characterized as "spatio-temporal" by their nature and can, thus, be classified as "geodata". As such, they allow for, comprehensive analysis and visualizations. Their geospatial and application potential has, however, not been fully unlocked so far. This paper deals with the ongoing research on these new kinds of massive geodata. It presents an approach to process and visualize this data for context-sensitive applications. Cartographic visualization is a particularly effective means to make the enormous stock of machine-recorded data available to human perception, exploration and analysis.

1 Introduction

In our wired world, modern automotive vehicles have developed into complex electronic systems. They are equipped with a large number of sensor devices essential for smooth technical operation (controlling, e.g., vehicle speed or engine revolutions) and environmental monitoring (measuring, e.g., barometric air pressure, ambient air temperature). The increase in the number of electronic components in automobiles is coupled with a growing number of electronic control units (ECU), in which each ECU is equipped with an intelligent, software-driven micro-controller designed for a specific task or activity area and linked through an in-vehicle data-bus network system (esp. CAN [Controller Area Network]). Such constantly acquired data are indispensable for a growing number of so-called Advanced Driver Assistance Systems (ADAS). Automotive sensor data are a prerequisite for semi-autonomous and autonomous driving systems currently under development and testing. In this context, the company Intel recently estimated the amount of produced data (raw sensor data; before the process of sensor fusion) inside one autonomous self-driving car of about four terabytes (4000 gb) per day [1].

Existing technical solutions in communications and bandwidth, coupled with a constant drop of transmission costs, have paved the way for using automotive sensor data in a variety of uses not or loosely linked to car-related applications. Therefore, these

© Springer International Publishing AG 2017
O. Gervasi et al. (Eds.): ICCSA 2017, Part IV, LNCS 10407, pp. 626–637, 2017.
DOI: 10.1007/978-3-319-62401-3_45

amounts of sensor data can help to identify and analyse hidden (urban) phenomena or to intensify existing databases. Prerequisites are a wide range of developments including communication models, such as vehicle-to-vehicle (v2v), vehicle-to-infrastructure (v2i), or vehicle-to-x (v2x) communication. In this context, so-called Extended Floating Car Data (XFCD) expand the existing concept of Floating Car Data (FCD). In fact, that XFCD data will play a pivotal role in future data-driven automobile developments. Currently cars are being turned into interconnected sensors (or, in other words, decentralized sensor networks) that collect and provide a vast amount of mobile data on vehicles, vehicle drivers, routes, traffic, transport infrastructure, and the environment. The enormous value of this massive data stock (big data) has only recently been recognized by the industry [2]. Because of ongoing developments, such as autonomous cars, (extended) floating car data will have a significant impact on our everyday life.

The ongoing research work presented in this paper aims at using the available automotive sensor data (XFCD in particular) as geodata to facilitate spatio-temporal analysis and geo-visualization for different application contexts, such as city climatology or traffic management evaluation. The overall aim is to aid the analysis e.g. of individual driving styles, environmental behaviour, or environmental conditions in a traffic network. For this an integrated and modular process framework (both on concept and implementation level) has been developed to handle XFCD based on the well-known visualization pipeline.

2   Car-Based Traffic Data

At the beginning, it is necessary to deal in more detail with the fundamentals of mobility respectively traffic data in general as well as the concepts of the specific data used in this ongoing research work. The recording of traffic data (specifically of automobiles) can be divided into the general recording of traffic and the recording of individual car routes or trajectories through incremental spatio-temporal tracking of a vehicle's position (e.g. by GPS [Global Positioning System]) in a given traffic network. Data on general traffic is mainly acquired by the monitoring of traffic flow (e.g. by induction loops, photoelectric barriers, camera surveillance systems). Constant traffic flow monitoring needs a network of localized and, in most cases, costly sensors. Individual FCD are taken by mobile sensors on random trajectories over defined time spans. Given the availability of multitudes of automotive sensor data, an obvious option is to examine whether individual FCD can augment and enhance the existing stationary traffic flow data. It can be assumed that by merging stationary point and linear mobile data a broader and deeper database will be available for promoting traffic-related research, applications and decision-making. The following sections are dedicated to individual (non-stationary) recoding procedures with special alignment to the concepts of FCD and XFCD as well as their technical implications and specifications.

2.1 Floating Car Data (FCD)

FCD record geo-positions and timestamps of the semantic parameters incrementally recorded during car drives. The result is a geo-located dataset of individual vehicle-operating states and selected environmental data for an individual space-time trajectory within the overall road traffic system [3]. According to this conception, the composition of a FCD data set can be described as follows:

$$FCD = position(coordinates) + time(timestamp) \tag{1}$$

The more FCD are generated, the more the database of the overall data system will grow, the more trajectories can be analyzed, and the more relevant the analysis result will tend to be. In this massive database single vehicles generating FCD can be identified as samples to access and evaluate the overall traffic situation. From a technical perspective, the main component of the FCD system is the so-called On Board Unit (OBU). The OBU is located in the vehicle. It features data binding (e.g. via the mobile phone network GSM [Global System for Mobile Communication]) and a central system or server to which the information is sent through programmed algorithms.

FCD data sets are point data determined by the acquisition at an incrementally defined position of the vehicle (geospatial reference) at an incrementally defined time (time reference). The spatial and temporal components of these data can be subjected to further processing [4]. For instance, travel time and driving progress can be calculated, the velocity of an individual vehicle can be determined, and so can the individual driving style regarding acceleration or braking. Information derived from the bulk of individual car data can help predict regional traffic status in an overall traffic system by the use of statistical methods. It needs to be noted that a large number of vehicles equipped with FCD systems is mandatory for any reliable automotive database compiled from individual recordings. Vehicle fleets, such as cab or bus fleets, provide the required data and are, hence, often used for traffic data acquisition.

2.2 Extended Floating Car Data (XFCD)

Already in the late 1990s, the German automotive company BMW developed the extension of an FCD concept by on-board sensor data from car electronics, permanently recording car aggregates' conditions. Without endorsing the commercial specification of BMW, it can be stated that XFCD amply demonstrates the potential generated by connecting FCD to spatio-temporal parameter recordings with aggregate status monitoring. In this manner XFCD can also be considered as typical FCD data sets extended with vehicle sensor data (one or more sensor device parameters combined with spatio-temporal reference):

$$XFCD = position(coordinates) + time(timestamp) + sensordata \tag{2}$$

$$XFCD = FCD + sensordata \tag{3}$$

In fact, all information on automotive electronics (such as ABS, ESP, rain sensors, etc.) is being used and analysed for different situations (traffic, weather, roads conditions, etc.). Along with other car manufacturers, BMW already produces modern cars equipped with specific OBUs and interconnection with the technical (cloud) infrastructure of the respective manufacturer. In this way modern automobile vehicles itself become mobile sensors (or sensor nodes) and are forming wide so-called geosensor networks (GSN): "a wireless sensor network that monitors phenomena in geographic space. [...]. A sensor is any device for measuring the physical qualities of the environment, such as humidity, CO_2 concentration [...]. Sensors effectively convert environmental stimuli, such as heat, light or electromagnetic radiations, into digital signals that can be processed by a computer" [5]. A division of the sensor devices can be achieved for example by a categorization according the sensors stimuli (e.g. in six categories: acoustic, chemical, electromagnetic, optical, thermal and mechanical). The common ground of all these possible car sensor data or parameters is given through the spatio-temporal relation of XFCD which allows a wide range of analysis applications [6].

2.3   Data Acquisition and Availability

Today, modern automobiles are equipped with an ever-growing number of car sensors. It can rightly be said that cars have turned into mobile sensors. Event and status data constantly recorded cannot only be used for traffic-related issues, such as traffic monitoring, but also for environmental issues, such as particulate emissions. Moreover, XFCD facilitate the development and implementation of traffic services. It is obvious that these data (and applications based on these) are of particular interest to groups or individual users which include:

- Private users or end-user,
- Planners (e.g. traffic and environment planning),
- Managers (e.g. fleet management),
- Decision-makers (e.g. politics and administration),
- Industry players (e.g. automaker, insurer).

In this context the question arise show mobility data in sense of XFCD can be acquired and used for different applications. In previous research work [7, 8] we could show that the acquisition of XFCD can performed within a smartphone-based approach and direct access to the vehicle data-bus, by using the mandatory On Board Diagnosis (OBD) interface. OBD is required by law in most countries of the world as gateway to the vehicle electronics system. On the smartphone, a mobile application is used for communication with the OBD hardware/interface to retrieve data (e.g. at defined time increments). This smartphone-based mobile application augments the acquired OBD data with real-time GPS coordinates and a time stamp of the respective acquisition time. The XFCD generated are either cached or transmitted from the automobile (identifiable by its vehicle identification number [VIN]) to an internet-connected server. Processing of the collected car sensor data on the server-side was used which significant increase data quality and content. Among the procedures applied the following operations are briefly named: map matching, generation of trajectories (polylines from point data), and anonymization. The last stage of the process allows the user to utilize the server-based application via the web browser (cross-platform). In addition, a complete visualization concept has been developed to fit the specific needs and (visual) analysis needs for predefined application scenarios, such as monitoring of traffic and environment.

Visualizations include cartographic presentations, user interface, and interaction design. For its generation, prototyping techniques, wireframes, and mock-ups were used. The outlined procedure provides a potential way for private users and small- to middle mid-sized car fleets to access the automotive electronics systems and collect spatio-temporal sensor data (XFCD). This is only limited by the availability of the in-vehicle sensor devices and the command set to access them. It is assumed that this possibility will be more widely used in the future. In this context it should be noted that the recently launched crowdfunding project "Macchina M2" [9], which provides an open and modular hardware platform for OBD access, gains in a short time more than triple of the required funding sum.

Open-Source projects (e.g. regarding open hardware and software platforms) can achieve a big contribution to enable and disseminate this data and its application for a wider public (and thus provide for everyone interested an insight in their own vehicles data). However, it can be assumed that the larger amount of this data treasure is already present at side of the car manufacturers companies. Unfortunately, these databases are currently widely locked for the interested public (e.g. for research and planning). Seen for the current situation in Europe (European Union) there exists at least one project which tries to initiate the necessary developments from a business orientated perspective. For example, the 'Automat' project (funded by the European Union's Horizon 2020 research and innovation program) aims to develop a common standardized data format for interchange (as necessary basis technical), a marketplace platform (and thus a monetarization possibility for the data), as well as service scenarios for innovative business ideas. This includes the following development objectives (selection) [10]:

- Creation of an open ecosystem for provisioning of manufacturer and service provider independent vehicle data
- Single point of data access for service providers via the Marketplace
- Definition of standardized and open interfaces for unconstrained data access
- Specification of the Common Vehicle Information Model (CVIM) data format that enables harmonized, generic vehicle data access
- Definition and prototyping of Vehicle Big Data Marketplace concept as mediator between vehicle data and cross-sectorial service providers

As long as these basic requirements for a general use and exchange of the data (which also includes legal questions about the data authorship/copyright) are not established, the car manufacturer companies, in particular, are in a preferred initial position. Of these, transparency and data protection (also effective data anonymization in particular) as well as standardization of data models prove to be problematic. To date, the largely proprietary nature of these data is already seriously affecting data exchange and wider data use in industry and science contexts.

3   Research Context

In order to produce effective visualizations from vehicle sensor data for traffic-related and environmental applications, demands and needs of the different targeted user groups have been discussed (in qualitative empirical form) with informed representatives (from research and commercial organizations). Utilizing the expertise gathered, their positive response indicates that visualizations based on spatio-temporal XFCD or geospatial databases augmented with these car sensor data are important to present and analyze car and traffic-related topics as well as for environmental issues.

It has been stated that effective cartographic visualization of these data facilitates decision-making processes in the respective application fields. To provide a context-aware formalization of the visualization generation process, which adequately deals with the technical implementation of the visualization process, the well-known visualization pipeline [11] is adapted in this ongoing research work. The visualization pipeline controls the processing of raw geospatial input data to generate a map graphic output through a sequence of processes, namely filtering, mapping and rendering (Fig. 1).

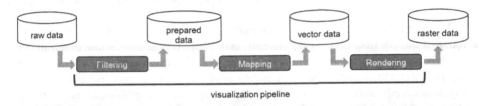

Fig. 1.   Schematic illustration of the visualization-pipeline and –process, adapted from [11].

It is obvious that the effective visualization of data is largely determined by the filtering component (included in XFCD). The mapping and rendering components are driven by rule bases from data-to-graphic conversion (vector data) and graphic-to-image conversion (raster data), respectively. Both rule sets are based on well-established map modelling principles of thematic cartography.

Applying the visualization pipeline to generate effective map graphics of traffic data can result in recurrent filtering, transformation and visualization tasks. These can be aggregated to patterns comprising a sequence of tasks and managed in a pattern library. Subject to the respective visualization goal, the visualization rule base determines the application and combination of patterns and additional single tasks to be executed automatically. The concept of design or GeoViz patterns [12] can be adapted for the development of car sensor data visualization patterns. In order to generate spatio-temporal visualizations based on cartographic methods and principles in a systematic way, the visualization process can be formalized and automated (Fig. 2).

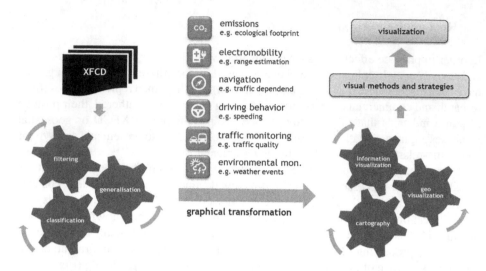

Fig. 2. Potential approach for formalization of manufacturing process (scheme).

The present has to be stated that this work directly connects to related research in automated quality map production systems, esp. [13]. The authors show that a major challenge is the integration of the GIS (Geographic Information System, a software system designed to capture, store, manipulate, analyze, manage, and display geographically referenced data) and VIS (Visualization System, a graphic-oriented software system providing wide-ranging drawing and design functions to emulate conventional map production, in which maps are stored as graphic data files only) components involved in the production process (for dynamic quality map-based visualizations). We consider the application of rule-based systems an appropriate way to automatically generate effective visualizations. Decision diagrams (as well as their connection and combination) help to formulate and display a set of decision rules required for the visualization process. In addition, we employ methods of software engineering, such as design patterns or libraries, service oriented architecture, and model view controller (MVC), together with a rule-based approach, to solve the issue. It has to be noted, however, that such approach is rather complex and will require additional research work.

4   Integrated Framework Approach

For a start, we devise a twofold approach by defining a 'conceptual' and an 'implementational' level. Combined, both will build an integrated framework approach. This will mean a direct transferability from the conceptual to the practical-oriented level. To do so, objects, parameters and processes need to be formalized to ensure generic usability. This facilitates context-aware adaptions, in particular, the interlacing of GIS and VIS process components. Included are the unification (or harmonization) of different data sources, which requires the creation of commonalities (on the basis of a common geodata model and the transfer to a common geodatabase storage or GDB) to provide for the generation of a primary (GIS/data) and secondary (VIS/map) representation model of the XFCD. While this research is currently an ongoing work in progress, we briefly outline relevant aspects of this framework below.

4.1 Conceptual Level

On a conceptual level, tasks and operations to be performed in the visualization process are defined. In loose analogy to the visualization pipeline these can be grouped by its function, namely data storage (database engine), data filtering (data querying engine), mapping (generation of vector data) and rendering (generation of raster data). In a more granular perspective, the main components and its modules can be listed as follows:

"(GIS) Data & Analysis" component

- preprocessing (of imported geodata to build a common geodata model),
- structuring (of imported geodatato storeinto a common geodatabase),
- modelling (of geodata in geodatabase to build a common GIS/data primary model).

"(VIS) Map Composition" component

- symbolization (allocation to graphical primitives),
- generalization (of imported data for map output),
- charts (generation and integration of linked charts),
- map composition (generation of professional map output),
- visualization composition (generation of interface and interaction elements output in dependence to map composition).

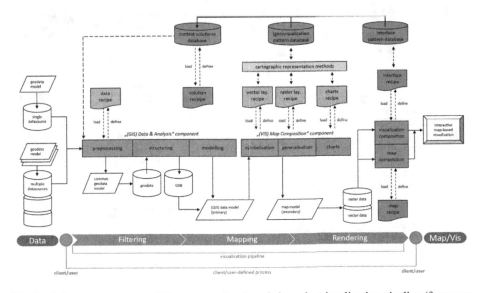

Fig. 3. Schematic overview of the process developed along the visualization pipeline (from raw data input to visualization output).

These components and their modules are to be used as generic building blocks in the visualization process (Fig. 3).

In part, this components-based approach can be aggregated by developing what we term rule-based visualization patterns. This reflects the fact that the seemingly abundant number of possible (cartographic) visualization options can be condensed to a limited number of recurring pattern solutions. Such patterns represent sample solutions or "recipe" for identical or similar visualization tasks. Visualization patterns are stored and managed in a pattern library. Depending on the visualization targeted solution, the patterns required are combined in an automated process. Any resulting pattern set can be characterized as a specific rule set applicable to a range of similar map visualizations. Different combinations of patterns from the pattern library allow for the visualization of a variety of geospatial data in various contexts or use cases.

The generation of a professional map output for a given topic is defined by a corresponding rule set or 'map recipe'. It consists of four sub-recipes with the following contents:

- data (selection, filtering and process of input data)
- vector layers (design and generation of vector layers for map output)
- raster layers (design and generation of raster layers for map output)
- charts (generation of charts liked to map data/content)

The generation of the interface and interaction elements of the visualization is defined by a 'interface recipe' which is connected and related to the 'map recipe'. The top-level of these rule sets is determinate by a 'solution recipe' in order to model individual application contexts. The resulting pattern libraries are eventually grouped into pattern databases for a better storage and management (Fig. 4).

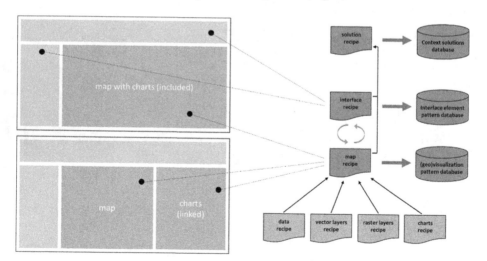

Fig. 4. Schematic overview of the use of pattern-based "recipes" for visualization tasks.

4.2   Implementational Level

On an implementation level, we define the technical implementation of the concept of visualizations pattern. The main task here is to separate the technical structure into a 'data core' (a raw database or -source) and a context-specific 'application shell' (analysis and visualization). This facilitates the adaptation of the above process to different application contexts. Resulting from the functional component structure adapted from the visualization pipeline it is possible to select and integrate any software application (open-source or proprietary) that complies with the component requirements (e.g. for faster generation), by encapsulating it into individual, connected services or modularized architecture. This concept draws on the recent software development paradigm of microservices, which we consider a powerful alternative to the traditional concept monolithic software architecture [14]. Using a microservice approach, we can directly transform the concept of visualization pattern into a technical implementation. Based on innovative software technologies, such as application virtualization (with application containers, e.g. environments like Docker, LXC), substantial flexibility is possible when it comes to, e.g.:

- Highly distributable operating,
- Platform-independent operation,
- Vertical and horizontal scalability,
- Exchangeability of the involved components.

Interchange between these (application-container based) microservices is facilitated by standardized interfaces and data formats (like REST, JSON). To connect, control, and manage individual services across the complete visualization process workflow, two strategies can be followed: service orchestration (centralized) and service choreography (decentralized) [15]. To achieve the advantage in flexibility mentioned above, a service choreography (e.g. with event stream) is investigated as a potential solution in further research work (Fig. 5).

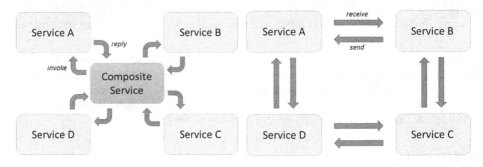

Fig. 5. Schematic illustration of "Service Orchestration" (left) vs. "Service Choreography" (right).

5   Conclusion and Outlook

This paper presents a concept to process and visualize car sensor data (XFCD, FCD), automatically acquired by a vehicle's onboard electronics while driving. It has been shown that these data possess an implicit spatio-temporal reference, in addition to their semantic attributes, thus allowing for geospatial analysis and visualization. XFCD, in particular, provide information on the current environmental situation in the geographic space, e.g. urban areas, passed through, either recorded directly or calculated during data processing. This way, a substantial amount of car sensor data can be collected and made available to further server- or client-side processing and subsequent analysis in various application fields, among which environmental issues rank first.

By now, FCD are already in use for traffic monitoring. XFCD, the extension of the FCD concept, allow a wide range of further applications, both on- and off-board. The environmental data recorded by XFCD outside a vehicle can be considered an added value, allowing for the spatio-temporal environmental analysis of road networks and their surrounding space. Applications include emissions, surrounding air quality, temperature or pressure. Provision and processing of the data mentioned can help to improve traffic and environmental planning issues and decision-making. We have shown that the visualization of floating vehicle sensor data can unlock access to these data for various audiences and applications by making them visible and thus perceptible to humans.

Hence visualization literally puts man as an actor into an original machine-to-machine communication setting. This way, data acquired without a car driver's involvement and/or knowledge are returned to use by its generators (in this case: car drivers) or a wider public. To make this succeed, the standardization of data recording and output is needed. Moreover, it is also crucial that the data are not only available to the car manufacturers or, to a lesser extent, insurance companies. From the research conducted so far, we conclude that it is essential to put the car driver, the active human generator of floating car data, into a position not only to determine its utilization but also gain insight into "his" data. This paper demonstrates that geo-visualization can play a useful role in communicating the information and making it available to further investigation.

Acknowledgements. This research work is part of a PhD project funded by the German Research Foundation (DFG) in the research training group 1539 "Visibility and Visualization - Hybrid Forms of Pictorial Knowledge" at the University of Potsdam. This support is gratefully acknowledged. The PhD project is supervised by Professors Dr. HartmutAsche (University of Potsdam) and Dr. Frank Heidmann (Potsdam University of Applied Sciences).

References

1. Nelson, P.: Just one autonomous car will use 4,000 GB of data/day. In: Network World. IDG Enterprise, Framingham (2016). http://www.networkworld.com/article/3147892/internet/one-autonomous-car-will-use-4000-gb-of-dataday.html. Accessed 05 2017

2. McKinsey: Big data: The Next Frontier for Innovation, Competition, and Productivity. McKinsey Global Institute, McKinsey & Company Inc., New York (2011). http://www.mckinsey.com/business-functions/business-technology/our-insights/big-data-the-next-frontier-for-innovation. Accessed 05 2017
3. Lorkowski, S.: Erste Mobilitätsdienste auf Basis von Floating Car Data. In: Beckmann, S., et al. (eds.) Stadt, Region, Land - 4. Aachener Kolloqium "Mobilität und Stadt" (AMUS). Institut für Stadtbauwesen der RWTH, Aachen (2003)
4. Treiber, M., Kesting, A.: Traffic Flow Dynamics – Data, Models and Simulation. Springer, Berlin (2013)
5. Duckham, M.: Decentralized Spatial Computing – Foundations of Geosensor Networks. Springer, Berlin (2013)
6. Schneider, S., et al.: Extended floating car data in co-operative traffic management. In: Barceló, J., Kuwahara, M. (eds.) Traffic Data Collection and its Standardization, pp. 161–170. Springer, New York. (2010)
7. Voland, P.: Webbasierte Visualisierung von Extended Floating Car Data (XFCD) - Ein Ansatz zur raumzeitlichen Visualisierung und technischen Implementierung mit Open Source Software unter spezieller Betrachtung des Umwelt- und Verkehrsmonitoring. Master thesis, University of Potsdam (2014). https://publishup.uni-potsdam.de/frontdoor/index/index/docId/9675. Accessed 05 2017
8. Voland, P.: Processing and geo-visualization of spatio-temporal sensor data from connected automotive electronics systems. In: Gervasi, O., Murgante, B., Misra, S., Rocha, A.M.A.C., Torre, C., Taniar, D., Apduhan, Bernady O., Stankova, E., Wang, S. (eds.) ICCSA 2016. LNCS, vol. 9788, pp. 290–305. Springer, Cham (2016). doi:10.1007/978-3-319-42111-7_23
9. Macchina Project: Introduction to M2. Macchina LCC, Minneapolis (2017). https://www.macchina.cc/m2-introduction. Accessed 05 2017
10. Automat Project. Automotive Big Data Marketplace for Innovative Cross-sectorial Vehicle Data Services. Project Coordination, Volkswagen AG (VW), Wolfsburg (2017). http://www.automat-project.eu/tags/project-description. Accessed 05 2017
11. Haber, R.B., McNabb, D.: Visualization idioms: a conceptual model for scientific visualization systems. In: Nielson, G., Shriver, B. (eds.) Visualization in Scientific Computing. IEEE Computer Society Press, Los Alamitos (1990)
12. Heidmann, F.: Interaktive Karten und Geovisualisierungen. In: Weber, W., Burmeister, H., Tille, R. (eds.) Interaktive Infografiken, pp. 66–67. Springer, Berlin (2013)
13. Asche, H., Engemaier, R.: From concept to implementation: web-based cartographic visualisation with cartoservice. In: Murgante, B., Gervasi, O., Misra, S., Nedjah, N., Rocha, A.M.A.C., Taniar, D., Apduhan, Bernady O. (eds.) ICCSA 2012. LNCS, vol. 7334, pp. 414–424. Springer, Heidelberg (2012). doi:10.1007/978-3-642-31075-1_31
14. Newman, S.: Building Microservices – Designing Fine-Grained Systems. O'Reilly Media Inc., Sebastopol (2015)
15. Peltz, C.: Web services orchestration and choreography. In: IEEE Computer, Issue January, vol. 36. IEEE Computer Society, Los Alamitos (2003)

Making Sense of Spatial Relationships Trough Local Knowledge Discovery in Social Media

Pasquale Balena[1](✉) ⓘ, Alessandro Bonifazi[1,2] ⓘ, Dino Borri[1],
and Caterina De Lucia[3]

[1] Polytechnic of Bari, Via Orabona 4, 70125 Bari, Italy
{pasquale.balena,dino.borri}@poliba.it
[2] ITERAS – Research Centre for Sustainability and Territorial Innovation,
Via C. Colombo 40, 70126 Bari, Italy
alessandro.bonifazi@iteras.org
[3] University of Foggia, Largo Papa Giovanni Paolo II 1, 71100 Foggia, Italy
caterina.delucia@unifg.it

Abstract. Over time, theories, models and methods have used scientific knowledge and structured data to model the relationships occurring across agents and places in a variety of domains. Recently, the diffusion of Social Networks is opening new research scenarios. Huge flows of data are being made available from Social Networks which contribute to the diffusion of local knowledge and to unravel several complex system dynamics.

The present work aims at advancing the understanding of how spatial relationships embedded in natural language communications may help harness local knowledge in planning- and decision-making processes. To that purpose, we developed a pilot study on disaster response in the Metropolitan Area of Bari (Italy), by administering an on-line survey focussed on social media use in emergency situations.

Main results suggest that the correct interpretation of local knowledge-laden natural language becomes a challenging problem when the role of tacit or implicit knowledge is taken into account. We argue in favour of acknowledging the importance of local knowledge for a full understanding of spatial relationships and calls for implementing spatial data science tools in such a way that local and tacit knowledge (including vernacular forms) may be adequately understood.

Keywords: Local knowledge · Spatial relationships · Social media · Natural language

1 Introduction

The current state of the art in information and decision studies highlights a long-term intellectual deadlock about local knowledge, which might explain why the international scientific community tends to refrain from carrying out (or to ignore the few existing) studies on local knowledge in several domains. On the one hand, this marginalization is due to long-standing cultural traditions in several scientific disciplines, which emphasize expert knowledge rather than local knowledge; on the other hand, the

© Springer International Publishing AG 2017
O. Gervasi et al. (Eds.): ICCSA 2017, Part IV, LNCS 10407, pp. 638–651, 2017.
DOI: 10.1007/978-3-319-62401-3_46

importance of technical-methodological complexities is such that local knowledge seems to be less attractive than expert knowledge from a computational point of view.

Over the last few years, the institutional attention towards public participation in urban and regional governance has gained momentum. Thus, the international scientific debate is becoming more interested in local knowledge as a key factor in collaborative decision-making processes. The recent evolution of Information and Communication Technology (ICT) and mobile devices has strongly encouraged public e-participation as a tool for decision-support systems. In the framework of environmental and spatial planning, most of these e-participation tools fall within the domain of Participatory Geographic Information System (PGIS). Recently, the use of these e-participation tools has also extended to several domains – such as natural disasters, humanitarian crises, political conflicts – with the main aim to help affected populations and provide useful information for survival.

Nonetheless, e-participation tools present some drawbacks for managing non-structured information retrieved from large databases and Social Networks. The limitations concern either the need to understand knowledge in (almost) real time and to share it with experts and decision makers, or to facilitate mutual understanding in the context of those events – such as humanitarian crises and natural disasters – that mobilize heterogeneous cultures, languages and organizations.

The present research dwells on the above limitations, to tie information, analysis, interpretation and sharing of local knowledge. The rationale of the work conducted in the present study arises from early results of a recent research [1] on disaster response. Based on a simulation analysis using social networks in which participants were asked to write a message with a request for/offer to help, in the aftermath of an earthquake, the author argues that the respondent makes use of several references to indicate a specific spatial location based on his/her local knowledge. Also, these spatial references are not available and cannot be retrieved from any geographical database.

The paper is structured as follows: Sect. 2 briefly reviews the forms of knowledge with a particular emphasis on local knowledge; Sect. 3 illustrates a discussion on the role of local knowledge in current literature and dwells on the analysis of spatial relationships embedded in natural language communications; Sect. 4 depicts the pilot survey carried out in the Metropolitan area of Bari (Southern Italy) using social media; and Sect. 4, covering a brief discussion on how local knowledge about spatial relationships may be harnessed in planning- and decision-making processes, concludes the paper.

2   Forms of Knowledge

Over time, researchers have treated and compared different types of knowledge, although they have been always aware that there is no borderline that can be used to sort knowledge into clear-cut classes. Nonetheless, knowledge may be articulated under several forms.

To this end, the study by [2], although originally aimed at reviewing the different understanding of knowledge in the field of environmental management, covers several

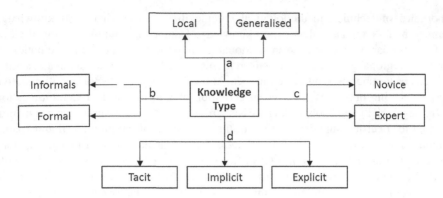

Fig. 1. Dimensions of knowledge types derived from the environmental management literature. Adapted from [2]

aspects that are relevant to our analysis. Figure 1 summarises the four main types of knowledge, which can be delineated as follows:

a. *Local* and *Generalised* knowledge which focuses on spatial aspects;
b. *Formal* and *Informal* knowledge which focuses on legal/administrative aspects;
c. *Novice* and *Expert* knowledge which focuses on the dimension/background aspects of knowledge;
d. *Tacit, Implicit* and *Explicit* knowledge which focuses on the degree of knowledge expression.

For the purposes of the present work, *Local, Informal, Novice* and *Tacit* knowledge play an important role since they are strongly rooted in the personal (and emotional) sphere of an individual, and hence difficult to formalise, share and transfer. The remaining forms of knowledge such as *Generalised, Formal, Expert* and *Explicit* are generally easier to understand and analyse because they incorporate words and numbers, scientific formulas, specifications, manuals [3–5].

It should be stressed that it is possible to have combinations between two or more forms of knowledge. For example, knowledge can simultaneously be treated as *Local, Expert* and *Informal*. Other scholars have instead framed the forms of knowledge as local, scientific and hybrid [2]. The author specifies the existence of two sub-categories of local knowledge: 'Personal Experience' and 'Traditional Cultural Rules and Norm'. Recently, it is this level of disaggregation that has received attention in the international literature. A detailed description of each relevant type of knowledge as classified by [2] is provided below. For the purposes of the present work, the term Local knowledge is used to include all such forms of knowledge.

Personal

This is a form of knowledge based on (individual) experiential processes that can be distinguished into different forms [4, 6].

Lay
It refers to informal knowledge which reflects the most common interpretation given by individuals about a specific situation [7–9].

Local or situated
This is a form of knowledge based on the understanding of local phenomena. It is often used to distinguish it from external expert knowledge. The latter, although rich in technical experience and expertise, lacks local views and nuances [10–12].

Tacit
It is an unconscious knowledge that is often latent, difficult to express. Therefore, it has a significant influence on the individual thinking and behaviour, because it is deep and closely linked to each person's worldviews, values, personal experiences and expertise [4, 10, 13].

Implicit
This form of knowledge is rooted in an individual but it is not accessible to others. It differs from tacit knowledge because it can be expressed [4, 14]. Some authors, including [15], argue that no difference exists between the two forms of knowledge (implicit and tacit), and that these are part of the same concept.

Informal
It is similar to personal and tacit knowledge. It refers to the knowledge acquired with different experiences, without structured processes (such as rules and procedures) and which is aimed at improving understanding and learning [16–18].

Non Expert, Novice
This form of knowledge generally does not incorporate the depth of experience and expertise which, in contrast, are clear features of expert knowledge [3, 4].

Expert
It is a form of knowledge which is represented by the degree of experience of an individual gained over the years through practice, not necessarily formalized in scientific frameworks or structured processes [19, 20].

Indigenous
Is it exclusively related to a specific culture and social groups, or indigenous peoples [21–23].

Traditional
It can be classified as a local knowledge handed down across generations [22, 23].

Specific knowledge is rooted in local populations and is important in response to complex systems such as, for example: (i) balancing natural, bio and climatic systems; (ii) conserving biodiversity to promote risk mitigation and to reduce vulnerability of territories; (iii) strengthening resilience to natural, climatic and environmental disasters [12, 22, 24, 25]. Also, specific knowledge is the result of experiences, awareness and sensitivity. Hence, it interweaves biophysical and social contexts, it facilitates the understanding of several local phenomena and it allows the assessment of priority interventions – as implemented through regional government policies and management practices [26, 27].

3   Understanding Local Knowledge of Spatial Locations from Natural Language Communications

As mentioned in Sect. 1, the present study is based on early results of a simulation analysis [1] on disaster response in the Municipality of Bari (Southern Italy) conducted in October 2016. The results suggested that specific elements of the natural and built environment in which respondents live (i.e., the city of Bari and its surroundings) assume some particular forms of natural language, often characterised by a poor lexical apparatus. Some information on spatial locations take the form of local or situational knowledge; and are considered as such only from those who are accustomed with that particular space, place or territory. The respondents assume that who is listening to their requests of help has the same tacit or implicit knowledge of spatial locations as the sender of the text message. A natural language of places and locations which cannot be retrieved from any geo-database.

In some specific contexts, such as risk or emergency domains, those who write a text message do not take into account the chance that the reader of the message could be unable to interpret the message correctly because he/she does not belong to that specific local community. The interpretation of text messages becomes even more complex if one considers that actual PGIS are not provided with intelligent systems which are able to retrieve data from local knowledge.

Suppose one wanted to extract information relating to the spatial location of a person who asks for help by sending a message on a social network. Messages captured via streaming processing could potentially incorporate the geographic location[1]. Recent literature suggests that 0.42% of posts contain GPS information [28] Information on the spatial or geographical location is provided directly (e.g. geographic coordinates, addresses) or indirectly by natural language (e.g. indication of known places). The latter case also occurs when additional topological indications are provided such as a position relative to a known place or object or area: For example 'Help! I am next to Saint Sabino church'. In this case 'church' (an object) defined as non-delimited space corresponds to thousands points on a map. 'Saint Sabino' is an instance of the church and its features make the church unique in a confined space. The spatial location is not always reported in a text message. This is because the user, in most cases, assumes that the reader knows about an event and the place where it has happened.

Much more complex is the conceptualization of spatial relationships, which, in the example above, are defined by the string 'next to'. Complexity arises because the word 'next to', often considered as an 'empty word', is central in several domains, particularly those related to emergency responses. Text analysis software usually confront

---

[1] This is true in the case in which the message is sent from a device equipped with GPS and the application used to send the post is turned on. The user authorises the activation of the application.

users with default dictionaries containing a list of empty words. However, there exist empty words that combined with others contribute to define a meaning.

In the Italian language, this is particularly true for the case of simple prepositions: 'di, a, da, in, con, su, per, tra, fra' (of, to, from, in, with, above/upon/on, for, between) and compound prepositions such as: 'dal, dalla, dagli, dallo, del' (from the). Similarly, for 'improper prepositions' such as: 'davanti' (or 'davanti a') (in front or in front of), 'dietro' (or 'dietro a') (behind), 'dopo' (after), 'fuori' (outside), 'lontano' (far), 'lungo' (along), 'mediante' (through), 'prima' ('prima che' or 'prima di') (before), 'sopra' (or 'sopra a') (above), 'sotto' (or 'sotto a') (below).

In the example above, if one considers a sequence of words where the preposition 'next to' is placed between two nouns, he/she obtains: 'The house next to the church'. Should the word 'to the' be considered as non-important, the remaining word 'next' could be mis-interpreted as an adjective of 'house'. This problem could cause loss of spatial location content in the text message. Similarly, this is the case for simple prepositions such as 'da' (from) and 'a' (to) that from a spatial point of view indicate a direction.

The methods to handle, retrieve and analyse information on spatial location from natural language are presented in next section.

4 Methodology

This section depicts a qualitative analysis carried out in the city of Bari (Southern Italy) with the adoption of an on-line survey using social media. The pilot survey pursues the following aims: i. To test local knowledge on given landmarks and help determine the spatial location of a random population; ii. To provide further information from local knowledge and improve the services offered by the spatial information system; iii. To determine the existence of local/tacit knowledge in natural language communications about spatial location; iv. To demonstrate the existence of subjective knowledge in the perception of spaces; v. To support the usefulness of natural language to the understanding of local knowledge in several domains (e.g. humanitarian crises, political fights, natural disasters).

The survey is structured to retrieve information on the use of natural language and to respond to the above aims. The first five questions inquire on terms such as 'the entrance of', 'end of street', 'in front of', 'behind' which may prove ambiguous when used to determine a specific spatial location. These terms refer to landmarks in Bari such as the 'Fiera del Levante' (Eastern Fairground), 'La Muraglia' (The Wall), 'Basilica di San Nicola' (Basilica of Saint Nicholas), Teatro Petruzzelli' (Petruzzelli Theatre), and 'Parco 2 Giugno' (2 June Park). Figures 2, 3, 4, 5 and 6 show the questions related to the above landmarks.

Each question also comprises a 3D-picture of the landmark taken by Google Map with the indication of the possible alternatives.

Figure 2 shows the following question: 'A person that you know asks for your help and he/she says that he/she is at the entrance of the Eastern Fairground. Which of the marked entrances would you reach to help your friend?'. The question clearly indicates the spatial location of the entrances (points B, G, R, M) on a geo-referenced map as well as shows a picture of each of the entrances.

Figure 3 asks respondents the following: 'A person that you know asks for your help and he/she says that he/she is at the end of the 'Wall' ('La Muraglia'). Which of the marked entrances would you reach to help your friend?' The question indicates the location of the entrances (points X, J and the 'do not know' alternative) and shows the pictures of each of the entrances.

Figure 4 asks respondents to provide an answer about their location with respect to the Cathedral of Saint Nicholas: 'A person that you know asks for your help and he/she says that he/she is in front of the Cathedral of Saint Nicholas. Which of the three marked entrances would you reach to help your friend?' The question indicates the location of the entrances (B, G, R) and shows the pictures of each of the entrances.

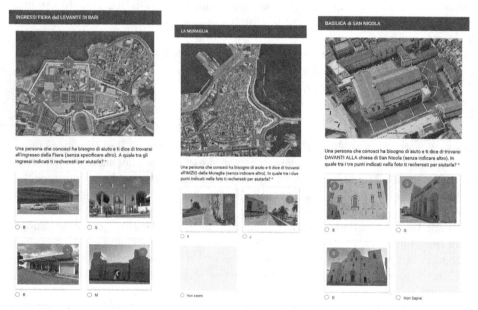

Fig. 2. Question 1 of the pilot-survey

Fig. 3. Question 2 of the pilot-survey

Fig. 4. Question 3 of the pilot-survey

Figure 5 asks respondents an enquiry about the Petruzzelli Theatre: 'A person that you know asks for your help and says that he/she is behind the Petruzzelli Theatre. Which of the four marked entrances would you reach to help your friend?' The question indicates the location of the entrances (B, G, R, M) and shows the pictures of each entrance.

Fig. 5. Question 4 of the pilot-survey

Fig. 6. Question 5 of the pilot-survey

Fig. 7. Question 6 of the pilot-survey

Figure 6 asks respondents an enquiry about a city park: 'A person that you know asks for your help and he/she says that he/she is in the building in front of the entrance of "2 June" Park. Which of the three marked entrances would you reach to help your friend?' The question indicates the location of the entrances (B, G, R, and the 'do not know' alternative) and shows pictures of each entrance.

The last three questions of the survey were designed to retrieve information on the use of the words 'near to/far from' (Figs. 7 and 8) and 'nearby' (Fig. 9). Figures 7 and 8 refer to 'Corso Vittorio Emanuele' (Vittorio Emanuele Avenue) one of the main streets in Bari; and Fig. 9 refers to the Central Station.

In particular, a first question (see Fig. 7) asked respondents the following statement: 'You are at the beginning of Vittorio Emanuele Street (next to Garibaldi Garden). A tourist asks you for the location of the Margherita Theatre. You tell him/her that he/she is at the end of the street and that the Theatre is: very near, quite near, near, quite far, far, very far, do not know'. The question that follows (Fig. 8) tests respondents on the perception of the distance between his/her/the tourist's location and that of the Margherita Theatre. Respondents provide an answer by choosing among 9 distance options (from 250 m-to more than 2 km) and the 'do not know' alternative.

Finally, Fig. 9 shows the last question which captures an understanding of the term 'nearby' by respondents. The figure shows a location of the Bari Central Station and ten ring zones. Each zone is 100 m distant from the station. In particular, the question

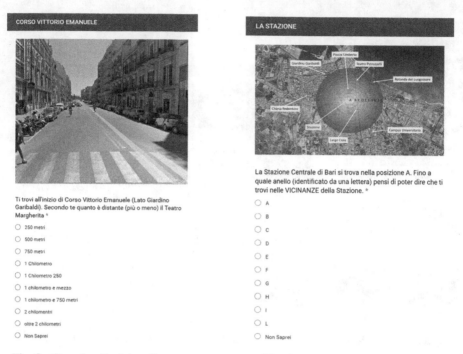

Fig. 8. Question 7 of the pilot-survey   **Fig. 9.** Question 8 of the pilot-survey

asks the following statement: 'Bari Central Station is located in A. Which area (identified by a letter) do you think can be defined as being nearby the station?'. The map also indicates some outlier landmarks such as Chiesa Redentore (Redentore Church), Giardino Garibaldi (Garibaldi Park) and Campus Universitario (University Campus).

5   Local Knowledge and Spatial Relationships: A Pilot Survey in the Municipality of Bari (Southern Italy)

The pilot-survey is based on a random sample of 150 people living in Bari. The final sample comprises of 123 observations after removing duplicates and incomplete records. Tables 1, 2, 3, 4, 5, 6, 7 and 8 summarise the results relative to questions 1–8 of the pilot-survey, which suggest that the interpretation of natural language to understand local knowledge is an important research issue. In turn local knowledge appears a relevant factor in disaster response. In detail, Table 1 shows that 65% of respondents argue that 'the' entrance of the Levante's Fair is that located at point G (which is the main entrance). Similarly, in Table 2 the end of the Wall ('La Muraglia') is that corresponding to point J for almost 84% of respondents. In addition, the almost totality of the sample agrees that in front of Saint Nicholas Basilica means the main entrance as indicated in point R (Table 3). For the majority of respondents being

Table 1. Frequency table Q1 – Eastern Fairground entrance

Alternative	Freq	%	Cum
B	5	4.07	4.07
G	83	64.48	71.54
M	22	17.89	89.43
N	10	8.13	79.56
R	3	2.44	100

Table 2. Frequency table Q2 - *End of* the Wall

Alternative	Freq	%	Cum
J	103	83.74	83.74
N	8	6.5	90.24
X	12	9.76	100

Table 3. Frequency table Q3 - *In front of* Saint Nicholas Basilica

Alternative	Freq	%	Cum
B	2	1.63	1.63
G	4	3.25	4.88
N	1	0.81	5.69
R	116	94.31	100

Table 4. Frequency table Q5 - *Behind* Petruzzelli Theatre (Teatro Petruzzelli)

Alternative	Freq	%	Cum
B	9	7.32	7.32
M	27	78.86	86.18
N	2	1.63	87.80
R	15	12.20	100

behind the Petruzzelli Theatre means to be located at point M (Table 4). Finally, as for question in Table 5 the distribution of respondents is mostly bimodal on the entrances G (about 30%) and R (about 30%).

As for Tables 6 and 7 the responses seem somehow consistent. 38% of respondents think that Margherita's Theatre and Garibaldi Garden are far away from each other (Table 6). This perceived 'distance' corresponds to 750 m for the majority of the sample (32.5%) (Table 7). In Table 8 the nearby distance from the Central Station coincides with 400 m for 39% of respondents.

Table 5. Frequency table Q4 - *In front of* Largo 2 June Park (Parco Largo 2 Giugno)

Alternative	Freq	%	Cum
B	19	15.45	15.45
M	36	29.27	44.72
N	32	26.02	70.73
R	36	29.27	100

Table 6. Frequency table Q6 - How far is Margherita's Theatre from Garibaldi Garden

Distance	Freq	%	Cum
Quite far	18	14.63	14.63
Quite near	41	33.33	47.97
Far	7	5.69	53.66
Very far	2	1.63	55.28
Very near	5	4.07	59.35
Near	3	2.44	61.79
Don't know	47	38.21	100

Table 7. Frequency table Q7 - The perceived distance between the Margherita's Theatre and Garibaldi Park

Distance	Freq	%	Cum
100 m	3	2.44	2.44
200 m	11	8.94	11.38
300 m	28	22.76	34.15
400 m	48	39.02	73.17
500 m	13	10.57	83.74
600 m	8	6.50	90.24
700 m	9	7.32	97.56
900 m	1	0.81	98.37
1000 m	2	1.63	100.00

Table 8. Frequency table Q8 - The *nearby* distance from the Central Station

Distance	Freq	%	Cum
250 m	3	2.44	2.44
500 m	19	15.45	17.89
750 m	40	32.52	50.41
1000 m	32	26.02	76.42
1250 m	6	4.88	81.30
1500 m	20	16.26	97.56
2000 m	3	2.44	100

6 Discussion and Concluding Remarks

The present study tries to grasp the exclusively local linguistic subtleties, and to put their inherent ambiguities to the test – as it is the case with regard to the direction of the Wall ('La Muraglia') promenade in Bari illustrated in Table 2, according to which a start and an end of the wall could be identified. This is a crucial issue since in everyday communication, terms are being used which do not fall into a universally defined domain, but rather shift form one context-specific domain to another, and their meaning is fully and univocally understandable only when the involved agents share the same relevant knowledge base.

The empirical work carried out for the present paper seem to confirm the potential of local knowledge to support decision-making processes. The analysis of messages collected in simulated contexts has highlighted two main aspects:

- firstly, even in emergency situations, human communication seems to be imbued with culturally mediated and place-based understanding of spatiality, relationality and actions;
- secondly, natural language appears to be locally articulated (in vernacular and dialectal forms) and thus using terms that can only be understood within specific networks or communities.

Hence, the accuracy of any text mining methodology to assist planning and decision making is strongly dependent upon its ability to detect and decode the peculiarities inherent to these personalized, informal and context-laden languages.

The correct interpretation of local knowledge-laden natural language becomes an even more challenging problem, when the role of tacit or implicit knowledge is taken into account, as agents restrain themselves from declaring those concepts or information which they consider would be taken for granted within their group or community. This attitude is especially relevant in risk-related planning and management, since a mismatch between the cognitive frames of emergency response teams and victims or exposed citizens may jeopardize the effectiveness of rescue operations.

Indeed, while there exist several studies on risk and expert knowledge (especially in computer science literature), the relationships between risk and local knowledge are still erratically investigated and poorly understood. Following a long-standing distrust of local knowledge, scholars are now turning to it with ever-increasing interest: while acknowledging the difficulties in bridging the divide between local and expert knowledge [29] there is a growing awareness of the wealth of information being embedded into local knowledge, all the more so when they are strictly linked to behaviours, beliefs, and lifestyles, pertain to highly sensitive domains (like risk), or concern spatial knowledge and territoriality [10].

A few recent trends seem to be converging in that direction, such as Volunteered Geographical Information and PGIS, as well as the use of all-purpose social networks (Twitter, Facebook, etc.) to send out disaster-related messages that could reach well beyond the institutional body in charge of traditional top-down frameworks, to the wider internet community. To further advance, it appears that distributed crowdsourcing methods, combined with collaborative hypertext editors (wikis), may be effective in many fields (Imran et al. 2014).

Therefore, and based on the pilot work that has been carried out, the present paper argues in favour of acknowledging the importance of local knowledge in planning and decision making – consistently with the position of many scholars [2, 3, 5] – and calls for implementing spatial data science tools (databases, vocabularies, maps, models, etc.) in such a way that local and tacit knowledge (including vernacular forms) for spatial relationships based from natural language may be adequately understood and modelled.

References

1. Balena, P.: Local knowledge and social sensor: integrated models of text analysis for disaster response. Ph.D. Thesis. Technical University of Bari (2017)
2. Raymond, C.M., Fazey, I., Reed, M.S., Stringer, L.C., Robinson, G.M., Evely, A.C.: Integrating local and scientific knowledge for environmental management. J. Environ. Manage. **91**(8), 1766–1777 (2010)
3. Nonaka, I., Konno, N., Toyama, R.: Emergence of "Ba": a conceptual framework for the continuous and self-transcending process of knowledge development of business organizations. In: Nonaka, I., Nishiguchi, T. (eds.) Knowledge Emergence: Social, Technical and Evolutionary Dimensions of Knowledge Creation. Oxford University Press, Oxford (2001)
4. Fazey, I.R.A., Proust, K., Newell, B., Johnson, B., Fazey, J.A.: Eliciting the implicit knowledge and perceptions of on-ground conservation managers of the Macquarie Marshes. Ecol. Soc. **11**(1), 25 (2006)
5. Olaide, I.A., Omolere, O.W.: Management of indigenous knowledge as a catalyst towards improved information accessibility to local communities: a literature review. Chin. Librarianship Int. Electron. J. **35**(2005), 87–98 (2013)
6. Polanyi, M.: Personal Knowledge: Towards a Post-critical Philosophy. The University of Chicago Press, Chicago (1962)
7. Jones, O.: Lay discourses of the rural: developments and implications for rural studies. J. Rural Stud. **11**(1), 35–49 (1995)
8. Halfacree, K.H.: Talking about rurality: social representations of the rural as expressed by residents of six English parishes. J. Rural Stud. **11**(1), 1–20 (1995)
9. Hansen, J., Holm, L., Frewer, L., Robinson, P., Sandøe, P.: Beyond the knowledge deficit: recent research into lay and expert attitudes to food risks. Appetite **41**(2), 111–121 (2003)
10. Smith, E.: The role of tacit and explicit knowledge in the workplace. J. Knowl. Manage. **5**(4), 311–321 (2001)
11. Robertson, H.A., McGee, T.K.: Applying local knowledge: the contribution of oral history to wetland rehabilitation at Kanyapella Basin, Australia. J. Environ. Manage. **69**(3), 275–287 (2003)
12. Kettle, N.P., Dow, K., Tuler, S., Webler, T., Whitehead, J., Miller, K.M.: Integrating scientific and local knowledge to inform risk-based management approaches for climate adaptation. Clim. Risk Manage. **4**, 17–31 (2014)
13. Kumar, A.J., Chakrabarti, A.: Bounded awareness and tacit knowledge: revisiting challenger disaster. J. Knowl. Manage. **16**(6), 934–949 (2012)
14. Frappaolo, C.: Implicit knowledge. Knowl. Manage. Res. Pract. **6**, 23–25 (2008)

15. Ambrosini, V., Bowman, C.: Tacit knowledge: some suggestions for operationalization. J. Manage. Stud. **38**(6), 811–829 (2001)
16. Van Herzele, A.: Local knowledge in action - valuing nonprofessional reasoning in the planning process. J. Plan. Educ. Res. **24**(2), 197–212 (2004)
17. Pasquini, M., Alexander, M.: Soil fertility management strategies on the Jos Plateau: the need for integrating "empirical" and "scientific" knowledge in agricultural development. Geogr. J. **171**(2), 112–124 (2005)
18. Bond, A.J., Viegas, C.V., Coelho de Souza Reinisch Coelho, C., Selig, P.M.: Informal knowledge processes: the underpinning for sustainability outcomes in EIA? J. Clean. Prod. **18**(1), 6–13 (2010)
19. Kuhnert, P.M., Martin, T.G., Mengersen, K., Possingham, H.P.: Assessing the impacts of grazing levels on bird density in woodland habitat: a Bayesian approach using expert opinion. Environmetrics **16**(7), 717–747 (2005)
20. Pollock, M.L., Legg, C.J., Holland, J.P., Theobald, C.M.: Assessment of expert opinion: seasonal sheep preference and plant response to grazing. Rangeland Ecol. Manage. **60**, 125–135 (2007)
21. Mackay, E.: Indigenous traditional knowledge, copyright and art - Shortcomings in protection and an alternative approach. Univ. South Wales Law J. **32**(1), 1–26 (2009)
22. Mercer, I., Kelman, L.: Taranis et, S., Suchet-Pearson, J.: Framework for integrating indigenous and scientific knowledge for disaster risk reduction. Disasters **34**(1), 214–239 (2010)
23. Howden, K.: Indigenous traditional knowledge and native title. UNSW Law J. **24**(1), 60–84 (2011)
24. Olsson, P., Folke, C.: Local ecological knowledge and institutional dynamics for ecosystem management: a study of Lake Racken watershed, Sweden. Ecosystems **4**(2), 85–104 (2001)
25. Newport, J.K., Jawahar, G.G.P.: Community participation and public awareness in disaster mitigation. Disaster Prev. Manage. **12**(1), 33–36 (2003)
26. Berkes, F., Folke, C.: Back to the future: ecosystem dynamics and local knowledge. In: Gunderson, L.H., Holling, C.S. (eds.) Panarchy: Understanding Transformations in Human and Natural Systems, pp. 121–146. Island Press, Washington, D.C. (2002)
27. Picketts, I.M., Curry, J., Rapaport, E.: Community adaptation to climate change: environmental planners' knowledge and experiences in British Columbia, Canada. J. Environ. Planning Policy Manage. **14**(2), 119–137 (2012)
28. Sui, X., Chen, Z., Wu, K., Ren, P., Ma, J., Zhou, F.: Social media as sensor in real world geolocate user with microblog. In: Zong, C., Nie, J.Y., Zhao, D., Feng, Y. (eds.) Natural Language Processing and Chinese Computing. CCIS, vol. 496, pp. 229–237. Springer, Heidelberg (2014). doi:10.1007/978-3-662-45924-9_21
29. Gaillard, J.C., Mercer, J.: From knowledge to action: bridging gaps in disaster risk reduction. Prog. Hum. Geogr. **37**, 93–114 (2013)

Spatial Function of Influence on Center Optimal Location Based on L_p-Norms

Didier Josselin[1,2]($\boxtimes$), Julio Rojas-Mora[3], and Marc Ciligot-Travain[4]

[1] UMR 7300 ESPACE, CNRS, Université d'Avignon et des Pays de Vaucluse,
Avignon, France
didier.josselin@univ-avignon.fr
[2] Laboratoire d'Informatique d'Avignon, Université d'Avignon et des Pays de
Vaucluse, Avignon, France
[3] School of Informatics, Universidad Católica de Temuco, Temuco, Chile
[4] Laboratoire de Mathématique d'Avignon, Avignon, France

Abstract. We propose a sensitivity analysis using generalized L_p-norm (Minkowski distance) applied on center optimal location (1 facility). The results show that there exists in one dimension an underlying (log)linear relation between influence and distance of the demand points on the center. New L_p-norms are emphasized with interesting properties in statistics (*e.g.* with *p=3*) although they are not used in location optimization. The law we enhance is of interest in both statistics and and spatial analysis domains and highlights in a new way the impact of the metrics choice on the center location, through the induced spatial influence function, those metrics aiming at spatial equity (L_∞), equality (L_2) or efficiency (L_1).

Keywords: Spatial influence function · Lp-norm · Center optimal location · Sensitivity analysis

1 Introduction

Positioning a resource center or a facility in an optimal way is a well studied and know process in urban planning [3]. Generally, planners know about the center function and then choose the appropriate metrics to locate it, according to ground availability, building costs, accessibility and political constraints. Thus a health-care center or a hospital should be located in such a way to minimize the maximum time to access to it, whereas a logistics center or a transport station should be as close as possible to the concentrated users population to minimize the averaged distances. The decision process has to deal with *equity vs. efficiency* [1]. Those choices are fixed using the appropriate distance, that is to say a L_p-norm, if the metrics are within this mathematical framework. In networks and transportation optimization, the most used metrics is the *1-median* with the *minisum* operator (or *k-median* generalized for *k* facilities, sometimes called the *p-median*) [2,14]. Then comes the *1-center* (*vs.* *k*-center or *p*-center) with a *minimax* operator. Far behind is paradoxically the gravity center, although it is

© Springer International Publishing AG 2017
O. Gervasi et al. (Eds.): ICCSA 2017, Part IV, LNCS 10407, pp. 652–661, 2017.
DOI: 10.1007/978-3-319-62401-3_47

the main norm used in statistics and optimization in general, except in facilities optimal locating.

The remaining of this paper is organized as follows. We first explain the process to estimate the demand point influence in one dimension and then in space (two dimensions). To do so, we developed a sensitivity analysis in optimal location [5], using generalized L_p-norm applied on *1-facility* optimal location, in two dimensions. We use a large series of different values of x, p from several L_p-norms. Then we depict and discuss the clear relationship in one dimension between the distance to the center and the point influence, according to the different studied metrics. Indeed, new L_p-norms show very interesting properties in statistics (e.g. with *p=3*). Actually, in one dimension, there exists a (log)linear relationship between distance separating the demand point from the center and the influence (or weight w_i) of the point in fixing the center location, whatever the exponent p of the L_p-norm. The law we enhance is a mix between statistics and space and highlights the impact of the metric choice on the center location, through the induced spatial influence function, those metrics aiming at spatial equity (L_∞), equality (L_2) or efficiency (L_1) or intermediate objectives that would benefit to be explored and experienced in spatial urban planning.

2   Distance de Minkowski, L_p-Norm

A simple distance can be expressed by the following formula:

$$d_{ic} = (|x_i - x_c|^p + |y_i - y_c|^p)^{\frac{1}{p}} \tag{1}$$

with (x_i, y_i) the demand point coordinates i, (x_c, y_c) the centered facility coordinates c, p the type of L_p-norm considered.

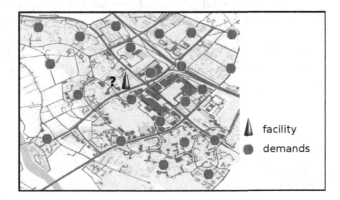

Fig. 1. Where is located the optimal center to respond a set of demand points in the town?

The problem we tackle is related to the 1-*facility* optimal location problem in an isotropic space (cf Fig. 1), which a particular case of *k-facilities* optimal location problem with n-demands [6,9]. For a generalization of this kind of *min-isum* issues, see [10,14]. Other authors presented a clear behavior of the center location according to different well-known norms in spatial econometrics [11,12].

Given a value of p and its corresponding computed norm, let us consider the distance d_{ic} to be processed such as the sum of the distance from each demand point i to the centered facility c should be minimal according to p. Let us notice that this sum is also affected of an exponent related to p: i.e. $\frac{1}{p}$.

$$c^* = min \left(\sum d_{ic}^p \right)^{\frac{1}{p}} \tag{2}$$

With $p = 2$, we get the Euclidian distance and the gravity center. With $p = 1$, we get the *Median* by the Manhattan distance and the *minisum* operation. When $p \to \infty$, we get the *Center* by the *minimax* operator. Due to the fact that, except for $p = 2$, there does not exist any exact solution to locate the center c, c^* is then approximated using nonlinear programming functions based on gradient descent, for instance.

3   Estimation of Demand Point Influence on a Center

We propose an algorithm of sensitivity analysis of the center location according to demand change location. We proceed by locally moving the set of demand points and then assess how much the center location was changed. This algorithm is applied according to different L_p-norms. The objective is to assess the derivative $\delta_{x_c}/\delta_{x_i}$. When this elasticity is low, this mean the center is not sensitive to micro-changes of demand location. When the value of this elasticity increases, this means that the influence w_i of the demand point(s) is stronger [4,7]. To estimate w_i, we use a local filter that allows to compute changes of location is several directions around each point neighbor. This approach can be extended to optimal location on networks as proposed in [8]. For each demand point i among a set of n points and for each iteration k of a location change related to a direction change, i becomes i' and c becomes c', and the optimal center is recalculated recording its location change. The global demand points influence w_i is then averaged and normalized using the following formula:

$$w_i = \frac{\frac{1}{n} \sum_k \frac{\delta_{c \to c'}}{\delta_{i \to i'}}}{\sum_i \left(\frac{1}{n} \sum_k \frac{\delta_{c \to c'}}{\delta_{i \to i'}} \right)} \tag{3}$$

with w_i the averaged demand point influence i, n the number of demand points, k the number of local changes in different directions in the point neighborhood, $\delta_{i \to i'}$ the local change of point location which is fixed (i moved to i'), $\delta_{c \to c'}$ the change of center location which is observed (c moved to c').

We tested our algorithm on different sets of data according to several statistical distributions (Gaussian, Uniform, Random, etc.) with different values of k and finally fixed k to 36 in practice to ensure a sufficient local density for a smoothed computation. For any distribution, the global shapes of the curves are similar, but they are sometimes asymmetric when dealing with asymmetric distributions. These results are not depicted in this paper. In any case, we notice that the influence w_i mainly depends on the topological structure of the demand in space and on the value of p of the Minkowski distance.

Our method is developed in R and requires the package *nloptr* for non linear optimization.

4   Relation Between w_i and p in one dimension

In 1 dimension, with a batch of data, the picture is very clear as depicted in the Fig. 2, which crosses the influence with the distance, according to a series of L_p-norms. p varies from 1 to 25 (including non integer norms) on the same set of data x_i. What we notice here are the different shapes of the curves depending on which case is considered. On both sizes of $p = 2$ (the sample mean), the curves show progressive opposite curvatures. With $p = 1$, the points close to the median (the central value minimizing this norm), have a strong influence, whereas when p increases (here $p = 25$), almost only the farthest points have an

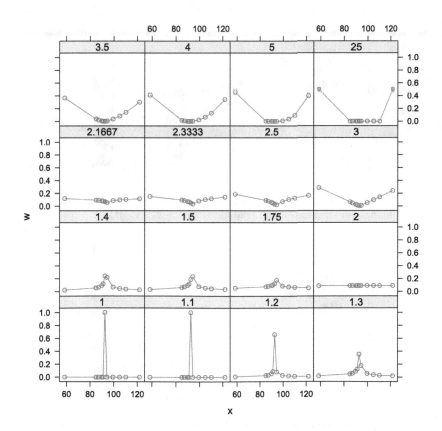

Fig. 2. Demand point influence w in one dimension according to the L_p-norm (value of p written on the top of each plot) on a batch of 10 data (x).

influence on the center location (minimax center). Between those two extreme cases, we observe a curvature continuous and smoothed process. Let us especially remark the cases with $p = 1.5$ showing a smoothed curve with a moderate peak and $p = 3$ disclosing a perfect straight line. Let us notice that, despite this property, in operations research, mathematics, spatial econometrics or quantitative geography, this norm is totally ignored. This will be discussed afterwards.

5   Mapping the Demand Point Influence in an Isotropic Space

In two dimensions, we observe similar phenomena. Instead of having a single dimension making two opposite directions on both sides of the case $p = 2$, we have to consider successive circular distances around the geographical center and the order in which each demand point appears within a centrifugal counting process. With $p = 2$, there is no effect of the distance on the influence, which is perfectly constant, making a geographical equality of influence (cf Fig. 3).

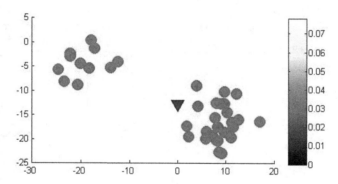

Fig. 3. Mapping the demand point influence on the *gravity center*; darker the points, lower the influence on the center; the triangle is the center location.

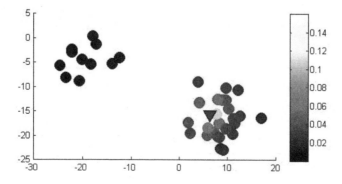

Fig. 4. Mapping the demand point influence on the *1-median*; darker the points, lower the influence on the center; the triangle is the center location.

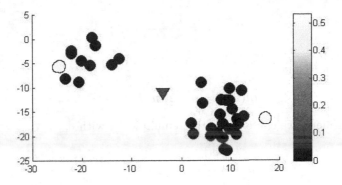

Fig. 5. Mapping the demand point influence on the *1-center*; darker the points, lower the influence on the center; the triangle is the center location.

It is rather different when considering $p = 1$ and $p \to \infty$. With $p = 1$, the points close to the center have a string influence due to the objective of efficiency (cf Fig. 4). With $p \to \infty$, only the most peripheral demand points weight on the center location (cf Fig. 5). None of the other points has any influence due to the *minimax* operator.

6   Generalization of the Influence Function in One Dimension

6.1   Generalized Functions in One Dimension

Once observed this regular change of the relation between the influence (weight w_i) of the demand points on the center, we tried to generalize the relation at least in one dimension. Dealing with two dimensions is considered in current work. We found that there exists a clear log-linear relation between point influence and distance to the center. Whatever the L_p-norm considered with its associated optimal center, the relation is similar to the ones presented as examples in Figs. 6 and 7 with $p = 4$ and $p = 7$ respectively. Processing many simulations of randomized series of points using different statistical distributions, as explained before, we notice that the correlation R^2 values are very high in any case, showing a very well adjusted fit between the model and the function. Thence, the law seems to be generalized among all the norms and all the types of data. More precisely, an interesting result is in the value of the line slope, which is systematically equal to $p - 2$ when considering integer values of p.

The general relation between influence w_i and distance d_{ic} from the point to the facility can be expressed as follows and is directed linked to the Minkowski derivative function in two dimensions, including a remainder r and depending on the L_p-norm:

$$w_i = \frac{d_{ic}^{(p-2)}}{e^{-r}} \tag{4}$$

with $d_{ic} \geq 0$,
which is equivalent to:

$$ln(w_i) = (p-2)ln(d_{ic}) + r \tag{5}$$

In complement, we can express the remainder r, with $d_{ic} \neq 1$:

$$r = \frac{ln(w_i)}{(p-2)ln(d_{ic})} = \frac{1}{p-2}log_{d_{ic}}(w_i) \tag{6}$$

We can remark that:

- the distance from the point to the center provides the *log base* (*scale*) in the remainder value calculation (r),
- the weight or influence is the variable,
- the value of p plays on the factor of the *log*,
- $p-2$ can be considered as a *fractal dimension* because it is the slope of a straight line crossing $ln(w_i)$ with $ln(d_{ic})$.

6.2   Application to Different L_p-norms

With $p = 1$, the demand point influence is conversely proportional to the distance to the center. It is the case of the *median* that would correspond in 2D to the Fermat/Weber point [15], considered as an efficient center in terms of cost. It corresponds to the minimal cumulated distance from all the points to the center. In this case, the center is located in the most concentrated area of points.

$$w_i = \frac{1}{d_{ic}e^{-r}} \tag{7}$$

and

$$r = -\frac{1}{2}log_{d_{ic}}(w_i) \tag{8}$$

With $p = 2$, we verify that influence is constant, that is to say that each demand point has the same impact on the center location. It is the mean or average center, which minimizes the squared distances. r cannot be calculated because $d_{ic} = 1$, which is obvious because the weight is constant whatever the distance from the point to the center.

$$w_i = \frac{1}{e^{-r}} \tag{9}$$

With $p = 3$, we observe a very clear linear relation between influence and distance, already observed in the Fig. 2. Farther a point to the center, lower its influence.

$$w_i = \frac{d_{ic}}{e^{-r}} \tag{10}$$

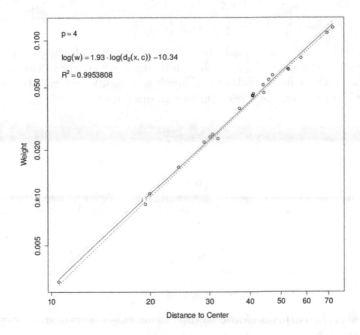

Fig. 6. Relation between point influence and distance to the center with $p = 3$.

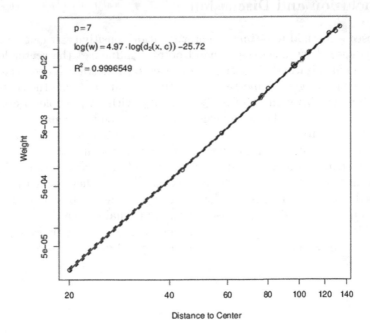

Fig. 7. Relation between point influence and distance to the center with $p = 7$.

and
$$r = log_{d_{ic}}(w_i) \tag{11}$$

With $p = 4$, we obtain a quadratic relation between influence and distance. We get closer to the norm L_∞, which would illustrate equity in two dimension [13], e.g. the farthest individuals are as much as possible unfavored and so own the highest influence on the center (*minimax* operator) :

$$w_i = \frac{d_{ic}^2}{e^{-r}} \tag{12}$$

and
$$r = \frac{1}{2}log_{d_{ic}}(w_i) \tag{13}$$

With $p = 1.5$, the square root plays an inverse role in the influence function:

$$w_i = \frac{d_{ic}^{-0.5}}{e^{-r}} = \frac{1}{e^{-r}\sqrt{d_{ic}}} \tag{14}$$

and
$$r = 2.log_{d_{ic}}(w_i) \tag{15}$$

Many other L_p-norms could be studied using this generalization, depending on the urban planning evolution and forecasting.

7   Conclusion and Discussion

We proposed a method to estimate center location sensitivity. It can be used to accurately assess how much the demand points "influence" the center location through the optimization computing given a certain metrics. Indeed the choice of the L_p-norm is of great importance in optimal location, fixing the center purpose and function between *efficiency* and *equity*, with all possible intermediate meanings. We presented the (log)linear relation between the demand point influence and distance to the center for the case of oner dimension. We emphasized the properties of well-known and new L_p-norms. We finally wonder why other L_p-norms (e.g. $p = 3$ or $p = 1.5$) are not more often used in urban planning, that sometimes could better fit the planner aims. We believe that the method we designed in two dimensions and the generalization we proposed in one dimension open on more tuned approaches to design optimal centers, with thoughtful and suitable compromises between spatial *efficiency*, *equality* or *equity*. In further works, more experiments will be done using real data to assess the method usability.

References

1. Beguin, H.: Efficacité et équité en aménagement du territoire. L'Espace Géographique **5**, 335–336 (1989)
2. Brimberg, J., Love, R.F.: Global convergence of a generalized iterative procedure for the minisum location problem with lp distances. Oper. Res. **41**(6), 1153–1163 (1993)
3. Chan, Y.: Location Transport and Landuse. Modelling Spatial-Temporal Information. Springer, Heidelberg (2005)
4. Ciligot-Travain, M., Josselin, D.: Impact of the norm on optimal locations. In: Gervasi, O., Taniar, D., Murgante, B., Laganà, A., Mun, Y., Gavrilova, M.L. (eds.) ICCSA 2009. LNCS, vol. 5592, pp. 426–441. Springer, Heidelberg (2009). doi:10.1007/978-3-642-02454-2_30
5. Drezner, Z., Hamacher, H.: Facility Locations. Application and Theories. Springer, Heidelberg (2004)
6. Hakimi, S.: Optimum locations of switching center and the absolute center and medians of a graph. Oper. Res. **12**, 450–459 (1964)
7. Josselin, D., Ciligot-Travain, M.: Revisiting the optimal center location, a spatial thinking based on robustness, sensitivity, and influence analysis. Environ. Plann. B, Plann. Des. **40**(5), 923–941 (2013)
8. Josselin, D., Rojas-Mora, J., Blanke, D., Gourion, D., Ciligot-Travain, M.: Influence of the metrics on discrete facility location. toward a pertinent lp norm targeting a transport objective. In: Transportation Research Arena 2014 (2014)
9. Labbé, M., Peeters, D., Thisse, J.F.: Location on networks. In: Handbook of Operations Research and Management Science, North Holland, Amsterdam (1995)
10. Nickel, S., Puerto, J.: Location Theory. A Unified Approach. Springer, Heidelberg (2005)
11. Peeters, D., Thomas, I.: Distance-lp et localisations optimales. simulations sur un semis aléatoire de points. Les cahiers scientifiques du transport **31**, 55–70 (1997)
12. Peeters, D., Thomas, I.: Distance predicting function and applied location-allocation models. Geogr. Syst. **2**, 167–184 (2000)
13. Rawls, J.: A Theory of Justice. Belknap Press of Harvard University Press, Cambridge (1971)
14. Scott, A.J.: Location-allocation systems: a review. Geogr. Anal. **2**, 95–119 (1970)
15. Weber, A.: Theory of the Location of Industries. The University of Chicago Press, Chicago (1909)

Deep-Seated Gravitational Slope Deformation in Urban Areas Matching Field and in-SAR Interferometry Surveys: The Case Study of the Episcopia Village, Southern Italy

Mario Bentivenga[1], Salvatore Ivo Giano[1], Lucia Saganeiti[2], Gabriele Nolè[3], Giuseppe Palladino[4], Giacomo Prosser[1], and Beniamino Murgante[2(✉)]

[1] Dipartimento di Scienze, University of Basilicata, 85100 Potenza, Italy
{mario.bentivenga,ivo.giano,giacomo.prosser}@unibas.it
[2] School of Engineering, University of Basilicata,
Viale dellAteneo Lucano 10, 85100 Potenza, Italy
lucia.saganeiti@gmail.com, beniamino.murgante@unibas.it
[3] CNR-IMAA, C.da S. Loja, Tito Scalo, 85050 Potenza, Italy
gabriele.nole@imaa.cnr.it
[4] Geology and Petroleum Geology, University of Aberdeen, Aberdeen, UK
giuseppe.palladino@abdn.ac.uk

Abstract. A limited sector of the left side Sinni River, including Episcopia village, has been investigated matching geological and geomorphological data to In-SAR Interferometry analysis. A large Deep-Seated Gravitational Slopes (DSGSD), affecting the Episcopia slope, has been documented for the first time. The DSGSD largely develops within phyllites belonging to the Liguride Units and, in the upper portion of the slope, within the sandy and conglomerate deposits of the Sant'Arcangelo Basin. Field survey has shown typical DSGSD features as well as trenches at the top and an evident bulge at the base corresponding to the Sinni River. These data allow us to hypothesize a listric geometry of the DSGSD plane reaching a depth of about 700 m.

Keywords: Deep-Seated Gravitational Slopes · In-SAR Interferometry Analysis · Episcopia southern Italy

1 Introduction

DSGSD is an acronym of the Deep-Seated Gravitational Slope Deformation referring to gravity-induced slope mass movements that affect high relief mountain slopes over long periods of time and at low rates [1–7]. It is classified between landslides and a faulting process that affects the slopes and displaces rock mass downward for several kilometres squares and up to 100 m depth, and the detailed processes responsible for their genesis are not well understood yet [6, 8, 9]. The typical DSGSD features are double ridges, trenches, tension cracks, uphill facing scarps (counter scarps or antislope scarps), downthrown blocks, buckling folds, toe bulging, and secondary mass movements [6, 10].

The DSGSDs are word wide recognized [10] and are peculiar phenomenon of the Italian Alp and Apennine chains [5, 6, 8, 9, 11–14]. All over the world there are a lot of

O. Gervasi et al. (Eds.): ICCSA 2017, Part IV, LNCS 10407, pp. 662–674, 2017.
DOI: 10.1007/978-3-319-62401-3_48

experiences of satellite images classification in the field of geology [40–44]. The aim of the study is to investigate the Episcopia DSGSD, already recognized by Bentivenga et al. [15], using a multidisciplinary approach that consists on a matching of field survey (geological and geomorphological investigations) supported by aerial photogrammetry and cartographic interpretations and In-Sar Interferometry technique.

The DSGSDs area that affects the whole Episcopia urban settlement is characterized of many landslides and is bounded by the Monaco and Confine Streams on the left and the right, respectively. Aerial photogrammetry interpretation confirmed by field surveys have revealed the typical morphological features of DSGSD that involves the whole slope until to the Sinni River valley and the urban settlement of Episcopia producing severe damage buildings.

2 Geological Setting

The southern Apennines chain (Fig. 1), a Miocene to Pleistocene fold-and-thrust belt, is composed of east-verging tectonic units [16] overlapping on the Apulian Platform and is characterized by large duplex geometries [17].

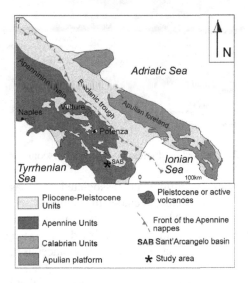

Fig. 1. Geological sketch map of southern Apennines.

The study area is located in the eastern sector of the south-Appennine chain and is formed by the Mesozoic to Cenozoic Apennines Unit successions overlapped by Plio-cene to Pleistocene clastic deposits (Fig. 1). The Apennines units are represented by the Liguride Unit [18] composed of different tectonic units named Frido, Crete Nere, Sara-ceno and Albidona formations [19–21].

The Frido Formation is the highest tectonic unit; it is divided in two tectonic subunits, Cretaceous to Oligocene in age [22, 23], and is composed of polydeformed metamorphic rocks with associated blocks of ophiolite-bearing and continental-type rocks (Fig. 2).

The ophiolitic rocks are mainly represented by serpentinized peridotite and metabasite [19] [243].

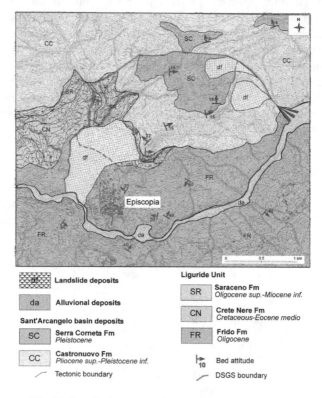

Legend:

df Landslide deposits

da Alluvional deposits

Sant'Arcangelo basin deposits

SC Serra Corneta Fm
Pleistocene

CC Castronuovo Fm
Pliocene sup.-Pleistocene inf.

Tectonic boundary

Liguride Unit

SR Saraceno Fm
Oligocene sup.-Miocene inf.

CN Crete Nere Fm
Cretaceous-Eocene medio

FR Frido Fm
Oligocene

Bed attitude

DSGS boundary

Fig. 2. Detailed geological map of the Episcopia area.

Dark-green cataclastic serpentinite and associated metabasite rocks marks the tectonic contact between the phyllite and calc-schist subunits.

The Crete Nere, Saraceno and Albidona formations are the tectonic units underlying the Frido one. The Crete Nere Formation [20, 25] is a deep-sea water succession, Cretaceous to Eocene in age, formed by quartzarenites and arenaceous limestones interbedded to black shales (Fig. 2).

It is stratigraphically covered by the Saraceno Formation that is composed of calcareous turbidites mainly formed by thin layers of limestones, marls, and clay. Finally, an angular unconformity divides the Saraceno Formation, on the bottom, and the Albidona, on the top.

This latter is formed by turbidite facies that vary from arenaceous to pelite in the bottom to conglomerate-arenaceous toward the top (Fig. 2). This succession represents the infill of the Miocene thrust-top/foredeep basins developed in the frontal sector of the southern Apennines accretionary wedge.

Starting from the Eocene the area was affected by four tectonic events that were developed at several crustal levels and with different metamorphic grade [22, 25–28].

The lower Miocene tectonic event generated NE-verging fold-and-thrusts involving both the Ophiolite and siliciclastic units. Differently, during the middle Pleistocene it was active a NW-SE-oriented normal faulting that partially re-activate the older structures.

The Liguride unit successions are lying by the marine to continental clastic deposits of the Sant'Arcangelo basin "Auctt.", a Pliocene to Pleistocene basin filled by up to 2500 m thick deposits [24, 29, 30].

The sedimentary succession in the study area is formed from bottom to top by Late Pliocene to Early Pleistocene polygenetic conglomerate with yellow sandy matrix that constitutes the Castronuovo Formation. This latter is overlapped by the fluvial conglomerates and sands with red sand matrix of the Middle Pleistocene Serra Corneta Formation [24].

3 Geomorphological Setting

From a geomorphological point of view the fold-and-thrust belt of the Southern Apennines can be roughly divided into three zones (inner, axial, and outer belts) parallel to its NW-SE-elongation axis (Fig. 1). The inner belt corresponds to the Tyrrhenian side of the formed Cilento Promontory, with a maximum elevation reached at Cervati Mt. (1900 m a.s.l.). Transverse incised fluvial valleys drive westward the main rivers toward the Tyrrhenian Sea, locally producing narrow gorges of one hundred meters deep.

The axial belt corresponds to the highest mountains peaks that are up to 2000 m a.s.l. and includes the remnants of the Pliocene to Pleistocene erosion landsurfaces uplifted and dismembered by Quaternary faults [23, 31]. Also block-faulted mountains bounded by high-angle fault scarps retreated by slope replacement processes [34] are present.

They are alternated with tectonically controlled basins filled by fluvial to lacustrine deposits [33, 34]. The fluvial network follows the regional dip of the chain and often transversally cut the bedrock to flow into the Tyrrhenian, Adriatic, or Ionian seas. The outer belt of the chain is characterized by a general passive north-eastward tilting as a consequence of the uplift of the axial zone of the chain [35, 36].

This is also supported by the drainage network that often flows perpendicularly to the main tectonic structures, in agreement with the regional slope of the belt [37–39]. The outer belt displays a landscape with a lower elevation than the axial belt and does not exceed 1100 m a.s.l.; the fluvial valleys are oriented from NE-SW in the northern sector to E-W in the southern sector and transversally cut the plain bending of the chain.

4 Data and Methods

The investigation of the Episcopia slope has been conducts by means of a multidisciplinary approach starting from a geological field survey that has revealed large slope deformation not only attributable to surficial landslides but rather than to more deep mass movements.

As a consequence, a more detailed geomorphological analysis has been carried out on the whole slope using 1:5000 contour maps and 1:33000 aerial photos that furnished a wide distribution of the features associated to the mass movements.

With the aim to investigate the kinematics and the morphological evolution of the area a multitemporal analysis by means of I.G.M.I. aerial photos relative to the 1954/55, 1992/93, and 2003 years has been carried out. All the results of the geological and geomorphological analyses are illustrated in the Figs. 2 and 3.

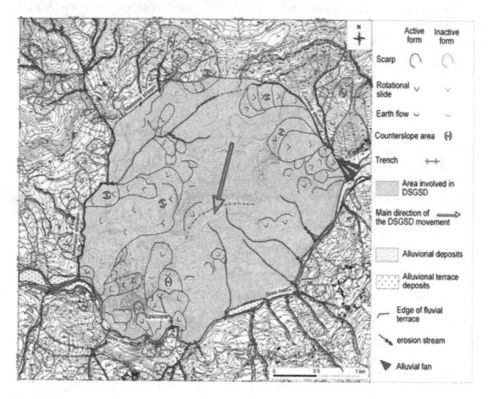

Fig. 3. Geomorphological map of the Episcopia area showing the landslides and the morphological features associated to the DSGSD landform.

Moreover, applications based on SAR data may be a further step in the study of the area. For the Differential Interferometry Synthetic Aperture Radar (DInSAR) analysis, 24 images of single look complex (SLC) were downloaded free of charge from the Copernicus site[1].

The TOP-SAR images captured by sentinel satellites 1 A and B were used, of which 18 interferograms were generated following the steps: co-registration [45], interferogram formation [46, 47], topographic phase removal, phase filtering [48], and phase unwrapping [49, 50] (Table 1).

---

[1] Copernicus https://scihub.copernicus.eu/dhus/#/home (2017).

Table 1. Dataset used for interferometric analysis.

Dataset	Sentinel 1A/B
Acquisition dates	From 01/11/2014 to 01/05/2017
Format	SLC
Polarization	VV
Pass direction	Ascending
Incidence angle	~41°
Radar frequency	5.405 MHz

These interferometric pairs were combined to improve the Signal to Noise Ratio SNR [51]. Finally, the Coherent Pixels Technique (CPT) [52, 53] was used for the analysis of displacements based on the estimation of the mean of coherence. This method allows to extract the deformation during large time spans from a stack of interferograms.

4.1 Geomorphological Analysis of the Study Area

Geomorphological analysis of the southern area of the Timpa Rossa site allowed the recognition of some trenches laterally jointing to stream channels and some others placed at the base of the main slopes.

The Episcopia village is placed on the left side of the Sinni River where many landslides of different wideness are located (Fig. 2). The wider landslides are found on the left side of the Monaco Stream and their main scarps have involved in the movement the Pleistocene conglomerates and sands deposits of the Sant'Arcangelo basin. Lower minor scarps affected also deposits of the Liguride units. In the right side of the Confine Stream the main scarp of the landslides involved only the conglomerates and sand of both the Serra Corneta and Castronuovo formations. On the Episcopia slope some head landslides show slope deposits arranged on a convex downward symmetry how the morphology of the main scarp.

The wider landslides of the study area have been interpreted as rotational slide because of the occurrence of backward tilting terraces, and also as complex landslides formed by rotational slide in the head and by earth flow in the toe [54–56].

The smaller landslides affected the urban area of the Episcopia village and surroundings, the south-east sector and the whole base slope of the Sinni River, on its right side. In this case only the deposits of the Liguride Unit are involved in the movement. The landslides affecting the study area are shown in Fig. 3, specifying type of movement and state of activity. This latter parameter came from both the field morphological surveys and the built damages evaluation. The active landslides are mainly located along the valley-side of the Monaco and Confine streams, in the urban area of the Episcopia Village and at the base slope of the right side of the Sinni River (see Fig. 3 for details). The fluvial pattern of the Episcopia slope is dendritic in the upper reach and radial in the middle to lower one. In fact, the western streams are tributary of the Monaco Stream, the eastern streams of the Confine Stream, and the southern ones of the Sinni River.

4.2 The Deep-Seated Gravitational Slope Deformation of the Episcopia Village

The identification of the Episcopia DSGSD came from the analysis of geological and geomorphological data that have shown in the Figs. 2 and 3. In order to analyse the geological area we understood the extent of reduction and the rotation endured by the interested sector of DSGSD following the stratigraphic horizons guide (Figs. 2 and 3). The stratigraphic boundary, between Serra Corneta Fm and the underlined Castronuovo Fm turns out to be easily to observe and to map because the first deposits have a reddish colour whereas the second is yellow. This stratigraphic limit turns out to be sub-horizontal throughout the top of the slope, whereas right after the main trench viewed upstream from DSGSD, is rotated in counter-gradient slope of about 10°.

It has been taken into consideration some important morphological clues as the evident trenches upstream of the slope of Episcopia. In this sector there are two evident trenches characterized by an arcuate trend with the concavity towards the valley. The main trench has an E-W trending direction in the south of Tempa Rossa site and then curving laterally towards the valley and there making a connection with the waterways affluent on the left of the river Sinni. In particular, the main trench joins laterally to the streams of the skein to the west and to the stream border to the east.

The second trench, mapped on the southern side, has a same trend of the previous one and is connected to the west with a left tributary of the Monaco Stream and to the east meets the first and so it follows the Confine Stream. At the base of the slope flows the Sinni River that follows a pathway characterized by an arcuate trend with a pronounced convex to the south, especially in the stretch at the base of the Episcopia village [38]. In addition, throughout the arcuate portion of the watercourse are not present terraced alluvial deposits, detected and mapped before and after. This further morphologic evidence has allowed us to accurately define the area involved by DSGSD that turns out to be equal at about 6 km². The upstream bounds of the DSGSD coincide with the main trench, laterally to the Matassa and Monaco streams to the east and the Confine Stream to the west and south with the deviated section of the Sinni River. The size of the deep gravitational movement that involved the slope of Episcopia corresponds to an average width of 2.5 km and an average length of about 2.4 km. The depth of the DSGSD was derived from geometric reconstructions and taking account of the involved mass, it was found that there is considerable as estimated at about 700 m from ground level. The geometry of the sliding surface, which is connected to the upstream trench and the most advanced part of the movement of the foot that has interested the valley floor, it can be hypothesized as listric [38]. The clear geological evidence, tied to the rotation counter slope of the boundary between the Serra Corneta Fm and the underlying Castronuovo Fm and the presence of well-preserved morphological evidence as the upstream trenches, erosion streams, the absence of river terraces along the arcuate portion of the Sinni River and the tendency to unseat for lateral erosion of the right side of the same leads to belief that the gravitational movement is active. Further support to this hypothesis is also the distribution of active landslides that are more focused along the streams and bund them laterally and in the urban area of the Episcopia village (Fig. 3).

5   In-SAR Interferometry Analysis

The elaborations carried out with the DInSAR analysis show congruent results with geological and geomorphological studies.

A 0.40 [57] (Mora et al. 2003) threshold was applied to the mean coherence layer to detect ground displacement of highly coherent pixels whose electromagnetic response remains stable over time. The no-coherent pixels represent areas that change more frequently, mostly in cultivated or woody areas. Thus, the interferometric phase in vertical displacement has been transformed [58]. An external reference point was chosen in the study area that was considered stable respect to the time span in question. Figure 4 shows that vertical displacements are within to the southwestern area of the red perimeter and in the northeast part. The first shows mostly negative values, whereas the second only recorded positive values. Interferometric analysis confirms the downward slow and the detectable gravitational motion of the area using very long observation intervals.

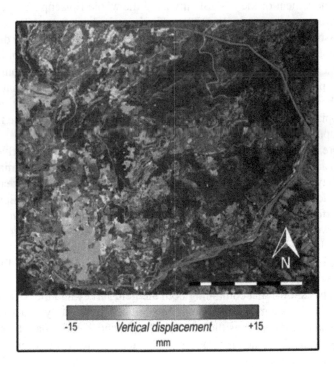

Fig. 4. Vertical displacement in the area of Episcopia village. Red line shows the bound of the DSGSD.

6   Discussion and Conclusions

The Episcopia area is located in the axial zone of the southern Apennines and has been affected by a strong regional uplift starting from Middle Pleistocene that was responsible for the high relief of the area [23, 59, 60]. As a consequence, a deep fluvial vertical incision and large landslides were activated in the whole site, and in the occurrence of a high uplift rate the Episcopia slope was affected by the DSGSD movement. The downward movement of the DSGSD modified the slope producing an upslope trench and in the downslope a clear deviation of about 800 m toward the south of the Sinni river channel occurred (Fig. 3).

As a result, the Sinni river valley become transversally asymmetric, the right side valley is steeper than the left one and is affected by many landslides focused in front of the Episcopia village.

A clear field evidence of the downward movement of the DSGSD is also the break of the Sinni fluvial terraces arrangement [34]. Moreover, two streams bound the DSGSD, both left tributaries of the Sinni River, the Fosso del Monaco Stream on the west-side and the Fosso del Confine on the east-side. They are entrenched and their valley-sides are affected by many active landslides, such as that in the Fosso del Monaco Stream affecting the north-eastern area of the Episcopia village.

An older movement of the DSGSD involved the whole Episcopia slope from NNE to SSW, whereas a younger one partially affecting the slope from NW to SE thus to forms the Fosso Lomea trench. These movements are also highlight by the displacement and the rotation of about 10° toward the SW of the stratigraphic horizon between the Serra Corneta and Castronuovo Fms. On these bases, we have reconstructed the displacement plane of the DSGSD by means of geological sections that allowed to measure at about 700 m of depth its thickness. The vertical displacement in the upside of the Episcopia slope and the horizontal translation in its downside are the features that allowed to suppose a listric geometry of the subsurface plane [61].

Furtermore, the recent surveying has shown the occurrence of many active landslides with seasonal activity in the south-eastern sector of the DSGSD. They are mainly placed along the valley sides of the Fosso del Monaco and Fosso del confine streams and is a strong field evidence that led us to consider still active the DSGSD of the Episcopia area [34]. The interferometric analysis is a preliminary result that shows the consistency with geological surveys, i.e., the stability of the north area and a movement of the south-west area that includes the urban zone. In the case of the Episcopia DSGSD, it would be wise to expand the observation dataset and use more accuracy methodologies for Persistent Scatterers (PS) choice and analysis of the low coherence pixel.

The paper has shown that combining both the field survey and the SAR-interferometry technique analysis a more detail could be obtained in the study of active processes that affect the landscape such as the DSGSD. Furthermore, these data together with a multitemporal analysis of aerial photo are relevant for the recognition of landscape modification, overall in the last decades.

References

1. Engelen, G.B.: Gravity Tectonics in the North-Western Dolomites (N. Italy). Geol. Ultraiectina **13**, 1–92 (1963)

2. Goguel, J.: Scale-dependent rockslide mechanisms, with emphasis on the role of pore fluid vaporisation. In: Voight, B. (ed.) Rockslides and Avalanches, Develop in Geotechnical Engineer, 14a. Elsevier, Amsterdam (1978)
3. Dramis, F.: Aspetti geomorfologici e fattori genetici delle deformazioni gravitative profonde di versante. Atti I Sem. DSGS, Boll. Soc. Geol. It. **103**, 681–687 (1984)
4. Sorriso-Valvo, M.: Presentazione. Atti I Sem. DSGS. Boll. Soc. Geol. It. **103**, 667–669 (1984)
5. Cavallin, A., Crescenti, U., Dramis, F., Prestininzi, A., Sorriso-Valvo, M.: Tipologia e diffusione delle deformazioni gravitative profonde di versante in Italia. Boll. Soc. Geol, It (1987)
6. Agliardi, F., Crosta, G., Zanchi, A.: Structural constraints on deep-seated slope deformation kinematics. Eng. Geol. **59**, 83–102 (2001)
7. Pasuto, A., Soldati, M.: Lateral spreading. In: Shroder, J.F., Marston, R.A., Stoffel, M. (eds.) Treatise on Geomorphology Mountain and Hillslope Geomorphology, vol. 7, pp. 239–248. Academic Press, San Diego (2013)
8. Agliardi, F., Crosta, G., Zanchi, A., Ravazzi, C.: Onset and timing of deep-seated gravitational slope deformations in the eastern Alps, Italy. Geomorphology **103**, 113–129 (2009)
9. Agliardi, F., Zanchi, A., Crosta, G.: Tectonic vs. gravitational morphostructures in the central Eastern Alps (Italy): constraints on the recent evolution of the mountain range. Tectonophysics **474**, 250–270 (2009)
10. Panek, T., Limes, J.: Temporal behavior of deep-seated gravitational slope deformations: a review. Earth Sci. Rev. **156**, 14–38 (2016)
11. Forcella, F., Orombelli, G.: Holocene slope deformations in Valfurva, Central Alps, Italy. Geogr. Fis. Dinam. Quat. **7**, 41–48 (1984)
12. Berardino, P., Costantini, M., Franceschetti, G., Iodice, A., Pietranera, L., Rizzo, V.: Use of differential SAR interferometry in monitoring and modelling large slope instability at Maratea (Basilicata, Italy). Eng. Geol. **68**, 31–51 (2003)
13. Guerricchio, A.: Tectonics, deep seated gravitational slope deformations (DSGSDs) and large landslides in the calabrian region (Southern Italy). Giornale di Geologia Applicata **1**, 73–90 (2005)
14. Di Martire, D., Novellino, A., Ramondini, M., Calcaterra, D.: A-differential synthetic aperture radar interferometry analysis of a deep seated gravitational slope deformation occurring at Bisaccia (Italy). Sci. Total Environ. **550**, 556–573 (2016)
15. Bentivenga, M., Laurita, S., Palladino, G., Prosser, G., Saroli, M.: Studio geologico e geomorfologico della DGPV di Episcopia (PZ) (Basilicata Centro-Meridionale). Rend. Online Soc. Geol. It. **6**, 47–48 (2009)
16. Pescatore, T., Renda, P., Schiattarella, M., Tramutoli, M.: Stratigraphic and structural relationship between Meso-Cenozoic Lagonegro basin and coeval carbonate platforms in southern Appennines, Italy. Tectonophysics **315**, 269–286 (1999)
17. Patacca, E., Scandone, P.: Geology of the Southern Apennines. Boll. Soc. Geol. It. (Ital. J. Geosci.) **7**, 75–119 (2007). Special Issue
18. Amodio Morelli, L., Bonardi, G., Colonna, V., Dietrich, D., Giunta, G., Ippolito, F., Liguori, V., Lorenzoni, S., Paglionico, A., Perrone, V., Piccarreta, G., Russo, M., Scandone, P., Zanettin Lorenzoni, E., Zuppetta, A.: L'Arco Calabro-Peloritano nell'Orogene Appenninico-Maghrebide. Mem. Soc. Geol. It. **17**, 1–60 (1976)
19. Vezzani, L.: La Formazione del Frido (Neocomiano-Aptiano) tra il Pollino ed il Sinni (Lucania). Geol. Rom. **VIII**, 129–176 (1969)
20. Bonardi, G., Amore, F.O., Ciampo, G., De Capoa, P., Micconet, P., Perrone, V.: Il complesso Liguride. Auct.: stato delle conoscenze e problemi aperti sulla sua evoluzione pre-appenninica ed i suoi rapporti con l'Arco Calabro. Mem. Soc. Geol. It. **41**, 17–35 (1988)

21. Monaco, C., Tansi, C., Tortorici, L., De Francesco, A.M., Morten, L.: Analisi geologico-strutturale dell'Unità del Frido nel confine calabro-lucano (Appennino meridionale). Mem. Soc. Geol. It. **47**, 341–353 (1991)

22. Monaco, C., Tortorici, L.: Tectonic role of ophiolite-bearing terranes in the development of the Southern Apennines orogenic belt. Terra Nova **7**, 153–160 (1995)

23. Schiattarella, M., Giano, S.I., Gioia, D., Martino, C., Nico, G.: Age and statistical properties of the summit palaeosurface of southern Italy. Geografia Fisica Dinamica Quaternaria **36**, 289–302 (2013)

24. Vezzani, L.: Il bacino plio-pleistocenico di S. Arcangelo (Lucania). Atti Acc. Gioenia Sc. Suppl. Sc. Geol. s. VI **18**, 207–227 (1967)

25. Knott, S.D.: The Liguride complex of Southern Italy a Cretaceous to Paleogene accretionary wedge. Tectonophysics **142**, 217–226 (1987)

26. Schiattarella, M.: Tettonica della Catena del Pollino (Confine Calabro-Lucano). Mem. Soc. Geol. It. **51**, 543–566 (1996)

27. Sansone, M.T.C., Rizzo, G.: Pumpellyite veins in the metadolerite of the Frido Unit (southern Appennines-Italy). Periodico di Mineralogia **81**, 75–92 (2012)

28. Laurita, S., Prosser, G., Rizzo, G., Langone, A., Tiepolo, M., Laurita, A.: Geochronological study of zircons from continental crust rocks in the Frido Unit (Southern Apennines). Int. J. Earth Sci. (Geol. Rundsch.) (2014). doi:10.1007/s00531-014-1077-7

29. Hippolyte, J.C., Angelier, J., Roure, F., Casero, P.: Piggyback basin development and thrust belt evolution: structural and palaeostress analyses of Plio-Quaternary basins in the Southern Apennines. J. Struct. Geol. **16**, 159–173 (1994)

30. Pieri, P., Sabato, L., Loiacono, F., Marino, M.: Il bacino di piggyback di Sant'Arcangelo: evoluzione tettonico-sedimentaria. Boll. Soc. Geol. It. **113**, 465–481 (1994)

31. Giano, S.I.: Geomorphology of the Agri intermontane basin (Val d'Agri-Lagonegrese National Park, Southern Italy). J. Maps **12**(4), 639–648 (2016)

32. Giano, S.I., Schiattarella, M.: Age constraints and denudation rate of a multistage fault line scarp: an example from Southern Italy. Geochronometria **41**(3), 245–255 (2014)

33. Aucelli, P.P.C., D'Argenio, B., Della Seta, M., Giano, S.I., Schiattarella, M.: Intermontane basins: quaternary morphoevolution of Central-Southern Italy. Rend. Fis. Acc. Lincei **25**(Suppl. 2), 107–110 (2014)

34. Giano, S.I., Gioia, D., Schiattarella, M.: Morphotectonic evolution of connected intermontane basins from the southern Apennines, Italy: the legacy of the pre-existing structurally-controlled landscape. Rend. Fis. Acc. Lincei **25**(Suppl. 2), 241–252 (2014)

35. Giano, S.I., Giannandrea, P.: Late Pleistocene differential uplift inferred from the analysis of fluvial terraces (southern Apennines, Italy). Geomorphology **217**, 89–105 (2014)

36. Bentivenga, M., Capolongo, D., Palladino G., Piccarreta, M.: Geomorphological map of the area between Craco and Pisticci (Basilicata, Italy). J. Maps (2014). doi:10.1080/17445647.2014.935501

37. Cinque, A., Patacca, E., Scandone, P., Tozzi, M.: Quaternary kinematic evolution of the Southern Apennines. Relationships between surface geological features and deep lithospheric structures. Ann. Geofis. **36**, 249–260 (1993)

38. Bentivenga, M., Coltorti, M., Prosser, G.: Il movimento gravitativo profondo di Craco (Basilicata Ionica). Il Quaternario, Ital. J. Quat. Sci. **17**(2/2), 613–625 (2004)

39. Scorpio, V., Aucelli, P.P.C., Giano, S.I., Pisano, L., Robustelli, G., Rosskopf, C.M., Schiattarella, M.: River channel adjustments in Southern Italy over the past 150 years and implications for channel recovery. Geomorphology **251**, 77–90 (2015)

40. Pascale, S., Bellanova, J., Losasso, L., Perrone, A., Giocoli, A., Piscitelli, S., Murgante, B., Sdao, F.: Geomorphological Fragility and Mass Movements of the Archaeological Area of "Torre di Satriano" (Basilicata, Southern Italy). In: Murgante, B., Misra, S., Rocha, Ana Maria A.C., Torre, C., Rocha, J.G., Falcão, M.I., Taniar, D., Apduhan, Bernady O., Gervasi, O. (eds.) ICCSA 2014. LNCS, vol. 8582, pp. 495–510. Springer, Cham (2014). doi:10.1007/978-3-319-09147-1_36

41. Sarma, J.N., Acharjee, S., Murgante, B.: Morphotectonic study of the Brahmaputra basin using geoinformatics. J. Geol. Soc. India **86**(3), 324–330 (2015). doi:10.1007/s12594-015-0318-0. Springer

42. Nath, B., Acharjee, S., Kumar Mitra, A., Majumder, D., Murgante, B.: A geospatial approach to determine lake depth and configuration of Reingkhyongkine (Pukur Para) Lake, Rangamati Hill District, Bangladesh with multi-temporal satellite data. J. Environ. Acc. Manage. **3**(3), 243–258 (2015). doi:10.5890/JEAM.2015.09.004

43. Pascale, S., Parisi, S., Mancini, A., Schiattarella, M., Conforti, M., Sole, A., Murgante, B., Sdao, F.: Landslide Susceptibility Mapping Using Artificial Neural Network in the Urban Area of Senise and San Costantino Albanese (Basilicata, Southern Italy). In: Murgante, B., Misra, S., Carlini, M., Torre, Carmelo M., Nguyen, H.-Q., Taniar, D., Apduhan, Bernady O., Gervasi, O. (eds.) ICCSA 2013. LNCS, vol. 7974, pp. 473–488. Springer, Heidelberg (2013). doi:10.1007/978-3-642-39649-6_34

44. Partheepan, K., Acharjee, S., Thayanath, S., Murgante, B.: A Remote Sensing and Geo-Informatics Approach in Watershed Planning of Irrigation Tanks Connected with Batticaloa Lagoon: A Case Study of Unnichchai Watershed. In: Boştenaru Dan, M., Crăciun, C. (eds.) Space and Time Visualisation, pp. 195–206. Springer, Cham (2016). doi:10.1007/978-3-319-24942-1_12

45. Press, W.H., Teukolsky, S.A., Vetterling, W.T., Flannery, B.P.: Numerical Recipes in C: The Art of Scientific Computing, 2nd edn. (1992)

46. Prati, C., Rocca, F., Monti-Guarnieri, A., Damonti, E.: Seismic migration for SAR focusing: Interferometrical applications. IEEE Trans. GRS **28**(4), 627640 (1990)

47. Gabriel, A., Goldstein, R.: Grossed orbits interfere metry: theory and experimental (1998)

48. Goldstein, R.M., Werner, C.L.: Radar interferogram phase filtering for Geophysical applications. Geophys. Res. Lett. **25**, 4035–4038 (1998)

49. Small, D., Schubert, A.: Guide to ASAR Geocoding, RSL-ASAR-GC-AD, Issue 1.0 (2008)

50. Derauw, D., Orban, A.: Baseline combination for INSAR DEM altimetric resolution enchancment. In: Proceedings of the FRINGE 2003 Workshop (ESA SP-550) (2003)

51. Costantini, M.: A novel phase unwrapping method based on network programming. IEEE Tran. Geosci. Remote Sens. **36**, 813–821 (1998)

52. Mallorquí, J.J., Mora O., Blanco P., Broquetas A.: Linear and non-linear long-term terrain deformation with DInSAR (cpt: coherent pixels technique). In: Proceedings of the FRINGE 2003 Workshop (ESA SP-550) (2003)

53. Blanco-Sanchez, P., Mallorquí, J.J., Duque, S., Monells, D.: The coherent pixels technique (CPT): an advanced DInSAR technique for nonlinear deformation monitoring. Pure. appl. Geophys. **165**, 1167–1194 (2008)

54. Varnes, D.J.: Slope movement types and processes. In: Schuster, R.L., Krizek, R.J. (eds.) Landslides, Analysis and Control, Transportation Research Board, Special report no. 176, pp. 11–33. National Academy of Sciences (1978)

55. Carrara, A., D'Elia, B., Semenza, E.: Classificazione e nomenclatura dei movimenti franosi. Geologia Applicata e Idrogeologia **20**, 223–243 (1985)

56. Bentivenga, M., Palladino, G., Caputi, A.: Development of the Pietra Maura landslide and interactions with the Marsico Nuovo dam (Basilicata - Italy). Geografia Fisica e Dinamica Quaternaria **35**, 13–22 (2012). doi:10.4461/GFDQ.2012.35.2

57. Mora O., Mallorqui, J.J., Broquetas A.: Linear and Nonlinear Terrain Deformation Maps From a Reduced Set of Interferometric SAR Images (2003)
58. Ferretti, A., Monti-Guarnieri, A., Prati, C., Rocca, F., Massonet, D.: InSAR Principles: Guidelines for SAR Interferometry Processing and Interpretation, ESA TM-19 (2007)
59. Amato, A., Aucelli, P.P.C., Cinque, A.: The long-term denudation rate in southern Apennines Chain (Italy): a GIS – aided estimation of the rock volumes eroded since middle Pleistocene time. Quatern. Int. **101–102**, 3–11 (2003)
60. Schiattarella, M., Di Leo, P., Beneduce, P., Giano, S.I.: Quaternary uplift vs tectonic loading: a case-study from the Lucanian Apennine, southern Italy. Quatern. Int. **101–102**, 239–251 (2003)
61. Hutchinson, J.N.: General report: morphological and geotechnical parameters of landslide in relation to geology and hydrogeology. In: Proceedings of 5th I.S.L. Landslides 1, Lausanne (1988)

Integrating Supervised Classification in Social Participation Systems for Disaster Response. A Pilot Study

Pasquale Balena[1](✉) [iD], Nicola Amoroso[2] [iD], and Caterina De Lucia[3] [iD]

[1] Polytechnic of Bari, Via Orabona 4, 70125 Bari, Italy
pasquale.balena@poliba.it
[2] University of Bari, Via Orabona 4, 70125 Bari, Italy
nicola.amoroso@ba.infn.it
[3] University of Foggia, Largo Papa Giovanni Paolo II 1, 71100 Foggia, Italy
caterina.delucia@unifg.it

Abstract. The recent evolution of Information and Communication Technology (ICT) and mobile devices has strongly encouraged social participation as a tool for decision-support systems. These social participation tools are labelled as Participatory Geographic Information System (PGIS). The use of these tools has also extended to several domains – such as natural disasters, humanitarian crises, political conflicts – with the main aim to help affected populations and provide useful information for survival.

Nonetheless, social participation tools present some drawbacks for managing non-structured information retrieved from large databases and Social Networks. The limitations concern either the need to understand knowledge in (almost) real time or data classification according to a specific domain.

The present work aims at understanding the use of supervised classification models in situations of emergencies (i.e. disaster response) to classify message requests asking for/offering to help. To achieve the above aim we use machine learning techniques to compare classification models and evaluate their effectiveness and potentials to integrate them into existing PGIS systems.

Main results suggest the existence of a relatively high accuracy of test and training classification by employing Random Forest, Neural Networks and Support Vector Machine (SVM) models. We argue in favour of supervised classification for its usefulness as a tool to be integrated in social participation for disaster response.

Keywords: Supervised classification · Social participation · Disaster response

1 Introduction

The latest social changes due to the rapid development of ICT, have primarily affected social interactions through countless applications oriented to share textual and multi-media content. There has been a growth of various initiatives to involve public participation in the decision making process.

© Springer International Publishing AG 2017
O. Gervasi et al. (Eds.): ICCSA 2017, Part IV, LNCS 10407, pp. 675–686, 2017.
DOI: 10.1007/978-3-319-62401-3_49

Web 2.0 technology platforms like Ushahidi[1] and OpenStreetMap[2] have witnessed the rise of terminologies including geospatial and participatory aspects such as Volunteered Geographic Information (VGI), PGIS, neogeography, citizen sensing, crisis mapping, crowdmapping, and citizen science [1–3]. In particular, PGIS and VGI find application for several governmental activities on specific issues [4].

Also, the rapid development of social networks like Twitter and/or Facebook has increased citizen participation on a number of questions for policy, economics, or environmental debates to cite a few. This type of participation on social networks is somehow not oriented to discuss a given issue/problem as is the case of PGIS platforms.

However, while these new tools and social media open new collaborative scenarios, they still leave some complex issues unresolved. Critical issues concern: the interpretation of information structured as texts and expressed in natural language; the reliability and quality of data collected through crowdsourcing [1, 6] and social media.

Based on the latter aspect, the aim of the present paper is to overcome this limitation and proposes a conceptual framework which integrates supervised classification of text messages from social media in existing PGIS tools. To test the efficacy of supervised classification in the proposed framework, we use machine learning algorithms applied to the domain of emergencies such as natural disaster events.

Over the last decade, there has been an increasing use of social media in disaster events such as the fires in California and Australia, the hurricanes in the USA, the earthquakes in Haiti, Italy, China or Indonesia, the floodings in UK and central Europe. In these contexts, social media play an important role to support the prompt management of humanitarian aid from governmental and non-governmental organizations and respond to affected populations. We argue that if assessed information is promptly read and/or observed by the rescue team, it can save human and animal lives and the ecological system.

The present work is structured as follows: Sect. 2 describes the use of crowdsourced data with particular emphasis on social media in disaster event and highlights the conceptual model and the machine learning techniques used in the pilot study; Sect. 3 illustrates the obtained results; Sect. 4 presents a brief discussion; and finally, Sect. 5 concludes the work.

2   Material and Method

For several years the growth of geo-referenced data was due to private firms providing their services to governmental organizations [7].

With the introduction of web 2.0 technology and diffusion of mobile devices endowed, through user friendly interfaces, with global position system (GPS) technology, the decision making process evolves to include the digital social participation. The exchange of data through these new technologies provides detailed information [8–10] and supports the diffusion of local geo-referenced knowledge [11].

---

[1] www.ushahidi.com.

[2] www.openstreetmap.org.

Over the last 15 years, PGIS/PGIS and VGI have been the main technologies used for social participation. Both technologies although based on similar information architectures pertain different aims such that the literature has confined them in two different domains. The former aims to reinforce local active participation and achieves detailed regional/territorial analysis. The latter aims to the implementation of methodologies oriented to large scale data acquisition [12, 13]. From a methodological point of view, PGIS are based on geographical information systems known as Participatory Learning and Action (PLA) [14]. The term VGI was introduced for the first time by [8]. It refers to a set of approaches, systems and methods for the collection of local knowledge and organization, based on architectures that use techniques such as user-generated content (UGC)[3], Web 2.0, Geoweb[4] in which the geo-spatial component plays a key role [8, 15, 16].

The term social media refers to a type of communication that uses web platforms where users discuss and share general topics. The platforms include blogging and micro-blogging, social networking sites, platforms, and wikis. Social media has nowadays reached a global level such to occupy all areas of public life [17].

Social media applications have radically changed the lives of millions of people, influencing the interaction between people and playing an important role in sharing crisis information [18].

The late nineties witnessed the first experience of using social networks to collect and share information from citizens being in an emergency, crisis or protest. One of the first websites with message board was created soon after the Indian Ocean tsunami of December 26 in 2004 to support the relief efforts of the affected population [19]. A similar experience was repeated a year later by the citizens of New Orleans on Myspace platform immediately after the devastation of the city caused by Hurricane Katrina [20].

Twitter was used for the first time in disaster event in 2007 during the fires in the areas surrounding San Diego, California (United States). Since then, Twitter is one of the most used platforms by affected people in disaster response aiming at collecting and disseminating information and supporting relief operations [19, 21].

The case of the Haiti earthquake of 2010 is perhaps the most cited in the literature [16, 22, 23]. The magnitude and the severe impact on populated areas, led initially to a local response that was crucial to support rescuing operations and to guide the search of missing people. At a second stage, Twitter was also central to organise international humanitarian aid.

According to a recent study by [19] it is possible to identify the main factors influencing the content of messages during an event. In particular, the content of a message may be characterized by several factors as described below:

- By application type: This considers the social network or messaging service used.
- By event type and information provided: The type of the event and its magnitude affect the content of the message.

---

[3] UGC are Website platforms, where citizens can publish their own comments, photos, videos, and more online such as YouTube, Facebook, Twitter, and Wikipedia [34].

[4] Geoweb is defined as a distributed set of geographic services that are user-controlled and available on the internet [35].

- By factual, subjective or emotional content: The message may report objective facts or subjective and emotional contents.
- By information source: Messages can be posted by individuals playing different roles in disaster response.
- By credibility: This feature refers to actors (individuals and organizations) that can be associated with a degree of reliability to the information contained in the message, which in turn, can be more or less credible or plausible.
- By location: The message, although relating to the event, can be sent by people who are nearby or far away to the area of the event. The perception and knowledge of the event affects the degree of knowledge of the event itself.
- By time: The phases of an event affect the content of the message. Messages sent ex-ante to an event have a different content than messages sent ex-post. The latter focuses on the request for help, while the former on reporting the probability of the occurrence of the event.

Several platforms such as Ushahidi are active in supporting disaster response and are seen as best practices for social participation. Figure 1 illustrates the conceptual model used in our work.

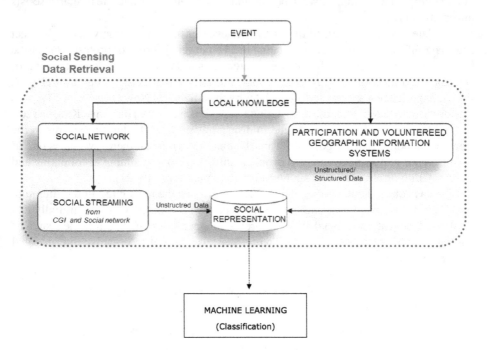

Fig. 1. Methodological framework

Information retrieved through a social network can be stored in a database. However, some limitations exist due to memo's fields in which information is stored as text with no input-constraints. A further limitation of the social representation is that the user should get to know with the application and install it on his/her mobile device. To solve this problem several platforms add new modules and link these ones to social networks, to capture further information and data. This process is attainable through application programming interface (API)[5] which are dedicated libraries between the platform and the social network (e.g. Twitter, Facebook). The social streaming captures, saves and stores text messages containing keywords such as for example 'earthquake' with the corresponding indication of location.

How to treat data with no input constraints from social streaming?

We carry out a pilot study with the use of PGIS technologies. These platforms (e.g. Ushahidi) retrieve geo-referenced data either directly (through specific functions of the platform) or indirectly (through social network streaming processing).

In a first step we retrieve unstructured data through a simulation analysis in the metropolitan area of Bari (Southern Italy) in which we use an open-ended web survey (Fig. 2). The on-line survey, after illustrating a hypothetical earthquake, asks participants to write request for or offer to help messages (max 140 characters). A set of 314 observations contains messages from the aftermath of the simulated earthquake (Fig. 3).

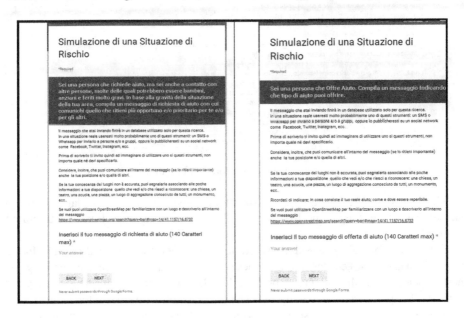

Fig. 2. Survey forms (in Italian)

---

[5] API is a set of software libraries and available procedures to execute a series of functions.

COD	DESCRIZIONE
Q	sono sotto ponte via cavour bari serve cibo e acqua
Q	Aiuto!Sono davanti la cattedrale di san sabino a Bari.Siamo 4 adulti di cui 2 anziani e 1 bambino di 3 anni.Abbiamo provviste per altri 2 gg
Q	sono rimasto bloccato nel sottopassaggio di Via Quintino Sella con la cinquecento, il livello dell'acqua sale e mia moglie mi picchia
Q	ho degli hamburger col ketchup nel tre ruote, li vendo a soli 10 euro l'uno, vista la situazione, servizio a domicilio
Q	Ci sono due donne (di cui una anziana) con tre bambini vicino la chiesa di Santa Lucia che hanno bisogno di viveri
Q	Sono nel borgo antico, posso offrire cibo, acqua e coperte
Q	Disponibile a soccorrervi: datemi coordinate gps
Q	Posso offrire sostegno per fornitura e consegna di beni di prima necessità
Q	Offro il mio supporto tecnico
Q	vi prego corrette ho due bambini con me nella palestra palacarrassi
Q	Sono a bari, San Girolamo, vicino canalone, ci sono persone bloccate sotto le macerie, si stimano 12 adulti e 3 bambini,si richiede aiuto.
Q	Una bambina col suo fratellino sono sotto le macerie affianco alla Cattedrale. Stanno bene ma hanno tanta paura e tanto freddo !!
Q	Ci stiamo Attivando per aiutarvi, per cercare di risolvere questa tragedia
Q	Siamo isolati all'interno di un palazzo crollato nei pressi dello stadio. Non c'è luce e fa molto freddo.
Q	Mi trovo in auto in corso Cavour davanti a me c'è un'altra macchina schiacciata dalle macerie dell'edificio adiacente sento lamenti
Q	Siamo circa una cinquantina di persone di tutte le età, siamo negli edifici vicino l' ospedale militare Via Petraglione e ci sono feriti.
Q	sono vicino alla Coop Via Fanelli, posso aggregarmi ad altri soccorritori in zona
Q	IMPORTANTE!!! All'angolo tra corso Cavour e via Putignani c'è un amico con una gamba bloccata da una maceria. Chi può venire ad aiutarci?
Q	Sono con altre persone vicino ad una chiesa
Q	Mi trovo vicino il Castello e attorno a me sento dei lamenti, io riesco a muovermi

Fig. 3. A subset of the earthquake simulation sample (In Italian)

In a second step we use unstructured knowledge on 'territorial issues' retrieved from a social participation platform. The latter data consists of 1000 observations (Fig. 4).

COD	DESCRIZIONE
S	tutto il patrimonio, di valore storico ed artistico, della città vecchia reso pubblico
S	un porto turistico e commerciale e non più industriale
S	un recupero identitario che miri a potenziare l'attravità del centro storico.
S	una città vecchia ripoplata con una forte vocazione turistica e artistica basatasul mestieri legati al mare
S	una città vecchia sperimentale nelle pratiche legate alla sostenibilità e i centri storici
S	utilizzare i palazzi antichi come laboratori culturali per divulgazione della cultura antica, le tradizioni ,il mare e il paesaggio
S	utilizzare viabilità via mare per raggiungere la città vecchia
S	valorizzare centro storico (ristrutturare creare luoghi di aggregazione
S	valorizzare i siti archeologici come laboratori universitari per le materie idonee alla storia del territorio
S	valorizzare la città vecchia organizzando eventi e attrazioni riguardanti la cultura del territorio e la storia
S	valorizzazione della rete di ipogei e dei beni archeologici della città vecchia. apertura di un museo diffuso dell'acropoli
S	zona porta napoli, cementir... costruire una piastra intermodale, punto di convergenza sia per un grande snodo stradale per tradizioni fe
S	conversione dell'economia del territorio da industriale ad agricola tecnologica, turistica, energia rinnovabile
S	abbattimento mura arsenale e restituzione dlle zone prospicienti alla citta' (ospedale militare, villa ammiraglio)
S	acqua potabile
S	adeguamento sistema e programmazione sanitaria in linea con i problemi derivanti dall'inquinamento industriale

Fig. 4. A subset of general territorial information (In Italian)

Third, we build the database for classification analysis by mixing the data of the two datasets, assuming they come from data collection from structured and unstructured knowledge.

Data should be validated and classified at a later stage by appointed experts. In the context of natural disasters, the timing of these operations can last several days and suggest inefficiencies, should the community proceed with the elaboration of information in disaster response. The proposed model of machine learning attempts to overcome this limitation.

The subsequent data analysis is performed with the use of methods implemented in open source data mining tools as R[6] and RapidMiner[7] that implement models such as: classification, segmentation, association, correlation and prediction.

---

[6] www.r-project.org.

[7] www.rapidminer.com.

We use Rapidminer to perform data cleaning operations for texts analysis as follows: (i) Tokenization allows to select the main words (token) included in a document; (ii) Stopwords allow to drop all irrelevant words listed in the stopword dictionaries (i.e. Italian dictionary); (iii) Replacing tokens replace compound words with single words; and (iv) Stemming reduces the number of words that have in common the same root in a single token [24] or more tokens (n-gram).

Whereas, we use R to perform classification with different models.

The obtained output of the text-mining approach is of two types: (1) The first one is a vector of lexical elements. The elements of the vector could be formed by a single word or several words; (2) The second one is a data matrix to run the predictive model. The columns of the matrix represent the parts of the document with a specific meaning (i.e. nouns, verbs and adjectives); the rows (the observations) identify each text message in which 1 indicates the presence of the lemma and 0 otherwise.

This representation yields to an N-dimensional feature space, the features interweave relationships that in principle can be both linear or non-linear. Thus, we proceed with classification analysis and investigate on the detection of an optimal separation between the classes (i.e words belonging to the disaster domain and viceversa) and study whether this separation is significantly dependent on the supervised model employed.

Given the dummy nature of the features adopted, we firstly investigate a tree-based classifier: Random Forest. Random Forests [25] is a state-of-the-art classifier based on the idea of combining simple tree classifier predictions in a unique model; the strength of this technique is its robustness and simplicity, as it requires substantially no tuning.

Besides, we compare the results obtained with Random Forests with other machine learning approaches. Specifically, we investigate a boosting algorithm, such as AdaBoost, which has already demonstrated its effectiveness in text categorization tasks [26]; the Naïve Bayes model which is widely used in literature [27]. And, finally, two state-of-the-art approaches for classification tasks which are Support Vector Machines and Neural Networks. Both are supervised model which have been widely adopted in several classification tasks with outstanding performances, also in the field of text categorization [28, 29].

To fairly compare the classification performance of the five classifiers mentioned above, we adopt a cross-validation framework. The goal is to provide a mean classification and error performances to compare the different results. In general, cross-validation procedures distinguish n-fold and leave-one-out cross-validation [30]. The former is carried out with a nested approach and is the algorithm included in R. Data is split into n-folds of equal size and trained and tested n-times. Of these n-subsets, a single subset is hold as input of the testing sub-procedure, and the rest of the n − 1 subsets are then applied as training data in the subsequent reiteration (i.e. as input of the training sub-procedure). The cross-validation is repeated n-times treating the n-subsets as holdout sets each time. The cross-validation procedure then predicts how sensitive is the model (i.e. how well performs the model) to a hypothetical holdout dataset.

Analogously, leave-one-out cross-validation uses the whole data sample for training, except one example which is kept out for test; it is known that leave-one-out tends to perform biased predictions, in particular it tends to overestimate the classification performance; leave-one-out is generally used when the sample size is small. As this is

not the case of the present study, n-fold is the preferred technique used for cross-validation.

3   Results

A set of classification experiments is designed with a 5-fold cross-validation. 50 cross-
validation rounds are performed for each classification model: AdaBoost, Naïve Bayes,
Neural Networks, Random Forest and Support Vector Machine.

For the simulation analysis, we create a training set of about 200 observations. A
sub-sample of 100 messages is taken from the on-line survey and a sub-sample of 100
messages is taken from the generic dataset about 'territorial issues'. The remaining
observations are used as test set.

Classification accuracy on the training and test sets has been compared. Training
accuracy is obtained by averaging the cross-validation performances. Each trained
model is also used on the test set.

The following Table 1 summarizes the obtained results.

Table 1. The comparison of the different models in terms of training and test accuracy. For each
model mean and standard deviations are reported

Method	Training accuracy	Test accuracy
AdaBoost	92.1 ± 1.4%	87.4 ± 1.3%
Naïve Bayes	81.6 ± 2.3%	73.3 ± 1.8%
Neural Networks	93.2 ± 1.6%	95.2 ± 1.1%
Random Forest	94.1 ± 1.5%	96.5 ± 0.8%
Support Vector Machine	92.8 ± 2.1%	94.4 ± 3.5%

The Random Forest and the Neural Network emerged as the two most successful
classifiers. The former yielded a training and test accuracy of, respectively, 94.1 ($\pm$ 1.5)%
and 96.5 ($\pm$ 0.8)%. For the latter, the figures were 93.2 ($\pm$ 1.6)% and 95.2 ($\pm$ 1.1)% for
training and test sets, respectively.

4   Discussion

The obtained results suggest that no matter what supervised model is employed it is
possible to reach satisfying levels of accuracy; this is an important measure of the reliability of the collected data. Besides, the cross-validation procedures granted a good
agreement between training and test performances: there are no great differences
between training and test results.

As expected, Random Forests were able to achieve the highest accuracy, even if the
difference with Neural Networks and Support Vector Machine is really subtle. The use
of dummy variables helped the tree classifiers of Random Forest to obtain this level of
accuracy; on the other hand, the complexity of feature space, in particular the high
dimensionality, helped Neural Networks and Support Vector Machine to be performing

too. It is worth noting that the poorest performance is obtained with the Naïve Bayes model. Probably this result suggests that in this field (i.e. disaster response) the contraction of a reliable probabilistic model depends on the acquisition of huge amount of data.

The obtained results and the use of machine learning can lead us to formulate some thoughts.

Firstly, as disaster response is likely to happen in unpredictable conditions where different types of threats interact to cause an array of direct and indirect, complex effects [31], the relationships among these factors should be carefully conceptualized and fully modelled. With climatic and environmental catastrophes being the threats most likely to trigger further socio-economic and ecological effects on the affected population, this study points to text analysis as being key to disentangle relevant information from messages that are often the only available direct source of messages sent by survivors and aid workers alike.

Secondly, the present research added to the evidence in favour of using machine learning techniques as being an adequate approach to disaster response.

A third aspect that may be singled out by reflecting on the empirical analysis is the effectiveness of predictive models to classify information from text messages. In line with the outcomes of other studies [28, 29], the chosen models proved to be reliable enough in sorting data over two domains, when a matrix detecting the presence or absence of a set of terms was applied.

5   Conclusion

The present study tries to overcome critical issues arising with crowdsourcing and social participation with a focus on disaster response domain. In particular, it constructs a conceptual model which integrates supervised classification in social participation technology tools. The rationale of the assessment of social participation in disaster response is that in such domains, should the assessed information be promptly read and/or observed by the rescue team, can save human and animal lives and the ecological system.

Main results from the classification analysis suggest that the employed predictive models appear effective to classify information from text messages. In particular, through a 5-fold cross-validation framework of 50 iterations across Adaboost, Random Forest, Support Vector Machine, Neural Networks, and Naïve Bayes models, the following was obtained: (i) The Random Forest and the Neural Network emerged as the two most successful classifiers; (ii) The former yielded a training and test accuracy of, respectively, 94.1 ($\pm$ 1.5)% and 96.5 ($\pm$ 0.8)%. For the latter, the figures were 93.2 ($\pm$ 1.6)% and 95.2 ($\pm$ 1.1)% for training and test sets, respectively. The results from the proposed pilot study suggest the existence of potential integration of supervised classification in social participation technologies.

5.1 Future Prospects

The use of classification functions as those implemented in R and Rapidminer could be integrated, in the near future, in PGIS and VGI platforms and more generally on decision support systems to develop, simultaneously, data streaming of risk events.

Classification from structured and unstructured knowledge could also be integrated with other models such as ontological models [32]. The creation of taxonomies and ontologies in a disaster response domain arises from the need to build conceptual models including all elements that somehow come into play. This is particularly relevant for the definition and interpretation of 'needs' to save lives.

The use of taxonomies and ontologies also arises with the aim of creating a strong reference for further developments such as application designs providing adequate indications to satisfy the needs which are universally shared and accepted about people and places. The creation of an ontology for a post-disaster event, aims to help solving complex problems that entail lack of understanding between actors and matching help requests with offers of assistance, through exchange of messages by the affected population. These forms of requests generally communicate a need for survival by including other information (not just basic information) – such as reference to places, other actors, objects, actions.

The above gaps may widen, as a result of demographic dynamics involving populations from heterogeneous ethnic groups with different languages, cultures and knowledge backgrounds. This diversity implies changes of social, cultural and language contexts and, while the transition is ongoing, it is complex to manage in terms of knowledge understanding. For this reason, the use of ontologies is predicated on the need to improve semantic interoperability of natural disaster domain models. Also, ontologies limit potential misunderstanding among rescue operators and strengthen the effectiveness and reliability of decision support systems.

The central role played by ICT in supporting disaster response requires cooperation between governmental bodies and other agencies, while operating on different software platforms to share the same type of information. Regardless of the technologies used for the exchange and sharing of information, it is relevant to have a common understanding of concepts and meanings of shared entities, in order to facilitate the functioning of decision support systems and make them interoperable [33].

More precisely, on the semantic level, interoperability calls for specific requirements, including common vocabularies and links between machine-understandable concepts to facilitate the interpretation and sharing of knowledge [19].

References

1. Elwood, S.: Volunteered geographic information: future research directions motivated by critical, participatory, and feminist GIS. GeoJournal **72**, 173–183 (2008)
2. Fast, V., Rinner, C.: A systems perspective on volunteered geographic information. ISPRS Int. J. GeoInf. **3**, 1278–1292 (2014)
3. Kar, B., Sieber, R., Haklay, M., Ghose, R.: Public participation GIS and participatory GIS in the era of geoweb editorial public participation GIS and participatory GIS in the era of GeoWeb. Cartogr. J. **53**, 296–299 (2016)

4. Verplanke, J., McCall, M.K., Uberhuaga, C., Rambaldi, G., Haklay, M.: A shared perspective for PGIS and VGI. Cartogr. J. **7041**, 1–10 (2016)
5. Bishr, M., Janowicz, K.: Can we trust information? - The case of volunteered geographic information. In: Toward Digital Earth Search Discovery Share Geospatial Data Work. Future Internet Symposium, vol. 6 (2010)
6. Flanagin, A.J., Metzger, M.J.: The credibility of volunteered geographic information. GeoJournal **72**, 137–148 (2008)
7. Goodchild, M.F., Glennon, J.A.: Crowdsourcing geographic information for disaster response: a research frontier. Int. J. Digit. Earth **3**, 231–241 (2010)
8. Goodchild, M.F.: Citizens as sensors: Web 2.0 and the volunteering of geographic information. GeoFocus **7**, 8–10 (2007)
9. Gill, A.Q., Bunker, D.: Crowd sourcing challenges assessment index for disaster management. In: 18th Annual Conference on Information System, AMCIS 2012, vol. 6, pp. 4428–4438 (2012)
10. Horita, F.E.A., Degrossi, L.C., Assis, L.F.F.G., Zipf, A.: The use of volunteered geographic information and crowdsourcing. VGI Disaster Manag. Syst. Lit. Rev. 1–10 (2013)
11. Frommberger, L., Schmid, F.: Crowdsourced bi-directional disaster reporting and alerting on smartphones in Lao PDR (2013)
12. Tulloch, D.L.: Is VGI participation? From vernal pools to video games. GeoJournal **72**, 161–171 (2008)
13. Sieber, R.E., Haklay, M.: The epistemology(s) of volunteered geographic information: a critique. Geo Geogr. Environ. (2015)
14. Rambaldi, G., Kyem, P.A.K., McCall, M., Weiner, D.: Participatory spatial information management and communication in developing countries. Electron. J. Inf. Syst. Dev. Countries **25**, 1–9 (2006)
15. McCall, M.K., Martinez, J., Verplanke, J.: Shifting boundaries of volunteered geographic information systems and modalities: learning from PGIS. ACME **14**, 791–826 (2015)
16. Xu, J., Nyerges, T.L.: A framework for user-generated geographic content acquisition in an age of crowdsourcing. Cartogr. Geogr. Inf. Sci. **406**, 1–15 (2016)
17. Poell, T., Dijck, V.: Understanding social media logic. Media Commun. **1**, 2–14 (2013)
18. Bruns, A.: Crisis communication. In: The Media and Communications in Australia, pp. 351–355 (2014)
19. Imran, M., Castillo, C., Diaz, F., Vieweg, S.: A processing social media messages in mass emergency: a survey (2015)
20. Shklovski, I., Burke, M., Kiesler, S., Kraut, R.: Technology adoption and use in the aftermath of Hurricane Katrina in New Orleans. Am. Behav. Sci. **53**, 1228–1246 (2010)
21. Vieweg, S., Hughes, A.L., Starbird, K., Palen, L.: Microblogging during two natural hazards events: what twitter may contribute to situational awareness. In: CHI 2010 Cris. Informatics, 10–15 April 2010, pp. 1079–1088 (2010)
22. Blum, J.R., Eichhorn, A., Smith, S., Sterle-Contala, M., Cooperstock, J.R.: Real-time emergency response: improved management of real-time information during crisis situations. J. Multimodal User Interfaces **8**, 161–173 (2014)
23. Haworth, B., Bruce, E.: A review of volunteered geographic information for disaster management. Geogr. Compass. **9**, 237–250 (2015)
24. Verma, T.: Tokenization and filtering process in RapidMiner. Int. J. Appl. Inf. Syst. **7**, 16–18 (2014). Found. Comput. Sci. FCS, New York, USA. ISSN 2249-0868
25. Breiman, L., Cutler, A.: Breiman and Cutler's random forests for classification and regression. Packag. "randomForest.", vol. 29 (2012)

26. Schapire, R.E., Singer, Y.: BoosTexter: a boosting-based system for text categorization. Mach. Learn. **39**, 135–168 (2000)
27. McCallum, A., Nigam, K.: A comparison of event models for Naive Bayes text classification. In: AAAI/ICML-98 Workshop on Learning for Text Categorization, pp. 41–48 (1998)
28. Lam, W., Ruiz, M., Srinivasan, P.: Automatic text categorization and its application to text retrieval. IEEE Trans. Knowl. Data Eng. **11**, 865–879 (1999)
29. Tong, S., Koller, D.: Support vector machine active learning with applications to text classification. J. Mach. Learn. Res. **2**, 45–66 (2001)
30. Basari, A.S.H., Hussin, B., Ananta, I.G.P., Zeniarja, J.: Opinion mining of movie review using hybrid method of support vector machine and particle swarm optimization. Procedia Eng. **53**, 453–462 (2013)
31. Coburn, A., Ralph, D., Tuveson, M., Ruffle, S., Bowman, G.: Cambridge System Shock Risk Framework A Taxonomy of Threats for Macro-Catastrophe Risk Management (2013)
32. Ianella, R.: Emergency information interoperability frameworks, 1–25 (2009)
33. Hiltz, S.R., Diaz, P., Mark, G.: Introduction: social media and collaborative systems. **18**, 1–6 (2011)
34. Hermida, A., Thurman, N.: A clash of cultures. J. Pract. **2**, 343–356 (2008)
35. Scharl, A., Tochtermann, K.: The Geospatial Web (2007)

Knowledge of Places: An Ontological Analysis
of the Social Level in the City

Rossella Stufano[1](✉), Dino Borri[1], Domenico Camarda[1], and Stefano Borgo[2]

[1] Politecnico di Bari, Bari, Italy
mariarosaria.stufanomelone@gmail.com
[2] Laboratory for Applied Ontology ISTC CNR, Trento, Italy

Abstract. The present paper proposes to enrich standard methodologies to interpret places with new information coming from other forms of place interpretation and description. We develop this proposal investigating geographical places since these are complex spatial environments well suited for the exploitation of different paradigms. The new approach we explore is based on ontological analysis. This approach, we believe, is very useful to integrate a cognitive stand within the traditional analytical and organizational views of complex spatial environments, in particular aiming to facilitate decision-making processes.

The overall rationale of this paper is twofold. From the one hand, the introduction of ontological levels is rather useful for organizing the modeling of complex systems. On the other hand, while these levels are informative, our understanding of space cannot be reduced to the ontological elements *per se* since they lack the contextual perspective. Therefore, deeper studies and research are needed to develop formal frameworks that really integrate standard and ontological methodologies for general modeling purposes.

Keywords: Spatial cognition · Ontological analysis · Cognitive modeling · Planning

1 Introduction

Places are landscapes seen from far away, are cities lived from the inside, are cities imagined from the outside, are ecological ecosystems and much more. This richness of the notion has always been a challenge for the modeler which has available only limited methodologies and modeling techniques and, yet, is asked to identify and manage a large variety of information and viewpoints.

We pick up this challenge by focusing our attention on *lived places*. Underlying there is a notion of physical place which in turn is composed of a concept of space and a concept of place. Each of these concepts has different declinations and for each declination there is a possible definition. Still, none of them is simple. From a cognitive or designer perspective, for example, space itself is something that develops and that changes with the agent. Space is not just a 3-dimensional geometrical entity [1].

A place is even more complicated: it is an interpreted space, a reasoned space, a space that raises feelings, the result of an aesthetic fruition. We can say that a place

© Springer International Publishing AG 2017
O. Gervasi et al. (Eds.): ICCSA 2017, Part IV, LNCS 10407, pp. 687–694, 2017.
DOI: 10.1007/978-3-319-62401-3_50

comes with a set of mental images, with a representation including an architecture of cognitive processes. The essence of place lies in the quality of being somewhere specific, the knowing that you are "here" rather than "there" [2]. For example, enclosure (or better the status of *being enclosed*) becomes a very important aspect of the making of a place.

We understand places mostly through cognitive contexts. This is the reason we read *places we live in*. We can interpret our being in a space as an objective proposition according to geometrical rules/indications. Nonetheless, our being in a place is defined only via a richer description. Every single person in a place has a subjective point of view and it is that point of view that characterizes that place as such. Points of view and contexts are results coming out from a historical – cognitive – cultural selection. Our knowledge of places can derive from experiences, from stories that structure ideas and feelings about them. When we talk about 'subjective knowledge' of places, what are we really dealing with? 'Subjective knowledge' is a kind of representation of places, and a representation vary from subject to subject and even across one's life [3]. "Knowledge of a place—where you are and where you come from—is intertwined with knowledge of who you are. Landscape, in other words, shapes mindscape" [3].

In literature there are many attempts to get a definition of representation of space. Ontological research [4] is increasingly seen as providing methodologies and tools to move forward in this direction. One advantage is that these systems are typically specified in languages that abstract away from data structures and implementation strategies. The languages of ontologies are closer to first-order logic than languages used to model databases. In computer and information science, an ontology is a technical term denoting a conceptual artifact that is designed for a purpose, which is to enable the modeling of knowledge about some domain, real or imagined [5].

2   About Planning

Today's awareness of the complexity of social and natural environments implies that in using state-of-the-art techniques to model these complex systems we must accept a dramatic, and perhaps discouraging, level of uncertainty. The traditional deterministic and quantitative approaches to urban planning and design in risky contexts seem to increasingly fall short of expectations in environmental domains; and this is now widely recognized [6].

Planning tries to manage complexity as the result of a recurring interaction between collective knowledge and the desired results: a position that requires sharing as the foundation of a necessary political dimension of contemporary design [7]. An urban project as a plan or as a strategy has to evolve over time, it can't stay frozen [8]. The planner, like the urban designer, has always to look at changes of the territory and has to read the different relationship between built space and complex urban organization. Architecture, social sciences or anthropology have an active role in the thinking and the development of urban projects. In the anticipation game, a city is a relational system that must be thought as a whole, not a mere composition of districts [9]. For these reasons a rich and reliable modeling of the place is an essential starting point for the planner.

3   Carving up Geographical Places

Humans live, move in and sense complex spatial environments using different paradigms. Their interaction with space is sophisticated. It continuously changes over time and relies on a variety of information types that can be classified in as many types as topology, geometry perspective, dynamics, affordance, society, culture and so on. Perhaps due to the richness of this interaction, humans are not aware of how their understanding of and interacting with space is realized. Ontological analysis, the study of what is at the core of our view on reality, can help to recognize, clarify and organize the essential elements and features of places that is crucial to humans in terms of objects, properties and processes. Searching for a general framework where to discover and organize this kind of information, we can list a few levels that seem quite relevant. Without aiming at an exhaustive list, we propose to subdivide these levels as follows: spatial, artifactual, cognitive, social, cultural and processual. These levels, in turn, can be subdivided in finer levels as we can see from these cases.

3.1   The Spatial Level

This is perhaps the most studied level since it is in large part independent of the subjective perspective easily leading to a formal analysis [10, 11]. Here we can recognize the *mereological* level within which one understands space in terms of parts, e.g., recognizing the distinction between an area and its neighborhood. A second level is the *topological* one within which one understands space in terms of contact and unity, e.g., recognizing the contiguity between neighborhoods and the unity of a city. Another level is the *geometrical* where one understands space in terms of shapes, e.g., recognizing that the shape of a city is constrained by that of the valley where it is located. Finally, the *geographical* level in which one understands space in terms of locations and their descriptions, e.g., distinguishing being along a valley or having a radial disposition in space.

3.2   The Artifactual Level

This is the level where one recognizes the physical realm and how human activities can change it. Here we have the *material* level where one understands space in terms of materiality, e.g., seeing the presence of wood, concrete, water. Then the *structural* level that allows to understand space in terms of qualified components, e.g., distinguishing natural vs manmade and a residential are vs a production area. The *artifactual* level adds an intentional aspect to the environment [12], e.g., looking at a garden as an intentionally modified environment. The next level is the *functional* one where one understands space in terms of functionality, e.g., recognizing a building as a shelter. Finally, the *production* level looks at entities as manipulation sites, e.g., seeing a farm as production site.

3.3 The Cognitive Level

At this level the specific capabilities of humans take the lead. The basic *cognitive* level allows to understand space in terms of experience, e.g., perceiving how to move across objects in space. Instead, the *representation* level leads to understand space in abstract terms, e.g., perceiving the relationships among areas in an airport. The *observation* level is where one understands space in terms of how things in it may change, e.g., perceiving the change in the transportation system. Next, we have the *phenomenological* level where one understands space as a moving entity, e.g. perceiving a city as evolving. The *perspectival* level allows to understand space from a perspectival viewpoint, e.g., differentiating a square depending from where one is looking at it. At the *conceptual* level space is seen as a collection of realized concepts, e.g., perceiving space as the manifestation of natural and artificial objects. Finally, the *action* level where one understands space as an entity in which to act, e.g. perceiving the changes that one can enforce on things.

4   The Case Study

Our ontological analysis of places starts from the data collected for the making of the Taranto's strategic plan to 2065. The data were collected via a series of nine community-based, interactive processes of knowledge exchange, aimed at building future scenarios for the new plan. The interactive processes of knowledge exchange were carried out in Taranto, southern Italy during spring and summer in 2014. They were carried out to support policies and decisions on urban socioeconomic as well as environmental domains and organized as a sequence of face-to-face brainstorming forums aimed at cooperatively singling out strategic lines to build alternative development scenarios. From a methodological point of view, it was a 2-step *scenario-building* activity [13] (Khakee et al. 2002). First, agents were invited to report problems they faced in their town districts. Then, each agent was invited to generate a reflection about the future of the district, particularly concerning expectations of future changes. Such sessions were organized in all town districts, indoor or outdoor, with participants divided in groups each of them sitting around a dedicated desk. A municipal representative coordinated each desk without taking part in the generative session, she/he had only the task of transcribing in linear charts concerns, problems, expectations and desires presented by the participants at the desk.

In order to manage the results in real time (synthesis and refinement), the interactive process was supported by the use of conceptual maps drawn using dedicated software tools (Decision explorer, Inspiration) [14] (Heft, 2013) (Fig. 1). This resulted in a real/virtual hybridization of the process, following well-established research trends, as reported in a number of case studies [13, 15]. Results achieved during the nine organized meetings were very different from one another. In particular, the first meeting was organized in the Città Vecchia (inner city district) with its great historical, environmental and cultural resources as well as significant environmental, physical and social degradation problems. In the Città Vecchia session the citizen participation was very high. About 80 stakeholders joined form different societal domains: residents, merchants, students, tourists, visitors. These agents, gathered around 6 desks and about 150 instances were collected.

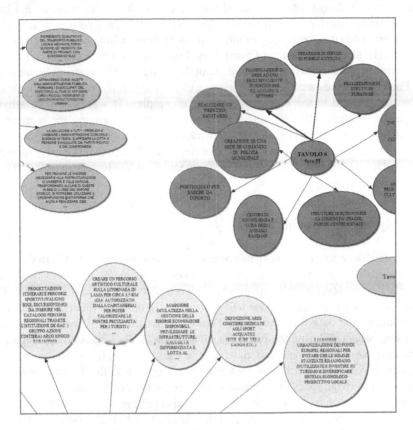

Fig. 1. Cognitive map example (excerpt)

The database collected during this session resulted interestingly rich and articulated. For this reason, it is a significant and valuable source for the present research effort.

The process naturally leads to two general types of instances: a. contextual problems; b. future visions. These two set of instances are about each quarter of the city as well as about the city in general. From an analysis of the data emerges that the environment is the most recurring issue in the groups. It is present in community problems and/or expectations, but also in the perceptions of the physical reality of the city. The industrial problem, on the contrary, is often absent from the discussed issues.

A first common character across the groups is the natural environment that persists in many city representations, so apparently resisting the consequences of an industrial culture. A second one is related to a structural relationship that the city has with the sea, intended as an element of both union and communication. A third is the potential of the city as tourist attraction which is linked to different characters in relation to the different peculiarities of the area. The industrial problem often seems idiosyncratically absent from protocols, but it is difficult that findings can be used for strategies disregarding industrial relations.

There was an almost total absence of participants in the forum session held in the industrial district, perhaps given the disillusionment with past policymaking. Other issues are related to the inadequacy of urban and metropolitan linkages to the city center, as well as related to the recovery of many illegal settlements. Other instances are about the inadequacy of the urban services and about the inadequacy of metropolitan connections. Further instances are about the recovery of unauthorized coastal settlements.

The session held in the inner city was quite complex. It was held with a hybrid computer-based and traditional, rather conflictual interaction among the participants. Outcomes showed a clear prevalence of visions on mere problems: important issues were the unstopped relationship with the sea (for touristic aims and/or city infrastructuring) and the enhancement of Taranto as archaeological and historical center (Magna Graecia colonization).

5   Analyzing the Social Level

Now that the theoretical framework has been outlined and the case study introduced, we proceed to analyze the levels one at the time. Generally speaking, this analysis is useful to identify if every level is well structured or if it is necessary to model additional information. Later in this research line we will proceed to characterize the specific sub-level.

Admittedly, the data we have about Taranto is not meant for research objectives since it was collected during the participation activities belonging to the strategy planning process. Nevertheless we think that it can be useful to start from this data for a first delineation of 'objects', 'attributes' and 'relations' populating the different levels. We decide to start from the social ontological level since the material collected in the Taranto case study is very rich from this perspective. We also believe that the material could be useful to analyze the cultural and process levels but this has not been evaluated yet. These views are not studied in this paper. Finally, the material collected in Taranto does not seem suitable for an analysis of the remaining levels, e.g., cognitive and spatial.

First of all, since 'social' has a broad connotation, we have to limit the boundary of this first analysis. Here we focus primarily on social practices, i.e., the way people live a city and its parts. Still, we include also the quality of the interactions between people and how they change in time. Note also that at the social level it can be difficult to elicit the distinction between formal and informal knowledge because the social knowledge is principally informal, tacit and implicit. For this reason, our work in this paper should be considered preliminary under several aspects.

We start by singling out references to places and landmarks for the relevance they have in social practices and by listing the relevant entities and the relationships that were expressed between them. Then we look at how inhabitants use those places and the social habits they implicitly or explicitly expressed. Finally, we classify the collected entities in ontological terms following the DOLCE foundational ontology [4].

Analyzing the social level it clearly emerges that the objects of the city are not just building, locations and landmarks. They are complex cognitive objects enriched with a set of different meanings/signifiers that can acquire different meanings depending on the time and even on the person. This analysis shows that at some point it will be necessary to investigate complex entities' definitions. Also, several objects that a technician would image essential key points for the sociality were not mentioned in the discussions, for instance: the San Cataldo cathedral, the S. Domenico church, the Ringhiera, the doric columns, the Aragonese castle, Fontana square, the stone bridge, the Ponte girevole and even the town hall. Instead we find *places* and *landmarks* like the beachfront, the bathing establishments, the area of Porta Napoli, the new Aeropolio, the inland and the piers. These entities are separated from other *objects* which are taken at their face value like buildings of low interest, the cruise ships and, from some aspects, the sea itself. Indeed, the same term can occur with different meanings, e.g., as a landmark and as a generic building. These lists do not cover the whole range. Many entities have special social *roles* like the city itself as the capital of Magna Grecia, the convergence point (a place where roads and railways converge), the service center or the old city seen as an eco-museum. At this point, we have the *service* level that includes public services like restaurants, cafes and shops, bathing establishments (this time the term denote the service, not the physical entity nor the landmark), the service center, the university and the pedestrian network across the city (mainly identified in special areas like the water-front). Finally, the identified the desired features which can be presented as functional objects, reassessment of existing objects, services, norms or generic topics. Here we find work, areas close to traffic, primary and secondary infrastructure, regulation of public spaces.

Moving to the relational aspects, we point out the difficulties to classify the above elements since the data are only partially qualified for our analysis. This leads to some uncertainty regarding the relationships holding across these elements. We find strong relational bounds between the space and the city in terms of districts, between space and objects in terms of locations, space and landmark or role, space and services (the location of needs), landmark and social practices as well as between social practices.

6   Analyzing the Social Level

There is a strong perspectival aspect in the way we live in places, a kind of description (mostly implicit) of the place that includes what are for us the relevant elements in it and their relationships. Thus, a perspective provided by a place is an information entity that contains: a (typically partial) description of the place, what there is in it and how the place is evolving (e.g. things moving, leaving or arriving, agents acting and trans-forming them etc.) and possibly the potential interactions between us and what is in the place. A place is grounded, as opposed to a generic location, is a context that refers to one or more actual/existing entities.

A place is also full of links that can be elicit via ontological analysis and the classifica-tion of what we use for understanding places in general and the actual place that we are experiencing. For this reason, the analysis has to include the physical elements (e.g. location and objects), the material components and layout (e.g. enclosed spaces, object distribution); agentive figures (e.g. habitants, organizations, social roles) the relationships across them and the objects (e.g. generic dependences and actual goal or habits).

Due to the material at hand, we decided to start from the highest level in the given ontological list, i.e., the social level. Here we have reported the very first achievement of a complex ontological analysis aimed to unravel the complex knowledge that forms the city.

References

Freksa, C., Nebel, B., Hegarty, M., Barkowsky, T. (eds.): Spatial Cognition IX. Springer, Heidelberg (2014)

Rapoport, A.: Human Aspects of Urban Form: Towards A Man-Environment Approach to Urban Form and Design. Pergamon, Oxford (1977)

Orr, D.W.: Ecological Literacy: Education and the Transition to a Postmodern World. SUNY Press, New York (1992)

Borgo, S., Masolo, C.: Ontological foundations of DOLCE. In: Poli, R., Healy, M., Kameas, A. (eds.) Theory and Applications of Ontology Computer Applications, pp. 279–295. Springer, Heidelberg (2010)

Gruber, T.R.: A translation approach to portable ontology specifications. Knowl. Acquis. **5**(2), 199–220 (1993)

McConnell et al. (2010)

Formato, E., Russo, M.: Re-use/re-cycle territories, TeMA INPUT 2014 (2014). Print ISSN 1970-9889, e- ISSN 1970-9870

Gregotti, V.: L'architettura del realismo critico. Laterza, Roma (2004)

Ingallina, P.: L'attractivité des territoires: regards croisés, Ministère de l'Ecologie, de l'Energie, du Développement Durable et de l'Aménagement du Territoire Ministère du Logement Direction Générale de l'Aménagement, du Logement et de la Nature PUCA - Plan Urbanisme Construction Architecture (2007)

Bateman, J., Borgo, S., Lüttich, K., Masolo, C., Mossakowski, T.: Ontological modularity and spatial diversity. Spat. Cognit. Comput. **7**(1), 97–128 (2007)

Borgo, S.: How formal ontology can help civil engineers. Stud. Comput. Intell. **61**, 37–45 (2007)

Borgo, S., Franssen, M., Garbacz, P., Kitamura, Y., Mizoguchi, R., Vermaas, P.E.: Technical artifact: an integrated perspective. Front. Artif. Intell. Appl. **229**, 3–15 (2011). IOS Press

Khakee, A., Barbanente, A., Camarda, D., Puglisi, M.: With or without? Comparative study of preparing participatory scenarios using computer-aided and traditional brainstorming. J. Future Res. **6**, 45–64 (2002)

Heft, H.: Environment, cognition, and culture: reconsidering the cognitive map. J. Environ. Psychol. **33**, 14–25 (2013). doi:10.1016/j.jenvp.2012.09.002

Borri, D., Scandale, L.: Aspetti cognitivi e organizzativi di campagne politiche come strumenti di visioning e pianificazione strategica. Evidenze dal caso dei Forum per Bari. In: Bruzzo, A., Occelli, S. (eds.) Le Relazioni tra Conoscenza e Innovazione nello Sviluppo dei Territori, pp. 100–121. Franco Angeli, Milano (2005)

Computer-Aided Drafting of Urban Designs for Walkability

Ivan Blecic[1](✉), Arnaldo Cecchini[2], and Giuseppe A. Trunfio[2]

[1] Department of Civil and Environmental Engineering and Architecture, University of Cagliari, Via Corte d Appello 87, 09124 Cagliari, Italy
ivanblecic@unica.it
[2] Department of Architecture, Planning and Design, University of Sassari, Palazzo Pou Salit, Piazza Duomo 6, 07041 Alghero, Italy
{cecchini, trunfio}@uniss.it

Abstract. We present a design support tool which generates outlines of urban projects targeting user-defined walkability objectives. The tool is part of our ongoing research effort to develop not only evaluative, but also generative tools, to be used *during* the design process, assisting architects and urban planners in designing more walkability of cities. The tool couples the capability-wise walkability score (CAWS) evaluation method with the NSGA-II multi-objective genetic algorithm, to generate a set of non-dominated solutions whose properties and expected effects can be explored within the software tool.

Keywords: Walkability · Urban design · Design support systems · Walkability explorer · Multi-objective genetic algorithms

1 Introduction

In this work, we explore the prospect of embedding formal evaluation of walkability *into the designing process* in urban planning and design.

There has of late been a pullulating of studies proposing methods and tools to evaluate the walkability of urban environment. This operational effort reflects the growing interest among scholars, practitioners, and public-policy makers for pedestrian-centred urban design and planning [1–9]. In this scholarly debate as well as in practice, the concept of walkability has come to occupy a pivotal theoretical and operational role. From being considered a mere question of accessibility applied to pedestrians, the concept has through debate and practice evolved into a richer, more nuanced, and intrinsically multidimensional description of the relationships and interactions among pedestrians, urban space, and its social practices of use.

Hence the proliferation of attempts to operationalise the concept of walkability, to develop formal metrics, audit protocols, evaluation methods, and tools [6, 10–12]. In this effort, many recent technological developments have been beneficial to scholars and analysts, from the abundance of (open) geodata, to the increasing sophistication of computational techniques and data-processing tools, to the growing capabilities of computers in general.

© Springer International Publishing AG 2017
O. Gervasi et al. (Eds.): ICCSA 2017, Part IV, LNCS 10407, pp. 695–709, 2017.
DOI: 10.1007/978-3-319-62401-3_51

All this commendable work of many has produced a wealth of methods and tools primarily for the evaluation of urban walkability, be it that currently on the ground, or that expected as outcomes of urban plans and designs to implement. However, little has yet been done to build a more effective bridge between the evaluation of walkability and the practice of "designing" in urban planning and design. We are undoubtedly quite far behind the kind of human-computer collaboration we see emerging in architecture, and growingly in many other design practices. So, in a way, our Thesis Eleven here is: the analysts have hitherto only evaluated the walkability of cities and plans, the point is to design them for walkability.

In practice, our design support tool generates project *outlines* of public works and improvements of the street network and public spaces, in order to target specific user-defined walkability objectives. This opens up for the possibility of applications other than the common use-case of evaluation tools as decision support where *given* urban projects get assessed for walkability (e.g. by estimating their impact on some walkability score or indicator, and comparing it to the current situation). Rather, our tool addresses, as it were, the inverse problem: given some user-defined walkability objectives and constraints, the tool sketches out a set of projects to best satisfy them. So rather than evaluative, we aim at developing *generative procedures* to assist architects and urban planners design urban projects for walkability.

For the walkability assessment in our design support tool, we adopt the capability-wise walkability score (CAWS); an evaluation methodology we developed in the past [9, 13, 14]. That evaluation model – briefly presented in Sect. 2 – underlies the formalisation of our "inverse problem", which turns out to be of a great computational complexity. Indeed, given the high number of combinatorial options and thus a vast search space of solutions, the problem must be approached with a search heuristic, namely in our case, a multi-objective genetic algorithm – whose formalisation and adaptation is covered in Sect. 3. We give the tool a test drive on the streets of the city of Alghero in Italy, and we present the results thereof in Sect. 4. We end the paper with a few concluding remarks.

2 Evaluating Walkability

Let us first recall the essential features of the CAWS evaluation methodology, and of the software Walkability Explorer (WE) which implements it. The main purpose of this paper is to present the "inverse problem" and a computational approach we experimented to tackle it. That is why we will provide just the essential modelling of the CAWS evaluation method, sufficient for reader's understanding of the "inverse problem", without discussing the rationale and the implications of the modelling choices in CAWS. For a more detailed presentation and discussion of CAWS and WE, we refer the reader to few our previous papers [9, 13, 14]).

In the CAWS approach, rather than evaluating how much a specific place is *in itself* walkable, the walkability score reflects how, and where to, a person can walk *starting from* that place; in other words, not how much walkable in itself, but rather what is the *walkability the place is endowed with*. Therefore, the capability-wise walkability score of a point in space is an aggregate combining three factors: (1) the number of destinations/urban opportunities reachable by foot; (2) their distances from that point; and (3) the quality of the pedestrian routes towards those destinations. The quality of the pedestrian routes is evaluated on several attributes relevant for walkability, related to the features of streets and of the surrounding environment, which may contribute to make walking efficient, pleasant, secure and attractive.

Formally, the street network is represented as a graph $\mathcal{G} = \langle \mathcal{E}, \mathcal{V} \rangle$ composed of a set of edges $\mathcal{E}$ and a set of nodes $\mathcal{V}$. Each edge $e_k \in \mathcal{E}$ is described on a vector $a_k = \left\{ a_{k1}, \ldots, a_{kq} \right\}$ of q edge attributes a_{kl} relevant for walkability.

In Table 1 we report the list of edge attributes we adopt in our study, chosen with particular care for the spatial and urban design features relevant to the comfort and efficiency of the walk, elements that generate the sense of safety and influence the pleasantness of walking and the attractiveness of the path and its surroundings (for a detailed discussion and motivations see [9, 13, 14]).

For walkability evaluation in WE all the nodes are considered possible origins of walks, while the destinations are assumed to be the nodes nearest to the attractors (the nearest node in case of point attractors, such as schools, centroid in case of areal attractors, such as urban parks).

The basic assumption of the evaluation model is that a person/inhabitant living at a point in space would be able to walk a certain number of times towards the available destinations, and would from than obtain a benefit β defined by the following constant-elasticity-of-substitution (CES) function:

$$\beta(\mathbf{x}) = \left(\sum_{i=1}^{n} x_i^{\rho} \right)^{\frac{1}{\rho}} \tag{1}$$

where n is the number of available destinations, x_i is the number of times the person visits the i-th destination and $1/(1 - \rho)$ is the elasticity of substitution among destinations. Our choice to model the benefit in this way is tightly connected to the way we conceptualise walkability. Equation (1) exhibits convex preferences, which in our case means that the benefit deriving from multiple visits to a destination is marginally decreasing. It also incorporates the hypothesis of differentiation among destinations of the same type. For example, two urban parks are not considered perfect substitutes (otherwise, the optimal individual behaviour that would derive would be to always visit only the nearest one). We impose the following constraint on the pedestrian:

$$\sum_{i=1}^{n} c_i x_i \leq \mu \tag{2}$$

where c_i is the "cost" the pedestrian foregoes to reach the destination i, and μ is the available budget with a conventional constant value. Finally, it is necessary to define the "cost" term of a route (c_i in Eq. (2)), which in our case takes into account both the length and the attributes relevant for its *quality* for pedestrians. Therefore, the cost of a route composed of m edges is defined as:

Table 1. Edge attributes

Attributes	Weight	Scale values
Physical features		
Cyclability	2/30	Exclusive lane (0.8); off-road lane (0.5); on-road lane (0.3); not possible/prohibited (0.1)
Width of the roadway	1/30	Pedestrian way (0.8); one car lane (0.6); 2 car lanes (0.5); 3 car lanes (0.3); >3 car lane (0.1)
Car speed limit	2/30	Pedestrian way (0.8); 20 km/h (0.7); 30 km/h (0.5); 50 km/h (0.3); 70 km/h (0.1)
One way street	1/30	Pedestrian way (0.8); yes (0.5); no (0.1)
On-street parking	1/30	Prohibited parking (0.8); permitted (0.5); illegal parking (0.1)
Width of sidewalk	2/30	Wide (0.8); comfortable (0.7); minimum (0.5); inadequate (0.3); lacking (0.1)
Separation of pedestrian route from car roadway	2/30	Marked/strong (0.8); weak (0.5); lacking (0.1)
Path slope	2/30	Smooth (0.8); light (0.5); rise (0.1)
Paving (quality and degree of maintenance)	2/30	Fine (0.8); cheap (0.5); bumpy (0.1)
Quality of urban design features		
Lighting	1/16	Excellent (0.8); good (0.6); inadequate (0.3); lacking (0.1)
Shelter and shade	1/16	Strong (0.8); weak (0.5); lacking (0.1)
Sedibility	1/16	Extended (0.8); thin (0.5); lacking (0.1)
Frequency of services/activities	1/16	Abundant (0.8); somewhat (0.6); rare (0.3); no services/activities (0.1)
Attractiveness from an architectural and urban viewpoint	1/16	Prevalence of pleasant elements (0.8); presence of a few pleasant elements (0.6); lack of pleasant or disturbing elements (0.4); presence of a few disturbing elements (0.2); prevalence of disturbing elements (0.1)
Attractiveness from an environmental point of view	1/16	Prevalence of pleasant elements (0.8); presence of a few pleasant elements (0.6); lack of pleasant or disturbing elements (0.4); presence of a few disturbing elements (0.2); prevalence of disturbing elements (0.1)
Transparency and permeability of the public-private space	1/16	Permeable (0.8); filtered (0.5); separated (0.1)
Urban texture	1/16	Dense (0.8); park or green space (0.6); low density (0.4); undeveloped land (0.1)

$$c = \bar{c} + \sum_{k=1}^{m} l_k \eta_k \tag{3}$$

where $\bar{c}$ is the fixed cost, l_k is the length of the k-th edge in the path, and η_k is a *cost factor* defined as:

$$\eta_k = \left[1 - \left(\sum_{j=1}^{q} \gamma_j a_{kj}^r \right)^{\frac{1}{r}} \right] \tag{4}$$

In the latter equation, q is the number of edge's attributes, $a_{kj} \in [0, 1]$ is the value of the j-th attribute, γ_j is the weight of the attribute (with $\sum \gamma_j = 1$), and r is a parameter with $1/(1 - r)$ being the elasticity of substitution among attributes. Note that the cost factor η_k is 1 when all attributes are at their minimum (i.e. 0), and it approaches 0 when all attributes approach the maximum of 1. The weights of attributes γ_j we use in Eq. (4) to calculate the cost are shown in Table 1.

Among all the alternative routes between an origin and a destination, the least costly one is used in Eq. (2). To determine the cheapest route, WE uses an efficient variant of the well-known Dijkstra search algorithm [15].

Finally, the *walkability score* attributed to the point in space corresponds to the maximum benefit the person located at that point may attain, given the assumptions of the behavioural model in (1), (2) and (3). As we have said, this procedure is executed for each node of the graph, and thus the evaluation model attributes a walkability score w to every node, such that $w = \max \beta(x)$ under the constraint (2).

To determine the walkability scores for a given urban area, WE performs the following procedure:

1. determine all the least costly routes, in the sense of Eq. (3), between all the origin nodes in the area, and all the available destination nodes reachable by foot;
2. next, compute the walkability score for each origin node, using least costly routes towards all the destinations available from that node;
3. finally, given that the street network graph does not cover all the pedestrian-accessible areas, interpolate the walkability scores of nodes on a raster grid of a given resolution. In the current implementation of WE, the interpolation is performed using the Inverse Distance Weighting method.

3   Design Support: The Generative Algorithm

The distinctively design-support, as opposed to mere evaluation, feature of WE resides in its capability to generate a set of project outlines, in terms of improvements of the street network for walkability. Specifically, WE presents to designers and decision makers a set of Pareto-efficient project outlines over two objectives: walkability improvement and effort. In the following, we formulate the bi-objective search problem and describe the solution procedure.

A project outline (a "design") for walkability improvement is formalised as:

$$\mathcal{P} = \left\{ \langle e_1, \Delta \eta_1 \rangle, \ldots \langle e_q, \Delta \eta_q \rangle \right\} \tag{5}$$

where $e_i \in \varepsilon$ is an edge of the street network and $\Delta \eta_i \in \,]-1, 0[$ is the reduction of the walkability cost (defined in Eq. (3) above) of the i-th edge due to a series of improvements of the respective street. These improvements aim at increasing the values of some of the edge attributes (a_i in Eq. (4)) For example, according to Table 1, the action of improving the quality and degree of maintenance of paving for an edge e_i from 'bumpy' to 'fine', would increase the value of the corresponding attribute from 0.1 to 0.8. This, in turn, would reduce the cost η_i of that edge by a certain amount $\Delta \eta_k$ according to Eq. (4). It is worth noting that, in general, a given reduction $\Delta \eta_k$ of the walkability cost for an edge e_k can be obtained in many ways, through different combinations of attribute improvements $a_k = \left\{ a_{k1}, \ldots, a_{kq} \right\}$. To search for efficient designs we assign to each candidate solution P a fitness in terms of its effectiveness in improving the walkability score. In particular, the fitness $W(\mathcal{P})$ of $\mathcal{P}$ is evaluated as follows:

1. we consider a set $\mathcal{V}_O \subseteq \mathcal{V}$ of origin nodes, which represent the targeted urban areas, whose walkability need to be improved, and a set of nodes $\mathcal{V}_D \subseteq \mathcal{V}$ representing relevant destinations to be considered for quantifying the walkability performance;
2. we virtually apply the design $\mathcal{P}$ to the graph representing the street network;
3. we use the WE evaluation procedure outlined above for computing the walkability score w_i of all the nodes in $\mathcal{V}_O \subseteq \mathcal{V}$;
4. then, the fitness value $W(\mathcal{P})$ is defined as the average value of all the computed walkability scores w_i.

In our model, each design $\mathcal{P}$ is also characterised by an implementation *effort* $E(\mathcal{P})$, which, depending on the purpose, design requirements and policy-making context, may represent financial costs, time, consensus, or other kind of "resources" necessary for the implementation of the improvements. To evaluate the effort, we assume that for each edge e_k, there exists a function $\in_k(\mathcal{P})$ that provides the minimum effort required to achieve a given decrease $\Delta \eta_k$ of the cost factor. Such a function may simply be estimated by experts, on the basis of the condition of the street, which is represented by its current vector of attributes a_k. Alternatively, it can be pre-computed using an optimisation process on the basis of Eqs. (3) and (4), by assigning a cost to each variation of the attributes a_{ki}. We define the effort $E(\mathcal{P})$ of a design $\mathcal{P}$ as the sum of all the efforts required by the involved edges.

Using the automatic evaluation procedure in WE, it is straightforward to evaluate the effects of a "manually designed" design affecting some edges of the street network. However, manually devising efficient designs, in which the benefit $W(\mathcal{P})$ in maximised and the effort $E(\mathcal{P})$ is minimised, is much more difficult on the typical graph representing an urban street network. Indeed, the set of all possible $\mathcal{P}$s, even considering a constraint on the available effort, grows rapidly with the number of edges. Also, the effects of an intervention on an edge within a complex graph are not always straightforwardly intuitive, so some suitable solutions may not be trivial. For these reasons, a manual trial-and-error procedure rarely results in an efficient design solutions.

Here arises the main purpose of our tool, to support the design process through an automatic search procedure capable of providing a sets of possible design outlines $\mathcal{P}$ which efficiently maximise the benefit $W(\mathcal{P})$ while minimising the effort $E(\mathcal{P})$. So, the problem can be formalised as the following bi-objective constrained optimisation:

$$
\begin{cases}
\max_{\mathcal{P} \subset \Pi} W(\mathcal{P}) \\
\min_{\mathcal{P} \subset \Pi} E(\mathcal{P}) \\
\bar{\eta}_k < \eta_k + \Delta\eta_k < 1 \quad \forall \langle e_k, \Delta\eta_k \rangle \in \mathcal{P}
\end{cases}
\tag{6}
$$

where $\Pi = \mathcal{E} \times \,]-1, 0[$ is the set of all possible couples $\langle e_k, \Delta\eta_k \rangle$, and $\bar{\eta}_k$ indicates the minimum achievable value for the cost factor of e_k, depending on the physical conditions of the streets.

To address the problem in Eq. (6), we do not aggregate over the two objectives (benefit and effort), but rather generate a set of non-dominated (i.e. Pareto-optimal) solutions to present to designers and decision makers for further exploration, comparison, and ultimately choice. In particular, given two candidate solutions $\mathcal{P}_i$ and $\mathcal{P}_j$, we say that $\mathcal{P}_i$ dominates $\mathcal{P}_j$ if the first is not inferior to $\mathcal{P}_j$ on both objectives, and, additionally, there is at least one objective on which it is better. As shown below, this allows us to generate a set of non-dominated (or efficient) solutions instead of a single solution. The idea is to allow the decision maker to choose solutions from the produced set by exploring the trade-offs between the overall improvement of walkability and the corresponding implementation effort of the project.

3.1   The Evolutionary Multi-objective Search Algorithm

For the bi-objective problem seen in Eq. (6), a typical graph representing the street network of an average city can easily lead to very large decision spaces. Indeed, even considering only designs $\mathcal{P}$ containing a limited number of elements, the corresponding number of possible subsets of the set of edges $\mathcal{E}$ is given by the binomial coefficient $|\mathcal{E}|$ choose $|\mathcal{P}|$. Furthermore, since each element of $\mathcal{P}$ can be the object of actions with different intensities of effort, it is easy to see the challenging nature of the problem in Eq. (6). To address it, in this study we propose the use of an evolutionary algorithm [16, 17], namely the well-known multi-objective Genetic Algorithm (GA) NSGA-II [18–20], with specifically designed recombination and mutation operators.

To improve the computational efficiency, given the aforementioned large size of the search space, we restrict the search to account for the specific way in which the fitness function $W(\mathcal{P})$ is computed. In fact, the improvement of the walkability score between an origin node $v_i \in \mathcal{V}_O$ and a destination node $v_j \in \mathcal{V}_D$ implies a reduction of the current minimum cost $c_{ij}^{(0)}$ to be used in Eqs. (1) and (2). However, such a reduction can be achieved either by improving the edges of the current best path between v_i and v_j (i.e., the one with the least cost according to Eq. (3)), or by improving an alternative path. The latter should have a length ranging from the minimum distance $l_{ij}^{(min)}$ between v_i and v_j to the maximum length $l_{ij}^{(max)}$ such that:

$$l_{ij}^{(max)} = \bar{c} + \sum_{k=1}^{m} l_k \, \bar{\eta}_k \leq c_{ij}^{(0)} \tag{7}$$

where m is the number of edges in the path, l_k is the length of each edge e_k and $\bar{\eta}_k$ is the minimum achievable value for the cost factor of e_k, already introduced above. Therefore, for each origin node $v_i \in \mathcal{V}_O$ and a destination node $v_j \in \mathcal{V}_D$ we restrict the search for improvements of walkability on a sub-graph $\mathcal{G}_{ij}$ composed of all the shortest paths connecting the two nodes v_i and v_j having length between $l_{ij}^{(min)}$ and $l_{ij}^{(max)}$, as defined by Eq. (7). The whole search space of the problem in (7) then becomes based on a graph $\mathcal{G}_{OD}$ obtained as the union of all sub-graphs $\mathcal{G}_{ij}$, being $v_i \in \mathcal{V}_O$ and $v_j \in \mathcal{V}_D$. In practice, this requires two steps: (i) the computation of all the values $c_{ij}^{(0)}$ for the current state of the graph; (ii) the use of a suitable algorithm for finding all the best paths with maximum length $l_{ij}^{(max)}$.

The second step is accomplished using a k-shortest path routing algorithm, which is a generalisation of the standard shortest path problem. This algorithm not only finds the shortest path, but also the $k - 1$ other paths in a non-decreasing order of length. In particular, to obtain the top k shortest paths connecting a pair of vertices, we use an implementation of the Yen's algorithm [21], which has the advantages of being incremental (i.e. we can increase the value of k step-by-step, up to the desired maximum length).

At the beginning of the procedure, we store all the candidate paths $p_{ij}^{(k)}$ between each pair of vertices $v_i \in \mathcal{V}_O$ and $v_j \in \mathcal{V}_D$. Subsequently, we use a GA to evolve a randomly initialised population of n_p candidate designs represented by a data structure containing two components:

1. an array of triplets $\langle i, j, k \rangle$, where i and j refer to a couple origin-destination and k refers to a previously computed candidate path $p_{ij}^{(k)}$; the same triplet $\langle i, j, k \rangle$ can be included in an individual only once;

2. a list $\mathcal{L}$ of improvements for the edges composing all the $p_{ij}^{(k)}$ included in the candidate design; the list $\mathcal{L}$ contains couples $\langle e_t, \Delta\eta_t \rangle$, where e_t refers to one of the edges of the paths $p_{ij}^{(k)}$ and $\Delta\eta_t$ is the corresponding improvement fulfilling the constraint in Eq. (7).

It is worth noting that two different paths included in the array of triplets can have one or more edges in common. This is properly considered in the management of the evolved individual.

The population to be evolved is initialised for each candidate individual $\mathcal{P}$ by selecting a random number of triplets, within a prefixed maximum. Then, for each triplet to be inserted into $\mathcal{P}$:

1. the origin index i and the destination index j are randomly drawn considering the vertices in $\mathcal{V}_O$ and $\mathcal{V}_D$ respectively and having care to avoid repetitions of the same couple origin-destination in $\mathcal{P}$;
2. the index k of one of the candidate shortest paths computed before is randomly selected in order to generate the element $\langle i, j, k \rangle$;
3. all the edges e_t belonging to the path $p_{ij}^{(k)}$ are inserted into the list $\mathcal{L}$ with randomly generated $\Delta \eta_t$.

After the population has been initialised, the individuals are evolved according to the standard NSGA-II algorithm, through a predefined number of generations, in order to obtain a suitable set of non-dominated design outlines. At each generation, two individuals can be selected and recombined to form offspring individuals and the latter can be mutated to compete with the previous population. More in details, each generation involves the creation of a hierarchy of Pareto fronts, which are subsets of non-dominated individuals. The fronts are created using the Goldberg's *non-dominated sorting* procedure [22], which works as follows:

1. all the non-dominated individuals in the current population are inserted in the first front Φ_1, which corresponds to the highest fitness;
2. these individuals are virtually removed from the population and the next set of non-dominated individuals are inserted in a second front Φ_2, corresponding to the second-highest fitness;
3. phases 1–2 are reiterated until all of the individuals have been assigned to a fitness rank.

When all fronts Φ_i have been created, the so-called *crowding distances* are assigned to every individual $\mathcal{P} \in \Phi_i$, to be used in the selection phase with the purpose of promoting a uniform sampling of the Pareto set.

At each generation, n_p selected individuals are recombined to generate n_p offspring individuals. Selection is performed by binary tournaments [18, 19]: between two randomly drawn individuals, the one belonging to the front with the lowest rank wins. This is because, according to the non-dominated sorting procedure described above, the fronts with lower ranks contain better individuals from the point of view of non-dominance. If the randomly drawn individuals come from the same front, the one with the highest crowding distance wins, since a high distance to the closest neighbours indicates that the individual is located in a sparsely populated part of the front.

In particular, the recombination operator, which is applied with probability ϵ_c, is defined as follows: first we merge the two selected parents $\mathcal{P}_1$ and $\mathcal{P}_2$ into a single candidate design $\mathcal{P}^* = \mathcal{P}_1 \cup \mathcal{P}_2$, having care to avoid duplicates both in terms of triplets $\langle i, j, k \rangle$ and in terms of the elements of the resulting lists $\mathcal{L}^*$; subsequently, we randomly split $\mathcal{P}^*$ into two new candidate solutions $\mathcal{P}_1^*$ and $\mathcal{P}_2^*$, again attributing the elements of $\mathcal{L}^*$ to the offspring by considering to which path each edge in the couples $\langle e_t, \Delta \eta_t \rangle$ belongs. Note that in this phase the same couple $\langle e_t, \Delta \eta_t \rangle$ can be attributed to both $\mathcal{P}_1^*$ and $\mathcal{P}_2^*$ if two paths of $\mathcal{P}^*$ having e_t in common are assigned to different individuals.

After the recombination operator, for each $\mathcal{P}^*$ we apply the following mutation operators with small probabilities:

1. *path replacement*: the index k of a best path in a triplet $\langle i,j,k \rangle$ can be changed with probability $\in_s$. The list $\mathcal{L}^*$ is update accordingly.
2. *origin-destination insertion*: with probability $\in_a$, a new random triplet $\langle i,j,k \rangle$ is added as in the population initialization described above. Proper elements $\langle e_t, \Delta\eta_t \rangle$ are randomly generated and added to $\mathcal{L}^*$;
3. *origin-destination removal*: with probability $\in_r$, an existing triplet $\langle i,j,k \rangle$ is removed and the list $\mathcal{L}^*$ is updated accordingly (i.e., the corresponding elements are removed if not referred to by other paths in $\mathcal{P}^*$);
4. *random variation of cost factor reduction*: for each element of $\mathcal{L}^*$, the value of $\Delta\eta$ is randomly changed, in accordance with the bound constraint, with probability $\in_e$.

The offspring population and the parent population are merged and the above described non-dominated sorting procedure is used to rank all the $2n_p$ individuals. The ranks and the crowding distances mentioned above are used to select n_p individuals for the next generation. More details on the NSGA-II algorithm can be found in [18, 19].

It is worth noting that the evaluation of new individuals at each generation does not require a Dijkstra's search as in the standard walkability score evaluation performed in WE. In fact, we operate directly on the pre-computed candidate best paths linking each origin node $v_i \in \mathcal{V}_\mathcal{O}$ with each destination node $v_j \in \mathcal{V}_\mathcal{D}$. This allows to considerably speed up the computation.

At the end of the evolutionary search, a set of non-dominated designs is available. The user interface of WE allows the user to analyse in detail the found solutions, by visually selecting them along the approximate Pareto front. For each solution, the involved couples origin-destination are available and the edges object of intervention are highlighted. Moreover, it is possible to apply one of the proposed designs in order to perform a standard WE analysis on a virtual street network affected by the proposed actions of walkability improvements. This allows for the evaluation of the overall effects of the design on the city-wide walkability score.

4 An Example Use Case

As an example of a design-support use case, we present a test run on the city of Alghero, a coastal town of about 40.000 inhabitants in the North-Western Sardinia, in Italy. The underlying dataset with the street attributes has been collected during a contingent filed survey of the entire city in January 2016 [23].

Once all the datasets have been imported, WE through a visual user interface lets the user select a series of representative origin nodes whose walkability to maximise. An example is shown in Fig. 1, with the selected nodes shown in red and all the available destinations (attractors) as yellow (commerce) and green (services) dots and areas.

Now the search procedure can be executed to generate a set of non-dominated project outlines in terms of the two objectives: walkability score and estimated project

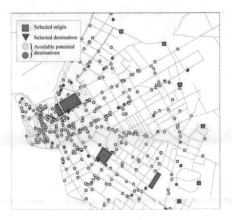

Fig. 1. Initial setup scenario: selection of representative nodes whose walkability to maximise. (Color figure online)

implementation effort. The solutions generated for our example origins are presented in the Pareto frontier in Fig. 2.

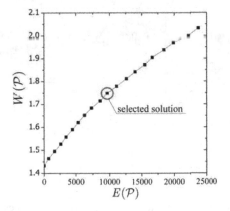

Fig. 2. A set of non-dominated solutions generated by WE.

The user now has the possibility to better explore each proposed solution and to see what each entails in terms of the suggested interventions on the street network. Figure 3 shows an example of a solution selected on the graph in the window (red square). Once selected, WE shows (in the table and on the map) all the edges implicated in the solution and their required improvements in terms of walkability cost.

It is further possible to examine if there are expected changes to the route due to the implementation of the project. For example, in Fig. 4 we see two cases of origin-destination couples where the best path after the project is expected to change (from blue to red paths, both paths have in common the green edges).

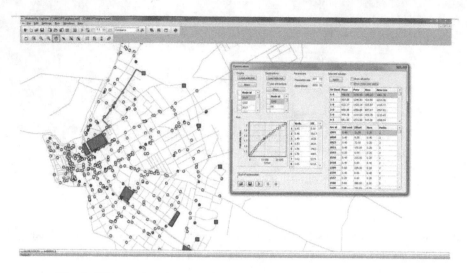

Fig. 3. WE user interface: exploration of solutions. (Color figure online)

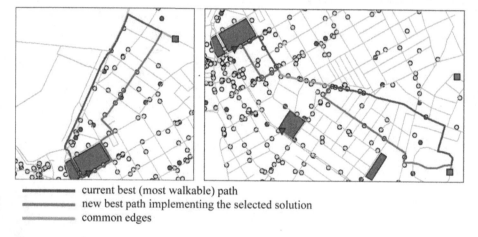

======== current best (most walkable) path
======== new best path implementing the selected solution
======== common edges

Fig. 4. Expected changes in best routes from an origin to a destination node after the implementation of the solution. (Color figure online)

Finally, WE also calculates the overall variation in the walkability scores over the whole area/city related to each proposed solution. The example solution we have selected above yields variation in the walkability scores shown in Fig. 5.

This brief illustration of WE's features exemplifies how the tool may be useful as a design support, to use within the "designing" process, especially during the initial phases of project outlining. After setting walkability policy objectives for the project (e.g. to improve the walkability of a neighbourhood), the software suggests a set of non-dominated solutions, where each solution is a project outline defined as a set of street edges whose walkability cost has to be lowered by a specified amount.

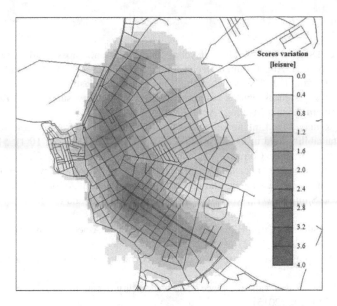

Fig. 5. Expected variation of walkability scores due to the proposed solution.

The designers and policy makers can then further explore in WE the required effort, as well as other features, implications and expected effects on walkability, of each suggested project outline. This use scenario thus guides them towards the final selection of one (or more than one) outline as a project candidate for further development, and for more detailed treatment of urban and architectural design.

5 Conclusions

We have proposed a tool, coupling a walkability evaluation methodology and an evolutionary search algorithm, to support urban planning and urban design process. Its distinctive quality resides in its capability not only to evaluate, but also to generate project proposals, given a user-defined walkability objective.

Although we are of course still quite far from having computers "do urban design", we believe there is a promising perspective for tools to assist urban design processes, centred on accessibility and walkability of places. Such a focus in urban design goes way beyond the standard problem of road network graph optimization since, as we have seen, the concerns for walkability require a "thicker", highly multidimensional description of the urban environment.

However, such a description significantly raises the bar of computational complexity for modelling. We have explored here a possible route to formalise and reduce the problem to make it computationally more tractable, but further research is necessary to more systematically investigate if and what other approaches and search heuristics may perhaps prove to be better suited for the task. Given the potential service such tools may offer for the future urban design and planning, it seems to us a research line worth pursuing.

References

1. Cervero, R., Duncan, M.: Walking, bicycling, and urban landscapes: evidence from the San Francisco bay area. Am. J. Public Health 93(9), 1478–1483 (2003)
2. Livi, A.D., Clifton, K.J.: Issues and methods in capturing pedestrian behaviors, attitudes and perceptions: experiences with a community-based walkability survey. In: Transportation Research Board Annual Meeting, April 2004
3. Porta, S., Renne, J.L.: Linking urban design to sustainability: formal indicators of social urban sustainability field in Perth, Western Australia. Urban Des. Int. 10(1), 51–64 (2005)
4. Frank, L.D., Sallis, J.F., Conway, T.L., Chapman, J.E., Saelens, B.E., Bachman, W.: Many pathways from land use to health: associations between neighborhood walkability and active transportation, body mass index, and air quality. J. Am. Plann. Assoc. 72(1), 75–87 (2006)
5. Clifton, K.J., Smith, A.D.L., Rodriguez, D.: The development and testing of an audit for the pedestrian environment. Lanscape Urban Plann. 80, 95–110 (2007)
6. Speck, J.: Walkable City: How Downtown Can Save America, One Step at a Time. Macmillan, New York (2012)
7. Paez, A.: Mapping travelers attitudes: does space matter? J. Transp. Geogr. 26, 117–125 (2013)
8. Forsyth, A.: What is a walkable place? The walkability debate in urban design. Urban Des. Int. 20(4), 274–292 (2015)
9. Blečić, I., Cecchini, A., Congiu, T., Fancello, G., Trunfio, G.A.: Evaluating walkability: a capability-wise planning and design support system. Int. J. Geograph. Inf. Sci. 29(3), 349–374 (2015)
10. Capp, C.J., Maghelal, P.K.: A review of existing pedestrian indices. J. Urban Reg. Inf. Syst. Assoc. 23(2), 5–19 (2011)
11. Saelens, B.E., Handy, S.L.: Built environment correlates of walking: a review. Med. Sci. Sports Exerc. 40(7), 550–566 (2008)
12. Talen, E., Koschinsky, J.: The walkable neighborhood: a literature review. Int. J. Sustain. Land Use Urban Plann. IJSLUP 1(1), 42–63 (2013)
13. Blečić, I., Cecchini, A., Congiu, T., Fancello, G., Trunfio, G.A.: Walkability explorer: an evaluation and design support tool for walkability. In: Murgante, B., et al. (eds.) ICCSA 2014. LNCS, vol. 8582, pp. 511–521. Springer, Cham (2014). doi:10.1007/978-3-319-09147-1_37
14. Blečić, I., Cecchini, A., Congiu, T., Fancello, F., Fancello, G., Trunfio, G.A.: Walkability explorer: application to a case-study. In: Gervasi, O., et al. (eds.) ICCSA 2015. LNCS, vol. 9157, pp. 758–770. Springer, Cham (2015). doi:10.1007/978-3-319-21470-2_55
15. Dijkstra, E.W.: A note on two problems in connexion with graphs. Numer. Math. 1(1), 269–271 (1959)
16. Coello Coello, C.A., Van Veldhuizen, D.A., Lamont, G.B.: Evolutionary Algorithms for Solving Multi-Objective Problems. Kluwer Academic Publishers, New York (2002)
17. Fonseca, C.M., Fleming, P.J.: An overview of evolutionary algorithms in multiobjective optimization. Evol. Comput. 3(1), 1–16 (1995)
18. Deb, K., Agrawal, S., Pratap, A., Meyarivan, T.: A fast and elitist multiobjective genetic algorithm: NSGA-II. IEEE Trans. Evol. Comput. 6(2), 182–197 (2002)
19. Jensen, M.T.: Reducing the run-time complexity of multiobjective EAs: the NSGA-II and other algorithms. IEEE Trans. Evol. Comput. 7(5), 503–515 (2003)
20. Blečić, I., Cecchini, A., Trunfio, G.A.: A decision support tool coupling a causal model and a multi-objective genetic algorithm. Appl. Intell. 26–2, 125–137 (2007)

21. Yen, J.Y.: Finding the K shortest loopless paths in a network. Manag. Sci. **17**(11), 712–716 (1971)
22. Goldberg, D.: Genetic Algorithms and Evolution Strategy in Engineering and Computer Science: Recent Advances and Industrial Applications. Wiley, New York (1998)
23. Blečić, I., Canu, D., Cecchini, A., Congiu, T., Fancello, G.: Factors of perceived walkability: a pilot empirical study. In: Gervasi, O., et al. (eds.) ICCSA 2016. LNCS, vol. 9789, pp. 125–137. Springer, Cham (2016). doi:10.1007/978-3-319-42089-9_9

City Dashboards: The Case of Trieste

Trieste Overview

Oscar Brunetto[✉]

Port Network Authority of the Eastern Adriatic Sea - Port of Trieste, Trieste, Italy
oscar.brunetto@outlook.com

Abstract. The paper talks about the concept and the development of a city dashboard for Trieste named "Trieste Overview". This tool is created with the purpose of informing users, through the social network's institutional profiles and the links to the main smart instruments, about activities and services offered by Trieste. The project integrates the process undertaken by the municipality to achieve the technological standards of a smart city.

Keywords: City dashboard · Institutional communication · Trieste · Citizens science · Urban indicators

1 Introduction

We need just a look around us to see ourselves surrounded by machines, devices and technology in general. Often when we interact with the world our needs are anticipated, such as walking to a door which is opening, the air conditioner automatically adjusts the temperature of a room to make it comfortable, cameras that follow our movements to ensure safety, etc. Day after day everything become normal and these devices start to make works and actions previously did by people. In recent decades we seen a great developed of technological tools that provide services in an invisible way, for example sending and receiving inputs and signals of frequencies that we can't see, or controlling objects remotely and networking them together.

Cities now hide a vast underworld of computers and software, and internet hosts part of them and its citizens collecting an infinite amount of information. Everything flow into a huge stream of data that if represented effectively can help to find solutions to old and new problems. In a smart city problems can be solved, among other things, also with instruments of this nature, thanks to data that give new life to inspire analysis and new points of view, making interaction faster and solution more modular [5].

The information revolution allows everyone to actively participate in the construction of new projects [1]. The essence and the democracy of internet lies in its freedom of expression. People are no longer a cog in a big machine but rather become part of the organizational mind of the smart city. Each of us has in his pocket a smartphone that unwittingly cast himself in the building cities of the future.

The organization of a smart city starts from the bottom drive by internet and the web. The information revolution has taken place for several reasons inherent in the concept

© Springer International Publishing AG 2017
O. Gervasi et al. (Eds.): ICCSA 2017, Part IV, LNCS 10407, pp. 710–721, 2017.
DOI: 10.1007/978-3-319-62401-3_52

of internet. This instrument uses existing technologies and can be integrated with different solutions, such as georeferencing, that multiply the possibilities of development. The web has become one of the first sources of information because it is open and accessible for everyone in real time, especially today with the release of several devices that allow multiplatform access. Now this space is fundamental to study, learn and inquire and will make possible to express directly and have comparisons and connections quickly and easily with people.

Summing up the web is positioned between different reality thanks to some key feature that characterize its nature:

- hyperconnectivity: capability of connecting multiple subjects and objects together;
- open: anyone can access in real time;
- it allows to publish easily.

Carlo Ratti, a professor at the Massachusetts Institute of Technology in Boston, reminds the substantial difference between the first public appearance of Pope Benedetto XVI in 2005, greeted by a crowd waving joyfully hands, and that of Pope Francesco, in 2013, welcomed from a smartphone sea ready to immortalize it. This icon makes us understand the degree of harmonization of technology development today, the spread of electronic devices connected to the network allows the city to become an intelligent space that gives solutions to citizens. This is possible thanks to a perception of needs done through receiving data and processing them with very high performance computers, tablets, etc.... The sensitivity, in other words the ability to implement what happens around us and react dynamically, is now more and more performing thanks to the new perception systems that invade every urban space. Nowadays you can create a traffic map using data collected by the telecommunications network, create an air pollution map using quality air measuring instruments, such as the Copenhagen Wheel developed by Superdestrian, or get an amazing picture of the labyrinthine waste management system revealed by the Trash Track Project in Seattle, installing microdevices for geolocalize rubbishes. Another great innovation, made real by smartphones, is the possibility to make people sensors capable to collect data through a lot of applications that allow to be located, to map and to indicate a phenomenon or even communicate their needs, as booking a taxi or find out events near you. In this way data comes voluntarily by citizens making them more and more active in sharing.

Since the first building projects of cities, scientists and engineers tried to rationalize the chaotic nature of urbanization. During the nineteenth century industrial revolution, the planning of cities became a matter able to generating benefits for the community, such as the improvement of public health building drainage systems or optimization of housing in very crowded areas. Meanwhile the study of urbanization became more complex and now engaged very different disciplines [2]:

- Science vs. design: this dimension is constituted by the contrast between science and design. The first explains the world by universal laws while the second identifies the reason that makes unique every single place. Everyone knows that, for example, New York is different from Los Angeles, Tokyo from Albuquerque, etc.... The purpose is to understand what are the main factors that make them quite different. These two realities have to live together in the best way. Cities cannot be composed of single individuals but these must conglomerate creating an added value.

- New ideas from particular realities: the complexity of urban environments has pushed many researchers to study these phenomena. Therefore brilliant researchers ventured in the development of theories using analytical tools to work in the complexity of urban science.

- The computational strength: in this era, driven by digital technologies and IT innovations, it be fixed a strong bond between urbanization and digital data. This intersection gave rise to a branch of study called "urban informatics" which treats the collection, classification, storage, retrieval and dissemination of data and their features.

2   The Smart City

During the last two decades it has took place two important phenomena: urbanization and development of information and communication technologies. The technological and economic development contributes to the increase of well-being in urban centers causing the progressive abandonment of rural areas. On one hand this meant a high level of education and new jobs, on the other hand, this concentration in cities has worsened the traffic conditions and lead to higher level of pollution and waste. Under these conditions amplified the idea of environment conservation causing an increase of sensitivity to the sustainable material. On one side it should be emphasized the strong link between the concept of smart city and the concept of sustainability, on the other side it is important to consider the city in its whole. Obviously a city to be sustainable does not have to be smart, the smart way is the one that uses ICT's tools. Is there a smart city model? How it should organize the city government that aims to become smart? The concept goes beyond just adopting digital initiatives that facilitate access to information and the use of services by citizens [13]. Smart City is a new way of conceiving the city government where the production of services is not understood as the exclusive prerogative of local administrators in a classic top-down model, but as a collaborative process that includes citizens and companies. In this sense there is no single model to follow rather different facets to be considered together:

- net city: the cities are flexible centers able to relate both to their own population and to international flows of finance, economy and culture, with the ambition to act as a liaison between the local and the global dimension. From this perspective, the city becomes the tool to mobilize and develop human resources and skills to optimize global competition. To do this, first of all, it must be comfortable and able to attract the creative class in innovation and researching.

- Open city: the city that gives priority to the transparency of its work. The communication of its activities is not mediated but is direct: online publication of all acts, live stream broadcast of council meetings. With the adoption of open data this approach finds its maximum expression.

- Sentient city: the city aims to improve operational efficiency and sustainability of development by creating the infrastructure conditions to produce and manage information in priority areas such as mobility, energy resources, environmental quality. The collection of information is not only linked to the spread of new urban instruments in the form of sensors, but the new projects involve citizens who, as users or beneficiaries, they become active participants in the city monitoring. The city is able to remember, correlate and anticipate events. Basically it is a place in which the human experience is settled.

- Wiki city: in this context the communication is designed to encourage the involvement of citizens in the management of public affairs. From the first experiments of e-democracy to the recent experiences of public contest and wiki-government, citizens are called upon to become an active part in decisions affecting the city.
- Creative city: the city face to the redevelopment of urban areas. It is the city which gives space for communication that comes from the bottom of artistic production format. The neighborhoods become laboratories for research and development.
- Resilient City: resilience is a term stolen from materials technology. In simple words, it indicates the ability of a material to absorb and release the energy that could deform it, returning to the initial state. It has to do with the elasticity. Resilience in social organizations indicates the ability to predict damage or possible attacks, to respond in an appropriate way, to carry out quick. In summary it is a city that helps citizens better understand the risks of its territory, especially related to climate change, through training and awareness, and to share information in threatening events. It is a city capable of reacting to external disasters by sharing information [9].

The city is a complex ecosystem made up of many micro-ecosystems where various organizations, public agencies, private citizens, companies, co-inhabit, interact and influence each other through activities and interdependent needs. The city government is the over-structure which facilitates the coordination of these activities and the evolution of the ecosystem.

3   E-Government

Administrators often define themselves smart because they propose to implement systems for which the car parks can be found with the smartphone, or garbage collection is carried out at a time when the sensors signal the attainment of the maximum level of the container or even suggest that the lamps are equipped with solar panels. But the issue is wider and does not concern a different way of doing politics but a different way of being politic [4]. Each city is inevitably different from each other so there cannot be a homogenization even on technologically level. It is certain that the project of intelligent cities have same goals for all, such as energy conservation, social cohesion etc., but it is essential an in-depth analysis of resources, uses and vocations of each territory.

Internet has provided very interesting tools to reinvent the territory management, allowing you to transform traditional bureaucratic paradigms, involving standardization and fragmentation of departments, and cost efficiency based on the reduction of operations in the electronic government paradigms (e-government) that emphasize the network working, the collaboration and the comparison with the internal or external reality entity, and the optimization of the service for the customer. This process has spurred a transformation in the philosophy and organization of governments [15]. E-government has many meanings, some of which translate into operations, such as receiving information through innovative tools or creating shared databases between different entities. In a broader view, the electronic government concerns the introduction of technological tools and the emergence of new opportunities, the incentive to create new services, the desire to increase citizen participation and the goal of creating a national information infrastructure. Mark Forman, associate director for technology information and e-government at the US Federal Office of Management and Budget, has thus defined e-government as the use of digital technologies to transform operations and improve effectiveness, efficiency, and service delivery.

New ICT tools are revolutionizing the way in which administrations, citizens and businesses interact. New channels, provided by the internet and web-based tools, are improving both the performance of top-down unidirectional communication and the processes of mutual influence between users and administration. Major issues such as social identity, representation and, above all, how to be citizens are brought into play. It redefines major issues such as social identity, representation and, above all, how to be citizens.

4   Social Media in Public Administration

The ICT's revolution doesn't change only the daily life of people but also the way citizens and government interact. With it began a new form of public organization aimed to redefine the system for gathering and disseminating data. In this process social networks have an important role because they allow active collaboration, sharing information and managing resources by the collective intelligence based on the union of different skills in different places. So social networks contribute to an open administration that makes government more transparent, more accountable and more credible.

Social media can be considered disruptive technologies for government because they generate overwhelming innovations as regards the digitalization of government models, services delivery and administrative processes. To better develop these channels, administrations must build strategies and models to use the available technologies and implement all aspects of administration: providing services, making policy decisions, analyzing and developing democracy. In recent years we are witnessing the extension of the communication mix of public bodies through the creation of participatory sites and platforms based on a multichannel perspective.

At the same time, digital technologies, and in particular social media, by promoting greater transparency of public bodies [10], seem to encourage the development of colloquy administration, enabling citizens to participate not only as users of services, but also to involve them in the design and delivery of duties and in defining public policies. For these reasons, the web has gradually become a place of intense connections between administrators and citizens. Following this, administrators launched citizens oriented projects, and many institutions colonized social networking platforms.

We should, however, consider that, according to current legislation, this is for the public administration a choice because there are no obligations that push this way. The number of entities that are gearing up for a presence on such platforms is growing steadily. This phenomenon occurs for a multitude of reasons, mainly because nowadays users are less inclined to looking for information navigating through corporate and public administration websites. The site and the public portal are necessary but not sufficient if you want to reach the fullest of the citizens who live in the network. A time to inform the citizens was enough to make the billings on the walls, but progressively the tools and places to inform have changed and today they often correspond to social networks. These new platforms that allow immediate dialogue between citizens and administrators stimulate the emergence of new opportunities, but of course also new responsibilities. Being in the network and managing social networks does not just mean to learn the rules of using a new communication tool to provide public offices. Being on the net, for a public administration, means dealing with a profound cultural change that involves not only ways of providing services and information, but also and principally how to deal with the citizen and his role. This implies opening, listening and dialogue skills, interaction orientation, and willingness to change [16].

5 City Dashboards

Indicators, benchmarks, and dashboards assume a dimension that seems to be external to reality and operate independently by it. These elements seem to be able to accurately and objectively measure the world and reveal its reality through a description of statistics and visualize it by graphs and maps [14]. These tools inspire a new way of knowing the city with indicators studied to be essential and very representative of what needs to be measured. The detectors are faithful, abstract and objective, so they can be compared to each other as a fact is nothing more than a fact. For example, in a city there are a certain number of people, a certain number of death in a year, a certain number of unemployed, the trains have a certain minutes' amount of delay and the level of pollution is equal to a certain level. All of these measures can be compared with others and with the same in other cities. Where people play a key role in collecting data, strict rules and mechanical methods have to be established to ensure objectivity, transparency and impartiality of data with regard to mistakes, preferences, culture and knowledge of researchers [11]. From this perspective, the great potential of such tools is to be able to transform the city into a set of elements composed of automated facts that can be traced, viewed, analyzed and interpreted.

On the other hand, observing critically the philosophy behind the data, it must recognize that they do not exist independently of ideas, tools, practices, contexts, knowledge, and systems used to generate and analyze them. Data is produced by many minds working in different situations, contexts, and structures. As we approach the data, how we measure them and what we do to them generate a certain information frame [8]. Information related to the same phenomena can be collected and recorded in different ways and interpreted through several different lenses. However, it must be considered that the method by which the data is generated is influencing, protocols, organizational and operational processes, measures, categories and standards are negotiated and discussed, so the data cannot be defined as totally neutral. This is one of the major political, ethical and normative criticisms that restrict the adoption of such tools in analysis, interpretation and management choices.

From this perspective, these tools and analyzes are not an end in themselves but become socially and technically complex data gathering initiatives, consisting of inevitably interwoven elements [6]. This is the main motivation for which there are many different projects in this field that use aggregated data in a different way and for various purposes. In summary, dashboards can be defined as neutral, essential and objective, but unpredictable, twisted, and context-sensitive.

Cities are very complex systems, often subject to accidental events, composed of very different realities and open and dynamic entities. Is it therefore conceivable to summarize a kind of scenario like this with some indicators? Can inherent errors, reliability, and uncertainty be considered negligible in this process? How much a city dashboard has to do with the concept of transparency and what about the will to provide a tool for governance? How can data be best presented? What are the results that indicators-based actions might hide? What are the mistakes hidden in the indicators? Can the indicators be exploited by any political will? Are urban indicators and dashboards really useful to inform you?

These questions reveal perhaps the most critical aspects of the indicators-based projects. The complexity of the realities complicates the process leading to the detection of the drivers needed to describe the city as it really is, objectively. The ultimate goal is to standardize the subjective look of every individual on the city. But how many limitations can result in an objective view? Are you likely to exclude some important variables?

One possible way is to allow the indicators to assert the various potentialities: to spread the knowledge of the city and to highlight what is best for it thanks to the logical basis that a definite representation of the information allows. It is possible to justify certain political and legal actions related to city issues, or to avoid criticism of solutions based on purely technical analysis [3]. These lines summarize the reasons why these types of projects can make good local democracies and provide the opportunity to learn about the local society. It is also noted that the dashboards have great utility, offer many opportunities, provide insights and data to participate in debates and argue the thesis, but if the value of these initiatives should not be understood and its limits openly recognized and valued higher than benefits? Such projects have great usability but do not represent the remedy capable of solving all the issues of administration. A dashboard is simply a way of presenting a source of knowledge to understand and handle the complex reality of cities [12]. It is necessary to recognize the importance of planning the structure and activities of an urban reality for the development of communities and companies and the promotion of a new managerial approach to the protection of particular common interest and the reduction of inequalities and injustices.

5.1 A City Dashboard for the City of Trieste

The project was born approximately in April of the year 2015 after some meetings organized by the University of Trieste in collaboration with the municipality of Trieste. During these times, the municipal administrators expressed the willingness to adopt innovative ideas for developing tools that could improve and streamline communication between public administration and citizen. The City of Trieste, aware that technological evolution multiplied the possibilities of access to the web, is currently using social networks, both to provide information in a top-down view and to increase relations with citizens, thus facilitating the satisfaction of both explicit and above latent users' needs. We believed that push information is fundamental because it communicates in a spontaneous way by updating to facts not expressly sought for.

In order to meet these communicative needs, we have begun to conceive the idea of a city dashboard that is easily interpretable and accessible by any device (personal computer, smartphone or tablet).

5.2 The Design Phases

The design of the dashboard was created in March 2015 initially to face the confusion of social networks' users. We observe a certain level of misunderstanding about the nature of the various social profiles, in particular in identifying institutional ones from others. The main cause of this was the low level of familiarity with Twitter. So the social media manager of the municipality of Trieste has since been interested in listening to innovative ideas in order to improve social communication. In the subsequent meetings the concept was conceived and after the technical approval we start the operational phase of designing and implementing the dashboards.

Initially, we carried out an analysis of twitter accounts pertaining to the city of Trieste by verifying the follow-up, the resonance created and the refresher frequency, and thus generally the degree of profile activity. After a first skimming, we focused on the main accounts concerning the spread of events, natural and landscape beauties, news both via radio and television and journalism.

Successively, by carefully looking at profiles, the phenomenon of content redundancy was identified, since the information was often the same with different styles. For this reason, only the profiles in the next section were selected for the institutional function of the project. For public administration, it is compulsory to offer the same opportunities to all actors in the area. If there were private entities performing the same function, it would not be acceptable to enter an operator's work in the dashboard excluding others. In order to guarantee this right, to highlight the nature of the project and to ensure non-injurious and offensive content, only institutional twitter profiles were chosen for users.

The idea behind the project was to create a simple and straightforward platform that could provide a wide range of information to any subject related to the city of Trieste. The dashboard wants to give the viewer a sensation of a panoramic view of the city. In other words an idea of what the place offers daily to its guests and a review of smart tools usable in the territory. For this purpose, the city dashboard is made up of just one page so you can have a light look and an overview of the content through a quick glance. The choice of the platform's name took place after a careful analysis of what have to be inspired in the observer, that is, the idea of a city view and a smart instrument. For this reason, after verifying the availability of the domain, we decided for the name "Trieste Overview".

5.3   The Architecture of Trieste Overview

The platform consists of three main parts:

The headline that contains the title and a sober gradient that recalls the main colors of the page. Just below this header you can see a bar containing some references to the pages that offer the link to the main smart tools available to users in the city of Trieste. The purpose of this placement is primarily the spread of such smart methods of living the city. They are visible in Fig. 1:

- A drop-down menu that presents a collection of the informatics tools useful for navigating the city by public transport. The first link refers to the service provided by Trieste Trasporti S.p.A. called "point to point" through which you can have all the information regarding the bus line, the stop and the journey time to reach a certain place. The second link goes to the page of the famous "Moovit" application, which is a real personal transport assistant. The third and last link refers to the application "Trieste Bus" that allows you to quickly and easily access city bus times and request information from the internal community within the application.
- The second section is entitled "Paga il parcheggio" and consists of a link to the "EasyPark" service that allows you to pay the parking ticket using an application available for every type of smartphone. This solution allows you to pay for the actual stop time and to avoid the obligation to return to the car to extend the parking time if the stopping takes longer than expected.
- The third tool is "Comunichiamo", a warning system that the citizen can use to detect problems in the city through a pre-set format that can be compiled both by an application available for every smartphone and the web.
- A link to the web page of the "Qurami" application capable of performing the queue virtually and thus facilitating the user.
- The last area is reserved for the Acegas service called "Rifiutologo" through which you can find clear explanations on how to split the materials to be thrown, and it is possible to send environmental reports by a photo retraining a problem that concerns the services carried out by the company.

TriesteOverview

Muoviti con i mezzi pubblici ▾   Paga il parcheggio   Segnala i problemi   Fai la fila con Qurami   Il Rifiutologo: App Raccolta Diff.

Fig. 1. Header and menu (Source: Own processing by http://progettots.altervista.org/)

The body of the city dashboard presents a map developed with Google maps' instruments that contains all hotspots for Wi-Fi present in the city of Trieste. These hotspots allow you to access the public Wi-Fi of the city. The locations are graphically highlighted on the map and listed, by the address, in the disappearing menu. In this section there is also a graphical reference to the weather in the city that proposes a three-day forecast (Fig. 2).

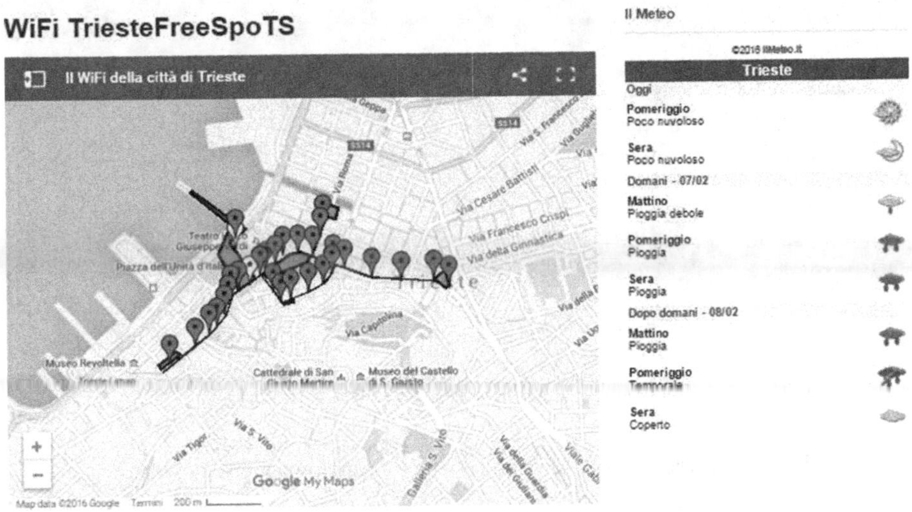
WiFi TriesteFreeSpoTS
Il WiFi della città di Trieste
Via Cesare Battisti
Via Francesco Crispi
Via della Ginnastica
Piazza dell'Unità d'Italia
Museo Revoltella
Cattedrale di San Giusto Martire
Museo del Castello di S. Giusto
Via Capitolina
Via S. Vito
Via Tigor
Google My Maps
Il Meteo
©2016 ilMeteo.it
Trieste
Oggi
Pomeriggio
Poco nuvoloso
Sera
Poco nuvoloso
Domani - 07/02
Mattino
Pioggia debole
Pomeriggio
Pioggia
Sera
Pioggia
Dopo domani - 08/02
Mattino
Pioggia
Pomeriggio
Temporale
Sera
Coperto

Fig. 2. Wi-Fi map and weather (Source: Own processing by http://progettots.altervista.org/)

In the lower section there are four Twitter feeds that provide a real-time preview of the profiles that can be observed in Fig. 3:

- Trasporti (@TriesteTrasporti): the public transport company operating in the province of Trieste. The information provided is indispensable for both citizens and tourists, to be always up to date on any strikes, route modifications and various issues related to public transport;
- Comune di Trieste (@ComunediTrieste): the official account of the municipality of Trieste;
- Protezione Civile (@ProtCivTrieste): is the official civil protection account of Trieste that thanks to the use of Twitter effectively manages communication during weather alerts;
- Divulgazione Units (@UniTwitTs): managed by the University of Trieste, proposes initiatives and meetings related to didactics, research and culture. Being Trieste a scientifically recognized city, it is essential to introduce this account to disseminate and promote all the cultural initiatives.

The selection of the profiles was defined considering the institutional value of the project, so only relevant themes' profile, with a considerable activity on the territory, were chosen.

Trieste Overview combines information from various sources in an intuitive and simple way. Its added value therefore identifies not so much with data exclusivity, but rather with the way these are presented and the ability to aggregate information from different sources by creating an orderly structure where there is confusion and disorder. Trieste Overview connects different areas of information and makes them live with complementarity. There are some areas that are very relevant in the city dashboard; these are the public and private transport area, and the information one intended for Twitter. The peculiarity of this type of dashboard is the large space reserved for Twitter,

Fig. 3. Twitter feed (Source: Own processing by http://progettots.altervista.org/)

considered by the City of Trieste as the social network for excellence in the dissemination of news and information, thanks to its immediacy and its native dedication to content rather than authors.

Trieste Overview is designed and organized so that it does not have to engage operators for its function. The underlying technology of the project and the way in which content is embedded is such that it works individually and provides an automatic real-time update. The content structure allows a wide range of customization. Widgets within it are easily repository and replaceable with the tools provided by Wordpress.

6   Conclusion

The analysis of the paper aims at deepening the progress of the cities arriving at the phenomenon of smart cities, observing how this not only implies technological evolution in the urban sphere, but also a functional change in the ranges of a urban reality. The main ICT tools used in public administrations were then analyzed, examining the major problems and emerging issues.

Public operators, managing an ever-increasing amount of information can lead the individual's privacy. However, it has been noted that such tools bring direct improvements in the coordination of public resources, thanks to the collective participation and constant monitoring of the city's infrastructure systems, resulting in faster reaction times and greater accessibility to the city's own management by the individual. In fact, greater involvement can be translated into an active commitment to contribute to improving urban living, growing environmental awareness or involvement in governmental decision-making processes. This was followed by an in-depth study of the dynamics of e-government, paying particular attention to the social networks widely used by the municipality of Trieste, namely Facebook and Twitter, the latter being relevant in designing the city dashboard Trieste Overview. Subsequently, the main tools for displaying data and then strategic policy planning, dashboards, have been studied, by looking at the main applications of these tools with some examples.

In this context, the nature of information available in the public administration was analyzed, observing the main sources and opportunities arising from the big data and the open data. Subsequently, the route was completed by exposing the process of developing a city dashboard for the city of Trieste. This tool seeks to give importance to the favorite channels of the municipality of Trieste, spreading smart tools and developing the transparency and dissemination of data. The public administration organization is developing in this direction, the citizen is, increasingly, an integral part and participatory in the management choices. The phenomenon of e-government makes the use of information and communication technologies (ICT) as essential for making public administrations more effective and in keeping with the times, able to offer innovative services and to get closer to the citizen. These themes are the priority challenges for the European Union that supports and encourages the transformation of processes and practices to meet the demands of citizens and businesses and to capitalize on the opportunities offered by new technologies [7].

References

1. Batty, M., Axhausen, K., Fosca, G., Pozdnoukhov, A., Bazzani, A., Wachowicz, M., Ouzounis, G., Portugali, Y.: Smart cities of the future. UCL Working Paper Series, Paper 188, Ottobre 2012
2. Batty, M.: The New Science of Cities. The MIT Press, Cambridge (2013)
3. Block, T., Assvche, J., Goeminne, G.: Unravellingurban sustainability: how the Flemish city monitor acknowledges complexities (2015)
4. Bonomi, A., Masiero, R.: Dalla Smart City Alla Smart Land. Marsilio, Venice (2014)
5. Borruso, G., Murgante, B.: Smart Cities in a Smart World (2014)
6. Brown, M., Garson, G.: Public Information Management and E-government – Policy and Issues. IGI Global, Hershey (2013)
7. Cocchia, A.: Smart and digital city: a systematic literature review. In: Dameri, R., Rosenthal-Sabroux, C. (eds.) Smart City. Progress in IS. Springer, Cham (2014)
8. Davis, K., Fisher, A., Kingsbury, B., Merry, S.: Governance by Indicators – Global Power Through Quantification and Rankings. Oxford University Press, Oxford (2012)
9. Dominici, G.: Smart cities e communities: l'innovazione nasce dal basso (2012)
10. Faccioli, F.: Comunicazione pubblica e cultura del servizio, Carocci (2007)
11. Kitchin, R.: The Data Revolution: Big Data, Open Data, Data Infrastructures and Their Consequences. Sage, Thousand Oaks (2014)
12. Kitchin, R., Lauriault, T.P., McArdle, G.: Urban indicators and dashboards: epistemology, contradictions and power/knowledge. Reg. Stud. Reg. Sci. 2 (1), 43–45 (2015)
13. Murgante, B., Borruso, G.: Smart cities or dumb cities? Città dall'alto, città dal basso, GEOmedia n. 6 (2013)
14. Scipioni, A., Mazzi, A., Mason, M., Manzardo, A.: The Dashboard of Sustainability to measure the local urban sustainable development: the case study of Padua municipality. Ecol. Indic. 62(4), 434–444 (2008). Elsevier Ltd.
15. Tat-Kei Ho, A.: Reinventing local governments and the e-government initiative. Public Adm. Rev. 62(4), 434–444 (2002)
16. Vademecum – Pubblica Amministrazione e social media

Change Detection and Classification of Seismic Damage with LiDAR and RADAR Surveys in Supporting Emergency Planning. The Case of Amatrice

Lucia Saganeiti[1], Federico Amato[1], Michele Potleca[2], Gabriele Nolè[3], Marco Vona[1], and Beniamino Murgante[1(✉)]

[1] School of Engineering, University of Basilicata,
Viale dellAteneo Lucano 10, 85100 Potenza, Italy
lucia.saganeiti@gmail.com,
{federico.amato,marco.vona,beniamino.murgante}@unibas.it
[2] Civil Protection of Friuli Venezia Giulia, Palmanova, Italy
michele.potleca@protezionecivile.fvg.it
[3] Italian National Research Council, IMAA, C.da Santa Loja, 85050 Tito Scalo, Potenza, Italy
gabriele.nole@imaa.cnr.it

Abstract. The spread of new satellite and LiDAR data is recently leading to the development of effective methodologies to support the monitoring and management of disaster risks, assessing the level of damages in the very early post-event phase. The increasing availability of SAR images and the diffusion of LiDAR data due to technologies such as solutions such as drones offers the opportunity to experiment new techniques for monitoring the territory. The paper will examine the case study of Amatrice (Central Italy), the Municipality most affected by the seismic swarm started in August 2016, and discuss the results obtained with the technique of interferometric differentiation and detection of change.

Keywords: RADAR · LiDAR · SAR · Seismic risk · Interferometry · Change detection

1 Introduction

Risk in generally defined as the likelihood that an uncertain event of an uncertain nature occurs; it may be produced by natural or anthropic causes. Among the natural risks, this paper analyzes the factors arising from seismic one. This is a matter of crucial importance in Italy, given the high seismicity of the entire national territory. Even though the presence of anti-seismic regulations, emergency plans and territorial monitoring tools, Italy is still not efficaciously prepared to the occurrence of seismic events. Emergency management requires effective planning [1–4]. This can be structured within a cyclical model defined by the following stages: early warning, disastrous event, first impact, recovery, attenuation, and preparation. From this cyclical model emerges the need to keep a constant focus on seismic risk - an attention that will continue over time regardless of whether or not the event is happening [5].

© Springer International Publishing AG 2017
O. Gervasi et al. (Eds.): ICCSA 2017, Part IV, LNCS 10407, pp. 722–731, 2017.
DOI: 10.1007/978-3-319-62401-3_53

Spatial analysis and geographical modelling can have a role of absolute importance in managing pre and post seismic events, through the application of well-known and widely validated methodologies [6–9].

This paper discusses an innovative spatial analysis tools based on RADAR and LiDAR data to support the post-emergence management phases. The methodology is applied to the case study of Amatrice (Central Italy), one of the Municipality most affected by the seismic swarm started in Italy from August 2016. The outcomes will show the usefulness of the proposed approach in assessing seismic damage, highlighting the contribution that these techniques can provide to the monitoring of territorial transformations in the pre-event phases.

2   Materials and Methods

In this paper, RADAR and LiDAR technologies will be analyzed with the purpose of obtaining information to deal with a seismic emergency in the best possible way.

The RADAR data used for a large-scale preliminary analysis is satellite data provided free of charge by the European Space Agency (ESA) in conjunction with the Copernicus European project. These have allowed the evaluation of the displacements of the soil right after a seismic event. LiDAR data, granted by its entities for research purposes only, is, instead, proprietary data. Their use allowed the development of a change detection to identify the most damaged areas [10].

2.1   Study Area

Amatrice is a Municipality located in the Province of Rieti in the Lazio Region, Italy (Fig. 1). Its territory is characterized by the presence of mountainous area with an altitude ranging between 900 and 2500 m. The city rises at the center of the high river basin of the River Tronto. According to the Italian Seismic Classification, the Municipality of Amatrice falls in Zone 1 [11].

This is the most dangerous area in which the probability that there will be strong seismic events is very high. The earthquake that occurred on August 24, 2016 has been the result of a persistent seismic swarm of several days with shocks of various magnitudes. The earthquake epicentered in the Apennine area between the Laga Mountains and the Sibillini Mountains had a magnitude of 6.2 and completely destroyed the historic settlement of Amatrice.

2.2   Data Acquisition

The RADAR data used in the following processing was downloaded free of charge from the Copernicus website [12]. It was chosen to use TOP-SAR images captured by Sentinel Satellites 1A and B. The Sentinel Application Platform (SNAP 5.0) distributed by ESA was used for data processing.

For each image, the following characteristics were chosen:

Satellite Platform: Sentinel 1A and B.

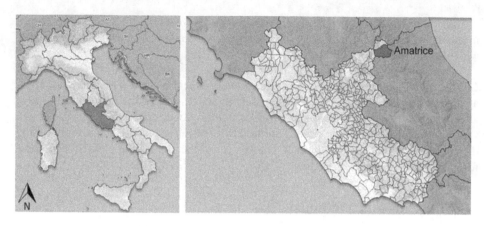

Fig. 1. The location of the Lazio Region in Italy (left) and the location of the Municipality of Amatrice within the region (right) are highlighted in red. (Color figure online)

Product Type: Single Look Complex (SLC). These products are characterized by SAR focusing, geo-referenced using orbital path data and slant-range geometry. Slant-range is the observation of the actual distance of the radar signal from the satellite defined as the line of sight between the radar and each reflective object.

Polarization: VV. As in this paper the aim is the creation of an interferogram, it is advisable to use homogeneous polarizations i.e. VV or HH.

Sensor acquisition mode: Interferometric Wide Swath (IW). It is the main land acquisition mode. It acquires data with a 250-km swath (scan width) and spatial resolution of 5 to 20 m.

Orbit Number: 22.

Direction of Passage: descending.

LiDAR data are instead proprietary data. Regarding the pre-earthquake data of August 24, 2016, the LiDAR survey was carried out by [13]. The data can be consulted on the [14] through WMS services and can be downloaded through a specific request. Data features are:

Date: 2008.

Relief Motif: waterway monitoring.

Data Type Provided: DSM first, DSM last, DTM, intensity, points in.xyz.

Ground Point Resolution: 1 × 1 m.

The LiDAR post-earthquake data were obtained from a survey carried out by the [15]. These data was provided following a specific request and can only be used for study and research purposes.

Data features:

– Date: August 29, 2016.
– Relief Motif: mapping of areas affected by the earthquake of August 24, 2016.
– Data Type Provided: points clouds in .las and .laz.
– Ground Point Resolution: 1 × 1 m.

2.3   Methodology

The RADAR dataset was processed with the SNAP software that allowed to perform an interferogram considering the Sentinel 1A images of August 22, 2016, and Sentinel 1B of August 27, 2016. The data processing process involved the co-registration of the stereo pair, the creation of the interferogram, burst removal, phase topography removal with Topographic Phase removal, application of goldstein and multilooking corrections and phase development. The Phase to Displacement algorithm was then applied to the developed phase, and the oblique component of the LOS was transformed into vertical displacement.

The LiDAR dataset was used to develop Digital Elevation Models. Generally, a Digital Surface Model (DSM) can be obtained from a point cloud of LiDAR data. In the post-processing phase, DSM points classification and filtering may result in a Digital Terrain Model (DTM), i.e. a DSM cleaned up of all the anthropic and vegetative elements. A DEM generally indicates a model that can be both a DTM and a DSM. It is a 3d model whose main feature is to contain information about the height of each point on the detected surface. Each point in a DEM will contain information about the X, Y and Z coordinates.

2.3.1   RADAR Technologies: Differential Interferometry to Monitor Terrain Displacements

Using differential interferometry technique it is possible to evaluate the land displacements along the LOS of two captured satellite images at different times and with the minimum possible time interval. This technique is useful for monitoring soil movements due to earthquakes, landslides, or other faulty movements [16], and to detect centimeter shifts. Since the LOS is not perpendicular to the Earth's surface, the differential interferometer returns the oblique component of the ground displacement. Through appropriate algorithms, it is possible to calculate the vertical displacement component so that subsidy is obtained. Therefore, the process is divided into:

– S1-TOPS Co-registration: Co-registration [17] was performed with a bilinear interpolation of two images. The S1-TOPS Co-registration operator allows to co-register two SLC products (Master and Slave) Sentinel 1 on the same sub swath using the orbit paths of the two products and a DEM. We chose the sub swath IW2, VV polarization and, concerning the DEM, we chose the 3 s automatic 3-sec download with bilinear interpolation. The co-registration process has as output the co-recorded bands of master and slave in i/Q and intensity format.
– Interferogram Formation: The phase of an image SAR provides information about moving a target or the ground when this is observed from two different angles. Therefore, by combining two SAR images, it is possible to determine the magnitude and direction of the target or soil displacement. The difference between the phases of two or more SAR images acquired on the same area but at different times is an interferogram [18]. The phase of a SAR image is mainly determined by the distance between satellite antennas and ground targets. By combining the phase of the two previously co-recorded images, users can generate an interferogram whose phase is

highly correlated with the topography of the ground. The interferogram is formed by multiplication between the master image and its slave conjugate complex. The amplitude of both images is multiplied while the new interferometric phase is representing the phase difference between the two images [19]. The interferometric phase $\Delta\varphi$ of each pixel in the SAR image depends on the orbital trajectory difference (Δr) of the two captures. Therefore, it is proportional to the ratio between a whole cycle of the phase in radians and the wavelength transmitted λ.

Considering that a whole phase cycle in radians corresponds to 2π and that $\Delta r = 2r$ as wavefront return path has to be considered, it is possible to demonstrate the relationship:

$$\Delta\varphi = \frac{2\pi\Delta r}{\lambda}$$

and therefore, being $\Delta r = 2r$

$$\Delta\varphi = \frac{4\pi r}{\lambda}$$

Through the creation of the interferogram, the sources of error are eliminated and the processing related to the elevation and displacement is retained. Given the periodic nature of the sinusoidal signal, values of Δr that differ in wavelengths from a whole multiple of λ, always introduce the same phase difference corresponding to a whole cycle 2π. This implies that the phases are not distinguishable between them. In other words, the phase of the SAR signal corresponds to the measurement of the fraction of Δr which is smaller than the wavelength of the transmitted signal.

Consequently, interferometric fringes represent a complete cycle 2π. These appear on the interferogram as arbitrary color cycles, and a complete cycle (repetition of all image colors) corresponds to the half-wavelength of the sensor. In mathematical terms, if

$$\Delta\varphi = 2\pi,$$

from the previous definition of $\Delta\varphi$ we can write

$$r = \frac{\lambda}{2}$$

The greater is the tension on the ground, the greater will be the closeness of the fringes. The tension on the ground depicts a shift.

- Corrections: TOPSAR images need a series of corrections to improve their quality. In this study, S1-TOPSAR Deburst, Topographic Phase Removal, Goldstein Phase Filtering [20] and Multi Loo-King [21] were applied.
- Phase unwrapping: The phase values as they appear in the interferogram are nor useful for an understandable reading. The interferometric phase is ambiguous and is

known only within a 2π radius expressed in radians. The correlation between the interferometric and the topographic phases is solved with phase unwrapping. Thus, this technique solves this ambiguity by integrating the phase difference between adjacent pixels [22]. After eliminating any full number of ambiguous quotas (equal to a full phase 2π cycle), the phase shift between two points on the flattened interferogram will correspond to a real altitude variation.

- Ground Movement Model - Phase to Displacement: This operator allows the location of land moves over the time interval between the two SAR observations by converting the interferogram into a displacement map [23]. As already mentioned, the shift that is obtained is along the LOS, thus knowing that the interferometric phase change-displacement contribution is:

$$\Delta\varphi_d = \frac{4\pi}{\lambda}d$$

Where λ the transmitted wavelength and d is the LOS displacement; we can derive d:

$$d = -\frac{\lambda}{4\pi}\Delta\varphi_d$$

The vertical component can be calculated as:

$$d_v = -\frac{\Delta\varphi_d \lambda}{4\pi cos\theta}$$

where:
- d_v: vertical displacement;
- $\Delta\varphi_d$: Interferometric phase variation regarding displacement contribution;
- λ: wavelength
- θ: angle of incidence to calculate the vertical component.
  SNAP calculator also allows the addition of the vertical displacement band to the interferogram.

2.3.2 LiDAR Technologies for DEM Analysis

The output of a LiDAR is a point cloud i.e. a set of points defined by their position in a coordinate system and by any associated intensity values. Through the laser beam pulses it is possible to define the classes to which each point belongs. This operation is called classification and allows the location of points belonging to the soil, to the vegetation or to the built-up areas. The most common types of soil cover classification divide the points into: bare ground, forest, shrubs, urbanized and thick grass, spruce, undergrowth or crops.

These classifications allow the identification of points of interest by eliminating the superfluous ones that might obstruct the results of the analysis. The American Society for Photogrammetry and Remote Sensing (ASPRS) proposes a more analytical classification method that associates a number in each category. This classification has been implemented in several point cloud processing algorithms. Thus, a given figure presents itself as a sown sparse of points that must be transformed into a surface by connecting points in a coherent manner and according to a specific logic. For the purposes of this study, point cloud processing aimed at the creation of a DEM. This could be organized into three different data structures: GRID, TIN and Contour Lines [24]. In the proposed case we chose to organize the point cloud according to a GRID, resulting into a raster matrix in which each point was stored with its relative dimension.

3   Result and Discussion

3.1   Vertical Displacement – RADAR Dataset

From the processing of the interferogram obtained with the satellite data, the vertical displacement of the terrain was analyzed following the earthquake of August 24, 2016. In the Municipality of Amatrice between August 22 and August 27, displacements between 0.25 and 10 cm were measured (Fig. 2).

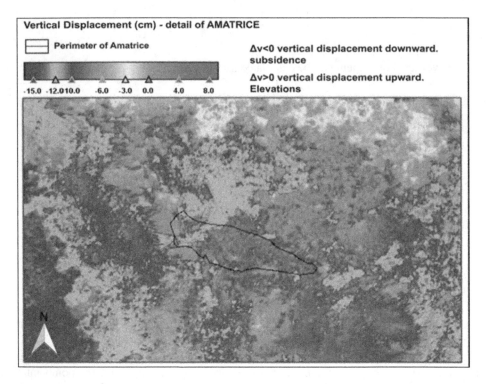

Fig. 2. Vertical displacement in the Amatrice area; the boundaries of the historical settlement of the Municipality are highlighted with a black line.

The recorded displacement is negative and therefore corresponds to a land sinking phenomenon along the vertical direction.

3.2   Change Detection, Triple Change Mask – LiDAR Dataset

From the difference between the pre-earthquake DSM obtained with the 2008 LiDAR data and the post-earthquake DSM obtained with the 2016 LiDAR data, a change detection [25] represented by the triple change mask [26] was performed. This is exemplified by a raster whose pixels have a size of 1×1 m. Despite the errors evaluated in a range of $-0,4$ and $0,4$ m, it is therefore possible to locate and distinguish all the points belonging to (Fig. 3):

- Positive variations: all pixels whose altitude attribute has a positive value of between 0.4 and 20 m. In the specific case, positive variations detect, on the map, an altitude decrease, and they therefore correspond to building collapses.
- Null variations: all pixels whose altitude attribute is zero or close to zero, i.e. between -0.4 and 0.4 m. The null variations identify, on the map, all the areas that have not been subject to elevation changes due to the seismic event.
- Negative variations: All pixels whose altitude attribute is negative, or between -0.4 and -20 m. In the specific case, negative variations reveal, the presence of rubble after collapsing on the roads being examined.

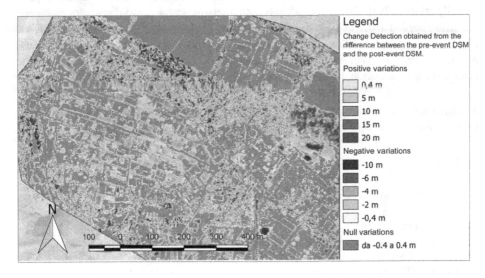

Fig. 3. Change detection - triple change mask on Amatrice historical settlement.

The proposed methodology undergoes to several considerations. The interferometry obtained with the RADAR dataset as well as identifying the areas most affected when a seismic event occurs, if periodically carried out, returns the ground movements and thus allows to monitor a those areas which are most prone to seismic movements. Analyzing ground displacements is useful to have an immediate feedback on the areas that could have been damaged after a seismic event. However, these data only allow large scale analysis. Nevertheless, positive and negative variations obtained with change detection techniques allow a more in-depth analysis aiming at the single building evaluation. Indeed, the LiDAR relief enables the location of an area or building that is struck by the earthquake with extreme precision.

4   Conclusions

This paper proposed an analysis of RADAR and LiDAR technologies as tools for monitoring the territory and assessing damages in the immediate post-earthquake phases. The RADAR dataset has been used to evaluate the displacement of the terrain following the seismic event, while the LiDAR dataset has been used to make a 3D change detection. The case study examined was that of Amatrice's historical settlement. The use of the proposed methodologies highlighted how the use of RADAR and LiDAR technologies can be useful both for the non-emergency period to monitor seismic-affected areas and for the immediate post-earthquake phases to assess the effects it has caused.

A long-lasting monitoring of the territory is of central importance, since only knowing its behavior over time can be prevented, or rather mitigated, the damage caused by an earthquake. Differential interferometry is an effective way to perform a first evaluation of the effects of a seismic event. Moreover, it may become a form of area monitoring if it is periodically effected. In the hours immediately after a seismic event, up-to-date cartography and media are needed to detect the state of damage of buildings as soon as possible. The LiDAR reliefs or helicopter reliefs are good techniques for this purpose. From the positive and negative variations evaluated through the change detection, users can quickly identify the priorities for intervention, identify collapsed buildings, and inaccessible roads.

Acknowledgements. Authors are grateful to the Civil Protection of Friuli Venezia Giulia region, for providing LiDAR dataset analyzed in this paper.

References

1. FAO: The state of the world's land and water resources for food and agriculture (SOLAW) - Managing systems at risk. Rome and Earthscan. Food and Agriculture Organization of the United Nations, London (2011)
2. Casas, G.L., Scorza, F.: Sustainable planning: a methodological toolkit. In: Gervasi, O., et al. (eds.) ICCSA 2016. LNCS, vol. 9786, pp. 627–635. Springer, Cham (2016). doi: 10.1007/978-3-319-42085-1_53
3. Amato, F., Martellozzo, F., Nolè, G., Murgante, B.: Preserving cultural heritage by supporting landscape planning with quantitative predictions of soil consumption. J. Cult. Heritage **23**, 44–54 (2017). doi:10.1016/j.culher.2015.12.009
4. International Guidelines on Urban and Territorial Planning. Nairobi (2015)
5. Amato, L., Dello Buono, D., Izzi, F., La Scaleia, G., Maio, D.: HELP - an early warning dashboard system, built for the prevention, mitigation and assessment of disasters, with a flexible approach using open data and open source technologies (2016)
6. Scardaccione, G., Scorza, F., Casas, G.L., Murgante, B.: Spatial autocorrelation analysis for the evaluation of migration flows: the Italian case. In: Taniar, D., Gervasi, O., Murgante, B., Pardede, E., Apduhan, B.O. (eds.) ICCSA 2010. LNCS, vol. 6016, pp. 62–76. Springer, Heidelberg (2010). doi:10.1007/978-3-642-12156-2_5

7. Murgante, B., Tilio, L., Lanza, V., Scorza, F.: Using participative GIS and e-tools for involving citizens of Marmo Platano-Melandro area in European programming activities. J. Balk. Near East. Stud. **13**(1), 97–115 (2011). doi:10.1080/19448953.2011.550809. Taylor & Francis, London. ISSN 1944-8953

8. Las Casas, G., Murgante, B., Scorza, F.: Regional local development strategies benefiting from open data and open tools and an outlook on the renewable energy sources contribution. In: Papa, R., Fistola, R. (eds.) Smart Energy in the Smart City: Urban Planning for a Sustainable Future, pp. 275–290. Springer, Heidelberg (2016). doi:10.1007/978-3-319-31157-9_14. ISBN 978-3-319-31155-5

9. Las Casas, G., Scorza, F.: Discrete spatial assessment of multi-parameter phenomena in low density region: the Val D'Agri case. In: Gervasi, O., et al. (eds.) ICCSA 2015. LNCS, vol. 9157, pp. 813–824. Springer, Cham (2015). doi:10.1007/978-3-319-21470-2_59

10. Sarma, K., Dey, K.S., Bahuguna, S., Shah, A., Nayak, D., Bhattacharyya, S.R.: Application of remote sensing for the study of mangrove assemblages in Sunderbans, West Bengal. In: IAPRS, Hyderabad, India, vol. XXXIV, Part 7, published on CD (2002)

11. Testo Unico delle Norme per l'edilizia: Classificazione sismica del territorio italiano adottata in seguito al Decreto Legislativo n. 112 del 1998 e Decreto del Presidente della Repubblica n. 380 del 2001 (2001)

12. Copernicus, February 2017. https://scihub.copernicus.eu/dhus/#/home

13. Ministry of the Environment and the Protection of the Territory and Sea (MATTM), Extraordinary Environmental Remote Surveillance Plan (PST-A) and Of its Extension (PST-A Extension 2008) (2008)

14. Geo Portale Nazionale, February 2017. http://www.pcn.minambiente.it/mattm/

15. Region, Civil Protection of Friuli Venezia Giulia (2016)

16. Lasaponara, R., Murgante, B., Elfadaly, A., Qelichi, M.M., Shahraki, S.Z., Wafa, O., Attia, W.: Spatial open data for monitoring risks and preserving archaeological areas and landscape: case studies at Kom el Shoqafa, Egypt and Shush, Iran. Sustainability **9**, 572 (2017). doi:10.3390/su9040572

17. Press, W.H., Teukolsky, S.A., Vetterling, W.T., Flannery, B.P.: Numerical Recipes in C: The Art of Scientific Computing, 2nd edn. Cambridge University Press, New York (1992)

18. Goldstein, R., Gabriel, A.: Grossed orbits interferometry: theory and experimental (1998)

19. Prati, C., Rocca, F., Monti-Guarnieri, A., Damonti, E.: Seismic migration for SAR focusing: interferometrical applications. IEEE Trans. GRS Geosci. Remote Sens. **28**(4), 627–640 (1990). New York

20. Goldstein, R.M., Werner, C.L.: Radar interferogram phase filtering for geophysical applications. Geophys. Res. Lett. **25**, 4035–4038 (1998)

21. Small, D., Schubert, A.: Guide to ASAR Geocoding, RSL-ASAR-GC-AD, Issue 1.0 (2008)

22. Costantini, M.: A novel phase unwrapping method based on network programming. IEEE Tran. Geosci. Remote Sens. **36**, 813–821 (1998)

23. Massonet, D., Monti-Guarnieri, A., Prati, C., Ferretti, A.: InSAR Principles: Guidelines for SAR Interferometry Processing and Interpretation, ESA TM-19 (2007)

24. Qin, R., Tian, J., Reinartz, P.: 3D change detection – approaches and applications. ISPRS J. Photogram. Remote Sens. **122**, 41–56 (2016)

25. Singh, A.: Digital change detection techniques using remotely-sensed data. Int. J. Remote Sens. **10**, 989–1003 (1989)

26. Tian, J., Chaabouni-Chouayakh, H., Reinartz, P., Krauss, T., d'Angelo, P.: Automatic 3D change detection based on optical satellite stereo imagery. Int. Arch. Photogram. Remote Sens. Spat. Inf. Sci. **38**(Part 7B), 586–591 (2010)

Storm Model Application at Indonesian Tropical Ocean

Fredhi Agung Prasetyo[1], Mohammad Arif Kurniawan[1], Siti Komariyah[1],
Rudiyanto[2], and Tutut Herawan[3,4(✉)]

[1] Research and Development Division, Biro Klasifikasi Indonesia,
Yos Sudarso 38-39-40, Tg. Priok, Jakarta 14320, Indonesia
fredhiagung@bki.co.id
[2] Biro Klasifikasi Indonesia, Jakarta, Indonesia
rudiyanto@bki.co.id
[3] Universitas Teknologi Yogyakarta, Yogyakarta, Indonesia
tutut@uty.ac.id
[4] AMCS Research Center, Malang, Indonesia

Abstract. The ocean phenomenon consists of mixed types of wave condition. In order to simulate the actual ocean phenomena, Tomita proposed "storm model" in which take into account the changing of wave history during ocean voyage. The wave history is modeled based on "storm" and "calm-sea" condition while in storm is configured from crescendo de crescendo amplitude wave blocks, and calm-sea are configured by time random history. Tomita developed storm model from actual wave height history determined from the ships in which voyage along North Pacific Ocean. The period of 2010 to 2013, one of the author members developed the advanced of Storm model so that can configure storm profile, simulate variation of storm duration and generate equivalent short sea sequence from variable observation period data. Since that the development both of storm model is on the basis of wave data of non Tropical Ocean, that is North Pacific and North Atlantic Ocean, the wave history of Indonesian ocean area as a part of tropical area, in which positioned across between two continents; Australia and Asia, and two oceans; Indian Oceans and Pacific Ocean are examined in this work. This paper presents an analysis of wave history on the chosen tropical ocean by using the storm model. The analysis of storm duration and its changing nature is examined. The storms configuration, the number of storm classes, and the changing nature of amplitude wave block in each storm class are determined based on these wave histories.

Keywords: Ocean phenomenon · Storm model · Indonesian tropical

1 Introduction

The main components that to be considered during design and assessment process of ship structures is stated by 4 parts that defined as a state beyond which the structure no longer satisfies the applicable requirement [1]. Those are serviceability limit state (SLS), ultimate limit state (ULS), fatigue limit state (FLS) and accidental limit state (ALS). The limit state mostly is dependable to the load applied to the ship structure, and the

© Springer International Publishing AG 2017
O. Gervasi et al. (Eds.): ICCSA 2017, Part IV, LNCS 10407, pp. 732–745, 2017.
DOI: 10.1007/978-3-319-62401-3_54

main component of the ship load is based on the load of environmental. The example as mentioned in the above paragraph is fatigue limit state. The accuracy of assessment of the FLS ship is dependable to description of the fatigue load. Here, the accuracy of fatigue load is represented to the ability of the generation on actual ocean condition and the changing nature of ocean wave during ship operations.

In order to represent the real ocean wave, Tomita [2–4] developed the storm model to simulate the changing nature of wave during its voyage operation. The wave is recorded during the ship sailed on the North pacific ocean. The storm model consider two wave conditions, there are storm and calm-sea. Further advance development of storm model conducted by Prasetyo [5–9] by adding additional wave area, North Atlantic. In his advanced, the storm model has capability to take into account automation storm profile configuration, various storm duration and various measurement period of wave data histories.

As presented in previous paragraph, the storm model is mainly developed based on North atlantic and North pacific ocean, this means that the storm model might be applied on the non-tropical ocean area. Furthermore, in order to shows the capability of storm model on the tropical ocean area, as well as his based ocean area, the Indonesia tropical ocean are chosen. Therefore, this paper presents an analysis of wave history on the chosen tropical ocean by using the storm model. The analysis of storm duration and its changing nature is examined.

The rest of this paper is organized as follow: Sect. 2 presents related wave data. Section 3 presents storm model. Section 4 presents obtained results and following by discussion. Finally, the conclusion of this work is given in Sect. 5.

2 Wave Data

The tropical area are located between 25°N and 25°S. The area that is located in the middle of North Pacific and North Atlantic ocean, could be chosen for this purpose. This study choose Indonesian tropical ocean as depicted on Fig. 1. The wave data histories are only collected from ocean area that is located in the range of 90°E to 140°E and 10°N to 10°S. This area also used by Kurniawan [10–12] in order to define the wave characteristic along Indonesian waterways in term of wave spectrum specific and its statistical representation.

Furthermore, this study uses the measured hindcast data that is provided from the European centre for medium-range weather forecasts (ECMWF) [14]. These data are collected from 1979 to 2015 in four period collections per day i.e. 06.00 am, 12.00 am, 06.00 pm and 12.00 pm. The wave data that are provided from ECMWF is significant wave height H_W, mean period T_W, and wave direction θ_W. Only the two data will be utilized for the analysis on this paper.

3 Storm Model

This section presents storm model comprises analysis of wave data, storm model, and analysis of storm duration.

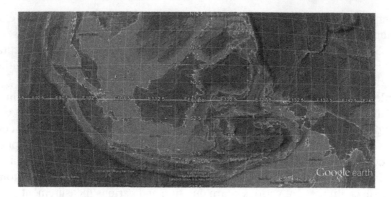

Fig. 1. The Indonesian tropical ocean. The area in which locate between 90°E to 140°E and 10°N to 10°S are used in the study.

3.1 Analysis of Wave Data

The wave data histories of Indonesian tropical ocean are prepared from the chosen coordinate, 90°E to 140°E and 10°N to 10°S. The chosen coordinate are divided in grid point with 0.25° lattice accuracy. Since the huge wave data histories are collected from ECMWF at chosen location, the range of grid points are simplified by choosing grid point with 0.75° and 1.0° interval, with the total of grid points is 43680 points.

Kurniawan [10–12] conducted a study to analysis and define the wave characteristics of Indonesian waterways area. He divided the Indonesian area by using two typical

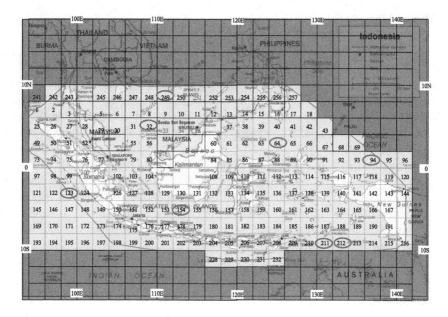

Fig. 2. The Indonesian waterways area, as defined by Kurniawan [10–12]. The area has 2° × 2° spatial.

Table 1. The sampling of area that the wave data histories are collected

No.	Area	Longitude range	Latitude range
1	1	140°E–142°E	10°N–8°N
2	2	140°E–142°E	10°N–8°N
3	3	140°E–142°E	10°N–8°N
...			
90	86N	120°E–122°E	2°N–1.35°N
91	86S	120°E–122°E	0.25°N–0°N
...			
107	99NW	98°E–99°E	0°N–1°S
108	99NE	99°E–100°E	0°N–1°S
109	99SW	98°E–99°E	1°S–2°S
110	99SE	99°E–100°E	1°S–2°S
...			
305	264	140°E–142°E	10°N–8°N

criteria, i.e. The areas are divided based on 2° × 2° spatial; ii. For the closed waterways area, the divided area are re-defined in the finite area by considering the geographical location. This criteria was developed in order to take into account the specific local geographic location of Indonesian archipelago. The area as Kurniawan's definition is shown in Fig. 2.

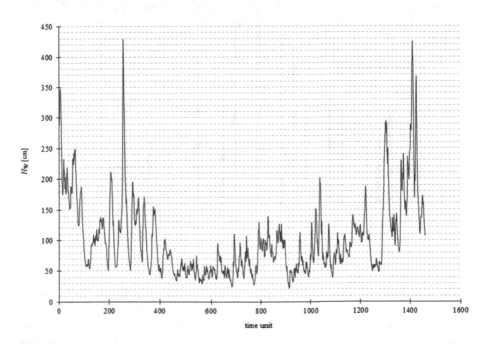

Fig. 3. The example of significant wave height histories during 2005 at point located on 110°E 5°N.

This work also divides the chosen location as the areas. The areas are divided in the same as well as Kurniawan's method that be explained in previous paragraph. Total area are used in this work is 305 areas. The sampling of area, in which divided are presented in Table 1. The wave data histories are collected from points (with interval 0.75 and 1.0) located inside of each area. Figure 3 shows the example of wave history during 2005 at point located on 110°E 5°N.

3.2 Storm Model

Storm model, 1G storm, was developed by Tomita [2–4], by considering that the real ocean could be simulated by two type of wave. The first type of wave is calm-sea and the other is storm. 1G storm was assumed that the period duration of storm is 3.5 days and it is remain unchanged for all storm class and conditions. 1G storm consist crescendo de crescendo amplitude individual waveform (h_W). 1G storm is figured as Fig. 4. 1G storm divide into 5 (five) storm classes and calm-sea condition. 1G storm classes are (1) storm F with maximum h_W 15.0 m; (2) storm E with maximum h_W 11.0 m; (3) storm D with maximum h_W 9.0 m; (4) storm C with maximum h_W 8.0 m; (5) storm B with maximum h_W 7.0 m; (6) storm A with maximum h_W 6.0 m; calm-sea with maximum h_W 5.0 m. Since the seakeeping theory does not take into account in the modelling process of 1G model, this model will not account the relation between sea state and stress response.

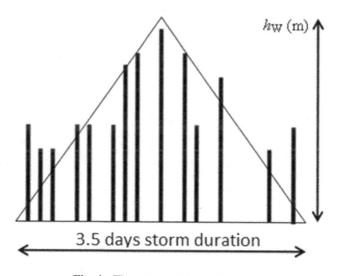

Fig. 4. The representation of 1G storm.

The next phases of storm model development are conducted by Kawabe [15], Osawa [16] and Prasetyo [5] in order to take into account the coupling process of sea keeping theory. The storm nature is configured based on the relative frequency of H_W in a storm and its statistical function, that is tail of the long-term probability density distribution of H_W and H_W is changed linearly in time. The storm profile is assumed that H_W increased and decreased linearly with time and number of storm will be decrease monotonically inline with the increase in maximum H_W in storm. Both of Kawabe and Osawa model, their storm model have indication that manual adjustment is still needed when configured the storm profile by operator.

Instead of Kawabe and Osawa models, Prasetyo introduced the automatic storm profile configuration include with the adaptive function of the profile configuration procedure [5] on the variation of storm duration and the variation of collection period of the wave data. Here, this storm model calls as 2G storm.

Figure 5 shows the example of H_W sequence on the 2G storm profile in certain period of history time. The storm profile is configured from different period of collection period in the same locations. The periods of wave data collection are 2 h and 6 h.

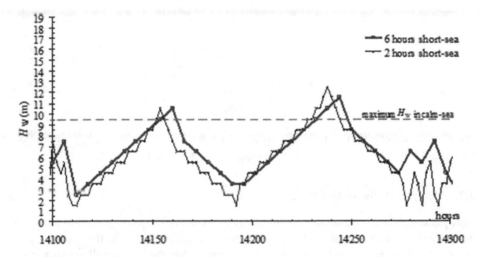

Fig. 5. The example of H_W sequence of 2G storm profile. The different period of observation of wave data are presented. The first data is collected in every 6 h, and the second one is 2 h.

The 1G and 2G storms was developed on the basis of location area, that is shown in Fig. 6. These figures show both of North Pacific and North Atlantic area, that the wave data histories was used to developed both storm model. In this paper, the storm profile configuration are not discussed. However, the storm duration analysis on the tropical and sub-tropical area that used in storm model development will be extensive examined in following paragraph.

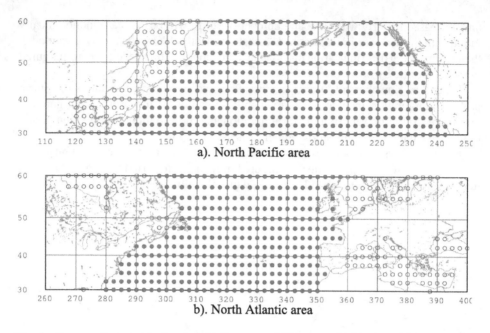

Fig. 6. The area that used to developed 1G storm and 2G storm. (a) North pacific area, 30°N–60°N and 110°E–110°W; (b) North Atlantic area, 30°N–60°N and 80°W–10°E.

3.3   Analysis of Storm Duration

This paragraph will discuss the methodology to examine the storm duration from the wave data histories. As described in previous, the storm profile is the increase and decrease step in H_W linearly with time. This means that the storm will starting from certain H_W in certain period increase to his maximum H_W in storm. After the storm reach to its peak, it will be gradually decrease to the remaining H_W in end of storm.

Boccoti [17] introduced the equivalent triangular storm, by assuming that the storm will occur if exceed the 2.0 times of mean value of H_W and this condition will not fall below to the threshold in a certain time. Both of these assumption are applied in order to examine the duration of storm for different wave data histories location.

The storm profile is examined from wave data histories, and its changing nature are presented in Fig. 7. The targets points from all chosen area, North Pacific and North Atlantic area (Fig. 6) as the representative of sub-tropical zone and Indonesian tropical ocean area as a part of Tropical zone (Fig. 2) are analyzed by using these changing nature and following procedure:

a.   The original wave data histories are smoothed based on weighted moving average method, as formula (1).

$$H_W[i] = \sum_{k=1}^{3} \left\{ \frac{H_W[i-3+k] * k}{6} \right\} \qquad (1)$$

b. Examine the local maximum of H_W ($H_{max,j}$) and be numbered in consecutive order of storm.

c. Once $H_{max,j}$ is identified, the other attribute, local minimum H_W just before $H_{max,j}$; $t_{B,(j)}$ and that of after $H_{max,j}$; $t_{E,(j)}$. The storm [j] is identified from its $H_{max,j}$, $t_{B,(j)}$ and $t_{B,(j)}$.

d. The storm duration ($d[j]$) is determined as:

$$d[i] = t_{E,j} - t_{B,j}. \tag{2}$$

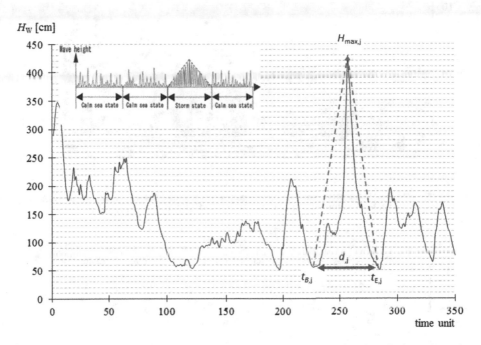

Fig. 7. The definition of storm based on description of storm model and equivalent triangular storm [17].

4   Results and Discussion

The storm duration is one of important to be examined since that 1G storm assumed that storm duration is fixed, 3.5 days, and 2G storm assumed that the storm duration is dependency variable based on its wave data histories location.

Three specific area that is representation of sub tropical zone and tropical zone are conducted. These areas are North Pacific area (30°N–60°N and 110°E–110°W), North Atlantic area (30°N–60°N and 80°W–10°E), Indonesia tropical ocean area (10°N–10°S and 90°E–140°E).

Figure 8 shows the scatter plotting of storm duration that is examined in the North Pacific area, while for the North Atlantic area is presented in Fig. 9. It is comparable with that of fixed storm duration, 3.5 days, and it is found that the difference between the average storm duration in North Pacific area (3.398 days) and in North Atlantic area

(3.988 days) are not in acceptable limit. Furthermore, when we consider the Indonesian ocean area, the average storm duration (ranged from 2.0 days to 2.857 days) is shorter than 3.5 days, with the individual storm duration is ranged from 0.5 days to 8.75 days.

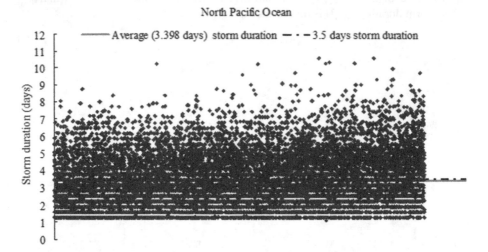

Fig. 8. Examined Storm duration in North Pacific area [5, 7, 8].

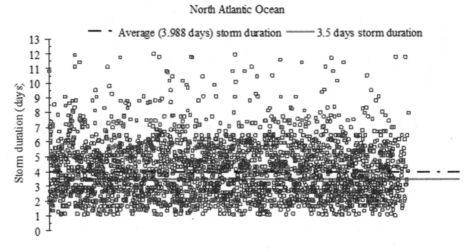

Fig. 9. Examined storm duration in North Atlantic area [5, 9].

Figures 8, 9 and 10 show that the idealism correlation with scatter of storm duration could be estimated based on the examination results. As consequently, for the practical engineering, the storm duration might be assumed by using several kind of statistical distribution approach.

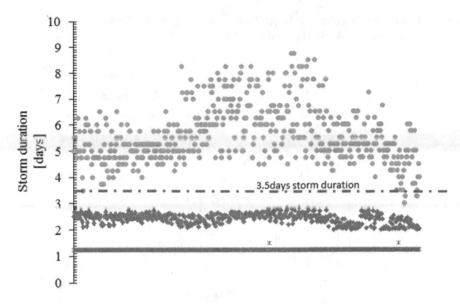

Fig. 10. Examined storm duration in Indonesian tropical ocean area [13].

Figures 11 and 12 show the frequency distribution of storm duration in North Pacific area and North Atlantic area. The assumed normal distribution is also plotted in these figures. It is shown that the fitness of storm duration and its frequency distribution is reasonable, by using the variable of normal distribution that produced from the statistical data for each, North Pacific and North Atlantic area. The mean

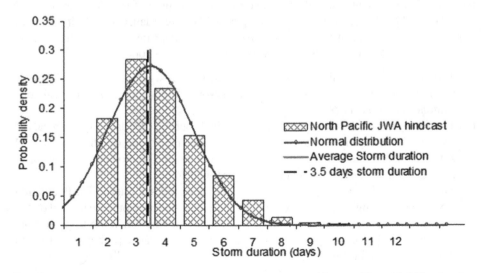

Fig. 11. Frequency distribution of storm duration for North Pacific area. The probability density function is approached by using Normal distribution [5, 7, 8].

value μ and the variance σ² for North Pacific area are 3.398 days and 1.446, and for North Atlantic area is 3.988 days and 1.822.

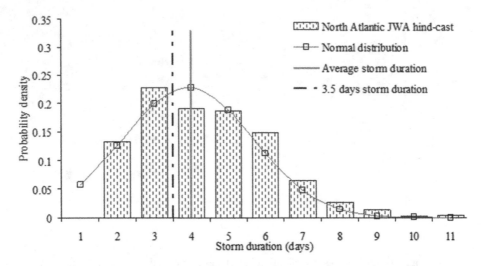

Fig. 12. Frequency distribution of storm duration for North Atlantic area. The probability density function is approached by using Normal distribution [5, 9]

Since 1G storm and 2G storm was developed in sub tropical zone (North Pacific and North Atlantic area), Fig. 13 shows the plotting of probability density of storm duration in tropical zone (Indonesian ocean area). The assumed approach of exceedance probability of storm duration in Indonesian tropical ocean area is presented in Fig. 14. This figure shows that the assumed approach that is representation for storm duration in North Pacific & North Atlantic area do not have the same accuracy for Indonesian tropical ocean area. Thus, the reasonable fitting of log normal of exceedance probability of storm duration for Indonesian tropical ocean area could be linear interpolation than that of normal distribution. As discuss above, we could conclude as following:

a. The procedure to examine storm duration that is analysis from wave data histories in sub tropical zone (North Pacific area and North Atlantic area) and tropical zone (Indonesian tropical ocean area) is proposed.
b. The average storm duration occurs in sub tropical zone is 3.398 days for North Pacific area and 3.988 days for North Atlantic area. The average storm duration for tropical zone is ranged from 2.0 days to 2.857 days. The storm duration occurs in tropical zone is relative shorter than that of in sub-tropical zone.
c. The storm of sub tropical and tropical zone are fluctuated in duration. The fluctuation storm duration might be assumed by using statistical distribution. The normal distribution is have good correlation when regress the storm duration in sub-tropical zone. However, the linear interpolation of lognormal of exceedance probability of storm duration has good fitting in the tropical zone.

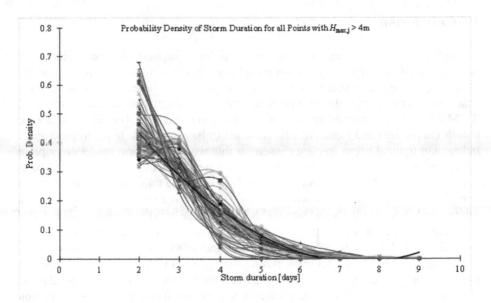

Fig. 13. Probability density of storm duration for all points in the chosen location of Indonesian tropical ocean area [13]

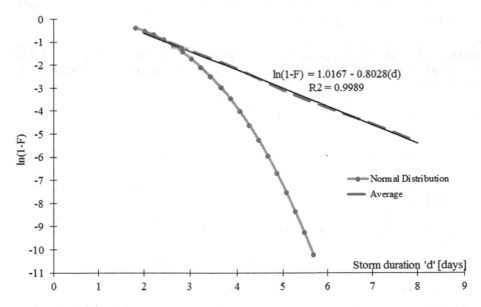

Fig. 14. The plotting of exceedance probability of storm duration for average storm duration in Indonesian ocean area. The assumed normal distribution and assumed linear formula are comparable [13]

5 Conclusion

The actual ocean phenomena is examined in order to support the design phase and operational safety analysis. The storm model is proposed to have the capability to the modelling of the actual ocean phenomena. The model was developed based on wave data histories that is provided by European centre for medium range weather forecasts (ECMWF). The storm model application that was developed based on sub tropical zone (North Pacific area and North Atlantic area) are to be expandable to the tropical zone. Indonesian tropical ocean area are chosen for this work. The storm model description and in combination with equivalent triangular storm are used to analysis the storm duration for sub tropical zone and tropical zone. As results, the following is concluded: (1) The procedure to examine storm duration that is analysis from wave data histories in sub tropical zone (North Pacific area and North Atlantic area) and tropical zone (Indonesian tropical ocean area) is proposed; (2) The average storm duration occurs in sub tropical zone is 3.398 days for North Pacific area and 3.988 days for North Atlantic area. The average storm duration for tropical zone is ranged from 2.0 days to 2.857 days. The storm duration occurs in tropical zone is relative shorter than that of in sub-tropical zone; (3) The storm of sub tropical and tropical zone are fluctuated in duration. The fluctuation storm duration might be assumed by using statistical distribution. The normal distribution is have good correlation when regress the storm duration in sub-tropical zone. However, the linear interpolation of lognormal of exceedance probability of storm duration has good fitting in the tropical zone.

Acknowledgment. This research is supported by Biro Klasifikasi Indonesia. The work of Tutut Herawan is supported by Universitas Teknologi Yogyakarta Research Grant no vote O7/UTY-R/SK/0/X/2013.

References

1. IACS: Common Structural Rules for Bulk Carriers and Oil Tankers. IACS (2015)
2. Tomita, Y., Kawabe, H., Fukuoka, T.: Statistical characteristics of long-term wave-induced load for fatigue strength analysis for ships. In: Proceedings of 6th PRADS, vol. 2, pp. 2792–2805 (1992)
3. Tomita, Y., Hashimoto, K., Osawa, N., Terai, K., Wang, Y.: Study on fatigue design loads for ships based on crack growth analysis, ASTM STP 1439
4. Tomita, Y., Matoba, M., Kawabe, H.: Fatigue crack growth behaviour under random loading model simulating real encountered wave condition. Mar. Struct. **8**, 407–422 (2015)
5. Prasetyo, F.A.: Study on advanced storm model for fatigue assessment of ship structural member, Doctoral dissertation, Osaka University Suita Japan (2013)
6. Prasetyo, F.A., Osawa, N., Sawamura, J.: Study on the effect of storm duration fluctuation on the accuracy of fatigue assessment of ship structural member. In: Proceedings of 21st ISOPE Conference, vol. IV, pp. 921–928
7. Prasetyo, F.A., Osawa, N., Sawamura, J.: Study on load history generation method based on storm model with consideration of fluctuation in storm duration. In: Proceedings of 25th TEAM Conference (2011)

8. Prasetyo, F.A., Osawa, N., Kobayashi, T.: Study on preciseness of load history generation based on storm model for fatigue assessment of ship structure members. In: Proceedings of 22nd ISOPE Conference (2012)

9. Prasetyo, F.A., Osawa, N.: Study on the applicability of load history generation method based on storm model in North Atlantic route for fatigue assessment of ship structure members. In: Proceedings of 26th TEAM Conference (2012)

10. Kurniawan, M.A., Prasetyo, F.A., Komariyah, S.: Study on wave scatter mapping of Indonesia waterways based on hind-cast data. In: Proceedings of Asian-Pacific Technical Exchange and Advisory Meeting (TEAM 2014) (2014). ITU Published

11. Kurniawan, M.A., Komariyah, S., Prasetyo, F.A.: Initial preview on re-mapping wave scatter area of Indonesian waterways. In: Proceedings of RINA ICSOT (2014)

12. Kurniawan, M.A., Prasetyo, F.A., Komariyah, S.: A comparison of three different water areas and its influence for development of rules regulation. In: Proceedings of Asian-Pacific Technical Exchange and Advisory Meeting (TEAM) (2016)

13. Prasetyo, F.A., Kurniawan, M.A., Komariyah, S.: Study on the analysis of rouge waves in Indonesian waterways. In: Proceedings of Asian-Pacific Technical Exchange and Advisory Meeting (TEAM) (2016)

14. European Centre for Medium-Range Weather Forecasts (ECMWF). www.ecmwf.int

15. Kawabe, H.: Contribution of supposed wave condition on the long-term distribution of a wave-induced load. J. Mar. Sci. Technol. **6**, 135–147 (2002)

16. Osawa, N., Hashimoto, K., Sawamura, J., Rokutanda, A.: Construction of the storm model with consideration to the sea area and the season. In: Proceedings of 2nd PAAMES and AMEC (2006)

17. Boccoti, P.: Wave Mechanics for Ocean Engineering. Elsevier Oceanography series. Elsevier, Amsterdam (2000)

Author Index

Printed in the United States
By Bookmasters